Professional Responsibility

Carolina Academic Press
Context and Practice Series
Michael Hunter Schwartz
Series Editor

Administrative Law
Richard Henry Seamon

Civil Procedure for All States
Benjamin V. Madison, III

Constitutional Law
David S. Schwartz and Lori Ringhand

Contracts
Michael Hunter Schwartz and Denise Riebe

Current Issues in Constitutional Litigation
Sarah E. Ricks, with contributions by Evelyn M. Tenenbaum

Employment Discrimination
Susan Grover, Sandra F. Sperino, and Jarod S. Gonzalez

Evidence
Pavel Wonsowicz

International Women's Rights, Equality, and Justice
Christine M. Venter

The Lawyer's Practice
Kris Franklin

Professional Responsibility
Barbara Glesner Fines

Sales
Edith R. Warkentine

Torts
Paula J. Manning

Workers Compensation
Michael C. Duff

Professional Responsibility

A Context and Practice Casebook

Barbara Glesner Fines

University of Missouri-Kansas City
School of Law

Carolina Academic Press
Durham, North Carolina

Library of Congress Cataloging-in-Publication Data

Fines, Barbara Glesner.
 Professional responsibility : context & practice / Barbara Glesner Fines.
    p. cm.
 Includes bibliographical references and index.
 ISBN 978-1-59460-650-2 (alk. paper)
 1. Legal ethics--United States. 2. Attorney and client--United States. 3. Practice of
law--United States. I. Title.

 KF306.F52 2012
 174'.3--dc23   2012023661

Carolina Academic Press, LLC
700 Kent Street
Durham, NC 27701
Telephone (919) 489-7486
Fax (919) 493-5668
www.cap-press.com

Printed in the United States of America
2016 Printing

Contents

CONTENTS

Table of Principal Cases

Series Editor's Preface

Welcome to a new type of law text. Designed by leading experts in law school teaching and learning, Context and Practice casebooks assist law professors and their students to work together to learn, minimize stress, and prepare for the rigors and joys of practicing law. **Student learning and preparation for law practice are the guiding ethics of these books.**

Why would we depart from the tried and true? Why have we abandoned the legal education model by which we were trained? Because legal education can and must improve.

In Spring 2007, the Carnegie Foundation published *Educating Lawyers: Preparation for the Practice of Law* and the Clinical Legal Education Association published *Best Practices for Legal Education*. Both works reflect in-depth efforts to assess the effectiveness of modern legal education, and both conclude that legal education, as presently practiced, falls quite short of what it can and should be. Both works criticize law professors' rigid adherence to a single teaching technique, the inadequacies of law school assessment mechanisms, and the dearth of law school instruction aimed at teaching law practice skills and inculcating professional values. Finally, the authors of both books express concern that legal education may be harming law students. Recent studies show that law students, in comparison to all other graduate students, have the highest levels of depression, anxiety, and substance abuse.

The problems with traditional law school instruction begin with the textbooks law teachers use. Law professors cannot implement *Educating Lawyers* and *Best Practices* using texts designed for the traditional model of legal education. Moreover, even though our understanding of how people learn has grown exponentially in the past 100 years, no law school text to date even purports to have been designed with educational research in mind.

The Context and Practice Series is an effort to offer a genuine alternative. Grounded in learning theory and instructional design and written with *Educating Lawyers* and *Best Practices* in mind, Context and Practice casebooks make it easy for law professors to change.

I welcome reactions, criticisms, and suggestions; my e-mail address is michael. schwartz@washburn.edu. Knowing the authors of these books, I know they, too, would appreciate your input; we share a common commitment to student learning. In fact, students, if your professor cares enough about your learning to have adopted this book, I bet s/he would welcome your input, too!

Professor Michael Hunter Schwartz, Series Designer and Editor
Co-Director, Institute for Law Teaching and Learning
Associate Dean for Faculty and Academic Development
Washburn University School of Law

Preface

Dear Students:

My primary goal in writing this text and in teaching professional responsibility is that, by the end of the course, you will believe that issues of attorney ethics and regulation are very important to every attorney and that you will feel confident that you can identify and respond to any ethical issue that might arise in your practice.

Overall, the text has the following major learning outcomes that recur throughout the chapters.

First, you should know the law that regulates attorneys. You should be able to explain the relationship between bar-generated disciplinary codes and other sources of law, such as cases, statutes, and regulations. You should be able to identify the core issues and governing law in any troublesome situation and be able to analyze complex professional responsibility problems in the primary areas of concern for attorneys:

- The four C's of the attorney-client relationship: Competence, Communication, Confidentiality, and Conflict-free representation;
- The three C's of the attorney-court relationship: Candor, Compliance, and Civility;
- The FAIR rule for the attorney's relationship with everyone else in society: Fairness, Access, Integrity, and Responsibility.

You should be able to recognize the tensions and gaps among these concepts, which are inherent in the regulation of attorneys.

Second, you should be able to learn more. You should be able to read rules of professional conduct and extract their meaning. You should be able to research issues of professional responsibility and be aware of sources for additional help.

Third, you should have acquired a habit of thinking of the values underlying professional issues and how your own personal values relate to those values. You should recognize the value of personal reflection and collaborative work in addressing issues of professional responsibility.

Fourth, you should be able to avoid getting yourself, your fellow attorneys, and your clients into trouble, by having learned some practical strategies for avoiding common professional pitfalls.

The text provides opportunities for you to assess your own learning and to practice a range of skills important to effective professional lawyering: reflection, collaboration, research, risk assessment, effective written and oral communication with clients, and a range of office management practices.

A word about one of the learning goals you may have for this course. Many students take the Multistate Professional Responsibility Exam (MPRE) during law school and so presume that the primary goal of the Professional Responsibility course should be to prepare them for this exam. While there is a substantial overlap in subject matter between the professional responsibility course and the MPRE, the law school course is not designed as a "bar prep" course for the MPRE for three reasons.

First, the MPRE tests some materials that are easily mastered without a law school course. That is not to say that you need not prepare for the MPRE. You must read all the rules and comments of both the Model Rules of Professional Conduct and the Code of Judicial Conduct and take a practice exam (at a minimum) in order to pass the MPRE. The appendix to the text provides general advice on preparing for and taking the MPRE.

Second, the MPRE tests only a small portion of the knowledge required to practice law professionally and ethically. The MPRE necessarily cannot test doctrines for which there is substantial uncertainty or controversy regarding their meaning or application nor can it test notions of "best practices." Yet this is the very knowledge that attorneys must call upon in their day-to-day practice.

Third, you do a great disservice to yourself in preparing for practice if your approach to learning in a course of Professional Responsibility is to focus only on preparing for the MPRE. One of the easiest matters to test on a multiple-choice test is exactly where the lines between permitted and prohibited conduct lie. But attorneys who make a career out of walking on that line, rather than aiming for higher standards of practice, are at continual risk of losing their licenses, reputations, and careers. As Professor Kordesh observed, "lawyers do not practice in a multiple-choice world." Maureen Straub Kordesh, *Reinterpreting ABA Standard 302(f) in Light of the Multistate Performance Test*, 30 U. Mem. L. Rev. 299, 310 (2000).

I am interested in any comments or suggestions you have about the text. My email address is glesnerb@umkc.edu.

Peace,

Barbara Glesner Fines

Acknowledgments

Over 2000 of my students have learned professional responsibility in my classes using some portion of this textbook. To the extent it is a useful learning tool, it is because of their insights, contributions, questions, and confusions. I am especially grateful to my research assistants who proofread and indexed the text: Kristin Jacobs (Class of 2011); Ashley Williams (Class of 2012); and Bree Berner (Class of 2014).

This text surely would not have been possible without the support of my colleague, co-teacher, and Dean Ellen Suni. It was she who first developed her own teaching materials for the course and, over the past fifteen years, we have shared those materials back and forth so much that there is very little in this text that does not have origins in those discussions. In particular, her influence is evident in the chapter on current client conflicts and the selection of the Dresser case (still a great learning tool after all these years); the chapter on advertising and the approach to teaching that material through a constitutional history approach; and the many problems set in the context of criminal representations. Finally, in her role as Dean, she encouraged this work with support for travel and research stipends. I owe her an enormous debt of gratitude.

Other colleagues here at UMKC have played an important role in the text as well. Our immediate past Dean, Burnele Powell, also a professional responsibility scholar and teacher, was equally supportive in my development of expertise in the field. My newest colleague, Professor Marcia Narine, co-taught the course with me, tested the materials through her own course, contributed her expertise from a well-established career in corporate compliance, and shared her perspectives as a new faculty member teaching the course for the first time. The chapter on counseling compliance was especially influenced by her contributions. Thanks as well to my librarian colleagues: Professor Paul Callister, Michael Robak, and Larry MacLachlan for their insights and assistance in the research instruction lessons throughout the text. Exercises and narrative discussions of ethical issues in the context of family representation were enriched by my ongoing collaborations with my family law colleagues: Professors Mary Kay Kisthardt, Mary Kay O'Malley, and June Carbone. My former colleague Dean Irma Russell inspired me to pay more careful attention to the ways in which practice area context shapes ethics issues and their resolution. My colleagues in the legal writing program, Professors Wanda Temm, Barbara Wilson, Judy Popper, Daniel Weddle, and Aaron House all instruct me regularly on the nuances of teaching drafting and thereby informed the skills exercises throughout the text. Finally, one of my earliest colleagues, Professor Judith Maute, introduced me to the value of reflective journal writing over twenty years ago and my clinical colleagues from around the country have informed my continuing efforts to incorporate this important clinical pedagogy into my teaching.

My teaching is constantly informed by the many colleagues who have lent countless hours of conversation and collaboration over the years. In particular, many of the materials in the text were informed by my work with the Center for Computer-Assisted Legal Instruction. I am exceedingly grateful for the time and passion the John Mayer and Deb Quentel have brought to supporting my work in developing these unique learning materials. I have learned more about structured learning through the opportunities to author lessons and work with other faculty members in CALI projects than in nearly any other collaboration.

So many of my colleagues in the field have enriched my understanding and influenced my teaching, including the many I have quoted or cited many in the text. I am especially grateful for permission from the authors of the following articles, which I have included in more sizeable excerpts in the text:

John Leubsdorf, *Legal Ethics Falls Apart*, 57 Buffalo L. Rev. 959, 959-62 (2009).

Jean R. Sternlight & Jennifer Robbennolt, *Good Lawyers Should Be Good Psychologists: Insights for Interviewing and Counseling Clients*, 23 Ohio St. J. on Disp. Resol. 437, 487-491, 499-504 (2008).

Andrew Perlman, *Civil Procedure and the Legal Profession: The Parallel Law of Lawyering in Civil Litigation*, 79 Fordham L. Rev. 1965, 1971-1973 (2011).

I have been especially intellectually enriched and inspired by my many colleagues and friends from the American Association of Law Schools Professional Responsibility and Teaching Methods Sections and the National Institute for Teaching Ethics and Professionalism. I will commit the sin of omission to them collectively so as to avoid the insult of inadvertently omitting any one individually.

Finally, I am exceedingly honored and grateful to have been invited to join the Context and Practice series by Professor Michael Hunter Schwartz. Both he and Professor Gerry Hess have been spirited cheerleaders, gentle cajolers, tactful editors, and inspiring role models. My editors at Carolina Academic Press as well have been a delight: endlessly patient and supportive. I am especially grateful to Tim Colton for his inspired work in translating my amateur efforts at capturing critical ideas in graphics into professional and effective images.

The problems that remain are my own alone.

A word on editing. All cases are edited. Citations have been removed or shortened, however, I have indicated with ellipses only those omissions of significant substantive text. I have chosen to include state rules of professional conduct rather than ABA Model Rules, to reinforce the message that the governing disciplinary standards are not from a bar association but from the state. However, I have deliberately chosen state versions that closely track the ABA Model Rules and have highlighted any significant variations. In this way, I hope to reinforce the centrality of the rules of professional regulation. I look forward to suggestions and comments.

Last, but most importantly, like any book author, my family has paid most dearly for this project with my missed dinners, reams of paper strewn throughout the house, distracted listening and endless claims of "almost done." Thank you Dave and Dan. Your love and support mean more to me than words on paper can ever capture.

Peace,
Barbara Glesner Fines

Professional Responsibility

Learning About Professional Responsibility

Goals of Unit One

Before we begin studying the details of any particular doctrine that regulates your practice as an attorney, we will learn about the profession of law, who regulates it, and how each of us fit into that picture. By the end of this unit, you should be able to describe what it means to be a lawyer, the skills and values that characterize professionalism, and your vision of yourself in the profession of law. You should be able to identify the many sources of law that may regulate an attorney's conduct and begin to be able to research those sources efficiently and effectively. Finally, you should have a systematic approach to reading a rule of professional conduct.

Pretest

To gauge your assumptions about the materials covered in this unit, decide whether you think the following statements are true or false.

1. White males over the age of 45 represent the largest demographic group of attorneys.

2. About half of all attorneys in private practice are in solo practice.

3. More attorneys represent entities (such as corporations) than represent individuals.

4. Less than 1% of attorneys work full-time serving clients whose incomes are so low that they qualify for free legal services.

5. A civic professional is an individual with specialized knowledge and skill who uses that knowledge and skill to serve others.

6. Being able to collaborate with other attorneys is a key skill for professional success and satisfaction.

7. Attorneys are increasingly being regulated by a complex web of state, federal, and international law.

8. Attorneys are admitted to practice law in the first instance by state supreme courts.

9. The American Bar Association (ABA) Model Rules of Professional Conduct are not primary law, but are only suggested standards that the states may or may not adopt as their regulation governing lawyers.

10. An attorney practicing exclusively federal law is also subject to the regulation of the state in which that attorney is licensed.

11. Attorneys in nearly all specialized areas of practice can obtain ethical guidance for the particular issues that arise in their practice from voluntary professional organizations; however, this guidance ordinarily does not have the force of law.

12. Persons seeking admission or readmission to practice law have the burden to prove that they have good moral character.

13. One of the most important professional skills in serving clients is the ability to listen.

14. A non-lawyer professional may not own an interest in a for-profit law firm except for limited circumstances when an attorney has died.

15. In most of Europe, there are no restrictions on unauthorized practice of law or on non-lawyer ownership of law firms.

16. Limitations on sharing fees with non-lawyers and non-lawyer ownership of law firms do not apply to non-profit law firms or organizations.

Chapter One

What Is a Professional?

Learning Objectives

After you have read this chapter and completed the assignments

- In analyzing a professional responsibility issue, you should be able to raise questions about the practical consequences (technical professionalism) and the consequences to the client, the courts, and the public (civic professionalism) of an attorney's conduct. (By the end of the course, you should be able to answer most of the questions you raise.)

- You should begin to develop a personal career plan that accurately assesses the market possibilities in light of the demographics of the profession.

- You should perceive the value of reflection in improving your own professionalism.

Rules to Study

This chapter is primarily about the profession, rather than the rules that regulate it. However, you will find that reading the preamble and scope of the ABA Model Rules of Professional Conduct will give you a useful overview of the predominant view of what it means to be a professional.

Preliminary Problem

Before you read the chapter, close your eyes and think of a professional. Better yet, draw a picture of a professional (don't worry if you aren't an artist—the important thing is that you know what you are representing in your drawing). Ask some non-lawyer friends to do the same thing. Compare your pictures.

What do you see?

What does your professional look like? How is the professional dressed?

What is the environment around the professional? Are there other people in the picture?

What is the professional doing?

What are the sources of your conception of a professional? How does that conception affect your decisions as an attorney? How has that conception changed during law school, if at all?

1.1 Who Are Lawyers and What Do They Do?

As we consider our picture of professionals, let's begin with some basics. How much do you know about who lawyers are and what they do? The first and perhaps most important professional choice you have is what kind of practice you will pursue, in what setting, with whom, and for whom. Thoughtful consideration of the demographic and economic facts of your profession can help you to make better choices. See if you can answer the following questions (answers are provided on the following page, with links for web resources for more current data).

1. About how many licensed lawyers were there in the United States as of 2010?
   a. 750,000
   b. 1.2 million
   c. 1.7 million

2. What percentage of lawyers in 2000 were women?
   a. 47%
   b. 37%
   c. 27%

3. What was the median age of lawyers in 2000?
   a. 39
   b. 41
   c. 45

4. What percentage of attorneys in 2000 were members of a racial or ethnic minority group?
   a. 5%
   b. 11%
   c. 22%

5. In 2000, what percentage of attorneys were in private practice?
   a. 68%
   b. 74%
   c. 85%

6. Of these attorneys in private practice in 2000, what percentage were in solo practice?
   a. 28%
   b. 48%
   c. 68%

7. About what were the median annual earnings of all lawyers employed by others in 2008?
   a. $75,000
   b. $110,000
   c. $165,000

8. What was the median starting salary for the 2009 graduates of United States law schools, based on those working full-time and reporting a salary nine months after graduation?
   a. $98,000
   b. $72,000
   c. $45,000

9. What proportion of attorneys represent entities (corporations and institutions) rather than individuals?
   a. Most attorneys represent entities
   b. About an equal proportion of attorneys represent entities and individuals
   c. Most attorneys represent individuals

10. What is the proportion of legal aid lawyers to low-income individuals in 2005?
    a. One lawyer for every 7,000 people
    b. One lawyer for every 3,000 people
    c. One lawyer for every 500 people

11. What is the approximate mean total of hours worked for a first-year attorney in a law firm in 2007?
    a. 2140
    b. 2070
    c. 1890

12. What percentage of entry-level associates in firms leave the firm within the first 16 months?
    a. 8
    b. 12
    c. 16

Much of this demographic information can be found on the American Bar Association website: http://new.abanet.org/marketresearch/Pages/StatisticalResources.aspx.

How well informed were you about your chosen profession?

Number of lawyers (Question 1 — answer b)

According to the ABA Market Research Department, in 2010 there were 1,225,452 licensed lawyers in the United States. The U.S. Department of Labor Bureau of Labor Statistics has a somewhat smaller number for lawyers, but this number does not include judges and other undefined "legal services workers." Regardless of which number you consider, there has been a substantial growth in legal employment over the past 25 years. The Bureau of Labor Statistics forecasts growth of jobs in law at a rate of about eleven percent during the years 2010–18, about as fast as the average for all occupations:

> Growth in the population and in the level of business activity is expected to create more legal transactions, civil disputes, and criminal cases. Job growth among lawyers also will result from increasing demand for legal services in such areas as healthcare, intellectual property, bankruptcy, corporate and security litigation, antitrust law, and environmental law. In addition, the wider availability and affordability of legal clinics should result in increased use of legal services by middle-income people. However, growth in demand for lawyers will be constrained as businesses increasingly use large accounting firms and paralegals to perform some of the same functions that lawyers do. For example, accounting firms may provide employee-benefit counseling, process doc-

uments, or handle various other services previously performed by a law firm. Also, mediation and dispute resolution are increasingly being used as alternatives to litigation.

U.S. DEPARTMENT OF LABOR, OCCUPATIONAL OUTLOOK HANDBOOK, LAWYERS (2010–11 Ed.) http://www.bls.gov/oco/ocos053.htm.

Demographics of lawyers: Gender (Question 2 — answer a)

According to the American Bar Foundation in the 2004 edition of *The Lawyer Statistical Report*, 27% percent of lawyers were women in 2000. (The latest issue of the report was still under development at the time this text was published.) It appears that women have come a long way since 1872 when Supreme Court Justice Bradley concluded that, "[t]he natural and proper timidity and delicacy which belongs to the female sex evidently unfits it for many of the occupations of civil life." *Bradwell v. Illinois*, 83 U.S. (16 Wall.) 130, 141 (1873) (Bradley, J., concurring). However, women still face barriers to advancement in the legal profession. The National Association of Women Lawyers conducts an annual survey of the status of women in the nation's largest law firms. In its 2011 survey, it concluded that:

> Not only do women represent a decreasing percentage of lawyers in big firms, they have a far greater chance of occupying positions — like staff attorneys, counsel, and fixed-income equity partners — with diminished opportunity for advancement or participating in firm leadership. We recognize that the current economy has led to continuing challenges for big firms. Nevertheless, those challenges explain neither the uneven progress made by women lawyers compared to their male counterparts nor the backward slide of gender equity in law firms.

NATIONAL ASSOCIATION OF WOMEN LAWYERS, 2011 NATIONAL SURVEY. The full NAWL Survey Report can be accessed by visiting the NAWL website at http://www.nawl.org/ and following the link for *Publications* and then *NAWL National Surveys*. For more information on this issue, see the materials at the website of the ABA Commission on the Status of Women in the Profession at http://www.abanet.org/women/.

Age (Question 3 — answer c)

The three choices reflect the median age of lawyers in 1984 (39), 1991 (41), and 2000 (45). Obviously, this aging of the profession will have a profound impact on how the legal professional develops in coming years. To read more about this aspect of the profession, see the classic study on this issue, Marc Galanter, *"Old and in the Way": The Coming Demographic Transformation of the Legal Profession and Its Implications for the Provision of Legal Services*, 1999 WIS. L. REV. 1081 (1999).

Race/Ethnicity (Question 4 — answer b)

In 1990, 7.4% of attorneys were members of a racial or ethnic minority group; by 2000, that percentage had grown to 11.2%. (Source: 1990 and 2000 U.S. Census, Bureau of the Census). The American Bar Association's Commission on Racial and Ethnic Diversity and the Harvard Law School Program on the Legal Profession issues regular reports on the status of minorities in the legal profession. The conclusions of the most recent study (2004) were:

1. Minority representation in the legal profession is significantly lower than in most other professions.

2. Minority entry into the profession has slowed considerably since the 1980s and mid-1990s.

3. The initial employment of minority lawyers still differs significantly from that of whites.

4. Minorities remain grossly underrepresented in top-level private sector jobs, such as law partner and corporate general counsel.

5. Progress has been especially slow for minority women in the profession.

6. Minorities in general continue to face significant obstacles to "full and equal" participation in the legal profession.

ELIZABETH CHAMBLISS, MILES TO GO: PROGRESS OF MINORITIES IN THE LEGAL PROFESSION (2004) (American Bar Association Commission on Racial and Ethnic Diversity in the Profession). For a thought-provoking discussion of racial identity and white lawyers read Professor Russell G. Pearce, *Symposium: Critical Race Lawyering: White Lawyering: Rethinking Race, Lawyer Identity, and Rule of Law*, 73 FORDHAM L. REV. 2081 (2005).

Practice Setting (Question 5 — answer b)

The percentage of attorneys in private practice has grown from 68% in 1980 to 74% in 2000.

Practice Setting (Question 6 — answer b)

Of the attorneys in private practice, nearly half were in solo practice and another 22% were in firms of 2–10 lawyers. For more general demographic and practice setting information, read Quintin Johnstone, *An Overview of the Legal Profession in the United States, How that Profession Recently Has Been Changing, and Its Future Prospects*, 26 QUINNIPIAC L. REV. 737 (2008).

Average Earnings (Question 7 — answer b)

In May 2008, the median annual wages of all wage-and-salaried lawyers were $110,590. The middle half of the occupation earned between $74,980 and $163,320. BUREAU OF LABOR STATISTICS, U.S. DEPARTMENT OF LABOR, OCCUPATIONAL OUTLOOK HANDBOOK, LAWYERS (2010–11), http://www.bls.gov/oco/ocos053.htm.

New Lawyer Earnings (Question 8 — answer b)

Consider the graph depicting the salary distributions for new attorneys on the next page. According to NALP, the national median salary for the Class of 2009, based on those working full-time and reporting a salary, was $72,000 and the national mean was $93,454. However, as the NALP study makes clear, there are actually few attorneys earning starting salaries near the median or mean. Rather, starting salaries are distributed along a bi-modal curve, reflecting the vastly different starting salaries for attorneys in public practice or smaller firms and those working for large corporate law firms. To provide a more realistic picture of starting salaries, NALP now provides an "adjusted mean" which compensates for differences in the availability of salary data from large firms and small firms or solo practice.

Professor William Henderson has studied the dynamics behind the development of this curve and suggests that the "Cravath Model" responsible for the very high starting salaries among elite law firms cannot be sustained. William Henderson, *Are We Selling Results or Résumés?: the Underexplored Linkage between Human Resource Strategies and Firm-Specific Capital*, http://papers.ssrn.com/sol3/papers.cfm?abstract_id=1121238.

Salary Distribution for New Attorneys

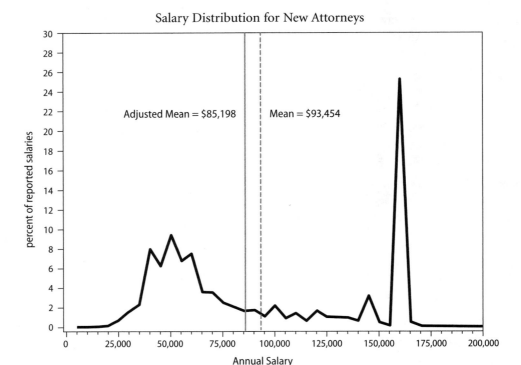

Source: NALP *http://www.nalp.org/startingsalarydistributionclassof2009*

Whom do we represent? (Question 9 — answer a)

Researchers of the Chicago bar have provided considerable insight into the social strat-ification of law practice. In their book, JOHN P. HEINZ AND EDWARD O. LAUMANN, CHICAGO LAWYERS: THE SOCIAL STRUCTURE OF THE BAR (1982), the researchers advanced the hy-pothesis that there were two hemispheres of lawyering: that most attorneys either work in large firms representing entities or in solo and small firm practice serving individuals. Their follow-up survey and research in 1995 confirmed their original hypothesis of a di-vide between entity and individual representation. The survey also revealed a significant shift in the relationship between these two hemispheres of practice. More attorneys today represent entities (corporations and institutions) rather than individuals. Their more re-cent study also suggested that there was even more specialization within the bar. JOHN P. HEINZ, ROBERT L. NELSON, REBECCA L. SANDEFUR, & EDWARD O. LAUMANN, URBAN LAWYERS: THE NEW SOCIAL STRUCTURE OF THE BAR (2005). These studies focus on lawyers in Chicago. For a contrast, *see* DONALD D. LANDON, COUNTRY LAWYERS: THE IMPACT OF CONTEXT ON PROFESSIONAL PRACTICE (1990).

The consequences of this shift for access to justice are that increasingly middle-income Americans are unable to afford legal services.

Delivering affordable legal services to the middle class is a challenge that the legal profession has been unable to meet. Advice on topics of daily importance in the lives of individuals, such as landlord/tenant law, child custody disputes, and tes-tamentary dispositions is priced beyond the reach of millions of working Amer-icans. Equal Justice Under the Law is an ideal whose pursuit is becoming increasingly futile. Wealthy individuals and large organizations have the financial means to purchase the legal services they need, while members of the middle class and small business owners are left to struggle in a legal maze from which extrication is almost impossible.

Mary C. Daly, *The Structure of Legal Education and the Legal Profession, Multidisciplinary Practice, Competition, and Globalization*, 52 J. Leg. Ed. 480, 484 (2002).

Access to legal representation (Question 10 — answer a)

Recent studies by the Legal Services Corporation analyzing the number of attorneys in legal aid practice revealed the following:

> Nationally, there are well over ten times more private attorneys providing personal legal services to people in the general population than there are legal aid attorneys serving the poor. While there is only one legal aid lawyer (including all sources of funding) per 6,415 low income people in the country, this report estimates that there is one lawyer providing personal legal services (that is, services aimed at meeting the legal needs of private individuals and families) for every 429 people in the general population.

Legal Services Corporation, Documenting the Justice Gap in America: The Current Unmet Civil Legal Needs of Low-Income Americans 19 (2009), http://www.lsc.gov/sites/default/files/LSC/pdfs/documenting_the_justice_gap_in_america_2009.pdf.

Most legal needs of low-income individuals are not met.

> According to most estimates, about four-fifths of the civil legal needs of low-income individuals, and two- to three-fifths of the needs of middle-income individuals, remain unmet. Less than one percent of the nation's legal expenditures, and fewer than one percent of its lawyers assist the seventh of the population that is poor enough to qualify for aid. Our nation prides itself on a commitment to the rule of law, but prices it out of reach for the vast majority of its citizens.

Deborah Rhode, *Access to Justice: Connecting Practices to Principles*, 17 Georgetown J. of Leg. Ethics 369, 371 (2004).

Work life—Hours (Question 11 — answer b)

The average number of hours worked in 2007 in private practice for new associates was 2068. National Association of Law Placement, *How Much Do Associates Work?* NALP Bulletin (April 2009) http://www.nalp.org/may07billablehrs.

(Question 12 — answer b)

According to the National Association for Law Placement, 8.4% of entry-level associates leave their firm within the first 16 months. Mid-sized firms of 251–500 reported the highest rate of attrition. The annual attrition rate for entry-level associates was 13.8%, with firms of more than 500 attorneys experiencing a lower rate of departures (11.6%) and mid-sized firms of 251–500 attorneys a higher rate (17.2%). The highest attrition rate was for minority men, who left firms at the rate of 17.5% annually, the highest for any group. The most common reason for departures (20.4% of all associates) was "unmet performance standards," followed closely by geographic preference (16.8%), advancement opportunities (7.4%), and billable hour pressures (6.1%). NALP Foundation, Keeping the Keepers II: Mobility and Management of Associates— Entry-Level and Lateral Hiring and Attrition 1998–2003. http://www.nalp foundation.org/webmodules/articles/anmviewer.asp?a=89. To read more about the work life and job satisfaction of attorneys, see Nancy Levit & Doug Linder, The Happy Lawyer (2010).

1.2 What Is a Professional?

The title of this text is *Professional Responsibility*. But who, exactly, is a *professional* and how is a professional's responsibility different from that of any other person? Consider your own conception of the term professional. Reconsider the picture you drew (or imagined) at the beginning of this chapter. Now consider this definition of "profession" from the Merriam-Webster's Dictionary: "a calling requiring specialized knowledge and often long and intensive academic preparation."

Does your picture reflect this definition? For nearly everyone, a professional is someone who has devoted themself to becoming an expert in a particular field. To the extent that long and intensive academic preparation is becoming necessary for more and more careers, one might consider that all jobs have become "professions" in some sense.

Yet this definition leaves out an important question. For what purpose does one undertake this long and intensive academic preparation? Many people picture a professional as someone who uses her specialized knowledge and skill to attain social status and financial success. In this vision of professionalism, the ability to achieve individual success is the defining characteristic. We may think of the term "professional" mostly in contrast to "amateurs" — many talented amateurs have developed significant expertise in their hobby, but they are not paid for their knowledge, skills, and talent, and so are not professionals. What role do status and money play in your conception of what makes a professional?

In his study of the professions, William M. Sullivan terms this vision of professionalism: "technical professionalism." He contrasts that concept with what he terms "civic professionalism." William M. Sullivan, Work And Integrity: The Crisis And Promise Of Professionalism In America 5 (2d ed. 2005). The difference between these two concepts is not to be found in the expertise or education, but in the reasons for this expertise. For civic professionals, the primary purpose of their specialized knowledge is service to the public good:

> The term 'profession,' it should be borne in mind, as a rule is applied to a group of people pursuing a learned art as a common calling in the spirit of public service where economic rewards are definitely an incidental, though under the existing economic conditions undoubtedly a necessary by-product. In this a profession differs radically from any trade or business which looks upon money-making and personal gain as its primary purpose. The lawyer cannot possibly get away from the fact that his is a public task. In all probability the professional relation of a lawyer to his client arose out of status rather than contract. It called, and still calls, for something more than a mere merchant-customer contact. It was, and still is, based on ideas more nearly akin to that of a fiduciary relationship than one which originated from the principle of caveat emptor. The general public has need for a professional man in whom it can repose a particular type of confidence whenever it is faced with some distressing problems, often of a very personal nature. Hence the most important aspect of the practice of law is the fact that it is, and the inherent nature of things demands that it always shall be, a profession.

State ex rel. Wolff v. Ruddy, 617 S.W.2d 64, 65–66 (Mo. banc 1981), *cert. denied*, 454 U.S. 1142, 102 S.Ct. 1000, 71 L.Ed.2d 293 (1982) (quoting Anton-Hermann Chroust, 1 The Rise of the Legal Profession in America x–xi (1965).

Recall the dictionary definition of "profession." Note that the term "calling"—the first definition of profession in that dictionary—relates to taking religious vows. The notion of civic professionalism has deep roots in this notion of vocation. Historically, three callings that were termed "professions" were the clergy, medicine, and law. Each of these professions required specialized knowledge and training. Entrance into each was strictly regulated by the members of the profession itself. Each transformed a person—becoming a clergyperson, doctor, or lawyer, an individual would become "Pastor" or "Doctor" or "Esquire." And perhaps most distinctive, each was responsible for serving some critical aspect of society's needs: clergy cared for the public's spiritual health; doctors cared for society's physical and mental health; and lawyers cared for society's relationships.

If the care of society's relationships is the job of a lawyer, look again at your picture. Where is the client in your picture? If your picture doesn't have a client, why not? Can you be a professional without a client? If your picture does have a client, what is the relationship between the client and the lawyer? Who else is in your picture? A judge or jury? The public generally? Compare your conception of professionalism with that of the Council of Bars and Law Societies of Europe (CCBE), the collective of bar associations of the 31 European countries:

> In a society founded on respect for the rule of law the lawyer fulfills a special role. The lawyer's duties do not begin and end with the faithful performance of what he or she is instructed to do so far as the law permits. A lawyer must serve the interests of justice as well as those whose rights and liberties he or she is trusted to assert and defend and it is the lawyer's duty not only to plead the client's cause but to be the client's adviser. Respect for the lawyer's professional function is an essential condition for the rule of law and democracy in Society.

CCBE Code of Conduct for European Lawyers, article 1.1.

The irony in this tension between technical professionalism and civic professionalism is that the more that you align your practice and conception of yourself as a professional to the needs and interests of others, the more likely you are to attain the social and material success that will make you satisfied. In contrast, a self-centered drive toward technical professionalism undercuts the public's perception of attorneys and trust in the legal system and thus undermines the very foundation from which individual success can be built. In other words, civic professionalism (in the sense of an orientation to the client and the public good) is also good business. That doesn't mean that you must take vows of poverty and abandon all business sense—but it does mean that you must operate from a clear sense of what defines your relationship with your client, the public, and the rule of law.

Of course, avoiding pure selfishness is a pretty basic starting point for ethical analysis. In nearly every culture, one can find some version of the Golden Rule. The more difficult ethical questions in applying that rule come from the tensions inherent in service. Whose interest—the client, the public, the legal system itself—gets priority and how much? As you will see in this course, much of the regulation of the legal profession is an attempt to wrestle with this balance. But there is much room for individual discretion in striking this balance. Scholars disagree about the relationship between regulation and ethical or moral decision making. You can read more about this debate in the articles and books cited at the end of this chapter. As a practical matter, if you clarify where the client and others are located in our picture of yourself as a professional, you will make the exercise of ethical discretion clearer, if not easier.

Reflective Practice

Perhaps you have thought about your career planning as something separate from your academic preparation for the practice of law. A critical part of this course, however, requires that you think deeply about what kind of work you would like to do after law school (whether practicing law or an alternative to law practice), where you would like to do that work, with whom, and with what goals. Taking time to reflect on your career choices is an important professional responsibility skill.

In his book, *The Reflective Practitioner*, David Schon suggests that professional behavior is guided by theory. Schon describes two types of theories: "theories of action," which are the values, strategies, and underlying assumptions that affect behavior, and "theories-in-use," which are the theories implicit in one's habitual actions. In other words, professionals don't always behave in ways that are consistent with how they talk about their professional values and beliefs. Through reflection, professionals can examine their own theories (both explicit and implicit) and align their behavior and theory.

Often the most useful way to incorporate regular reflection into your professional development is through reflective writing. Because writing engages your thoughts in a different (and sometimes deeper) manner than just thinking about a topic, a journal or log can be an important tool to improving your professionalism. Try your hand at some reflective writing this semester. Throughout the text you will find reflective practice topics to prompt deeper thinking about the materials on a personal or professional level.

Examine your theories in action and theories in use regarding collaboration. Traditional legal education trains you to work independently and competitively. Rules that prohibit collaboration on papers and explicit "ranking systems" may lead you to believe that this is the world of practice as well—every person for himself. While there is no denying the degree of individual responsibility you have in law practice and the amount of competition there may be for clients or cases, it is simply not true that attorneys never collaborate. As you saw in the demographics in this chapter, only about a third of attorneys are in solo practice. But even attorneys who have a solo practice rely on a network of mentors and colleagues to whom they turn for advice, collaboration, and backup.

This networking reduces risk and increases quality and satisfaction. Susan Bryant, *Collaboration in Law Practice: A Satisfying and Productive Process for a Diverse Profession*, 17 Vt. L. Rev. 459 (1993). As Professors Levit and Linder suggest in their work on career satisfaction:

> If the best elixir isn't money, but people—and one of the best ways to make people happier is to help them create strong and supportive personal relationships—law schools should work to increase social bonds. The practice of law is increasingly interdisciplinary and multi-discipli-

nary. Law schools should create team players, by developing more collaborative projects and assignments.

Nancy Levit & Douglas O. Linder, *Happy Law Students, Happy Lawyers*, 58 SYRACUSE L. REV. 351, 363–64 (2008).

Likewise, in his study of the legal profession, Professor Henderson has built upon extensive empirical studies of knowledge workers at Bell Labs to suggest that law firms develop different models for recruiting and training new lawyers—models that rely less on numerical accomplishments (grades, billable hours) and more on qualities that extensive empirical study had demonstrated to be associated with high performance. William Henderson, *Are We Selling Results or Résumés?: The Underexplored Linkage between Human Resource Strategies and Firm-Specific Capital*, Indiana Legal Studies Research Paper No. 105, http://papers.ssrn.com/sol3/papers.cfm?abstract_id=1121238). Those qualities included several that relate directly to collaboration such as networking ("tapping into coworkers' expertise and shar[ing] their own knowledge"); perspective ("understanding jobs within the larger context of the organization and analyzing problems from the viewpoint of customers, managers and team members"); followership ("setting aside their own agendas and using their talents to help other leaders accomplish the organization's goals"); and teamwork ("assum[ing] joint 'ownership' of goal setting, group commitments, work activities, schedules, and defusing conflict among group members").

Write a short reflection regarding your attitudes toward and experiences of collaboration in law school or in legal practice. Is your behavior consistent with your theory?

To Learn More

In addition to the books and articles cited in this chapter, you may consider the following books and law review articles about the role of attorneys:

DAVID LUBAN, THE GOOD LAWYER: LAWYERS' ROLES AND LAWYERS' ETHICS (David Luban Ed. 1983).

MARY ANN GLENDON, A NATION UNDER LAWYERS: HOW THE CRISIS IN THE LEGAL PROFESSION IS TRANSFORMING AMERICAN SOCIETY (1996).

Nathan M. Crystal, *Developing a Philosophy of Lawyering*, 14 NOTRE DAME J.L. ETHICS & PUB. POL'Y 75 (2000).

Charles Fried, *Lawyer as Friend: The Moral Foundations of the Lawyer-Client Relation*, 85 YALE L.J. 1060 (1976).

Russell G. Pearce, *Revitalizing the Lawyer-Poet: What Lawyers Can Learn from Rock and Roll*, 14 WIDENER L.J. 907 (2005).

Stephen L. Pepper, *The Lawyer's Amoral Ethical Role: A Defense, a Problem, and Some Possibilities*, 1986 AM. B. FOUND. RES. J . 613 (1986).

Another excellent way to help shape your vision of yourself as a professional is to find a mentor in the legal profession. Speak with a professor in your field, get involved in your local bar association, or find other routes to meet experienced and reputable attorneys from whom you can learn more about the choices attorneys make over a career that define their vision of professionalism.

Chapter Two

What Laws Govern Attorney Conduct?

Learning Objectives

After you have read this chapter and completed the assignments, you should be able to:

- Explain how an attorney disciplinary action starts and what outcomes might result from that action.

- Read and interpret a reporting rule and apply it to a range of situations in which you have information about another attorney's conduct.

- Recognize issues of professional responsibility as implicating multiple sources of regulation so that, when faced with an issue of professional responsibility, you will be able to brainstorm a thorough list of possible legal constraints and conduct the necessary research to guide your conduct.

- Perceive the increasing role of statutory and administrative regulation that regulates attorney conduct and be able to identify the constitutional issues raised by this regulation.

- Access and evaluate specialized sources of regulation and guidance in your particular practice area.

Rules to Study

We will study the ABA Model Rule of Professional Conduct, Rules 8.3 and 8.4 in this chapter. However, as you can see from the learning objectives for this chapter, part of the point of this chapter is that the state disciplinary rules do not provide the sole or even most important regulation of the legal profession. The challenge for you will be to keep in mind all these other external sources of regulation as you study the profession's standards for self-regulation.

Preliminary Problems

A. You have missed a deadline in answering a complaint filed against your client. What law governs your decisions about the next steps you can and should take?

B. You have conducted a significant amount of research and investigation on behalf of a client and have prepared a complaint for the client. However, the client has now decided that she wants to proceed on her own and fires you. The client has not yet paid for your representation but is demanding that you give her the file on her matter, including the products of your research and drafting. ABA Model Rule 1.16(d) directs that you must surrender papers and property "to which the client is entitled" and also notes that an attorney may retain papers relating to the client "to the extent permitted by law." What "law" will you research to determine whether you must give the client the file? What other considerations will guide your choice?

C. You are preparing to open a solo law practice. Your last name is long, difficult to spell and pronounce, and you believe it will make it more difficult to market your practice. You would like to use a trade name for your practice using a name more common to your community. You are thinking of something like "Arthur Brown and Associates." What source of law will you consult to determine the legal implications of your plan? What personal ethical issues does this plan raise for your consideration?

2.1 What Sources of Law Regulate the Legal Profession?

For most of its history in the United States, the legal profession was regulated by informal professional norms more than by the force of law. Guided by aspirational canons, unwritten community norms, and individual ethical standards, the attorney who questioned his own conduct or duty would consult colleagues, reflect, and come to a decision. Attorneys were admitted by committee without extensive character and fitness applications and the few cases of professional sanction either followed criminal convictions or other blatantly egregious behavior. States controlled the practice of law and there was little federal law involved in regulating attorneys.

Then, things started to change. The profession began to regulate itself with formal rules. By 1970, the ABA had promulgated the Model Code of Professional Responsibility and made recommendations for the professionalization of disciplinary enforcement. States quickly adopted versions of the ABA Model Code as their own disciplinary standards to regulate attorneys. With the emergence of formal state legal regulation, the federal courts also began to police that regulation for constitutionality. In *Goldfarb v. Virginia State Bar,* 421 U.S. 773 (1975), the court held that attorneys were engaged in "trade or commerce" and thus, were not exempt from antitrust laws. In *Bates v. State Bar of Arizona,* 433 U.S. 350 (1977), the Court held that attorney advertising was commercial speech protected by the First Amendment, striking down state regulation that banned nearly all advertising.

Today, some attorneys still rely primarily on "common sense" and the informal norms of their practice community to resolve professional responsibility issues. But this approach is fraught with risk. Given the increasing diversity and mobility of the profession, an individual attorney's standards of practice are not as likely to coincide with the norms of the professional community as they once were. Rather, professional regulation has become more precise and objective and it reaches a broader range of conduct than in the past. The competitiveness and diversity of today's legal community weakens (but does not eliminate) the impact of informal controls such as reputational harm. In addition, consumer activism has led to greater regulation of the providers of legal services. The increased media access to and knowledge of attorney conduct makes this activism easier to engage.

Increasingly, regulation is aimed at general categories of service providers, some of whom might be attorneys. Attorneys are subject to the same regulations that govern similar service industries: whether that is general consumer protection laws or more specific regulation of particular services such as debt collection or corporate reporting. Especially at the federal level, those industries are being regulated in ways that directly affect how attorneys represent their clients, including legislation targeting the advice and information attorneys can give to their clients and the actions they can take on their behalf.

If we widen our lens to look at how attorneys are regulated globally, we can see that statutory and administrative regulation is likely to increase. The United States has negotiated fifteen international trade agreements that apply to legal services in recent years, including the North American Free Trade Agreement (NAFTA) and the General Agreement on Tariffs and Trade. These treaties speak of attorneys as "legal service providers" and will bring increasing pressure to measure regulation of the profession for its impact as a "barrier to trade." Laurel S. Terry, *From GATS to APEC: The Impact of Trade Agreements on Legal Services*, 43 AKRON L. REV. 875, 969-78 (2010).

The result of these trends is that attorneys can find themselves subject to discipline, sanctions, or liability more often, for more reasons, than ever before. With this increased risk comes an increased need for rigorous and thorough research and analysis to answer issues of professional conduct.

Each of the central themes of professional responsibility is regulated by rules of professional conduct, but each also is governed by other sources of law. When researching an issue of professional responsibility, attorneys must take care to recognize the regulatory context in which the issue is being addressed. Answers to an attorney's questions regarding her professional responsibility might be found in state or federal legislation, in common law standards, in rules and procedures of a court or tribunal, or in standards of national, state or local professional associations. Especially when assessing conduct to determine possible liability or sanction, it is crucial that an attorney not overlook one of these major sources of law and keep in mind the context in which he is considering the issue.

For example, consider the table at the top of the next page and think about all the standards that might apply when an attorney makes a mistake in representing a client.

The context for a professional responsibility issue is not always intuitively obvious, but is critical to accurate assessment of the liability and disciplinary parameters for conduct. The researcher must recognize that the procedural context can change the meaning of the professional responsibility standard. For example, the confidentiality standards of disciplinary codes are not identical to the confidentiality standards of the evidentiary attorney-client privilege or the work-product protections of rules of procedure. Similarly, conflict of interest standards are most often applied by courts in cases addressing disqualification of counsel, but because those courts are considering the impact of disqualification on a particular case, they may interpret the standards differently than might a court considering whether an discipline for a conflict of interest.

Source of Law	Consequence to Attorney
Rules of professional conduct adopted by the highest court in the state	State attorney disciplinary agency imposes discipline on attorney for incompetence.
Court rules of civil or criminal procedure	Attorney seeks relief from error or is subject to sanction.
Inherent power of the court	Trial level court holds attorney in contempt or requires attorney forfeit fees.
General common law	Client sues for damages (under tort or contract suit for malpractice or suit for breach of fiduciary duty).
Statutes	Clients may sue for damages (under codified common law standards or under additional legislative bases, such as consumer protection laws).
Malpractice insurance contract	Insurer increases malpractice rates or declines coverage.
Reputational regulation	Client fires attorney and doesn't pay for the representation. Client, other attorneys, and court will not refer other clients.

Researching Professional Responsibility 2-A: Brainstorming Search Terms

One of the first steps to researching an issue of professional responsibility is to brainstorm the words that describe both the facts and the possible sources of law and doctrines that might apply to the conduct in question. A good way to avoid overlooking important sources of regulation is to ask yourself the question: what law would govern this behavior if I were not an attorney? While the terms you need to research may be clear, you may often find that you need to think about analogous areas of law or generate multiple synonyms for your research terms in order to be sure you have identified all the relevant law.

Practice brainstorming research terms for these problems.

Suppose your client has fired you. You have done substantial research and drafting for the client, which the client now wants you to turn over to a new attorney. The client has not paid all that she owes you. Moreover, there are memos in your file that you wrote when you were considering withdrawal because the client was so difficult to work with. What terms might you use in researching whether you have to turn over the entire file to your client?

Consider the accompanying graphic of some search terms you might use. Notice that you might research the law of personal property (bailment, ownership); the rules of civil procedure (work product) or evidence (privilege); copyright law; the rules of discipline (withdrawal); and specialized statutes or common law rules that your research in these other areas might uncover (shop-right doctrine, attorney retaining liens). Notice that you must be able to brainstorm analogous doctrines from other areas of law, because few matters of attorney regulation are governed solely by rules of professional conduct.

interests
entitled reasonable
bailment possession withdrawal
papers retention
attorney privilege costs **lien** ownership
copy paid **possessory** retain
property **work product**
discovery shopright doctrine
retaining **file** original **client**
copying surrender discharged
copyright

Now you try it. You are representing a client in a securities matter based on financial records the client has provided to you. You have filed reports to the SEC, and have brought claims and made defenses in district court all based on these records. However, you have now discovered that your client has lied to you and falsified these records. What are your obligations if you continue to represent this client without correcting the statements made to the SEC and the courts? Brainstorm all the areas of law and search terms that might be relevant in researching this issue.

2.2 What Are Rules of Professional Conduct?

We begin our examination of the many sources of attorney regulation by looking at rules of professional conduct. There are two misconceptions to avoid in studying these rules.

First, do not presume that the ABA Model Rules are the law. Because the multistate professional responsibility exam (MPRE) tests the ABA Model Rules and because many textbooks and study guides focus on the ABA Model Rules, students sometimes forget that these are just what they are titled: models. They are not primary authority. Like any other "model" code, the ABA Model Rules do not have the force of law unless the state or federal court adopts them as official regulations.

That being said, the rules of professional conduct in most jurisdictions are drawn largely from the ABA's Model Rules of Professional Conduct. First adopted in 1983, they now provide the basis for the state court rules of conduct in all states except California. In addition, some states retain specific rules drawn from the older ABA Model Code of Professional Responsibility. These state adoptions are the source of disciplinary regulation of attorney conduct at the state level (and usually by incorporation in the federal courts as well). These rules are adopted as court rules in some states and as legislation in others. However, no state has adopted every one of the ABA Model Rules without some variation. In this text, the rules we focus on for study are drawn from state law. Often the state version will be identical to the ABA Model Rules but sometimes the state version will have some important or common variation.

A second misconception about the rules of professional conduct is that they are a comprehensive source of regulation of attorneys. However, the rules are designed for discipline and discipline is only one part of the picture of attorney regulation. Civil liability, administrative regulation, court control and sanction through the powers of contempt and disqualification, criminal law—all these can be important sources of regulation. Sometimes courts will allow the rules of professional conduct to be introduced as evidence in these other actions, but the rules are not sources of private causes of action.

We will begin by reading a version of Rule 8.4 Misconduct. Consider the following guidelines for reading any rule of professional conduct and apply these guidelines to reading 8.4.

2.3 Reading the Rules: Basic Guidelines for Reading a Rule of Professional Conduct

In practice, you will find many situations in which you must locate a statute or rule governing your situation and you will need to understand its meaning and application without benefit of any other sources to help guide your understanding. How do attorneys approach reading a rule to understand its meaning and application? In reading any rule, attorneys look for context, relationships, structure, and reasons. They often will "diagram" the rule or find some other way to visualize the rule. Finally, they will use their imaginations to conceive how the rule might apply.

We will use Missouri Supreme Court Rule 4-8.4 as our first rule on which to practice our rule reading skills. This version of Rule 8.4 is identical to ABA Model Rule 8.4 except for the italicized subsection. First read through the entire rule one time.

Rule 4—Rules Governing the Missouri Bar and the Judiciary— Rules of Professional Conduct
4-8.4 Maintaining the Integrity of the Profession—Misconduct

It is professional misconduct for a lawyer to:

(a) violate or attempt to violate the Rules of Professional Conduct, knowingly assist or induce another to do so, or do so through the acts of another;

(b) commit a criminal act that reflects adversely on the lawyer's honesty, trustworthiness, or fitness as a lawyer in other respects;

(c) engage in conduct involving dishonesty, fraud, deceit, or misrepresentation;

(d) engage in conduct that is prejudicial to the administration of justice;

(e) state or imply an ability to influence improperly a government agency or official or to achieve results by means that violate the Rules of Professional Conduct or other law;

(f) knowingly assist a judge or judicial officer in conduct that is a violation of applicable rules of judicial conduct or other law; or

(g) manifest by words or conduct, in representing a client, bias or prejudice based upon race, sex, religion, national origin, disability, age, or sexual orientation. This Rule 4-8.4(g) does not preclude legitimate advocacy when race, sex, religion, national origin, disability, age, sexual orientation, or other similar factors, are issues.

Now, go back through the rule using the following system to guide your reading:

Context

As with any rule or statutory provision, the place to start is to place the rule in context of the larger set of rules. The rules of professional conduct are divided into sections with numbers 1 — 8. The rules in section 8 are labeled "Maintaining the Integrity of the Profession." What does that tell you about how you might read this rule?

Relationships

Especially with regard to the rules of professional conduct, be aware of the relationship between the rule and other rules and law that may regulate attorneys. What is the relationship between Rule 4-8.4 and the remainder of the rules of conduct? Look carefully at 4-8.4(a). The remaining provisions of Rule 4-8.4 refer to other standards. Where would you find those other standards?

Structure

Read with a sense of structure. Read the entire rule before you begin to interpret any one part. One of the dangerous reading habits we acquire in our electronic search world is the habit of "mining" rather than reading. That is, we look for key language in a case, statute, or article and then read only the brief information around that key language. This approach to reading a statute or rule is a road to malpractice, however. More often than not, a particular statute or rule contains qualifying language at the beginning or exceptions at the end. If you read only a subsection, you will simply get it wrong. This is true not only for an individual statutory or rule section but for the chapter or set of rules as a whole. Most state rules of professional conduct adopt the organization of the ABA Model Rules of Professional Conduct, with comments following the rules, separate sections providing definitions (*see* Rule 1.0 Terminology), and rules for interpreting the statute or rule (the Preamble to the Model Rules, for example, identifies the role of the rules and the comments). Many states also provide additional state-specific comments, legislative history, and comparisons between the state rule and the ABA Model Rules.

Reasons

Ask why. The best way to clear up ambiguities in a rule (or at least to understand the nature of those ambiguities) is to understand the purpose or purposes of the rule. Obviously, these purposes will not always be clear or explicit. Time spent conceiving the purpose for a rule can go a long way toward increasing your understanding of the rule itself.

Visualize

Often complex rules are best unraveled by diagramming the rule so that you can visually see the structure between the different parts of the rule. This is particularly so for those with strong visual learning preferences. For anyone, no matter their learning preference, to the extent that you work with the rule in some active way and make it your own, you will increase learning.

Some rules, like 4-8.4, are simply lists (in this case, a list of situations that define "misconduct"). One important consideration in reading any list is determining the relationship between the parts. Is the list more like a menu, in which you can pick one subsection and apply it on its own, or is it more like a recipe in which all subsections are necessary to meet the definition? The answer is usually found in the "and" or the "or" at the end of the penultimate subsection.

A second consideration applies when reading lists. Do not automatically assume that each subsection is only one item in the menu or one ingredient in the recipe. There are seven subsections in this rule, but some of those subsections are themselves lists (like subsection a). Rewriting a rule into a structure that allows you to see each distinct part is an excellent way to make the rule your own.

Consider the following visual organization of Rule 8.4. Complete the chart.

Misconduct =
    Violate a rule
        Yourself
            Actual violation
            Attempted violation
        Through another
            Knowingly assist another to violate
            Knowingly induce another to violate
            Violate through the acts of another;
OR   Criminal act that
        Reflects adversely on the your honesty or trustworthiness
        Reflects adversely on your fitness as a lawyer in other respects;
OR   Conduct involving
        Dishonesty
        Fraud
        Deceit, or
        Misrepresentation;
OR …

Visually breaking up the rule's elements forces you to consider each element separately and determine the relationship among elements. For example, why does "knowingly" modify only "assist or induce"? Does this mean if you personally violate the rules, it doesn't matter if you do so knowingly? Why do you suppose the drafters chose the list of conduct in part c of the rule? Wouldn't the term "dishonesty" alone include all the other terms in the list?

Imagine

Read with your imagination. When you are reading a rule or statute to find the answer to a particular problem, you already have a set of facts that will help you to think about the rule and its application. But when you are simply trying to familiarize yourself with a statute or rule to guide future conduct (whether your own or your current or future clients), you must imagine the facts that will go with the rules. What would be an example of "conduct prejudicial to the administration of justice"? What would be a criminal act that would NOT "reflect adversely on the lawyer's honesty, trustworthiness, or fitness as a lawyer in other respects"? For each key term in the rule, think of clear examples of what falls within the rule and outside the rule and then think of examples of the gray areas in between.

Test Your Understanding

How do you know what you know? One important way to test your understanding of a rule is to simply see how much you recall after you have finished studying. Stop and close your book. Write or say as much of the rule as you can remember. Explain the meaning of key terms and the purposes of the rule. Then go back and re-read the rule and see what you have missed. This practice of recalling knowledge is one of the best ways to truly learn a subject and will provide you with more long-term learning than simply reading again or even taking more notes or otherwise working from the text.

Problems for Practice

1. Arnold Attorney is a member of the Missouri bar. He is also licensed as a real estate broker. Recently, Arnold was called before the Real Estate Commission for violating the rules against purchasing property without disclosing that he was a licensed broker. The Commission placed Arnold on probation for six months. Is he subject to discipline under Rule 4-8.4? *[handwritten: misrepresentation]*
   A. Yes, because his actions involve dishonesty or misrepresentation.
   B. Yes, because his actions violate the law.
   C. No, because his action was not in his capacity as an attorney.
   D. No, because his action did not result in a criminal conviction.

2. Attorney has a brand new sports car and has gotten three speeding tickets in the past month (each is a misdemeanor violation), resulting in a six-month suspension of her driver's license. She did not cause any damage due to the speeding, she paid for all the tickets in a timely fashion, and she has not driven while her license is suspended. Is Attorney also subject to discipline?
   A. Yes, because she has a criminal conviction.
   B. Yes, because her repeated violations demonstrate conduct prejudicial to the administration of justice.
   C. No, because speeding is not conduct that reflects adversely on Attorney's honesty, trustworthiness, or fitness.
   D. No, because the Double Jeopardy clause of the Constitution would prohibit punishing her again for the same actions.

3. Attorney has a drinking problem that has become reflected in his repeated arrests for driving while intoxicated. However, through aggressive representation by his lawyer and a willingness to plead to and pay high fines for reckless driving or other non-alcohol related offenses, Attorney also has managed thus far to avoid conviction for driving while intoxicated. Is Attorney subject to discipline? *[handwritten: pled down]*
   A. Yes, because his plea bargaining to alternate driving infractions is conduct prejudicial to the administration of justice.
   B. Yes, because driving while intoxicated is criminal conduct that reflects adversely on Attorney's fitness.
   C. No, because attorney has not been convicted of a crime that would reflect adversely on Attorney's honesty, trustworthiness, or fitness.
   D. No, because attorney's conduct was not in the course of representing a client.

4. Attorney recently lost a major discrimination action for firing his secretary because she was "too attractive and was a distraction to him" and she refused to go out with him after work. He regularly refers to other female employees as "honey" and "sugar" and comments on their appearance. He does not often represent women but that is as much a function of the gender representation

in the construction industry he represents as his own practices. He has never had a complaint about his treatment of women clients, witnesses, or attorneys. Is Attorney subject to discipline?

A. Yes, because Attorney manifests bias based on sex.

B. Yes, because Attorney's conduct is prejudicial to the administration of justice.

C. No, because his attitudes do not interfere with his competent representation of his clients.

D. No, because his biased conduct is not in the course of representing a client.

Analysis

1. The best answer is A. The key to understanding this question is to recognize that each of the subsections of 8.4 is a separate basis for misconduct. The remaining incorrect choices should reinforce your understanding that not all violations of the law are misconduct, while, at the same time, conduct needn't be criminal and needn't be in one's capacity as an attorney to constitute misconduct.

2. The best answer is C. Speeding is not likely to be considered conduct that reflects adversely on Attorney's honesty, trustworthiness, or fitness. The fact that the rule does not make all criminal conduct a basis for misconduct means that the drafters were looking for some connection to the practice of law. While speeding might not be a good thing, and in some instances might reflect a larger disregard for law, it is hard to establish a close link between mere speeding and any behaviors that would lead an attorney to harm clients or the legal system. You might make an argument that speeding is "conduct prejudicial to the administration of justice" but as a practical matter this standard is nearly always applied to conduct which also at least arguably fits one of the other categories of misconduct. While broad and open-textured, the standard has generally withstood constitutional challenge. *See, e.g., In re Keiler*, 380 A.2d 119, 126 (D.C. 1977) ("a rule setting guidelines for members of the bar need not meet the precise standards of clarity that might be required for rules of conduct for laymen.") Answer D is not correct because discipline is not considered punishment for the purposes of the Double Jeopardy clause.

3. The best answer is B. (Notice that the subsection b says "commit a criminal act" not "be convicted of a criminal act" — so a charge and conviction are not necessary). In most states, if an attorney is convicted of a felony, this will result in expedited discipline and is a *per se* violation of this section (unlike the misdemeanor convictions, such as speeding, that must be independently analyzed for whether they reflect adversely on honesty, trustworthiness, or fitness in other respects). You can debate the relevance of the crime (is drunk driving really something that reflects on an attorney's fitness?) but given the prevalence of alcoholism in the profession and its close connection with discipline, you are unlikely to prevail. Likewise, you might argue that the common practice of plea bargaining in traffic offenses cases is dishonest or unjust; however, it is such an integral part of the system that it is unlikely that participating in that system would be considered misconduct.

4. The best answer is B. C may be true as a matter of fact, but it does not reflect the definitions of misconduct and so it not the best answer. A is also true as a matter of fact, but again it does not reflect the rule accurately. D is the reason that 8.4(g) would not provide the basis for misconduct. This is an interesting addition to the rules and very narrowly drawn as you can see by this problem.

It was proposed as an addition to the Model Rules but was eventually only included as a comment to the Rule 8.4 (comment 3). But just because the narrower definition of misconduct does not apply, that doesn't mean another provision won't apply. While many jurisdictions do not have this rule as part of their definition of misconduct, nonetheless they do impose discipline for biased conduct under the standard of "conduct prejudicial to the administration of justice"—usually for conduct that has occurred in connection with client representation but not necessarily so. *See, e.g., In re Peters*, 428 N.W.2d 375 (Minn. 1988) (neither conviction for crime nor attorney-client relationship are necessary to support discipline for attorney's sexual harassment of employees). *See generally*, Gregory G. Sarno, Annotation, *Sexual Misconduct as Ground for Disciplining Attorney or Judge*, 43 A.L.R. 4th 1062 (1986, 2011 Supp.) (collecting cases).

2.4 What Is the Significance of Law as a Self-Regulated Profession?

When an attorney violates a rule of professional conduct, how does this misconduct come to the attention of regulatory authorities? Courts, which in most states are responsible for administering the disciplinary structure, do not have an enforcement staff to investigate and unearth misconduct. Rather, it is through the reports of clients, the courts, and attorneys themselves that misconduct is brought to light.

Attorneys have the duty to police each other's conduct. Using the same guidelines you applied to reading Rule 8.4, read Rule 8.3 of the Model Rules of Professional Conduct in your rule supplement or online. A helpful way to diagram this rule might be to use the journalists' investigation questions. For example, ask yourself:

Whose conduct must be reported?
What does an attorney have to report?
When does the reporting duty arise?
When must the report be made?
To whom must the report be made?

In reading the rule, you will see that there are several key terms that require interpretation in order to apply the rule to any given situation. Notice as well that part (c) of the rule provides two exceptions to the duty to report: when information is protected by the attorney's duty of confidentiality to a client and when the information was gained while participating in "an approved lawyers assistance program." The following case provides an excellent example of the attorney's reporting obligation. Pay particular attention to the court's resolution of some of the issues regarding the reporting obligation.

In re Riehlmann

cancer telk friend he lied on case

891 So. 2d 1239 (La. 2005)

This disciplinary matter arises from formal charges filed by the Office of Disciplinary Counsel ("ODC") against respondent, Michael G. Riehlmann, an attorney licensed to practice law in Louisiana.

Underlying Facts

Respondent is a criminal defense attorney who was formerly employed as an Assistant District Attorney in the Orleans Parish District Attorney's Office. One evening in April 1994, respondent met his close friend and law school classmate, Gerry Deegan, at a bar near the Orleans Parish Criminal District Court. Like respondent, Mr. Deegan had been a prosecutor in the Orleans Parish District Attorney's Office before he "switched sides" in 1987. During their conversation in the bar, Mr. Deegan told respondent that he had that day learned he was dying of colon cancer. In the same conversation, Mr. Deegan confided to respondent that he had suppressed exculpatory blood evidence in a criminal case he prosecuted while at the District Attorney's Office. Respondent recalls that he was "surprised" and "shocked" by his friend's revelation, and that he urged Mr. Deegan to "remedy" the situation. It is undisputed that respondent did not report Mr. Deegan's disclosure to anyone at the time it was made. Mr. Deegan died in July 1994, having done nothing to "remedy" the situation of which he had spoken in the bar.

Nearly five years after Mr. Deegan's death, one of the defendants whom he had prosecuted in a 1985 armed robbery case was set to be executed by lethal injection on May 20, 1999. In April 1999, the lawyers for the defendant, John Thompson, discovered a crime lab report which contained the results of tests performed on a piece of pants leg and a tennis shoe that were stained with the perpetrator's blood during a scuffle with the victim of the robbery attempt. The crime lab report concluded that the robber had Type "B" blood. Because Mr. Thompson has Type "O" blood, the crime lab report proved he could not have committed the robbery; nevertheless, neither the crime lab report nor the blood-stained physical evidence had been disclosed to Mr. Thompson's defense counsel prior to or during trial. Respondent claims that when he heard about the inquiry of Mr. Thompson's lawyers, he immediately realized that this was the case to which Mr. Deegan had referred in their April 1994 conversation in the bar. On April 27, 1999, respondent executed an affidavit for Mr. Thompson in which he attested that during the 1994 conversation, "the late Gerry Deegan said to me that he had intentionally suppressed blood evidence in the armed robbery trial of John Thompson that in some way exculpated the defendant."

In May 1999, respondent reported Mr. Deegan's misconduct to the ODC. In June 1999, respondent testified in a hearing on a motion for new trial in Mr. Thompson's armed robbery case. During the hearing, respondent testified that Mr. Deegan had told him that he "suppressed exculpatory evidence that was blood evidence, that seemed to have excluded Mr. Thompson as the perpetrator of an armed robbery." Respondent also admitted that he "should have reported" Mr. Deegan's misconduct, and that while he ultimately did so, "I should have reported it sooner, I guess."

On September 30, 1999, respondent gave a sworn statement to the ODC in which he was asked why he did not report Mr. Deegan's disclosure to anyone at the time it was made. Respondent replied:

> I think that under ordinary circumstances, I would have. I really honestly think I'm a very good person. And I think I do the right thing whenever I'm given the opportunity to choose. This was un-questionably the most difficult time of my life. Gerry, who was like

a brother to me, was dying. And that was, to say distracting would be quite an understatement. I'd also left my wife just a few months before, with three kids, and was under the care of a psychiatrist, taking antidepressants. My youngest son was then about two and had just recently undergone open-heart surgery. I had a lot on my plate at the time. A great deal of it of my own making; there's no question about it. But, nonetheless, I was very, very distracted, and I simply did not give it the important consideration that it deserved. But it was a very trying time for me. *And that's the only explanation I have, because, otherwise, I would have reported it immediately had I been in a better frame of mind.* [Emphasis added.]

Disciplinary Proceedings

[The Office of Disciplinary Counsel filed formal charges against Deegan, for violations of Rules 8.3(a) and 8.4(d). A formal hearing before a committee was held. The hearing committee recommended a public reprimand for violation of Rule 8.4(d). Both respondent and the ODC filed objections to the hearing committee's recommendation, so the case proceeded to the Disciplinary Board.]

Discussion

In this matter we are presented for the first time with an opportunity to delineate the scope of an attorney's duty under Rule 8.3 to report the professional misconduct of a fellow member of the bar. Therefore, we begin our discussion with a few observations relating to the rule and its history.

At the time the formal charges were filed in this case, Louisiana Rule 8.3(a) provided:

> A lawyer possessing unprivileged knowledge of a violation of this code shall report such knowledge to a tribunal or other authority empowered to investigate or act upon such violation.

Thus, the rule has three distinct requirements: (1) the lawyer must possess unprivileged knowledge of a violation of the Rules of Professional Conduct; (2) the lawyer must report that knowledge; and (3) the report must be made to a tribunal or other authority empowered to investigate or act on the violation. We will discuss each requirement in turn.

Knowledge

... [A]bsolute certainty of ethical misconduct is not required before the reporting requirement is triggered. The lawyer is not required to conduct an investigation and make a definitive decision that a violation has occurred before reporting; that responsibility belongs to the disciplinary system and this court. On the other hand, knowledge requires more than a mere suspicion of ethical misconduct. We hold that a lawyer will be found to have knowledge of reportable misconduct, and thus reporting is required, where the supporting evidence is such that a reasonable lawyer under the circumstances would form a firm belief that the conduct in question had more likely than not occurred. As such, knowledge is measured by an objective standard that is not tied to the subjective beliefs of the lawyer in question.

The attorney says that, but for the distraction of his personal problems, he surely would have reported. Yet, one can imagine the bonds of friendship would have provided a significant disincentive to reporting as well. Can you think of other reasons attorneys might be reluctant to report another's misconduct?

Notice that the knowledge relates to the "conduct in question" — Suppose an attorney knows of conduct, but is not sure whether that conduct violates the rules? Why does the court adopt an objective measure here?

When to Report

Once the lawyer decides that a reportable offense has likely occurred, reporting should be made promptly. Arthur F. Greenbaum, *The Attorney's Duty to Report Professional Misconduct: A Roadmap for Reform*, 16 Geo. J. Legal Ethics 259, 298 (2003). The need for prompt reporting flows from the need to safeguard the public and the profession against future wrongdoing by the offending lawyer. *Id.* This purpose is not served unless Rule 8.3(a) is read to require timely reporting under the circumstances presented.

Why isn't the court more specific about a timeliness requirement? Could you improve this definition to make the standard clearer? Is a clearer standard necessarily better?

Appropriate Authority

Louisiana Rule 8.3(a) requires that the report be made to "a tribunal or other authority empowered to investigate or act upon such violation." The term "tribunal or other authority" is not specifically defined. However, as the comments to Model Rule 8.3(a) explain, the report generally should be made to the bar disciplinary authority. Therefore, a report of misconduct by a lawyer admitted to practice in Louisiana must be made to the Office of Disciplinary Counsel.

Determination of Respondent's Misconduct and Appropriate Discipline

Applying the principles set forth above to the conduct of respondent in the instant case, we find the ODC proved by clear and convincing evidence that respondent violated Rule 8.3(a). First, we find that respondent should have known that a reportable event occurred at the time of his 1994 barroom conversation with Mr. Deegan. Stated another way, respondent's conversation with Mr. Deegan at that time gave him sufficient information that a reasonable lawyer under the circumstances would have formed a firm opinion that the conduct in question more likely than not occurred. Regardless of the actual words Mr. Deegan said that night, and whether they were or were not "equivocal," respondent understood from the conversation that Mr. Deegan had done something wrong.

Is knowing that an attorney had done "something wrong" is the same thing as knowing that an attorney had violated the rules? Does the court simply presume that every attorney knows the prosecutor's Brady obligations? Should it?

Respondent admitted as much in his affidavit, during the hearing on the motion for new trial in the criminal case, during his sworn statement to the ODC, and during his testimony at the formal hearing. Indeed, during the sworn statement respondent conceded that he would have reported the matter "immediately" were it not for the personal problems he was then experiencing. Respondent also testified that he was surprised and shocked by his friend's revelation, and that he told him to remedy the situation. There would have been no reason for respondent to react in the manner he did had he not formed a firm opinion that the conduct in question more likely than not occurred. The circumstances under which the conversation took place lend further support to this finding. On the same day that he learned he was dying of cancer, Mr. Deegan felt compelled to tell his best friend about something he had done in a trial that took place nine years earlier. It simply defies logic that respondent would now argue that he could not be sure that Mr. Deegan actually withheld Brady evidence because his statements were vague and non-specific.

Would it have been improper for him to wait until his friend had died in order to spare him the pain of disciplinary proceedings?

We also find that respondent failed to promptly report Mr. Deegan's misconduct to the disciplinary authorities. As respondent himself acknowledged, he should have reported Mr. Deegan's statements sooner than he did. There was no reason for respondent to have waited five years to tell the ODC about what his friend had done.

In his answer to the formal charges, respondent asserts that he did comply with the reporting requirement of Rule 8.3(a) because he promptly reported Mr. Deegan's misconduct to the District Attorney and the Criminal District Court through the attorneys for the criminal defendant, John Thompson. Respondent has misinterpreted Rule 8.3(a) in this regard. The word "tribunal" must be read in the context of the entire sentence in which it appears. The proper inquiry, therefore, is what authority is "empowered" to act upon a charge of attorney misconduct. In Louisiana, only this court possesses the authority to define and regulate the practice of law, including the discipline of attorneys. La. Const. art. V, §5(B); *In re Bar Exam Class Action*, 99-2880 (La. 2/18/00), 752 So. 2d 159, 160. In turn, we have delegated to disciplinary counsel the authority to investigate and prosecute claims of attorney misconduct. Supreme Court Rule XIX, §4. Furthermore, while a trial court bears an independent responsibility to report attorney misconduct to the ODC, *see* Canon 3B (3) of the Code of Judicial Conduct, only this court may discipline an attorney found guilty of unethical behavior. Therefore, respondent is incorrect in arguing that he discharged his reporting duty under Rule 8.3(a) by reporting Mr. Deegan's misconduct to Mr. Thompson's attorneys, the District Attorney, and/or the Criminal District Court. It is undisputed that respondent did not report to the appropriate entity, the ODC, until 1999. That report came too late to be construed as "prompt."

Having found professional misconduct, we now turn to a discussion of an appropriate sanction. In considering that issue, we are mindful that the purpose of disciplinary proceedings is not primarily to punish the lawyer, but rather to maintain the appropriate standards of professional conduct, to preserve the integrity of the legal profession, and to deter other lawyers from engaging in violations of the standards of the profession. The discipline to be imposed depends upon the facts of each case and the seriousness of the offenses involved, considered in light of any aggravating and mitigating circumstances.

Respondent's actions violated the general duty imposed upon attorneys to maintain and preserve the integrity of the bar. *In re Brigandi*, 02-2873 (La. 4/9/03), 843 So. 2d 1083 (*citing Louisiana State Bar Ass'n v. Weysham*, 307 So. 2d 336 (La. 1975)). While we adhere to our observation in *Brigandi* that an attorney's failure to comply with the reporting requirement is a "serious offense," in the instant case, we find that respondent's conduct was merely negligent. Accordingly, Standard 7.3 of the ABA's Standards for Imposing Lawyer Sanctions provides that the appropriate baseline sanction is a reprimand.

Notice that the ABA Standards — another "Model" — are cited as authoritative

The only aggravating factor present in this case is respondent's substantial experience in the practice of law. As for mitigating factors, we adopt those recognized by the disciplinary board, placing particular emphasis on the absence of any dishonest or selfish motive on respondent's part. Notwithstanding these factors, however, respondent's failure to report Mr. Deegan's bad acts necessitates that some sanction be imposed. Respondent's knowledge of Mr. Deegan's conduct was sufficient to impose on him an obligation to promptly report Mr. Deegan to the ODC. Having failed in that obligation, respondent is himself subject to punishment. Under all of the circumstances presented, we conclude that a public reprimand is the appropriate sanction.

A dissenting judge would have imposed harsher sanctions. What do you think was the appropriate discipline for the attorney's conduct in this case? Why?

Accordingly, we will reprimand respondent for his actions.

Conclusion

Reporting another lawyer's misconduct to disciplinary authorities is an important duty of every lawyer. Lawyers are in the best position to observe professional misconduct and to assist the profession in sanctioning it. While a Louisiana lawyer is subject to discipline for not reporting misconduct, it is our hope that lawyers will comply with their reporting obligation primarily because they are ethical people who want to serve their clients and the public well. Moreover, the lawyer's duty to report professional misconduct is the foundation for the claim that we can be trusted to regulate ourselves as a profession. If we fail in our duty, we forfeit that trust and have no right to enjoy the privilege of self-regulation or the confidence and respect of the public.

Decree

Upon review of the findings and recommendations of the hearing committee and disciplinary board, and considering the record, briefs, and oral argument, it is ordered that Michael G. Riehlmann, Louisiana Bar Roll number 2072, be publicly reprimanded. All costs and expenses in the matter are assessed against respondent in accordance with Supreme Court Rule XIX, § 10.1, with legal interest to commence thirty days from the date of finality of this court's judgment until paid.

Notes

1. As you may have noted, there are several differences between the ABA Model Rule of Professional Conduct and the Louisiana Rule that was in effect at the time this case was decided. Most states have some variations on the reporting requirement. At one end of the spectrum is Kansas, which requires a lawyer to report knowledge of "any action, inaction or conduct that in his or her opinion constitutes misconduct of an attorney under these rules." This rule requires reporting *any* misconduct by *any* attorney (including yourself). At the other end of the spectrum are states like Georgia, which use the standards of Model Rule 8.3 but make the rule aspirational rather than mandatory ("should" rather than "shall"). In between, states have a number of other variations of the who, what, and when of reporting. Which version of the rules do you think makes better policy sense? The choice is not insignificant. Professor Susan Daicoff, in her study of ethical decision making by attorneys, found that attorneys who reported a fellow attorney's misconduct most often relied on rules to justify their decision.

   > ... [I]f left to one's personal values and standards, the choice [to report a colleague] might be less ethical and less conservative than if one followed what the law or legal code of ethics requires.... When carrying out an unpleasant task, like reporting a colleague's misconduct, it may be easier to accept that the law or legal code of ethics requires some particular action than to justify taking action based on one's own personal stan-

dards. This would explain why attorneys tended to rely on laws and codes in justifying their more ethical, conservative choices [to report a colleague's clear misconduct].

Susan Daicoff, *(Oxymoron?) Ethical Decisionmaking by Attorneys: An Empirical Study,* 48 FLA. L. REV. 197, 246 (1996).

2. What if the misconduct is not by a friend but by an attorney in your firm? In addition to the risk of discipline for failing to report misconduct, you may also have a risk of liability to clients or reputational harm for your own association with this misconduct. If you are in a supervisory position relative to the attorney, you may also be subject to discipline under Rule 5.1.

   Reporting misconduct by senior attorneys in your firm presents its own risks. Jurisdictions that have addressed the issue are split over whether an attorney has a cause of action if they are fired for reporting under Rule 8.3. The Illinois courts have refused to recognize a cause of action for retaliatory discharge. *Jacobson v. Knepper & Moga,* 706 N.E.2d 491 (Ill. 1998). Similarly, the Texas court in *Bohatch v. Butler & Binion,* 977 S.W.2d 543 (Tex. 1998) found no cause of action for a partner of a law firm who was expelled from the partnership after reporting suspicions of overbilling. Later opinions have been more protective of attorneys who are whistleblowers. The New York court in *Weider v. Skala,* 609 N.E.2d 105 (N.Y. 1992) held that every law firm's employment contract with its associates contains an implied term that the firm will support compliance with the rules of professional conduct and a firm that interferes with this duty to report by firing an associate may be liable for breach of contract. Similar approaches can be found in the following unreported opinions: *Keeling v. Kronick, Moskovitz, Tiedemann & Girard,* Civ. No. JFM-00-133, 2001 WL 21224. 2001 U.S. Dist. Lexis 209 (D. Md. 2001) (applying California law) and *Matzkin v. Delaney, Zemetis, Donahue, Durham & Noonan PC,* No. CV044000288S,w6 2005 WL 2009277 (Conn. Super. Ct. 2005). To learn more about this issue, see Douglas R. Richmond, *Professional Responsibilities of Law Firm Associates,* 45 BRANDEIS L.J. 199 (2007).

   How can you know whether you are joining a firm that is likely to demand that you engage in or cover up unethical conduct?

3. There are two exceptions to the reporting requirement. One is for confidential client information. We will study the boundaries of the duty of confidentiality in the next unit, but for now you should understand that if you come to know of another attorney's misconduct through the representation of a client (for example, from the client himself or from your investigation of the client's case), you may still report the attorney, but in doing so you may not reveal confidential client information or report in a time or manner that would undermine the client's interest. RESTATEMENT (THIRD) OF THE LAW GOVERNING LAWYERS § 5, cmt i (2000).

   A second exception to reporting requirements is "information gained by a lawyer or judge while participating in an approved lawyers assistance program." Every state has a program to assist the profession in recognizing, preventing, and addressing chemical dependencies, stress, depression, and other emotional health issues. Find the website for your state or local lawyer assistance agency and survey some of the resources available there. A directory of these programs is available from the ABA Commission on Lawyer Assistance Programs at *www.abanet.org/legalservices/colap/lapdirectory.html*.

Researching Professional Responsibility 2-B: Finding Disciplinary Rules

The ability to locate relevant resources to guide your professional conduct is critical to ethical practice. How you tackle your research depends on the type of research problem you are facing. Sometimes, an ethical issue arises in the context of a particular set of laws that you already have identified as applicable — for example, you may want to know whether the particular conduct would provide a basis for sanctions under the discovery rules of civil procedure, or you may have a question about whether your conduct would subject you to discipline. For this kind of targeted research, you would research the law in much the same way as in any other area of law, looking for statutes, rules, administrative standards, and cases that apply to your situation.

You likely already are familiar with finding cases or statutes on a given topic, but finding rules of professional conduct may not be something you have practiced. As you recall reading, rules of professional conduct in most states are promulgated by the state supreme court. Where are the state rules of professional conduct found in your state? There are several easy routes to locating your state's rules: Online, you could simply use a search engine to search for "[your state] rules of professional conduct." Be sure that whatever you find through this general web search is an official and current version of the rules. Or you could begin with the American Bar Association Center for Professional Responsibility at www.abanet.org/cpr/links.html or the American Legal Ethics Library from Cornell's Legal Information Institute at *www.law.cornell.edu/ethics/listing.html*. Both of these online sources are free.

Online subscription services can also be excellent sources of research of course. Westlaw has databases for state professional responsibility standards, which you can most easily find by starting with the "Legal Ethics and Professional Responsibility" database. There you will find a listing of the court rules for each state, and their individual database identifiers are XX-RULES (with XX as the state's postal abbreviation). Likewise, in Lexis, by starting with the ethics library and following the path: "Legal > Area of Law—By Topic > Ethics > Find Statutes & Rules" you can locate the court rules that govern attorneys in your state. Note, however, that in both these approaches you will be searching in databases that contain other state court rules as well. Sometimes that is exactly what you might want to do, for example, if you want to use opinions interpreting a rule from other states, you will need to know that the other state has the same or a similar rule as your own.

One of the best sources of professional responsibility research is the ABA/Bloomberg BNA Lawyers Manual on Professional Conduct. The manual is available online through subscription, either directly through www.bna.com or as a special subscription through Westlaw or Lexis. The manual lists the ethics codes of each state with a link to a free, online web resource for the code. The manual also contains comparisons between the ABA Model Rules and state variations.

Of course, even without a computer you can find the law! For nearly all states, the book to start with is the most recent copy of your state supreme court's rules.

In some states, the rules of professional conduct are published as part of the state's statutes.

Practice researching the rules of your state by identifying the rule governing an attorney's obligations to report misconduct of other attorneys. Locate your state's rules of professional conduct and answer the following questions: What is the proper citation to your state's rule regarding reporting professional misconduct? What are the elements of the reporting obligation (or aspirational standard) in your state?

2.5. The Disciplinary Process

The Rules of Professional Conduct do not indicate what happens after a complaint or report is received. Rather, this is a matter for separate regulation. Once again, the ABA has been influential in this area, providing model guidelines. The "Standards for Lawyer Discipline," adopted in 1979, suggest procedures for discipline. A range of sanctions and guidelines for imposing these sanctions were adopted in the 1986 "Standards for Imposing Lawyer Sanctions." These standards have been adopted by some states as their official discipline system. Other states draw on the guidelines as sources to interpret their own discipline standards. As with the conduct rules, discipline procedures and standards may be found in state or federal codes, in court rules, or both.

Once a complaint or a report is received, disciplinary authorities will usually notify the attorney about whom the complaint or report has been made. Even though disciplinary actions are *sui generis*, neither criminal nor civil but designed for the protection of the public, attorneys do have some basic due process protections. For example, the U.S. Supreme Court in *In re Ruffalo*, 390 U.S. 544 (1968) held that a lawyer has a due process right to fair notice of the charges against him in disciplinary actions. In *Spevack v. Klein*, 385 U.S. 511 (1967), the Court concluded that the attorney could invoke the privilege against self-incrimination. The disciplinary authority may conduct further investigations and may then pursue several options, depending on the specific rules of the jurisdiction.

They may conclude that there is insufficient basis for bringing disciplinary charges. There may be a problem, but not one that amounts to a violation of the rules. In these instances, disciplinary authorities may refer the attorney or client to other services. Many complaints to disciplinary agencies from clients relate to fee disputes with the attorney or communication difficulties. Increasingly states have mediation services available to assist attorneys and clients in resolving these disputes without disciplinary intervention. In some instances, the complaint or report may not identify rule violations but may raise a generalized concern about the attorney's fitness due to addiction, depression, or other health states. Disciplinary authority may suggest that the attorney speak with the state lawyer assistance program for confidential assistance with these issues.

Disciplinary counsel may not have substantial or clear evidence of a violation, but may nonetheless feel there is a need for response to educate the attorney or reform his or her conduct. In a number of states, disciplinary counsel may enter into a "diversion agreement" with the attorney, providing that if the attorney successfully completes specific educational programs or oversight, no formal disciplinary charges will be filed.

When disciplinary authorities do file charges, the process then proceeds in a manner similar to criminal proceedings. A formal charge is filed to which the attorney must respond in a timely fashion or the charges will be deemed admitted. An attorney may choose to voluntarily surrender his or her license, in the hopes of heading off charges, but resignation does not prevent discipline. If the attorney does respond, there will then be an opportunity for discovery and some sort of trial or hearing. The disciplinary authority will then issue a recommendation of discipline, with which the attorney can either acquiesce or appeal. If the resulting discipline is a private reprimand, it is just that — not publicly published or available. However, the private record of that reprimand can become a basis for imposing increased sanction in any subsequent disciplinary actions. A public reprimand is reported, generally in the state bar publication or state court website.

Suspensions are more serious discipline — even if only for a brief period of time, a suspension requires that an attorney notify all his or her clients and the courts and engage in no practice of law whatsoever during the period of suspension. Violating a suspension order is contempt of court and itself a violation of the rules of professional conduct. Sometimes a disciplinary authority may place probationary conditions on an attorney's suspension, either during, after, or in lieu of the actual suspension itself. These might include education, reporting, supervision, or limitations on practice. Finally, the most serious discipline is disbarment. A disbarred attorney may, in some circumstances, apply for reinstatement, so that even this sanction need not mean an attorney may never practice law again.

Because the process for admitting attorneys to practice or disciplining them once admitted is designed to protect the public, it always involves a certain degree of prediction. The task for the courts in these proceedings is not merely to determine what are the historical facts — the "what happened?" — and then to provide compensation or punishment for that past act. Rather, past actions are merely some evidence the court will consider in determining what is going to happen in the future.

Read the following decision of the Oklahoma Supreme Court reinstating an attorney and think about that process of prediction. What, besides past actions, did the court consider? While none of us ever expects to find ourselves in attorney Whitworth's position, we can learn from his experience nonetheless. What lessons will you draw from his case?

In the Matter of the Reinstatement of Whitworth

Meth addict

2011 Okla. 79, __ P.3d __ (Okla. 2011)

Notice there are two different discipline processes involved here — A Rule 6 proceeding is discipline for misconduct and a Rule 10 proceeding is a proceeding for unfitness. Why do you suppose the court separates these?

Petitioner Whitworth was suspended for two years, beginning on June 26, 2006, following a disciplinary hearing brought by the Respondent Oklahoma Bar Association pursuant to Rule 6, Rules Governing Disciplinary Proceedings (RGDP), 5 O.S. 2001, Ch. 1, App. 1-A. This Court also ordered Petitioner's suspension under Rule 10, RGDP, having found he was personally incapable of practicing law because of his addiction to drugs and alcohol. Petitioner filed his Petition for Reinstatement pursuant to Rule 11, RGDP, on September 3, 2010.

Procedural History

On March 11, 2008, this Court suspended Petitioner John Matthew Whitworth (Whitworth or Petitioner) from the practice of law for two years following disciplinary proceedings brought by the Oklahoma Bar Association (the Bar). The suspension began to run on June 26, 2006,.... [T]his Court found Petitioner was personally incapable of practicing law due to his admitted addiction to methamphetamine and suspended him also under Rule 10. We ordered that "[u]pon regaining sobriety and upon the expiration of his [two-year] suspension period..., Respondent may seek reinstatement by demonstrating his sobriety and by meeting all the requirements for Rule 11 reinstatement."

Petitioner Complied With Rule 11, RGDP

Whitworth's petition for reinstatement, the subject of this proceeding, was filed on September 3, 2010.... Petitioner provided a copy of a cashier's check in the amount of $1,241.18, payable to the OBA for reimbursement of funds expended on his behalf from the Client's Security Fund of the OBA. He also provided a copy of a cashier's check in the amount of $300, payable to the OBA, representing costs incurred in the previous proceeding and further agreed to pay the costs of investigating and processing his petition for reinstatement and the cost of the original and one copy of the hearing transcript.

> A client security fund is provided by the supreme court in all states to reimburse clients for losses due to their attorney's unethical behavior.

... In this reinstatement proceeding, Petitioner contends he is sober and drug-free and wishes to return to the practice of law. [The Professional Responsibility Tribunal (PRT) investigated, held a hearing and recommended reinstatement.]

Jurisdiction, Standard of Review and Burden of Proof

This Court has the nondelegable and constitutional duty to regulate the practice of law and the ethics, licensure, and discipline of practitioners of the law. Our review of the record is de novo, and we are not bound by the findings of fact of the trial panel, or its view of the evidence or the credibility of witnesses. Pursuant to Rule 11.4, RGDP, an applicant for reinstatement must show affirmatively that, if the suspension from practice is removed, his or her conduct will conform to the high standards required of a member of the Bar. The burden of proof by clear and convincing evidence is on the applicant who will be required to present stronger proof of qualifications than an applicant seeking admission for the first time. The proof presented must be sufficient to overcome this Court's former judgment adverse to the applicant.

> The burden of proof is on applicants for admission and readmission but on the state for discipline. Why?

When ruling on a petition for reinstatement, we consider eight factors. They include: 1) present moral fitness; 2) consciousness of the wrongfulness and disrepute it brought upon the legal profession; 3) the extent of the petitioner's rehabilitation; 4) the seriousness of the original misconduct; 5) conduct after discipline; 6) time elapsed since the original discipline; 7) the petitioner's character, maturity, and experience; and 8) present legal competence. Although each factor is relevant when a suspension is the result of an incapacity to practice law, those weighing most heavily to the incapacity are: 1) the extent of rehabilitation of the affliction attributable to the incapacity;

2) the conduct subsequent to the suspension and the treatment received therefor; and 3) the time which has elapsed since the suspension.

Factual Summary and Evidence

Addictions are a common cause of the behaviors that cause discipline — the behaviors are ordinarily the basis for discipline rather than the addictions

Whitworth testified at his reinstatement hearing that he was suspended from the practice of law for his addiction to methamphetamine and alcohol and the consequences which arose from it. His disciplinary hearing was originally set because of other misconduct, the most frequent violation being his failure to respond to the Bar's allegations. However, he stated his addictions to methamphetamine and alcohol were not mentioned in the allegations, and he told the trial panel at his disciplinary hearing "that I was a drug addict addicted to methamphetamine and I was an alcoholic." He testified he did not know whether the Bar would have been otherwise aware of these addictions. He said he made it known because it was a fact, and he had an affirmative duty to report it.

Why did he have a duty to report this?

Petitioner described how his addiction to alcohol destroyed his professional and family life. It destroyed him "economically, mentally, spiritually and physically as well." He discussed having cirrhosis and hepatitis, being homeless, and going long periods of time without seeing his children. He stated his addictions created quite a "wreckage" in his personal life, involving the things "nearest and dearest" to him. He testified his professional life was even more neglected.

However, he stated he "reached bottom" and cried out for help by calling his mother, who called his ex-wife, who called his father. His ex-wife took him to his father's home. He stayed with his father who nursed him back to health from a liver condition which, based on a series of blood tests, would have soon required him to be hospitalized. He started spending time alone, removed from everything.

He credits this change with starting him down the right path. He admitted to his father and mother that his illness was caused by his methamphetamine addiction. He told his ex-wife who had custody of his two sons, that "I'm the person on the street you point at and tell your kids to stay away from." He stated it was a "real eye opener" for him and occurred a couple of months before his disciplinary hearing.

Why are these details important?

He also credits "the event of" his disciplinary hearing "[f]or the genesis of my walk through sobriety." He explained he was still very physically ill at the time and was experiencing mental and emotional discomfort, as well. He recalled talking to his older son who rode with him to the hearing. His son asked him if he would get to keep his license. Petitioner answered, " '[i]f there's any justice in the world, son, no. No. We're going to go down and we're going to tell them the truth ….' Professionally, I couldn't practice. I said 'I owe an obligation to my profession, to my clients, to the bar association and most importantly to you, your brother and myself, to look the world in the eye and tell them the truth.' " He described that event as the "opening of recovery for me…." He stated he had been so low that complete candor and honesty with the world was palatable to him. As he had heard a friend say frequently at AA meetings, "When the pain of changing or the fear of changing is less than the fear of the pain of staying the same, then people will be open … to change."

He chose honesty and to look people "in the eye" and tell them what's going on in his world and what type of person he is. He'll accept the consequences, which is the legacy he wants for his children, that "regardless of the mistakes you make, look the rest of the world in the eye and accept your consequences and I'll respect you as a man."

The witnesses who testified on his behalf all stated Petitioner was very candid about his addictions, losing his law practice, and his suspension. He was also very open about his treatment and experience with AA. The AA members who testified also spoke about Petitioner's extra involvement in AA, including sponsoring new members, serving as an officer, and attending "group conscience" meetings after the regular meetings. Joe Halley testified Petitioner shows he wants to effect change in his life and tries to help others at the meetings.

Petitioner testified he did not practice law during his suspension. He said he has been approached by lawyers in Bartlesville about working with them and has done legal research for some of them during his suspension. He adamantly denied doing any legal work in his part-time job for Sharon Leach, a friend who is a real estate agent, or her broker, or otherwise giving legal advice to them. His work involves simple jobs such as locking and unlocking houses or placing signs in the ground. He testified he appeared pro se in a legal dispute over custody of an infant daughter he learned he had. He obtained custody shortly after his daughter's first birthday. She lives with him and his two sons in a home he rents in Bartlesville.

… His plan for resuming the practice of law after reinstatement is to continue working part time at Lowe's on weekends and to take cases from local attorneys as they see fit to use him. He said this arrangement will allow him to integrate his family life with a busy employment schedule. While currently working at Lowe's on a full-time basis, his schedule rotates, sometimes requiring him to work late on week nights. When this happens, he spends time during the day with his daughter, running errands, getting her ready for day care. Then, either a friend or one of his sons transfers her to his home where a college student watches her until he gets home. Practicing law during the week and working at Lowe's part-time on the weekends will permit him to be home more evenings a week and provide stability and predictability for his family.

> Why is this plan for his family relevant to his fitness to be reinstated?

Petitioner testified that he had attended seminars sponsored by the Tulsa County Bar Association. He stated he had received 38 CLE hours in the last two years. He has done legal research for some lawyers and has read the Oklahoma Bar Journal. He represented himself in his disciplinary proceeding. As noted, he hired a lawyer to pursue his paternity suit. He appeared pro se in his custody case, but he did not give his Bar number in that case.

He stated he is a little "gun shy" about talking about legal matters, as this can be seen as the unauthorized practice of law. He says he is more diligent now about avoiding "coffee shop talk" and discussing what is going on at the courthouse than he was previously. He realizes that what happens in his community can become a story in the local newspaper.

The Presiding Master of the PRT raised the issue of Petitioner's taking on "full accountability." He responded, "Absolutely. I have to. There's no recovery without that for me." When asked about the stress involved in prac-

In fact, relapse is a common phenomenon among recovering alcoholics and addicts, with some studies indicating that relapse rates for addictive diseases usually are in the range of 50% to 90%.

ticing law and whether it could cause a relapse to drug and alcohol use, he answered that stress occurs in all aspects of life. He said AA has taught him how to deal with stresses and how to live life on life's terms, whether it involves a client, a relationship, health problems or challenges with children. He said you must deal with it proactively "by getting yourself in a condition to handle those things and you set your priorities." He agreed that no matter where the stress comes from, he has the tools to deal with it and relapsing is not part of the equation. He also stated he has passed every random drug test he has been given.

Stronger Proof of Qualifications Upon Reinstatement Than When First Admitted

Rule 11.4, RGDP, requires that an applicant seeking reinstatement "will be required to present stronger proof of qualifications than one seeking admission for the first time." Moreover, the proof presented "must be sufficient to overcome the Supreme Court's former judgment adverse to the applicant." Upon consideration of the reinstatement factors ... which weigh most heavily to a lawyer's incapacity, i.e., 1) the extent of rehabilitation of the affliction attributable to the incapacity; 2) the conduct subsequent to the suspension and the treatment received therefor; and 3) the time which has elapsed since the suspension, we find Petitioner has met his burden of proof for reinstatement.

Notes

1. Are you surprised by the readmissions process? Many people presume that disbarment is permanent.

2. Oklahoma provides a separate "discipline" track for attorneys who become unfit to practice due to issues such as addictions. If an attorney violates her duties to her clients because of alcoholism or drug addiction, should that be considered a mitigating factor in sanctions? *See, e.g., Petition of Johnson,* 322 N.W.2d 616 (Minn. 1982) (providing five-step test necessary in order for alcoholism to be considered a mitigating factor in attorney discipline proceeding).

3. Because drug and alcohol addiction is such a common problem in the profession and is so closely associated with discipline, all states have programs to provide free, confidential counseling for attorneys. These lawyer assistance programs also serve attorneys who are suffering from other addictive behaviors as well as other debilitating results of the stress of practice. Notice that Rule 8.3 provides an exception to reporting misconduct when attorneys learn about this conduct through a lawyer assistance program.

   In some states, the lawyer assistance programs have a separate role, monitoring attorneys who have been placed on probation as a condition of a suspension. Most recently, in 2008, the ABA House of Delegates approved a Model Rule on Conditional Admission to Practice Law. The purpose of the rule is protection of the public:

   Conditional admission is not intended to apply to all applicants who have rehabilitated themselves from prior conduct or other matters of concern to bar admissions authorities, but only to those whose rehabilitation or treatment is sufficiently recent that protection of the public requires monitoring of the applicant for a specified period. The availability of conditional admission does not preclude unconditional admission in cases where rehabilitation or treatment has been successful for a sustained time period; nor does it preclude denial or deferral of admission in cases where rehabilitation or treatment has been of shorter duration.

The rule requires monitoring of admitted attorneys. The ABA left up to the states the controversial question of whether conditionally admitted attorneys would be required to disclose their status to clients. Would such a program be helpful for attorneys such as Whitworth?

4. At what point are special rules for attorneys with addictions merely discrimination on the basis of disability? Is an attorney who is in recovery in some senses less of a threat than an attorney who does not yet admit that she has a problem? Should attorneys with repeated arrests for driving while impaired be required to submit to alcohol screening as a condition of retaining their licenses? *In re Kelley*, 801 P.2d 1126 (Cal. 1990).

5. Often flow charts or other visual devices will be very helpful to your understanding of a rule or system of law. The diagram on the next page provides an example of a disciplinary system. Your state's system may have additional or different bodies for investigation or appeal, or additional procedures. Compare this flowchart with your own state's disciplinary system and amend the chart to reflect the differences.

2.6 Obligations under General Law

Of course, attorneys are subject to the civil and criminal law just like anyone else. Accordingly, you should always examine any professional responsibility issue from the perspective of its general legality. In addition, when appearing before a tribunal, rules of procedure govern conduct before that tribunal. Procedural rules govern not only pleadings, discovery, and judgment, but also may regulate communications with the court, witnesses, or jurors; establish procedures for particular actions or motions; or provide standards of good faith and candor. Rules of evidence such as the evidentiary privileges, for example, may impact attorney ethics issues. Applicable standards for practice before a state trial court might be found in state codes, in rules of the supreme court of the state, and in local rules of court.

Finally, courts have the inherent authority to control their courtrooms and proceedings and to enforce their orders. Contempt is the disobedience of court authority. A court's power to enforce its orders and to control the courtroom is called the contempt power. When a court uses this power to issue a sanction, we speak of that person being held in contempt. Contempt can be classified in a number of ways: Contempt can be classified based on the degree to which the acts constituting contempt occur in the presence of the court: Direct contempt occurs in the presence of the court; Indirect (constructive) contempt occurs outside the court's immediate presence. Contempt sanctions can be classified as civil or criminal, depending on the purpose and effect of the sanction imposed. Civil contempt sanctions can be further classified as either compensatory

Sample Attorney Disciplinary Process

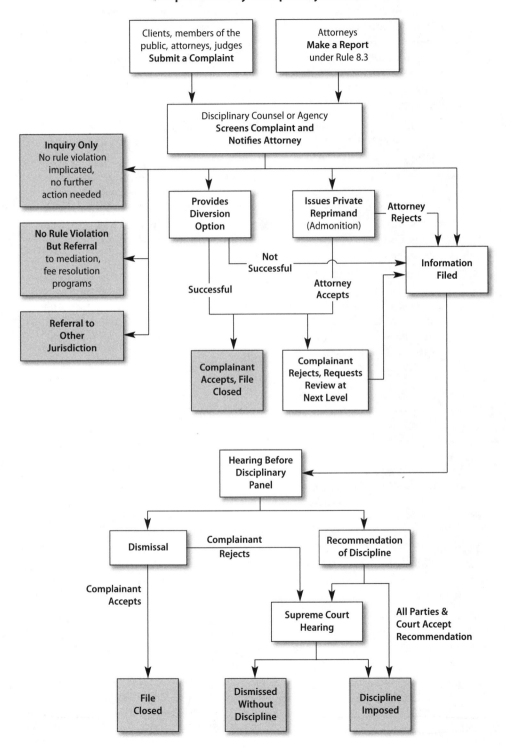

or coercive, depending again on the purpose and effect. Direct contempt is always considered criminal. Indirect contempt can be either civil or criminal.

Direct contempt interferes with court authority. Direct contempt occurs in the immediate view and presence of the court, though courts differ in their interpretations of this proximity requirement. Direct contempt need not necessarily involve disobeying a court order. It may result, for example, from the refusal of a non-privileged witness to testify in court, *United States v. Wilson*, 421 U.S. 309, 316-17 (1975) or an assault on a court officer, *Ex Parte Terry*, 128 U.S. 289, 298 (1888). The most controversial uses of direct contempt are for statements made by attorneys or litigants, particularly criticisms of judges, as these actions implicate the First Amendment. Louis S. Raveson, *Advocacy and Contempt—Part Two: Charting the Boundaries of Contempt: Ensuring Adequate Breathing Room for Advocacy*, 65 WASH. L. REV. 743 (1990).

Indirect contempt is any violation of a court order and can be either criminal or civil. The most dramatic sanction for violation of a court order is the imposition of criminal contempt sanctions: fines or imprisonment. Criminal contempt requires willful disobedience of a court order. Willfulness need not be with malice or bad faith—any violation of a court order that is merely knowing and not inadvertent is sufficient to trigger criminal contempt sanctions.

Violation of court orders can also result in civil contempt sanctions. These might include a judgment for the amount of damages caused to another because of the violation of the court. A powerful form of civil contempt is that which, rather than compensating for violation of an order, attempts to coerce the defendant into complying with an order. Coercive civil contempt sanctions are open-ended— for example, a court can order that an individual remain in jail until they are willing to comply with an order to reveal information or testify. This can result in extreme sanctions if an individual is committed to disobedience.

Liability in civil suits is another form of regulation. Of the common law standards that can result in civil liability for attorneys, the most common is legal malpractice. Almost any malpractice action is likely to be accompanied by other common law actions, including intentional torts, breach of fiduciary duty, or breach of contract claims. The American Law Institute has produced the Restatement (Third) of the Law Governing Lawyers, which attempts to summarize many of these common law standards. The influence of the Restatement on the development of attorney regulation remains to be seen, but it is certainly an important tool for researching issues of professional conduct.

Statutes may regulate attorney conduct. Examples include statutes governing conduct of attorneys working for a governmental body, or statutes governing attorney's fees (payment to appointed counsel, allowance of fees in certain actions, collection by attorneys of fees). Sometimes this legislation may provide very detailed regulation of many aspects of the attorney's work. The Legal Services Corporation Act (42 U.S.C. § 2996 *et seq.*) is one example of a statute extensively regulating attorney conduct. As a condition of receiving federal funding, the Act restricts Legal Aid offices using certain tactics (*e.g.*, cannot file class actions), representing certain clients (*e.g.*, cannot represent certain immigrants), and suing certain opponents (*e.g.*, cannot sue the government). This last requirement was held unconstitutional as content discrimination in *Velazquez v. Legal Servs. Corp.*, 164 F.3d 757, 773 (2d Cir. 1999), however most of the rest of these extensive regulations have not been challenged successfully.

Attorneys should also be aware of laws that, while not specifically addressing attorneys, nonetheless apply to the situations in which attorneys act. These laws include statutory and common law standards governing fiduciary relationships, professional corporations, personal service contracts, creditor/debtor rights, and the variety of fraud and misrepresentation laws found in the common law and statutes. Statutes and administrative regulation govern areas of practice in which attorneys share the market with other professionals such as tax advising, debt collection, bankruptcy, or mediation. For example, a federal statute that applies to attorneys is the Fair Debt Collection Practices Act. Originally the Act exempted attorneys from its scope. In 1986, Congress amended the Act, eliminating the attorney exemption. The United States Supreme Court thereafter held that the Act created no implied exceptions for attorneys. *Heintz v. Jenkins*, 115 S. Ct. 1489, 1492 (1995).

At the state level as well, consumer protection statutes are increasingly being applied to attorney conduct. For example, the Alaska Supreme Court recently applied its state Unfair Trade Practices and Consumer Protection Act to attorney conduct in debt collection. The attorney in this case was collecting a dishonored check and had mistakenly sent her demand letter to an incorrect address. The state law required that demand letters collecting dishonored checks be delivered personally or be sent via first-class mail to "the address shown on the dishonored check." The state supreme court reversed the trial court's dismissal of the debtor's suit against the attorney, finding that applying the act to lawyers did not unconstitutionally usurp the supreme court's exclusive authority to regulate the practice of law. "[T]he attorney disciplinary system and consumer protection laws can coexist as long as the legislature does not purport to take away this court's exclusive power to admit, suspend, discipline, or disbar." *Pepper v. Routh Crabtree APC*, Alaska, No. S-13042, 11/20/09. *See also*, *Heslin v. Connecticut Law Clinic of Trantolo*, 461 A.2d 939 (Conn. Sup. Ct. 1983) (application of the Connecticut Unfair Trade Practices Act to lawyers suspected of engaging in deceptive trade practices does not violate court's inherent authority to regulate profession).

Increasingly, attorneys are treated as indistinguishable from other professional service providers in regulation. This is especially so in regulations by Congress and, under its authority, federal agencies. Examples of federal agency regulations governing attorneys and other professionals who practice before that agency include:

- Patent and Trademark Office—The PTO is the only federal agency with separate admission requirements for attorneys and patent agents to practice before it. Regulations are found in 37 CFR Part 10.

- Office of Thrift Supervision—This office has considerable regulation for practice before it (12 C.F.R. §§ 513-590 (1992)).

- Security & Exchange Commission—The power of the SEC to discipline professionals was upheld in Touche Ross & Co. v. SEC, 609 F.2d 570 (2d Cir. 1979). Section 307 of the Sarbanes-Oxley Act of 2002 expressly directs the SEC to promulgate rules regulating the practice of attorneys "appearing and practicing before the Commission." 15 USC § 7245. These rules are at 17 C.F.R. §§ 205.1-205.7.

- Immigration—Attorneys who practice before the INS (Department of Homeland Security) are regulated by a number of administrative regulations. See, 8 C.F.R. §§ 292.3(a)-(g), 1003.1(d) (5), 1003.101, 1003.103-108 (2007). However, DHS attorneys who prosecute removal cases before the DOJ are not subject to these rules. *See* 8 C.F.R. §§ 292.3(a)(2), 1003.109 (2007).

- Treasury Department—Internal Revenue Service—The regulation of attorneys and others who "practice before the Internal Revenue Service" is governed by Circular 230 (31 CFR §§ 10.0-10.93).

- Bankruptcy Code—The Bankruptcy Code imposes various obligations on attorneys include advertising restrictions, restrictions on counseling clients, and frivolous pleading standards. 11 USC § 707(b)(4)(C).

Milavetz, Gallop & Milavetz, P.A. v. United States

130 S.Ct. 1324, 176 L. Ed. 2d 79; 2010 U.S. LEXIS 2206 (2010)

Congress enacted the Bankruptcy Abuse Prevention and Consumer Protection Act of 2005 (BAPCPA or Act) to correct perceived abuses of the bankruptcy system. Among the reform measures the Act implemented are a number of provisions that regulate the conduct of "debt relief agenc[ies]" — *i.e.*, professionals who provide bankruptcy assistance to consumer debtors. *See* 11 U.S.C. §§ 101(3), (12A). These consolidated cases present the threshold question whether attorneys are debt relief agencies when they provide qualifying services.

I.

In order to improve bankruptcy law and practice, Congress enacted through the BAPCPA a number of provisions directed at the conduct of bankruptcy professionals. Some of these measures apply to the broad class of bankruptcy professionals termed "debt relief agenc[ies]." That category includes, with limited exceptions, "any person who provides any bankruptcy assistance to an assisted person in return for ... payment ..., or who is a bankruptcy petition preparer." § 101(12A). "Bankruptcy assistance" refers to goods or services "provided to an assisted person with the express or implied purpose of providing information, advice, counsel, document preparation, or filing, or attendance at a creditors' meeting or appearing in a case or proceeding on behalf of another or providing legal representation with respect to a case or proceeding" in bankruptcy. § 101(4A). An "assisted person" is someone with limited nonexempt property whose debts consist primarily of consumer debts. § 101(3). The BAPCPA subjects debt relief agencies to a number of restrictions and requirements as set forth in §§ 526, 527, and 528. As relevant here, § 526(a) establishes several rules of professional conduct for persons qualifying as debt relief agencies. Among them, § 526(a)(4) states that a debt relief agency shall not "advise an assisted person ... to incur more debt in contemplation of such person filing a case under this title or to pay an attorney or bankruptcy petition preparer fee or charge for services performed as part of preparing for or representing a debtor in a case under this title."

II

The plaintiffs in this litigation—the law firm Milavetz, Gallop & Milavetz, P. A.; the firm's president, Robert J. Milavetz; a bankruptcy attorney at the firm, Barbara Nilva Nevin; and two of the firm's clients (collectively Milavetz) — filed a preenforcement suit in Federal District Court seeking declaratory relief with respect to the Act's debt-relief-agency provisions. Milavetz asked the court to hold that it is not bound by these provisions and thus may freely advise clients to incur additional debt....

III

A

We first consider whether the term "debt relief agency" includes attorneys. If it does not, we need not reach the other questions presented, as §§ 526 and

528 govern only the conduct of debt relief agencies, and Milavetz challenges the validity of those provisions based on their application to attorneys. The Government contends that "debt relief agency" plainly includes attorneys, while Milavetz urges that it does not. We conclude that the Government has the better view.

As already noted, a debt relief agency is "any person who provides any bankruptcy assistance to an assisted person" in return for payment. § 101(12A). By definition, "bankruptcy assistance" includes several services commonly performed by attorneys. Indeed, some forms of bankruptcy assistance, including the "[provision of] legal representation with respect to a case or proceeding," § 101(4A), may be provided only by attorneys. *See* § 110(e)(2) (prohibiting bankruptcy petition preparers from providing legal advice). Moreover, in enumerating specific exceptions to the definition of debt relief agency, Congress gave no indication that it intended to exclude attorneys. *See* §§ 101(12A)(A)-(E). Thus, as the Government contends, the statutory text clearly indicates that attorneys are debt relief agencies when they provide qualifying services to assisted persons.

In advocating a narrower understanding of that term, Milavetz relies heavily on the fact that § 101(12A) does not expressly include attorneys. That omission stands in contrast, it argues, to the provision's explicit inclusion of "bankruptcy petition preparer[s]"—a category of professionals that excludes attorneys and their staff, *see* § 110(a)(1). But Milavetz does not contend, nor could it credibly, that only professionals expressly included in the definition are debt relief agencies. On that reading, no professional other than a bankruptcy petition preparer would qualify—an implausible reading given that the statute defines "debt relief agency" as "*any person* who provides any bankruptcy assistance to an assisted person ... or who is a bankruptcy petition preparer." § 101(12A) (emphasis added). The provision's silence regarding attorneys thus avails Milavetz little. *Cf. Heintz v. Jenkins*, 514 U.S. 291, 294, 115 S. Ct. 1489, 131 L. Ed. 2d 395 (1995) (holding that "debt collector" as used in the Fair Debt Collection Practices Act, 15 U.S.C. § 1692a (6), includes attorneys notwithstanding the definition's lack of an express reference to lawyers or litigation).

Milavetz's other arguments for excluding attorneys similarly fail to persuade us to disregard the statute's plain language. Milavetz contends that 11 U.S.C. § 526(d)(2)'s instruction that §§ 526, 527, and 528 should not "be deemed to limit or curtail" States' authority to "determine and enforce qualifications for the practice of law" counsels against reading "debt relief agency" to include attorneys, as the surest way to protect the States' role in regulating the legal profession is to make the BAPCPA's professional conduct rules inapplicable to lawyers. We find that § 526(d)(2) supports the opposite conclusion, as Congress would have had no reason to enact that provision if the debt-relief-agency provisions did not apply to attorneys. Milavetz's broader claim that reading § 101(12A) to include attorneys impermissibly trenches on an area of traditional state regulation also lacks merit. Congress and the bankruptcy courts have long overseen aspects of attorney conduct in this area of substantial federal concern. *See, e.g., Conrad, Rubin & Lesser v. Pender*, 289 U.S. 472, 477-479, 53 S. Ct. 703, 77 L. Ed. 1327 (1933) (finding broad authorization in former § 96(d) (1934 Ed.) (repealed 1978) for courts to examine the reasonableness of a debtor's prepetition attorney's fees).

[Handwritten margin notes: "△ Arg →" ; "△ Arg leads to absurd results"]

[Margin note, left side:] Consider the broader consequences of the Court's treatment of this issue. Since in most states it is the courts that regulate the practice of law, is there not also a separation of powers argument? Why isn't that raised here? Does this decision sanction any legislative regulation of the practice of law?

Accordingly, we hold that attorneys who provide bankruptcy assistance to assisted persons are debt relief agencies within the meaning of the BAPCPA.

[The Court then goes on to interpret the scope of the Bankruptcy Code's restrictions on attorney advice to client and advertising. We will examine these issues in subsequent chapters.]

Researching Professional Responsibility 2-C: Professional Guidance in Your Practice Area

The practice of law has become increasingly specialized and the ethical issues presented to a transactional attorney in a large firm representing entities may be very different from the ethical issues presented to a solo practitioner representing individuals. Yet, specialized codes of regulation in the disciplinary context are the exception rather than the rule. As one noted scholar observed:

> The assumptions that all lawyers and all clients are the same have led to perhaps the most dramatic delusion inherent in the modern professional codes; namely, that a single set of rules should apply equally to, and can adequately govern, all legal representation. This premise finds justification only by reference to the notion that lawyers and clients simply could not understand or work with more nuanced professional standards. Yet the premise often leads to bad rules or to situations in which lawyers feel tempted to disobey the rules.

Fred C. Zacharias, *The Future Structure and Regulation of Law Practice: Confronting Lies, Fictions, and False Paradigms in Legal Ethics Regulation*, 44 ARIZ. L. REV. 829, 841 (2002).

As evidence of this diversity of specialized practice issues, for nearly every area of practice today, you can find a professional organization that provides guidance and support in your specialized practice area. For example, an attorney who specializes in regulation of lawyers might be a member of the ABA Center for Professional Responsibility (http://www.abanet.org/cpr/); the Association of Professional Responsibility Lawyers (http://www.aprl.net/); or the National Organization of Bar Counsel (http://www.nobc.org).

Many of these organizations have even produced specialized ethical guidelines to supplement, explain, or influence the formal rules of professional conduct. For example, in its "Standards Relating to the Administration of Criminal Justice" (1979), the ABA provides guidance for criminal defense attorneys and prosecutors. The courts regularly cite these standards in determining issues of ineffective assistance of counsel. Family law attorneys, for example, might look to the American Association of Matrimonial Lawyers' *Bounds of Advocacy* for guidance on specialized issues in their practice (http://www.aaml.org). Trusts and estates attorneys might look at the American College of Trusts and Estates Counsel's *Commentaries on the Model Rules,* available at the ACTEC website: www.actec.org. Even if an organization has not published a code of ethics, it may have a "practice manual" or it may issue regular ethics advice columns. For many areas of practice, allied professionals have ethical codes about which attorneys should be familiar. For example, tax attorneys should understand the standards of accountants; family law attorneys should understand standards governing social workers and mental health professionals.

A final source of guidance and regulation of attorney conduct may be the guidelines established by the attorney's client, partners, organization, or malpractice insurer. Sometimes these may be the very informal and unwritten norms of a practice community. In contracts, many large law firms have detailed policies for practice—determining the types of cases accepted, setting up office management procedures, and establishing guidelines for resolving issues of professional responsibility. These peer review systems have, in some cases, been ordered by a court as part of disciplinary proceedings or may have been implemented at the recommendation of a malpractice insurer.

Attorneys for government agencies or corporations likewise may be subject to policies that guide the scope of their conduct. For example, an attorney who has worked for the United States Department of Justice is subject to the federal conflict-of-interest provisions, which prohibit former executive branch employees from participating in certain kinds of matters. *See* 18 U.S.C. §§ 205-207; 5 C.F.R. § 2635. State and local legislation similarly guides attorneys for these governmental units.

A final note on regulation by employers and insurers: each attorney must maintain the ultimate responsibility for adhering to the standards for the profession. While third parties such as partners or insurers, and even clients, may suggest guidelines for the attorney's practice, these suggestions should not substitute for or infringe upon the attorney's own independent professional judgment.

Research and identify at least two professional organizations for your area of practice. What kinds of resources do these organizations provide to guide your practice and represent your practice area's viewpoint in professional regulation?

Identify an attorney who practices in your area of practice and interview her about the ethical issues that are most common and the issues that are most difficult in her area of practice. A good source for identifying these attorneys may be the local bar association's specialized practice committees.

Test Your Understanding

To assess your understanding of the breadth of the regulation of attorneys, consider the following problem.

You are a licensed attorney and also a licensed real estate agent. You have been approached by Frank, a fellow attorney you have known for several years. You and Frank are both attorneys at the law firm of Able, Baker & Charlie, Inc. His practice consists of business planning and he is an expert in forming syndications in particular, while your expertise is in real estate matters. Frank has asked you to join him in a business proposal involving one of his clients, named Book. Book came to Frank a month ago, seeking advice about an investment in a real estate opportunity (Evergreen). Frank took Book's Evergreen contracts and told him that he would look them over and provide Book with advice.

Frank is now proposing that you join him in forming a real estate investment business with Book. Frank proposed that Book would provide the investment funds and Frank and you together would provide the legal and real estate expertise. He says that he has already secured Book's oral agreement to the arrangement, in which you would divide ownership of the business 60% to Book (who will serve as president), 25% to Frank (who would be vice president), and 15% to you (who would serve on the board). You ask Frank if he has negotiated terms of profits, salaries, etc., and he indicates that "Book will agree to whatever I propose."

The proposal sounds extremely lucrative, but you are concerned about the ethical and legal ramifications of forming a business with a client. What areas of a law would you research to find guidance on whether this is a permissible and enforceable arrangement? If you conclude that the proposal is unethical, would you be required to report Frank?

[handwritten margin notes: – SEC – investments – financial Regulations – FINRA – real estate – ABA PR – state laws]

After you have brainstormed the possible legal standards that might apply to this problem, compare your ideas with the causes of action brought in *Fair v. Bakhtiari*, 195 Cal. App. 4th 1135 (Cal. App. 2011). Did you identify sources of law different than or in addition to those in the opinion?

To Learn More

For additional study and practice of Rule 8.4, see the CALI lesson on "Bases for Discipline," http://www.cali.org/lesson/657.

For more review of the regulation of legal practice, see the CALI lesson "Sources of Law Regulating the Practice of Law," http://www.cali.org/lesson/655.

To follow some of the recent developments in regulation of attorneys, subscribe to one of the following blogs:

The Legal Profession Blog, http://lawprofessors.typepad.com/legal_profession/

Legal Ethics Forum, http://www.legalethicsforum.com/

To read more about the structure of regulation of the legal profession, read one of these classic law review articles on the topic:

David B. Wilkins, *Who Should Regulate Lawyers*, 105 Harv. L. Rev. 801 (1992)

Charles Wolfram, *Lawyer Turf and Lawyer Regulation—The Role of the Inherent-Powers Doctrine*, 12 U. Ark. Little Rock L. Rev. 1 (1989-90).

Chapter Three

Who Should Be a Lawyer?

Learning Objectives

After you have read this chapter and completed the assignments:

- You should be able to explain to another person the following:
  - the routes to admission to practice law in most states?
  - the qualifications necessary for admission to practice law in most states?
- You should be able to research the particular requirements for admission in your state.
- In evaluating a particular set of facts involving personal conduct, you should be able to:
  - evaluate the risks that the conduct would preclude admission based on character and fitness issues, and
  - explain whether that same conduct, if engaged in by a practicing attorney, would subject that attorney to discipline.
- You should be able to interview a bar applicant to gain information necessary to identify character and fitness concerns and provide some basic counseling about how to best address those concerns.

Rules to Study

In this chapter, we will study Rule 8.1 and the rules governing admission to practice law.

Preliminary Problem

Miranda Medina is a citizen of Costa Rica and a permanent resident alien in the United States. Miranda graduated from the Universidad de San José — Facultad de Derecho and practiced law in Costa Rica for three years, working for an international non-governmental organization on environmental issues. She then came to the United States to attend law school (assume an ABA accredited law school) for a masters of law degree, emphasizing international environmental law. She recently became a permanent resident alien.

During her time in the United States, she has continued her involvement in environmental issues. Miranda has a very serious personality to begin with, but when it comes to environmental issues, she is relentless and passionate. She regularly writes letters to the editor and opinion columns online and in print media castigating leaders of industry and government for their actions or inaction on environmental issues. The letters are often strident in tone and just shy of slanderous. She has been arrested twice for civil disturbances arising out of protest demonstrations, though prosecutors dropped both cases. She has been active in recruiting individuals to join class action lawsuits on a variety of environmental matters and has been serving as a legal consultant to environmental groups challenging various trade agreements and international treaties. Her work may be considered to be the practice of law, but she has never been formally charged with unauthorized practice despite the high profile role she sometimes takes in these matters.

Miranda has applied for admission to practice law in your state. She has applied for admission without examination, based on her licensure in Costa Rica; however, she is willing to sit for the bar examination if that is required.

As you read the materials in this chapter, think about Miranda's prospects for bar admission. Consider as well your personal views on whether Miranda should be admitted to practice law. Do you have concerns about her application? Why?

3.1 Who Admits You to Practice Law?

In most states, the licensing of attorneys is in the primary (if not exclusive) control of the supreme court of the state. Only in a few states does the legislature play a role in the admission to practice law and only in Virginia does the legislature alone promulgate standards for admission. State bar associations may play an important role in this process but only upon delegation from the supreme court of the state. The power to regulate bar admission and attorney discipline is often considered one that is simply part of the inherent powers of the court. Most courts maintain that these inherent powers vest in the courts upon their creation. *Anderson v. Dunn*, 19 U.S. 204, 227, 5 L. Ed. 242 (1821); *Link v. Wabash R.R. Co.*, 370 U.S. 626, 630, 8 L. Ed. 2d 734, 82 S. Ct. 1386 (1962) (inherent powers are "necessarily vested in courts to manage their own affairs"). As one court commented: "This inherent power of the judicial branch of government to regulate the practice of law does not depend on any express constitutional grant or on the legislative will; rather, it exists because of the intimate connection between the practice of law and the exercise of judicial power in the administration of justice." *DeKrasner v. Boykin*, 54 Ga. App. 29, 35, 186 S.E. 701 (1936). Some state constitutions expressly provide that their supreme court has the power to make rules governing attorney admission and discipline. See, Ark. Const. Amendment 28 (1995), Fla Const. Art. V § 15, Ky. Const. § 116 (Michie 1996), N.J. Const. Art. VI § 2 3, Pa. Const. Art. 5, § 10 (1997), Mont. Const. Art. VII, Section 2(3) (1996). The admission to practice law, then, begins with admission within a particular state, and in most states, with the highest court of the state.

There are additional routes to admission for attorneys who already are licensed in one state. The federal courts also admit attorneys to practice before them. Most federal district courts require, as a precondition to admission, that you be a licensed member in good standing in the bar of the state in which the district court sits. Other district courts and the federal courts of appeals and supreme courts allow admission to be based on your prior admission to some other federal court first, thus indirectly requiring a state bar admission. Practice before federal agencies generally depends on state licensure as well. Only the US Patent and Trademark Office maintains separate admissions standards. The Agency Practice Act prohibits most other agencies from setting up separate admission standards. 5 U.S.C. § 500 (1997). *See McDaniel v. Israel*, 534 F. Supp. 367 (W.D. Va. 1982) (striking down a Social Security Administration requirement that attorneys are allowed to practice before the agency only if the client provided a signed appointment of representation).

Once an attorney has been practicing for some time in one state, he may apply for admission to practice in another state by motion — meaning that the requirement of the bar examination will be waived for that attorney. To be eligible for admission by motion, most states require four to five years of active practice, defined by many states as including law teaching, working for a government agency in a legal capacity, serving as a military lawyer, in-house attorney in a corporation, or acting as a judge for a court of record. For most states in which admission by motion is available, there are additional requirements. The most common requirement is reciprocity; that is, the attorney would have to have practiced in a state that would grant admission by motion to any attorneys from the state to which the attorney is applying for admission. *See generally*, Michael A. DiSabatino, Annotation, *Validity, Construction, and Effect of Reciprocity Provisions for Admission to Bar of Attorney Admitted to Practice in Another Jurisdiction*, 14 A.L.R.4th 7 (1991, 2008 Supp.) (collecting cases). Attorneys for admission by motion must meet all of the other educational and character requirements of the state just as applicants who will take the bar examination.

If an attorney licensed in one state wants to represent a client before another state's court for that case only, the attorney can apply to that court for *pro hac vice* admission. *Pro hac vice* admission is a matter of court discretion. There is no due process right for attorneys to be given this opportunity. *Leis v. Flynt,* 439 U.S. 438 (1979) *reh'g den.* 441 U.S. 956. (Attorneys have no right under the United States Constitution to appear *pro hac vice.* Any protected interest the out-of-state attorney might have must stem from an independent source such as state law.) Moreover, most courts will require the out-of-state attorney to associate with a local attorney. While this requirement has been challenged on a number of constitutional bases, it has been upheld on the rationale that the forum court must have a resident attorney, who is subject to the discipline of the court, responsible for the litigation.

In recent years, courts in states like California and New York, where the bar examination is a formidable obstacle to licensure in the state, have become increasingly concerned about the abuse of *pro hac vice* admission. *Pro hac vice* admission is intended to be an occasional accommodation for out-of-state attorneys, not an alternative route to regular practice in a state. While few courts track *pro hac vice* admissions or place any express limit on the number of motions an attorney may file, trial courts will deny admission to attorneys who are using *pro hac vice* admission for more than limited appearances. *Hanson v. Spolnik*, 685 N.E.2d 71 (Ind. Ct. App. 1997). *But see, Florida Bar. Keller Indus. v. Yoder*, 625 So. 82 (Fla. App. 1993) (attorney who had appeared before Florida courts three times in past three years did not appear so frequently as to justify trial court's denial of *pro hac vice* admission).

Finally, increasingly states have specialized licensing or "registration" rules that allow more limited practice for certain attorneys. The most common categories of limited admission are for in-house counsel, for foreign legal consultants, and for clinical faculty members in law schools.

The following graphic summarizes these many routes to licensure.

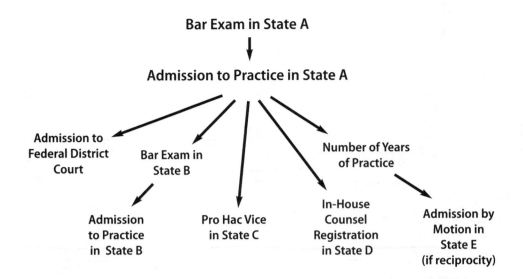

What about bar associations? We often talk about being "admitted to the bar" or speak as though it is the bar association, rather than the court, that administers admission and discipline. However, most bar associations are merely private associations. The American Bar Association, for example, is not a governmental agency and its Model Rules and Formal Opinions do not have the force of law (though they have been very influential in the development of law). Likewise, county and specialty bar associations are simply private organizations.

However, in over half the states, attorneys must join the state bar association as a condition of being admitted to practice law in the state. These mandatory state bar associations (sometimes also called "integrated" or "unified" bar associations) function not only as membership organizations, offering benefits such as malpractice insurance and educational programs, but also as quasi-governmental bodies who play a central role in regulating the profession. Constitutional challenges to mandatory bar membership have not met with success, except to the extent that mandatory bar dues may not be used for political or ideological purposes, such as lobbying for particular partisan legislation. *Keller v. State Bar of California,* 496 U.S. 1 (1990).

3.2 What Are the Qualifications Necessary for Admission to Practice Law?

In both federal and state courts, there are certain educational and character prerequisites that apply. Reasons suggested as justifications for these admission requirements include: to protect clients who often do not know much about the lawyer they consult; to protect courts from subversion and fraud; and to protect the professional image of lawyers. *In re Alexander,* 807 S.W.2d 70 (Mo. 1991). It is not unduly cynical to note that admission rules also protect attorneys from competition. Perhaps this is one of the reasons that the unauthorized practice of law is a frequent reason for denying admission. *See, e.g., In re Craig,* 190 Wis. 2d 494, 526 N.W.2d 261 (1995).

The state's power to regulate admission to the bar is subject to Constitutional restraint. Most challenges to bar admission requirements have arisen under the Fourteenth Amendment. Nonetheless, the Due Process Clause leaves a wide range of discretion to the state in establishing admissions standards. One of the historical prerequisites for admission — residence in the state — has been held unconstitutional. In three different cases, the United States Supreme Court held that these requirements violate the Privileges and Immunities Clause of the United States Constitution. In *Supreme Court of New Hampshire v. Piper*, 470 U.S. 274 (1985), the court invalidated a simple residency requirement that mandated residency at the date of admission. In *Virginia Supreme Court v. Friedman*, 487 U.S. 59 (1988), the Court applied *Piper* to invalidate a provision requiring nonresident attorneys to take a bar exam for admission but allowing resident attorneys to "waive into" the bar without examination. Finally, in *Barnard v. Thorstenn*, 489 U.S. 546 (1989), the Court invalidated a Virgin Islands requirement that applicants have previously resided for a year and intend to reside in the future. The Equal Protection Clause protects resident aliens as well as citizens. Just as state restrictions on the practice of law by non-resident attorneys have been held unconstitutional, so too a state may not constitutionally exclude persons from the practice of law based on their citizenship. See, *Application of Griffiths*, 413 U.S. 717, 93 S. Ct. 2851, 37 L. Ed. 2d 910 (1973), on remand to, 165 Conn. 807, 309 A.2d 689 (1973).

Today, most states have two major components to their licensing requirements: an educational component (typically a law degree and a bar exam) and a character and fitness component. We will consider each of these.

3.2.1. Educational Requirements

Educational requirements are designed to insure competence in attorneys. But how effective are these requirements? Many years ago, most attorneys qualified for licensure by studying in another attorney's law office. In a few states today, this avenue for bar admission is still available. Most states, however, require a law degree and a bar examination for new attorneys. In weighing the comparative value of law office study, law school, and bar examination requirements, consider how these requirements allocate power among various groups. Do law schools have different interests they might seek to advance as compared to the national or local bar associations? Consider the diploma privilege, in which one who has graduated from an accredited or approved law school within the state and who meets other conditions is entitled to admission without examination to that state's bar. This approach to bar admission has been tried and abandoned by thirty-three jurisdictions. Today, only one state (Wisconsin) recognizes the privilege. Why do you think that is? Think about these broader questions as we explore the specific requirements more carefully.

One of the goals of a bar admission process is to ensure that attorneys have a minimum competence to practice law. How does the admission process evaluate competence? How effective are these measures? What are the implications of using these measures of competence?

Educational prerequisites provide one method for measuring competency. Many states have some form of pre-legal education requirement, such as an undergraduate degree or its equivalent. Nearly all states require that initial applicants (those who have never been admitted to any bar) have a law degree. In almost all states that degree must come from an "accredited" or "approved" law school. These requirements have withstood a variety of constitutional challenges. *See, e.g., Nordgren v. Hafter*, 616 F. Supp. 742 (S.D. Miss. 1985) *aff'd* 789 F.2d 334 (5th Cir. 1985) *cert. den.* 479 U.S. 850 (1985) (Requirement of graduation from ABA approved law school not unconstitutionally vague, does not violate equal protection or due process rights, does not relate to residence and fundamental right of interstate travel, and thus does not implicate privileges and immunities clause.)

The power of the American Bar Association in the accreditation of law schools has been the subject of continuing challenge. In 1893, the American Bar Association established the Section of Legal Education and Admissions to the Bar as the Association's first section. The Section played the major role in creating the Association of American Law Schools in 1900, which, in turn, began some regulation by establishing requirements for a law school's membership. In 1921 the American Bar Association promulgated its first Standards for Legal Education, which became the basis for the law school accreditation process. Recent antitrust challenges to the ABA's involvement in accreditation have been somewhat successful. In June 1995, the United States Department of Justice filed a civil antitrust suit against the ABA, alleging violations of antitrust laws in the accreditation program. The civil suit was concluded by a final consent decree that was approved in June 1996. It includes a number of requirements concerning the Standards. For example, the ABA may not collect or consider information about compensation paid to faculty, deans, or staff in the accreditation process, unless there is a complaint about discrimination. The requirements of the consent decree apply only to the ABA in its accreditation function, not to an approved law school. The effect of this consent decree on the growth of unaccredited law schools is unclear, but since the decree many new law schools have become accredited and recent denials of accreditation have generated additional lawsuits.

The effect on the admission process is even more uncertain. Antitrust law generally does not apply to state actors. Challenges to the reliance on ABA accreditation as a condition of admission to practice law have not fared well. For example, in *Appeal of Murphy*, 482 Pa. 43, 393 A.2d 369, *cert. den. and app. dismd.* 440 U.S. 901 (1978), the Pennsylvania Supreme Court rule allowed admission without examination of practicing attorneys from other states if they had graduated from ABA accredited law schools. The rule was challenged based on an unlawful delegation of power under the state constitution. The court upheld the rule as reasonable, because undertaking the evaluation of every applicant's legal education would be "very impractical."

In addition to requiring a law degree, some states go even further in their educational requirements and require that initial applicants have successfully completed certain courses in law school or after law school. These courses tend to focus on ethics and professionalism training, and basic skills training. *See generally*, Robin Cheryl Miller, *Annotation, Validity, Construction, and Application of Enactment, Implementation, or Repeal of Formal Educational Requirement for Admission to the Bar*, 44 A.L.R. 4th 910 (1986, 2010 Supp.) (collecting cases).

3.2.2. Bar Examinations

All but four states also require first-time applicants (as opposed to attorneys from other jurisdictions seeking admission) to pass the Multistate Bar Examination combined with a state examination. Court challenges to the use of bar examinations have met with little success. For example, in *Applicant Number Five to Delaware Bar*, 658 A.2d 609 (D.C. 1995) a bar examinee who failed to pass bar examination petitioned for reconsideration of his exam grades. As a rule, courts will not interfere with decisions to deny such petitions for re-grading unless the Board of Bar Examiners has discharged its responsibility in arbitrary, fraudulent, or unfair matter. Here, the Court held that the Board did not act unfairly in its accommodation of a dyslexic examinee. The record failed to support granting of waiver of objective standards for examinee's admission to the Bar, although the examinee successfully passed another state's bar exam and received a high score on portions of the Delaware exam, where the examinee missed other criteria required to pass the exam.

Is the Multi-State Bar exam, the most common requirement of the states, a useful device for insuring competence? Critics of the MBE have attacked its relevance to determining competency. For example, one critic notes that, "Where the rigors of law practice often require protracted attention to a single, precisely defined issue, the MBE is premised on the fleeting and fragmented attention that 1.8 minutes allows for issues as numerous as they are replete with contrivance. The MBE tests no one's competence or intelligence. It tests only the ability to pass the MBE." Jeffrey Duban, *Rethinking the Exam: The Case for Fundamental Change*, Manhattan Lawyer, Jun. 1990, at 16-17. Other critics of bar examinations point to the potential for bias and unfairness in their construction and administration.

Some of the most recent challenges to the bar examination have been based on federal legislation such as the Americans with Disabilities Act. State bar examiners must comply with Title II of the Americans with Disabilities Act of 1990 (ADA), including changes made by the ADA Amendments Act of 2008 (P.L. 110-325), which became effective on January 1, 2009. That law prohibits discrimination by a public entity on the basis of a disability. In particular, 42 U.S.C. § 12132 provides that "Subject to the provisions of this subchapter, no qualified individual with a disability shall, by reason of such disability, be excluded from participation in or be denied the benefits of services, programs, or activities of a public entity, or be subjected to discrimination by any such entity." Title III of the act requires entities that offer licensing examinations to provide reasonable accommodations to disabled individuals. 42 U.S.C. § 12189 ("Any person that offers examinations or courses related to applications, licensing, certification, or credentialing for secondary or postsecondary education, professional, or trade purposes shall offer such examinations or courses in a place and manner accessible to persons with disabilities or offer alternative accessible arrangements for such individuals.")

3.2.3. Character and Fitness

Nearly all states have a generalized requirement that applicants have "good moral character" but, apart from specific disqualifications for applicants with criminal convictions, the boundaries of that requirement are somewhat unclear. One example of the breadth of this requirement can be found in *Hallinan v. Committee of Bar Examiners, State Bar*, 65 Cal 2d 447, 55 Cal Rptr 228, 421 P.2d 76 (1966), in which the court defined "moral turpitude," as "everything done contrary to justice, honesty, modesty, or good morals." Generally any evidence of prior misconduct in a professional role or any indications of dishonesty or disrespect for the law is relevant to this determination.

In the following case, the Supreme Court of Nebraska decided that Gary Lane should not be admitted on the basis that he lacked the character and fitness required for admission.

As you read the case, ask yourself the following questions:

What exactly are the facts that led the court to deny admission here?

Would this same conduct subject an attorney to discipline? Should it?

What interests is the court trying to protect by its decision?

If you had been advising Lane in preparing his initial application, what would you suggest he do to increase the chances of his admission?

Abrasive behavior / violent / sexist at Creighton Law school

Lane v. Bar Commission of the Nebraska State Bar Association

544 N.W.2d 367 (Neb. 1996).

Per Curiam.

Pursuant to Neb. Ct. R. for Adm. of Attys. 15 (rev. 1992), the applicant-appellant, Gary M. Lane, challenges the decision of the respondent-appellee, the bar commission of the Nebraska State Bar Association, to deny his application for readmission to the Nebraska bar through membership in the association.

Facts

[Lane was denied admission to the Nebraska bar on the basis that he lacked the character and fitness required for admission.]

Hostile, Threatening and Disruptive Conduct.

At the June 9, 1995, hearing, various witnesses testified to events which occurred during September 1994 and January through February 1995. Two of the events are worthy of discussion. The first concerns Lane's involvement at the Creighton University legal clinic. Catherine Mahern, an associate professor of law at Creighton, as well as the director of the clinic, and Connie Kearney, an adjunct professor at the clinic, testified that Lane had come to the clinic in the spring or early summer of 1994 and offered to volunteer after school started again. On his first day, September 19, 1994, Lane accompanied Kearney and two law students to a juvenile court hearing. Lane asked to sit with the students at counsels' table, but Kearney told him that he should remain behind the bar. Lane responded that he was a licensed attorney, that he was in good standing, and that he wanted to sit with the students. Kearney again told him that she wanted him to remain behind the bar, to which Lane responded, "I'll remember this." Kearney testified that she took this statement as a threat.

Mahern met with Kearney and Lane to discuss Lane's role in the clinic and to clear up any misunderstandings that might have occurred at the hearing. During the meeting, Lane stated that Kearney was the type of woman who does not know how to deal with men and is intimidated by them. He also admitted what he had said to Kearney at the hearing and that he did not take it back. He told Mahern that while he could work with students, he would not work with women students. Finally, Lane stated that "those people in Colorado" had gotten to Mahern, that what they had told her was not true, that the record had been expunged, and that they could not prove anything. The next day, Mahern called Lane into her office and asked him to leave the clinic. Lane became very irritated and said that Kearney and a student were on the phones in the back room talking to each other about him in whispered voices or in code. When Mahern stated that he must have been mistaken, he said in a loud voice, "Don't you accuse me of auditory hallucinations, I've been accused of that before and it's not true." On his way out, Lane passed by Kearney's desk and asked that she keep him out of her phone conversations from now on.

Lane testified that he did not intend to threaten Kearney at the juvenile court hearing; he had made the statement to her because he felt she was being deliberately discourteous to him as a lawyer from a neighboring jurisdiction. He also stated that he did not tell Mahern that he would not work with the female students, but, rather, that he would let them approach him if they wanted help and that he would just work with the male students "who apparently didn't find [Lane] very intimidating."

The second event occurred during the BAR-BRI review course at Creighton University law school. During one of the review sessions, Lane left approximately 10 minutes early. After the review session ended, Lane returned and demanded to know who had stolen his keys. Lane used strong and profane language in accusing the students in attendance of stealing his keys. After the students had left the room, Lane said to one of the students, Corby Gary, "We can take this outside and settle this." Lane went on to say to Gary, "I'll find out where you live." Gary testified that the latter statement caused him concern for himself and his wife.

Other events which were mentioned by witnesses at the hearing included intimidating and rude conduct directed at a security guard and a custodian at Creighton and abrasive behavior during the BAR-BRI review sessions.

In addition, there are other events alluded to in the evidence which cause some concern, especially his interactions with women. His employment history at AppleOne Colorado, Inc., indicates that he had "outbursts in lobby while filling out application," that he was very rude to female employees, and that he walked off one job, allegedly telling a supervisor to have all of his employees see a psychiatrist. Lane testified that he did not quit that shift early, but, rather, was asked to leave because he was "having another one of these disagreements with another one of these women who didn't apparently like me or my demeanor." Lane acknowledged that his being accused of behaving in an intimidating manner toward women is "part of a recurring problem that I've experienced," and that more women tend to find him intimidating than men.

Lane was also discourteous in his answers to various questions put to him by commission members at the hearing:

Q. Well, it was a stormy night that night, is that correct?

A. No, it was not. We're going to talk about the weather now[?] ...

Q. Aren't you glad you didn't go outside with him?

A. I think that's kind of a silly question....

Q. What's the title of the one that was published? ...

A ... I don't see what relevance this has....

Q. Were [the keys] lost? ...

Stop here and consider these facts carefully. How would you characterize Lane's behavior based on this description? Would these same facts subject an attorney to discipline? Consider Rules 8.1 and 8.4.

What additional information about Lane does this incident add? If this were the only incident in Lane's record, would it have been sufficient to deny him admission?

How is Lane's attitude toward women relevant to his ability to practice law?

A. I don't understand why this is so important.

Moreover, his correspondence with the commission during the investigation process evidences a sarcastic and cavalier attitude toward it and its responsibilities. One letter to Harold L. Rock, the chairperson of the commission, contains the following:

> I am sure you are cognizant of the ethical obligation attorneys have to be courteous to one another. Mr. Henshaw clearly disregards this obligation. If Mr. Henshaw does not have an undisclosed agenda perhaps he should be questioned concerning his unnecessary sarcasm. Perhaps my unemployment is not so difficult to understand after all, if this is the attitude of persons in positions of authority.

… Lane also implies that the commission was politically motivated in its investigation of his character and fitness. This assertion had been made earlier in a letter from Lane to the commission, in which he objected to the "inquisitorial approach to [his] Bar admission that [he] believes to be motivated by personal or political animosity." Furthermore, Lane is under the impression that all of the people who were in the BAR-BRI course were against him, allegedly because of racial animosity they felt toward him (Lane testified that he is part Hispanic, part Italian, and part "Anglo Irish"), and because they may have heard of his reputation.

While any one of the events described above, viewed in isolation, could perhaps be attributed to the pressures of taking the bar examination or perhaps a misunderstanding, taken together these incidents show that Lane is prone to turbulence, intemperance, and irresponsibility, characteristics which are not acceptable in one who would be a counselor and advocate in the legal system.

Accordingly, our de novo review of the record leads us to independently conclude that Lane has exhibited a pattern of acting in a hostile, threatening, and disruptive manner.

Having so determined, we turn our attention to Lane's claim that even so, the behavior does not constitute sufficient relevant conduct to deny admission under the provisions of Rule 3.

Rule 3 provides, in part, as follows:

> An attorney should be one whose record of conduct justifies the trust of clients, adversaries, courts, and others with respect to the professional duties owed to them. A record manifesting a significant deficiency in the honesty, trustworthiness, diligence, or reliability of an applicant may constitute a basis for denial of admission.

Apparently, Lane is arguing that abusive, disruptive, hostile, intemperate, intimidating, irresponsible, threatening, or turbulent conduct does not reflect on his "honesty, trustworthiness, diligence, or reliability." He is wrong.

Appendix A to rule 3 explains that "an attorney should be one whose record of conduct justifies the trust of clients, ~~adversaries,~~ courts, and others with respect to the professional duties owed to them." A record of conduct that shows a history of abusive, disruptive, hostile, intemperate, intimidating, irresponsible, threatening, or turbulent behavior is not the type of record that justifies the trust of others with respect to the professional duties owed them

If Lane had been courteous to authority but rude and sarcastic to everyone else, would that have changed the outcome in this case?

The dissent in this case disagreed, stating, "Obnoxious and rude behavior by definition simply do not reflect on one's character for honesty, trustworthiness, diligence, or reliability—let alone demonstrate a 'significant deficiency' in these traits, as required by rule 3." Do you agree?

Our Code of Professional Responsibility speaks directly to this issue. Canon 7, EC 7-10, provides that a lawyer is obligated to treat with consideration all persons involved in the legal process, and Canon 7, EC 7-37, provides that although ill feelings may exist between clients in an adversary proceeding, such ill feeling should not influence a lawyer in his or her conduct, attitude, and demeanor toward opposing lawyers. A lawyer should not make unfair or derogatory personal reference to opposing counsel. Haranguing and offensive tactics by lawyers interfere with the orderly administration of justice and have no proper place in our legal system.

The requisite restraint in dealing with others is obligatory conduct for attorneys because "the efficient and orderly administration of justice cannot be successfully carried on if we allow attorneys to engage in unwarranted attacks on the court [or] opposing counsel.... Such tactics seriously lower the public respect for ... the Bar." *Application of Feingold*, 296 A.2d 492, 500 (Me. 1972) . It necessarily follows that "an attorney who exhibits [a] lack of civility, good manners and common courtesy ... tarnishes the ... image of ... the bar...." *In re McAlevy*, 69 N.J. 349, 352, 354 A.2d 289, 291 (1976).

In addition, appendix A declares, in part, that "the public interest requires that the public be secure in its expectation that those who are admitted to the bar are worthy of the trust and confidence clients may reasonably place in their attorneys." When members of the public engage attorneys, they expect that those attorneys will conduct themselves in a professional and businesslike manner. Attorneys who routinely exhibit abusive, disruptive, hostile, intemperate, intimidating, irresponsible, threatening, or turbulent behavior toward others involved in the legal system are not worthy of such trust and confidence. What cannot be permitted in attorneys cannot be tolerated in those applying for admission as attorneys. *In re Martin-Trigona*, 55 Ill. 2d 301, 302 N.E.2d 68 (1973), *cert. denied* 417 U.S. 909, 94 S. Ct. 2605, 41 L. Ed. 2d 212 (1974).

Moreover, the qualities listed in the rule are merely illustrative; "the fact is that in reviewing an application for admission to the bar, the decision as to an applicant's good moral character must be made on an ad hoc basis." *In re Application of Majorek*, 244 Neb. 595, 606, 508 N.W.2d 275, 282 (1993). We therefore join other courts in holding that abusive, disruptive, hostile, intemperate, intimidating, irresponsible, threatening, or turbulent behavior is a proper basis for the denial of admission to the bar. *See, Board of Overseers of the Bar v. Campbell*, 663 A.2d 11 (Me. 1995); *In re Alexander*, 807 S.W.2d 70 (Mo. 1991), *cert. denied* 502 U.S. 885, 112 S. Ct. 241, 116 L. Ed. 2d 196; *Matter of Ronwin*, 139 Ariz. 576, 680 P.2d 107 (1983).

Even if we assume, arguendo, that Lane believes he is the victim of a conspiracy which encompasses various interests in Texas, various people in Colorado, and the commission itself, the sincerity of his belief in this supposed wide-ranging conspiracy against him cannot overcome the requirements for the practice of law. Belief unrelated to reason is a hallmark of fanaticism, zealotry, or paranoia rather than reasoned advocacy. The practice of law requires the ability to discriminate between fact and faith, evidence and imagination, reality and hallucination. While an applicant for admission to the bar is entitled to argue vigorously that the commission erred in its findings and recommendation, and this court would take seriously any substantiation of

Should the "image of the bar" provide a legitimate basis for denying admission to practice or for disciplining attorneys? Why or why not?

Do you agree with this analysis? Aren't there situations or clients groups who need and want a "fighter" working for them? Where is the line between being a vigorous advocate and being unprofessional?

behavior —
or
motives ??

what is the line for an advocate? climate change a hoax?

the existence of bias or misconduct on the part of the commission, a much stronger showing is needed than demonstrated by this record to warrant a conclusion that the commission had acted out of some type of political or personal animus. *See In re Demos*, 579 A.2d 668 (D.C. App. 1990).

Verbal abuse, unfounded accusations, and the like have no place in legal proceedings. While occasional lapses in decorum can be overlooked, Lane's transgressions exceed occasional incivility, anger, or loss of control. On this record, they form a pattern and a way of life which appear to be Lane's normal reaction to opposition and disappointment....

Our *de novo* review leads us to independently conclude, contrary to Lane's contention, that his egregious pattern of abusive, disruptive, hostile, intemperate, intimidating, irresponsible, threatening, or turbulent conduct is sufficient relevant conduct to deny him admission to the bar.

Lack of Candor.

Question 7 of the application read: "List every job you have held for the ten year period immediately prior to the date of this application or since the age of 18, beginning with your present employment, if any. Please include self-employment, clerkships, internships, temporary or part-time employment and military service." Lane explained that he had failed to list the Colorado temporary employment because he held simple common labor jobs, and he may have either misread the question or forgotten about the jobs. We agree with the commission's determination that such an explanation is not credible. The correspondence between Lane and Henshaw set out earlier establishes not only that Lane failed to list the employment, but that he originally denied having had any employment during the period in question.

In addition, not only did Lane fail to list his former membership in the Iowa bar, but he failed to reveal that he had previously been a member of the bar of this state, the very state whose bar he was again seeking to join. That piece of information was certainly one of the more important and relevant items he could have provided the commission. His explanation that he simply forgot to list it, or that he had run out of space, or that he did not think it was relevant or material, we find to be incredible, despite the somewhat contrary finding of the commission. Contrary to the commission's implication, we have never held that in order to be found to have lacked candor in filling out an application, an applicant must have had an intent to deceive. On the contrary, in *In re Application of Majorek*, 244 Neb. 595, 604, 508 N.W.2d 275, 281 (1993), we observed that "false, misleading, or evasive answers to bar application questions may be grounds for a finding of lack of requisite character and fitness." While an intent to deceive will reflect on whether such answers are false, misleading, or evasive, and would properly be considered by the commission, an applicant who recklessly fills out an application, as the consequence of which the application contains false answers, is just as culpable of lacking candor in the application process as is the applicant who intends to deceive the commission.

Accordingly, our *de novo* review of the record leads us to independently find that Lane lacked candor in filling out the application at issue. Moreover, contrary to Lane's contention, we independently find such conduct reflects on Lane's honesty, trustworthiness, diligence, and reliability, and thus provides an additional reason to deny him admission to the bar of this state.

* * *

Conclusion

For the foregoing reasons, we affirm the commission's decision to deny Lane's application to be readmitted to the bar of this state through membership in the Nebraska State Bar Association.

Affirmed.

Notes

1. No matter what the reason a bar admissions official may have for questioning an applicant's character and fitness, an applicant can easily make matters worse by responding to inquiries with anger, arrogance, or rudeness. Failing to cooperate with or attempting to inappropriately influence the bar admission process can provide a separate basis for denial of admission. For example, in *Matter of McLaughlin*, 675 A.2d 1101, 144 N.J. 133 (1996), Mr. McLaughlin's admission to the New Jersey Bar was denied in part due to insufficient disclosure of three prior events in his history: an arrest in Massachusetts, an arrest in New Jersey, and circumstances relating to personal automobile insurance. However, his real problem was his demeanor and expressions in correspondence that caused the Court to conclude that he had an insufficient appreciation for the proper administration of justice. He made "condescending and inappropriately sarcastic remarks" while addressing character committee members, and he "denigrated inquiries and resorted to extreme personal vilification" against court employees. He described the Assistant Secretary of the Board of Bar Examiners as "the odious Uberman" and "either a liar or an incompetent, perhaps both." *See also, In re Wagner*, 119 Ohio St. 3d 280, 893 N.E.2d 499 (Ohio 2008) (applicant's "unduly defensive" comments regarding her conviction for driving under the influence provided part of the basis for denial of application); *In re Application of Head*, 867 N.E.2d 824, 114 Ohio St.3d 29 (Ohio 2007) (attempt to exert inappropriate influence over board of bar examiners personnel resulted in denial of application for six months).

2. In the past, other bases that have been used to deny admission have included adultery, cohabitation without marriage, or homosexuality. *See generally,* Eric H. Miller, Annotation, *Sexual Activity or Sexual Orientation as Ground for Denial of Admission to Bar*, 21 A.L.R. 4th 1109 (1991, 2008 Supp.) (collecting cases). Obviously, such wide-ranging standards can raise concerns for potential bias and abuse in their administration. As Justice Hugo Black commented:

   > The term "good moral character" has long been used as a qualification for membership in the Bar and has served a useful purpose in this respect. However the term, by itself, is unusually ambiguous. It can be defined in an almost unlimited number of ways for any definition will necessarily reflect the attitudes, experiences, and prejudices of the definer. Such a vague

qualification, which is easily adapted to fit personal views and predilections, can be a dangerous instrument for arbitrary and discriminatory denial of the right to practice law.

Konigsberg v. State Bar of Cal., 353 U.S. 252, 262-63 (1957).

3. Read and be prepared to discuss the following problems. Would you admit this candidate? If your state permits conditional admission, what conditions would you impose on the admission under this rule? Think about the relationship between the admissions rules and the rules of professional conduct. Would the candidate's behavior, if it occurred in the context of law practice, provide a basis for professional discipline? Recall the United States Supreme Court's caution regarding admission standards: "A State can require high standards of qualification, such as good moral character or proficiency in its law, before it admits an applicant to the bar, but any qualification must have a rational connection with the applicant's fitness or capacity to practice law." *Schware v. Board of Bar Examiners*, 353 U.S. 232, 77 S. Ct. 752, 756 (1957). For additional information, see Aaron M. Clemens, *Facing the Klieg Lights: Understanding the "Good Moral Character" Examination for Bar Applicants*, 40 AKRON L. REV. 255 (2007).

Candidate A—Andrew is a thirty-year-old man who grew up in poverty in the inner city and had a record of several arrests from ages 14 to 22 for various drug-related crimes. He had only one conviction however, a felony conviction at age 22 for possession of 10 grams of marijuana. He was given a five-year suspended sentence. With the help of a friend from church, he got a job and worked his way through the local college. He completed probation three years ago, just before beginning law school, where he has been an exemplary student, and the recipient of the Pro Bono student volunteer of the year award from the local bar association. *See generally,* Donald M. Zupanec, Annotation, *Criminal Record as Affecting Applicant's Moral Character for Purposes of Admission to the Bar*, 88 A.L.R. 3d 192 (1980, 2008 Supp.) (collecting cases).

Candidate B—Barbara is a 40-year-old attorney who has been practicing law as a licensed attorney in the state of New York for 15 years, with an excellent record and reputation. In the wake of her recent divorce, she relocated to another state that does not allow admission by motion. She applied to take the bar examination. One week after submitting her application, she was arrested for public drunkenness, after neighbors called the police because she was wandering down the street in her residential neighborhood singing loudly. She pled guilty to the misdemeanor offense and served 24 hours in the local jail. She did not, however, immediately update her bar application to disclose the offense, as is required by the state rules. Nine months later, she passed the bar examination and was sent an attestation form, requiring that she affirm that all the information in her application was true and complete. In response, she notified the admissions authorities of her conviction. When asked why she did not report the information earlier, she indicated that she was embarrassed and unsure that she would even pass the bar exam. If she didn't pass the exam, her plan was to withdraw her application, so she thought she would spare herself disclosing the information until she knew she would have to do so. *In re Strzempek*, 962 A.2d 988 (Md. 2008).

Candidate C—Clarence, who is 27 years old, was expelled from a college dormitory due to continual derogatory slurs he aimed at students in the dorm whom he believes are homosexuals. He also regularly participates in picketing of public businesses with employees or customers, where he carries signs with slogans such as "Close Down Sodom" and "Don't Finance Fags." Emelie E. East, *Note: The Case of Matthew F. Hale: Implications for First Amendment Rights, Social Mores and the Direction of Bar Examiners in an Era of Intolerance of Hatred*, 13 Geo. J. Legal Ethics 741 (2000).

Candidate D — Dolores is a recent graduate who, in her third year of law school, fell behind on deadlines to complete her required research paper in time to graduate. She asked a fellow classmate to help her with the paper. Her professor discovered this and required that she start over with a different topic because the rules of the course prohibited collaboration on papers. Dolores wrote the second paper, but this time the professor discovered that she had copied, without attribution, three pages of the paper from a paper posted on the internet. The professor discounted those pages and gave her a grade penalty, resulting in a final grade of D- on the paper, but allowing her to graduate on time. She received no formal discipline from the law school as a whole. In response to the question "Regardless of whether the record has been expunged, canceled, annulled, or whether no record was ever made, have you ever been suspended, placed on probation, expelled, warned, reprimanded, or disciplined in any form for any academic or non-academic reasons at any post-secondary school, college, or university?" she answers "no" because she does not consider this to be discipline because it was all simply the professor's response. When the information is reported to the bar by her law professor, the applicant is remorseful and forthcoming with all information regarding the papers. *Application of Widdison*, 539 N. W. 2d 671 (S.D. 1995); *In re Bar Admission of Terry George Radtke*, 601 N.W.2d 642 (Wis. 1999).

Lies

Candidate E — Edmund is a 34-year-old entrepreneur, who has started and closed several businesses since he graduated from high school. He has also, during that time, accumulated crushing credit card debt and had several substantial judgments entered against him in collection suits and has a horrible credit rating. He currently has a student debt of approximately $145,000, in part because he has used student loans from both public and private sources to try to continue to finance his business enterprises while he went to school. *See generally*, George L. Blum, Annotation, *Failure to Pay Creditors as Affecting Applicant's Moral Character for Purposes of Admission to the Bar*, 108 A.L.R.5th 289 (2004, 2011 Supp.) (collecting cases).

Credit problems

Candidate F — Felicity is a 27-year-old unmarried woman with an 11-year-old daughter. Felicity worked her way through college as an "exotic dancer" and topless waitress. One of the professors in her law school left the school after his affair with her became public knowledge and his wife, a prominent and well-respected attorney in the community, divorced him. *Florida Bd. of Bar Examiners Re N.R.S.* 403 So. 2d 1315, 1317 (Fla. 1981). *See generally*, George L. Blum, Annotation, *Sexual Activity or Sexual Orientation as Ground for Denial of Admission to Bar*, 105 A.L.R. 5th 217 (2004, 2008 Supp.) (collecting cases).

Stripper w/ prof

Candidate G — Gerald suffers from bipolar disorder, which he was diagnosed with in college and has learned to manage with medications since then. He did have some challenges during the first semester of law school, when an episode of depression led him to drop out after eight weeks. However, with an adjustment to his medications, he returned and successfully completed law school.

bipolar

Few of his classmates or teachers know of his illness, though in part this is because he has kept to himself, not participating in any law school organizations or social activities, and maintaining a very low profile in classes.

3.3 Reading the Rules: Connecting Rules to Procedures

How does a state discover information about character and fitness matters? Primarily, states obtain this information from the applicants themselves. Moral character is assessed through an application process in which individuals seeking admission are asked a series of questions regarding their past work, education, finances, and health, among other questions. Applicants are required to disclose information that would otherwise be considered private or even privileged. Failure to cooperate in answering admissions questions is a frequent basis for denial of admission; however, it can also be a basis for discipline. Study Rule 8.1 to determine the role of attorneys in the admission process. The Nebraska rule on this issue is identical to ABA Model Rule 8.1

Nebraska Supreme Court Rules of Professional Conduct
§ 3-508.1. Bar admission and disciplinary matters.

An applicant for admission to the bar, or a lawyer in connection with a bar admission application or in connection with a disciplinary matter, shall not:

(a) knowingly make a false statement of material fact; or

(b) fail to disclose a fact necessary to correct a misapprehension known by the person to have arisen in the matter, or knowingly fail to respond to a lawful demand for information from an admissions or disciplinary authority, except that this rule does not require disclosure of information otherwise protected by Rule 1.6.

Context

Part of the context of this rule is its relationship, not only with the rest of the rules of professional conduct, but with other court rules regulating the profession. The rules of professional conduct provide standards for discipline of attorneys, but Rule 8.1 not only applies to attorneys but also to applicants to the bar. The rule can provide the basis for discipline for an attorney who has been admitted and about whom undisclosed information later comes to light. In *In re Jordan*, 478 N.E.2d 316 (Ill. 1985), for example, an attorney was disbarred for his failure to disclose on his bar application all of his former residences, the discipline that had been imposed while he was a police officer, 300 unpaid parking tickets, and a previous bankruptcy petition. More commonly, however, the rule is used to deny admission to those who lack candor in their applications for admissions.

Relationships

This rule requires candor in providing information relevant to the admissions process. This rule facilitates another set of rules entirely—the rules governing admission to practice. Jurisdictions vary in the specificity they provide for these standards, but all provide some requirement of character and fitness. Consider that evidence of moral character can include attitudes and reputation. How does that match with this rule's requirement of disclosure and candor relating to "statements of material fact"?

An important part of the character determination relates to criminal activity. Bar admission authorities are given a broad power to demand information from applicants—even information such as sealed juvenile court records or expunged criminal convictions that would otherwise be unavailable. For example, the Mississippi Supreme Court has held that an attorney may be asked to answer questions about criminal records that have been expunged, even though the state statute providing for expungement does not provide an exception for bar applications. The court stated that, because the state supreme court has the sole and exclusive authority to regulate the practice of law, its admission standards and procedures trump state legislation. *Stewart v. Mississippi Bar,* 2011 Miss. LEXIS 2 (Miss. Jan. 6, 2011) (denying reinstatement for failing to disclose expunged criminal record in application for reinstatement); *See also, In re Carroll,* 572 N.E.2d 657, 658 (Ohio 1991) (denying admission to applicant who failed to reveal expunged records of criminal convictions).

However even the court's authority to regulate the practice of law is subject to constitutional restrictions. Note this comment to Rule 8.1:

> This Rule is subject to the provisions of the Fifth Amendment of the United States Constitution and corresponding provisions of state constitutions. A person relying on such a provision in response to a question, however, should do so openly and not use the right of nondisclosure as a justification for failure to comply with this Rule.

Structure

This rule contains an important exception for confidential information relating to a representation (Rule 1.6). To which part of the rule does this exception apply? This is an especially tricky part of the rule to read because the exception comes at the end of the (b) subsection of the rule. Notice that subsection (b) has the conjunction "or" connecting "fail to disclose" and "knowingly fail to respond." The same sentence then has a subordinating conjunction "except that" cancelling out the previous duties.

Grammatically, this structure leaves you wondering if the exception applies to both of the preceding clauses or only the second clause. The exception clause itself provides the answer, in that it provides that "this rule" does not require disclosure. Since the entire set of laws at issue here are called "The Rules of Professional Conduct" and one regularly refers to a particular "Rule" (such as Rule 8.1), it seems most logical that the exception is meant to apply to the rule as a whole.

This exercise in parsing the sentence is one you should be able to do with any rule or statute, as many critical interpretations have turned on the structure of a rule.

Reasons

Why have disciplinary rules about admissions candor? Couldn't the court "cancel" a bar admission when it was secured through dishonesty or fraud? Would this necessarily have to be the same process as disbarment? (Think of an analogy to contract law here). To whom is this rule mostly addressed?

Visualize

Often one of the most useful ways to dissect a rule is to create a chart of the elements of the rule like the one that follows. Try translating Rule 8.1 into this chart. What questions does this exercise raise for you?

WHO
    1. _____
    2. _____
WHEN
      _____

WHAT (shall not ...)
    1. _____
    2. _____
    3. _____
EXCEPT IF
      _____

Imagine

Under what circumstances would a court ordinarily apply this rule? Think about a situation in which an attorney might have lied to gain admission to practice law. How would that information come to light? Notice that the rule does not appear to impose an affirmative requirement for attorneys to report information about applicants. Yet attorneys in most states (including Nebraska) do have an affirmative obligation to report a violation of the rules by individuals once they are licensed attorneys (recall the discussion of Rule 8.3 from Chapter Two). Does the combination of these two rules mean that if an attorney is aware that someone has lied in order to gain admission to practice, the attorney must report that fact?

Researching Professional Responsibility 3-A: Using Research Guides

Research the admission requirements for your state. Learn how one is admitted by examination and by motion. Identify whether your state has any other types of admission. For this research, you will find a research guide that can make your research much easier.

For many areas of Professional Responsibility, the American Bar Association or other national organizations provide helpful guides comparing the law of the several states. These are excellent resources for beginning research to locate a particular state's law or to get an overview of the national perspective on an issue.

For example, in researching the requirements for admission to practice in the state in which you plan on practicing, one of the easiest resources for quickly identifying qualifications for admission is through the NATIONAL CONFERENCE OF BAR EXAMINERS, COMPREHENSIVE GUIDE TO BAR ADMISSION REQUIREMENTS. This is available as a pdf document at their website: http://www.ncbex .org/bar-admissions/. The Guide provides tables, with supplementary comments, that outline a variety of requirements for all the U.S. States and Territories. You will find this resource very helpful as you prepare for admission to practice.

However, while useful in providing an overview, guides such as this are secondary authority. Particularly as admission requirements are changing among the states, you should read the court's rules, statutes, and regulations that govern admission in your own state. In all states, admission rules are promulgated by the state supreme courts. In a few states, the legislature also enacts admission rules. The bar admission authorities that implement those rules often promulgate additional regulations.

Professional Responsibility Skill 3-A: Interviewing a Bar Applicant

You are an attorney in the state of Central, which has adopted the current version of the ABA Model Rules of Professional Conduct. You have been contacted by a recent law school graduate, Pat Heart, regarding advice on an admissions issue. She has apparently been denied admission to the bar, after having requested accommodations for her learning disability, and would like your assistance.

Central's rules for admission are the same as those of your state. Central uses a standard form for its process of character and fitness screening. You can see an example of this form at the National Conference for Bar Examiner's website www.ncbex.org.

You will be meeting Ms. Heart for an initial interview. The intake form and correspondence in the file appear on the following pages. Your goals in this interview should be to determine:

What does Ms. Heart want?

Can you help her?

Would she like you to represent her?

Fees are not an issue — your senior partner has asked that you take on this representation pro bono. Time is an issue, however, as you don't want to be wasting your time or your client's pursuing goals that are unrealistic. Plan on speaking with Ms. Heart for no more than 45 minutes.

HEART 2011 YH 207   Telephone Intake

Date: August 16, 20xx
Time: 10:45 AM
Name: Pat Heart
Address: 500 East Main Street, Everycity, Central
Phone: (816) 235-0000 (home)
Email: pat.heart@yahoo.com
Employment: Midwestern Central University Law Library, clerk

Nature of problem: bar admission

Notes: Ms. Heart went to law school at MCU Law school and graduated this past May. Received disability accommodations on testing in law school. Requested accommodation for July bar exam but was denied. Now has to appear for hearing regarding her application to take the February bar. Would like advice on preparing for that hearing.

Other parties involved? Midwestern Central University Law School; Central Board of Bar Examiners

Consulted with other Attorneys? ✓ Yes __ No
Special program officer for Board of Bar Examiners; Chairman of Board of Bar Examiners (Terry Garrison)

Prior representation in this or related matter? __ Yes ✓ No
Intake by Pauline Paralegal

✓ Appointment confirmation letter sent 8-16, 20xx

__ Fee statement sent

__ Engagement letter sent

Appointment date and time: August 22, 20xx 11:00 am

✓ Calendared

HEART CASE # 2011BG3   **Conflict of Interest**

Potential Client's Name: Pat Heart

Employer: Midwestern Central Univ. Law Library

Potential Parties: Midwestern Central Univ. Law School

                              Board of Bar Examiners

Previous Representations:

    Chairman of Board of Bar Examiners (Terry Garrison)
    Matter: Bar Admission
    Possible conflicts: None
    Confirmed by: Yurnam Here

YURNAM HERE
ATTORNEY AT LAW

August 16, 20XX

Ms. Pat Heart
500 East Main Street
Everycity, Central

Re: Appointment with Yurnam Here

Dear Ms. Heart:

Thank you for your call today to request an appointment to discuss possible representation regarding your bar application. We will be meeting at my office on August 22nd at 11:00 am. At that time, we will discuss your situation and give you some more particular information about the types of services we might be able to provide to assist you. There is no charge for this first forty-five minute consultation. Our office is located on the fifth floor of the Core Street Building on the corner of 2nd and West Streets. Please contact my secretary, Sally Assist, at 816-235-0001 if we need to change the time for your appointment.

We can best assist you if you can bring to that meeting any documents or correspondence you have regarding your situation. Please do not send us any documentation before the meeting however.

Please be aware that we do not have an attorney-client relationship at this point. We do not represent you until you decide that you would like to engage our services, we agree that we can represent you, and you have signed and returned to us a mutually agreed-upon engagement letter or contract. We will discuss more when we meet.

I look forward to meeting you on August 22nd.

Sincerely,

Yurnam Here
Yurnam Here, Esq.

Test Your Understanding

Return to the preliminary problem in this chapter. Do you recognize that:

- Miranda's citizenship status does not prevent her from being admitted to practice law.

- Her license in Costa Rica might qualify her to register as a foreign legal consultant but would not, in most states, allow her to become licensed as an attorney unless the state was willing to recognize her foreign law degree (which would depend on how close Costa Rica's legal system is to the United States).

- Her Masters of Law, even though from an accredited law school, would not necessarily qualify her to be admitted in most states without some kind of waiver of the requirement of a JD.

- Her public letters that are "strident in tone and just shy of slanderous" would not by themselves be evidence of bad moral character so long as they did not actually cross the line to illegal conduct. What would be very influential to the bar admission authority would be how she conducts herself in applying for admission.

- Her arrests for protests would be relevant to the character determination because this might be seen as a failure to respect laws. That the arrests do not involve violence or dishonesty would help.

- Her litigation activity would be relevant to the character determination if the bar authorities consider that she has been engaged in the unauthorized practice of law. This can be a very negative factor in bar admission decisions. How she held herself out and whether anyone was hurt would be important additional considerations on this.

To Learn More

Remember that one of the best ways to learn material is to practice retrieving it. Take a few moments to see how much you can remember about who admits attorneys to practice, what the qualifications are for admission, and what types of routes to admission exist in most states.

To further review your understanding of the materials in this chapter, review the CALI lesson on The Law Governing Admission to Practice Law at http://www.cali.org/lesson/656.

Chapter Four

The Legal Services Industry

Learning Objectives

After you have read this chapter and completed the assignments:

- In analyzing the applicability of Rule 5.5 to a set of facts involving an attorney's practice, you should be able to analyze how likely it is that the facts would constitute the unauthorized practice of law and how, short of becoming licensed, the attorney involved could increase the chances it would not be unauthorized practice.

- You should be able to identify situations in which attorneys are at risk of discipline for permitting lay person involvement with the lawyer's delivery of legal services.

- You should be able to describe key trends in multijurisdictional and multidisciplinary delivery of legal services.

Rules to Study

We will examine Rules 5.4 through 5.6—rules of professional conduct that have been under considerable stress as the market for delivery of legal services expands and changes.

Preliminary Problem: The New World of Legal Practice

You have built up a boutique firm that serves alternative energy industries, with experts in energy and environmental regulation and the protection of business and intellectual property. You serve companies and entrepreneurs in setting up business ventures around the globe. You provide a range of legal, business, engineering, marketing, and intellectual property advising. Your clients have asked you to put together lobbying efforts to secure favorable legislation at the local, state, and national level.

Where are you practicing law? Where must you be licensed to practice? For some of these activities is it even wise or necessary to have a license? May you bring in allied professionals (accountants, engineers, patent agents, etc.) into your firm as full-time employees? If you do, may they serve clients who are coming to the firm solely for these other services and not for legal services? May they share an equity ownership interest in the firm?

4.1. How Is the Practice of Law Changing?

In Chapter One we examined the idea of a "Profession" and the notion of civic professionalism. In this model, the profession of law is comprised of lawyers and judges, self-regulated, highly educated, with an expansive duty to the public. In this chapter, we will examine another view of the legal profession, that is, as a legal services industry. That industry includes attorneys and judges, but also the many other persons and businesses that assist entities and individuals with their legal needs. As Professor William Henderson, who studies trends in the legal profession, predicts:

> The 21st century is sure to give rise to a new generation of legal entrepreneurs who create novel ways to adapt to the needs of clients. Successful innovators will grapple with the three interconnected forces that make change inevitable:
>
> 1) More sophisticated clients armed with more information and greater market power to rein in costs.
>
> 2) A globalized economy, which increases the complexity of legal work while exposing U.S. lawyers to greater competition.
>
> 3) Powerful information technology that can automate or replace many of the traditional, billable functions performed by lawyers.

William D. Henderson & Rachel M. Zahorsy, *Law Job Stagnation May Have Started Before the Recession — And It May Be a Sign of Lasting Change*, A.B.A.J (July 2011).

Think about each of these forces very carefully.

Sophisticated, Empowered Clients

Remember from Chapter One that most attorneys represent entities (corporations, associations, or governments). The individuals who purchase legal services for those entities are most often lawyers themselves, but they are also members of their entity — keenly aware of that entity's "bottom line" and operating culture. They can provide many legal services in-house or can act as a general contractor, engaging outside attorneys and other professionals to provide some or all of the services the entity requires. They can communicate with others like themselves to solve common problems and increasingly do so, eliminating the need for law firm assistance. Likewise, individual clients in the information age are increasingly willing to represent themselves. It has long been the rule that corporations, unlike individuals, do not have the right to represent themselves in judicial proceedings. *Osborn v. United States Bank,* 22 U.S. (9 Wheat.) 738 (1824). It is unclear how these restrictions will be affected by the United States Supreme Court's decision in *Citizens United v. Federal Election Commission,* 130 S.Ct. 876 (2010), in which the Court recognized the free speech rights of corporations in political campaigns. Even without constitutional pressure, however, as corporations increasingly hire in-house counsel to handle their own legal needs, and as corporate structures become more complex, one wonders how long the prohibition is likely to stand.

A Globalized Market for Legal Services

A telling footnote in a recent ABA Ethics 2000 Letter describes the global nature of large law firms.

> Of the sixty-seven U.S.-based law firms identified in the American Lawyer "Global 100" in 2010, which ranks the world's top 100 law firms by gross revenue, only

seven had offices exclusively in the United States. Two firms were structured as vereins and were therefore not identified as U.S.-based law firms for purposes of the American Lawyer survey. *See* Michael D. Goldhaber, "Empire Builders," *The American Lawyer* (October 1, 2011), *available at* http://www.law.com/jsp/tal/PubArticleTAL.jsp?id=1202516509353.

ABA Discussion Paper on Alternative Law Practice Structures (Dec. 2, 2011), http://www.americanbar.org/content/dam/aba/administrative/ethics_2020/20111202-ethics2020-discussion_draft-alps.authcheckdam.pdf.

Smaller firms and in-house counsel increasingly tap into a global market as well. Consider an example of an entity requiring assistance in putting together a transaction. Suppose, for example, a national retailer regularly requires assistance in purchasing or leasing real estate. In each instance, state laws must be researched and agreements (leases or real estate contracts) must be drafted. Perhaps some work might be undertaken by real estate professionals rather than attorneys. However, for most of this work, the company would likely want attorneys to provide this service. The company might hire attorneys in each state for this work, or might choose to have one firm or even in-house counsel undertake this work from a central office. Increasingly, businesses and firms are outsourcing this work to attorneys in countries such as India where routine document preparation and review can be completed at a fraction of the cost of domestic legal service providers. Companies such as Pangea3 (which was recently acquired by Thomson Reuters, which also owns West Publishing Co.) and Unitedlex are examples of the growth of this new industry of legal process outsourcing (LPO). While the individuals providing this service may all be attorneys, they may not be licensed in all the states in which they are practicing law.

Even practices that might seem purely local are affected—as the solo practitioner in the middle of the United States discovers when trying to trace products through a global supply chain to bring a products liability suit for a consumer or a family law attorney learns when trying to unravel the complexities of the Hague Convention in order to work out a transnational custody agreement. Increasingly lawyers find that they "aren't in Kansas anymore" and must structure their practices to reach outside their state's geographical boundaries.

Technology

With computerized forms and internet advice, and an increasing sophistication of artificial intelligence, the challenge to attorneys is to determine the "value added" of representation delivered in person or to find ways of harnessing technology to provide that same value added to clients remotely.

Considering these pressures, think more broadly as well about whether a state-by-state approach to regulating legal practice is the best and how you will manage these jurisdictional aspects of your own practice.

4.2 Where Do You Practice Law?

The ABA Model Rules of Professional Conduct prohibit attorneys from assisting in the unauthorized practice of law, but do not themselves define the practice of law. The American Law Institute, in drafting the Restatement (Third) of the Law Governing

Lawyers also was unable to provide a definition, likely because the case law is so conflicting and vague that "restatement" is not an option. RESTATEMENT (THIRD) OF THE LAW GOVERNING LAWYERS §4 cmt. c (2000) ("definitions and tests employed by courts to delineate unauthorized practice by nonlawyers have been vague or conclusory"). The most common single definition asks whether one is providing advice and assistance about the law to address particular facts or whether one is simply providing general information. For attorneys who are assisting others with legal matters, even that definition is likely too narrow, since many courts will presume that an attorney who is providing information about the law has engaged his or her legal training and judgment in choosing the information to provide. We explore the issue of unauthorized practice by lay persons more particularly in Chapter 25.

In this chapter, the question of regulating the unauthorized practice of law is not as much *who* as *where*. Rule 5.5 prohibits attorneys from practicing law in jurisdictions in which they are not admitted.

Since there is no national or international admission to practice law, attorneys must be licensed in each country and, within the United States, in each state where they plan to practice law. In recent years, with mobility of both clients and attorneys and the emergence of national and international law firms, the question of multijurisdictional practice has received increasing attention. Suppose for example that a large national retailer regularly requires assistance in purchasing or leasing real estate. In each instance, state laws must be researched and agreements (leases or real estate contracts) must be drafted. The company would like to outsource this work. Is this a problem?

A decision by the California Supreme Court focused the attention of the legal community in 1998: *Birbrower, Montalbano, Condon & Frank, P.C. v. Superior Court,* 17 Cal. 4th 119, 70 Cal. Rptr. 2d 304, 949 P.2d 1, *cert. denied* sub nom. *Birbrower, Montalbano, Condon & Frank, P.C. v. ESQ Business Servs., Inc.,* 525 U.S. 920, 119 S. Ct. 291, 142 L. Ed. 2d 226 (1998). In that case, ESQ Business Services Inc. was suing the Birbrower firm of New York for malpractice. ESQ was a California subsidiary of a New York company which had been Birbrower's client. The disputed representation involved a contract between ESQ and Tandem Computers Inc. The contract was based on California law. Lawyers from Birbrower made several trips to California to conduct negotiations, scheduled an arbitration, and advised ESQ. Birbrower did not have an office in California or any attorneys licensed in California.

The California court did not rule on the question of malpractice, but granted ESQ's request to be relieved of its more than $1 million in attorney's fees because Birbrower had engaged in the unauthorized practice of law. The court's decision sent shock waves through the legal profession, particularly since the attorney's conduct in Birbrower seemed so "safe" at the time. Birbrower did not open an office in California, it did not hold itself out as a California law firm or as having attorneys licensed in California, it was representing the subsidiary of a regular New York client, and its work was incidental to an arbitration rather than a local lawsuit. The court's test was not an easy one to apply going forward. The court held that, to constitute unauthorized practice, there must be "sufficient contact with the California client to render the nature of the legal services a clear legal representation." *Birbrower,* 17 Cal. 4th at 128, 70 Cal. Rptr. 2d at 309, 949 P.2d at 5.

In response, the ABA formed a separate Commission on Multijurisdictional Practice, which produced a series of recommendations for the states to facilitate multijurisdictional practice while protecting the rights of states to police the practice of law in their jurisdictions. These recommendations included amendments to the Model Rules of Professional Conduct, as well as model rules for *pro hac vice* admission, admission on motion, registration of in-house counsel (a more limited form of admission), and rules for reciprocal and interstate disciplinary enforcement. You can read more about each of these recommendations and follow their adoption by the states at the Commission's website at www.abanet.org/cpr/mjp/home.html.

4.3 Reading the Rules: Rule 5.5

Most states have adopted a version of Rule 5.5 with some variation. Arizona is one state that has adopted a version of Rule 5.5 that closely tracks the ABA Model. The italicized portions of the rule are provisions that Arizona added to the Model Rule.

Arizona Rules of Professional Conduct 5.5 (2009)
Unauthorized Practice of Law

(a) A lawyer shall not practice law in a jurisdiction in violation of the regulation of the legal profession in that jurisdiction, or assist another in doing so.

(b) A lawyer who is not admitted to practice in this jurisdiction shall not:

1) except as authorized by these Rules or other law, establish an office or other systematic and continuous presence in this jurisdiction for the practice of law: or

2) hold out to the public or otherwise represent that the lawyer is admitted to practice law in this jurisdiction.

(c) A lawyer admitted in another United States jurisdiction, and not disbarred or suspended from practice in any jurisdiction, may provide legal services on a temporary basis in this jurisdiction that:

1) are undertaken in association with a lawyer who is admitted to practice in this jurisdiction and who actively participates in the matter;

2) are in or reasonably related to a pending or potential proceeding before a tribunal in this or another jurisdiction, if the lawyer, or a person the lawyer is assisting, is authorized by law or order to appear in such proceeding or reasonably expects to be so authorized;

3) are in or reasonably related to a pending or potential arbitration, mediation, or other alternative dispute resolution proceeding in this or another jurisdiction, if the services arise out of or are reasonably related to the lawyer's practice in a jurisdiction in which the lawyer is admitted to practice and are not services for which the forum requires pro hac vice admission; or

4) are not within paragraphs (c)(2) or (c)(3) and arise out of or are reasonably related to the lawyer's practice in a jurisdiction in which the lawyer is admitted to practice.

(d) A lawyer admitted in another United States jurisdiction, or a lawyer admitted in a jurisdiction outside the United States, and not disbarred or suspended from practice in any jurisdiction, *and registered pursuant to Rule 38(i) of these rules,* may provide legal services in this jurisdiction that:

1) are provided to the lawyer's employer or its organizational affiliates and are not services for which the forum requires pro hac vice admission; or

2) are services that the lawyer is authorized to provide by federal law or other law of this jurisdiction.

(e) *An attorney who engages in the authorized multijurisdictional practice of law in the State of Arizona under this rule must advise the lawyer's client that the lawyer is not admitted to practice in Arizona, and must obtain the client's informed consent to such representation.*

(f) *Attorneys not admitted to practice in the State of Arizona, who are admitted to practice law in any other jurisdiction in the United States and who appear in any court of record or before any administrative hearing officer in the State of Arizona, must also comply with Rules of the Supreme Court of Arizona governing pro hac vice admission.*

(g) *Any attorney who engages in the multijurisdictional practice of law in the State of Arizona whether authorized in accordance with these Rules or not, shall be subject to the Rules of Professional Conduct and the Rules of the Supreme Court regarding attorney discipline in the State of Arizona.*

Now go back and carefully revisit the rule, considering its context, relationships, structure, and reasons. Graph or otherwise make the rule your own and imagine the ways it might come into play in practice.

Context

The rules numbered beginning with 5 are in the section of the rules governing "Law Firms and Other Associations"—rules that govern the relationships among lawyers and other professionals. Yet most of new Rule 5.5 has nothing to do with non-lawyers whatsoever. How are the policies relating to non-lawyer unauthorized practice related to the concerns over a lawyer's unauthorized practice?

Relationships

Sometimes the rules of professional conduct make explicit the relationship between these rules and other law that may regulate attorneys, as for example when a rule refers to a "crime or fraud." Sometimes the reference to other law is more cryptic. In this rule, for example, consider the exception in part (b) (1) *"except as authorized by these Rules or other law."* What other law or rules might create an exception? How could you find those exceptions? One place to start is in the comments to the rules, which will often direct you to specific rules or laws.

Structure

Each subsection of Rule 5.5 serves a separate function in the rule that you can capture with a brief label. For example, (a) might be labeled "UPL prohibited." Label the remaining subsections:

(b)

(c)

(d)

(e)

(f)

Reasons

The best way to clear up ambiguities in a rule (or at least to understand the nature of those ambiguities) is to understand the purpose or purposes of the rule. Obviously, these purposes will not always be clear or explicit. Time spent conceiving the purpose for which a rule is created can go a long way toward increasing your understanding of the rule itself. One of the questions you can ask in understanding Rule 5.5 is, "Whose interests are being protected and how?"

Visualize

This rule contains lists but the lists are safe harbors nested within prohibitions. You might visualize this rule as placing behaviors on a continuum from clearly permissible to clearly prohibited. Place the following behaviors on the spectrum.

Clearly Permitted ←————————————————————————→ **Clearly Prohibited**

1. Open an office in the other state
2. Target ads to clients in the other state
3. Represent multiple clients from the other state
4. Appear in the other state for legal transactions at least once a week over several months
5. Represent only one client on a single matter in the other state
6. Represent many clients from your own state about the law of the other state
7. Have a systematic and continuous presence in the state
8. Obtain pro hac vice admission in the state

Imagine

What would the "holding out" of section (b)(2) look like? When would practice be "reasonably related" to your home state practice? Think of clear examples of what falls within the rule and outside the rule and then think of examples of the gray areas in between.

Questions

1. Rank the following actions for the risk they present of your being subject to discipline for unauthorized practice of law in Arizona. If you would need more information in order to rank an item, state an assumption as part of your ranking. Compare your answers. What characterizes the low risk activities? What activities do you consider high risk? For those that are of uncertain risk, how could you lower the risks and still provide the requested legal services?

   a. A client in your home state is thinking of moving its business to Arizona and wants your advice regarding several aspects of Arizona law that might impact its decision.

   b. A client from Arizona calls you and is interested in moving its business to your home state and wants your advice regarding several aspects of your home state's law that might impact its decision.

   c. You've bought a winter vacation home in Arizona and decide to open a part-time office there to provide estate planning services.

d You regularly represent individuals from a particular foreign country in their petitions for asylum and other immigration matters. You represent an average of two clients each month before immigration court in Arizona. You do not have a regular office in the state.

e. You regularly vacation in Arizona and, while there, you have developed many friends who now call you regularly for legal advice about their business and personal decisions and disputes. Over the past three years, you have billed about 100 hours a year to these Arizona clients. None of the representations involve court appearances.

f. You are hired by an Arizona client to represent her in a criminal defense case. You advise the client and begin to negotiate a plea agreement while your motion for pro hac vice admission is pending.

g. You are in-house counsel for a major corporation, which owns a subsidiary in Arizona. You regularly consult with the legal staff and officers of the subsidiary regarding matters involving Arizona law.

h. You are a national expert in grandparent rights. You act as a consultant to an attorney in Arizona representing a grandparent seeking custody of her deceased daughter's child.

i. Your regular client from your home state has a contract dispute with a company in Arizona. The contract forum selection and choice of laws provisions specify Arizona. Client would like you to represent him in the arbitration required by the contract.

Obviously, there are areas of ambiguity in rule 5.5 that will have to be clarified by application of the rule. You, however, likely do not want to have to be the attorney involved in the disciplinary case that provides that clarification. So what do you do to reduce risks when you are providing legal services that may or may not constitute the unauthorized practice of law?

2. The Arizona rule adds provisions that emphasize that an attorney who practices law in Arizona without a license (whether permissible under the rules or not) is subject to the Arizona rules of professional conduct. Given that the sanctions available in disciplinary actions in most states are limited to reprimand, suspension, and disbarment, of what practical value is it to say that an attorney is subject to the disciplinary rules of a state in which she is not licensed? Remember that court disciplinary orders are enforced through the power of contempt.

   Model 5.5 was adopted in order to close the gap between the way attorneys were actually practicing law and the territorial-based rules of an earlier age. Many attorneys underestimated the seriousness and narrowness of the unauthorized practice restrictions and crossed jurisdictional borders to practice law in other states on routine basis, believing that their greatest risk was a loss of fees. Consider the consequences of that attitude to attorney Trester in the following case.

In the Matter of Trester
285 Kan. 404; 172 P.3d 31 (2007)

This is an original proceeding in discipline filed by the Disciplinary Administrator against respondent, Irwin S. Trester, an attorney admitted to the practice of law in Kansas in 1968. A hearing panel of the Kansas Board for the

Discipline of Attorneys conducted a formal hearing, as required by Kansas Supreme Court Rule 211 (2006 Kan. Ct. R. Annot. 284).

The hearing panel concluded that Trester violated Kansas Rules of Professional Conduct (KRPC) as follows: KRPC 5.5(a) (2006 Kan. Ct. R. Annot. 494) (unauthorized practice of law); KRPC 8.4(b) and (c) (2006 Kan. Ct. R. Annot. 510) (misconduct). Additionally, Trester was held to have violated Kansas Supreme Court Rule 202 (2006 Kan. Ct. R. Annot. 239) (grounds for discipline). The hearing panel unanimously recommended that Trester be indefinitely suspended from the practice of law in the state of Kansas.

Kansas: indefinitely suspended

Indefinite suspension is similar to disbarment, except a disbarred attorney seeking reinstatement faces a higher burden of proof than an attorney asking a court to lift a suspension

Hearing Panel's Findings of Fact

This action arose out of Trester's practice of law in the state of California where he does not have a license. Despite his admission to the Kansas Bar, Trester never practiced law in the state of Kansas and returned to California and took the California Bar examination on four occasions. Trester never passed the California Bar examination but was not dissuaded and, for nearly 40 years, practiced law in California. His office was advertised as "Law Offices of Irwin Trester." Much of his work was limited to the federal practice in the areas of immigration and labor law. Trester testified before the hearing panel that he was merely required to have a license to practice in some state, not necessarily in the same state where his office was located.

Friedman Bag Company (Friedman), a California company, retained Trester to represent it in the areas of labor and employment law. Trester never informed Friedman that he was not licensed to practice law in California. In 2002, Friedman sued both Trester individually and his business, the "Law Offices of Irwin Trester," in California Superior Court, alleging legal malpractice and fraud. The fraud claim was based on the fact that Trester represented Friedman without a license to do so.

What if Trester had followed the directions provided by Arizona's version of Rule 5.5 and had informed each client that he was not licensed to practice law in California?

In 2005, California prosecutors charged Trester with seven counts of grand theft ... and one count of unauthorized practice of law. The basis for the theft charges was Trester's acceptance of retainers without a license to practice law in the state of California. Trester subsequently entered a plea of no contest to three charges of felony theft and one charge of misdemeanor unauthorized practice of law. On October 26, 2005, the California court placed Trester on probation for 3 years and ordered him to perform 100 hours of community service, to pay restitution, and to refrain from practicing law in California. Then, in June 2006, the California court granted Trester's motion to reduce the felony convictions to misdemeanors under the California penal code.

theft charges

Does it surprise you to see unauthorized practice being characterized as grand theft?

Note that, because its purpose is protection of the public, discipline is not considered criminal punishment. Thus, constitutional protections against double jeopardy do not apply.

Hearing Panel's Conclusions of Law

... KRPC 5.5(a) states that a lawyer shall not "practice law in a jurisdiction where doing so violates the regulation of the legal profession in that jurisdiction." 2006 Kan. Ct. R. Annot. 494. Because Trester was convicted of engaging in the unauthorized practice of law in California, the hearing panel found him in violation of that rule.

The hearing panel found that Trester violated KRPC 8.4(b), which states: "It is professional misconduct for a lawyer to ... commit a criminal act that reflects adversely on the lawyer's honesty, trustworthiness or fitness as a lawyer

R 8.4(b)

in other respects." 2006 Kan. Ct. R. Annot. 510. Focusing again on Trester's three California theft convictions and one conviction of engaging in the unauthorized practice of law, the hearing panel concluded that theft and the unauthorized practice of law are crimes that reflect directly on his honesty and trustworthiness.

Finally, the hearing panel also found that Trester violated KRPC 8.4(c), which states: "It is professional misconduct for a lawyer to ... engage in conduct involving dishonesty, fraud, deceit, or misrepresentation." 2006 Kan. Ct. R. Annot. 511. The hearing panel concluded that Trester engaged in dishonest conduct when he held himself out as an attorney in California....

The Deputy Disciplinary Administrator recommended Trester be indefinitely suspended, and Trester requested published censure....

Standard of misconduct

Analysis

... Attorney misconduct must be established by substantial, clear, convincing, and satisfactory evidence. *In re Comfort*, 284 Kan. 183, 190, 159 P.3d 1011(2007); *In re Lober*, 276 Kan. 633, 636, 78 P.3d 442 (2003); Supreme Court Rule 211(f) (2006 Kan. Ct. R. Annot. 284)....

Violation of KRPC 8.4(c)

△ Arg

First, Trester argues that clear and convincing evidence does not support the hearing panel's finding that he violated KRPC 8.4(c). KRPC 8.4(c) provides that "[i]t is professional misconduct for a lawyer to ... engage in conduct involving dishonesty, fraud, deceit, or misrepresentation." ...

Rather than motivated by dishonesty, fraud, or deceit, Trester contends that his misconduct was motivated by the "mistaken belief" that he could hold himself out as an attorney because he was admitted to practice law in Kansas and had been admitted to practice law before the United States Supreme Court, the Ninth Circuit Court of Appeals, and the Tenth Circuit Court of Appeals. According to Trester, he has a "plausible explanation" justifying this mistaken belief.

Why was Trester's reliance on the advice of the attorney who was head of the ethics division not a sufficient defense? One reason may have been that the court did not believe that Trester had requested the opinion in good faith — that he had not accurately described his practice to the ethics attorney in securing the opinion.

Recall that Rule 5.5 of the ABA Model Rules of Professional Conduct permits attorneys to practice law if they are authorized by federal law to do so. If Trester had indeed limited his practice to exclusively federal law and federal tribunals, would he have nonetheless have faced charges in California?

Regarding this alleged "plausible explanation," Trester claims that before opening his California office, he solicited input from Los Angeles Attorney Ira Sherman, then head of the ethics division of the California Bar. In his testimony at the hearing, he indicated that the services he provided in California were consistent with the advice given to him by Sherman.

Before the hearing panel, Trester denied ever making any appearances as an attorney before the California Superior Court, Appellate Court, or Supreme Court, instead claiming that he only appeared in those courts as a mediator. Instead of appearing in a legal capacity in California state courts, Trester testified that he made regular appearances in federal immigration courts and before administrative agencies. When asked, however, what percentage of his practice in the last 10 years has related to immigration law, Trester answered: "It's varied from 15 to 20 percent to 50 and sometimes 60 percent." ...

Trester contends that he never told anyone he was a member of the California Bar. But, as the petitioner points out, Trester admitted he never told Friedman that he was not licensed to practice law in California, nor did he place his state of licensure on his business cards or stationery. Trester, instead, advertised that he was an "attorney at law" in the "Law Offices of Irwin Trester," which gave the impression that he was authorized to practice law generally in that state. The petitioner argues that Trester's admission and actions show the intent to deceive. We agree....

Recently, in *In re Pyle*, 283 Kan. 807, 825, 156 P.3d 1231 (2007), this court acknowledged the fact that, in fewer than 50 cases, we have found attorneys guilty of violating KRPC 8.4(c) in its current form. See, *e.g.*, *In re Singleton*, 279 Kan. 515, 111 P.3d 630 (2005) (attorney misrepresented documents to judge; indefinite suspension); *In re Rock*, 279 Kan. 257, 105 P.3d 1290 (2005) (attorney converted client funds, abandoned clients, and committed other misconduct; disbarment). We have no qualms, however, saying that holding oneself out as an attorney in a state in which he or she has no license to practice law and giving the impression the attorney is authorized to practice law generally in that state engages in conduct that violates KRPC 8.4(c).

Clear and convincing evidence supports the panel's finding that Trester violated KRPC 8.4(c).

[After examining aggravating and mitigating factors, the court imposed an indefinite suspension.]

Notes

1. Trester unsuccessfully raised an ethics opinion as his defense in this case. In every state, attorneys may request informal ethics opinions from state ethics authorities or from private bar associations in the state. In California, attorneys may request advisory opinions from the Standing Committee on Professional Responsibility and Conduct. Inquiries must be in writing and may be directed to the bar counsel or to any member of the committee. Opinions may address the application of the rules of professional conduct and advertising and solicitation issues but questions of law or judicial conduct are not addressed. If the chair of the committee determines that a simple or routine response is appropriate, a letter opinion will be issued. Letter opinions are drafted by the chair or an assigned committee member and circulated to all committee members. Unless two or more members object within ten days, the chairperson sends the letter opinion to the attorney. Those inquiries meriting formal opinion responses result in a more formal process of deliberation, drafting, approval by the Board of Governors, and publication. Despite this formality, these ethics opinions are not binding on state disciplinary authorities. What then, is the value of requesting an ethics opinion?

2. A second defense Trester raised was that he had a federal practice. The "federal practice" exception has proven to be one of the most controversial aspects of attorney multijurisdictional practice, especially for immigration and bankruptcy attorneys who represent individuals. Is it truly possible to limit your practice to only federal law? Doesn't even an immigration or bankruptcy attorney have to advise his or her clients about the effect of state law on their situation? If it is practical to limit your practice only to federal law, may you

then open an office in a state in which you are not licensed and advertise your legal services? What concerns do states have in conceding a "federal practice" exception to state licensing requirements?

4.4 What Are Some Alternative Business Forms for Legal Services Delivery?

Read Model Rules 5.4 and 5.7 and the comments to these rules. These rules are designed to prohibit attorneys from placing themselves in positions in which non-lawyers can influence their independent professional judgment. The general rule found in Rule 5.4 prohibits sharing fees with non-lawyers and does not permit lay persons to have an ownership interest in a for-profit law firm. Rule 5.7 presents the mirror image of the unauthorized practice issue—regulating attorneys involved in activities that are not technically treated as the practice of law. The rule does not prohibit attorneys from engaging in these "ancillary practices" or hiring other non-lawyer professionals to provide these services, but it requires attorneys to insure that clients of these services are given the same protections of the rules (competence, confidentiality, and loyalty, for example) as any other client. Where the rule draws the line is when the other professional working with the attorney becomes a partner rather than an employee, or shares fees from cases, or is otherwise placed in a position where he might influence or direct the attorney's judgment.

These rules are under significant pressure from clients, allied professional groups, and global regulation that permits these arrangements. Some exceptions to non-lawyer investment or direction of attorneys exist and more have been proposed. Of course, corporations are permitted to hire in-house counsel to represent their interests. Likewise, attorneys for government entities work at the direction of non-lawyer government officials. While theoretically, this is no different than any client who hires an attorney, practically, the role of an in-house or government attorney—serving one client and often involved in not only the client's legal decisions but its day-to-day operations—can be quite different than that of a private practice attorney.

Another circumstance that has put the rule under pressure is when nonprofit legal services organizations wish to hire attorneys to provide legal services to the clients of the organization. Notice that Rule 5.4 provides exceptions for these types of practice. How far do those exceptions extend? States that have addressed this circumstance have concluded that these arrangements do not violate the rules of professional conduct. For example, the New Jersey court in *In Re Educational Law Center, Inc.*, 86 N.J. 124 (1981) concluded that nonprofit corporations employing attorneys as staff to handle client matters are not engaging in unauthorized practice of law if the corporation's involvement is limited to that of a conduit to bring the attorney and client together, and the corporation takes special precautions to avoid interfering with the attorney's independent professional judgment in the handling of the matter.

But why limit non-lawyer involvement in law firms on an equal footing with attorneys? Europe has permitted so-called "multidisciplinary practices" for some time now. The 2007 Legal Services Act is designed to liberalize and regulate the market for legal services in England and Wales and to encourage more competition. The Act will allow non-lawyers to have ownership interests in legal services organizations and will permit multidisciplinary partnerships. Solicitors across England have already begun banding together to develop a marketing strategy to meet the challenge of competitions from banks, and even supermarkets. In fact, the Act is called by some the "Tesco Law," after the supermarket giant that many fear will be soon offering wills and conveyancing along with oranges and haircuts. A new regulatory agency, the Legal Services Board, will license all of these "alternative business structures." Will the United States follow suit? Wills by Walmart anyone?

In the United States, however, only the District of Columbia has liberalized its rule on multidisciplinary practice, primarily because so many law firms have non-lawyer lobbyists. The comments to the DC rule indicate some of the rationale for the liberalization.

[3] As the demand increased for a broad range of professional services from a single source, lawyers employed professionals from other disciplines to work for them. So long as the nonlawyers remained employees of the lawyers, these relationships did not violate the disciplinary rules. However, when lawyers and nonlawyers considered forming partnerships and professional corporations to provide a combination of legal and other services to the public, they faced serious obstacles under the former rules.

[4] This rule rejects an absolute prohibition against lawyers and nonlawyers joining together to provide collaborative services, but continues to impose traditional ethical requirements with respect to the organization thus created....

[7] As the introductory portion of paragraph (b) makes clear, the purpose of liberalizing the Rules regarding the possession of a financial interest or the exercise of management authority by a nonlawyer is to permit nonlawyer professionals to work with lawyers in the delivery of legal services without being relegated to the role of an employee. For example, the rule permits economists to work in a firm with antitrust or public utility practitioners, psychologists or psychiatric social workers to work with family law practitioners to assist in counseling clients, nonlawyer lobbyists to work with lawyers who perform legislative services, certified public accountants to work in conjunction with tax lawyers or others who use accountants' services in performing legal services, and professional managers to serve as office managers, executive directors, or in similar positions. In all of these situations, the professionals may be given financial interests or managerial responsibility, so long as all of the requirements of paragraph (c) are met.

[8] [The Rule] does not permit an individual or entity to acquire all or any part of the ownership of a law partnership or other form of law practice organization for investment or other purposes. It thus does not permit a corporation, an investment banking firm, an investor, or any other person or entity to entitle itself to all or any portion of the income or profits of a law firm or other similar organization. Since such an investor would not be an individual performing professional services within the law firm or other organization, the requirements of [the rule] would not be met.

[11] [the rule] permits a lawyer to share legal fees with a nonprofit organization that employed, retained, or recommended employment of the lawyer in the matter. A lawyer may decide to contribute all or part of legal fees recovered from the opposing party to a nonprofit organization. Such a contribution may or may not involve fee-splitting, but when it does, the prospect that the organization will obtain all or part of the lawyer's fees does not inherently compromise the lawyer's professional independence, whether the lawyer is employed by the organization

or was only retained or recommended by it. A lawyer who has agreed to share legal fees with such an organization remains obligated to exercise professional judgment solely in the client's best interests. Moreover, fee-splitting in these circumstances may promote the financial viability of such nonprofit organizations and facilitate their public interest mission.

Notice that the D.C. rules do not go as far as the European model in opening practice ownership to non-lawyers. What do you think about a rule permitting non-lawyers to form partnerships with lawyers or even own law firms? What are the risks? The benefits?

The North Carolina Bar Association's Taskforce on Multidisciplinary Practice examined the following hypotheticals and discussed whether these business arrangements were consistent with the values of the legal profession. See if you agree with the Bar Association:

- A traditional law firm creates a separate legal subsidiary to provide word processing services for other law firms and businesses.
- A large CPA firm hires a lawyer to draft legal documents to effectuate the merger and acquisition arrangements negotiated by the CPA.
- A law firm enters into a contract with a CPA firm to refer business to each other on a nonexclusive basis including referencing each other in their marketing brochures.
- A three-member law firm practicing elder law admits as a partner in the law firm a Medicare/Medicaid expert but the lawyers control the law firm in all ways and all partners must comply with legal ethics rules.
- A realtor and a lawyer split fees on selling and then closing real estate. They also provide credit life insurance for a commission to home buyers.

North Carolina Bar Association, Committee on Multidisciplinary Practice, Memorandum (2000) http://www.ncbar.org/about/committees/mdp.aspx.

While the commission was comfortable only with the first of these, it recognized that there might be some value in others, though it did not believe the law had yet evolved to the point that these arrangements would be permissible. Do you agree?

Test Your Understanding

Stephen Suem is a civil procedure expert, a professor at the University of Anystate, and an attorney licensed in the state of Anystate. He also has been admitted to practice in the federal district court for the district of Anystate and the 20th Circuit Court of Appeals (in which the Anystate district court is located). He has been approached by a group of Otherstate attorneys representing plaintiffs in various federal court actions to act as a consulting expert in their litigation.

Anystate has adopted Rule 5.5 of the Model Rules without variation. It does not have a statute regulating unauthorized practice of law. Otherstate has not adopted the newest version of Rule 5.5 but has the prior version of the rule, which prohibits only the unauthorized practice of law without definition. The Otherstate code has a statute that makes the unauthorized practice of law a misdemeanor. That statute defines the practice of law as "the exercise of professional judgment in applying legal principles to address another person's individualized needs through analysis, advice, or other [legal] assistance."

The plaintiffs want to consolidate their actions into the federal court of Otherstate, which is in the 20th Circuit. Suem is not licensed in the state of Otherstate, but has significant experience with federal litigation in other district courts in the circuit. They approached Stephen for his expertise in the hopes that he would manage the plaintiff's committee: coordinating the timing of discovery and advising and directing them on other strategic considerations in the federal procedure. The litigation is likely to take several years and require regular visits to Otherstate. Stephen agreed to do so at an hourly rate of $250. Since all the attorneys were acting on contingent fee basis, however, Stephen agreed that he would only bill the attorneys if they were successful in their suits.

a. What law determines whether Suem's actions are the unauthorized practice of law for the purposes of discipline? (See Model Rule 8.5).

b. What is Suem's best argument that he is not engaged in the practice of law?

c. What is the best argument that Suem is engaged in the practice of law?

d. If Suem's actions are considered the practice of law, what is his best argument that these activities are not unauthorized practice?

e. What are the risks to Suem for agreeing to this arrangement?

f. How would you advise Suem to reduce these risks?

To Learn More

To read more about the future of the legal profession, read RICHARD SUSSKIND'S THE END OF LAWYERS?: RETHINKING THE NATURE OF LEGAL SERVICES (Oxford University Press 2010); THOMAS MORGAN, THE VANISHING AMERICAN LAWYER (Oxford University Press 2010); or Laurel S. Terry, *The Future Regulation of the Legal Profession: The Impact of Treating the Legal Profession as "Service Providers"*, 2008 J. PROF. LAW. 189, 189 (2008). Part of your professional skills you should be practicing now is that of keeping informed of current trends and events in the world of law. Many of the changes in the legal profession are best followed in law media such as the ABA Journal or the National Law Journal.

Unit One Review

Revisit the true/false questions at the beginning of this unit. You should now recognize that all of these statements were true.

Reflective Practice

Think about what you have learned about the legal profession and its regulation in this unit. How does this affect your thinking about the meaning of "professional responsibility"? What do you think this means for your future career? How do you think the structure of the legal profession will change during your career?

Multiple Choice Review Questions

*[handwritten: * multi-disciplinary practices are not sanctioned]*

1. A divorce attorney entered into a partnership with a licensed clinical social worker. The partnership provided legal and other assistance to clients in connection with divorce, child custody, adoption, and other family law matters. The social worker provided therapy and counseling within her area of expertise and licensing. The attorney had a comprehensive system in place to protect confidentiality, loyalty, and other duties so that the social worker did not interfere with the attorney's compliance with his professional obligations as a lawyer.

    Is the attorney subject to discipline?

    A. Yes, because clients of the partnership are provided legal services. *[handwritten: — what if 2nd partnership]*

    B. Yes, because lawyers may not form partnerships with non-lawyers.

    C. No, because the social worker performed only work that she was authorized to perform as a licensed clinical social worker.

    D. No, because the attorney made reasonable efforts to ensure that the social worker did not interfere with the attorney's compliance with his professional obligations as a lawyer.

2. Rule 4.2 provides that "In representing a client, a lawyer shall not communicate about the subject of the representation with a person the lawyer knows to be represented by another lawyer in the matter, unless the lawyer has the consent of the other lawyer or is authorized to do so by law or a court order." Amanda Attorney wants to talk to Ralph Represented, the opposing party in a lawsuit, but Ralph's attorney will not give her permission to speak to Ralph.

Amanda's paralegal, knowing about the situation, says that Ralph is a member of her church and she could talk to him about the case. Amanda agrees and coaches the paralegal about what to say to Ralph when she next sees him. The paralegal tries to do so, but Ralph refuses to speak with her. Is Attorney subject to discipline?

A. Yes, because she tried to communicate with Ralph without his attorney's permission.

B. Yes, because the attorney assisted the paralegal in practicing law without a license.

C. No, because the paralegal did not succeed in speaking with Ralph, there was no violation of Rule 4.2.

D. No, because it was the paralegal's idea to speak to Ralph.

Analysis & Answers:

1. This question helps you to recognize that there are multiple problems that a multi-disciplinary practice can raise. Answer C is tempting if you were reading this rule as a question about assisting in the unauthorized practice of law. While it is true that Attorney would not be subject to discipline for this reason, there are other rules to consider. Answer D as well is tempting, particularly because the language of the explanation is a direct quote from Rule 5.7, Responsibilities Regarding Law-Related Services. However, this is not merely a law-related services problem—it is a true multidisciplinary practice and, thus far, the ABA has not approved these practice arrangements. Thus, the correct answer is A. Rule 5.4(b) provides that lawyers may not form partnerships with non-lawyers IF the activities of the partnership include practicing law. Answer B is incomplete in addressing this rule. Of course, attorneys can form partnerships with non-lawyers (I can open a hot-dog stand with someone).

2. The best answer is A. The key to understanding this question is to carefully read the several bases for misconduct that are nested in subsection (a) and the relationship between these. Amanda violated Rule 8.4(a) in several ways: she "attempted to violate" Rule 4.2 and she "knowingly assisted" another to "do so" (that is, to attempt to violate the rule). Answer D is not correct because, while it might mean that Amanda didn't "induce" another to violate the rule, notice that the phrase is "assist OR induce" so each is a separate ground for violation. Answer B is not correct because the paralegal was not practicing law (she is not giving advice, advocating, etc.). Answer C is not correct because attempts are violations.

Unit Two

The Attorney-Client Relationship

Goals of Unit Two

The Preamble to the Model Rules of Professional Conduct identifies three roles of the attorney: "representative of clients, an officer of the legal system and a public citizen having special responsibility for the quality of justice." In this unit we will examine the first of these three roles—the representative of clients. The goals for this unit are for you to understand how one becomes a client, the allocation of authority between attorney and client, the standards for competent representation; and the available options for being paid for that representation. These are not always clear-cut matters and the rules provide a large degree of discretion on some of these matters. You should strive to not only understand the legal doctrines, but also begin to fill in the blanks provided by the doctrine with your own personal understandings and ethics. You will practice two skills, communication and reflection, that are central to creating, maintaining, and ending the attorney-client relationship in a professional manner.

Pretest

To gauge your assumptions about the materials covered in this unit, complete the following statements:

1. You have an attorney-client relationship with someone

    if ___hired___ ,

    or if ___advise___ ,

    or if ___counsel___ ,

    but not if or if ___talk___ OR ___tell them you are not. advising___

2. An attorney must accept representation of a client if

    ___duty imposed___

    unless ___violates ABA / law___ .

3. An attorney must withdraw from representing a client if

_____ *Conflict of interest* _____

and may withdraw from representing a client if

_____ *difficult client* _____

unless _____ *bound to continue* _____ .

4. The most common source of regulation of attorney competence is

_____ *ABA* _____ .

5. An attorney must comply with a client's directions regarding

_____ *best interest* _____

unless _____ *violates law* _____ .

4. Informed consent means

_____ *Party understands risks and accepts* _____

5. Attorneys fees are reasonable and enforceable if

_____ *informed consent is given* _____ .

Chapter Five

Selecting and Rejecting Clients

Learning Objectives

After you have read this chapter and completed the assignments, you should be able to:

- Identify the three ways in which an attorney-client relationship is formed and methods of reducing the risk of unintentionally creating duties to a client.
- Explain why it is easier to reject a client than to withdraw from representation and be able to screen a client for common risky representations.
- Explain why it is important to screen potential clients and be able to identify those representations an attorney must reject.
- In various fact situations, apply the requirements for three categories of attorney withdrawal (mandatory, good cause permissive, and other permissive) and identify the limitations on withdrawal rights.
- Use forms properly to draft letters and agreements that clarify the attorney-client relationship (or the absence of that relationship).

Rules to Study

As you will see, the foundational question we will examine in this chapter — whether there is an attorney-client relationship — is not addressed by the ABA Model Rule of Professional Conduct. Instead, answers to this question can be found in common law standards from the law of negligence (malpractice), contracts, and agency, and, in some states, by statutory definition. A number of rules of professional conduct are relevant when the question is not whether there is an attorney-client relationship, but with whom that relationship exists. Those rules include:

Rule 1.18 (Prospective Client)

Rule 1.13 (Organization as a Client)

Rule 1.14 (Client with Diminished Capacity)

Rule 4.2 (Communication with Unrepresented Persons)

Rule 1.8(f) (third-party payors)

In addition two rules come into play when you are deciding whether to withdraw or decline a client:

Rule 1.16 (Declining or Terminating Representation)

93

Rule 6.2 (Accepting Appointments)

Preliminary Problems

In practice, you will talk to many people about legal issues, for example:

1. Amanda calls your office and speaks to your secretary about hiring you to represent her in a dispute with her tenant. You meet with Amanda but she decides not to hire you.

2. You are in-house counsel for XYZ Corporation. Barbara, one of the employees, comes to you to discuss her concerns that her manager in the company is overbilling customers. Barbara is concerned about her own liability and that of the company.

3. Clarence is a doctor who has been sued for malpractice. His malpractice insurance carrier has engaged you to defend him in the action.

4. Darryl has been charged with robbery and you have been engaged to represent him. Edward is a witness who is going to testify that Darryl was with him at home during the time the robbery occurred. You are preparing Edward for his testimony.

5. Felicia is an attorney who has been engaged by George to represent him in a divorce. Felicia has asked for your help in drafting a qualified domestic relations order to split George's pension.

6. You sit on the board of a local non-profit hospice organization. At a recent board meeting, you are asked about the organization's tax liability for certain fundraising activities.

7. You are appointed to represent Imogene, a 14-year-old charged with selling drugs. Imogene does not trust you and is not interested in your help.

Which of these persons is your client? What conversations, actions, and documentation will make the answer to that question clearer in each of these cases?

5.1 How Do You Form an Attorney-Client Relationship?

The choice whether to represent a particular client is one of the most critical choices for an attorney, affecting not only the attorney's responsibilities to that client but shaping future choices of clients as well. When has someone become your client? You will not find the answer to this question in the ABA Model Rules of Professional Conduct or in most state versions of the rules. Paragraph 17 of the Preamble to the Model Rules emphasizes that it is from the common law (primarily from malpractice cases and cases involving the attorney-client privilege) that one finds the definition of the attorney-client relationship.

In most jurisdictions, an attorney-client relationship can be established in one of three ways. First, you can expressly agree to represent the client. Second, you can act in such a way that the client reasonably assumes that you are representing her. Third, a court can appoint you to represent a client. You can remember these as the three As of the attorney-client relationship: *Agreement, Assumption,* or *Appointment.* We will address the first two of these in this chapter and we will address appointments in the unit on access to justice.

The first method of establishing an attorney-client relationship is the most obvious — agreeing to represent a client. However, some attorneys mistakenly believe that, unless a client has signed a representation agreement and paid an advance, the attorney has no duty to that individual. While a written fee agreement and payment clearly establish the presence of an attorney-client relationship, the absence of either a written agreement or an obligation to pay does not mean that no relationship exists. So, while it is very useful and important to use written representation agreements, be sure that your communication is consistent. If you will not represent clients until they have signed a representation agreement (and perhaps paid an advance on your fees), be sure you clearly communicate that to a potential client, lest they leave your office believing that you are representing them.

The second method of forming an attorney-client relationship is one that creates for attorneys an "accidental client." Anything short of clear communication regarding whether and when you will represent an individual presents the risks of unintentionally forming an attorney-client relationship by creating a circumstance in which it is reasonable for an individual to assume that you are representing him. What are the circumstances in which someone might reasonably believe that she is your client even if you did not intend and have not expressly agreed to represent her?

The most common risk for an accidental client is when a prospective client seeks your assistance. *Togstad v. Vesely, Otto, Miller & Keefe*, 291 N.W.2d 686 (Minn. 1980) remains the classic case on this issue. In that case, Mrs. Togstad consulted an attorney about a potential medical malpractice action. Mrs. Togstad got the impression that the attorney thought her case was weak but that he would consult other attorneys in his office and get back to her if he decided otherwise. A year later, having never heard from the attorney, Mrs. Togstad consulted with another attorney and learned that the statute of limitations would bar the claim. She sued the original law firm, which was held liable for $649,500.

The opinion was important because it emphasized to attorneys the risks of ambiguity in dealing with potential clients. The attorney in this case testified that he had warned Mrs. Togstad about the statute of limitations and had told her that his firm did not have extensive experience in medical malpractice cases, but she denied this. Of course, who said what to whom is a question of fact to be resolved by a jury. It should come as no surprise that, absent any documentation, the jury believed Mrs. Togstad. Since this case, most attorneys routinely send "non-engagement letters" to potential clients they turn down, documenting that they are not undertaking representation, and suggesting that if the client wishes to pursue the claim, he should be mindful that time limitations might apply.

The opinion also made clear that one need not have an express, written agreement in order to be deemed to represent someone. The opinion reviewed two different theories for establishing the attorney-client relationship. Under an implied contract theory of malpractice, when an attorney provides someone advice in his capacity as an attorney and that person reasonably relies on his advice, the attorney has created an attorney-client relationship. Similarly, under a tort theory of malpractice, an attorney-client relationship can be based on an attorney's advice given in circumstances in which the attorney could reasonably foresee harm to the client if the advice is negligently given. Under both the tort and contract approaches to implying an attorney-client relationship, the key element is reasonableness—without reasonably foreseeable harm or reasonable reliance, no attorney-client relationship will be implied.

Ever since *Togstad*, generations of law students have been presented with the "cocktail party" hypothetical, in which someone approaches you at a party and casually asks for some legal advice and you casually provide it, thereby setting you up for malpractice liability if your advice was in error. The cocktail party scenario aside, there are certainly many opportunities for attorneys to inadvertently create attorney-client relationships in their day-to-day lives. Attorneys may enter into a business arrangement, make investments, run non-legal businesses, or serve on boards of directors of non-profit organizations. Note that it is giving advice, as opposed to general information about the law, that is the key to the malpractice risk in these circumstances. A lawyer may answer a "general question about the law, for instance in a purely social setting, without a client-lawyer relationship arising." RESTATEMENT (THIRD) OF THE LAW GOVERNING LAWYERS § 14, cmt c (2000). However, as we saw when trying to define the practice of law, the line between information and advice is not a clear one.

Even if, for malpractice purposes, there is no attorney-client relationship, you may still have some duties to an individual who seeks your advice. For example, it may be perfectly clear to both you and the individual with whom you are speaking that you will not be representing her and that you have given her no advice. So, in these circumstances, you would be unlikely to have an attorney-client relationship for purposes of malpractice liability. But you may nonetheless have a duty of confidentiality and loyalty to that individual based on your receipt of confidential information. Where an individual conveys information to you in your capacity as an attorney, and has a reasonable expectation that you will keep that information confidential, you have a fiduciary obligation to honor that expectation. "A fiduciary relationship may result because of the nature of the work performed and the circumstances under which confidential information is divulged." *Westinghouse Elec. Corp. v. Kerr-McGee Corp.*, 580 F.2d 1311, 1320 (7th Cir. 1978). This fiduciary duty, long recognized by the courts, has been incorporated into Model Rule 1.18 regarding prospective clients. Read that rule and consider how it compares to the common-law theories you have learned. We will examine that rule again more carefully in chapters on confidentiality and conflicts of interest.

Another situation in which the identity of your client may be unclear is when you are representing a client and, as part of that representation, must interact with other individuals involved in that matter. A prosecuting attorney represents the public, but must communicate with and even advise a complaining witness or victim. An attorney representing a corporation represents the entity itself (see Model Rule 1.13(a)) but can only do so by interacting with the people who work for that entity. An officer or director (or even an employee) of that corporation may easily believe that the attorney represents him — that his conversations with the attorney are confidential or that the advice the attorney gives him is to protect his interests. If there is no conflict of interest between the individual and the entity, the attorney may indeed choose to represent both clients at the same time. (Model Rule 1.13(e)) This is especially common in closely-held corporations or partnerships. However, this possibility only increases the risks of role confusion.

Even if an attorney is not representing an entity, there can be role confusion. An attorney representing an individual in a particular role (a trustee for an estate or a public official for example) may be unclear about whether the client is the person or the role. An attorney for a child may represent the child but may also or instead represent the "best interests" of the child. Family members or insurers who are funding or assisting in the representation of a client may believe they have the right to direct the attorney or to receive information about the representation. Even opposing parties in litigation may look to you for advice if they are themselves unrepresented. Even more confusing, the law sometimes recognizes a legal duty to these third parties even though they are not clients. For example, a communication between an attorney and his client who is a trustee is not protected by the attorney-client privilege against the beneficiaries of the trust who would seek to discover that communication. *United States v. Jicarilla Apache Nation*, 131 S. Ct. 2313, 2321; 180 L. Ed. 2d 187; 2011 U.S. LEXIS 4381 (2011).

These situations of ambiguity regarding client identity are even more complicated than situations involving prospective clients. How do you reduce ambiguity in a relationship with someone with whom you must regularly communicate, especially when it is important that the individual trusts you and is willing to provide information to you necessary to your representation?

Rule 4.2 directs that resolving misunderstandings about your role is a fundamental duty to unrepresented persons, but the rule does not give a great deal of specific guidance about how to do that. You can reduce the risk of accidentally turning a prospective client into an actual client by limiting the information you receive from that person, refraining from conveying advice, and having no further interactions after you have declined the representation, other than sending a non-engagement letter.

Reducing Risk of prospective client

Professional Responsibility Skill 5-A: Drafting Non-Engagement Letters

1. Identify a situation of client ambiguity that you are likely to face in your practice area. Develop a list of suggestions for avoiding that ambiguity and clarifying misunderstandings when they do arise.

2. Consider the following letter sent by an attorney following an initial meeting with a potential client. Identify the sentence that best protects the attorney from liability or discipline. Identify the sentence that exposes the attorney to the most risk of liability or discipline.

January 20, 20xx
Ms. Maybe Client
1234 Fifth Street
Any City, Any State

Re: Non-engagement

Dear Ms. Client:

Thank you for meeting with me today regarding your interest in incorporating your business. After we briefly discussed the steps necessary to incorporate your business, you have indicated that you are not yet sure whether you would like to incorporate your business or remain a sole proprietorship. Please understand that I have not thoroughly reviewed your circumstances and have expressed no opinion to you regarding the optimal business formation strategy for you. Rather, you have indicated that you are not yet sure that you are interested in pursuing this decision at this time. Therefore, I will not be representing you and have no further obligations to you until you first contact me and indicate that you would like to proceed and second sign an attorney-client engagement contract.

If I have not heard from you within 30 days, I will assume you do not wish to proceed and I will close my file and return the papers you have given me to consider.

Sincerely,

Attorney

3. One of the best ways to prevent misunderstandings with potential clients whom you choose not to represent is to write a non-engagement letter. Consider this non-engagement letter.

> Dear NONclient:
>
> I don't represent you.
> I won't represent you.
> I have never represented you.
> Don't expect I will give you advice or represent your interests.
> Don't expect I will keep your information confidential.
> Don't expect I will avoid representing others whose interests conflict with yours.
>
> Sincerely,
>
> NOT your attorney

For each of the six statements in this letter, decide whether this is a message you want to send the client and whether you can send that message consistent with Rule 1.18. Then re-write the letter to express just as clearly but less harshly the messages you want to and are permitted to convey.

Researching Professional Responsibility 5-A: Finding Forms

As you have seen, documenting your relationship with a client (or lack of relationship) is a critical part of professional responsibility practice. In drafting their letters to clients, engagement contracts, and other essential written communications with clients, many attorneys work from examples of these documents or checklists. How do you find these drafting guides? One excellent source for letters and engagement letters can be your state bar association or state malpractice insurer. Many of these organizations provide free formbooks (often called "Client Keepers"), some of which are available online. The following are some examples:

The Alabama Bar Association Practice Management website has a collection of forms, checklists and handbooks of practice management, including a "Client Keeper" with sample letters. http://www.alabar.org/pmap/articles.cfm.

The Louisiana State Bar provides a variety of sample forms on its loss prevention website (includes a conflict checking form and screening checklist for new clients) http://www.lsba.org/2007Solo/GilsbarLossPreventionForms.pdf.

The Missouri Bar Association, Law Practice management site has a variety of resources, including a Client Keeper (consisting of forms for interviewing clients, fee agreements, in Word and PDF formats.) http://www.mobar.org/lpmonline.

The American Bar Association publishes law practice management books that provide sample letters and forms. Formbooks are available for general research as well, both in hard copy and in Lexis and Westlaw; however, many of these forms will not be as practical as the forms developed locally for your state's practice.

Regardless of where you find forms and checklists, never simply use a form without carefully reviewing it for currency and fit. Forms are not necessarily updated to reflect changes in the law, so compare any forms you find with the current requirements of the law. Likewise, few client communications are so generic that you can simply fill in the blanks on a form and be confident that it is communicating the information you need. Review the letter or agreement to be sure it fits the needs of your client and your representation.

Practice researching and evaluating examples of client letters by locating at least two sample client non-engagement letters. What do they have in common? How are they different?

5.2 Reading the Rules: Withdrawing from Representation

Sometimes you do not discover that a client is someone you should not or must not represent until after you have already undertaken the representation. You do not have an unlimited right to simply "fire" a client. Your rights to withdraw are limited by Rule 1.16.

Rule 1.16 governs the attorney's duty to avoid certain representations and the duty and right to withdraw from representation once undertaken. The rule is fairly dense and requires careful reading, but is an excellent rule for practicing your skill in deciphering a rule. Do yourself a favor and really struggle through the rule before you find a source that explains the rule for you.

Let's use Indiana's version of Rule 1.16 to practice reading this rule. (You will notice that Indiana has adopted the ABA Model with no substantial modifications.) First, read through the entire rule, paying particular attention to the function of each section of the rule.

Indiana Supreme Court Rules—Rules of Professional Conduct
Rule 1.16. Declining or Terminating Representation

(a) Except as stated in paragraph (c), a lawyer shall not represent a client or, where representation has commenced, shall withdraw from the representation of a client if:

> (1) the representation will result in violation of the Rules of Professional Conduct or other law;
>
> (2) the lawyer's physical or mental condition materially impairs the lawyer's ability to represent the client; or
>
> (3) the lawyer is discharged.

(b) Except as stated in paragraph (c), a lawyer may withdraw from representing a client if:

> (1) withdrawal can be accomplished without material adverse effect on the interests of the client;

(2) the client persists in a course of action involving the lawyer's services that the lawyer reasonably believes is criminal or fraudulent;

(3) the client has used the lawyer's services to perpetrate a crime or fraud;

(4) a client insists upon taking action that the lawyer considers repugnant or with which the lawyer has a fundamental disagreement;

(5) the client fails substantially to fulfill an obligation to the lawyer regarding the lawyer's services and has been given reasonable warning that the lawyer will withdraw unless the obligation is fulfilled;

(6) the representation will result in an unreasonable financial burden on the lawyer or has been rendered unreasonably difficult by the client; or

(7) other good cause for withdrawal exists.

(c) A lawyer must comply with applicable law requiring notice to or permission of a tribunal when terminating a representation. When ordered to do so by a tribunal, a lawyer shall continue representation notwithstanding good cause for terminating the representation.

(d) Upon termination of representation, a lawyer shall take steps to the extent reasonably practicable to protect a client's interests, such as giving reasonable notice to the client, allowing time for employment of other counsel, surrendering papers and property to which the client is entitled and refunding any advance payment of fee or expense that has not been earned or incurred. The lawyer may retain papers relating to the client to the extent permitted by other law.

Now, re-read the rule, using the guidelines for rule reading below:

Context

The first step in understanding many rules of professional conduct is deciding whether the rule prohibits, requires, or merely authorizes conduct. (See ABA Model Rules, Preamble para. 14). Which parts of Rule 1.16 are "must" or mandatory rules and which are "may" or discretionary? Remember to identify the Who, What, When, Where, and Why of the rule—in particular, when precisely do the duties in this rule arise? (See part (d)).

Relationships

Remember that this rule is a rule of professional conduct; that is, it provides standards for attorney discipline. To what extent does this rule constrain a court's discretion to deny withdrawal? If an attorney has entered an appearance on behalf of a client, the attorney must comply with any law that requires notice or permission of the court's permission to withdraw. If an attorney is required to withdraw under this rule, must the court grant the attorney permission to withdraw? Notice that the rule provides that, if the court refuses that permission, the attorney must continue the representation. How would that work if the reason the attorney was requesting to withdraw is because the client fired the attorney or continuing the representation would result in a violation of the law?

Structure

Do you see that there are three basic categories of withdrawal in the rule? Mandatory withdrawal (a) Permissive harmless withdrawal (b)(1), and Permissive good cause withdrawal (b)(2)-(6). A common error in reading 1.16(b) is assuming that all of the seven enumerated bases for withdrawal are parallel to one another. Examine the list carefully. How is 1.16(b)(1) different from the other bases? Look for other similarities and differences between the bases for withdrawal.

Perhaps you have elsewhere learned the maxim of statutory construction *Expressio Unius Est Exclusio Alterius* (the expression of one thing is the exclusion of another). This maxim is often used to conclude that, if a situation is not included in a statutory list, the drafters intended to exclude it. Does this maxim apply to the list provided in Rule 1.16(b)? In other words, was this list meant to be an exhaustive list of the situations in which an attorney may withdraw? How do you know?

Reasons

Why have a rule requiring withdrawal? Isn't it just common sense that an attorney would have to withdraw if she can't represent a client without violating the rules? What does this rule add? Why do you suppose the drafters provided specific examples of good cause for withdrawal? Who is this portion of the rule designed to protect? Read the comments in particular to help you understand the reasons for these rules.

Visualize

Try building a decision tree or flow chart that represents the series of questions you will need to ask any time you are thinking about withdrawal.

For example, look at the decision tree on the next page, which is designed to answer the question, "Must you withdraw?"

Now you try it. Create a decision tree to answer the question of whether you *may* withdraw. To get you started, consider the following questions. Which part of the rule does this question come from? In what order would you ask these questions? Would a yes or no answer lead to additional questions or to a final answer?

Have you entered an appearance before a tribunal?

Would withdrawal cause a material, adverse effect on your client's interests?

Have you warned the client that you will withdraw?

Imagine

Finally, identify ambiguities in the rule by trying to come up with an example for each situation of withdrawal listed there.

Professional Responsibility Skill 5-B: Choosing Clients

Apart from instances in which they are appointed to representation, attorneys are generally free to reject potential clients for any reason at all. There are several situations in which an attorney must or should reject representation. Once an individual becomes a client, even if the attorney later withdraws, the attorney owes duties of competence, confidentiality, and conflict-free representation. Those duties would not ordinarily have arisen had the attorney initially rejected that representation. Accordingly, attorneys should carefully screen clients for potential problems that might later cause the attorney to be required to withdraw.

Perhaps even more important is avoiding representations that would not necessarily provide a good cause for withdrawal but are going to be a continual problem to you. All attorneys have clients, cases, or transactions that they wish they had not accepted. These representations present significant risks of malpractice and discipline just because they are so unpleasant that you will be tempted to avoid giving them the diligent attention they require. How do you avoid these?

Many attorneys will tell you that your list of "red flag" clients should include those who set off your intuitive alarm bells, even if you can't precisely identify why. However, early in your career your "client selection" judgment is unlikely to be as refined as after you have had more experience. Accordingly, a conscious protocol for rejecting clients will be helpful to you. Brainstorm a number of categories of clients you would want to avoid and then identify how you would screen for these clients. What would you ask or investigate before accepting a representation? For example, unless you have already determined that you will represent a particular client pro bono, you will not want to represent a client who cannot afford your services. How would you know that?

You are in a situation in which you believe you may have to withdraw from a representation.

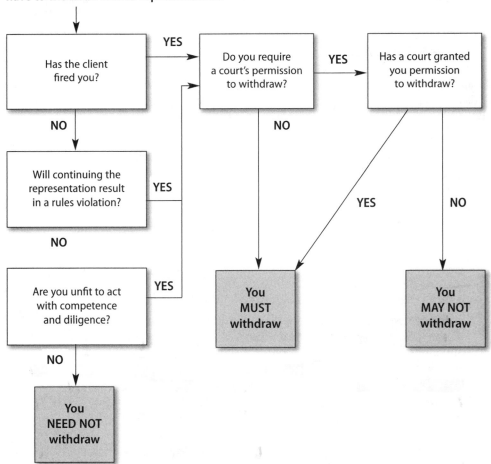

Reflective Practice: Saying Yes, Saying No

Unless you begin your own practice when you graduate, you are unlikely to be in a position of choosing most of your clients at the beginning of your career. Thus, you may find yourself representing individuals whom you would otherwise prefer not to represent or wishing you could represent individuals that your supervising attorneys decline. These conflicts between the clients you have and the clients you wish you had can undermine your effectiveness. Understanding your own risk preferences and vulnerabilities ahead of time can help. Think about circumstances in which you have had to work with people you don't like. What were the characteristics of those people that you found difficult? What made it easier to work with them? What made it harder? What insights does that provide to you that might help you when working with clients you would prefer not to represent?

Test Your Understanding

1. Attorney is asked to bring an action on behalf of Paula Plaintiff for breach of contract against Darren Defendant. After about 25 hours of work on the case, Attorney discovers that Paula has lied about a key aspect of the contract that makes her action frivolous. The statute of limitations is about to run on the action in two weeks. Attorney immediately calls Paula and tells her that he will withdraw from the case because of her dishonesty. Paula pleads with the attorney to help her and promises that she will be more honest; however Attorney is not interested in working with her any further. Paula asks Attorney to at least give her a copy of the petition he has drafted on her behalf. Attorney refuses and Paula is unable to secure alternate counsel in time to file the action. Paula files a disciplinary complaint against attorney.

   How would you defend attorney?

2. Choose one of the preliminary problems that fits the type of practice you are interested in pursuing. Make a checklist of the steps you will take to clarify the identity of your client.

To Learn More

For more practice in identifying clients, see the CALI lesson "Client or Not?" at http://www.cali.org/lesson/660.

For additional review of Rules 6.2 and 1.16, see the CALI lesson "Choosing and Withdrawing from Representation" at http://www.cali.org/lesson/658.

Chapter Six

Providing Competent Lawyering

Learning Objectives

After you have read this chapter and completed the assignments, you should be able to:

- Describe the many public and private sources of regulation of attorney competence including the elements of competence, diligence, and communication in the rules of professional conduct; the basic elements of a legal malpractice case; and the applicability and standards of ineffective assistance of counsel.
- Describe how you manage mistakes responsibly.
- Explain what to do when you make a mistake in client representation.
- Recognize the extent to which you can be held responsible for the mistakes of others.
- Discuss mistakes with others.
- Locate secondary sources that help you to understand professional responsibility issues.
- Identify your own risks for discipline or liability, based on your own strengths and weaknesses and the risks of your chosen practice area, and plan ways to reduce those risks.

Rules to Study

Rules of professional conduct provide standards for competence, diligence, and communication, and rules that govern an attorney's responsibility for the competence of others. However, overall, the doctrines that most often truly regulate attorney competence are found in the common law of agency, malpractice (negligence or contract), and ineffective assistance of counsel. To a lesser extent, we will consider rules of procedure providing relief from judgment and sanctions for frivolous actions.

Preliminary Problem

Donald is a partner in a small practice and you are the newest associate in the firm. However, you have been close friends with Donald and his wife for some years. Donald is on your firm's management committee, taking primary responsibility for the trust accounts and billings with an efficiency that has kept the firm's finances stable and secure for many years now. He is also the firm's internet expert. Anyone stuck on investigating a case, researching a legal issue, or even just tracking down a bit of trivia knows to ask Donald, who will almost miraculously have the answer within minutes. Donald relies on e-mail to contact colleagues and clients and uses online databases to conduct legal research. His efficiency and productivity have been amazing.

Lately, however, you have noticed that Donald has been cancelling appointments and missing deadlines. The quality of his work has fallen considerably, and you have personally bailed him out of a couple of situations that would have been a disaster for the clients and the firm had you not stepped in. All this is happening even though Donald seems to be in the office more than ever. Donald is usually at the office before you arrive and no matter how late it is when you leave, he is still there at his computer. In fact, when you ran into Donald's wife at the grocery store recently and mentioned how hard he's been working, she became upset and confided that their marriage was in trouble and that she thought he was staying away from home to avoid facing their relationship and financial issues.

A couple of days ago, you came into Donald's office to ask for some advice on how to find a particular resource on the web. You noticed that Donald quickly clicked to a blank window on his computer. As he was showing you some websites he had found to help answer your inquiry, you noticed the taskbar at the bottom of the screen listed several windows with some odd titles. You ignored the matter at first, but that afternoon you once again had to drop everything and help him finish a brief that was due at the end of the day. It was clear to you that even though Donald said he had been working on the brief for weeks, he had done almost no work at all. You go home worried about Donald more than ever. At home, you look up a couple of the names of websites you'd seen on Donald's computer and discover they are online gambling sites.

Over the course of the next ten days, Donald handed off three different problems for you to "fix"—all involving botched deadlines, ineptly drafted documents, or incomplete work. In each case, you were able to correct the errors without harm to the clients, but you are very worried. You are more convinced than ever that something is seriously wrong with Donald. You strongly suspect that he is engaged in some risky investment trading or perhaps addicted to online gambling. You believe this is causing him to neglect his clients. Worst of all, you fear that his access to client trust money could be too much temptation if he is in serious financial trouble.

Today, Donald calls you and asks you to fill in at the last minute on a closing for a client who is buying some property. Donald assures you that all the work is complete and you need only meet the client at the closing, do one last read through of the documents, and wrap up the deal. Your experience of the previous week has your nervous. You ask Donald if the closing couldn't be delayed to give you time to come up to speed on the deal, but he insists that it's not necessary and would potentially cause the deal to fall through.

1. Has Donald committed malpractice by his previous errors? Has he violated a rule of professional conduct?

2. Do you have any obligation to do anything to prevent Donald from violating the rules of professional conduct or to help him address any problem he may have that risks violations? If so, what will you do?

3. Do you have an obligation to report Donald's conduct? If so, to whom?

4. Can you step in for Donald on the transaction? What are your options?

As you will see in this chapter, the regulation of competence is a matter that is addressed in a range of laws—disciplinary regulation, liability, procedural standards in both civil and criminal law, as well as the private law of malpractice insurance and rules within firms and among partners. In this first section, we will learn how to avoid circumstances in which our own conduct might put us at increased risk of costly mistakes. We will then briefly review the basic doctrines that provide regulation of competence.

6.1 Why Do Lawyers Make Mistakes and How Should They Respond?

Hopefully your career will never require that you test the limits of the doctrines regulating competence or experience first-hand their application. Certainly you must know the standards for minimum competence, but knowledge alone is not enough to prevent falling below those standards. Rather, you must also consider and put into practice the skills and attitudes that will reduce your risks. That requires understanding why mistakes happen and what to do when they occur.

More important than knowing how to prosecute or defend a malpractice action or respond to a disciplinary inquiry is the ability to know what your risks are and how to reduce those risks. Malpractice, discipline, and sanction are not necessarily a product of inexperience or ignorance in the law, but of failing to pay attention to your clients and to know yourself and manage your work flow. These are skills, rather than knowledge, and do not require a particular class or practice experience to improve them. When attorneys face malpractice or disciplinary actions, there are some fairly common excuses one hears to explain the reason for the error.

[handwritten margin note: Excuses for malprac + disciplining actions]

1. *Time got away from me*—the number one cause of malpractice claims is a missed deadline. The errors that lead to missed deadlines include failing to know the deadline, failing to calendar the deadline, and failing to meet the deadline. Think about your own time and work management system you have developed in law school. Do you have realistic expectations for yourself or do you take on more work than you can handle? Do you plan work and maintain a work schedule that allows you to complete work in a timely and professional manner or are you prone to procrastination or poor planning? Do you have an effective system for calendaring your obligations or do you lose track of deadlines? What is your risk for malpractice if you continue to follow the system you now use? Procrastination is also fertile territory for discipline. *People v. Maynard*, 238 P.3d 672 (Colo. O.P.D.J. 2009) (suspending attorney who "established a pattern and practice of filing matters at the last possible minute as a tactic to delay proceedings"); *In re Lober*, 204 P.3d 610 (Kan. 2009) (Attorney suspended for neglecting case to the point that it was dismissed).

2. *Practicing law would be great if I didn't have to deal with clients*—Law is a service profession and communication skills are at the heart of good client service.

more than half of malpractice actions

Failure to communicate with clients or unclear communication is at the root of many other instances of malpractice. Indeed, together, communications and time management are the two groups of errors that make up more than half of all malpractice actions.

3. *It's all too much* — In the background of many disciplinary and malpractice cases, one can find an attorney who is suffering from depression or excessive stress or who may be coping with the stress of practice with addictions. So common is this problem and so central to competence in the profession that every state has a Lawyers Assistance Program, designed to help educate the profession concerning emotional health and provide prevention and recovery assistance to attorneys. The ABA Commission on Lawyer Assistance Programs maintains a directory of these programs and hosts annual conferences addressing these issues.

4. *I had no idea* — Malpractice risk increases the more you "dabble" in the law. Attorneys who believe that some areas of law are simple enough to "pick up a case now and then" underestimate the extent to which all areas of law today have multiple layers of differing laws and practice standards. Perhaps one of the areas of law attorneys are most likely to believe can be practiced "by the seat of their pants" is the subject matter of this course — professional responsibility. Attorneys who would never think to advise a client on a matter of substantive law without researching the topic will nonetheless resolve issues of professional discipline or liability by consulting their common sense and no more.

5. *I had a feeling , ..* — Attorneys sued for malpractice often "had a feeling" about a particular client but simply ignored it. The client screening protocol you developed in Chapter Five is a critical risk management tool. Likewise, you should have a system for screening types of cases — for the time, skill, and resources the case will take. The pressure for attorneys in private practice to generate hours or fees can lead them to feel that they cannot afford to say no; however, the costs of taking on too much work are far greater than the lost opportunity costs of a managed caseload.

6. *I was just trying to help* — Some attorneys can't say no because they are "only trying to help." Often these attorneys find that their good-hearted efforts to help lead them to take on representations that are beyond their competence or that violate rules regarding conflicts of interest or unauthorized practice. Attorneys in public practice — public defenders, guardians *ad litem*, legal aid attorneys — are especially susceptible to saying yes to the desperate needs for legal representation presented to them, with the result that they often labor under staggering caseloads. A series of ABA Formal Opinions issued between 1981 and 2006, in response to crises in funding for legal representation of indigents, all emphasized that attorneys have an affirmative duty to restrict the size of their caseloads, that underfunding of representation does not excuse attorneys for indigent clients from their duty of competence and diligence, and that attorneys must decline excessive representation. ABA Comm. on Ethics and Prof'l Responsibility, Formal Opinions 347 (1981), 96-399 (1996), and 06-441 (2006).

7. *I wasn't getting paid* — Because we tend to use the language of contract to talk about the attorney-client relationship, some attorneys believe that the duty of competence applies only to clients who are paying for a legal representation. They may believe that, until the client pays, or if a client stops paying, they need not take any steps to protect the client's interest. Or they may believe that pro bono clients

need not be given the same level of basic competence as paid clients because they are better off with some representation (no matter how poor) than none. However, the attorney representing an indigent client pro bono or as a court-appointed attorney owes the same duty of competence to that client as does the attorney for a wealthy entity. As you may recognize, of course, standards of ineffective assistance of counsel and immunity for attorneys in some public positions may eliminate some forms of competence regulation, but that does not mean that the standard of competence is lessened.

8. *I was only trying to get paid*—Often lawyers instigate malpractice claims by suing clients for unpaid fees. The client defends and counter-claims for malpractice. The Model Code's EC 2-23 discourages attorneys from suing for fees. The fact that these suits generate malpractice claims is yet another good reason for that caution.

9. *I was just doing what I was told*—We will examine Rules 5.1 and 5.2 more carefully later on in this chapter. For now, you should recognize there is no "following orders" defense in the rules of professional conduct if the conduct being ordered unarguably violates the rules

10. *I didn't say that!*—Sometimes, an attorney truly has not done anything wrong except to be so unaware of the risks of liability as to never document any of her advice, conclusions, actions, or directions. When malpractice liability turns on a "he said, she said," attorneys who do not document their representation are rarely in a favorable position.

No matter how much you understand your own risks for these ten mistakes and work to lower those risks, mistakes are bound to happen. What do you do when you make a mistake? The natural human tendency is to react with a stress response: fight, flight, or freeze. But these instinctive responses are the very ones you must avoid. Flight or freeze might take the form of ignoring or trying to cover-up the mistake. But trying to hide a mistake is always unethical, can ruin careers, and frequently magnifies damages. Indeed, the classic pattern of discipline in this area is one of a domino effect. An attorney takes on too much or too complex work, with insufficient resources, then makes a mistake (often missing a deadline), then avoids dealing with the mistake by refusing to communicate with the client, sometimes leading to attempts to cover up the error by lying about the mistake and attempting to "pay off" the client. *See, e.g., In re Helman*, 640 N.E.2d 1063 (Ind. 1994).

Perhaps even more common but equally bad judgment is the fight response—blaming someone else—often the secretary or paralegal. There is no ground to be gained in passing off an error. Even if a secretary or non-lawyer assistant did make a mistake, you are very likely responsible for that error if it resulted from your sloppy supervision. Attorneys are responsible not only for their own competence but for the competence (or lack thereof) of any attorneys or non-lawyer personnel under their supervision.

Clearly, the first step in addressing a mistake is the hardest: that is, admitting that you have made a mistake and telling the appropriate people. Who are those people? First you should notify your client. If the lawyer's conduct of the matter gives the client a substantial malpractice claim against the lawyer, the lawyer must disclose that to the client. *Leonard v. Dorsey & Whitney*, 553 F.3d 609 (8th Cir. 2009). *See generally*, Benjamin P. Cooper, *The Lawyer's Duty to Inform His Client of His Own Malpractice*, 61 BAYLOR L. REV. 174 (2009). Likewise, supervising attorneys should be notified, both so you can

(3) Notify insurer

have assistance in managing the mistake and so that the firm can fulfill its own independent duties to the client. Finally, your malpractice insurer should be notified of the error. Nearly all policies have a "notice of claim" provision, requiring attorneys to notify the insurer when an error that could give rise to liability has occurred. Failure to comply with this notice requirement will lead to a denial of coverage. One last possibility for reporting your mistake: Do you ever have an obligation to report your mistake to disciplinary authorities under Rule 8.3? You may recall that in most states, as in the ABA Model Rule, you have a duty to report only "another lawyer."

Fix error (4)

The next step is to try to fix the error. Even if a client's interests have been threatened or harmed in some way by your error, you need not necessarily withdraw. Especially if the error is one the attorney can mitigate or correct, both the attorney and client's interests are aligned. Even if the attorney can't fix the problem, the client may not always want the attorney to withdraw and the attorney would continue to have a significant incentive not to commit any further errors. Lawyers need only withdraw from representation if the error reflects a more generalized incompetence, if the client fires the lawyer, of if the lawyer believes his breach has broken down his relationship with the client sufficiently that his representation will be materially limited.

withdrawal circumstance

Withdrawal

What about compensating the client for any harm caused? An attorney may negotiate for a release of a malpractice claim but only if the client is advised in writing of the advisability of independent counsel. Attorneys may not settle a potential malpractice claim with an unrepresented or former client unless the client is advised to obtain an attorney and given an opportunity to do so. See Model Rule 1.8 (h).

Reflective Practice: Thinking about Mistakes

Think about a situation in the past in which you made a mistake that had consequences for someone other than yourself. Write a page or two of reflection about that experience. What led to the mistake? How did you respond? What does your reflection on that experience tell you about your ability to manage mistakes in your professional practice?

6.2 Reading the Rules: Rule 1.1 — Disciplinary Regulation of Competence

The twenty-four words of Wisconsin's Rule 1.1 (which is identical to the ABA Model Rules) do not provide a good deal of guidance regarding its application. Nonetheless, you should approach reading it with the same degree of care as any other rule, with attention to the context, structure, relationships, and reasons and by applying your imagination and visualizing the rule.

Wisconsin Supreme Court Rules of Professional Conduct for Attorneys
Rule 20:1.1 Competence

A lawyer shall provide competent representation to a client. Competent representation requires the legal knowledge, skill, thoroughness and preparation reasonably necessary for the representation.

Admission requirements do not guarantee competence, especially as the profession moves toward increased specialization and the law becomes increasingly complex. Competence, diligence, and communication problems are some of the greatest challenges to the legitimacy of self-regulation. Notice that this is the first rule, a deliberate choice by the drafters, designed to emphasize its importance in the rules. But there is not much to it. Where do you go for further explanation?

As the Preamble to the rules notes, "The Comment accompanying each Rule explains and illustrates the meaning and purpose of the Rule" (Preamble, Para 21). One question the comments help to clarify in particular is how one can ever take on a representation in a novel area. Read comments 1–4 carefully. Often one of the ways in which comments are especially helpful is in translating the rule into its practical application. For example, when an attorney is faced with a request for representation that is beyond the attorney's area of competence, you can see from the comments that there are three ways to respond. You can decline the representation, or "refer the matter to, or associate or consult with, a lawyer of established competence in the field in question" or undertake the "necessary study" to become competent.

If novel area/no competence =
(1) decline
(2) refer
(3) study

In addition to Rule 1.1, competence is regulated by other rules. Rule 1.3 requires that an attorney be diligent in representation. Why, when Rule 1.1 talks about "thoroughness," is there a need for an additional rule about diligence (Rule 1.3)?

One of the most important considerations in understanding Rule 1.1 is its relationship to other sources of competence regulation, such as the relationship between Rule 1.1 and malpractice. In most states, the preamble to the rules indicates that violation of the rules does not "itself" provide a basis for a cause of action. No state provides a private cause of action for breaching rules of professional conduct. However, many do allow for some use of the rules in proving the standard of care in a malpractice action. Michigan, for example, allows proof of a violation of the rules to create a rebuttable presumption that there has been a breach in the standard of care. *Lipton v. Boesky*, 313 N.W.2d 163, 166 (Mich. Ct. App. 1981); *See also, CenTra Inc. v. Estrin*, 538 F.3d 402 (6th Cir. 2008). At the other end of the spectrum are those few jurisdictions that keep a strict separation between the two systems, holding that rules of professional conduct are inadmissible in malpractice actions. *See, e.g., Orsini v. Larry Moyer Trucking Inc.*, 833 S.W.2d 366 (Ark. 1992); *Bross v. Denny*, 791 S.W.2d 416 (Mo. Ct. App. 1990). Nonetheless, even in these jurisdictions, experts testifying as to the standard of care are likely to look to the standards created by the rules, even as they are prohibited from citing the rule as their source. Most jurisdictions permit the rules to be admitted as evidence to prove malpractice. "[B]ecause the [rules of conduct] reflect a professional consensus of the standards of care below which an attorney's conduct should not fall, it would be illogical to exclude evidence of the professional rules in establishing the standard of care." *Mainor v. Nault*, 101 P.3d 308 (Nev. 2004). *See generally*, Kathleen J. McKee, Annotation: *Admissibility and Effect of Evidence of Professional Ethics Rules in Legal Malpractice Action*, 50 A.L.R. 5th 301 (1997, 2012 Supp.) (collecting cases).

breach of ABA rules may lead to malprac.

rule breach ↓ evidence

What about the influence of malpractice law on discipline cases? Is a single act of negligence a violation of Rule 1.1? Read the language of the rule. Does it appear to make an exception for the single act of incompetence? Theoretically any single instance of malpractice could also be the basis for discipline for incompetence. However, as a practical matter, a single instance of malpractice is rarely the basis for discipline. Most often discipline is imposed when the court finds an overall pattern of incompetence or a single instance of incompetence is combined with other violations relating to the attorney's honesty or fitness. Generally, to be subject to discipline for incompetence an attorney must demonstrate "indifference and a consistent failure to carry out the obligations assumed to his client or a conscious disregard for the responsibilities owed to his client." ABA Comm. on Ethics and Prof'l Responsibility, Formal Op. 335, n.1 (1974). Does this seem an appropriate interpretation of the standards? *See* Susan R. Martyn, *Lawyer Competence and Lawyer Discipline: Beyond the Bar?* 69 Geo. L.J. 705, 716 (1980).

Especially as you think about the relationship between malpractice, other forms of regulation, and discipline, consider the purposes of these regulatory schemes. Malpractice is a civil tort designed to compensate; whereas professional discipline is a private regulatory system designed to protect the public in general (not to punish wrongdoers or compensate victims). How do those purposes affect the way these doctrines might be applied? Unlike malpractice actions, when disciplinary counsel finds incompetence or neglect, there is no defense available based on the fact that the client was not harmed or prejudiced by the error. How does the presence of one of these sets of regulations impact the creation, interpretation, and application of other regulations?

The comments to Rule 1.1 suggest that, when asked to take on a representation for which you feel you have inadequate knowledge or skills, you have three options. One way to remember these options is by creating a mnemonic device to cue each of these options. Mnemonics are helpful only if they represent a key to a much larger understanding. The risk of mnemonics is that they oversimplify or distort concepts. That means it is often better for you to create mnemonics yourself than to rely on those created by others. With that caveat, here is at least one way to visualize your options when faced with a novel area of law: "Refuse, Refer, or Research."

REFUSE. Just say no. This simple answer seems very difficult for some attorneys. Why?

REFER. Associate with an attorney of established competence who can guide you sufficiently to insure your own competence. The attorney may act as co-counsel or may simply be a mentor who will provide uncompensated advice. In either instance, you will want the client to know that this is your plan and secure his or her consent to the involvement of another attorney. In its August 2012 amendments to the Model Rules, the ABA added comments to Rule 1.1 to emphasize that the decision to refer work to attorneys outside the firm is one that must be motivated by the desire to provide better representation of the client. The comment exphasizes that "[t]he reasonableness of the decision to retain or contract with other lawyers outside the lawyer's own firm will depend upon the circumstances, including the education, experience and reputation of the nonfirm lawyers; the nature of the services assigned to the nonfirm lawyers; and the legal protections, professional conduct rules, and ethical environments of the jurisdictions in which the services will be performed, particularly relating to confidential information."

Most new attorneys will be working in a firm or agency where senior attorneys can provide guidance. Of course, these new attorneys must be willing to ask for guidance. New attorneys in solo practice or without mentors are at special risk. *See, e.g., In re Willer*, 735 P.2d 594 (Or. 1987) ("classic scenario of an inexperienced lawyer who accepts work beyond her competency and capacity and, when faced with almost certain disaster, continues to dig herself further into trouble rather than seeking help.")

RESEARCH. Do the extra work necessary to bring yourself up to the level required to provide competent representation. In the first years of your practice, this will be necessary for many if not all of your representations. One of the judgment calls you have to be able to make when taking on a new case outside your field of experience and expertise is how much study will be required to make yourself competent. Here again, consulting with an attorney of more experience can help you determine whether you can become competent with reasonable preparation and study.

This will also help you to determine what a reasonable fee for your services is. You are ill-advised to try to charge your clients for excessive amounts of preparation that are required simply because you have no experience in the area. It cannot be that an inexperienced lawyer is entitled to charge three or four times as much as an experienced lawyer for the same service. "Clients should not be expected to pay for the education of a lawyer when he spends excessive amounts of time on tasks which, with reasonable experience, become matters of routine." *In re Estate of Larson*, 694 P.2d 1051, 1059 (Wash. 1985). So, for example, in determining the reasonableness of a fee in fee shifting cases, a court might account for the additional work by reducing the hourly fee or by discounting the hours charged. *Olympia Inc. v. Chayer*, 639 N.W.2d 802 (Wis. App. 2001).

6.3 Regulation of Attorney Competence through Civil Liability

Even more than disciplinary regulation, the threat of civil liability is likely the most potent regulation of attorney competence. As Professor Leubsdorf concludes in his article, *Legal Malpractice and Professional Responsibility*, 48 Rutgers L. Rev. 101, 102 (1995).

> The time has come to consider legal malpractice law as part of the system of lawyer regulation. In recent decades, that system has been transformed. Increasingly, professional ideals have been turned into enforceable law, and self-regulation by the organized bar has become regulation by courts and legislatures. The civil liability of lawyers obviously has a role to play in promoting the goals of this regulatory system. These goals include ensuring that lawyers fulfill their fiduciary duties to clients, restraining overly adversarial behavior which is harmful to non-clients, and promoting access to legal services.

> Malpractice law is likely the single greatest source of civil liability for attorneys. Malpractice law is a highly developed field of practice, the description of which consumes multi-volume treatises. Ronald E. Mallen & Jeffrey M. Smith, Legal Malpractice (2010) (also available on Westlaw). Studies of malpractice rates appear to indicate that up to twenty percent of attorneys may face a malpractice suit. See Manuel R. Ramos, Legal Malpractice: The Profession's Dirty Little Secret, 47 Vand. L. Rev. 1657, 1664-68 (1995). At one time, even the client with a viable malpractice claim would find it very difficult to find a lawyer who would take the case or expert witness attorneys to testify against the attorney. Today, there are attorneys who specialize in professional malpractice. While cases are more easily brought today, there are still few trials. Lawyers (and insurance carriers) generally prefer to settle the case and avoid adverse precedent and publicity.

The ABA projects that lawyers entering practice today can expect to face three malpractice lawsuits over the course of their practices. Certain areas of law and practice settings increase that risk. For example, solo and small firm attorneys face higher risks than attorneys in larger practice settings. Attorneys in private practice have a 4% to 17% chance of being sued for malpractice each year, depending on their jurisdiction and area of practice, according to the American Bar Association's (ABA) Lawyer's Desk Guide to Legal Malpractice. A 2007 study of legal malpractice claims by the American Bar Association (ABA) indicates that some practice areas and activities present more malpractice claims than others: 21.5% of the claims reviewed arose from plaintiff personal injury law practice (a decrease from the previous study in 2003); 20% from real estate cases (an increase from 17% in previous studies); 10.3% from family law; 9.7% from estate, trust, and probate work; and 7.3% from collections and bankruptcy cases. Am. Bar Ass'n Standing Comm. on Lawyers' Prof'l Liab., Profile of Legal Malpractice Claims 2004–2007, at 6 (2008).

The Elements of Malpractice

The law of legal malpractice is complex and could occupy an entire course. However, a basic overview of the doctrine is important to understanding your professional responsibility. One of the most important things to learn about malpractice is that it is a doctrine that contains multiple theories of liability. If you do not recognize these multiple roots, you may overlook significant liability risks in your practice.

Most commonly, malpractice can be framed as a tort sounding in negligence law. Restatement (Third) of the Law Governing Lawyers § 48 (2000). The elements, then, are those of any other negligence cause of action: duty, breach, cause, proximate cause, and damages. Negligence defenses such as contributory or comparative negligence can apply and damages can include those recoverable for any negligence tort.

Under a tort theory, the standard of care is that of a minimally competent attorney under the circumstances. The duty owed by attorneys is to act with the degree of care, skill, professional knowledge, and diligence ordinarily possessed by attorneys under similar circumstances. 1 R. Mallen & J. Smith, Legal Malpractice 857 (3rd Ed. 1989). Usually, the standard of care is established by expert testimony. Some errors are so obviously below the standard of care—missing deadlines is a good example—that no expert testimony will be required. At the other end of the spectrum are those errors that rarely result in malpractice. For example, if an attorney exercises poor judgment in making choices about strategy and thereby loses a case, that poor choice is generally not sufficient to establish a breach of the duty of care. Courts have long held that when an attorney exercises "informed judgment" in the face of uncertainties in the law, facts, or tactical choice, the attorney will not later be held liable if that judgment turns out to wrong. *Savings Bank v. Ward*, 100 U.S. 195 (1879). This is sometimes referred to as the "barrister's rule." *Woodruff v. Tomlin*, 616 F.2d 924 (6th Cir. 1980) (en banc), *cert. denied*, 449 U.S. 888 (1980).

The causation elements of tort theory are what make malpractice lawsuits so difficult to prove. If the malpractice arises out of an attorney's representation in litigation, for example, showing that the plaintiff could have won the lawsuit if the attorney had been competent often requires a "trial within a trial." The plaintiff must prove that the plaintiff would have achieved a different and better outcome if the attorney's failure had not occurred. Finally, in a tort theory, damages is a prima facie element of the claim. The practical consequence of this element is that many errors are simply not actionable. This also distinguishes malpractice from incompetence—a competent attorney (or someone for whom he is responsible) can make a simple mistake that results in significant harm, but it is not necessarily the result of incompetence. Likewise, incompetent attorneys may commit a multitude of errors that do not result in provable harm and so may escape liability.

Alternate Basis of Liability

While malpractice lawsuits are based on a negligence theory, occasionally, a plaintiff may premise the suit against the attorney on a breach of contract theory. The premise of this type of malpractice action is that the lawyer agreed to perform a specific duty or (rarely and unwisely) warranted a particular result (e.g., to properly consummate the sale of a business). Sometimes attorneys are simply using "marketing" language in a client engagement letter (e.g., "we will provide you with the highest quality, personalized professional representation"), not realizing that they may be held later to have agreed to a higher standard of care than tort theory would impose. Since the attorney contracted for a specific standard, the reasonable attorney standard is irrelevant and one may not need expert testimony on standard of care because the lawyer assumed a duty beyond ordinary care. The plaintiff does still need to prove breach and causation. The contract cause of action may have different defenses than the tort cause of action and, in most jurisdictions, a shorter statute of limitations.

Finally, given that attorneys are considered agents for their clients, malpractice can also be framed as a breach of their fiduciary duty claim. In some circumstances, a plaintiff might choose to rely on this theory rather than other bases of liability. For example, when the client is trying to establish liability based on advice an attorney gave in an initial interview, even though the attorney declined the representation at the end of the interview, this would be an appropriate instance in which to rely on law governing fiduciaries. If there is no privity of contract, in most states neither contractual nor malpractice liability will be available. Fiduciary duties may attach when an individual entrusts an attorney with confidential information. Courts will often require that attorneys forfeit their fees because of breaches of fiduciary duty, even if no other harm has occurred. In some states, these actions must be brought as malpractice; there is no separate cause of action for fiduciary breach. *Donohoe v. Shughart, Thomson & Kilroy*, 900 S.W.2d 624, 629 (Mo. banc 1995). For a more complete description of the breach of fiduciary duty cause of action and a criticism of its use in situations of negligence, see Charles W. Wolfram, *A Cautionary Tale: Fiduciary Breach as Legal Malpractice*, 34 Hofstra L. Rev. 689 (2006).

Perhaps the most important contribution malpractice law has made to our understanding of our professional responsibility is in determining to whom we owe duties of care. As you will recall, the rules of professional conduct do not define who is a client. Yet, in general, an attorney owes a duty only to a client. It is the law of malpractice that established the doctrines that a client can be created by contract (if you agree to represent a client) or by tort or agency law (if the client reasonably assumes you represent her).

Most courts have created some exceptions allowing tort actions beyond the strict confines of the attorney-client relationship. A number of states apply third-party beneficiary doctrine to find a duty. Here, the attorney and client both intend that the reason for the representation is to confer a direct benefit on a third party. Some courts use a balancing test to establish duty, weighing a number of factors in determining whether to permit an exception to the rule requiring privity between attorney and client. These factors include the extent to which the transaction was intended to benefit the third party, the foreseeability of harm to that party, the degree of certainty that the third party suffered injury, the closeness of causation, the moral blame attached to the attorney's conduct, and the policy of preventing future harm. In *Lucas v. Hamm*, 56 Cal. 2d 583, 364 P.2d 685, 15 Cal. Rptr. 821 (Cal. 1961), *cert. denied*, 368 U.S. 987, 7 L. Ed. 2d 525, 82 S. Ct. 603 (1962), the California Supreme Court established this test. That case involved a legal malpractice action against an attorney by his client's trust beneficiaries for negligently drafting a "pour-over will" (a will that bequeaths property to an existing trust). The court held that the balance of several factors determined whether an exception to privity existed: (1) the extent to which the transaction was intended to affect the plaintiff; (2) the foreseeability of harm to him; (3) the degree of certainty that the plaintiff suffered injury; (4) the closeness of the connection between the defendant's conduct and the injury; (5) the policy of preventing future harm; and (6) whether imposing liability placed an undue burden upon the legal profession. *Lucas*, 364 P.2d at 687-88. The *Lucas* case has been very influential in third-party malpractice actions, especially arising in estate planning practice.

Just as liability for malpractice has been extended to third parties in some areas of practice, in other areas of practice attorneys are not readily subject to civil liability for malpractice at all. Prosecutors, for example, are absolutely immune from civil liability for actions taken within the scope of their duties. *Arzeno v. Mack*, 39 A.D.3d 341, 833 N.Y.S.2d 480 (1st Dep't 2007). Similarly, military attorneys are given immunity by federal legislation. 10 U.S.C. § 105 (2010). Lawyers may have judicial or governmental immunity when they are appointed by the court to represent judicial or governmental interests, such as trustees in bankruptcy, *Bennett v. Williams*, 892 F.2d 822 (9th Cir. 1989), public school districts, *Closs v. Goose Creek Consolidated Independent School District*, 874 S.W.2d 859 (Tex. Ct. App. 1994), or the best interests of children as guardians *ad litem*, *McKay v. Owens*, 937 P.2d 1222 (Idaho 1997); *Tindell v. Rogosheske*, 428 N.W.2d 386 (Minn. 1988); *State ex rel Bird v. Weinstock*, 864 S.W.2d 376 (Mo. App. E.D. 1993). States disagree on whether public defenders enjoy governmental immunity from suit. Annotation, *Public Defender's Immunity From Liability For Malpractice*, 6 A.L.R. 4th 774 (1991, 2009 Supp.). Attorneys in these settings will usually be regulated by removal from appointments or by their governmental employer.

We will return to these theories of liability in future chapters, as an attorney may find herself a defendant in these actions when violating other duties besides competence.

Researching Professional Responsibility 6-A: Using Secondary Sources

In any research task, often the very best place to begin is with secondary sources. Why reinvent the wheel when someone may have already done all your research? Using the topic of liability for attorney errors as an example, what types of secondary sources might you consult to find answers to issues that arise in this context? For example, suppose you have missed a deadline in filing a claim on behalf of your client. The substantive claim was a strong one and the demand of $500,000 was a fair estimate of the damages. Now you are facing a malpractice action by your former client. You have just discovered that the defendant in the underlying action has filed for a "no asset" bankruptcy action. It appears that even if the client had won a judgment in her case, she would not have actually been able to collect any money at all. Does that mean there are no damages, so there is no claim for malpractice? If the client's ability to actually enforce a judgment is relevant, who has the burden of raising or proving the issue?

You might research this question by looking at cases in your jurisdiction on malpractice. However, this would be an excellent issue for which a secondary source might save you considerable time and effort. Some excellent secondary sources include treatises, ALR annotations, journals, and web blogs.

When the question is legal malpractice, the leading secondary authority is the multi-volume treatise by Ronald E. Mallen & Jeffrey M. Smith, *Legal Malpractice,* which is published annually. Your own jurisdiction might have practice guides or desk books on this topic as well. American Law Reports (ALR) annotations cover a number of professional responsibility issues, including malpractice standards. Annotations collect and describe cases on a particular issue. Using ALR gives you not only an overview of the issue but citations to cases on either side of the issue. ALR annotations also provide a "Total Client Service Library" which gives cross references to encyclopedias, case reporters, treatises, finding aids, and practice guides on various topics. The process for researching professional responsibility issues in ALRs is similar to general legal research. The ALR Quick Index provides citations to annotations in the ALR 2nd through 6th series and the ALR Federal Series. ALR annotations gather state and federal case law but do not generally state rules or advisory opinions of ethics panels.

Law journals and periodicals can also be important starting points for research on a specific issue. Today, many articles are available on the web, either in online journals or through services such as the Social Science Research Network. A generalized search engine can uncover many of these articles, but a search engine such as Google Scholar will provide more focused research results.

No matter what secondary source you use, recognize that these resources are simply an efficient starting point for understanding the issue and identifying primary authority. Always read the cases you find through these sources for yourself and check to insure that your research is current.

6.4 Other Regulation of Attorney Conduct

Courts can regulate attorneys directly in proceedings through the court's power of contempt and court procedural rules. Attorneys who disobey orders of court or miss court dates may face contempt charges. The rules of civil procedure also provide sanctions for conduct that is, at base, incompetence. Sanctions under Rule 11 of the Federal Rules of Civil Procedure often involve conduct that is incompetent: filing a complaint without supporting facts (incompetence in investigation) and filing a complaint without a good faith legal basis (incompetence in research). Likewise, discovery sanctions, sanctions for violations of pretrial orders, and other rule-based sanctions regulate competence just as readily as they sanction more intentional abuses of the legal system.

In litigation, errors may lead to judgments against clients that the clients may later seek to escape. In civil litigation, motions to obtain relief from judgment must generally meet very stringent standards. For example, under Rule 60(b) of the Federal Rules of Civil Procedure one might seek relief from judgment for "mistake, inadvertence, surprise or excusable neglect," or "other reasons justifying relief." As a general principle, clients are bound by the actions of their attorneys and cannot justify relief from judgment by simply blaming their attorney's error. As the Supreme Court stated in reviewing the dismissal of a plaintiff's cause of action because the attorney had failed to appear at a pretrial conference:

> Petitioner voluntarily chose this attorney as his representative in the action, and he cannot now avoid the consequences of the acts or omissions of this freely selected agent. Any other notion would be wholly inconsistent with our system of representative litigation, in which each party is deemed bound by the acts of his lawyer-agent and is considered to have "notice of all facts, notice of which can be charged upon the attorney."

Link v. Wabash Railroad Co., 370 U.S. 626, 633-34 (1962). Nonetheless, most courts are held to have a wide range of discretion in deciding motions for relief from judgment.

In criminal litigation, clients must show that their attorney's rendered ineffective assistance of counsel in order to be given relief from judgment. The Court in *Strickland v. Washington*, 466 U.S. 668 (1984) established a two-pronged test for ineffective assistance. First, the defendant must overcome a "strong presumption of effectiveness" and prove that the attorney did not provide "reasonably effective assistance." Some commentators have noted that courts are extremely deferential in their application of this standard, willing to "attribute any conceivable strategy to the performance, even if there is no evidence that the attorney pursued that strategy."

Second, a defendant must prove "a reasonable probability that, but for counsel's unprofessional errors, the results ... would have been different." Just as with malpractice, if there is no proof of damage resulting from an attorney's deficient conduct, there is no ineffective assistance of counsel. In determining whether prejudice exists, courts of appeal often consider the evidence supporting the verdict, independent of the attorney's error, and if that evidence supports the outcome of the trial, there is no prejudice. In some cases, prejudice may be presumed, but based on only the most egregious of errors. These include sleeping during trial, (*Javor v. United States*, 724 F.2d 831, 833 (9th Cir. 1984)); being absent at critical stages without the client's informed consent, (*Olden v. United States*, 224 F.3d 561, 569 (6th Cir. 2000)); or failing to participate in the proceeding, (*Harding v. Davis*, 878 F.2d 1341, 1344 (11th Cir. 1989)).

How do these standards relate to malpractice and discipline? In the criminal defense setting, malpractice standards are modified to reflect the standards of ineffective assistance of counsel. Recall that for a conviction to be overturned for ineffective assistance of counsel, there must be proof of prejudice—which in most states requires proof that the defendant would have prevailed had it not been for the attorney's incompetence. In most states, in order for a defendant to maintain a malpractice claim against his defense attorney, he must successfully appeal his conviction based on ineffective assistance of counsel. Some states go even further, requiring plaintiffs to prove actual innocence of the underlying offense in order to win a criminal malpractice action. See, Susam M. Treyz, *Note: Criminal Malpractice: Privilege of the Innocent Plaintiff?*, 59 Fordham L. Rev. 719 (1991). What is the rationale for this different treatment of criminal defendants?

Other forms of regulation of competence fall under the category of education and oversight rather than sanction. Most jurisdictions have mandatory continuing legal education requirements. Some proposals have come before the ABA to strengthen these requirements by including testing. Further education is common as a condition of reinstatement in many discipline cases.

Some large corporations have begun to audit their outside counsel. Would some system of peer review be an effective measure? While major law firms often still have in-house mentoring programs for new associates, in smaller firms, the tradition of mentoring relationships has declined. In response, some state and local bar associations have established mentoring programs in which experienced attorneys are matched with newer attorneys. In some of these programs, the participating attorneys receive CLE credit for their work together. Some programs require that one or both attorneys carry professional liability insurance; some require that the attorneys negotiate a plan for meetings and topics; some require that the protégé sign a disclaimer and release agreeing not to sue the mentor, the bar association, or any related person or entity for the consideration of services rendered through the program. What kinds of implications do these programs raise for delivery of legal services to clients?

6.5 Reading the Rules: Rules 5.1 and 5.2— Responsibilities to Other Attorneys

Are you ever responsible for the competence of others? To what extent may you excuse your own errors by pointing to the direction given you by a supervisor? To the extent all attorneys sometimes have an obligation to report other attorneys when they violate rules, there is a general duty to police one another. However, more specific rules govern the allocation of responsibility between supervisor and subordinate lawyers. Read Oklahoma's Rule 5.1 Responsibilities of Partners, Managers, And Supervisory Lawyers and Rule 5.2 Responsibilities of a Subordinate Lawyer. (These Oklahoma rules are identical to the ABA Model Rules.)

Oklahoma Rules of Professional Conduct
O.S. § 5, Chap. 1, App. 3-A

Rule 5.1. Responsibilities of Partners, Managers, and Supervisory Lawyers

(a) A partner in a law firm, and a lawyer who individually or together with other lawyers possesses comparable managerial authority in a law firm, shall make reasonable efforts to ensure that the firm has in effect measures giving reasonable assurance that all lawyers in the firm conform to the Rules of Professional Conduct.

(b) A lawyer having direct supervisory authority over another lawyer shall make reasonable efforts to ensure that the other lawyer conforms to the Rules of Professional Conduct.

(c) A lawyer shall be responsible for another lawyer's violation of the Rules of Professional Conduct if:

(1) the lawyer orders or, with knowledge of the specific conduct, ratifies the conduct involved; or

(2) the lawyer is a partner or has comparable managerial authority in the law firm in which the other lawyer practices, or has direct supervisory authority over the other lawyer, and knows of the conduct at a time when its consequences can be avoided or mitigated but fails to take reasonable remedial action.

Rule 5.2. Responsibilities of a Subordinate Lawyer

(a) A lawyer is bound by the rules of professional conduct notwithstanding that the lawyer acted at the direction of another person.

(b) A subordinate lawyer does not violate the rules of professional conduct if that lawyer acts in accordance with a supervisory lawyer's reasonable resolution of an arguable question of professional duty.

Context

You can see from Rule 5.1 that attorneys are responsible for the misconduct of other attorneys if the attorney ordered or ratified the misconduct or if the attorney had some supervisory authority. Very early in your career, you are unlikely to be in a position to supervise other attorneys, and so are more likely to be protected by Rule 5.1 than subject to discipline for its violation.

Just how far does that protection extend? Comment 1 to the rule notes as an example that, "if a subordinate filed a frivolous pleading at the direction of a supervisor, the subordinate would not be guilty of a professional violation unless the subordinate knew of the document's frivolous character." So does that mean the junior attorney need not worry about investigating documents he is asked to sign or file? Clearly not. The comment is designed to illustrate the rule in context, and must be read in context of the entire set of rules. Reading Rules 5.1 and 5.2 together makes it clear that the junior attorney's responsibility is the same as that of his supervisor's duty and it is only when the question of duty is unclear that the junior attorney may safely defer to his supervisor's "reasonable resolution."

Relationships

If an attorney signs a pleading that is frivolous, that attorney will be held responsible by the court under rules of civil procedure or the court's general authority to regulate conduct in its courtroom (by reprimanding the attorney, holding the attorney in contempt, or issuing other appropriate orders). Consider the comments of the court in a case in which an associate had, at the direction of her supervising attorney, filed a number of frivolous motions:

> Associates may not blindly follow commands of partners they know to be wrong. Rule 19 of our Local Rules requires that counsel not act negligently thereby proximately causing the filing or maintenance of frivolous or harassing motions which unnecessarily multiplies the proceedings and results in an increase in the costs of litigation. Rule 19 requires a lawyer who elects to sign a paper to take responsibility for it, even if that responsibility is shared. Rule 19 does not speak in terms of associate and partner or lead and primary counsel; no distinction is made by the rule, nor may one legitimately be implied for different standards of conduct. No lawyer may disclaim responsibility for his/her own actions or for a paper bearing his/her name. When others are involved in misconduct with counsel, degrees of culpability may vary but ultimate responsibility does not....
>
> Before filing any motions and then pursuing them an attorney, by virtue of Rule 19, has an obligation to make certain that the motions not only possess a good faith basis in fact and law, which the six consolidated motions did not, but also must make certain that they are necessary and could not have been achieved through amicable discussions. This responsibility, among others, may not be passed blindly from one lawyer to another up the extensible chain of command, with each lawyer claiming it was not his or her job to ultimately review that motion.

Roberts v. Lyon, 131 F.R.D. 75, 84 (E.D. Pa. 1990).

When it comes to malpractice liability, the principle of *respondeat superior* may result in a supervising attorney being held responsible for a junior attorney's errors, but that doctrine will certainly not insulate the junior attorney from liability.

Structure

Rule 5.1 provides a variety of levels of responsibility for the conduct of other attorneys. Rule 5.3, which describes an attorney's responsibility over non-lawyer personnel in a firm, has a very similar structure.

Part (a) of the rule describes the duty to have policies in place to ensure professional conduct. What might these policies be? They could include everything from law office management systems such as calendaring systems, billing practices, and conflicts of interest systems, to structures and systems that encourage consideration of broader ethical questions, such as ethics counsel or CLE series. Often the most important policies are ones that do not, at first glance, appear to be directly tied to ethical concerns. These might include billable hours requirements and business development rewards that create incentives to cut corners and lie to clients. Cut-throat competitive systems in which one attorney's achievement or mistake is considered another attorney's loss or gain undermine the entire ethical culture of a law firm.

Part (b) of the rule describes the responsibility of one attorney for another. How do you distinguish an attorney's responsibility under (a) and (b)? In a larger firm, in-house counsel staff, or government attorney office, there are often persons designated as responsible for the management of the firm (usually the equity partners) who have the policy-setting responsibilities of part (a), while any attorney who supervises another attorney on a project, case, or practice area has the responsibility described in section (b). In a smaller firm or practice, parts (a) and (b) may be more difficult to distinguish, as policies and lines of authority are less formal. In these settings, attorneys who have any authority would be wise to consider that they have responsibility not only for the attorneys they supervise directly but for the overall policies of the practice as well.

Notice that parts (a) and (b) can subject an attorney to discipline even if the attorney did not direct the misconduct or even know that it occurred. Part (c), in contrast, requires knowledge, though it does not necessarily require that the supervising attorney have ordered the misconduct.

Keep in mind that Rule 5.3 imposes a similar structure of responsibility for supervising non-lawyer conduct in a firm. Thus, even if it will be years (although you will be surprised how few) before you find yourself supervising another attorney, you are likely to be supervising non-lawyers from the very beginning of your practice. Under Rule 5.3, much like rule 5.1, if a paralegal engages in conduct that, if performed by a lawyer, would constitute a violation of the Rules of Professional Conduct, then the lawyer is responsible if the lawyer orders or ratifies the conduct. The lawyer also may be responsible for the paralegal's actions if the lawyer has "direct supervisory authority," knows of the conduct in time to remedy it, and fails to do so. If an attorney fails to exercise appropriate supervision, the attorney, rather than the paralegal, will suffer the legal repercussions, which can include procedural sanctions, suspensions, and even disbarment. *See, e.g., Spencer v. Steinman*, 179 F.R.D. 484, 489 (E.D. Pa. 1998) (when paralegal issued subpoena duces tecum on non-parties without prior notice to defendant in violation of Fed. R. Civ. P. 45, the lawyer was sanctioned under Rule 11 for not "assuring himself that [the paralegal] had adequate training" and for his failure to "adequately supervise her once he assigned her the task of issuing subpoenas"); *Matter of Discipli-*

nary Action Against Nassif, 547 N.W.2d 541 (N.D. 1996) (disbarment for failure to properly supervise which resulted in the unauthorized practice of law by office paralegals). Keep in mind, then, these three types of responsibility for supervision: making sure policies are in place, making sure the subordinate is aware of and complies with these policies, and directing subordinates ethically and correcting their misbehavior when it occurs.

Reasons

The rules primarily envision attorneys as independent agents but the practice of law is, in fact, highly collaborative. This collaboration increases efficiency and quality but it also allows wrongdoing to be diffused to the point that no one can be held effectively responsible. Professor Ted Schneyer has suggested that professional discipline systems should be able to target entire firms, with fine structures that provide effective deterrence. Ted Schneyer, *Professional Discipline for Law Firms?* 77 CORNELL L. REV. 1 (1992); Ted Schneyer, *A Tale of Four Systems: Reflections on How Law Influences the "Ethical Infrastructure" of Law Firms*, 39 S. TEX. L. REV. 245 (1998). Only New York and New Jersey have adopted this proposal however. Why is there such a resistance to law firm responsibility?

Visualize / Imagine

An effective way to think about this rule is to place it in the context of an actual firm or practice setting. The following are some of the attorneys in a firm and their general responsibilities:

> Attorney A is a one of the founding partners in the firm. He is semi-retired and doesn't take much of an active role in managing the firm any longer and maintains his own book of long-term clients. When he needs help on cases, he generally enlists the assistance of one of the new associates, whom he enjoys mentoring.

> Attorney B is an equity partner in the firm. He directs the firm's management committee. He also maintains the firm's close relationship with ABC Corporation, one of the firm's largest clients, though he doesn't necessarily work on ABC representation directly. With these business development and management functions, he has a fairly minimal caseload during his tenure in these positions.

> Attorney C is an equity partner in the firm who serves as the department head of the employment litigation department of the firm. There are two equity partners, two non-equity partners, four associates in the department, four paralegals, and two secretaries in this department.

> Attorney D is a non-equity partner in the firm who manages the firm's pro bono program, either taking over appointments made to other attorneys in the firm or directing other attorneys in their own pro bono representations.

> Attorney E is a fifth-year associate in the firm, who works in the employment litigation department with Attorney C.

> Attorney F is a first-year associate in the firm. The firm rotates new associates through three different departments in their first year and encourages their participation in the pro bono program.

> Attorney G is a contract attorney who works part-time for the firm, doing document review and emergency research projects.

Paralegal H is a paralegal who has been with the firm for 25 years. She works in the employment litigation department.

Place the attorneys on an organizational chart that shows who is responsible for whom.

Professional Responsibility Skill 6-A: Difficult Conversations

Your responsibility as an attorney is likely to involve many difficult conversations, and few are more difficult than the conversations in which you must discuss a mistake. Sometimes the conversation involves your acknowledgement of your own errors. Model Rules 8.3, 5.1, and 5.2 point out that sometimes these conversations will have to be about another attorney's mistake. While Rule 5.2 allows a subordinate attorney to defer to a supervisor's "reasonable resolution" of an "arguable" question of professional duty, determining whether a question is arguable or a resolution is reasonable can be challenging for a new attorney. The place to start, in addition to independent research, is a conversation with the supervisory attorney. If that conversation does not resolve concerns adequately, the attorney may talk to others in the firm, especially if there is an attorney in the firm who is designated as "ethics counsel" or if there is a firm ethics committee.

Whether admitting your own error or questioning the conduct or direction of another attorney, the conversation will be difficult. How do you best approach these conversations effectively and professionally?

In their book *Difficult Conversations*,[1] Douglas Stone, Bruce Patton, and Sheila Heen point out that every difficult conversation is actually three conversations:

The "What Happened?" conversation, in which you disagree about the facts;

The Feelings Conversation, in which emotions influence the conversation, whether addressed directly or not; and

The Identity Conversation, which is our own internal conversation about how the situation affects our own view of ourselves.

The authors have several suggestions for making difficult conversations more productive.

1. Shift to Learning Stance

In a learning stance you do not assume you know the other person's perceptions, intentions, and interests. Without giving up your own emotions and perceptions, you are respectful of the dignity and interests of the other person and approach the conversation from a stance of forward-looking learning and problem solving rather than backward-looking blame.

2. Listen

Try to see the situation from the other person's point of view *before* you try to communicate your point of view. Use the essentials of active listening:

- Ask open-ended questions. "Tell me more …" "Help me understand …"

---

1. D. Stone, B. Patton, & S. Heen, *Difficult conversations: how to discuss what matters most.* (New York: Penguin. 1999). This is an excellent book and well worth reading in its entirety.

- Paraphrase for clarity. Express to the other person, in your own words, what you think you have heard.

- Acknowledge the other person's feelings. Feelings left unacknowledged will cause trouble in a conversation. Do not assume you know what another feels, but when he makes his feelings clear, acknowledge those feelings.

3. Adopt the "Yes, And ..." Stance

The perceptions, emotions, and values of the other person have value AND so do yours. You are unlikely to impose yours on the other person. The critical component is that you allow yourself to express your view *and* listen to the other person's view as well. Once you have reached this stage, you can say: "Now that we really understand each other, what's a good way to resolve this problem?"

4. Recognize the Story You Bring to the Conversation

In the "What Happened?" Conversation, you may assume you already know everything that happened, what was intended, and who should bear the blame. If you approach a difficult conversation with these assumptions, you will not have a conversation, you will have a blaming session. Instead first change your assumptions that you cannot know the other person's perceptions and intentions until you ask and listen and that there are few situations in which one person is solely and completely at fault.

In the Feelings Conversation, an assumption that feelings are irrelevant and should be ignored (or that only your feelings count) is counterproductive. As the authors discuss, "Feelings are the heart of the situation." Address feelings (yours and theirs) before trying to problem solve.

In the Identify Conversation you or the other person may find the conversation challenging to their identity as good or bad or competent or incompetent. Adopting the assumption that both of you are complex and neither is perfect can help maintain balance in the conversation.

5. Focus on Contribution, not Blame

Focus on the factors that created the problem (including your own) in a forward-looking "how do we fix this" attitude.

Try applying these principals to the introductory problem in this chapter. Practice the conversation you would have with Donald.

Review Problem

Analyze the following problems to test your understanding of the relationship among the various sources of regulation of competence we have discussed thus far.

1. Years ago, Arnie Attorney helped his client Henry to form a small business (ReadySign) that makes signs and banners. In the subsequent years, he has continued to provide legal services to Henry, charging Henry for each of these representations. Arnie provided Henry some advice on building code restrictions when he remodeled the store last year, and defended him in one unemployment compensation hearing. In addition, each year he has prepared Henry's taxes for the business. Arnie undertook all of these representations without

written representation agreements, since Henry knew well how Arnie charged and they agreed orally on the scope of the representation.

Arnie and Henry are friends as well, and every few weeks or so, they get together for lunch. At many of these lunches, Arnie inevitably ends up answering a few questions or giving Henry some simple advice on ongoing legal aspects of the business. Last year, at one of these lunches, Henry mentioned to Arnie that he was upset about another sign company that had opened up in the next major metropolitan area (about 200 miles away), using the name "Readdy Sign." Not only was the name very similar to Henry's but it was styled in the same colors and font. Henry said he wasn't terribly worried because the company wasn't really cutting into his business, he was just irritated by the presumption. He asked Arnie if he should do anything. Arnie said, "Well, I don't know much about trademark law, but I know this, the chances this business will be open in six months are slim and it will be expensive to litigate this, so if you aren't really being hurt in your business, there's no need to start a war right way. Better to just wait and see if they actually cause you any real trouble."

Fortunately, Arnie's business prediction was correct and the competing business folded within the year. Unfortunately, his legal advice was just plain wrong—doing nothing could have cost Henry his ability to protect his mark and to recover the infringer's profits. Given this, is Arnie subject to discipline or liability for this advice?

2. Client asks attorney to take over a case that was started by another attorney, but whom the client had fired because the attorney would not communicate with the client. After assuring himself that the prior attorney had indeed withdrawn from the case, attorney agrees to take on the case. After two hours of research, attorney concludes that the case is frivolous given recent legislation. After discussing the matter with client, attorney concludes that the previous lawyer was unaware of this legislation and expended many hours of unnecessary work because of this oversight. Attorney concludes that this conduct would state a claim for malpractice against the prior attorney. Does Attorney have a duty to make a disciplinary report? Does Attorney have a duty to advise client about a possible malpractice action against the prior lawyer?

3. Attorney represented Client in defending a criminal charge of embezzlement in state court. Attorney made several errors that demonstrated significant incompetence in his representation, resulting in Client's conviction and sentence. Suppose that the state disciplinary authority has sanctioned Attorney for incompetence based on this representation. What additional consequences might flow from that decision? Could the client sue Attorney for malpractice? Could the client's conviction be overturned for ineffective assistance of counsel? Could the client defend against an action to enforce the Attorney's fees?

Researching Professional Responsibility 6-B: Getting Advice on Your Professional Duty

Reconsider the preliminary problem at this point. In particular, consider what your duties are under the Rules of Professional Conduct. You could begin by researching the rules themselves in your jurisdiction. You might consider your state's version of Rule 5.2 or Rule 8. However, you would find that neither rule truly answers the question of what you must or may do to help Donald and protect his clients.

For many difficult questions about how the rules apply, ethics opinions provide helpful guides. The ABA Standing Committee on Ethics and Professional Responsibility publishes opinions interpreting the Model Rules and Code. These opinions do not have the force of law but may be persuasive authority in litigation or discipline and are useful guides for conduct. These opinions are divided into formal and informal opinions, much like federal regulatory opinions. Formal opinions deal with broader, more generally applicable issues while informal opinions are limited to analysis of a particular set of facts.

Unfortunately, the full text of ABA formal and informal opinions is not generally available on the web. You must either use books in the library or online subscription databases. These include the ABA/BNA Lawyer's Manual on Professional Conduct (either in hardcopy, through subscription to the BNA website (http://www.bna.com), or on LEXIS, by searching in the Area of Law library, by topic under Ethics (Treatises & Analytical Materials) or in WESTLAW under the directory ABA-BNA). LEXIS and WESTLAW also provide access to ABA Ethics opinions directly as well as through the ABA/BNA Manual. In LEXIS, one can find these in the library: Legal > Area of Law—By Topic > Ethics > Administrative Materials & Regulations > Legal Ethics Opinions. In WESTLAW, the directory is ABA-ETHOP.

Like the ABA, many state and local bar committees also give opinions interpreting the attorney regulations. Almost all jurisdictions limit these opinions to prospective conduct and will not review conduct that has already occurred, is ongoing, or is the subject of litigation or discipline proceedings. Most states also will respond only to attorneys requesting opinions as to their own conduct, rather than the conduct of others. Finally, most opinions will limit themselves to the application of state rules of professional conduct and will not pass on questions of law. Some states will issue only formal written opinions addressing hypothetical issues; others limit their opinions to private advisory responses to individual attorneys. Most states provide both private and formal opinions.

The process of issuing these opinions varies greatly from state to state. In one common version of this process, an individual attorney will request an opinion regarding the ethics of his or her proposed conduct. Occasionally the bar grievance committee or the state court may request an opinion regarding recurrent issues stated in a hypothetical format. The chair of the ethics committee may screen these requests to determine whether they are appropriate for committee response. The chair will then appoint one of the members of the committee to draft an opinion, which the full committee will then review and edit or approve. The committee may also decide what form of response should be provided: formal public opinions or informal opinions (private advisory letters).

The authority of the state ethics opinions also varies, depending in large part on the source of authority for the ethics committee and on whether the state has an integrated bar association. In some states, for example, the body that produces ethics opinions is an arm of the state supreme court and the opinions are authoritative interpretations of the law. In states in which opinions carry some authority, a process of appeal may exist: to the ethics committee or to the state supreme court for example. In most states, though, the ethics opinions are advisory only, having no binding authority over the state disciplinary system. Even in those states, however, an attorney's reliance on an ethics opinion may serve as evidence of a good faith attempt to comply with a reasonable resolution of a disputed issue.

In most states, the full text of ethics opinions is published in state bar newsletters or journals, is distributed to law libraries within the state, or is available by calling the state bar. An increasing number of state and local bar associations publish their ethics opinions on the internet as well. The National Organization of Bar Counsel provides a directory of these resources at http://www.nobc.org/State_Ethics_Opinions.aspx. The ABA/BNA Lawyers Manual on Professional Conduct also provides summaries of state ethics opinions.

Finally, remember that, in most states, the rule governing confidentiality of client information has an exception that permits attorneys to disclose information in order to get advice about their professional duty. Consequently, you are free to consult ethics experts, whether state ethics counsel, a bar association ethics attorney, or even your former professional responsibility professor, without fear of violating your client's confidentiality. Of course you should always take care when disclosing client information to be sure that you disclose only as much as is necessary to secure your advice and only in the most private way you can.

Research the preliminary problem to find an ethics opinion that will guide you in understanding your responsibility to address your concerns about Donald's conduct.

6.6 Beyond Mistake Management and Risk Avoidance

Avoiding discipline and malpractice is an admirable goal, but most of us strive for more than simply avoiding trouble. What kinds of skills and knowledge do attorneys need to be excellent? When practicing lawyers are asked what they believe to be the most important lawyering skills, among the highest ranked are:

- honesty
- integrity
- the capacity to act ethically
- the ability to perform legal research

ALI-ABA, *A Model Peer Review System:* Discussion Draft at 11 (April 15, 1980).

Surprised? Obviously, with the exception of the last, we don't expend much effort studying these skills in law school. Yet most attorneys believe that the members of the profession should exhibit these qualities.

According to the ALI-ABA survey, experienced lawyers think some very important ethical and interpersonal traits are noticeably absent among new attorneys. These include:

Judgment

Maturity

The ability to deal effectively with others

The capacity to be thorough in accomplishing a task

Other qualities which young attorneys are short on: tolerance and patience, understanding of human behavior, and self-confidence.

In his book, FROM CLASSES TO COMPETENCIES, LOCKSTEP TO LEVELS (2007), Attorney Peter B. Sloan describes how one large law firm (Blackwell, Sanders, Peper, Martin) changed its system of associate evaluation from a "lockstep" system in which each class of new attorneys progresses at the same rate to a "level" system in which attorneys are evaluated individually on a matrix of competencies. Among these competencies are some of the criteria mentioned in the ALI-ABA study. More and more large law firms are moving toward this model of associate evaluation.

Reflective Practice: Self-Evaluation and Planning for Professional Development

In a major research project funded by the Law School Admissions Council, law professor Marjorie Shultz and psychology professor Sheldon Zedeck interviewed hundreds of lawyers, law faculty, law students, judges, and clients and asked them what qualities they look for in a good lawyer. They categorized these qualities into 26 criteria, falling under 8 general categories.

1. Intellectual & Cognitive (Analysis and Reasoning; Creativity/Innovation; Problem Solving; Practical Judgment)

2. Research & Information Gathering (Researching the Law; Fact Finding; Questioning and Interviewing)

3. Communications (Influencing and Advocating; Writing; Speaking; Listening)

4. Planning and Organizing (Strategic Planning; Organizing and Managing One's Own Work; Organizing and Managing Others (Staff/Colleagues))

5. Conflict Resolution (Negotiation Skills; Able to See the World Through the Eyes of Others)

6. Client & Business Relations — Entrepreneurship (Networking and Business Development; Providing Advice and Counsel and Building Relationships with Clients)

7. Working with Others (Developing Relationships within the Legal Profession; Evaluation, Development, and Mentoring)

8. Character (Passion and Engagement; Diligence; Integrity/Honesty; Stress Management; Community Involvement and Service; Self-Development)

Marjorie M. Shultz and Sheldon Zedeck, Final Report: Identification, Development, and Validation of Predictors for Successful Lawyering 26-27(September 2008) available at http://www.law.berkeley.edu/files/LSACREPORTfinal-12.pdf.

Review these categories and consider where your strengths lie and those areas that you would like to develop further. Write a short (1-2 pagese- to) reflection on one of the areas you would like to further develop and the ways in which you think you can do so.

Test Your Understanding

Consider these statements about competence. Are these accurate statements of an attorney's duty of competence?

Attorneys who are providing their services for free have a lesser duty of competence than those who are paying for the attorney's services.   *No*

The higher your grade point average upon graduation from law school, the less likely you are to face a malpractice action.   *No*

The only mistakes that really present a risk to your career are those that you can't correct.   *No*

To Learn More

Professional organizations dedicated to your specialized area of practice provide excellent resources for maintaining and improving competence. Likewise, many malpractice insurers provide significant support to attorneys with practice management advice and resources. Search the web to locate the resources available to your practice area and region. Here, as in other areas, some of the most important resources are the people around you. If you do not have a network of trusted and competent individuals to help you in your practice, you should take steps to establish that network now.

Chapter Seven

Fees, Files, and Property

Learning Objectives

After you have read this chapter and completed the assignments, you should be able to:

- Explain the relationship between fees and other central duties in the attorney-client relationship.
- Explain the reasons it is important to keep track of your time in practice and maintain time records that communicate work completed and time spent and identify your own attitudes toward time that will make that easier or harder.
- Analyze a fee for reasonableness.
- Analyze billing and collection practices for conformity with rules of professional conduct and agency principles.
- Explain the essential elements of a client trust account and describe the funds that must be deposited or kept in a trust account.
- Differentiate an advance on fees and a retainer and identify the ethical risks of pure retainers.
- Identify the various approaches to ownership of client files.
- Identify common drafting problems in an agreement regarding fees and file retention.

Rules to Study

The two primary rules of professional conduct we will study in this chapter are Model Rules 1.5 and 1.15. Rule 1.8 has a number of rules that are relevant to the subject of financial transactions with clients as well. Obviously, any financial or property transaction will also be governed by common law doctrines of contract, agency, and bailment. In addition, misbehavior in this area will implicate a host of tort, criminal law, and statutory laws.

Preliminary Problem

Which of the following actions would subject the attorney to discipline?

1. Lawyer finds it possible to schedule court appearances for three clients on the same day. He spends a total of four hours at the courthouse, the amount of

can't double dip ↰

time he would have spent on behalf of each client had it not been for the fortuitous circumstance that all three cases were scheduled on the same day. His clients understand that they will be billed on the basis of time spent, so he bills each of the three clients for the four hours he spent at the courthouse.

↳ 2. Lawyer is flying cross-country to attend a deposition on behalf of one client, expending travel time she would ordinarily bill to that client. She decides not to watch the movie or read her novel, but to work instead on drafting a motion for another client. She charges both clients, each of whom agreed to hourly billing, for the time during which she was traveling on behalf of one and drafting a document on behalf of the other.

can't charge both ↰

3. Attorney researches on a particular topic for one client that later turns out to be relevant to an inquiry from a second client. The firm bills the second client, who agreed to be charged on the basis of time spent on his case, the same amount for the recycled work product that it charged the first client.

4. Attorney bills in 15-minute increments. Regardless of how long Attorney actually works on a matter, she rounds up the time to the next 15-minute increment and charges on that basis.

5. Attorney is representing an individual seeking a divorce, custody, and child support. The individual cannot afford to pay for the attorney's representation out of her available funds, so the attorney agrees that he will represent her on a contingent fee basis, in which he will recover as his fee 35% of the value of the funds and property distributed to her in the divorce.

6. Attorney receives a $5,000 advance on her fees from a client and places those funds in the client trust account. Attorney works over 80 hours on the case, over a period of several months, earning $1,600 in fees, but gets behind in her billing, so she has not withdrawn those funds from the trust account. She has an immediate bill for office equipment due, so she simply writes a check for $1,600 from the trust account to pay for the equipment.

Does it surprise you to discover that all of these actions could subject the attorneys involved to discipline, and, in many cases, the most severe discipline of disbarment?

7.1 Setting Fees

Law is not only a profession, it is a service industry. Like any other service industry, we have nothing more or less to sell but our time and our expertise. How do you go about setting a fee for that service? For most new attorneys, the question is answered by someone else, but the answer has profound implications. How we charge for that time and expertise influences broader ethical and professional issues. Among the public generally, concerns about the cost of legal services drive much of the public's distrust of attorneys. Access to justice is affected by the standards relating to the reasonableness of fees, the rights and duties regarding communication with clients about fees, and the availability of contingent fees or other fee agreements. The integrity and independence of the profession is critically influenced by the standards regarding an attorney's ability to recover fees, division of fees with others, and contingent fee limitations. How you set your fees can affect your ability to perform work competently and without conflict of interest, as well as your satisfaction with your work/life balance.

Where does one look to determine what fee is appropriate? One place may be to simply ask other attorneys. Prior to 1975, many private local and state bar associations had fee schedules that provided attorneys with recommended minimum fees for common legal services. The Supreme Court in *Goldfarb v. Va. State Bar*, 421 U.S. 773, 781-82, 792-93 (1975) held that these fee schedules violated federal antitrust law. Today, a new attorney might simply ask a trusted mentor for advice on common ranges of rates.

Of course antitrust law does not apply to the government when regulating fees and there is a rich jurisprudence governing attorneys' fees to be awarded under statutes in various settings. When fees are set by the courts under many fee shifting statutes, a traditional method of calculating those fees is referred to as the lodestar method. Under this method, the courts determine the attorney's reasonable hours spent in the representation and multiply that by the reasonable hourly fee for that type of representation. The result can be increased or decreased for other factors that have not otherwise gone into the calculation. Read the following description of that method:

> The lodestar method has its roots in accounting practices adopted in the 1940s to allow attorneys and firms to determine whether fees charged were sufficient to cover overhead and generate suitable profits. W. Ross, THE HONEST HOUR: THE ETHICS OF TIME-BASED BILLING BY ATTORNEYS 16 (1996).... Hourly records initially provided only an internal accounting check. The fees actually charged might be determined under any number of methods: the annual retainer; the fee-for-service method; the "eyeball" method, under which the attorney estimated an annual fee for regular clients; or the contingent-fee method, recognized by this Court in *Stanton v. Embrey*, 93 U.S. 548, 556 (1876), and formally approved by the ABA in 1908. As it became standard accounting practice to record hours spent on a client's matter, attorneys increasingly realized that billing by hours devoted to a case was administratively convenient; moreover, as an objective measure of a lawyer's labor, hourly billing was readily impartable to the client. By the early 1970's, the practice of hourly billing had become widespread.
>
> The federal courts did not swiftly settle on hourly rates as the overriding criterion for attorney's fee awards. In 1974, for example, the Fifth Circuit issued an influential opinion holding that, in setting fees under Title VII of the Civil Rights Act of 1964, 42 U.S.C. § 2000e-5(k) (1970 ed.), courts should consider not only the number of hours devoted to a case but also 11 other factors. *Johnson v. Georgia Highway Express, Inc.*, 488 F.2d 714, 717-719 (5th Cir. 1974). The lodestar method did not gain a firm foothold until the mid-1970's and achieved dominance in the federal courts only after this Court's decisions in *Hensley v. Eckerhart*, 461 U.S. 424 (1983), *Blum v. Stenson*, 465 U.S. 886 (1984), and *Pennsylvania v. Delaware Valley Citizens' Council for Clean Air*, 478 U.S. 546 (1986).
>
> Since that time, "the 'lodestar' figure has, as its name suggests, become the guiding light of our fee-shifting jurisprudence." *Burlington v. Dague*, 505 U.S. 557, 562 (1992). " ... [W]here settlement between the parties is not possible, 'the most useful starting point for [court determination of] the amount of a reasonable fee [payable by the loser] is the number of hours reasonably expended on the litigation multiplied by a reasonable hourly rate.' "

Gisbrecht v. Barnhart, 535 U.S. 789, 800-802 (2002).

Reasonable fee method (handwritten margin note)

In *Gisbrecht*, the Court was interpreting 42 USC § 406(b), which provides fees for representation before the social security administration. That act provides that an attorney who represents a prevailing claimant may recover "a reasonable fee for such representation, not in excess of 25 percent of the total of the past-due benefits to which the claimant is entitled by reason of such judgment" and that "no other fee may be payable or certified for payment for such representation ..." The Court determined that the lodestar method was not appropriate for fee awards under this statute, particularly since so many attorneys use contingent fees in these cases:

Alternative to lodestar (handwritten margin note)

> Contingent fees, though problematic, particularly when not exposed to court review, are common in the United States in many settings. Such fees, perhaps most visible in tort litigation, are also used in, e.g., patent litigation, real estate tax appeals, mergers and acquisitions, and public offerings. *See* ABA Formal Opinion 94-389 (1994). *But see id.*, at n. 3 (quoting observation that controls on contingent fees are needed to "reduce financial incentives that encourage lawyers to file unnecessary, unwarranted, and unmeritorious suits"). Traditionally and today, "the marketplace for Social Security representation operates largely on a contingency fee basis." SSA Report 3; *see also id.*, at 15, 66, 70; App. to Pet. for Cert. 56, 60, 88, 89, 91 (affidavits of practitioners).

> ... we again emphasize, the lodestar method was designed to govern imposition of fees on the losing party. In such cases, nothing prevents the attorney for the prevailing party from gaining additional fees, pursuant to contract, from his own client.... By contrast, § 406(b) governs the total fee a claimant's attorney may receive for court representation; any endeavor by the claimant's attorney to gain more than that fee, or to charge the claimant a noncontingent fee, is a criminal offense. 42 U.S.C. § 406(b)(2) (2001).

Gisbrecht v. Barnhart, 535 U.S. 789, 803-809 (2002).

Whether using a lodestar method or some other "reasonableness" measure, the courts ultimately determine reasonableness on a case-by-case basis. The rules of professional conduct give guidance for that determination in the context of discipline.

7.2 Reading the Rules: Rule 1.5

Rule 1.5 provides a baseline for determining how to set fees and a variety of regulations regarding fee agreements in different settings. Nearly all states have some variations on the ABA Model Rule, but most follow the Model Rule's organizational scheme: The rule has three basic parts. Parts (a) and (b) apply to all fee agreements and govern the how much and how to communicate about fees. Parts (c) and (d) relate to contingent fees and part (e) is about fee splitting. While each part of the rule presents its own challenges and you should study each part carefully, we will consider here Rule 1.5(a) in particular, which provides the rules regarding how much to charge. Arkansas has adopted the Model Rule with a variation most states have included. That is the introductory phrase "A lawyer's fee shall be reasonable" which was part of the Model Rules until 2002.

Arkansas Supreme Court Rules of Professional Conduct
Rule 1.5(a)

Rule 1.5(a) *A lawyer's fee shall be reasonable.* A lawyer shall not make an agreement for, charge, or collect an unreasonable fee or an unreasonable amount for expenses. The factors to be considered in determining the reasonableness of a fee include the following:

(1) the time and labor required, the novelty and difficulty of the questions involved, and the skill requisite to perform the legal service properly;

(2) the likelihood, if apparent to the client, that the acceptance of the particular employment will preclude other employment by the lawyer;

(3) the fee customarily charged in the locality for similar legal services;

(4) the amount involved and the results obtained;

(5) the time limitations imposed by the client or by the circumstances;

(6) the nature and length of the professional relationship with the client;

(7) the experience, reputation, and ability of the lawyer or lawyers performing the services; and

(8) whether the fee is fixed or contingent.

Context

This rule is again one of the basic rules governing the attorney-client relationship. How one interprets this rule often reflects one's predominant view of the profession — as a business and as a calling — that we considered in Chapter One. Under the common law predating the Code of Professional Responsibility, attorneys were subject to discipline only if their fees were unconscionable. Here is one court's explanation of that standard:

> We think that supplying amplifying phrases such as "shocking to the conscience," "monstrously harsh," "exceedingly calloused," and other expletives, adds little or nothing to the definitive qualities sought to be established by the law. They depend largely for their meaning upon who is speaking and who is listening. When the courts use the expression "unconscionable" in classifying a fee, we think they mean an amount under the circumstances which neither lawyer nor client can sensibly argue to be otherwise. A legitimate dispute could well arise between an attorney and his client concerning whether or not an attorney's fee, either claimed or kept, is unreasonable or excessive or even exorbitant, thus requiring the intervention of the civil court and the hearing of expert witnesses on both sides to reach a fair decision. It may be that the client is ignorant of the research involved in the problems presented, of the long and tedious hours of investigation represented by the lawyer's work. It may be that the lawyer places too high a value upon his services, that he too well remembers the long and arduous hours spent in acquiring a legal education and passing the bar examination, or that he assesses too high a charge with too little an experience. However, these are all factors which are subject to review by the courts in an action in contract.
>
> Where, however, ethical considerations take us from one end of the spectrum marked "reasonable" through categories designated successively as unreasonable, excessive, immoderate, inordinate, exorbitant, and unconscionable, we move in a direct line from the civil arena into a disciplinary forum. Differences of opinion can legitimately arise as to whether or not a fee is reasonable or unreasonable, or even excessive or exorbitant; but we find that sensible differences of opinion do not arise where the fee is palpably unconscionable.

In re *Greer*, 380 P.2d 482, 487 (Wash. 1963).

The adoption of the ABA Code of Professional Responsibility set the standard for regulation of fees as a prohibition of "clearly excessive" fees, which, in practice, did not raise the bar above the common law that preceded it. However, by moving from a prohibition of excessive fees to a standard of reasonableness, the Model Rules of Professional Conduct were intended "to impose a stricter standard on lawyers who would charge too much." ABA Comm. on Ethics and Prof'l Responsibility, Informal Op. 1509 (1984).

Nonetheless, the *Greer* court's distinction between a standard for enforceability of an attorney's fees and that for imposing discipline still appears to apply today. As the Restatement notes, "For a variety of reasons, discipline might be withheld for charging a fee that would nevertheless be set aside as unreasonable in a fee-dispute proceeding." Restatement (Third) of the Law Governing Lawyers § 34, cmt. a (2000). Some state disciplinary rules continue to apply the "clearly excessive" standard of the past, while others, in adopting the reasonableness standard, make explicit the distinction between the standard for enforcement and that of discipline. For example, Kansas Supreme Court Rule 226, which adopts a version of the ABA Model Rules, provides in Rule 1.5(c) that "A lawyer's fee shall be reasonable but a court determination that a fee is not reasonable shall not be presumptive evidence of a violation that requires discipline of the attorney." Regardless of your state's standard in its rules of professional conduct, when researching standards for reasonableness of fees, it is critical to remember this distinction between a fee that is enforceable and one that will subject you to discipline.

[handwritten margin note: unreasonable fee is not sufficient for discipline]

Relationships

Fees impact the attorney's other primary duties to client. Think about the relationship between fees and competence for example. In addition, you can see the relationship between fees and the duty of confidentiality in Rule 1.6(b)(5), which allows attorneys to reveal confidential information in order to establish a claim or defense (which would most commonly be a claim for fees). Likewise, fee arrangements can raise significant issues of conflict of interest, addressed especially in Rules 1.8 and 5.4.

In terms of the relationship between this rule and other law, there are many areas of law that might impact a fee issue: contracts, the law of agency, consumer protection and fee statutes, or procedural rules that provide fee consequences. The reasonableness of fees might be reviewed in a disciplinary case, but also in fee-shifting cases, such as divorce, environmental, or civil rights litigation; in class actions in which attorneys' fees have been awarded; or in bankruptcy cases where the attorney's fees are recovered from the estate. At the extremes, criminal actions might be brought against attorneys for fraudulent billing practices.

Structure

Rule 1.5(a) has two separate parts. First, there is the prohibition—notice that there are three actions that the rule targets: agreeing, charging, and collecting. Why does the rule specify these three aspects of fees? Second, there is the definitional aspect of the rule—the list of factors that determine reasonableness. You have already considered other lists in the rules. How does this list function? Notice that it is not a list of separate examples, or independent bases, but is a list of factors that are used to judge the very open-textured term "reasonable."

Reasons

At first glance, one might presume that the entirety of this rule is designed to protect clients, but look at each part of the rule and the comments more carefully. Do you see other interests addressed?

Visualize

Often reasonableness tests operate as balancing tests, with some factors favoring one decision and others favoring another. Using the concept of a scale and separate weights, think about the factors in Rule 1.5(a).

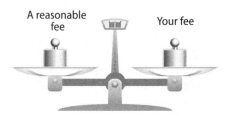

In a balance scale, the grocer (or scientist or customs officer) places a known weight (say one pound) on one side of the scale and then adds the goods to the other side until the scale balanced. Think of this analogy when considering how you would measure the reasonableness of fees. What might be considered the "scale weight" against which your own fee would be measured?

Are there some factors that are more likely to be used to determine the "standard weight" of a reasonable fee? While the rule does not itself indicate that some factors are more important than others, in practice you can imagine that some are always going to be very influential. Among these is the degree to which the client has understood and freely agreed to the fee arrangement. Time spent and hourly rate will generally be the starting point in evaluating the fee.

Students sometimes expect to find a degree of predictability in this rule that is simply not present in most balancing tests. Each case will be judged on its own merits. You can, however, draw some broad generalizations. A fee is more likely to be considered reasonable if it is similar to fees customarily charged in the community, if it is not disproportionate to the value of the case as a whole, and if the client has some options in arriving at the fee agreement. Fees are more likely to be considered unreasonable if they appear duplicative, do not represent work performed, or if the attorney has engaged in any misrepresentation or overreaching. Researching case law for similar types of cases can help to provide some additional guidance, though do not expect to find a large number of discipline cases involving fees. While courts do not easily find that a fee is unreasonable for purposes of discipline, where they do, they do not hesitate to impose sanctions. *See, e.g., In re* Dorothy, 605 N.W.2d 493 (S.D. 2000) (in which an attorney was reprimanded for charging a client $60,000 in a child custody action which did not present any especially novel facts or law and in which the other attorneys in the case had charged less than $20,000).

Imagine

Notice that the list of factors determining reasonableness is not exclusive (see the term "including"). What other factors can you think of that might influence the reasonableness of a fee? Is there an hourly rate or a percentage contingent fee that you could imagine is always going to be unreasonable?

Reflective Practice: Your Relationship with Money

In her article "Lying to Clients," Professor Lisa Lerman describes practices of deception and fraud in attorney billing practices: charging for unnecessary work or even for leisure, inflating hours, pressuring clients to settle in order to meet cash flow needs, etc. She describes these practices in all areas of law practice. Particularly in large firms, she notes,

> ... earning money is valued above all else. Lawyers give up their private lives, consoling themselves with lavish salaries, perks, and fringe benefits. The pressure and the isolation combine to compel lawyers to accept deception to whatever extent it is accepted in the firm, so that lawyers come to believe, in Nietzsche's words, that "lies are necessary in order to live." The structure of the work in large law firms places large firms on an institutional collision course with many humanistic values such as truthfulness and altruism.

Lisa G. Lerman, *Lying To Clients*, 138 U. Pa. L. Rev. 659, 769 (1990). Reflect on Professor Lerman's description. What is your relationship with money? How do you define financial success and how important is that value to you?

7.3 How Do I Bill Clients?

How you charge for your legal services depends to a large extent on the setting in which you are practicing and the types of clients you represent. Each method presents its own ethical risks.

While it was not always so, today the billable hour method is the most commonly used method for charging for legal services. The hourly rate may vary by individual in the firm or by type of activity (for example, some attorneys have a different rate for court appearances than for other time). The billable hour has come under increasing criticism for inflating costs, discouraging collaboration, and creating inefficiencies. In the recent recession, many businesses have demanded that their outside counsel charge for a large percentage of their services using flat fees or other alternative billing methods.[1]

Attorneys who work for entities such as in-house counsel and government attorneys are generally paid a salary. These attorneys, particularly public defenders, face pressures to provide larger and larger amounts of representation for very limited resources. The challenge for these attorneys is to insure that they control their caseloads so that they can continue to provide competent representation. However, how does a public defender easily turn down multiple court appointments? Can the office simply adopt a policy that it will no longer represent certain types of defendants? *State ex rel. Mo. Pub. Defender Comm'n v. Pratte*, 298 S.W.3d 870 (Mo. 2009) (holding that State Public Defender System did not have authority to deny representation to a class of defendants in order to control caseloads).

---

1. Nathan Koppel & Ashby Jones, *'Billable Hour' Under Attack*, Wall Street Journal, August 24, 2009 at A1, *available at* http://online.wsj.com/article/SB125106954159552335.html.

Attorneys in private practice representing individuals who have claims that may result in substantial awards or in causes of action for which fee shifting is possible, may charge on a contingent fee basis. A fee is contingent if the payment of the fee depends on the outcome of the representation. A typical contingent fee is one in which an attorney represents a plaintiff in a damages claim and charges a percentage of the damages recovery if the suit is successful. However, defendant's attorneys might charge a contingent fee based on a percentage of the money saved in successfully defending a suit. Conceivably, even a transactional attorney could use a contingent fee—charging a client a fee (either a designated amount or a percentage of savings) only if a deal is successfully concluded. The primary criticisms of contingent fee awards are that they create incentives for attorneys to stir up litigation that is unnecessary or frivolous, and that attorneys recover fees that are excessive in light of the work they perform in the individual case. Defenders of contingent fee arrangements argue that these fee arrangements allow access to justice for individuals who might not otherwise be able to afford representation and that the amounts charged are reasonable in light of the risk the attorney is taking of having no recovery whatsoever.

Rule 1.5 prohibits contingent fees in criminal defense and some aspects of family law practice because of dangers of overreaching with particularly vulnerable clients and because contingent fees might create an incentive for attorneys to counsel clients against plea bargains (in criminal cases) or reconciliation (in divorce). Contingent fees may be prohibited by statute or regulation in certain other practice settings. Comment 3 to Rule 1.5 states, "When there is doubt whether a contingent fee is consistent with the client's best interest, the lawyer should offer the client alternative bases for the fee and explain their implications." Notice that contingent fees, where they are permitted, must be in writing. In particular, attorneys should be sure to specify any expenses or fees that are not included in the contingent aspect of the fee agreement.

If an attorney is fired or withdraws before a contingent fee representation has concluded, the attorney may still be able to recover fees from the client. If the client's case successfully concludes—through settlement or judgment—the discharged attorney may be able to charge for the time spent on the case under a theory of *quantum meruit*. To recover, the attorney must be able to prove the time spent on the case, and an hourly rate, both of which must meet the standard of reasonableness.

No matter what the billing method, attorneys in private practice have two additional concerns. First, attorneys must address how expenses (filing fees, costs of experts, etc.) will be paid. Rule 1.8(e) generally prohibits an attorney from paying a client's expenses, with two exceptions: an attorney charging on a contingent fee basis may advance these expenses contingent on the outcome and attorneys representing indigent individuals on a pro bono basis may pay these expenses without a repayment obligation. Some expenses are simply part of overhead—the costs of maintaining an office and staff; practice management tasks such as bill preparation and conflicts checking; general clerical work such as photocopying and organizing; and general professional development, such as ongoing training and oversight. Generally, these expenses should be incorporated into the base hourly rate or contingent fee percentage rate. Some expenses are attributable to a particular representation, such as filing fees and expert witness costs.

Attorneys who bill on an hourly basis should insure that the clients understand what types of expenses will be billed separately. Some courts take the position that in-house expenses, such as clerical, photocopying, and the like, must be considered part of the overhead cost and cannot be billed as separate expenses. *See, e.g., In re Ireland*, 706 P.2d 352 (Ariz. 1985). However an ABA Formal Opinion on Billing for Professional Fees, Disbursements and Other Expenses concludes that this practice might be permissible if the overall fee was reasonable, if the method of charging for these activities was clearly explained to the client in advance and if the attorney used an accounting method that fairly and accurately allocated overhead associated with these activities. ABA Comm. on Ethics and Prof'l Responsibility, Formal Op. 93-379 (1993).

A second general concern regarding fees arises if your client is involved in criminal activity, even if the criminal activity is unrelated to your representation. If your client's funds come from criminal activities, they can be subject to forfeiture, even after the client has paid those funds to you. Forfeiture provisions exist in a number of federal and state criminal statutes for a variety of criminal activities, but most commonly drug violations and fraud schemes. For many of these statutes, the government need not wait until a conviction, or even an indictment to seize the funds. All that is required is for the government to show probable cause that the asset is substantially connected to the illegal activity. Under the "relation back" doctrine of this statute and other civil forfeiture statutes, the government's property interest in the proceeds of criminal transactions vests upon the commission of the crime. The government can trace these assets into the hands of third persons, including attorneys. Even if the government can provide a connection between the assets or funds held by a third party and the criminal activity, third parties may defend against forfeiture by proving that they are "a bona fide purchaser for value of such property who at the time of purchase was reasonably without cause to believe that the property was subject to forfeiture." The Supreme Court upheld forfeiture of attorney's fees in *Caplin & Drysdale, Chartered v. United States*, 491 U.S. 617 (1989).

You cannot necessarily avoid forfeiture by avoiding criminal defense practice. Criminals buy property, get divorced, have accidents, and engage attorneys for a full range of legal services just as do any other individuals. The best way to reduce your risk of forfeiture is to know how your client is financing your representation. If you can clearly identify the source of funds for your fees as coming from the proceeds of a legal transaction, whether by timing or source, and you memorialize that understanding, you have powerful evidence that you are "reasonably without cause to believe that the property was subject to forfeiture." Additionally, do not accept large cash fees. It is hard to argue that you didn't suspect illicit sources for fees when you are accepting bundles of cash. Moreover, any cash transaction over $10,000 requires that you file a Form 8300 with the IRS, which raises its own challenges.

Consider the type of practice you would like to pursue. What are the most common methods of compensation for that practice area? What ethical risks do these compensation methods raise? How can you reduce those risks?

Professional Responsibility Skill 7-A: Timekeeping

Even if you do not charge on an hourly basis, there are important reasons to keep track of the time you spend in representing clients. The practice of keeping time records is an important management tool for monitoring efficiencies, comparing productivity, and justifying fees determined on other bases. Good timekeeping is a skill that must be mastered with practice. The essentials of good timekeeping are:

Contemporaneous timekeeping—waiting until the end of the day and trying to reconstruct the time spent on a particular matter will inevitably result in inaccurate—and thus unethical—billing. You can keep time using a simple paper-and-pencil method, an electronic notepad on your computer, phone, or other electronic device, or timekeeping software. Regardless of the method, the key task is the same—note down the beginning and ending time for each task you perform.

"*Billable time*"—not every minute of every day of legal practice is spent in work for a particular client; yet, it is important to know how those additional hours are actually spent—whether it is attending a CLE or other professional development activity, client development and networking, or simply managing the practice. These hours are part of your overhead, which go into the determination of your hourly rate. You may not charge a particular client for these general overhead tasks, but you should nonetheless record your time on these tasks. Getting into the habit of recording all your time allows you to see why an eight-hour day gave you only five billable hours.

Itemized task records—Even if you spend an entire day working on one case, you may have completed several different tasks—investigating, consulting, researching, and writing for example. A record that reads "7.2 hours—interviewed client, researched legal issue, phoned records department, drafted motion" is simply no longer acceptable to most courts and clients. Rather, you should describe each separate task and the time spent on that task. The American Bar Association, in cooperation with other professional organizations, has developed a "Uniform Task-Based Management System," which provides code sets for discrete tasks and activities to systematize budgeting and billing. You can see an example of this system for litigation practice, at the ABA litigation section website at http://www.abanet.org/litigation/utbms/.

Billing increments—while you could simply charge on a per-minutes basis, most attorneys keep their time in larger increments, with one-tenth of an hour being the most common. In this approach, if you spend three minutes on a phone call for a client, you would round that time up to six minutes. Attorneys who use increments of larger than one-tenth of an hour may be significantly overcharging their clients. For example, the Kansas Supreme Court recently disciplined an attorney who routinely rounded up all time to the nearest hour. *In re Myers*, 127 P.3d 325 (Kan. 2006).

Some billing practices, designed to inflate billable hours, are plainly unethical, though these methods are very tempting methods to gain an edge in a competitive practice setting, to fulfill what are essentially unrealistic hours expectations, or to simply satisfy a desire for more profit. These practices include:

- "churning" (generating unnecessary or duplicative work simply to run up hours);

- "chipping" (breaking down a task into multiple small entries that add up to more time than the task should have taken);

- "double charging" (charging twice for the same task, frequently by having more than one person repeat the task or by charging more than one client for the same time);[2]

---

2. ABA Comm. on Ethics and Prof'l Responsibility, Formal Op. 93-379, *Billing for Professional Fees, Disbursements and Other Expenses* (December 6, 1993) (That opinion concludes that "The practice of billing several clients for the same time or work-product, since it results in the earning of an unreasonable fee, therefore is contrary to the mandate of the Model Rules. Model Rule 1.5.").

- "padding" (charging for more time than is actually spent on the task, sometimes a result of excessive "rounding up" of time segments).

As consumers of legal services become increasingly sophisticated and competition for legal business continues to increase, they will police attorney billing methods for these and other unethical or simply inefficient practices.

Reflective Practice: Your Relationship with Time

Try keeping your time spent on law school for one week. Consider each class, organization, or office a separate "client."

After you have tried some timekeeping for a few days, stop and reflect on the experience. Did you find it difficult to keep track of your time? Did the process of keeping time affect the way you worked? How? Were you tempted to "cheat" and inflate or estimate your time?

7.4 Collecting Fees

Charging for your services is only half of the business task — you must also be able to collect on your charges. You can increase the chances a client will actually pay your bills by communicating clearly at the outset your expectations for payment and by billing regularly and in a way that charges fairly and communicates clearly the work you have performed. What if, despite your best efforts, a client does not pay? You may not simply curtail services (or threaten to do so) or otherwise prejudice your client's case as a way to coerce payment. You may, however, have the option to withdraw, but your choice is to either withdraw or to represent — there is no middle ground of "temporary withdrawal" or "suspended services." Remember also that once you have entered an appearance on behalf of a client, you may not withdraw without permission of the court.

You should let the client know from the very beginning the circumstances upon which you will request to withdraw for failure to pay. While it is important to let your client know that you may request to withdraw if he does not pay your fees, trying to secure a client's advance consent to a withdrawal for nonpayment is neither effective nor ethical. Under Model Rule 1.16 and its state counterparts, an attorney may withdraw from representation if a client has failed to fulfill a substantial obligation and has been given a warning that the attorney may seek withdrawal. To the extent a fee agreement purports to give an attorney the right to withdraw for any nonpayment of fees and without any further notice to the client, the agreement misrepresents the attorney's discretion. Moreover, even with a client's consent, a court may not approve an attorney's withdrawal. A court may be unwilling to grant that permission if you could have known from the beginning that the client would not be able to afford your services or if it is simply too late in the representation to withdraw without significantly prejudicing both the client and the judicial process. Finally, even if withdrawal may be premised on a client's consent, advance consent is unlikely to be sufficiently informed to be considered reasonable. Accordingly, you may inform a client that the rules permit attorneys to seek withdrawal for non-payment of fees, but that is a different statement than asking the client to consent to your withdrawal based on circumstances that have not yet arisen.

When disputes regarding fees arise, attorneys may use a variety of approaches to resolution. Increasingly, states offer mediation or arbitration of fee disputes. In some states,
attorneys are required to submit fee disputes to these alternative dispute mechanisms before they can bring a suit for unpaid fees. *See, e.g., Cunningham v. Selman*, N.C. Ct. App.,
No. COA09-199, 12/8/09 (court has no jurisdiction to hear fee dispute action until state
fee mediation program has concluded). You may wish to include a provision in your fee
agreement requiring the use of these dispute resolution methods should a fee dispute
arise. As a last resort, you may choose to sue your client for your fee; however, beware.
Remember that fee collection claims have a way of generating malpractice counter-claims.

The best approach, of course, is to avoid trouble in the first instance by carefully screening your clients, communicating with them regarding fees at the outset and regularly
thereafter, and documenting these communications with written fee agreements and detailed billing statements. Practically, one of the best ways to insure that you will not en-
counter collection difficulties with a client is to collect your fees in advance. Perhaps the
most important rule to keep in mind with advances is that you must never commingle
client funds with your own. Until you have actually earned a portion of the advance, keep
the advance in the client trust account. As you earn the fees, you must notify the client
and then withdraw the portion that you have earned. Any unearned fees at the end of
representation need to be refunded. Simple enough, but neglecting this accounting task
provides the basis for the most serious of discipline.

Some attorneys charge clients retainer fees. A true retainer is not the same as an advance—it is a nonrefundable sum paid simply to engage an attorney's services. State
courts vary in the evaluation of the ethics of these nonrefundable fees. Attorneys defend
these fees by arguing that every time an attorney agrees to represent a client, the attorney has taken on the potential for conflicts of interest and the commitment of time and
resources that may preclude other more lucrative employment. Thus there is a "lost opportunity" cost to the attorney in simply agreeing to represent a client. Additionally attorneys will argue that there is value to a client in simply being able to say that she has
hired an attorney—especially if the attorney has a widespread and quality reputation.
Nonetheless, most state courts have rejected these arguments and have held that nonrefundable retainers violate public policy and are unethical unless there is some specific,
identifiable employment that would be precluded by the client's engagement of the attorney.
Columbus Bar Ass'n v. Halliburton-Cohen, 832 N.E.2d 42 (Ohio 2005)*; In re Kendall*, 804
N.E.2d 1152 (Ind. 2004).

If a client cannot afford to pay your fees, can you assist him to obtain financing? An
increasing number of attorneys allow clients to pay their fees by credit card. This allows
attorneys to collect their fees in a timely manner, insuring a more regular cash flow, and
shifting the costs of collection to the credit card companies. Older ethics opinions in the
states and from the ABA had forbidden or discouraged the practice. These opinions cited
a number of concerns: loss of confidentiality (as credit card companies gain information
about which of their customers are paying for legal services); promotion of litigation (as
attorneys advertised credit card payment plans); sharing of fees with non-lawyers (since
the attorneys would be required to pay a charge to the credit card agencies for processing the payments); and inflating fees unreasonably (as attorneys might increase their fees
to cover the costs of using credit card companies and clients would be paying interest on
the charges).

More recent ethics opinions have concluded that, so long as an attorney's advertisements regarding credit cards are honest, and the client consents to this payment method,
there is nothing inherently improper in using credit cards. ABA Comm. on Ethics and Prof'l

Responsibility, Formal Op. 00-419 (2000). If an attorney sets up a plan in which a client's credit card will be directly billed as fees are earned, the client should be given the opportunity to review the bill before the attorney charges the credit card. A few states continue to discourage the practice however, so, as with all areas of professional regulation, you should research the rules and ethics opinions in your state to determine its position.

7.5 Client Funds and Property

As fiduciaries for their clients, attorneys have the highest duty of trust in regard to handling the funds and property of the clients or third persons. When might an attorney have these funds or property? A client may pay an advance for the attorney to draw from as fees are earned. In other circumstances, the client might pay funds to the attorney that need to be paid to another, such as court costs or fines, expenses associated with experts or inspections, or funds to be conveyed upon closing a transaction. Finally, sometimes an attorney might receive funds from a third person that must be dispersed in whole or part to the client or others, such as settlement proceeds or awards.

The basic principles behind the rules governing funds and property are fairly straightforward. First, attorneys have a duty to guard their clients' funds (by having a client trust account) and property (by keeping it properly stored and identified). Second, attorneys must separate client funds from the attorney's personal or business operating account and from other fiduciary accounts.

State courts take this duty very seriously, imposing the most severe of discipline on those who violate the rules regarding client funds and property. If you're an honest person and don't steal from your client's account, you have nothing to worry about right? That may be what the attorney believed in *In re Williams*, 711 S.W.2d 518 (Mo. banc 1986). The attorney had delegated his bookkeeping to his wife and had not supervised her work, resulting in several dishonored checks and commingling of attorney and client funds. The court disbarred the attorney, noting that:

> The misappropriation of a client's funds is a serious matter. It is always a ground for the disbarment of an attorney that he has misappropriated the funds of his client, either by failing to pay over money collected by him for his client or by appropriating to his own use funds entrusted to his care. That respondent has made restitution of the converted funds is no defense to these charges. Neglect of duty to one's client also justifies disciplinary action.
>
> … Respondent's offer of his ignorance as mitigation to harsh punishment must fail where he had knowingly and intentionally failed to correct the ongoing problems with the trust account, given that he knew of the account problems. It is readily apparent from the evidence that respondent is not the innocent victim of an errant employee-spouse. We cannot allow an attorney to escape ultimate responsibility for mishandling of a client's funds where he knowingly and intentionally ignores trust account problems and demonstrates an almost total disregard for the protection of those funds.

Obviously, you must be sufficiently aware of how trust accounting works to be able to supervise anyone to whom you might delegate the actual bookkeeping functions.

Lawyers often hold funds in trust or escrow for their clients. When the funds the lawyer holds for a particular client are substantial in amount or will be held for a long period of time, clients are entitled to the interest on these funds. In these circumstances, the lawyer ordinarily will open up a separate federally-insured, client trust account for these funds only. In most circumstances, however, the funds an attorney must hold for a client or third person are so small or will be held so briefly that the administrative costs of establishing and maintaining a separate interest-bearing account for each individual client would exceed the interest earned. Attorneys could not place all these funds in a pooled interest-bearing account and keep the interest, because lawyers are ethically barred from benefiting from the use of their client's money, including earning interest on it. Today, in all states, attorneys must open one interest-bearing trust account for all these funds, paying the interest to a tax-exempt, non-profit organization that exists in all states. These pooled interest-bearing accounts are called IOLTA ("Interest on Lawyers Trust Accounts") accounts, and the IOLTA organization administers the funds generated to provide financial assistance to various non-profit agencies that provide legal aid to the poor.

IOLTA programs were established in the early 1980s and operated without significant challenge until the 1990s, when litigation challenged the legality of these programs in several states. The most common claim in these cases was that IOLTA violated the Just Compensation Clause of the Fifth Amendment to the Constitution. In *Brown v. Legal Foundation of Washington,* 538 U.S. 216 (2003), the United States Supreme Court upheld constitutionality of IOLTA, holding that even if the rules requiring a transfer of interest constituted a per se taking, it was for a valid public purpose and the amount of just compensation due to individual clients was zero.

In addition to maintaining client funds, in any representation you will also be collecting and generating numerous documents. What are your responsibilities regarding the client's file? Your first responsibility is to maintain your client files. Rule 1.15 provides that attorneys must retain records of fund and other property for five years after termination of the representation. The rule does not obviously apply to the documents that are generated by the attorney during the representation, but an attorney is wise to have a clear policy for document retention. Some attorneys have begun to operate "paperless offices" scanning all documents into electronic files. However, the originals of those documents belong to the client and should not be destroyed without the client's consent. Rule 1.16(d) indicates that, upon withdrawal, an attorney must return all papers to which the client is "entitled" and "may retain papers relating to the client to the extent permitted by other law." What is this "other law?" Why might an attorney want to keep a client's file rather than turn it over?

One circumstance in which an attorney might want to keep a file is as a device to collect fees. Historically, there has existed in many jurisdictions something called an Attorney's Common Law Retaining Lien which permits an attorney to retain a client's file if the client has not yet paid for the representation. Thomas G. Fischer, Annotation, *Attorney's Assertion of Retaining Lien as Violation of Ethical Code or Rules Governing Professional Conduct,* 69 A.L.R. 4th 974 (1991, 2008 Supp.). However, in many jurisdictions today, the courts have held that an attorney may not assert this lien to the detriment of the client. Obviously, if the only circumstances in which you can withhold a client's file are ones in which it will not affect the client, the lien becomes a toothless tool in fee collection. Other jurisdictions appear to reject the lien outright. So, for example, Missouri Formal Opinion #115 (1988) opined that "the file belongs to the client, from cover to cover" and an attorney may not withhold any portion of the file in order to enforce payment of expenses.

Another circumstance in which an attorney might seek to retain some or all of a client file is against a request by others to turn over the file. The court in the following case discussed the question "Who owns the documents in a legal file, the attorney or the client?"

Swift, Currie, McGhee & Hiers v. Henry

581 S.E.2d 37 (Ga. 2003)

Ordinarily, document discovery issues arise in the context of a discovery request brought by an opposing party. See, e.g., *Hickman v. Taylor*, 329 U.S. 495, 67 S.Ct. 385, 91 L.Ed. 451 (1947); *McKinnon v. Smock*, 264 Ga. 375, 445 S.E.2d 526 (1994); OCGA § 9-11-26(b)(3). Document discovery issues are rare when it comes to matters between attorney and client. But it is just such a discovery issue which must be resolved in this case. Boiled down to its essence, the question is this: Does a document created by an attorney in the course of representing a client belong to the attorney or the client?

Jurisdictions which have considered this question have given different answers. A minority of courts have ruled that a document belongs to the attorney who prepared it, unless the document is sought by the client in connection with a lawsuit against the attorney. *See Corrigan v. Armstrong, Teasdale, Schlafly, Davis & Dicus*, 824 S.W.2d 92 (Mo.App.1992); *BP Alaska Exploration v. Superior Court &c.*, 199 Cal.App.3d 1240, 245 Cal.Rptr. 682 (1988). These jurisdictions often employ a work product analysis and take the position that an attorney can raise the work product privilege vis-à-vis the client. If the work product privilege applies, the client cannot compel the attorney to disclose the document.[2]

A majority of courts have ruled that a document created by an attorney belongs to the client who retained him. *See, e.g., Resolution Trust Corp. v. H—, P.C.*, 128 F.R.D. 647 (N.D.Tex.1989); *In the Matter of Kaleidoscope, Inc.*, 15 B.R. 232 (Bankr.N.D.Ga.1981); *In the Matter of Sage Realty Corp. v. Proskauer, Rose, Goetz & Mendelsohn LLP.*, 91 N.Y.2d 30, 666 N.Y.S.2d 985, 689 N.E.2d 879, 883 (1997). Under this approach, courts presume that a client is entitled to discover any document that the attorney created during the course of representation. *Id.* However, good cause to refuse discovery would arise if disclosure would violate an attorney's duty to a third party. Good cause might also be shown if the document assesses the client himself, or includes "tentative preliminary impressions of the legal or factual issues presented in the representation, recorded primarily for the purpose of giving internal direction to facilitate performance of the legal services entailed in that representation." *Id.* at 883, 666 N.Y.S.2d 985, 689 N.E.2d 879.

Although much can be said for the minority view, we think the majority approach is better. It places the burden on the attorney, the party who is best able to assess the "discoverability" of the document. It is, after all, the attorney who possesses the document and knows its contents. The client, on the other hand, who does not know what the document contains, can only make a general case for discovery. *Id.* at 882, 666 N.Y.S.2d 985, 689 N.E.2d 879. Thus, it would be unfair, and perhaps unproductive, to put the burden on the client.

---

2. Under the minority view, however, some documents, such as pleadings, wills, contracts, correspondence, and other papers made public by the attorney, are not considered work product. These documents, deemed "end product," are owned by the client. *Federal Land Bank v. Federal Intermediate Credit Bank*, 127 F.R.D. 473, 480 (S.D.Miss. 1989).

Perhaps more importantly, the majority view fosters open and forthright attorney-client relations. An attorney's fiduciary relationship with a client depends, in large measure, upon full, candid disclosure. That relationship would be impaired if attorneys withheld any and all documents from their clients without good cause, especially when the documents were created at the client's behest. *See State Bar of Georgia, Formal Advisory Opinion* No. 87-5 (September 26, 1988) (attorney may not, to the prejudice of client, withhold client's papers as security for unpaid fees).

Finally, insofar as the minority view employs a work product analysis, we think it is out of place in cases of this kind. Simply put, "the work product doctrine does not apply to the situation in which a client seeks access to documents or other tangible things created or amassed by his attorney during the course of the representation." *Spivey v. Zant,* 683 F.2d 881, 885 (5th Cir.1982); Resolution *Trust Corp. v. H—, P.C., supra.*

[handwritten margin note: critique of work product minority]

Adopting the majority view, we hold, therefore, that [the client] is presumptively entitled to discover the memorandum which [his attorney] had prepared ... Barring a showing by [the attorney] of good cause to refuse access to the memorandum, [the client] must be given an opportunity to inspect and copy it.

FLETCHER, Chief Justice, concurring.

Although I generally agree with the majority's opinion, I write separately to identify a few of the issues that may arise on remand, or in future cases. First, an attorney could have a valid claim of work product protection against his client in a document that was prepared in anticipation of litigation between the client and the attorney. Second, I believe whether the client has been charged for the creation of the document should be a significant factor in deciding whether the client owns the document. Third, the document at issue in this case apparently memorializes what may be described as compromise negotiations and, therefore, would be inadmissible under OCGA § 24-3-37. On remand, the trial court should consider whether the document is inadmissible under OCGA § 24-3-37 and, if so, if it is nonetheless discoverable.

Notes

Noted professional responsibility scholar Fred Zacharias observed that confusion in the law regarding attorney files is common:

> On the one hand ... jurisdictions emphasize client protection and assert that ownership of work product belongs to clients. On the other hand, the decision makers do not entirely believe their own proclamations, sensing that attorneys too have some ownership interests. The relative importance of the client and lawyer interests may change, and become even more confusing, when the work-product issues arise in contexts other than direct attorney-client disputes. The failure to fully analyze the work-product privilege and the reasons why control of work product might be given to one or the other party has prevented the decision makers from identifying a coherent doctrine. Hence, the decisions express standards that later opinions seem to undercut.

Fred Zacarias, *Who Owns Work Product*, 2006 U. Ill. L. Rev. 127.

A good rule of thumb is to consider the overall policy behind Rule 1.16(d)'s description of your obligations when ending an attorney-client relationship. You should put your client in such a position that she can reasonably continue the matter with another attorney. That means any document or information you have gathered or created in the course of representing the client should be given to the client if it is reasonably necessary to her ability to continue. Thus your own internal memoranda regarding staffing or conflicts checks would not be part of the file, but personal notes evaluating the matter would be.

7.6 Communicating About Fees and Property

Since an attorney's fee is not displayed on a menu at the front door, attorneys have a fundamental duty to communicate with their clients about fees. Model Rule 1.5(b) requires communicating your fee and responsibilities for expenses "before or within a reasonable time after commencing the representation." Likewise, your duty to maintain a client's property and funds requires that you "promptly notify" the client when you receive funds or property belonging to him. Rule 1.15(d).

At the beginning of each representation, you should speak with the client about the costs of legal representation, the timing and methods of payment of those costs, and the client's ability to pay. For many new attorneys, these are not easy conversations. New attorneys may have no basis for estimating time and expense involved in even routine representations. Often, your most honest answer to "How much is this going to cost?" must be "I don't know." Nonetheless, it is your responsibility to raise the issue and speak with the client early on. Of course, the fee discussion need not be the first words out of your mouth, but clients should not be the ones to have to raise the issue, nor should you waste your client's time in collecting extensive case information or explaining other aspects of your representation if the client ultimately cannot afford your services.

Though not necessarily required by the rules of conduct (check your state for its approach), you should think twice before ever undertaking a representation without a written agreement. A written fee agreement serves many purposes: it reduces the chances of client surprise or misunderstanding about fees; emphasizes the seriousness of the matter of retaining an attorney; increases enforceability by the attorney; and provides evidence of the attorney's compliance with the duty to communicate fees clearly.

Communication about fees does not end with the agreement—you should bill clients regularly. Regular billing is an important tool in communicating with the client regarding the progress in the representation and the ongoing costs. It is also one of the best methods of insuring that you will be paid. Billing statements should communicate what work has been done, who has completed that work, the time spent and the total charged. Billing statements can include reminders of your payment policy and prompts for clients to contact you if they have concerns.

Likewise, communication about documents is an important part of keeping the client informed. Many attorneys send copies of pleadings, letters, and other documents, to the client during the representation. This is not a substitute for maintaining or returning the original file, however.

Professional Responsibility Skill 7-B: Documentation

Consider the following paragraphs from a client representation agreement. Decide whether these clauses accurately reflect the law, are enforceable, and are written clearly, precisely, simply, and concisely.

Fees:

1. By signing this document I (client) agree to the billable hour method to calculate and formulate a bill for the case of _____. Upon signing this agreement I (client) agree and promise to pay the amount determined by the billable hour method. Law firm will maintain an itemized task record of the time spent on the case and will round the billable hours to the nearest 1/10 of an hour.

2. Fees shall be collected by the law firm upon the rendering of legal services to the client. The client shall deliver the fees in a reasonably timely manner.

a) Rendering of legal services occurs when the client's legal issue has been resolved to the best of the law firm's ability. Rendering of legal services is not determined by the outcome of a dispute, but only upon its resolution.

b) Delivery of the fees may be done in a reasonable manner previously agreed upon by the law firm and the client. If the client fails to deliver the fees, the law firm may pursue fees through the use of debt collecting agencies.

c) Fees shall be delivered by the client to the law firm no later than 14 days after the rendering of legal services.

d) All provisions of fee collecting may be modified with mutual consent of the client and the law firm.

Files:

All documents that relate to clients in any manner that are obtained or created during the course of firm's representation belong to clients. However, clients agree and understand that all personal notes made by the attorney are the property of the attorney and the firm unless otherwise agreed. These documents constitute the client file. Upon termination of the attorney-client relationship for any reason, at any time, clients will have the right to request and accept possession of the client file within a reasonable time. If clients elect not to have said documents returned to them, the documents will be deemed abandoned after three years and shall be destroyed in keeping with the firm's retention policy. The firm has the right to maintain duplicates of any portion of the client file at the clients' expense. The firm shall retain all documents paid for by the firm in which the firm incurred costs the client has not yet reimbursed.

Criteria for editing attorney-client contract clauses:

- *Who's who.* Does the provision use clear and consistent names for the parties (e.g., "Client/Lawyer" or "You/We")? Or does it use different shorthand names for the parties or names that are unclear (e.g., "party of the first part")?

- *Representations.* Are any necessary background statements or representations included and are they clearly phased as statements of fact rather than statements of obligation? Or are necessary factual representations absent, confused, or written in language that confuses their purpose?

- *Purpose and effect.* Does the provision appropriately create an obligation (shall), an option or right (may), or a condition precedent (must)? Does it imply rather than express obligations, rights, or conditions? Does it create obligations, rights, or conditions that are not likely to be what was intended?

- *Consistency with law.* Is the provision a permissible term for negotiated agreement? Does the provision attempt to create obligations, rights, or conditions that the law does not permit or that would be unenforceable? Does the provision simply restate the default rule provided by the law? Is there a good reason for that redundancy?

- *Clarity of language.* Is the provision written grammatically correct, in plain English, using active voice, with concrete and well-defined terms? Or does the provision use legalese, vague terms, convoluted construction, and poor grammar?

- *Consistency.* Is the provision internally consistent—are the same terms used for the same ideas throughout the provision? Or does it make representations or create obligations, rights, or conditions that are inconsistent with one another or confuse the reader in an attempt to create "elegant variation"?

- *Depth.* Does the provision provide sufficient detail, at the appropriate level of generality, to guide performance and ensure enforceability? Or does the provision inappropriately omit key issues, speak in such general terms as to be unenforceable, or provide unnecessary detail that interferes with overall readability?

- *Organization.* Is the provision organized in a way that the structure aids understanding and the relationship between items is clear (especially in the use of numbering, punctuation, and connector words)? Or does the provision lack clear organization or create ambiguity because of incorrect punctuation or vague use of connector words?

Researching Professional Responsibility 7-A: Fees, Files, and Property

Spend some time researching the rules and procedures of the state in which you intend to practice. What variations from the Model Rules does its version of Rule 1.5 contain? Does your state have a fee dispute resolution system? What are its characteristics? What is your state's position, if it has taken one, on the ownership of the client file?

Test Your Understanding

You should be able to confidently answer the following questions about Fees, Files, and Property. If you are not confident you can answer each, go back through the chapter or discuss the questions with your peers.

1. Can you trade goods or services as payment? *Yes, unless state says no*
2. Can you use billing methods other than hourly or contingent fees? *sometimes states may allow*

3. What is a reasonable fee? *lodestar depends on circumstance* → *court will support reduce more than*

4. Can you discount or increase according to ability to pay? *yes, if reasonable*

5. Why are contingent fees so controversial? *potential for abuse dragging of things*

6. Why can't you charge contingent fees in a divorce case or a criminal case? *incentive against people will want to go*

7. What is the lodestar method? *reasonable fee × hours*

8. What fee agreements must be in writing? *Contingent fees*

9. Why keep time if you aren't billing on an hourly basis? *keep track + break down 4 client*

10. How do you keep time? *paper / electronic*

11. What are some examples of unethical time-based billing? *dragging / padding, clipping,*

12. What is the difference between a retainer and an advance? *non-refundable / double*

13. How do you make sure clients will pay? *be upfront + disclose / screen* *make them pay in advance* *charging*

14. If you have a contingent fee and the client fires you before the case settles, can you still collect? *Yes*

15. What is an IOLTA account and who has to have one? *every lawyer, fees for client that generates int. for*

16. Why do you have to turn over files to a client who hasn't paid just so she can give those files to some other attorney? *client entitled rights* *no prsf*

17. Do you have to report another attorney's overbilling? *duty to ABA*

18. How do you share fees with another attorney?

To Learn More

For additional review, see the CALI lesson on Fees at www.cali.org.

Chapter Eight

Communication and Authority

Learning Objectives

After you have read this chapter and completed the assignments, you should be able to:

- Identify whether a decision is one for the attorney, the client, or is one in which the law provides uncertain allocation of authority.
- Identify the type and degree of communication necessary for different decisions in a representation.
- Articulate the policy tensions inherent in laws defining the attorney's duty to counsel a client regarding matters outside the scope of representation.
- Recognize that substantive legal standards outside the rules of professional conduct may constrain the attorney in advising or assisting a client. Be able to locate those standards through research.
- Articulate your conception of what constitutes an ethical and effective relationship between attorney and client regarding decisions and be able to explain that to a client.
- Use the Restatement (Third) of the Law Governing Lawyers as a research tool.

Rules to Study

ABA Model Rules 1.2, 1.4, and 2.1 and the common law of agency will be our primary focus in this chapter.

Preliminary Problem

You received the following email today:

From: Arnold Attorney [aattorney@aattorney.net]
Sent: Friday, February 10, 2013 5:17 PM
To: Associate, Junior
Subject: Wilkins settlement

Classification: Confidential internal

As you know we are representing David Wilkins in his wrongful termination action against his former employer, Ourstate Industries. Last week at our pretrial conference, the trial court ordered that we appear this week for a day of mediated settlement discussions and ordered that each party have someone with settlement authority in attendance throughout the mediation. I gave a copy of the court's order to Wilkins and he agreed to attend the mediation, which began yesterday at 9:00 a.m. The president of Ourstate Industries, his attorney, Wilkins, and I met together and the mediator went over the ground rules, including the court's requirement that each side have someone present with settlement authority. We met together for about an hour and then the mediator split us into two separate rooms. The defendants' attorneys were in one room and Wilkins and I were in another. The mediator shuttled offers and counter offers back and forth until by noon we had agreed on a number of terms, including that Wilkins would not seek reinstatement, that his employer would remove anything from his employment file indicating that he had been fired or that he had engaged in any misconduct, and that he would be given the value of his accumulated sick leave and vacation pay in addition to any other financial settlement.

We then took a one-hour break for lunch. During lunch, Wilkins and I talked about how the negotiations were going. He was very impatient with the entire process, but told me that he was very happy with the agreements we'd obtained so far and that if he could get a financial settlement of at least $200,000 he would feel that he had won. I have the notes of that lunch meeting but nothing signed by Wilkins.

When we went back after lunch, Wilkins was increasingly impatient. Offers were being traded back and forth in very small increments, but we were slowly moving toward $200,000. By 2:30 we were only $10,000 apart, with the defendant offering $198,000. Wilkins got up from the room we were working from and said something like, "I'm leaving. You handle it." He went into the room where the defendant's attorney was sitting, picked up his briefcase, and left. After that, the defendant offered $208,000 and I told the mediator that was agreeable. The employer's attorney agreed to draft the agreement and I went to look for Wilkins but couldn't find him.

The settlement agreement arrived in my email inbox this morning and I tried to locate Wilkins. I finally was able to reach him this afternoon and told him that we had settled on the terms he wanted. Wilkins now says that he wants an accountant and another attorney to review the terms and he's decided that he might want to ask for reinstatement after all. I tried to explain to him that I had negotiated exactly as he had directed, but he didn't want to talk about it on the phone. We set a meeting for Monday morning at 8:00 am. Please let me know what the legal status of this settlement is. I think Wilkins can't back out of it now, but I'm afraid he's going to be very upset if I give him that news. He can be a hothead and I suspect he might file a disciplinary complaint against me, so research whether I've done anything to be concerned about.

8.1 The Scope of Representation

Just as attorneys need not accept all clients, in representing a client, an attorney need not represent that client on all matters or issues the client is facing. To so limit a representation requires the "informed consent" of the client. In no case can a client give up the right to discharge the attorney, the right to competent representation, the right to reasonable diligence and promptness, or the ultimate right to settle or terminate the representation or the litigation. However, it is not uncommon for an attorney to agree to represent a client at trial but not on appeal, or to form a business but not pursue litigation arising out of that business formation.

Clear definitions of the scope of representation are important for several reasons. The scope of representation you describe in an agreement with your client will prevent subsequent client misunderstandings and disappointment (and the malpractice actions that might generate). If a client sues you, your duties will be defined by your agreement with the client. If you are assessing the degree to which your current representation presents a conflict of interest, your representation agreement will provide important evidence. An open-ended or vaguely defined scope of representation may leave open the question of whether your representation has ended — making any conflicts analysis subject to the more stringent requirements for avoiding conflicts with current clients. Even if the representation has obviously ended, the scope of that representation will determine whether your former client's matter is the "same or substantially related" to your current client's matter. Accordingly, best practice requires you to carefully draft and clearly communicate the scope of your representation in your engagement letter or representation agreement with your client.

What are some of the essentials in drafting an agreement regarding the scope of representation? Make the identity of your client crystal clear, including identifying anyone that you do not represent if there is any ambiguity. If you are representing a company, are you also representing its affiliates or subsidiaries? Comment 34 to Rule 1.7 indicates that representation of one member of a corporate family will not necessarily conflict the attorney out of representation adverse to other members of the corporate family. But if your engagement letter indicates that you represent a business and "its affiliates" that presumption will be overcome and you will be subject to disqualification more easily. *Avocent Redmond Corp. v. Rose Elecs.*, 491 F. Supp. 2d 1000 (W.D. Wash. 2007). As the court in *Cliff Sales Co. v. Am. S.S. Co.*, 2007 U.S. Dist. LEXIS 74342 (N.D. Ohio Oct. 4, 2007) noted, defining who the client is in an engagement letter is "necessary in today's business world because so many companies are related in some way that law firms would have substantial conflict issues if a law firm was considered to have an attorney-client relationship with all of a client corporation's related corporations and entities." Likewise clearly and specifically address any other situation in which the identity of the client may be unclear, the scope of authority of the client's agent may need clarifying, or a third-party payor's role in the representation may need limiting.

Describe as clearly and plainly exactly what you will do for the client. Define the factual as well as legal issues. If there are time, jurisdictional, or remedial limits to your representation, be sure to include these.

The Kutak Rock law firm in Kansas learned the importance of a clearly defined scope of representation when it was sued for malpractice. The firm had been hired by an investment company Reimer and Koger (R&K) that was making investments for the Kansas Public Employee Retirement System (KPERS). R&K hired Kutak Rock to prepare the documents to complete an investment in Sharoff, a food service and distribution company. The company later went bankrupt and KPERS sued the Kutak Rock for failing to advise them regarding whether the investment was prudent.

Kutak Rock's engagement letter with the investment company described the scope of their representation in this way:

> We [Kutak Rock] will perform all services customarily performed by counsel in domestic transactions of the nature contemplated herein, including among other services, the drafting, negotiating and preparation of a preliminary agreement, or commitment letter, outlining the basic terms of the investment and a definitive agreement for the purchase by Reimer and Koger, on behalf of the Investors,

of subordinated Debentures, shares of Preferred Stock and Warrants to purchase Common Stock, of Sharoff, as well as all other documents necessary to effect the investment. In addition, we will perform such due diligence inquiries and activities as may be required by the investors in connection with its investment. We further understand that we may be called upon to render corporate, securities and tax advice in structuring the transaction.

The only due diligence that R&K asked Kutak Rock to perform was to insure that Sharoff was a company in good standing in Colorado, which the firm did. R&K performed the financial due diligence investigation. Because the engagement letter clearly identified Kutak Rock's scope of representation, the malpractice action against them was dismissed on summary judgment and affirmed on appeal. *KPERS v. Kutak Rock*, 44 P.3d 407, 415 (Kan. 2002).

Commentators have suggested that if Kutak Rock's engagement letter had been even more specific, it might have avoided litigation altogether. 1 MALLEN & SMITH, LEGAL MALPRACTICE § 2.10, at 122–23 (2008 ed.). In what way could the agreement have been more specific? Should the firm have amended its engagement letter when the scope of its "due diligence" duties was clarified by the client's agent? Often amendments to engagement letters are necessary and important to reflect the evolving understanding of the issues and tasks necessary for the representation. Even if you do not formally amend your engagement letter, be sure to document these evolving understandings with your client.

Often one of the most important statements you can provide in an engagement letter is a description of what you will *not* do. The Kronish Lieb law firm benefitted from this approach when it was sued by its client in connection with the formation of a business and preparation of a private placement memorandum. The firm's engagement letter explained that it would not be representing the client in "regulatory matters," which it described as "[National Association for Security Dealers (NASD)] filings and the like," and noted that plaintiffs had indicated that they would hire another, less expensive law firm to handle these issues (which plaintiffs did hire). When the NASD later brought an action against the clients for regulatory violations, the clients sued Kronish Lieb for malpractice. The New York Supreme Court granted Kronish Lieb's summary judgment motion, based on the specificity of the scope of its engagement. *Smookler v. Kronish Lieb Weiner & Hellman LLP*, 2006 N.Y. Misc. LEXIS 3982 at *10 (N.Y. Sup. Ct. Jan. 11, 2006). Think of the trouble the firm would have been in if it had relied on a standard form engagement letter that simply said the firm would be representing the client "in connection with the formation of a business" instead of tailoring the engagement letter to the specific facts of the client's representation.

Of course there are limits to how narrowly you can describe your representation. Recall that attorneys cannot easily ask clients to waive malpractice liability (Rule 1.8(h)), nor can the scope of representation be limited so much that the attorney is agreeing to provide less than competent representation (Rule 1.2). An attorney acting as local counsel for another attorney who has been admitted *pro hac vice*, for example, might want to limit the scope of his representation to basic tasks of accepting service or acting as a communication conduit. However, many local court rules require that local counsel be involved in the active management of the case. Thus, an attorney could not waive that rule's duties in an engagement letter.

8.2 How Are Decisions Allocated Between an Attorney and a Client?

Some decisions belong to the client and an attorney is required to follow the client's directions as to those decisions. Conversely, there are some client directions an attorney may not ethically follow. Finally, most decisions fall somewhere in between, where the attorney has a good deal of discretion in building the relationship with the client.

Rule 1.2(a) of the ABA Model Rules of Professional Conduct provides that there are some questions that always require a client's consent: settlement decisions, and, in criminal matters, pleas, jury trial waiver, and whether the client testifies. Some courts have read this rule to extend beyond the enumerated decisions to a range of ultimate decisions and other states expressly add additional matters to this list of decisions reserved to clients. "Rule 4-1.2(a) requires a client to be in control of the decisions that have the capacity to affect the client profoundly, specifically referencing the decision whether to accept a settlement of the case...." *In re Coleman*, 295 S.W.3d 857, 864 (Mo. 2009) (citing, *Parents Against Drunk Driving v. Graystone Pines Homeowners' Ass'n*, 789 P.2d 52, 55 (Utah Ct. App. 1990)). What would be matters that "affect the client profoundly?"

For example, suppose that an attorney represents an employer in a wrongful termination action brought by a former employee. The attorney would like to first defend the action in a motion to dismiss based on a procedural argument such as failure to exhaust administrative remedies. The employer would prefer to meet the action on the merits, concerned about the reputational harm if he does not defend the termination. Must the attorney forgo the procedural defense? Or consider a criminal defense client who wants her attorney to advance a self-defense theory (for which there is little evidence other than defendant's own testimony) and who does not want to raise the insanity defense (for which there appears to be some considerable evidence). Must the attorney defer to the client's decision regarding these issues? Does it matter that this is a criminal rather than civil case? Does it matter that the attorney believes there is evidence to support an insanity defense?

For those matters, such as settlement or plea decisions, just exactly what does it mean for a client to be in charge? From a disciplinary standpoint, this means that attorneys must respect a client's right to decide these matters and may not ask a client to waive his or her right to decide a settlement, *In re Grievance Proceeding*, 171 F. Supp. 2d 81 (D. Conn. 2001); *In re Lansky*, 678 N.E.2d 1114 (Ind. 1997). An attorney who compromises a client's substantive rights by settling a case without actual authority or entering a plea without the client's consent can be subject to discipline and liability. Consider the following clause in a contingent fee agreement:

> In consideration of one-third (1/3) of any recovery, I agree to forego my hourly rate, and instead, agree to accept one-third of any recovery. However, because I am taking a risk with you on this case, and because I am more familiar with the legal trends relative to judgments, settlements, and summary disposition, you agree I shall have the exclusive right to determine when and for how much to settle this case. That way, I am not held hostage to an agreement I disagree with.

Would such an agreement be ethical? Enforceable? In re Coleman, 295 S.W.3d 857 (Mo. 2009).

In criminal representation, the right to decide whether to accept a plea agreement is a fundamental right of the defendant. The United States Supreme Court has held that when a defense counsel "allowed a formal plea offer to expire without advising the defendant or allowing him to consider it, defense counsel did not render the effective assistance the Constitution requires." *Missouri v. Frye*, 566 U. S. ___ (2012). In concluding that a defense counsel's communication of a plea offer is an essential aspect of effective representation, the Court cited rules of professional conduct and noted that, "Though the standard for counsel's performance is not determined solely by reference to codified standards of professional practice, these standards can be important guides." The American Bar Association recommends defense counsel "promptly communicate and explain to the defendant all plea offers made by the prosecuting attorney," ABA Standards for Criminal Justice, Pleas of Guilty 14–3.2(a) (3d ed. 1999), "and this standard has been adopted by numerous state and federal courts over the last 30 years." *Id.*

Just as there are some decisions that an attorney may not take away from the client, there are also some client directions that the lawyer simply may not follow. Most of the actions attorneys cannot take on behalf of their clients violate other laws in addition to the rules of professional conduct. A lawyer always has actual authority to take action that he or she reasonably believes is necessary to comply with the law or a court order. Filing a frivolous pleading or motion on behalf of your client violates state versions of Model Rule 3.1 as well as the applicable court's rules of civil procedure (such as Federal Rule of Civil Procedure 11). Consequently, an attorney may withdraw from representation and refuse to take these actions or, if the attorney has already submitted a pleading or motion violating these rules, the attorney may withdraw the paper, even if the client objects. Rule 4.4 prohibits attorneys from taking actions designed merely to harass others, as do tort standards for abuse of process or malicious prosecution. Even without Rule 1.2(d) to tell us, we could know that attorneys may not assist clients with objectives that are criminal or fraudulent, given the criminal laws of aiding and abetting. The overlap with these legal standards is not perfect of course. We will examine more carefully the relationship between civil and criminal actions against attorneys for crime and fraud in later chapters. For now, it is sufficient for you to recognize that there is no general "following client orders" defense that will permit an attorney to break the civil or criminal law or violate court rules, orders, or the rules of professional conduct.

Rule 1.2(d) provides a qualification to the general prohibition on assisting a client's crime or fraud. An attorney may provide a client information about the legality of his conduct or proposed conduct. If attorneys had to be concerned that instructing their clients in the limits of the law might be deemed to be assisting in a crime or fraud whenever the clients choose to step over the line, the heart of the attorney-client relationship— providing legal advice and counsel—would be damaged.

In between the relatively clear allocations of authority we have examined thus far lies a vast area of discretion. Rule 1.2 provides the general guideline that clients are in charge of "objectives" and attorneys are in charge of determining the "means" to obtain those objectives. However, what is an objective and what is a means is not always clear. You can help to make this line clearer when you first establish an attorney-client relationship, by talking with your client about the kinds of "means" decisions you will be making and the manner in which you will communicate those decisions to your client. So, for example, you may wish to have the client agree that you have the authority to determine scheduling, lest an angry client view your agreement to a continuance as an act of disloyalty. *Purtle v. Comm. on Professional Conduct*, 878 S.W.2d 714 (Ark. 1994). As a matter of agency law, if a client instructs an attorney not to pursue a particular strategy or investigation, the attorney may not simply ignore the client's objection, even if the action would otherwise be legal or even necessary to the representation. For example, in *McInnis v. Hyatt Legal Clinics*, 461 N.E.2d 1295 (Ohio 1984) an attorney was held liable for violating an agreement with his client to keep the client's divorce out of the newspaper, even though service of process required some form of publication. If you believe you can represent the client competently and diligently without pursuing the objectionable means, you may continue the representation. Otherwise, you must withdraw from the representation.

When the question is one that is reserved solely to the client, the client may still give the attorney express authority to act on the client's direction in this matter. This express authority need not be written, though that will provide clear evidence of the client's intent. However, because a client can withdraw the attorney's authority at any time, an attorney should reaffirm even express written authority before exercising decisions on the client's behalf.

The attorney also can have actual authority to act on a client's behalf if it is reasonable to infer that authority from the circumstances. However, as a matter of best practice, attorneys should avoid relying on implied authority if they can obtain express authority. If the client disagrees with the attorney about the facts creating the implied authority or changes his or her mind about the decision, the attorney will be faced with proving that the circumstances implied that the client had indeed delegated his or her decision to the attorney.

While attorneys should always obtain a client's actual authority before acting on a client's behalf, the attorney may have the power—if not the authority—to act on the client's behalf in certain circumstances. First, if the client is happy with the attorney's decision, the client may ratify the attorney's actions after the fact. An informed client who ratifies the attorney's decisions is bound by those decisions (and is unlikely to complain to disciplinary counsel). Second, even if the client doesn't ratify the attorney's actions, the attorney acting without actual authority might have bound the client to the decision nonetheless. You may recall from other classes that the law of agency recognizes not only express and implied authority but also "apparent authority." An attorney can have apparent authority even if the client did not intend to give the attorney actual authority. If a client says or does something that causes a tribunal or third party to reasonably believe that the client has delegated authority to the attorney on a matter, the attorney's actions will bind the client. RESTATEMENT (THIRD) OF THE LAW GOVERNING LAWYERS § 27 (2000). While an attorney who has apparent authority can bind a client to a decision, the attorney may be subject to discipline and liability for doing so. As one classic statement of the doctrine explains:

> The power is real and not merely apparent. The agent is indeed a wrongdoer in exercising the power. He possesses the power but not the legal privilege of using it. Likewise, the authority (meaning the action of the principal creating the agent's power) is real. It is only the intention of the principal to create such a power that is merely apparent (i.e., non-existent).

WILLIAM R. ANSON, PRINCIPLES OF THE LAW OF CONTRACT 510 n.1 (Arthur L. Corbin ed., 3d Am. ed. 1919).

Jurisdictions disagree considerably about just what the circumstances are that would communicate apparent authority. Some cases do not recognize apparent authority in the context of the attorney-client relationship at all, while others presume apparent authority merely from the fact that a client has retained an attorney. Decisions turn on the court's weighing of important policy issues and the individual facts of each case. To read more about the various approaches to this issue, see Grace M. Giesel, *Enforcement of Settlement Contracts: The Problem of the Attorney Agent*, 12 GEO. J. LEGAL ETHICS 543 (1999).

The lesson here is that an attorney who acts on a client's behalf without clear, current, and written authority is taking a significant risk. If the attorney is wrong, and the client rejects the decision, the attorney will face a variety of troubles. The client may be able to void the settlement or withdraw the plea, but the attorney will still suffer reputational costs and possible disciplinary action.

Researching Professional Responsibility 8-A: Using the Restatement as a Research Tool

For issues of professional responsibility that are governed by agency law, the Restatement (Third) of the Law Governing Lawyers is an excellent starting point, not only for understanding the law, but also for researching case law interpretations. Though part of the Third restatement series, this restatement is actually a new addition to the restatement series (that is, there is no first or second Restatement of the Law Governing Lawyers). The American Law Institute began a project to restate the common law governing attorney conduct in 1986. The official Restatement of the Law (Third), The Law Governing Lawyers was published in 2000. Like other restatements, this restatement attempts to "comprehensively address those constraints imposed upon lawyers by law—that is, official norms enforceable through a legal remedy administered by a court, disciplinary agency, or similar tribunal." The form follows that of other Restatements, with black-letter standards, followed by Comments, Illustrations, and Reporter's Notes. The Reporter's Notes section can be a useful resource for further research. The Restatement also provides tables of cases and of codes, rules, and standards, parallel tables showing the corresponding section numbers from earlier drafts of the project, cross-references to the West Digest System and ALR annotations, and an index. The Restatement is available in hardcover and through Lexis, Westlaw, and HeinOnline's American Law Institute Library.

Because the Restatement addresses common law doctrines regulating attorney behavior, it is likely to become an increasingly important resource, especially for questions that the rules of professional conduct do not address. Locate a copy of the Restatement and provide the call number, database identifier, or URL for the copy you have located. Annotations of cases citing a Restatement section can be found in the appendices of the Restatements in print. They are updated with pocket parts, cumulative annual supplements, and semiannual pamphlets called Interim Case Citations. Alternately, you can find case citations by using Shepard's Restatement of the Law Citations, or you can KeyCite your Restatement Rule on Westlaw, or Shepardize it on Lexis.

Find the Restatement section that addresses an attorney's apparent authority and, starting with that section, see if your state courts have addressed the issue of an attorney's apparent authority. How would you characterize your state's approach to this question?

8.3 Reading the Rules: Rule 1.4—Communication with Clients

Regardless of how the rules of conduct allocate authority for a decision, the attorney must communicate with clients about those decisions. For decisions that are reserved to

clients, such as decisions regarding settlement or pleas, attorneys must communicate sufficient information for clients to give their informed consent. For client directives that ②
an attorney is prohibited from following, the attorney has the duty to counsel the client
about the limits of her role if she knows that the client expects her to step over the bounds
of the rules or law. For all other matters in which attorneys have some discretion to make ③
decisions as to the means to achieve the client's goals, the attorney need only "reasonably
consult" and keep the client "reasonably informed." In this area of uncertainty regarding
authority, the safest approach for attorneys is to make the lines clear for themselves and
their clients regarding what the attorney believes is "reasonable" consultation.

These requirements of consent, consultation, explanation, and communication are
addressed in Rule 1.4. In December 2008, New York became one of the most recent states
to have adopted a version of the ABA Model Rules of Professional Conduct (Maine adopted
the Model Rules in February 2009 and California has not yet adopted the rules). Like
some other states, the courts adopted the rules only—the preamble, scope, and comments to the rules were not officially adopted. Read New York's version of Rule 1.4

22 NYCRR Part 1200—New York State Unified Court System
Rules of Professional Conduct
RULE 1.4: Communication

(a) A lawyer shall:

   (1) promptly inform the client of:

      (i) any decision or circumstance with respect to which the client's informed
      consent, as defined in Rule 1.0(j), is required by these Rules;

      (ii) *any information required by court rule or other law to be communicated
      to a client; and*

      (iii) *material developments in the matter including settlement or plea offers.*

   (2) reasonably consult with the client about the means by which the client's
   objectives are to be accomplished;

   (3) keep the client reasonably informed about the status of the matter;

   (4) promptly comply with *a client's* reasonable requests for information; and

   (5) consult with the client about any relevant limitation on the lawyer's conduct when the lawyer knows that the client expects assistance not permitted
   by these Rules or other law.

(b) A lawyer shall explain a matter to the extent reasonably necessary to permit
the client to make informed decisions regarding the representation.

Context

New York's version of Rule 1.4 is identical to the ABA Model Rules of Professional
Conduct except for the more specific direction provided in the italicized portion of the
rule. To a large degree, these additions to the rule simply make explicit that which is an
implicit part of the general requirement to promptly inform clients of matters requiring
their consent. Twenty-one states have adopted the ABA rule without modification, but
the rest add or subtract additional details about communication. For example, prior to
2002, Model Rule 1.4 contained only those portions of New York's rule: 1.4(a)(3) ("reasonably informed") and (4) ("comply with requests") and 1.4(b) ("informed decisions").
Many states have this trimmed-down version of the rule and decided not to adopt the

additional provisions after the ABA amended the rule in 2002. Several states have a specific requirement like New York requiring attorneys to disclose information about settlement or plea offers. Others require that attorneys disclose whether the attorney has malpractice insurance (e.g., Alaska, Ohio, Pennsylvania, and South Dakota). New Jersey requires attorneys to "fully inform a prospective client of how, when, and where the client may communicate with the lawyer." Why do you think courts continue to add additional specific categories of communication requirements to this rule?

Relationships

Stop and consider the relationships among the ethical duties of communication, the agency doctrines of actual and implied authority, and the concept of informed consent? Notice that Rule 1.4(a)(1) requires an attorney to inform a client when there are decisions the client must make and that Rule 1.4(b) requires the attorney to give the client enough information to make an informed choice about those matters. Can a client provide actual authority to an attorney if he does not have sufficient information to provide informed consent to that delegation? A client's delegation of authority to an attorney is a decision for which standards of informed consent apply. That means a client must be advised of the advantages, disadvantages, and options for his choices. Informed consent isn't based on whether the client's decision is a good one. A client has a right to be "pigheaded" and "to tilt at windmills." *McKnight v. Dean*, 270 F.3d 513, 519 (7th Cir. 2001). It does, however, have everything to do with communication.

You may be familiar with the term "informed consent" from its use in the medical profession. In fact, there was some objection to using this term in the rules precisely because of the way the medical profession has treated the duty to obtain a client's informed consent in the past. The most consistent criticism of the informed consent standard in the medical profession has been that it does not work to protect patients. One commentator, reflecting on previous studies of medical practice, concluded that: 1) "doctors do not tell patients what tests they are performing or why;" 2) "doctors can frame the information they provide patients and quite successfully generate the physician-desired consent or refusal of the treatment;" and 3) "only about half of patients recall being informed of serious risks of interventions, such as the risk of death." Sandra H. Johnson, *End-of-Life Decision Making: What We Don't Know, We Make Up; What We Do Know, We Ignore*, 31 IND. L. REV. 13, 14 (1998).

For some attorneys, the term "informed consent" is synonymous with a "signed waiver." However, a written document may facilitate and provide evidence of the communication necessary to insure informed consent, but it is, in many instances, neither necessary nor sufficient to insure that a client has truly given informed consent. Consent need not be written unless the rules specify, though attorneys bear the risk if they infer silence as consent. *Turner v. Gilbreath*, 599 P.2d 323 (Kan.Ct.App.1979) (fact that client was widow of another lawyer does not warrant inference of informed consent to dual representation from her silence when present lawyer did not explain nature of conflict to her). In some instances, most notably for waivers of conflict of interest, a client's consent must be "confirmed in writing," but written or not, the requirement of informed consent requires that a client have sufficient information on the available choices and the risks and benefits of each option.

An attorney would be foolish to presume that a client's decisions are informed, and should always communicate with the client about those decisions. Comments to the rule emphasize that "the communication necessary to obtain such consent will vary according to the Rule involved and the circumstances giving rise to the need to obtain informed consent." Ordinarily informed consent requires disclosing to the client the situations raising the issue of consent, the advantages and risks of consent, and the alternatives available. The comments detail a list of factors to determine the extent of necessary communication, including the sophistication of the client.

Some clients would prefer that their attorneys simply "take care of the problem" and make all the decisions. They may indicate that they "trust your judgment" to "get the best settlement you can." However, an attorney who accepts such broad and vague authority runs the risk that the client may not agree after the fact that the attorney's choices were the right ones. Vague or implied grants of authority to a client may be enough to empower an attorney to bind a client to a decision, but may still subject the attorney to discipline for failing to communicate with the client sufficiently to permit the client to make an informed decision.

Risks of Vague grants of authority

Structure

Notice in particular the verbs and the timing in each subpart of the rule. What is the difference between "informing" a client, "explaining" to a client, and "consulting" with a client?

Reasons

It's easy enough to understand why communication with clients is important to effective representation. Yet there are additional policy justifications for the communication rules. Poor communication with clients is one of the most frequent complaints to disciplinary authorities. Might poor communication be a good proxy for even more serious conduct? Does the legal profession have a general interest in enforcing good communication with clients? See, for example, the court's statement in *In re Harris*, 890 S.W.2d 299, 302 (Mo. banc 1994) ("it is irritating to clients and damaging to the public perception of the legal profession when clients are not given timely and adequate information regarding the status of their case.") What about some of the more specific communication requirements? For example, what purpose is served by a requirement that attorneys disclose malpractice insurance?

Visualize

There are four categories of communication mandated by this rule: inform, consult, explain, and respond. Complete the following chart to better see the differences among these standards.

	About what?	When?
Inform		
Consult		
Explain		
Respond		

Imagine

The American Bar Association Standing Committee on Lawyers Professional Liability reported that 17% of all malpractice claims result from poor attorney-client relationships. ABA STANDING COMMITTEE ON LAWYERS PROFESSIONAL LIABILITY, THE LAWYERS

DESK GUIDE TO PREVENTING LEGAL MALPRACTICE (1999). In most jurisdictions, the most common basis for disciplinary complaints is poor communication. Why is failure to communicate adequately such a pervasive problem? Why won't attorneys return phone calls promptly? Why won't they explain procedures or strategies? Why won't they explain risks of decisions? Are there certain topics, clients, or types of practice that you would imagine might have special challenges in meeting the requirements of Rule 1.4?

Professional Responsibility Skills 8-A: Explaining the Attorney-Client Relationship

Many of the professional responsibility issues we have addressed in this unit are a critical aspect of the initial client interview. Many attorneys have developed standard ways of talking about fees, authority, expectations, and other aspects of the attorney-client relationship in this interview. These become "scripts" for these interviews. Think about an area of practice you are interested in. Talk to some attorneys in this field about how they explain their approach to an attorney-client relationship to potential clients. Develop your own script and practice using that script with another student.

8.4 What are Some Models of the Attorney-Client Relationship?

When a client walks in your office, what are you going to assume will be the terms of the relationship? How would you describe your role and the role of your client? Who are the clients your firm is likely to be representing? What are their expectations likely to be regarding their relationship with attorneys?

Read each of these statements and circle the one statement you think represents the best approach to counseling your clients:

- An attorney who tries to convince a client that the client's goals or motives are personally (not legally) unwise or unjust will be out of business.
- A lawyer's first duty to his clients is to give them the broadest range of advice regarding their actions, even if that advice requires consideration of non-legal matters.
- People do not hire attorneys for their practical or moral wisdom. When someone hires an attorney, he or she wants advice only on the technicalities of the law.
- Only a client knows what she really wants: lawyers should not be second guessing a client's motives or goals. A lawyer's job is simply to help a client reach those goals.
- An attorney who simply follows a client's directions, even if the attorney disagrees with the personal (not legal) wisdom or justice of those directions, will be out of business.
- A lawyer must never forget that he is the master. He is not there to do the client's bidding. The lawyer must serve clients' legal needs as the lawyer sees them not as the client sees them.
- Lawyers should never give advice to clients about moral, psychological, or economic decisions because lawyers are not clergy, psychologists or financial experts.

The effective practice of law rests on empowering clients. A good lawyer is one who facilitates the client's communication and problem solving rather than simply communicating and solving problems for the client.

Compare your choice to others. Does your choice depend on the types of clients you will represent? Why? For ethical and effective practice, attorneys must be aware of their own personal philosophy of the relationship between attorney and client and be able to communicate that vision to the client.

How we perceive our role as an attorney is a critical aspect of lawyering. It will guide our ethical decision-making in ways that no rules can ever significantly change. Who's in charge of your representation? Should you counsel a client, broadly and actively engage the client in constructing the purposes and goals of the representation? Or should you limit your advice to a technical application of the law to the extent relevant to advance the client's legal goals? What is the answer to the question asked of attorneys who represent unpopular or even despicable clients, "How can you represent those people?" What kind of responsibility does an attorney have for the extra-legal consequences of the representation? These are very important foundational questions for you to consider and reconsider throughout your career.

The answers are found in your overall philosophy of lawyering and your relationship with each individual client. This philosophy of lawyering is especially important when you are addressing issues that are not controlled by law. What if the client asks you to provide legal justifications for actions you consider immoral? Will the government undertake torture of prisoners? Will a business structure its business transactions in ways that cause harm to the local economy or environment? Will a divorcing spouse insist on a legal position that is not good for his or her children or other family members? What role should the lawyer play regarding these questions?

In recent decades, three general schools of thought have emerged among legal ethicists and legal clinicians concerning the lawyer's role in the counseling relationship. One approach to the lawyer's role advocates a more directive lawyer, a lawyer who is willing to assert control of moral issues that arise during legal representation. When considering this approach, ask yourself how the directive lawyer avoids imposing her values on the client. How does this model work practically when the client refuses to agree with the attorney's moral assessment of a decision?

A second approach, the "client-directed" model of representation, puts the client in charge. The lawyer should not act in ways that will influence the client's choice, apart from those choices that are clearly illegal or profoundly immoral. The client-directed model of representation recognizes the influence attorneys can have over their clients' choices and lives and argues that attorneys should resist the temptation to exercise that influence, valuing client autonomy instead. The classic statement regarding the impact of this role on the lawyer's ethical responsibility has been outlined by Richard Wasserstrom:

> The job of the lawyer ... is not to approve or disapprove of the character of his or her client, the cause for which the client seeks the lawyer's assistance, or the avenues provided by the law to achieve that which the client wants to accomplish. The lawyer's task is, instead, to provide that competence which the client lacks and the lawyer, as professional, possesses. In this way, the lawyer as professional comes to inhabit a simplified universe which is strikingly amoral— which regards as morally irrelevant any number of factors which nonprofessional citizens might take to be important, if not decisive, in their everyday lives.

Richard Wasserstrom, *Lawyers as Professionals: Some Moral Issues*, 5 Hum. Rts. 1, 8 (1975).

What's the difference between being a client-centered lawyer and merely acting as a "hired gun" in the hands of the client? How does this model work when the client has limited ability (a child, an individual with limited decision-making capacity, etc.)? Note that the Model Rules of Professional Conduct provide very little clear direction on this latter question. ABA Model Rule 1.14.

No matter how much Rule 1.2(b) suggests that you are independent from your client's goals and no matter how much you might wish to distance yourself from the consequences of your client's decisions, you need to realize how powerfully you can influence a client. Social science has told us that clients look for and defer to even subtle cues from attorneys about how they should proceed. "Even where they think of themselves as merely providing information for clients to integrate into their own decisions, lawyers influence clients by myriad judgments, conscious or not, about what information to present, how to order it, what to emphasize, and what style and phrasing to adopt." William H. Simon, *Lawyer Advice and Client Autonomy: Mrs. Jones's Case*, 50 MD. L. REV. 213, 217 (1991). *See also,* Robert W. Gordon, *The Independence of Lawyers*, 68 B.U. L. REV. 1, 30 (1988) ("Lawyers who say they just provide technical input and lay out the options while leaving the decisions and methods of implementing them up to their clients are kidding themselves....").

A third approach is the collaborative lawyer or "lawyer as friend" model. IN LAWYERS, CLIENTS, AND MORAL RESPONSIBILITY (1994), Professors Thomas Shaffer and Robert Cochran argue that the lawyer should approach difficult moral decisions in consultation with the client, in the same manner as a friend would approach a friend. This approach does not require the attorney to ignore moral issues, but asks the attorney to communicate with the client in a dialogue in which the client's own moral reasoning is engaged to consider the fairness of his positions and the effect of others. As a practical matter, however, is there really time for moral discourse in the hourly-billing-driven practice of today? Should a client pay for advice he doesn't want?

Which of these three approaches seems most appropriate to you and the types of clients you will be representing? When you study the rules of professional conduct, you see that attorneys have a good deal of discretion to answer these questions in different ways.

8.5 Reading the Rules — When Is a Rule Not a Rule?

Let's look at a very peculiar rule to examine this question of the relationship between attorney and client. Look carefully at Rule 1.2(b) of the Wisconsin Supreme Court's Rule 20 "Rules of Professional Conduct for Attorneys." (Wisconsin, like nearly all states, has adopted this rule verbatim from the ABA Model Rules.)

(b) A lawyer's representation of a client, including representation by appointment, does not constitute an endorsement of the client's political, economic, social or moral views or activities.

Context

Rule 1.2 defines the basic character of the attorney-client relationship and subsection (b) is a strong and unequivocal statement. Yet if you examine the remainder of the rule, you see a good deal of equivocation. Subsection (a) says a client is in charge of objectives and the attorney need only consult with the client about means; *however,* the comments hint that "other law" (primarily the law of agency) makes this allocation of authority less than clear. Subsection (c) allows an attorney to limit the scope of representation; *however,* the degree to which that can occur is not clear at all. Subsection (d) prohibits assisting a client in a crime or fraud; *however,* it does allow giving advice about legal consequences. Why do you think the boundaries of the attorney client relationship are so difficult to define in absolute terms? Why is subsection (b) so different?

Relationships

Consider the relationship between this rule and Rule 2.1, which provides that an attorney *may* advise a client on relevant extra-legal considerations. What "moral, economic, social, and political" values are relevant when counseling a client? Can Rule 2.1 be read to allow attorneys to express their own value judgments in a representation? But if 1.2(b) says that an attorney's representation is not an endorsement of the client's goals, does that mean that the attorney's own values are irrelevant and so should not influence the attorney's advice? Read the comments to Rule 2.1 and explore further your own philosophy of whether and to what extent an attorney's own values should play a role in the representation. If an attorney's own values are not relevant, how can an attorney avoid bringing those values into the representation?

Structure

Notice that this "rule" doesn't look much like a rule, or even a guideline. There is no "must" or "shall not" or even a "may." Instead this rule is really just a declarative statement of a conclusion, rather than an imperative or permissive direction. "Representation does not constitute endorsement." So what is the function of a declarative statement in a set of rules? Is this just poor drafting and the rule is intended to direct behavior? Does this statement mean attorneys should *not* identify with their clients? We know that many attorneys do identify strongly with their clients and even work to strengthen that identification in order to attract more clients. Are those attorneys acting unethically?

A common role for declarative statements in rules is to provide definitions as, for example, those in Rule 1.0. Rule 1.2(b) does not appear to be a definition in the sense of defining a word or phrase that is used elsewhere in the rules. It does, however, describe what it means to represent a client (or rather what it does *not* mean).

Reasons

To whom is this rule directed? What is its purpose? One place to look for purpose in any enacted law is, of course, in legislative history. The American Bar Association publishes a legislative history of the Model Rules of Professional Conduct. That legislative history suggests that the rule was written to provide support to attorneys who accept representation of unpopular clients. As you have seen, Rule 6.2(c) provides that attorneys may seek to avoid appointment if "client or the cause is so repugnant to the lawyer as to be likely to impair the client-lawyer relationship or the lawyer's ability to represent the client." Rule 1.2(b) was designed to provide a counterweight to this rule.

Visualize

Sometimes the best way to understand a rule such as this, that expresses a broad and fundamental perspective, is to identify a person who embodies that principle or a situation that forcefully illustrates the principle in action. Popular films and novels can provide engaging portraits for helping us to visualize these positions. Try watching one of the following films and concentrate in particular on the role of the attorneys in these films and their relationships with their clients:

- *To Kill a Mockingbird* (MCA-Universal 1962). Atticus Finch defending his poor, black client Tom Robinson against charges that he raped a white girl in the Depression-era South.

- *Guilty By Suspicion* (Warner Bros. 1991). Movie studio lawyer Felix Graff advises David Merrill, a movie director who has been blacklisted by the House Un-American Activities committee, to "take the easy way out."

- *Philadelphia* (1993). Attorney Joe Miller overcomes his initial bias and fear to represent Andrew Beckett, an attorney who was fired by his firm after learning of his homosexuality and AIDS.

- *The People v. Larry Flynt* (1996). Attorney Alan Isaacman's lengthy and tumultuous representation of his client, Hustler publisher Larry Flynt.

- *A Civil Action* (1998). Attorney Jan Schlichtmann representing a class of clients in a toxic tort case.

- *I Am Sam* (2001). Attorney Rita Harrison represents a mentally challenged father who wants to regain custody of his child.

- *Michael Clayton* (2007). Michael Clayton as the firm's "fixer" trying to reel in the firm's partner Arthur Edens who has had a psychological breakdown and is working to destroy one of the firm's clients.

- *The Conspirator* (2010). Based on the true story of the lone female charged as a co-conspirator in the assassination trial of Abraham Lincoln and the attorney who defends her.

Imagine

In what kinds of circumstances might you invoke Rule 1.2(b)? To whom would you be speaking?

Reflective Practice: Your Model of the Attorney-Client Relationship

Some of the most powerful lessons one can learn about what it means to represent a client come from the role models we choose to emulate. Do you have a personal role model who helps you define your vision of a professional? Write a short reflection about how your role model interacts with clients and why that approach is one you wish to emulate.

Test Your Understanding

1. Identify a typical representation in your preferred area of practice. Using the following chart, identify who would have the authority to make some of the decisions you would need to make in that representation.

Attorney may make these decisions without client consent	Decision authority could be either the attorney or the client, depending on their agreement	Client has the sole authority to make these decisions

2. Client is a parent in a divorce. Client wants attorney to pursue sole custody of the couple's child. Attorney becomes aware that Client is not truly interested in having sole custody. Rather, attorney concludes that Client believes that the other parent will agree to whatever financial settlement is offered if custody is at stake. May Attorney refuse to pursue sole custody? May Attorney withdraw if Client continues to insist on pursuing sole custody? The American Academy of Matrimonial Attorneys provide in their Bounds of Advocacy that an attorney should not assist her clients by using children as a weapon or bargaining chip. How does an attorney make that limitation clear to the client?

3. Client is a landlord. Client wants attorney to draft a provision in all new leases that tenants will be assessed a late fee that would amount to about 2% of the rent each month for each day rent is late, which is chargeable against their next month's rent payment if not paid on time. This represents a change in the terms of the lease. Attorney believes that under state law, it is unclear whether the clause would be enforceable but attorney believes there is a fair probability that it would be. Attorney would prefer that the clause include a disclaimer indicating the uncertain enforceability of the provision, and advises the landlord so. Landlord disagrees and directs attorney to include the provision because it will deter tenants from making late payments and tenants will be unlikely to challenge the provision. May Attorney refuse to include the term? May attorney withdraw from representation if Client insists on the term?

4. Attorney represents Client in a criminal trial. During the testimony of one of the key witnesses for the prosecution, Client continually whispers to Attorney that he should object to the witness's statements. Attorney refuses to do so. Has Attorney violated a duty to the client?

To Learn More

The doctrines we have discussed in this chapter have their greatest impact in attorney-client counseling. While communicating with a client is not a skill that one can easily learn by reading alone, there are some excellent resources that, in combination with practice in communication, can improve your skills and refine your understanding of what it means to be a lawyer. Two excellent texts for you to consider are:

Robert F. Cochran, Jr., John M. DiPippa & Martha M. Peters, The Counselor-at-Law: A Collaborative Approach to Client Interviewing and Counseling (Lexis 1999).

David A. Binder & Susan C. Price, Lawyers as Counselors: A Client-Centered Approach (West 1990).

Unit Two Review

Practice Context Review

1. The engagement contract

Review the following engagement letter. Using the paragraph numbers in the left hand column, identify those portions of the letter that raise potential issues of discipline or liability. How would you redraft the letter to reduce those risks?

¶ 1 Barbara Glesner Fines & Associates
25088 West Shawnee Mission Parkway
Shawnee Mission, Kansas

¶ 2 September 20, 20xx
Clarence Client
500 East 52nd Street
Kansas City, Missouri

Re: Engagement Letter

Dear Clarence:

¶ 3   We were pleased to have the opportunity to speak with you about your property ownership dispute today and to discuss our filing suit on your behalf. We look forward to working with you and we promise to provide you the highest quality legal services in a responsive, efficient manner.

¶ 4   The purpose of this letter is to clarify and confirm the terms and conditions of our representation. You asked us to represent you in connection with your ownership interest in land located in Clay County, Missouri, which is currently occupied by Mr. John Jones, who has operated a farm on that property for the past five years. You believe that a substantial portion of the land Mr. Jones is occupying in fact belongs to you, under the terms of your recent inheritance from your mother. You would like us to represent you in securing your claim to this property.

¶ 5   I will be the attorney primarily responsible for the representation, with the assistance of my paralegal Paula Para. You authorize us to incur all reasonable costs and to retain any investigators, consultants, or experts necessary in our judgment to pursue your claims. We may engage the services of another attorney if we feel that his or her assistance is called for.

¶ 6   When questions or comments arise about our services, staffing, billings, or other aspects of our representation, please contact Paula. Her direct telephone number is 816-500-5474. It is important that you are satisfied with our services and responsiveness at all times. We will return your phone call within 24 hours.

¶ 7   To enable us to effectively represent you, you agree to cooperate fully with us in all matters relating to the preparation and presentation of your case, to disclose all facts fully and accurately to us,

171

and to keep us informed of new developments. You agree that we have the sole discretion to determine negotiation, discovery, and litigation strategy and approve causes of action and parties to any litigation. We will send you copies of any legal documents filed on your case that reflect these decisions. You agree to cooperate with us in determining acceptable terms of any compromise, settlement, or agreement.

¶ 8   Our fees will be based primarily on the amount of time spent by attorneys and paralegals on your matter. Your attorney, Barbara Glesner Fines, has an hourly billing rate of $350 an hour based generally on her experience and special expertise in this area. Barbara's paralegal Paula has a billing rate of $150 an hour. The rate multiplied by the time spent on your behalf, measured in quarters of an hour, will be evaluated by the billing attorney as the basis for determining the fee. From time to time, I will confer with Paula or with any other attorney I engage on your behalf and two or more of us may attend meetings or proceedings on your behalf.

¶ 9   These rates may be adjusted from time to time generally to reflect increased experience and special expertise of the attorneys and paralegals and cost increases affecting our practice, and the adjusted rates will apply to all services performed thereafter. In addition to our fees, we will expect payment for any disbursements we make on your behalf.

¶ 10   Before we will begin your representation, you will deposit $2,000 with us to secure our services. No part of this deposit will be used for disbursements or charges or shall represent security for payment of our fees. You agree that, upon our review of the case, we will have the right to request additional deposits as advances on our fees based on our estimates of future work to be undertaken.

¶ 11   Once a trial or hearing date is set, we will require you to pay all amounts then owing to us and to deposit with us the fees we estimate will be incurred in preparing for and completing the trial, as well as jury fees likely to be assessed. If you fail to timely pay any additional deposit requested, we will have the right to cease performing further work. Your failure to pay required fees or deposits constitutes your consent to our withdrawal from the representation.

¶ 12   The fees and charges billed to you are your responsibility whether or not a court awards attorneys' fees against an opposing party. Courts may award attorneys' fees which they consider reasonable under the applicable statutes, but which are less than the amounts billed to you. In such cases, you continue to be obligated to pay us for our actual fees and charges even though the court awards less.

¶ 13   If a monetary judgment or award is made in your favor, we shall have a lien on the proceeds to the extent of any unpaid fees, disbursements, or other charges.

        If you agree to these terms and conditions of our representation, please confirm your acceptance by signing the enclosed copy in the space provided below and return it and the required retainer to me. If this letter is not signed and returned, you will be obligated to pay us the reasonable value of any services we may have performed on your behalf. We are pleased to have this opportunity to be of service and to work with you.

¶ 14   Very truly yours,

        Barbara Glesner Fines

¶ 15   I/we read and understand the terms and conditions set forth in this letter (including the attached General Provisions) and agree to them.

_____

Client

2. The Closing Letter

Alice Attorney works in the seven-attorney Kansas City branch office of a national law firm. Attorney's client Dan Dollars has come to her with a real estate development proposal. Anticipating "green zone" developments in the city, he wishes to start a business (GreenWater Inc.) to develop energy efficient water management systems for small businesses and residences. He has a number of investors and financing options and has several inventions that he would like to market through the business.

Alice agrees to represent Dan. She believes this will be an opportunity to develop an excellent long-term client and to develop her practice.

Dan has asked you about the licensing of a patent for a special water filter for GreenWater's product. The patent for this part is held by Precision Parts Inc. You are embarrassed to admit that you know nothing about patent law. You call a friend in another firm, Paul Patent, and ask him for some help in reviewing the license agreement proposed by Precision Parts. He meets with you and reviews the file. He then conducts some research, reviews the proposed license agreement, makes a couple of suggestions, and provides you with a short memo describing the issues he sees in the license. Paul doesn't charge you for this help because you often provide the same service for him regarding business law issues. Because you felt that it would be unethical to charge for your basic education in patent law, you did not tell Dan about the consultation or charge him for the time you spent learning about patent law from Paul.

Was your action in asking for Paul's help proper?

Suppose that you complete the necessary paperwork and filing to create GreenWater Inc. for Dan and you assist him in purchasing manufacturing facilities and equipment, obtaining business licenses and permits, and completing all other necessary business and legal steps to begin business operations. Dan is the President of GreenWater.

You then send the following letter:

Dear Dan:

It has been a pleasure working with you and helping to make GreenWater, Inc. a reality. I have now completed all the work I had agreed to provide for you on this matter and my representation has concluded. Thank you for your prompt payment of fees in this matter. I have enclosed a final accounting for your records.

You have asked if I would continue to serve as the business's attorney on an "as-needed" basis to handle any further ongoing business law matters. I would be happy to do so. Simply contact my office and we can negotiate a suitable representation agreement for any future matters you might have. If I am unable to help you with a particular matter, I will be happy to engage other counsel for you. I look forward to working with you in the future and to a very successful partnership!

Sincerely,

Attorney
Attorney

Is GreenWater, Inc. still your client?

Multiple Choice Review

1. Attorney A was approached by Sam who asked for assistance in filing an admittedly fraudulent claim for personal injuries. A refused the representation and counseled Sam that filing a false claim would be a violation of several different laws. He told Sam, "Do what you want, but I'm advising you strongly not to file this claim. I won't represent you. If you want an attorney to help you, you'll have to find someone else because I can't and won't put my license on the line for this." Sam immediately obtained the services of Attorney B for the filing of the claim, however, by the time Attorney B got the case filed, the statute of limitations had run and the case was dismissed. Is Attorney A subject to discipline?

    A. Yes, because Attorney A referred Sam to another attorney, which furthered his plan to file a frivolous action.
    B. Yes, because Attorney A did not advise Sam of the statute of limitations.
    C. No, because he counseled the client regarding the limitations on his conduct.
    D. No, because there was no harm to the insurance company.

2. On January 1, Client hired Attorney to handle a nuisance and trespass case against Client's neighbor. The statute of limitations would run on September 1. Attorney told Client he would begin work on the suit right away. However, Attorney became busy with other matters and did not work on Client's case. In mid-March, Client started calling Attorney's office regularly to inquire about the case. Each time, Attorney assured Client that he would be starting work on the case soon. On June 1, Client ran out of patience and fired Attorney and hired another lawyer who was able to get the suit filed by September 1. Though Client had not paid Attorney any money he reported the matter to the state bar. Is Attorney subject to discipline?

    A. Yes, because Attorney's delay and failure to keep the client informed violated his duties of diligence and communication to his client.
    B. Yes, because Attorney told the client he would begin work on the case right away.
    C. No, Attorney is not subject to discipline because he received no fee from the client.
    D. No, Attorney is not subject to discipline because the client was still able to file his suit within the statute of limitations period.

3. Attorney agreed to represent a client in a suit against his landlord. The client has limited funds and agreed to pay attorney $100 a month every month until the total fees are paid. After three months, Attorney had filed the pleadings and conducted substantial discovery, but client had yet to pay anything. Client says he has found an Attorney who will take over the representation for free and fires Attorney, owing $3,000 in fees. Attorney tells the client that he refuses to withdraw (and thus to allow the other attorney to enter his appearance on behalf of client) until the client pays at least $300 of the fees owed. Is Attorney subject to discipline?

    A. No, because the client breached his duty of fair dealing to Attorney.
    B. No, because Attorney must have the court's permission to withdraw.
    C. Yes, because Attorney must seek to withdraw if the client discharges him.
    D. Yes, because Attorney did not give the client adequate warning that he had failed to fulfill a substantial obligation.

4. Attorney represents ABC Corporation in a products liability action. Attorney discovers that the corporation has been destroying financial records that are potential evidence in a securities fraud case pending against it. (Attorney does not represent ABC Corp in securities matters.) Attorney discusses the matter with ABC and insists that the company begin to comply with the law regarding document retention or he will withdraw.

ABC responds that this is not Attorney's business and he should stick to the products liability suit. If Attorney withdraws at this point, ABC's ability to prevail in the products liability action will be significantly harmed.

A. Attorney may not withdraw from the representation because withdrawal would cause material adverse effect.

B. Attorney may not withdraw from the representation because he does not represent ABC in securities matters.

C. Attorney may withdraw from the representation because his client insists on continuing to destroy potential evidence.

D. Attorney must withdraw from the representation because his client insists on continuing to destroy potential evidence.

"may" not "must"
withdrawal is not required

5. Attorney has been approached by Client, who has just been fired from her job. Client believes that her employer discriminated against her on the basis of her age. Attorney has done some workers compensation cases, but has never handled an employment discrimination case. She is unsure whether she should help the Client file a grievance with the Client's union, a complaint to a state or federal agency, or a lawsuit. Attorney has a good friend (Frank) who is an expert in employment discrimination cases. Consider the following options for Attorney. Which would be proper for Attorney to do (more than one answer may be correct):   *could end @ any time*   *not paid, no k, not great*

A. Accept the employment and, with her client's consent, get continuing but uncompensated advice from Frank on how to handle the case.

B. Accept the employment and, without mentioning it to her client, agree with Frank that he will serve as her co-counsel with a reasonable fee to be divided between them in proportion to the services performed and the responsibility assumed by each.

C. Accept the employment, neither consult nor split fees with Frank, and immediately begin negotiations with the lawyer for Client's employer, hoping to work out some accommodation between the parties without the necessity of formal action.   *no clue what she's doing*

D. Decline the employment and refer Client to Frank.

6. In which of the following representations would the attorney be subject for discipline for failing to have a written fee agreement? (More than one may be correct.)   *not unethical to not have written fee agmt*

A. Attorney has not regularly represented a client and agrees to take on the client's divorce.

B. Attorney and a lawyer from another firm are taking joint responsibility for representing a client in a complicated civil fraud case. The two attorneys will be sharing the fee from the case in proportion to the work they do.

C. Attorney is representing a client in a small claims action on a contingent fee basis.

D. Attorney is taking on representation of a complicated business negotiation that will not be concluded within one year's time.

7. Arnold Attorney has been retained by David Defendant to represent him in an action brought by his girlfriend to obtain an adult abuse order of protection against him. Arnold's fee arrangement called for an initial retainer of $1,000 (which was paid). Attorney would charge $150 an hour and bill against the retainer, with client agreeing to pay for any work in excess of the retainer. However, the agreement also provided that this initial $1,000 retainer was nonrefundable, regardless of the work performed or the outcome of the case. Finally, the client agreed to pay attorney a bonus of $500 if the case was dismissed or the court refused to enter the order. Client's girlfriend entered a voluntary dismissal of the action the following day. Attorney had performed one hour of work on the case at that point. Attorney billed Client for the $500 bonus. Client refused to pay. Attorney then sued client for the $500 and Client counterclaimed

[handwritten margin note: not a true ... coust·fee]

for a refund of the $850. Which of the following statements is TRUE (more than one may be correct)?

A. Arnold is subject to discipline for entering into a contingent fee agreement in this type of case.

B. Arnold is subject to discipline for charging a non-refundable retainer. *[handwritten: not a problem everywhere, but when it was arrayed it was not true vert]*

C. Attorney is subject to discipline for suing his client over fees.

D. Attorney will prevail in the suit over fees because this was a valid contract.

8. Attorney, a sole practitioner, receives a check for $20,000 from an insurance company in settlement of Client's personal injury case. The check is made out to both Attorney and Client. Client is out of the country for a week and cannot be reached, but Attorney has a power of attorney from Client and can endorse the check for both herself and Client. Attorney, under a written agreement with Client, is entitled to 1/3 (or $6,666) as her fee. Tomorrow Attorney has to make a payment of $7,500 on a note executed by her for a land purchase. Due to her ex-husband's failure to make his child support payments for several months, Attorney has a cash flow problem. It is proper for Attorney to (choose one answer only):

A. Deposit the $20,000 in her Clients' Trust Fund account and withdraw her $6,666 fee.

B. Deposit the $20,000 in her Clients' Trust Fund account, execute a demand note to Client for $834, and then withdraw from the Clients' Trust Fund account the $7,500 needed to make her loan payment.

C. Take the action described in B, if she restores the $834 to the Clients' Trust Fund Account before Client returns.

D. Take the action described in B, inform Client upon Client's return, and refund any interest due Client on the $834.

9. Barbara is a first-year associate in a large national law firm. The firm has cut its training program for associates to save money and most senior partners have little time for mentoring. Associates are encouraged to take on pro bono work as a way of honing their skills, though the firm gives very little credit toward the billable hours requirement for this work. In the hopes of acquiring some courtroom experience and raising her profile with the partners, Barbara volunteered to take a criminal defense appointment for Arthur, the senior partner in her department. Arthur withdrew and Barbara substituted herself as attorney of record. Although she had almost no background for criminal defense work and barely enough time to handle the case, she managed to meet with the client, prepare a strategy, and defend the client through trial. She did not ask Arthur for any advice or assistance because it was clear that the reason she was taking the appointment was to relieve him of the time and responsibility. Her client was convicted. Later the conviction was overturned for ineffective assistance of counsel due to the many fundamental errors in the defense provided. Barbara was reprimanded by state disciplinary counsel for a violation of Rule 1.1 Competence.

Is Arthur subject to discipline?

A. No, because Barbara took over his appointment and he had no further responsibility.

B. No, because the client's conviction was overturned.

C. Yes, because Arthur did not make reasonable efforts to ensure that Barbara was competent to take over his case.

D. Yes, because Arthur did not provide Barbara guidance on how to handle the case.

Analysis & Answers:

1. Attorney would not be subject to discipline. A did not refer the client to B specifically nor was his statement designed to help client find an attorney who would further his scheme. B is also not a basis for discipline. While attorneys regularly do advise that "time limitations may apply" in their non-engagement letters, in order to avoid malpractice liability, this is not an ethical requirement. C is correct. Remember that Rule 1.2(d) provides that (d) A lawyer shall not counsel a client to engage, or assist a client, in conduct that the lawyer knows is criminal or fraudulent. Be careful about answer D. Remember that just because the client was not harmed, does not mean a violation doesn't exist. Discipline cases aren't like malpractice. Damages is not an element of the case. It may, of course, be relevant to the sanction imposed.

2. The best answer is A. Attorney violated Rule 1.4 by not communicating with his client for months and he likely violated Rule 1.3 by putting off the case—especially nuisance/trespass where evidence could disappear or change over time and waiting to build up damages sometimes is a basis for waiver in these types of cases. B identifies a problem, but it is only a small subset of the larger problem identified in A. C is there to remind you that pro bono attorneys owe their clients no less duty than paid attorneys and D is to remind you that damages are unnecessary to proof of a violation of the rules.

3. C is the correct answer. Rule 1.16(a) requires withdrawal if the client fires you, regardless of the reasons. While B is a correct statement of the rule, the fact that an attorney must seek permission to withdraw doesn't mean the attorney doesn't have to seek that permission. A is an unlikely interpretation of the facts, but even if it were true, the remedy is not to hold the client hostage for fees. D would only be relevant if the attorney were seeking to withdraw for nonpayment of fees. Here the attorney is seeking to block his own withdrawal as a means of forcing the client to pay.

4. The best answer is C. Attorneys may withdraw because the client is persisting in a course of action that the attorney considers repugnant, which is a permissive basis for withdrawal. Since there is a good cause basis for withdrawal it does not matter that withdrawal would cause material adverse effect (answer A). Moreover, it does not matter that the client's actions are not ones the attorney is involved in assisting or promoting (answer B), though that does mean the withdrawal is not mandatory (answer D).

5. A is just what Rule 1.1 suggests. B violates Rule 1.5(e) (and even if it didn't, Rule 1.4 should tell you that you can't do this without at least telling the client). C is incompetent. D is perfectly alright.

6. B (Rule 1.5(e)) and C (Rule 1.5(c)) are correct. D is not correct. While the statute of frauds may make this agreement unenforceable, it's not unethical. A is not correct, though it is best practice to have a writing.

7. A is likely False—this looks like a domestic relations case or a criminal case—types of cases in which contingent fees are prohibited, but it is technically neither. One could argue as a policy matter that the rule's prohibition should be extended to this type of case (anyone care to make that argument?). B is likely true. Most courts have found non-refundable retainers unreasonable (a Michigan court just decided the other way, but it's a bad decision). C is false—attorneys can sue their clients. They are discouraged from doing so and have to be very careful not to harass, but they can. Fee dispute resolution programs offered by the bar are a better choice. D is not necessarily true—remember that attorney fee contracts (indeed any business deal with an attorney) are

enforceable only if the attorney can meet his or her burden of proving the fairness of the contract both substantively and procedurally.

8. A is the only correct choice. Rule 1.15.

9. This question requires you to apply the standards of Rule 5.1 Responsibilities of Partners, Managers, and Supervisory Lawyers. The best answer is C, which paraphrases the standard of Rule 5.1(b) regarding a lawyer having direct supervisory authority over another. D is tempting; however, providing Barbara guidance is only one way Arthur could have exercised reasonable efforts to supervise Barbara. For example, he could have refused to let her take the case or he could have provided additional resources (people, time, education, etc.) to permit her to be able to handle the case. Answers A and B are both based on misconceptions about the rules. A ignores the entire message of Rule 5.1, which is that supervisory attorneys can be responsible for the mistakes of other attorneys. B makes an assumption that there is a "no harm, no foul" exception to rules violations. The given fact that Barbara had been disciplined should have alerted you to avoid this assumption.

UNIT THREE

Confidentiality — A Defining Duty

Suppose you are a public defender, representing Andrew Wilson, who was arrested for shooting and killing two police officers. When police arrested Wilson for killing the officers they found a shotgun linked to a shell at the scene of a different murder, that of security guard Lloyd Wickliffe at a McDonald's. However, police had already arrested two other men, Alton Logan and Edgar Hope, for Wickliffe's murder based on eyewitness identification, so the police did not charge Wilson for Wickliffe's murder. Logan's co-defendant, Hope, however, told his attorney that Logan was not involved in the murder, and that Wilson was the actual shooter. Suppose that Hope's attorney gave this information to you.

You confront Wilson with Hope's statement and he nods and says, "That was me."

What can you do with this information? Does it matter if Logan is actually convicted? What if he is sentenced to death?

This is the situation two public defenders faced in 1982, when representing Wilson. They concluded that their ethical duty of confidentiality required that they remain silent unless their client directed them to reveal the information. They obtained permission from their client to reveal the information only after his death, which occurred after Alton Logan had been in prison for 26 years for a crime he did not commit. Even then, there was some question whether their statements regarding Wilson's confession would be admissible in court or whether they fell within the protections of the attorney-client privilege.

(You can watch the interview with Alton Logan and Wilson's attorneys on a CBS *60 Minutes* interview at http://www.cbsnews.com/stories/2008/03/06/60minutes/main3914719.shtml.)

What is the purpose of a rule that requires attorneys to keep secrets like this? What kinds of exceptions should the rule have? Do you think that only public defenders find themselves having to keep secrets like this?

Goals of Unit Three

There is perhaps no more fundamental duty of the attorney to the client than the duty to protect the client's information. Yet the duty is also one of the most controversial and confusing of the duties of the attorney. This is true because the duty to guard a client's

179

information is found in many different legal doctrines, whose boundaries are drawn differently among various jurisdictions. Moreover, the duty is often in tension with other fundamental duties to the courts and third parties, which necessitates exceptions. In this unit, we will be exploring the rules governing the attorney's duty to protect client information and the exceptions to that duty. Master the rules as thoroughly as you can, being careful to keep separate your understanding of the ethical, evidentiary, and procedural rules. Also, work to consider whether you agree with the premises of these rules and the degree to which you will find these rules a challenge to follow.

Pre-Test

Are the following statements TRUE or FALSE under the ABA Model Rules of Professional Conduct?

1. For an attorney to have a duty of confidentiality regarding a conversation with a client, the client must have a reasonable expectation of privacy regarding that conversation.

2. If information relating to a representation is available in a public record, the attorney has no duty to refrain from disclosing that information, so long as he does not do so in a way that harms the client.

3. The attorney's ethical duty of confidentiality is basically a codification of the attorney-client evidentiary privilege.

4. If a client discloses information about the representation to third persons, he waives the protections of the ethical duty of confidentiality.

5. A client's advanced waiver of confidentiality is enforceable if it is in writing and that client is given time to seek outside legal advice regarding the waiver.

6. Even if an attorney reasonably believes that revealing a client's confidential information could prevent a death, the attorney would not be subject to discipline if she chose not to reveal that information.

7. An attorney may not reveal a client's financial fraud that is reasonably certain to result in substantial financial injury, even if revealing the fraud would prevent that injury, if the client had not used the attorney's services to further that fraud.

8. If a client does not pay his lawyer as agreed, the lawyer may use or reveal the client's confidential information because the client has abused the fiduciary relationship.

Answers

Statements 1–4 are all false and all reflect a common confusion between the ethical duty of confidentiality and the protections of the attorney-client privilege in the law of evidence.

Statement 1 is false because, absent the client's consent or an exception in the rules, an attorney must keep confidential a conversation with the client, even if the client does not have an expectation of privacy.

Statement 2 is false because even information in a public record is subject to the duty of confidentiality.

Statement 3 is false because the ethical duty is much broader in its protections of client information than the privilege, which protects only confidential communications between the attorney and client for the purposes of securing legal advice.

Statement 4 is false because, while this disclosure can waive the attorney-client privilege, an attorney must keep a client's information confidential even if the client does not.

Statements 5–8 all sound quite sensible as rules; however, only statements 6 and 7 are true. This is an example of why your own personal ethical analysis cannot substitute for knowing the rules and the exceptions to the rules.

Statement 5 is false—the standard for enforceability of a client's waiver of confidentiality is "informed consent"—while a written waiver and an opportunity to seek legal advice are good ideas, they aren't the standard and they aren't sufficient by themselves to make a waiver enforceable.

Statement 6 is true. While some states do require an attorney to reveal information in order to save a life, and surely most attorneys would want to do so, the ABA Model Rules make that decision discretionary.

Statement 7 is true. As you will see, an attorney's duties regarding confidentiality in the face of financial fraud is one of the most controversial areas of the rules, with many states having different versions of this rule.

Statement 8 is false because it is too broad a statement. While an attorney may use or reveal a client's information to "establish a claim" on the lawyer's behalf, he may do so only to the extent that disclosure is reasonably necessary to establish that claim.

Chapter Nine

Confidentiality, Privilege, and Related Doctrines

Learning Objectives

After you have read this chapter and completed the assignments, you should be able to:

- Define and distinguish the major doctrines defining an attorney's obligation not to disclose or use a client's information and identify when these doctrines apply in factual settings.

- Research issues of the scope of the duty of confidentiality, the attorney-client privilege, and the work-product doctrine.

Rules to Study

As you will see, there are a number of doctrines that regulate the attorney's duties to keep a client's information safe. We will study in particular:

ABA Model Rules of Professional Conduct

Rule 1.6 (Confidentiality),

Rule 1.18 (Prospective Client), and

Rule 1.9(c) (Former Clients).

We will also study the common-law attorney-client privilege (and related federal rule of evidence), and the work-product doctrine from the rules of civil procedure.

Preliminary Problem

Every day in your practice, you will be receiving information from and about your client. Some of that information will be secret, perhaps known only to you and the client; some will be freely available and widely known. What is your obligation to guard that information from disclosure or to refrain from using it? Consider the following everyday uses and disclosures:

- Phoning the client and leaving a message about the representation on the answering machine or discussing the matter with the client's roommate or spouse.
- Identifying clients in a law firm brochure.
- Revealing the identity of a client by processing a credit card payment.
- Telling a story to friends about a recent trial without revealing the client's identity or any other fact not contained in the public record.
- Taking a client file or discovery documents to the local photocopy shop.
- Listing "best" clients in Martindale-Hubbell.

Does it surprise you to know that in each one of these situations, even if the client is not harmed, you may have breached your duty of confidentiality if you did not have the client's permission to disclose this information or it was not necessary to further your client's interests? Nevada State Bar Standing Comm. on Ethics and Professional Responsibility, Formal Op. 41 (6/24/09).

9.1 Reading the Rules: Rule 1.6 and the Duty of Confidentiality

Rule 1.6 governs the attorney's duty of confidentiality. In this chapter, we will look only at the scope of the duty of confidentiality; in subsequent chapters, we will examine the exceptions to that duty. The scope of the duty can be found in the opening clause of Rule 1.6(a) as adopted by a majority of the states: "A lawyer shall not reveal information relating to representation of a client unless …".

Context

As you saw in the preliminary problem, the duty of confidentiality is extremely broad. The duty of confidentiality is further protected in conflict of interest rules. Yet it seems like you can hear attorneys talking about their clients and their clients' cases all the time. It is easy to assume that that there is little need to be scrupulous in your use or disclosure of client information unless that information is truly a "secret." The best attorney recognizes, however, that the client's information belongs to the client—not to the attorney—and that as a fiduciary, the attorney has a duty to protect that information and refrain from using it for personal gain. Scrupulous concern for a client's privacy conveys something about the care and devotion an attorney will give all of the other duties an attorney owes to the client.

Relationships

The ethical duty of confidentiality is only one of several doctrines that protect a client's information in the attorney-client relationship. However, each of these other doctrines may have a very different scope than the ethical duty. For example, the law of agency provides that the agent's fiduciary duty includes a duty to keep the principal's secrets and not to injure the principal; in the law of evidence, the attorney-client privilege shields confidential communications between attorney and client from compelled disclosure; the law of civil procedure provides degrees of immunity from discovery for attorney work product. Distinguishing among these doctrines is very important to your understanding of your ethical duty.

Structure

Rule 1.6's definition of confidential information is "information relating to the representation." It is easy to overlook those crucial five words when they are immediately followed by a laundry list of exceptions. However, think about that definition for a minute. It is breathtakingly broad. It is easiest to understand just how broad when you consider what the rule doesn't say.

It does not provide any prerequisites for the duty to attach. The rule applies **automatically** once an attorney begins to represent a client—whether or not the client asks the attorney to keep information confidential. The duty can even apply to someone who is not strictly a client. For example, a duty may exist if an individual provides information to an attorney, and the attorney has created a reasonable expectation that the attorney will maintain the confidentiality of that information. Likewise, as you will see under Model Rule 1.18, attorneys owe a duty of confidentiality to a prospective client even if the attorney declines the representation.

It does not matter **in what form** the information comes to you. "Information" can be documents, things, conversations, observations, facts, or data.

Nor does it matter **from whom** you gain this information. It might be from the client, it might be from your investigation, it might even be from your adversary.

Nor does it really matter **when** you acquire the information. Notice that the rule doesn't say "information *gained during* the representation." You almost certainly will have gained information related to a client's representation before the individual became a client, in the initial interview, for example, or in the context of a referral. In addition, you may gain additional information relating to the representation after it has formally concluded. Regardless of when the information was acquired, if it relates to the representation, it is confidential.

However, in some states, the scope of confidentiality is somewhat narrower than that provided by the model rules. Under the 1968 ABA Model Code of Professional Responsibility, DR 4-101(A) defined confidential information as "confidences and secrets … gained in the professional relationship." If the relationship had ended, information would be less likely to fall within this definition. Among the 49 states that have adopted the Model Rules of Professional Conduct, many have variations relating to the scope of confidentiality. For example, Arkansas, District of Columbia, New York, North Carolina, and Virginia all limit the scope of the duty of confidentiality to information "gained in the professional relationship" (or similar language). Accordingly, for any rules of professional conduct, but most especially for confidentiality rules, you should check your own state's version for variations.

To a certain extent, it does not even matter **why** you have gained the information. If you would not have received information but for the fact of the representation, it does not matter if the information is tangential to the ultimate objective—it ought to be considered confidential.

Moreover, it applies to **all information**, even if the information is not particularly harmful or secret. Look again at the definition—any information that relates to the representation is confidential. A client need not consider information "private" for the attorney to have a duty to keep that information confidential. Under the Model Code, the duty of confidentiality extended to "confidences" (which was interpreted as those communications protected by the attorney-client privilege) and "secrets" (anything a client wouldn't want revealed, regardless of source). Model Rule 1.6 simply uses "information relating to representation." In practice, however, the Model Code was interpreted as broadly as the language of 1.6 implies. The breadth of the definition can be seen in ABA Comm. on Ethics and Prof'l Responsibility, Informal Opinion 1287 (June 7, 1974) in which even the names and addresses of clients of a legal services office are secrets within 4-101[A].

Reasons

Why such a broad duty of confidentiality? An oft-cited rationale is that a broad protection of confidentiality promotes the trust necessary for the attorney-client relationship to be effective. An even more basic rationale is one grounded simply in privacy and ownership. The rule of confidentiality reminds us that when our clients come to us and share their stories, those stories and the information we gain because of that representation belong to the client. Clients do not share their stories for our profit or amusement.

That is not to say that there aren't exceptions to confidentiality that are designed to protect courts, the third persons, or ourselves. However, if there is no express exception, we should presume that information is confidential if it is from or about our clients and their cases. The rule of confidentiality is designed in the first instance to protect our clients from us. If our clients don't trust us, they will not provide us with the information we need to effectively counsel and represent them.

Visualize

Find a visual or an analogy that helps you to appreciate the breadth of the duty of confidentiality. For example, you could think about your client's information as a movie that is under production. All the characters, the entirety of the plot, the actors to be cast, and the location for shooting the film — all of the information about the movie — not just the spoiler — is confidential.

Imagine

Given the breadth of the duty of confidentiality, it is difficult to imagine information related to the representation that is not protected. Try.

You are likely to come up with one of three examples. The first is some category of information that you learned during the representation but is so generic as to be unrelated to the client specifically. For example, suppose you are representing a client from a foreign country. During the course of representation, you are likely to learn a great deal about that country, the people, culture, economics, and laws. This is generally available information that, while your motivation for learning the information was the representation, it is not in any sense information that is the property of the client. You obviously owe a client no duty to keep confidential or refrain from using this type of information.

A second scenario might be one in which there truly is not an attorney-client relationship. Be careful with this analysis. Remember that, even if someone is not a client for purposes of malpractice or other duties, you may still owe that person a duty of confidentiality if she conveyed confidential information to you with a reasonable expectation that you would keep it confidential.

The third scenario might be one in which you imagine an exception to the duty. However remember that, even when an exception applies, the duty has attached and an exception to the duty only allows disclosures of limited information in limited ways — an exception does not destroy the duty.

As you read the following case, think about how readily individuals share very private information with attorneys and how easy it can be to talk about that information if attorneys do not closely guard themselves.

In the Matter of Anonymous
932 N.E.2d 671 (Ind. 2010)

This matter is before the Court on the report of the hearing officer appointed by this Court to hear evidence on the Indiana Supreme Court Disciplinary Commission's "Verified Complaint for Disciplinary Action." The Respondent's admission to this state's bar subjects her to this Court's disciplinary jurisdiction. See IND. CONST. art. 7, §4.

We find that Respondent engaged in attorney misconduct by improperly revealing information relating to the representation of a former client. For this misconduct, we find that Respondent should receive a private reprimand.

Background

Respondent represented an organization that employed "AB." Respondent became acquainted with AB though this connection. In December 2007, AB and her husband were involved in an altercation to which the police were called, during which, AB's husband asserted, she threatened to harm him. In January 2008, AB phoned Respondent and told her about her husband's allegation and that she and her husband had separated. In a second phone call that month, AB asked Respondent for a referral to a family law attorney. Respondent gave AB the name of an attorney in Respondent's firm. (She also gave AB the names of two attorneys not associated with her firm.) Respondent then called this attorney to inform her of the referral and to give her AB's phone number. The attorney called AB that same day and arranged a meeting the following day, when AB retained the attorney. AB told the attorney about the December 2007 incident and directed her to file a divorce petition. Respondent was aware that AB had retained the attorney from her firm and had filed for divorce. AB and her husband soon reconciled, however, and, at AB's request, the divorce petition was dismissed and the firm's representation of AB ended.

In March or April 2008, Respondent was socializing with two friends, one of whom was also a friend of AB's. Unaware of AB's reconciliation with her husband, Respondent told her two friends about AB's filing for divorce and about her husband's accusation. Respondent encouraged AB's friend to contact AB because the friend expressed concern for her. When AB's friend called AB and told her what Respondent had told him, AB became upset about the revelation of the information and filed a grievance against Respondent.

The Commission charged Respondent with violating Professional Conduct Rule 1.9(c) (2), which prohibits revelation of information relating to the

This is a rather bare description of the facts giving rise to this action. For the story to be a lesson for us, we need to imagine ourselves in this attorney's shoes and reflect on our own motivations and reactions. What do you suppose were the details of this story?

Why do you suppose the attorney said something to AB's friend?

representation of a former client except as the Professional Conduct Rules permit or require. The hearing officer concluded that Respondent violated the rule as charged. The hearing officer found no facts in aggravation and the following facts in mitigation: (1) Respondent has no disciplinary history; and (2) Respondent was cooperative with the Commission.

Neither party filed a petition for review of the hearing officer's report. When neither party challenges the findings of the hearing officer, the Court accepts and adopts those findings but reserves final judgment as to misconduct and discipline. *See Matter of Levy*, 726 N.E.2d 1257, 1258 (Ind. 2000).

Discussion
Rules addressing revelation of confidential information.

The Rules of Professional Conduct ("Rules") contain several interrelated rules protecting the confidentiality of information relating to legal representations and consultations. Respondent is accused of violating Professional Conduct Rule 1.9(c), which sets forth the following duties owing to *former* clients:

> **A lawyer who has formerly represented a client in a matter or whose present or former firm has formerly represented a client in a matter shall not thereafter:**
>
> (1) use information relating to the representation to the disadvantage of the former client except as these Rules would permit or require with respect to a client, or when the information has become generally known; or
>
> (2) **reveal information relating to the representation** except as these Rules would permit or require with respect to a client.

(Emphasis added.)

Professional Conduct Rule 1.6(a), which covers duties to *current* clients, states: "A lawyer shall not reveal information relating to representation of a client unless the client gives informed consent, the disclosure is impliedly authorized in order to carry out the representation or the disclosure is permitted by paragraph (b)." Paragraph (b) allows disclosure under conditions not applicable to the current case, such as to prevent commission of a crime or to comply with a court order.

Professional Conduct Rule 1.18, which covers duties to *prospective* clients, states:

> (a) A person who discusses with a lawyer **the possibility of forming a client-lawyer relationship** with respect to a matter is a prospective client.
>
> (b) Even when no client-lawyer relationship ensues, **a lawyer who has had discussions with a prospective client shall not use or reveal information learned in the consultation**, except as Rule 1.9 would permit with respect to information of a former client.

(Emphasis added.)

Respondent's revelation of the information at issue was a violation of Rule 1.9(c)(2). Respondent argued to the hearing officer that AB initially gave her

the information at issue for the purpose of seeking *personal* rather than professional advice and only later phoned her again to ask for an attorney referral. Thus, she argued, the information was not confidential when AB first disclosed it to her, subsequent events did not change its nature, and she violated no ethical obligation in later revealing it.

The first January 2008 phone conversation did not include discussion of the possibility of forming an attorney-client relationship. If AB's communication with Respondent had ended with that phone call, revelation of the information at issue would not have been a violation of Respondent's ethical duties. "A person who communicates information unilaterally to a lawyer, without any reasonable expectation that the lawyer is willing to discuss the possibility of forming a client-lawyer relationship, is not a 'prospective client' within the meaning of paragraph (a)." Ind. Prof. Cond. R. 1.18 cmt. [2].

The information at issue, however, was disclosed to Respondent not long before the second call in which AB asked for an attorney referral and Respondent recommended an attorney from her firm. At that point, if not before, AB became a prospective client under Rule 1.18. The formation of an attorney-client relationship with Respondent's firm followed immediately thereafter, and the information at issue was highly relevant to the representation. Respondent then revealed the information with knowledge that her firm had been retained to represent AB in the matter. Under these circumstances, we conclude that once AB became a prospective client, the information became subject to the confidentiality protections of the Rules.

Respondent presented evidence that AB disclosed the information at issue to others, including some of AB's co-workers. Respondent argued to the hearing officer that AB's disclosure of the information to others indicated that AB's disclosure to Respondent in the first phone conversation was personal rather than professional in nature and not intended to be confidential. However, the fact that a client may chose to confide to others information relating to a representation does not waive or negate the confidentiality protections of the Rules, which we have found apply to the information at issue.

Respondent also argued to the hearing officer that revelation of the information at issue was not barred because it could be discovered by searching various public records and the internet. True, the filing of a divorce petition is a matter of public record, but Respondent revealed highly sensitive details of accusations AB's husband made against her to the police. There is no evidence that this information was contained in any public record. Moreover, the Rules contain no exception allowing revelation of information relating to a representation even if a diligent researcher could unearth it through public sources.[1]

Although we find it unnecessary in this case to explore the outer boundaries of the Rules concerning client confidences, the protection provided is broad.

We don't know much about the relationship between AB and the attorney. However, we do know that the attorney first met AB while representing AB's employer. Why wouldn't AB have a reasonable expectation that the attorney would be willing to represent her when she called the first time? If the attorney regularly practiced family law, do you think that would have made the first phone call sufficient to make AB a prospective client?

Consider the court's analysis carefully. If AB had never made the second phone call, apparently the court would not have held Respondent to the duty of confidentiality regarding the information. But after the second phone call, the duty of confidentiality apparently "related back" to the first phone call.

What if AB had gone to one of the other attorneys the Respondent had recommended, who was not in Respondent's firm, would Respondent still have a duty of confidentiality?

This is a very common misconception by attorneys — that if information isn't a "secret" it isn't confidential. The confusion may stem from the requirement of the attorney-client privilege in evidence law. For communications to be privileged under that doctrine, the communication must be in confidence or secret, and the privilege can be lost if revealed to third persons.

---

1. We note that Rule 1.9(c)(1) allows for *use* of information relating to a prior representation if the information has become *generally known*. Even if this were the provision at issue in this case, there is no evidence that the information relating to AB's husband's accusation, or even the divorce filing, was generally known.

The attorney-client privilege and work-product doctrine apply in judicial and other proceedings in which a lawyer may be called as a witness or otherwise required to produce evidence concerning a client. The rule of client-lawyer confidentiality applies in situations other than those when evidence is sought from the lawyer through compulsion of law. The confidentiality rule, for example, applies not only to matters communicated in confidence by the client but also to all information relating to the representation, whatever its source.

Ind. Prof. Cond. R. 1.6 cmt. [3] (emphasis added). An attorney has a duty to prospective, current, and former clients to scrupulously avoid revelation of such information, even if, as may have been the case here, the attorney is motivated by personal concern for the client.

Conclusion

The Court concludes Respondent violated Professional Conduct Rule 1.9(c)(2) by improperly revealing information relating to the representation of a former client. For Respondent's professional misconduct, the Court imposes a private reprimand. The costs of this proceeding are assessed against Respondent. The hearing officer appointed in this case is discharged.

The Clerk of this Court is directed to give notice of this opinion to the hearing officer, to the parties or their respective attorneys, and to all other entities entitled to notice under Admission and Discipline Rule 23(3)(d). The Clerk is further directed to post this opinion to the Court's website and Thomson Reuters is directed to publish a copy of this opinion in the bound volumes of this Court's decisions.

Note that the court had the discretion to simply issue discipline without a published opinion. Why do you think the Indiana Supreme Court chose to publish this opinion?

Notes

1. Recall that one of the most common responses of attorneys facing a disciplinary action is "I had no idea." The attorney here appeared to think that the rule was that, once a case is concluded, an attorney may discuss any information contained in the court files. The court made clear that the duty of confidentiality is much broader. Rule 1.9(c) does provide a "generally known" exception for information relating to the representation of a former client. However, that exception is only for *using*, not *disclosing*, information. Nonetheless, some courts do read the "generally known" exception to excuse disclosures in limited circumstances. Both the Restatement (Second) of the Law of Agency § 395 (1958) and the Restatement (Third) of the Law Governing Lawyers § 59 (2000) provide exceptions to the attorney/agent's duty of confidentiality for information that is "generally known" and some state rules and case law support this interpretation. Regardless of whether one reads the exception as applying only to use of information or to disclosure as well, the exception is extremely narrow — generally known requires a level of knowledge well above "publicly available." See, e.g., *Akron Bar Ass'n v. Holder*, 810 N.E.2d 426, 435 (Ohio 2004) ("an attorney is not free to disclose embarrassing or harmful features of a client's life just because they are documented in public records").

What further confuses attorneys is the narrower scope of the attorney-client evidentiary privilege. While all information relating to the representation is confidential, only private communications between attorney and client are privileged. The privilege is lost whenever a third person who is not part of the privileged relationship becomes privy to a communication between attorney and client. Thus, if attorney-client communications are revealed in court documents or other public sources, the privilege no longer protects those communications from discovery.

3rd party destroys privilege (evidentiary)

The very word "confidential" can cause confusion. The ethical duty of confidentiality applies to information that we might not, in ordinary parlance, think of as "confidential." To add to the confusion, a common definition of the attorney-client privilege speaks of communications "in confidence" between an attorney and client. The many different meanings of the word "confidential" can cause attorneys to confuse the broad ethical duty of confidentiality with the very narrow attorney-client privilege protections, leading to the kind of problems the attorney faced here.

2. Because of the broad scope and significant consequences of the attorney's duties of confidentiality, the doctrine is subject to abuse. Some clients have tried to take advantage of the disqualification effect of providing confidential information to an attorney, interviewing all the most qualified attorneys in a field so that they would be disqualified from representing an opponent. A recent ethics opinion from Virginia suggests that under these circumstances, there is no obligation of confidentiality. In that case Husband and Wife were planning a divorce. Husband interviewed all the divorce lawyers in their community on the pretense that he wanted to hire them. In each case he divulged confidences. Later Wife tried to hire one of the interviewed lawyers. The committee held that the lawyer could represent Wife, because Husband could not have had a "reasonable expectation of privacy," given the motive for the earlier interview. Va. Op. 1794 (June 30, 2004). In its August 2012 amendments to the Model Rules, the ABA expressly incorporated this interpretation into comment 2 of Rule 1.18, noting that "a person who communicates with a lawyer for the purpose of disqualifying the lawyer is not a 'prospective client'" and so would not create a disqualifying conflict. The difficulty in relying on this comment is proving the client's intent to "set up" a conflict.

Other clients attempt to attach confidentiality to their information for purposes other than representation, such as to shield illegal transactions. Some courts have allowed the presumption of confidentiality to be rebutted by an *in-camera* hearing in these instances. *B.F. Goodrich Co. v. Formosa Plastics Corp.*, 638 F. Supp. 1050 (S.D. Tex. 1986). If a client is attempting to use the duty of confidentiality to shield otherwise criminal or fraudulent activities, many states would allow an attorney to use or disclose the client's information to prevent substantial financial injury. Several states go further to permit an attorney to use or disclose confidential information to rectify past and completed client fraud. A few states actually require disclosure in at least some circumstances of client fraud. We will learn more about these exceptions to confidentiality in Chapter Eleven.

3. One of the ways in which attorneys and law students try to talk about client matters without breaching confidentiality is by speaking hypothetically. While comments to Rule 1.6 suggest that an attorney may use hypotheticals to dis-

cuss legal issues in order to get advice or suggestions about the law, you should not consider this an excuse for wide-ranging discussions about your client's sensitive factual information and certainly not as an opportunity for gossip. It is often easier than you might think for others to decipher the real facts behind the hypothetical, especially today when so much private information is readily accessible online.

9.2 When Must Attorneys or Clients Provide Information in Litigation?

When information is sought under government compulsion, an additional set of doctrines applies to protect some client information. These rules are the attorney-client privilege from the rules of evidence and the work-product doctrine from the rules of procedure. These are complex doctrines. From jurisdiction to jurisdiction, you can find significant variations on many of the central issues. At the federal level, questions of privilege and work product both are located in court rules, but are grounded in common law doctrines. Among the states, privilege and work-product questions might be addressed in the common law, court rules, legislation, or all three sources. Moreover, the doctrines may have different contours depending on whether they are raised in the criminal or civil context.

The procedural context in which these doctrines arise adds a further layer of complexity. When courts are scrutinizing the scope of the ethical duty of confidentiality, their review will take place after the information in question has already been disclosed, as in *In Re Anonymous*. However, when a judge is trying to decide whether the attorney-client privilege or the work-product doctrine shields information, the information is still a secret. If the information had to be disclosed in order to decide whether it is subject to these protections, the law would destroy confidentiality in order to protect it. Accordingly, courts have a variety of procedural methods for invoking these protections and proving their applicability. The complexities of these doctrines can fill volumes. Indeed you can find multivolume treatises that are designed to address each of these doctrines. For the purposes of this course we will focus on two objectives: understanding the essential elements of each doctrine and researching the issues that arise in applying those elements.

9.2.1. The Attorney-Client Privilege

The attorney-client privilege is an evidentiary rule developed at common law to protect client trust. The privilege is one of the oldest common law privileges protecting confidential communications. *Swidler & Berlin v. United States*, 524 U.S. 399, 403 (1998). You will sometimes see this doctrine referred to as the attorney-client "evidentiary privilege," "communications privilege," or "testimonial privilege." The scope and exceptions to privilege differ from state to state and in the federal courts. Privilege questions in federal court "shall be governed by the principles of the common law as they may be interpreted by the courts of the United States in the light of reason and experience" except when State law provides the rule of decision. Fed R. Evid. 501.

An attorney or client might invoke the attorney-client privilege in a number of settings. The client is asked a question in trial or in a deposition and her attorney objects, based on the privilege. An interrogatory asks about a communication between attorney and client. The attorney is concerned that discovery will seek privileged documents and brings a motion for a protective order. An attorney is subpoenaed to testify before a grand jury, legislative committee, or administrative tribunal about communications with a client. While the attorney cannot object to being compelled to appear, she can object to questions based on the privilege. Documents or computers are seized under a search warrant. The attorney moves to suppress the evidence and dismiss any actions based on that evidence. An attorney is required to report cash transactions in excess of $10,000 on an IRS Form 8300. The attorney asserts that the required disclosure would violate the attorney-client privilege.

In all of these circumstances, the attorney asserting the privilege has the burden of proof as to the application of the privilege as to each document or question. The Restatement defines the elements of the attorney-client privilege as "1) a communication (2) made between privileged persons (3) in confidence (4) for the purpose of obtaining or providing legal assistance for the client." RESTATEMENT (THIRD) OF THE LAW GOVERNING LAWYERS § 68 (2000). The following problem is designed to highlight some of the more common issues that arise in determining the scope of the attorney-client privilege.

Terrence Teadrop v. Teamist Distributors Inc.

You represent Teadrop Shop, a small tea shop, and its sole proprietor Terrence Teadrop. The tea shop is located in a shopping area that has about six shops and two restaurants on one block in a suburban neighborhood area. Terrence claims that one of his tea suppliers, Teamist Distributors Inc., did not deliver a shipment of specialty teas at the beginning of December, causing Terrence to lose substantial profits during the shopping area's annual holiday sales event. You have met with Terrence several times about the case and have conducted some informal discovery. You file a breach of contract action against Teamist. Now that formal discovery has begun, you are facing questions regarding the applicability of the attorney-client privilege.

---

a. *The privilege protects only a communication. It does not protect the underlying facts from compelled disclosure.*

This distinction can be very difficult to see in practice and courts sometimes err and protect facts simply because they were the subject of a communication. In part, this confusion might be the product of our understanding of another important privilege that does protect from disclosure of facts: the constitutional privilege against self-incrimination. If someone "takes the 5th" he is seeking the protections of a privilege that extends to facts, not just communications. The attorney-client privilege, however, protects only the communication process—the client may be compelled to reveal his knowledge of facts themselves. As the Supreme Court stated regarding the attorney-client privilege, that privilege:

> ... extends only to communications and not to facts. A fact is one thing and a communication concerning that fact is an entirely different thing. The client cannot be compelled to answer the question, 'What did you say or write to the attorney?' but may not refuse to disclose any relevant fact within his knowledge

merely because he incorporated a statement of such fact into his communication to his attorney.

Upjohn Co. v. United States, 449 U.S. 383, 395-396 (1981). Take a moment to think about this distinction carefully. Can you picture the distinction the *Upjohn* case presents? Here is one way to picture the difference between facts and communications about facts. Notice that the facts the attorney has are protected by the privilege whereas the facts the client has are not. Why is that? Because the only way the attorney has those facts is because of the communication, so compelling the attorney to reveal this information would also reveal the communication. On the other hand, compelling the client to reveal the information in his possession does not require disclosing the communication to the attorney and so is unprotected by the privilege.

[handwritten margin note: Communication is protected]

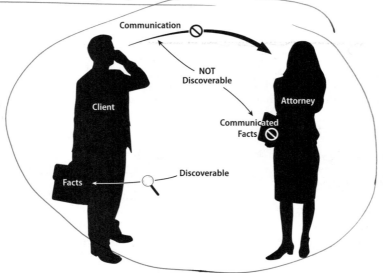

Suppose in our case that your client Terrence tells you that he was at his store for the entire period during which the goods were to be delivered. He admits, however that he does have a habit of stepping outside the back for a smoke or running next door to the restaurant for a snack regularly throughout the day, so it is possible that he might have missed someone attempting to make a delivery. You ask Terrence if he has spoken to others about his activity that day and he says that he has spoken to some of the other shop owners about whether they had seen the delivery truck and that he was afraid he might have missed it. You have interviewed the neighboring store owners and obtained statements from them about your client's activity in the store and his availability on the day in question.

Preparing for discovery, what is privileged? Only your confidential communication with Terrence would be protected by the attorney-client privilege. The information about his behavior or even his worries that he might have missed the delivery are not privileged; only his communication of that information to you. It does not matter that he may have spoken to others about his worry that he might have missed the delivery. As long as neither he nor you reveal that you and he had discussed this, your conversation is privileged and neither of you can be required to disclose the conversation.

However, the fact that Terrence may have been out when the delivery arrived is information that is not shielded from discovery. How might Teamist discover this information? They would be unlikely to ask you, since you are not really a witness (and would be ethically restricted in representing Terrence if you were—see Rule 3.7). However, the client can be asked to testify about his own behavior and beliefs. These *facts* are not privileged—only the client's confidential *communication* with you about those facts. The attorney's conversation with the client would be privileged, but the attorney's conversations with the store owners next door would not be privileged because they would not be between an attorney and client. The work-product doctrine would likely protect the attorney's interview notes with witnesses; but it would not shield those witnesses from being subpoenaed to testify about what they saw or knew.

b. The communication must be between privileged persons.

The attorney-client privilege applies to confidential communications between "privileged persons." Ordinarily that is the attorney and client. Suppose, for a moment, that Terrence, as an individual, is your client (we will revisit that assumption in just a moment). Obviously, communications between Terrence and you are between privileged persons. Suppose that Terrence has two employees in the store. One employee is Arnold Ackown, who helps Terrence with the books. You set up a meeting with Terrence to discuss the financial losses that likely resulted from Teamist's failure to deliver the specialty teas. Your paralegal will be present to take notes during the meeting. Terrence asks if he can bring Arnold along to the meeting. Terrence says that he trusts Arnold absolutely and that he really can't discuss the financial aspects of the business intelligently without Arnold's help. Is Arnold a privileged person?

The attorney-client privilege protects communications between attorneys and a number of other persons besides just the attorney and client. For example, when an attorney meets with an individual for the purposes of exploring the possibility of representation, that individual is not yet a client. Yet the attorney-client privilege protects these prospective clients as well. Because the purpose of the rule is to facilitate communication for the purposes of legal representation, it would be counterproductive if the privilege did not protect these communications. It is in the initial client interview that the attorney often must obtain some of the most critical information in order to counsel the client. Sometimes that counsel is the advice that the potential client's proposed course of action is illegal or unwise; sometimes the counsel is that an attorney is not necessary. In either case, if potential clients did not feel free to communicate with attorneys, much valuable legal advice would be lost.

Other individuals who could be considered privileged persons include an agent of the attorney who assists in the representation or an agent of either the attorney or the client who "facilitate[s] communications." RESTATEMENT (THIRD) OF THE LAW GOVERNING LAWYERS § 70 (2000). If a third person who is not a "privileged person" is present during an attorney and client communication, the attorney-client privilege does not attach to that communication. In this case, the paralegal would be the agent of the attorney for purposes of the representation and her presence would not affect the privilege. Arnold would be an agent of Terrence who would be necessary for Arnold to understand and communicate about the financial aspects of his business, and so his presence would not affect the privilege either.

As you can imagine, there are many instances in which it is not clear whether a third person is an agent for communication. The Restatement suggests the following test:

A person is a confidential agent for communication if the person's participation is reasonably necessary to facilitate the client's communication with a lawyer or another privileged person and if the client reasonably believes that the person will hold the communication in confidence. Factors that may be relevant in deter-

Factors for facilitation 3rd person ☆

mining whether a third person is an agent for communication include the customary relationship between the client and the asserted agent, the nature of the communication, and the client's need for the third person's presence to communicate effectively with the lawyer or to understand and act upon the lawyer's advice.

RESTATEMENT (THIRD) OF THE LAW GOVERNING LAWYERS, § 70 cmt f (2000).

You can visualize this aspect of the attorney-client relationship as the necessity to keep communications within a privileged circle. So long as everyone in the circle is a privileged person, the attorney-client privilege protects communications among the privileged persons for the purposes of securing legal advice. The privilege is destroyed by the presence of a third person who is not an agent of the attorney or an agent necessary for communication for the client.

c. Constituents of organizations and entities can be privileged persons.

There is another sense in which Arnold may be a privileged person. Suppose that your client is Teamist Company rather than Terrence (with a sole proprietorship, the difference is subtle but important). When the client is a business or other entity, the conversations with individuals who can speak on behalf of that entity client may all be considered privileged. Those persons can include not only the owners, directors, or officers of the entity but, in some jurisdictions, lower-level employees as well.

Suppose, for example, that Terrence's other employee is Yolanda, a shop assistant who works three evenings a week. She was not scheduled to work in the shop on the day the delivery was supposed to arrive but Terrence suggests that you speak to her about Teamist's usual delivery times and shop procedures generally. You interview her about Terrence's work and Teamist Company's practices. You learn that on the day that the Teamist delivery was supposed to have been made, Yolanda had stopped by the shop to pick up her sweater, which she had left there the day before. She came in the back door (she has a key) and Terrence wasn't in the shop. A "Be Right Back" sign was in the front window. She grabbed her sweater and left. You ask if she had been surprised to find the shop empty. She said that she was not because Terrence did a lot of "coming and going" throughout the day.

Are Yolanda's statements to you covered by the attorney-client privilege? The question of whether an employee is a "privileged person" is one of the most complicated issues in applying the privilege rules. The United States Supreme Court recognized that corporations, just as much as individuals, have the protections of the attorney-client privilege. *Upjohn Co. v. United States*, 449 U.S. 383 (1981). Partnerships as well may invoke the privilege. *See, e.g., In re Bieter Co.*, 16 F.3d 929, 935 (8th Cir. 1994) (discussing the applicability of the attorney-client privilege in the partnership context). While states vary in their approaches to the extent of that privilege, no jurisdiction fails to recognize the basic principle that corporations and other entities are protected by the privilege.

However, organizations or entities can only speak through people. Which people within an entity are agents of the entity when speaking with attorneys such that their conversations would be protected by the attorney-client privilege? Courts have traditionally applied one of two tests to determine the scope of the corporate attorney-client privilege: the "control group" test and the "subject matter" test. While the test is commonly called the "corporate attorney-client privilege" it has been interpreted to apply to other business and non-profit entities and organizations, including sole proprietorships. RESTATEMENT (THIRD) OF THE LAW GOVERNING LAWYERS § 73 (2000).

In the "control group" test, the only individuals whose communications with attorneys fall within the privilege are those employees who have authority to act on behalf of the corporation to implement the attorney's advice (generally senior management). The United States Supreme Court rejected the control group test because it "frustrates the very purpose of the privilege by discouraging the communication of relevant information by employees of the client to attorneys seeking to render legal advice to the client corporation. The attorney's advice will also frequently be more significant to non-control group members than to those who officially sanction the advice, and the control group test makes it more difficult to convey full and frank legal advice to the employees who will put into effect the client corporation's policy." *See Upjohn Co. v. United States*, 449 U.S. 383, 392 (1981). Nonetheless, some jurisdictions still adhere to this test. *See, e.g., Consolidation Coal Co. v. Bucyrus-Erie Co.*, 432 N.E.2d 250, 256-58 (Ill. 1982).

The majority of jurisdictions and the federal courts apply a test that looks to the subject matter of the conversation. A typical example of this test can be seen in the Eighth Circuit, where the test for when privileged communication attaches to an employee is one that looks to the purpose and direction of the contact. *Diversified Industries, Inc. v. Meredith*, 572 F.2d 592 (8th Cir. 1977). Under that test the privilege attaches if:

(1) the communication was made for the purpose of securing legal advice;

(2) the employee making the communication did so at the direction of his corporate superior;

(3) the superior made the request so that the corporation could secure legal advice;

(4) the subject matter of the communication is within the scope of the employee's corporate duties;

(5) the communication is not disseminated beyond those persons who because of the corporate structure, need to know its contents.

If you visualize the reach of the two tests, you can see how much greater the protection is under the "subject matter" test.

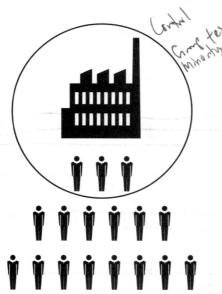

[handwritten: Control / Group test / minority rule]

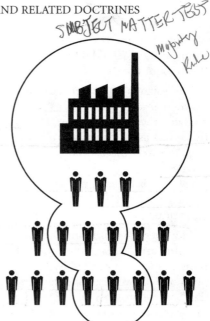

[handwritten: SUBJECT MATTER TEST / Majority Rule]

Corporation's
Attorney-Client Privilege
protects communications
with control group

Corporation's
Attorney-Client Privilege
protects communications
with a range of persons
in the corporation as needed
to provide the corporation
legal advice

[handwritten: Subject matter test / larger reach / scope]

Under the subject matter test, if Yolanda's statements to you were as an agent of the business and in confidence, they would qualify as privileged statements. Under the control group test, her statements would be much less likely to be protected communications.

d. The statement must be "in confidence" to be privileged.

This requirement of the privilege is likely what causes many attorneys to confuse the doctrine of privilege with the duty of confidentiality. The concept of "communication in confidence" simply means that the client has a reasonable expectation that the communication will be private. It does not mean that the facts themselves have been kept confidential. So, for example, when Terrence discusses his claim with you in your office, he would reasonably expect that the conversation would be private. But if you and Terrence were discussing the case in the neighboring restaurant, within earshot of others, that conversation could not be privileged, because Terrence could not reasonably expect that it was "in confidence." It would not matter that the subject matter discussed in that conversation was something that Terrence had discussed with others. So long as he did not tell others that he had communicated this with you, your conversation is protected.

[handwritten: reasonably expect confidentiality]

Moreover, as you will see in the next chapter, if a client or attorney does reveal an otherwise privileged communication to persons who are not subject to the privilege, the privilege will be deemed waived. Martha Stewart learned this when she forwarded to her daughter an email she had previously sent to her lawyer. Because there is no "mother-daughter" privilege and the daughter was not otherwise necessary to the representation so that she would be considered a privileged person, Martha Stewart waived the attorney-client privilege by sharing the communication with her daughter. *United States v. Stewart*, 287 F. Supp.2d 461 (S.D.N.Y. 2003).

e. The purpose of the communication must be to secure or provide legal assistance.

Suppose that you had known Terrence long before he engaged your services in the current dispute. Suppose you were a customer in the shop or that Terrence was your friend. If Terrence talked to you about the delivery problem simply to "vent" or to explain why certain products weren't available for your purchase, without intending to ask for your advice, those conversations would not be protected by the privilege.

Recall that the attorney in *In re Anonymous* claimed that the client's initial disclosures to her were for the purposes of "personal" rather than "professional" advice. The court noted that, if the client had never actually become a client, the duty of confidentiality might not have attached. However, since she did indeed become a client, even these personal conversations became subject to the duty of confidentiality. Not so for the privilege. If the purpose of the communication is "personal" or "business" and does not include the purpose to obtain legal advice or assistance, the privilege never attaches to that communication — even if there is an attorney-client relationship.

Once again, you can see how important it is to keep the duty of confidentiality and the attorney-client privilege separate. The duty of confidentiality applies to any information relating to the representation of a client — regardless of source or secrecy. The attorney-client privilege only protects communications between privileged persons, made in private, for the purposes of seeking legal assistance.

9.2.2. The Work-Product Doctrine

The attorney work-product doctrine was first developed by the United States Supreme Court as a way to protect attorneys' work and especially their mental impressions from unlimited discovery. *Hickman v. Taylor*, 329 U.S. 495, 510 (1947). It is now found in the rules of civil procedure at both the federal and state levels. The doctrine is sometimes referred to a privilege, but it provides less protection than evidentiary privileges, since it operates primarily as a limit on discovery. A similar doctrine exists in criminal procedure. Federal Rules of Criminal Procedure 16 provides work-product protection for documents prepared "during the case's investigation or defense" in criminal proceedings. Fed. R. Crim. P. 16(b)(2)(A).

This protection has two levels: first, there is a general protection for materials prepared in anticipation of litigation. The doctrine protects a document or tangible thing prepared in anticipation of litigation by or for a party, or by or for the party's representative. FED R. CIV. P. 26(b) (3). The breadth of this protection can be seen in the Restatement's description of work product:

> Work product includes tangible materials and intangible equivalents prepared, collected, or assembled by a lawyer. Tangible materials include documents, photographs, diagrams, sketches, questionnaires and surveys, financial and economic analyses, hand-written notes, and material in electronic and other technologically advanced forms, such as stenographic, mechanical, or electronic recordings or transmissions, computer data bases, tapes, and printouts.

Intangible work product is equivalent work product in unwritten, oral or re-membered form. For example, intangible work product can come into ques-tion by a discovery request for a lawyer's recollections derived from oral communications.

A compilation or distillation of non-work-product materials can itself be work product. For example, a lawyer's memorandum analyzing publicly avail-able information constitutes work product. The selection or arrangement of doc-uments that are not themselves protected might reflect mental impressions and legal opinions inherent in making a selection or arrangement. Thus, a lawyer's index of a client's preexisting and discoverable business files will itself be work product if prepared in anticipation of litigation. So also, the manner in which a lawyer has selected certain client files, organized them in pretrial work, and plans to present them at trial is work product.

RESTATEMENT (THIRD) OF THE LAW GOVERNING LAWYERS, § 87 cmt. f (2000). These doc-uments are not subject to discovery without showing that the information is substan-tially needed and unavailable without substantial hardship. Compare that level of protection to the attorney-client privilege, under which communications are not discoverable even if one has a special need for the material. The second level of protection in work-prod-uct doctrine is more akin to a privilege. That is the protection provided to an attorney's mental impressions.

Just as it is important to distinguish between the attorney-client privilege and the ethical duty of confidentiality, so it is important to understand the differences between the privilege and the work-product doctrine. Like the attorney-client privilege, work-prod-uct protection does not shield facts, but rather the attorney's work process in gathering, organizing, and analyzing those facts. The Massachusetts court provides this helpful summary:

With the attorney-client privilege, the principal focus is on encouraging the client to communicate freely with the attorney; with work product, it is on encourag-ing careful and thorough preparation by the attorney. As a result, there are dif-ferences in the scope of the protection. For example, the privilege extends only to client communications, while work product encompasses much that has its source outside client communications. At the same time, the privilege extends to client-attorney communications whenever any sort of legal services are being pro-vided, but the work-product protection is limited to preparations for litigation.

Suffolk Constr. Co. v. Division of Capital Asset Mgt., 870 N.E.2d 33,43 (Mass. 2007) (quot-ing EDNA SELAN EPSTEIN, THE ATTORNEY-CLIENT PRIVILEGE AND THE WORK-T DOC-TRINE 477 (4th ed. 2001).

There are additional differences between the doctrines. For example, the privilege ap-plies only to confidential communications between attorneys and their clients or their representatives. Work product applies to any material prepared in anticipation of litiga-tion—an attorney need not be involved for the work-product exception to take effect. Own-ership of the protection is another difference. Only the client has the right to waive the attorney-client privilege (though an attorney has the power to waive the privilege). How-ever, since the work-product doctrine is designed to protect the matters that are more within the attorney's authority and responsibility—that is, the preparation for litiga-tion—an attorney may choose to waive the work-product doctrine.

Is there any protection under the work-product doctrine for attorney impressions in documents that are prepared for representation aside from litigation? For example, suppose an attorney is representing a client in negotiating a business deal. The parties are working together well and there is no threat of litigation. If the attorney creates a document with strategies and mental impressions about the parties to assist in preparing for the negotiation, would that document be discoverable in a litigation that developed later on? *United States v. Textron Inc.*, 507 F. Supp. 2d 138, 152 (D.R.I. 2007), overruled on other grounds, 577 F.3d 21 (1st Cir. 2009). What exactly does "in anticipation of litigation" mean? Does it mean litigation must be imminent (a test based on timing) or does it mean thinking about potential litigation was part of the attorney's representation rather than in the ordinary course of business (a test based on purpose)?

Like most matters in discovery, the answer is unclear because courts have such broad discretion to fashion protective orders based on concepts like "overbroad" or "prejudicial" and appeals are rare because of the combination of the final judgment rule and the abuse of discretion standard. In the few appellate cases addressing the edges of the doctrine, one can find support for either the narrow timing approach or the broader purpose approach. The Second Circuit, for example, has adopted a fairly broad reading of "anticipation of litigation" to include attorney compliance and planning advice.

> The Second Circuit has adopted the "because of" approach to determining whether a document was prepared "in anticipation of litigation." Under this approach, a document is entitled to work product protection if it is prepared "because of" existing or expected litigation. The "because of" approach is more inclusive than the approach taken by those courts that require a document to be prepared "primarily or exclusively to assist in litigation." Under the latter approach, a document prepared primarily to assist in making a business decision would not be entitled to work product protection. On the other hand, under the "because of" approach, the Second Circuit found that a document containing a detailed legal analysis of a likely IRS challenge to a proposed business reorganization was prepared in anticipation of litigation, and did not lose its work-product protection merely because it was created primarily to assist in the making of a business decision about reorganization. Nevertheless, the Second Circuit emphasized that even the "because of" formulation withholds protection from documents that are prepared in the ordinary course of business.
>
> The "because of" approach adopted by the Second Circuit is the more persuasive view. Regular course of business and in anticipation of litigation are not always mutually exclusive and dichotomous fields. Many business decisions are made in anticipation of the inevitable litigation. The "because of" inquiry offers a more administrable standard, effectively resolving uncertainty at the margins in favor of work product protection. At the same time, protection is not unduly expanded if the document would not have been produced but for the anticipated suit. Evaluating the risks of litigation that a business plan will face is often integral to the plan and is in this sense generated in the course of business. There is no persuasive reason to deny work product protection because the document has these marks of business purpose, if it was prepared because of the anticipated litigation.
>
> Even if the anticipated litigation never is commenced, as long as the document was prepared in anticipation of litigation, it is entitled to protection. The non-occurrence of the events underlying the anticipated litigation, however, is a factor that the court may consider in deciding whether to order disclosure.

6-26 MOORE'S FEDERAL PRACTICE—CIVIL § 26.70 (2011) (footnotes deleted).

Researching Professional Responsibility 9-A: Rules of Evidence and Procedure

The attorney-client privilege and the work-product doctrine were both developed at common law. In some jurisdictions these doctrines are codified in rules of evidence and in rules of civil procedure. In most states, rules of procedure and evidence might be found in state statutes or in court rules or both. More than half of the states publish their rules of civil procedure in their statutory compilations. West publishes handbooks for many states collecting the rules of court for both state and federal practice in the state, which include rules of procedure and, in many instances, rules of evidence.

The court rules for all states are also available online through subscription databases. However, most states have their rules of procedure and evidence posted to a free official government website. To find your state's website, you can use a search engine or you can begin with a web directory such as the Legal Information Institute at http://www.law.cornell.edu/ wex/table_civil_procedure or LLRX at http://www.llrx.com/courtrules/.

However, in many states, the rules will provide very little guidance regarding the contours of the attorney-client privilege and work-product doctrine. Caselaw research will generally be required. State practice treatises can be especially helpful in locating cases and explaining trends and interpretations. If you are not familiar with the practice manuals series available for your state, ask your research librarian for assistance.

If your state's rules of procedure and evidence are modeled on the federal rules, searching for interpretations from the federal courts can be helpful as well. Two very useful multivolume treatises for federal procedure are:

CHARLES A. WRIGHT & ARTHUR R. MILLER, ET. AL., FEDERAL PRACTICE & PROCEDURE (3rd ed. 1998). The treatise is updated regularly and is available on Westlaw through the database FPP.

JAMES W. MOORE, ET. AL., MOORE'S FEDERAL PRACTICE (3rd ed.1997). Organized by each rule of the FRCP. Available online through LexisNexis in the database Federal Practice).

In addition, there are many fine treatises on the attorney-client privilege and work-product protections. For example, the American Bar Association publishes a two-volume treatise on these two doctrines: The ATTORNEY-CLIENT PRIVILEGE AND THE WORK-PRODUCT DOCTRINE (5th ed. 2007).

9.3 Comparing and Contrasting Doctrines

For any given item of information about your client, you might be called upon to say "it's confidential" or "it's privileged" or "that's work product" or even all three. As you saw from the prior case, it is important to be able to distinguish when you might invoke each of these doctrines. Attorneys are sometimes very sloppy in their use of the terminology, but the doctrines are quite distinct, apply in very different settings, for very different purposes, and with parallel but distinct exceptions. The following diagram represents all the information you might acquire from or about a client during the course of representation. As you can see, nearly all of that information is "confidential" — that is, you are re-

Attorney-Client Privilege:
"Confidential communication
between attorney and client
for the purpose of securing
legal advice."

Ethical Duty of Confidentiality:
"Information relating to
the representation."

Work-Product Protection:
"Documents prepared in
anticipation of litigation."

quired to protect that information from disclosure, unless the rules of professional conduct provide an exception to that duty.

Only when someone seeks information through judicial process, typically through a subpoena to produce documents or provide testimony, does the question of privilege or of work product arise. The scope of the attorney-client privilege is much narrower, applies to fewer communications, and an attorney has very little discretion to waive the privilege over a client's objection. Likewise, work-product protection applies only to documents and things prepared in anticipation of litigation and the court has considerable discretion in determining whether to allow or prohibit disclosure in discovery of these materials. While the ethical duty requires attorneys to invoke these doctrines to protect their clients, if the law or a court orders the disclosure of information, the ethical duty gives way to the duty to obey the law or the court.

You know that in litigation, rules of discovery and rules of evidence in general favor a very broad disclosure of information—bounded only by relevance and the balance of a few competing concerns like prejudice and fairness. Both the attorney-client privilege and work-product protection are narrow exceptions to this otherwise broad ability to gather information during litigation. Unlike the pressures that require an attorney to presume that a client's information must be protected unless there is a clear exception allowing use or disclosure, the presumption in litigation is that information should be freely available unless there is proof that a narrow protective doctrine prevents disclosure.

The pressures of client trust, privacy, and attorney loyalty all exert an outward pressure on the boundaries of confidentiality, keeping the scope broad.

In the setting of attorney-client privilege and work-product protection, the policy pressures are quite different. The need for efficient fact finding creates pressures to keep exceptions to disclosure quite narrow.

While the work-product protection is mostly to protect the attorney's litigation preparation, the duty of confidentiality and the attorney-client privilege both belong to and protect the client. How do these doctrines interact?

Notice that Rule 1.6 provides an exception to confidentiality when law or court order requires disclosure. So if an attorney or a client is asked to produce or testify to attorney-client communications, the attorney's ethical duty is to raise the attorney-client privilege objection. However, if that objection is overruled, once ordered or compelled by law to disclose, the ethical standards would be unlikely to be a defense to contempt or criminal charges of obstruction of justice, so the attorney should comply with the court order. However, once an attorney has been required to testify regarding attorney-client communications, or other information relating to the representation that is not covered by the privilege, that does not mean that the attorney no longer has a duty of confidentiality. Outside the court-ordered disclosure, the attorney must continue to protect his client's information unless some other exception to confidentiality applies.

In the past in many jurisdictions, the best course of action for an attorney faced with what he or she considers an erroneous, although binding, order to disclose client confidences or produce protected documents would be to attempt to appeal the decision rather than comply. This route is still available in many states, but in the federal system, the United States Supreme Court this term has held that a ruling on an attorney-client privilege objection is not one from which there is an immediate appeal under the collateral order doctrine. *Mohawk Industries, Inc. v. Carpenter*, 130 S. Ct. 599; 175 L. Ed. 2d 458; 2009 U.S. LEXIS 8942 (2009). The attorney would, in these courts, be required to reveal the information and appeal the ruling from an adverse judgment.

It is not only in litigation discovery that an attorney may need to raise the attorney-client privilege. Increasingly, attorneys are subject to reporting requirements or are being issued subpoenas to testify regarding their clients' activities. These requirements are the subject of intense controversy. Consider IRS Form 8300, which requires reporting the identity of any clients and the amounts and payment dates of any cash transactions in excess of $10,000. Most jurisdictions hold that subpoenas against attorneys requiring these disclosures are enforceable. See, *United States v. Sindel*, 854 F. Supp. 595 (E.D. Mo. 1994). Also *see*, *United States v. Monnat*, 853 F. Supp. 1301 (D. Kan. 1994) (court referred issues of duty to respond to form 8300 to Federal Court Committee on Attorney Conduct). Increasingly, prosecutors have used the subpoena power to compel testimony of defense attorneys. This use of subpoenas is not without criticism and some courts have adopted rules to limit the effectiveness of these subpoenas. *Whitehouse v. U.S. District Court*, 53 F.3d 1349 (1st Cir. 1995) (upholding a local rule requiring federal prosecutors to get advance judicial approval before issuing a subpoena).

Documents are particularly tricky because any given document might be confidential, privileged, and protected by work-product doctrine. Any document you have relating to your representation is confidential and you must protect it from disclosure. If that document is otherwise discoverable or admissible in litigation, however, you would ordinarily have to produce it unless it is either privileged or work product. So if a client gives a document to an attorney in anticipation of litigation, does that make it privileged and work product? No. For work-product protection to apply the document must have been *prepared* in anticipation of litigation. For the attorney-client privilege to apply, the document must constitute (or memorialize) a confidential communication between the attorney and client. As the Restatement states: "a client-authored document that is not a privileged document when originally composed does not become privileged simply because the client has placed it in the lawyer's hands." RESTATEMENT (THIRD) OF THE LAW GOVERNING LAWYERS § 69, cmt. J (2000). The United States Supreme Court explains the rule as follows:

> [P]re-existing documents which could have been obtained by court process from the client when he was in possession may also be obtained from the attorney by similar process following transfer by client in order to obtain more informed legal advice.... [W]hen the client himself would be privileged from production of the document, either as a party at common law ... or as exempt from self-incrimination, the attorney having possession of the document is not bound to produce.

Fisher v. United States, 425 U.S. 391, 404-405 (U.S. 1976). Recall that, even if the document itself is protected by privilege or work product, the client's information that is contained in that document remains discoverable.

Test Your Understanding

Complete the following chart to review your understanding of these three doctrines:

	Duty of Confidentiality	Attorney-Client Privilege	Work-Product Protection
What does it protect?			
Whom is it designed to protect against whom?			
What form of information is protected?			
For what purpose must the information have been gained?			
When must the information have been gained?			

1. Dan Defendant is sued by Vince Victim for an auto accident in which Dan ran into Vince's parked car while returning to work from lunch. Vince's complaint alleges that Dan "appeared inebriated" (though no police were called to the scene so there is no blood alcohol evidence). Dan insists that he had not had anything to drink that day but does admit that he had had very little sleep the night before and was probably too tired to be driving well. Attorney interviews Dan's friend Frank, who tells you that he and Dan had lunch that day and that Dan drank at least two martinis. Evaluate the following statements as either True or False:

   Dan's statements are both confidential and privileged.

   Frank's statements are confidential.

   Frank's statements are privileged.

2. Attorney was hired to represent Harry in a drunk driving charge. Harry is a minister in a local church and a well-respected member of the community who is socially involved with Attorney and the other partners in his firm. Harry requested that Attorney not disclose to Attorney's partners anything about the details of the charge and simply help him quietly settle the matter. Attorney left the file and notes of his interview with Harry open on his computer where they were read by Clarissa, a law clerk, who conveyed the information to the other partners.

   Can Attorney be subject to discipline for his actions?

   a. No, an attorney cannot agree to keep client confidences from his partners.

   b. No, Attorney made no affirmative effort to disclose the information.

   c. Yes, Attorney failed to take reasonable precautions to protect the confidences.

   d. Yes, but only if the information is circulated outside the firm.

To Learn More

To review the materials covered in this chapter complete the CALI lesson on The Attorney's Duty of Confidentiality & the Attorney-client privilege at http://www.cali.org/lesson/1202.

A number of ALR Annotations address the scope of the corporate attorney-client privilege. You might find reviewing these useful to your learning:

Alexander C. Black, *Determination of Whether a Communication is from a Corporate Client for Purposes of the Attorney-Client Privilege—Modern Cases*, 26 A.L.R. 5th 628 (1995, 2012 Supp.).

Alexander C. Black, *What Corporate Communications are Entitled to Attorney-Client Privilege—Modern Cases*, 27 A.L.R. 5th 76 (1995, 2012 Supp.).

Alexander C. Black, *What Persons or Entities May Assert or Waive Corporation's Attorney-Client Privilege—Modern Cases*, 28 A.L.R. 5th 1 (1995, 2012 Supp.).

Chapter Ten

Exceptions to Confidentiality and Privilege Based on Consent and Waiver

Learning Objectives

After you have read this chapter and completed the assignments, you should be able to:

- Explain the scope of the attorney's implied authority to disclose information to further the representation, give examples of situations in which attorneys would regularly use this authority, and reflect on your comfort with the responsibility to exercise judgment on another person's behalf.

- Identify common circumstances in which you would be more or less likely to ask for consent to disclose confidential information or for the client to waive the attorney-client privilege.

- Identify who can consent to disclosure or to waiver when the client is an entity.

- Obtain a client's informed consent to disclosure of confidential information in a situation of common representation and draft a waiver or consent.

- Explain the effects of inadvertent disclosure of a client's information and implement steps to avoid or rectify these disclosures.

- Recognize the effect of waiving the privilege on the duty of confidentiality and the effect of consenting to disclose confidential information on the protection of the attorney-client privilege.

- Research case law involving issues of professional responsibility.

Rules to Study

In addition to continuing to examine Rule 1.6 and its exceptions, we will study Model Rule 4.4(b) and Federal Rule of Evidence 502.

Preliminary Problems

1. *The Wrong Man*

Revisit the Logan problem that you read in the introduction to this unit. Suppose you found yourself in a situation in which your client was guilty of a crime for which another, innocent, person was about to be convicted and sentenced. Depending on the sentence that innocent person receives there may not be an exception to confidentiality that would allow you to unilaterally disclose your client's information that would exonerate the innocent defendant.

A. Could you obtain your client's consent to do so? If you did obtain his consent and he was later convicted for that crime, would you have provided ineffective assistance of counsel?

B. If you could not obtain your client's permission and no exception would permit disclosure, you could not even disclose this information after your client dies without his permission because the duty of confidentiality and the attorney-client privilege survive even the client's death. Recall that in the Logan case, the public defenders had obtained their client's permission to reveal his confession after he had died. However, even then the court was unsure about whether that consent was a valid waiver of the attorney-client privilege. How would you obtain consent that would be enforceable after your client's death?

2. *The Talkative Defendant*

Alvin Andrews is a long-time client of your firm, which has represented him in various business and real estate ventures over the past seven years. Several months ago, Alvin sold several thousand shares of stock in DataMed, Inc., a company that develops and sells computer programs for use in medical applications. The following day, DataMed announced that it was recalling its premier program, used to transmit data from remote locations (emergency sites, rural communities) to major hospitals. DataMed, Inc. stock is traded on the NASDAQ National Market System, an electronic market system administered by the National Association of Securities Dealers, Inc. After the announcement, the price of DataMed stock fell dramatically.

Soon thereafter, the Securities and Exchange Commission, the FBI, and the U.S. Attorney began investigations into Alvin's sale of stock. Alvin came to your firm for assistance. Alvin wrote an extensive email to you explaining the circumstances of his sale of DataMed stock. Alvin later that evening forwarded a copy of this email to his stock broker Sam Seller, who had assisted in his sale of the stock.

The SEC has brought a civil action against Alvin for violation of securities laws. Moreover a grand jury has convened to investigate the sale and determine whether any crimes were committed.

A. Suppose the SEC offers to settle the civil matter in exchange for Alvin's cooperation in tracking down the source of the insider information that caused him to sell his stock. How would you counsel Alvin in making this decision? Would a confidentiality agreement in which the SEC would not share the information with others provide any significant protection?

B. Did Alvin waive the protections of the attorney-client privilege or work-product protection when he sent Seller a copy of his email communication?

C. What if Alvin had mistakenly sent the email to Seller, thinking he was sending a similarly named, but entirely different in content, document to him?

D. Would it matter if Seller was under investigation as well and you had entered into a joint defense agreement with Seller's attorney to share information, research, and strategies?

E. What if your firm becomes a target of the SEC investigation? Suppose Alvin tells government investigators that he had consulted with a member of your firm regarding the legality of his sale of stock. Suppose the government claims that you illegally assisted in the sale of stock. What can you reveal to defend yourself?

These questions of voluntary and involuntary disclosure are the subject of this chapter. Both the duty of confidentiality and the privilege are designed to protect clients and preserve their trust in their attorneys. The ethical duty protects clients against their own attorneys, who might use or disclose information in ways that harm the client. The attorney-client privilege protects the attorney-client communications against third parties who would seek to obtain that confidential information. It is the client's right to decide whether an attorney discloses information about the representation and whether to assert or to waive the attorney-client privilege.

So critical is this protection of the client's information that both the ethical duty and the evidentiary privilege extend after the representation is over, indeed even after the client has died. In *Swidler & Berlin v. United States*, 524 U.S. 399 (1998), the United States Supreme Court was asked to apply a balancing test to determine whether the attorney-client privilege should continue after a client's death—balancing the need for the information against the need to promote client trust in communicating with the attorney. The case involved Deputy White House Counsel Vincent Foster who committed suicide shortly after Congress began to investigate the 1993 dismissal of certain White House Travel Office employees. Foster had met with his attorney James Hamilton nine days before his death and the attorney had taken three pages of notes, noting "privileged" as one of the first entries in the notes. Special Prosecutor Kenneth Starr was appointed to investigate the death and subpoenaed the notes, to which Mr. Hamilton responded by invoking the attorney-client privilege.

The Supreme Court recognized that there existed an exception to the privilege that would allow an attorney who drafted a will to testify regarding his deceased client's intent in the course of a will contest. However, the Court was unwilling to expand posthumous exceptions beyond this and rejected the balancing test the lower court had used in deciding on the motion. In holding that the attorney-client privilege survives even the death of the client, the Court emphasized the importance of the privilege to maintaining trust in the attorney-client relationship.

Knowing that communications will remain confidential even after death encourages the client to communicate fully and frankly with counsel. While the fear of disclosure, and the consequent withholding of information from counsel, may be reduced if disclosure is limited to posthumous disclosure in a criminal context, it seems unreasonable to assume that it vanishes altogether. Clients may be concerned about reputation, civil liability, or possible harm to friends or family. Posthumous disclosure of such communications may be as feared as disclosure during the client's lifetime.

524 U.S. 399 at 407.

However, clients may give up the protections of the attorney-client privilege and release the attorney from the duty of confidentiality. A client may expressly authorize an attorney to disclose information or may voluntarily disclose information himself. An attorney is inherently authorized to make disclosures needed to further the client's objectives in the representation. Even inadvertent disclosures can act to waive the attorney-client privilege; though if the attorney was the cause of the negligent disclosure, there may be a violation of the duty of confidentiality. Sometimes a client's objectives cause a waiver of the ethical and evidentiary protections. For example, if a client makes a claim that requires disclosure of attorney-client communications, the client has waived the privilege. This chapter examines these exceptions.

10.1 Disclosing Confidential Information to Further the Representation

To represent a client, you will have to use and disclose much of the information you receive. You will want to share information with your fellow attorneys, clerks, and paralegals in order to carry out the representation. You will need to share information in order to conduct negotiations. You will need to present your client's information to advocate your client's position before a tribunal. The rules of professional conduct provide that an attorney is "impliedly authorized" to disclose information "in order to carry out the representation." Thus, you need not request your client's permission to use or disclose information in these ways.

Sometimes, a client may direct you to keep confidential information that you would otherwise ordinarily share. In those instances, absent a legal duty to disclose that information, you must respect the client's wishes. For example, ordinarily attorneys are impliedly authorized to share information within the firm. But suppose a client has hired you on a highly sensitive and embarrassing matter and wants you to handle the matter personally and not share that information with others in your firm. Obviously, you would at least need the client's consent to provide your firm sufficient information to be able to conduct conflict of interest checks. But assuming your client would agree to this much disclosure and no more, and you agree to represent this client under these conditions, you must take care to preserve the client's information even from your staff and other attorneys.

When in doubt, the best course of action is to obtain the client's consent to disclosure. Especially if your disclosure does not obviously advance the client's interest, you need to make sure the client's consent is informed. Look at the definition of "informed consent" in Rule 1.0 of the Model Rules. Under that definition, for a client to give informed consent to disclosure of confidential information, the client must understand the alternatives to disclosure and the risks and benefits of the choice to consent to disclosure. Having the client sign a "consent" is neither necessary nor sufficient, because, as you read in Chapter Eight, "informed consent" is not a signature on a form, it is a process of communication. The paper should merely evidence the process. That process should be one that insures that the client's consent is completely voluntary and well informed. ABA Comm. on Ethics and Prof'l Responsibility, Informal Op. 1287 (June 7, 1974). Some clients will require more counseling and assistance to obtain their informed consent than others.

Reconsider the preliminary problem in this chapter regarding the client who committed a crime for which another person is about to be sentenced. How could you counsel that client to reveal this information in a way that would be consistent with loyalty to the client? May you bring moral or humanitarian arguments to bear in counseling the client to permit disclosure? Model Rule 2.1 permits an attorney to discuss with the client those "moral, economic, social and political factors that may be relevant." Most attorneys would presume that the client's objective in the representation is to avoid conviction. However, that may not necessarily be so. Professor Cochran, an advocate of the collaborative model of the attorney-client relationship, argues that attorneys who do not discuss the possibility of confession with their criminal defense clients "ignore the possibility that the client might seek goals other than freedom, such as forgiveness, reconciliation, and a clear conscience …" Robert Cochran, *Crime, Confession, And The Counselor-At-Law: Lessons From Dostoyevsky*, 35 Hous. L. Rev. 327 (1998).

R 2.1

However, even if your client does want to confess, your duty of competence and loyalty require care in counseling the client how and whether to do so. First, you should be sure that your client fully understands the consequences of his or her choice. If you doubt the capacity of your client to make a reasoned decision, Model Rule 1.14 permits you to bring others into the decision-making process to assist, including family members and mental health professionals. Second, you should work to find a way for your client to disclose the information that would permit exoneration of the innocent party while at the same time reducing or eliminating the risk that your client would simply be trading places. For example, you could negotiate with a prosecutor for immunity or pursuing clemency from the executive in exchange for the exonerating information. Prosecutors have a duty to insure that wrongful convictions are remedied. *See, e.g.,* Model Rule 3.8(g) & (h).

duty to client

R 1.14

Before disclosing client information, you must also consider carefully the effect that disclosure may have on the attorney-client privilege or work-product protections. Any time a client, the client's lawyer, or another authorized agent of the client voluntarily discloses a privileged attorney-client communication in a non-privileged communication, the privilege is then lost. *Smith v. Smith*, 839 S.W.2d 382 (Mo. App. 1992). Disclosure of work-product information may waive that protection when the disclosure "substantially increased the opportunities for potential adversaries to obtain the information." 8 Charles Alan Wright, Arthur R. Miller & Richard L. Marcus, Federal Practice & Procedure § 2024 (1994). Disclosing documents to adversaries or potential adversaries, such as government agencies, may waive the work-product protection against those adversaries and even against different adversaries in future cases. *United States v. Martha Stewart*, 287 F. Supp. 2d 461 (S.D.N.Y. 2003). Thus, in the preliminary problem involving Alvin's sale of securities, Alvin's choice to send his broker a copy of his attorney-client communications very likely waived the privilege as to those communications.

Consider effects of disclosure

Sending to 3rd parties likely disclose + waives privilege

However, an attorney's disclosure of confidential information in one circumstance — even if that disclosure waives the attorney-client privilege or work-product protection — does not release the attorney from the duty to maintain the confidentiality of that information in other settings. So, for example, a court might order an attorney to testify to confidential client communication in a trial or grand jury proceeding. That same attorney may not then disclose that information to others on the theory that the information is no longer "confidential."

When your client is an entity, such as a corporation, the question of voluntary disclosures is even more complex. As you learned in the previous chapter, an entity such as a corporation enjoys the protections of the attorney-client privilege just as an individual. Recall that whether a particular individual's communication with the entity's attorney will fall within the privilege is a question with varying answers among the states, depending on whether they use the "control group" or "subject matter" tests.

However, the question of which entity persons are covered by the attorney-client privilege is different than the question of which entity persons have the power to waive the privilege. In that context, courts agree that the power to waive the corporate attorney-client privilege rests with the corporation's management. Ordinarily that would mean that the officers and directors of an organization have the authority to invoke or waive the privilege.

Go back to the preliminary problem 2(A) involving Alvin's sale of securities and the SEC's proposal that he waive attorney-client privilege and cooperate in the investigation. Why might he decide to waive attorney-client privilege? Faced with investigations or allegations of misconduct, Alvin may choose to disclose privileged communications as a public relations strategy, in the hopes of mitigating sentencing in a criminal action, or as part of a plea agreement. Sometimes government agencies attempt to encourage corporations to cooperate in investigations by agreeing that the documents being handed over to the government are protected by the attorney-client privilege and the work-product doctrine. These agreements also state that the client does not intend to waive these protections, and that it shares a common interest with the government in obtaining information regarding the investigated problems. A few courts have recognized this doctrine of "selective waiver" *Diversified Indus. v. Meredith*, 572 F.2d 596 (8th Cir. 1977). However, in most courts, by turning over privileged documents, the client is found to have waived its privilege claims for these materials, despite these agreements. Private litigants are then able to request the production of these documents in shareholder and other actions. Given this state of uncertainty in the law, how would you counsel Alvin in response to the SEC's proposal?

Reflective Practice: Exercising Judgment

As you can see, in the course of representing a client, you must be able to decide what you can and should say. You can't ask your client to approve every statement you make in the course of a representation. How comfortable are you exercising judgment on behalf of another person? Write a short reflection about circumstances in your life in which you may have already been in a position to speak or act on behalf of another person. Was it an easy role for you? Were you effective?

10.2 Confidentiality, Privilege, and Shared Representations

The relationship between waiver of privilege and consent to disclose confidential information is especially important to understand in the context of joint representations. When parties are represented by the same attorney, the law implies a waiver of the attorney-client privilege among them. McCormick, Evidence (E.Cleary, ed., 2d ed. 1972) §91, at 190 ("the communicating client, knowing that the attorney represents the other party also, would not ordinarily intend that the facts communicated should be kept secret from him.") The privilege is retained as against the rest of the world, however. So if an attorney speaks to Client A while Client B is present, the presence of B does not waive the privilege as it would if B were any other third party.

A similar rule applies when different lawyers represent different clients, but share a common interest. For example, suppose toxic waste is discovered on a tract of land. Both A and B are sued in a civil action for contribution under Section 113 of the Comprehensive Environmental Response, Compensation, and Liability Act ("CERCLA"), 42 U.S.C. §9613. They each retain their own attorneys. However, they share a common interest in prevailing in the lawsuit. A and B might enter into a joint defense agreement, in which they would freely exchange information and preparation between themselves. Even if Client A speaks with Client B's attorney, the conversation would be privileged. The common interest or joint-defense privilege allows the clients to share privileged information in order to prepare their cases without losing the protections of the attorney-client privilege. The joint-defense privilege can protect communications between parties in a range of circumstances in which they share an interest in preparing their case. "Whether an action is ongoing or contemplated, whether the jointly interested persons are defendants or plaintiffs, and whether the litigation or potential litigation is civil or criminal, the rationale for the joint defense rule remains unchanged: persons who share a common interest in litigation should be able to communicate with their respective attorneys and with each other to more effectively prosecute or defend their claims." *In re Grand Jury Subpoenas, 89-3 & 89-4*, 902 F.2d 244, 249 (4th Cir. 1990). The same rule would protect the privilege when clients represented by different attorneys are working together on a common transaction, such as forming a business together.

What is the effect of this waiver of privilege on the attorney's duty to maintain confidentiality between the joint and common interest clients? A number of authorities conclude that joint representation alone does not create an implied authorization to disclose one client's confidences to another. Accordingly, any time an attorney undertakes a joint representation, he should obtain the express consent of each client to share all information relating to the representation with the other client. Otherwise, the attorney may find himself in a situation in which, no matter what he does, he will be violating a rule.

Problems for Discussion

1. How, practically speaking, do you go about obtaining a consent to waive confidentiality among jointly represented clients if you don't know what kind of confidential information they each may have? Suppose that Albert, Barry, and Corrine have approached you to incorporate a business for them to market a new product (a better mousetrap). Albert is an inventor, Barry is the person with the money, and Corrine has marketing expertise. Barry and Corrine are married. Decide how you will discuss confidentiality and privilege among them.

2. A special setting in which there may or may not be a common interest is in the insurer-insured relationship. Many insurance policies contain a "cooperation clause" which may require insureds to turn over various kinds of information to their insurers. Would such a clause waive the insured's communications with his or her attorney? Would that waiver require insureds to share attorney-client privileged information with the insurance company

in a later litigation between the two over coverage issues? The Illinois Supreme Court in *Waste Management, Inc. v. International Surplus Lines Insurance Co.,* 579 N.E.2d 322 (Ill. 1991) held that the clause removed any expectation of confidentiality as against the insurer and so no privilege attached. Other courts have disagreed. *See, e.g., Rockwell Int'l Corp. v. Superior Court,* 32 Cal. Rptr. 2d 153 (Cal. Ct. App. 1994); *Metro. Life Ins. Co. v. Aetna Cas. & Sur. Co.,* 730 A.2d 51, 63-64 (Conn. 1999); *E. Air Lines, Inc. v. United States Aviation Underwriters, Inc.,* 716 So. 2d 340, 342-43 (Fla. Dist. Ct. App. 1998). Which position do you support?

3. Joint defense agreements are complex arrangements. To see an example of some of the operative clauses in one of these agreements, refer to *City of Kalamazoo v. Michigan Disposal Serv. Corp.,* 125 F. Supp. 2d 219, 2000 U.S. Dist. LEXIS 19982 (W.D. Mich. 2000).

4. Given what you have now learned, look again at the preliminary problem involving Alvin. What would be the consequence if Seller was under investigation as well and, on behalf of Alvin, you had entered into a joint defense agreement with Seller's attorney to share information, research, and strategies?

Professional Responsibility Skill 10-A: Drafting a Waiver of Confidentiality

Suppose you are representing Frank and Jen, who want to start a web design business together. Frank and Jen have been friends since high school and attended the same college. Frank majored in computer engineering and business and Jen majored in graphic design and communications. If you represent them both in setting up their business, there will be no attorney-client privilege between the two of them as a matter of law. However, you will still owe a duty of confidentiality to each of them. Ordinarily, you will be able to disclose information from one to the other without concern because that disclosure would be impliedly authorized to carry out the representation. However, you can't necessarily predict the future and there may be circumstances in which you might have information from or about one client that you would conclude you have a duty to disclose to the other client. Without consent to that disclosure, you might find yourself in a situation in which, no matter what you do, you are violating a rule of professional conduct. Think about how you would counsel your clients about confidentiality and draft the clauses you would put in your representation agreement that would avoid this dilemma.

10.3 Waiver by Inadvertent Disclosure

You can see that the attorney's duty of confidentiality includes the duty to protect the client's attorney-client privilege. Do attorneys have any duty to protect the confidential information of other clients? The situation of inadvertent disclosures is a situation that has tested this question of an ethical duty to preserve confidentiality in the attorney-client relationship generally, with no clear consensus on the answer. Certainly one can disclose information by mistake. Accidently including the wrong document in response to a production of documents, failing to press the "mute" button on the telephone during a negotiation, pressing the wrong "autodial" button on the fax machine, or hitting "reply to all" on an email—any one of these situations could result in your client's smoking gun landing on opposing counsel's desk.

How should an attorney act when he or she inadvertently receives an opposing party's confidential document, sent or faxed by mistake? The 2004 Model Rules (Rule 4.4(b)) require that the receiver "shall promptly notify the sender" but the comments note that any further duties are beyond the scope of the Rules. However, the ABA had previously issued a formal ethics opinion (ABA Comm. on Ethics and Prof'l Responsibility, Formal Op. 92-368 (1992)) that advised lawyers not to review inadvertently disclosed material and instead to contact the sender for instruction. Nearly as many states considering the matter have rejected this approach as have adopted it. The August 2012 amendments to the Model Rules addressed this ongoing issue by including a new section in Model Rule 1.6: "(c) A lawyer shall make reasonable efforts to prevent the inadvertent or unauthorized disclosure of, or unauthorized access to, information relating to the representation of a client." New comments delineate the cost-benefit factors to be considered in determining the reasonableness of the lawyer's efforts. The comments also point out that other law, such as data privacy laws, may create additional duties to protect client information from inadvertent disclosure.

If a receiving attorney seeks to use the mistakenly sent information, the sending attorney might raise the privilege if the information is a confidential attorney-client communication. How should courts apply the doctrine of waiver when the disclosure was the result of an error? Here too, jurisdictions disagree. Some have held that inadvertent disclosure always destroys the privilege, e.g., *Wichita Land & Cattle Co. v. Am. Fed. Bank FSB*, 148 F.R.D. 456 (D.D.C. 1992). Others conclude that an inadvertent disclosure does *not* waive the privilege. *Mendenhall v. Barber-Greene Co.*, 531 F. Supp. 936 (S.D. Fla. 1991). Most take a position between these two extremes in which the court balances a number of factors on a case-by-case basis to determine waiver. *Elkton Care Ctr. Assocs. v. Quality Care Mgmt.*, 805 A.2d 1177, (Md. Ct. Spec. App. 2002) (discussing three approaches and adopting intermediate position; court identifies five factors to consider in deciding whether circumstances amount to waiver of privilege); *Amersham Biosciences Corp. v. PerkinElmer Inc.*, No. 03-4901 (JLL), 2007 WL 329290 (D.N.J. Jan. 31, 2007) (applying five-factor test to party's inadvertent disclosure of privileged metadata). The Restatement embraces the intermediate position. RESTATEMENT (THIRD) OF THE LAW GOVERNING LAWYERS § 79 cmt. h (2000) (Reporter's Note indicates that majority of courts "take the intermediate position" and "preserve the privilege unless, in effect, the client's own negligence produced the compromising disclosure").

In late 2008, the Federal Rules of Evidence were amended to address the issue. That amendment to Rule 502(b) clarifies that inadvertent disclosure does not result in waiver when the holder of the privilege "took reasonable steps to prevent disclosure" and "promptly took reasonable steps to rectify the error."

Consider the following case applying that new rule:

Peterson v. Bernardi

District of New Jersey (July 24, 2009)

Joel Schneider, United States Magistrate Judge

This matter is before the Court on plaintiff's "Motion to Compel the Return of Inadvertently Produced Documents Pursuant to Fed. R. Civ. P.

26(b)(5)(B)." The issue to be addressed is whether plaintiff waived any privilege or discovery protection applicable to documents that were inadvertently produced. The Court has received defendants' opposition, the documents in question for review in camera, and defendants' supplemental letter brief. The Court also conducted oral argument. For the reasons to be discussed, plaintiff's motion is GRANTED in part and DENIED in part.

Background

By way of brief background, plaintiff alleges he was wrongfully imprisoned for over eighteen (18) years based on a false conviction for murder and rape. The essence of plaintiff's claim is that his conviction was based on the defendants' wrongful conduct. With the assistance of the Innocence Project the charges against plaintiff were dropped in May 2006, after DNA sample results indicated that the samples from the crime scene evidence did not match plaintiff's DNA profile.

Plaintiff filed his motion after he discovered that he inadvertently produced allegedly privileged and irrelevant documents. Plaintiff argues the documents are protected by the attorney-client privilege and work product doctrine. Plaintiff also claims two documents are protected by the cleric penitent privilege. Plaintiff argues the documents should be returned because he took reasonable steps to prevent the inadvertent disclosure. Plaintiff alleges he was under time constraints to produce documents and his inadvertent production was only a small percentage of the total number of produced documents.[1]

Defendants argue that a weighing of the factors in *Ciba-Geigy Corp. v. Sandoz Ltd.*, 916 F. Supp. 404, 411 (D.N.J. 1996), compels the conclusion that plaintiff's motion be denied. Defendants argue plaintiff cannot establish that he took reasonable steps to prevent the inadvertent disclosure. Defendants also argue the number and extent of plaintiff's disclosures support a finding of waiver. In addition, defendants argue plaintiff delayed seeking to rectify his disclosure and that the interests of justice are not served by relieving plaintiff of his error. Defendants also argue that plaintiff has not established that the documents in question are privileged.

Discussion

Although not cited by the parties, plaintiff's motion is controlled by Fed. R. Evid. 502(b). This Rule was recently amended and reads:

> **Rule 502. Attorney-client privilege and Work product; Limitations on waiver**

---

1. Plaintiff's motion identified 156 allegedly privileged documents that should be returned. However, after the Court reviewed the documents in camera it was evident that some of the documents were not privileged. *See* June 24, 2009 Letter Order. [Doc. No. 59]. The Court then directed plaintiff's counsel to identify the documents genuinely at issue." *Id.* On July 1, 2009, plaintiff identified approximately 135 documents that should be returned. It is again apparent that plaintiff's counsel did not carefully review the allegedly privileged documents. By way of example, plaintiff's list includes numerous letters from law students advising of their office schedule, and other letters simply enclosing copies of public documents. For the reasons discussed herein, these documents are clearly not privileged.

(b) Inadvertent disclosure. When made in a Federal proceeding or to a Federal Office or agency, the disclosure does not operate as a waiver in a Federal or State proceeding if:

(1) the disclosure is inadvertent;

(2) the holder of the privilege or protection took reasonable steps to prevent disclosure; and

(3) the holder promptly took reasonable steps to rectify the error, including (if applicable) following Federal Rule of Civil Procedure 26(b)(5)(B).

When deciding whether inadvertently produced documents should be returned a two-step analysis must be done. First, it must be determined if the documents in question are privileged. It is axiomatic that FRE 502 does not apply unless privileged or otherwise protected documents are produced. Second, if privileged documents were inadvertently produced then the three elements of FRE 502(b) must be satisfied (1) the disclosure must be inadvertent; (2) the holder of the privilege or protection took reasonable steps to prevent the disclosure, and; (3) the holder promptly took reasonable steps to rectify the error, including (if applicable) following Fed. R. Civ. P. 26(b)(5)(B). The disclosing party has the burden to prove that the elements of FRE 502(b) have been met.

FRE 502 does not change applicable case law which places the burden of proving that a privilege exists on the party asserting the privilege, in this case plaintiff. *Louisiana Mun. Police Employees Retirement System v. Sealed Air Corp.* ("*Sealed Air*"), 253 F.R.D. 300, 305-06 (D.N.J. 2008). Except as to one category of documents discussed infra, the Court finds that plaintiff has not satisfied this threshold burden. Plaintiff's moving papers essentially make no attempt to establish that the documents in question are privileged or otherwise protected from discovery. Plaintiff simply attached a privilege log and assumed that all the listed documents are protected by the attorney-client privilege and work product doctrine. Plaintiff's burden of proof is not satisfied by his broad unsupported allegations. *See NE Technologies, Inc. v. Evolving Systems, Inc., C.A.* No. 06-6061(MLC), 2008 WL 4277668, at *5 (D.N.J. Sept. 5, 2008) (citation omitted) (boiler plate objections, without an accompanying affidavit, lack specificity and constitute a waiver of such objections).

The Court recognizes that many of the documents at issue involve communications between plaintiff and the New Jersey Office of the Public Defender and the Innocence Project. However, not all communications between a client and lawyer are privileged. The attorney-client privilege only insulates communications that assist the attorney to formulate and render legal advice. *See Westinghouse Electric Corp. v. Republic of the Philippines*, 951 F.2d 1414, 1424 (3d Cir. 1991). The privilege does not apply simply because a statement was made by or to an attorney. *HPD Laboratories, Inc. v. Clorox Company*, 202 F.R.D. 410, 414 (D.N.J. 2001). Nor does the privilege attach "simply because a statement conveys advice that is legal in nature." *Id.* The attorney-client privilege only applies to disclosures necessary to obtain informed legal advice which might not have been made absent the privilege. *Id.* (citations omitted).

[handwritten margin note: No evidence by Π of anticipation of litigation + purpose]

In addition to failing to establish the attorney-client privilege, plaintiff also did not submit evidence that the produced documents were prepared in anticipation of litigation and primarily for the purpose of litigation. Plaintiff, therefore, has failed to establish that his documents are protected by the work product doctrine. *In re Gabapentin Patent Litigation*, 214 F.R.D. 178, 183 (D.N.J. 2003); *Sealed Air*, 253 F.R.D. at 306-07. Given plaintiff's failure to establish the threshold requirement that his documents are protected from discovery, and except as otherwise discussed herein, plaintiff's motion is denied.

Even if plaintiff established that the documents in question were privileged, plaintiff's motion would still be denied except as to one category of documents. Plaintiff, not defendants, has the burden of proving that his documents were inadvertently produced. FRE 502(b) opts for a middle ground approach to determine if an inadvertent disclosure operates as a waiver. *See* Explanatory Note to FRE 502(b) (revised November 28, 2007).[2] This is essentially the same approach used in *Ciba-Geigy Corp. v. Sandoz Ltd.*, 916 F. Supp. 404, 411 (D.N.J. 1996), which has been applied in New Jersey. Under the Ciba-Geigy approach at least

[handwritten margin note: FRE 502b, Ciba-Geigy approach 5 factors]

five factors are analyzed to determine if a waiver occurred (1) the reasonableness of the precautions taken to prevent inadvertent disclosure in view of the document production; (2) the number of inadvertent disclosures; (3) the extent of the disclosures; (4) any delay and measures taken to rectify the disclosure, and; (5) whether the overriding interests of justice would or would not be served by relieving the party of its error. *Ciba-Geigy*, 916 F. Supp. at 411.

As to the first relevant factor for consideration, which is specifically referenced in FRE 502(b)(2), the Court finds that at best, plaintiff took minimal steps to protect against inadvertent disclosure. Plaintiff's moving papers only mention one step that was taken to prevent an inadvertent error "[a]t each time [document production], plaintiff's counsel engaged in a privilege review." However, plaintiff does not state when his review occurred, how much time he took to review the documents, what documents were reviewed, and other basic details of the review process. The Court does not accept plaintiff's bare allegation that he conducted a "privilege review" as conclusive proof that he took reasonable steps to prevent an inadvertent production.

[handwritten margin note: How do you suppose that happened?]

Plaintiff argues that in the course of his document review he identified a group of privileged documents, but the documents "were mistakenly not separated, and inadvertently produced to defendants." However, plaintiff did not proffer any facts to establish that reasonable precautions were taken to prevent this from occurring. Nor does plaintiff explain how other allegedly privileged documents come to be inadvertently produced. For the purpose of deciding plaintiff's motion, the Court does not question the sincerity of plaintiff's argument that he did not intend to produce the documents in question. However, plaintiff's subjective intent is not controlling. All inadvertent disclosures are by definition unintentional. *Ciba-Geigy*, 916 F. Supp. at 411.

---

2. The Note discusses a "multi-factor test for determining whether inadvertent disclosure is a waiver." These factors include the reasonableness of precautions taken, the time taken to rectify the error, the scope of discovery, the extent of disclosure and the overriding issue of fairness. Other factors are the number of documents to be reviewed and the time constraints for production. *Id.* No one factor is dispositive. "The rule ... is really a set of non-determinative guidelines that vary from case to case" and is designed to be "flexible." *Id.*

As to the other factors relevant to whether an inadvertent production occurred, the Court finds that on the whole they weigh in favor of waiver. Although on a total percentage basis the number of disclosures is small (approximately 135 out of thousands produced), the nature of the disclosures is relevant. Most of the documents in question are exchanges between plaintiff and his counsel. These communications warranted a significant level of scrutiny. Further, 135 documents is not an insignificant number. As to plaintiff's efforts to rectify his error, the Court finds this factor neutral. Although plaintiff did not alert defendants until months after his documents were produced when he was preparing for a deposition, plaintiff brought the error to defendants' attention within a week or two of his discovery. See *Heriot v. Byrne*, __ F.R.D. __, 2009 WL 742769, at *15 (N.D. Ill. March 20, 2009) ("how the disclosing party discovers and rectifies the disclosure is more important than when after the inadvertent disclosure the discovery occurs"). Plaintiff was not required to "engage in a postproduction review to determine whether any protected communication or information [was] ... produced by mistake." Explanatory Note, *supra*.

The interests of fairness and justice would not be served by relieving plaintiff of the consequences of counsel's error. *See Ciba-Geigy*, 916 F. Supp. at 414 ("the interests of justice would be served by a finding of waiver, whe, as here, a party's negligence has resulted in the inadvertent production of a privilege document"). Parties must recognize that there are potentially harmful consequences if they do not take minimal precautions to prevent against the disclosure of privileged documents. Further, in contrast to the documents discussed infra, no unfairness or injustice would result from finding that a waiver occurred.[3]

The Court rejects plaintiff's argument that his inadvertent disclosure should be excused because his privilege review was conducted under "extremely limited time constraints." Defendants' document request was served on November 27, 2007.... [T]he Court Ordered plaintiff to complete his document production by July 31, 2008, approximately eight months after defendants' document requests were served. Although plaintiff made a document production by July 31, 2008, as late as October, 2008, the production was not complete. On October 10, 2008, the Court Ordered plaintiff to complete his document production by October 31, 2008. Plaintiff's counsel contends he did not discover he inadvertently produced documents until sometime after February 9, 2009 when he was preparing for plaintiff's scheduled March 3, 2009 deposition. On February 19, 2009, plaintiff identified the inadvertently produced documents in his log produced to defendant. This background makes it clear that plaintiff had more than an adequate opportunity to respond to defendants' document request without feeling "rushed." Plaintiff's counsel only has himself to blame for the Court's insistence that he complete his doc-

---

3. The Court has reviewed all of the inadvertently produced documents. In the context of the primary issues to be litigated in the case, the documents will likely be inconsequential. (Nevertheless, as noted, they are discoverable). The Court reaches this conclusion because the documents generally discuss plaintiff's efforts from at least as early as 1990 to overturn his criminal conviction. This is not a disputed issue in the case. Further, on the whole the documents do not reveal any confidential information or attorney work-product that in the Court's opinion will have a material impact on the outcome of the case.

[Margin note: Nature of disclosures weigh in favor of disclosure]

[Margin note: Does eight months to review and produce thousands of documents seem extremely limited time to you?]

[Margin note: What should plaintiff's attorney have done when he knew at the end of July that he would not have all the documents produced?]

ument production by July 31, 2008 and October 31, 2008. The time constraints about which plaintiff now complains were self-imposed and do not excuse his careless actions. *Accord Ciba-Geigy*, 916 F. Supp. at 413.

Do you agree?

In sum, therefore, for all but a separate category of documents the Court denies plaintiff's motion. Since the documents are not privileged a FRE 502(b) analysis is not necessary.

Even if the documents were privileged, plaintiff has not established that all the elements of FRE 502(b) were met. Plaintiff did not demonstrate that the documents were inadvertently produced within the meaning of FRE 502(b)(1). Plaintiff also did not establish that he took reasonable steps to prevent disclosure within the meaning of FRE 502(b)(2).

Documents P006988-6996

Do you think the fact that the documents were prepared by student interns influenced the court's analysis? Should it have?

Despite the Court's ruling, however, the Court finds that documents P006988-6996 deserve special treatment. These nine (9) pages were prepared by student interns of the Innocence Project in 2003 and 2005 and describe in detail their litigation strategy and work product. The documents address in detail what plaintiff's attorneys and their representatives did to get plaintiff released from prison. In contrast to the other inadvertently produced documents, these documents are so obviously work product that no extrinsic evidence is necessary to establish this fact.

The Court's ruling is not made in a vacuum. The Court is mindful that the case involves plaintiff's claim that he was wrongfully imprisoned for eighteen years. It is undisputed that all charges against plaintiff were dropped in May 2006 even though he was convicted of rape and murder in 1989 and sentenced to life imprisonment. It is also undisputed that DNA tests in 2004 and 2005 on crime scene evidence did not match plaintiff. Given the nature of documents POO6988-6996, and the manner in which they were produced to defendants, the Court finds that the interests of fairness and justice are furthered by ruling that the work product protection attached to the documents was not waived.

What are the interests of fairness and justice the court was considering? What do you think of this interpretation of the rule?

The interests of fairness and justice are relevant factors to analyze to determine if inadvertently produced documents should be returned. Explanatory Note, *supra*; *Ciba-Geigy*, 916 F. Supp. at 411, 414. *See also* Fed. R. Civ. P. 1 (the Federal Rules should be construed and administered to secure the just determination of every action and proceeding). The Court rules that the interests of fairness and justice so overwhelmingly favor plaintiff with regard to documents POO6988-6996, that they outweigh the fact that at best plaintiff's counsel exercised minimal precautions to protect the documents from inadvertent disclosure.

The application of FRE 502(b) was designed to be flexible. This flexibility authorizes the Court to find that a waiver did not occur in circumstances in which an injustice to the client would result from a contrary ruling. It is rare that a Court will not find that a waiver occurred in an instance when a party presents only minimal evidence that it exercised reasonable precautions to prevent a waiver. This is one of those rare occurrences.

The Court does not believe that documents POO86988-6996 are determinative in the case. Although work product, the documents generally summarize events about which there is little dispute. In fact, an outside observer could reasonably opine that the documents help rather than hurt plaintiff's case. The Court would not be surprised if on reflection plaintiff decides to voluntarily produce the documents. Nevertheless, given the unusual circumstances of the case, the Court rules that plaintiff has the right to make an informed decision as to whether documents POO6988-6996 should be produced. The interests of fairness and justice demand no less.

Conclusion

Accordingly, for all the foregoing reasons, IT IS HEREBY ORDERED this 24th day of July, 2009, that plaintiff's Motion to Compel the Return of Inadvertently Produced Documents Pursuant to Fed. R. Civ. P. 26(b)(5)(B), is GRANTED in part and DENIED in part; and IT IS FURTHER ORDERED that pursuant to FRE 502(d) any privilege or discovery protection attached to documents POO86988-6996 is not waived by the inadvertent disclosure in this court. Pursuant to Fed. R. Civ. P. 26(b)(5)(B), defendants must destroy or promptly return all copies of the documents and any copies they have, and take reasonable steps to retrieve all copies of the documents they distributed; and IT IS FURTHER ORDERED that as to all other documents subject to plaintiff's motion, the motion is DENIED and all discovery privileges or protections applicable to the documents shall be deemed waived.

Questions

1. Notice that the means by which the plaintiff raised the privilege as to the documents was through a "privilege log." The Federal Rules of Civil Procedure require that:

> When a party withholds information otherwise discoverable under these rules by claiming that it is privileged or subject to protection as trial preparation material, the party shall make the claim expressly and shall describe the nature of the documents, communications, or things not produced or disclosed in a manner that, without revealing information itself privileged or protected, will enable other parties to assess the applicability of the privilege or protection.

Fed. R. Civ. Pro. 26(B)(5).

The failure to use the privilege log and to provide sufficient detail in that log can itself be a basis for waiving both the attorney-client privilege and work-product protection. One district court provides the following guidance in using privilege logs:

> A party seeking to avoid discovery cannot hide behind bald statements of "privilege" and "work-product" and expect the court to supply the rational to support the claims. *See Obiajulu v. City of Rochester Dep't of Law,* 166 F.R.D. 293, 295 (W.D.N.Y.1996). At the very least, the log should identify each document's author and recipient, as well as reasons why the information is claimed to be privileged. *See United States v. Construction Prod. Research,* 73 F.3d 464, 473 (2d Cir.1996). The priv-

ilege log is not simply a technicality, it is essential tool which allows the parties and the court to make an intelligent decision as to whether a privilege or immunity exists. *See Bowne v. AmBase,* 150 F.R.D. 465, 474 (S.D.N.Y.1993). Preparation of a privilege log is a critical step in discharging one's burden of establishing the existence of a privilege.

In asserting a claim of privilege, counsel should take care not to withhold unprivileged information. It is not proper to withhold an entire document from discovery on grounds that a portion of it may be privileged. Where a document purportedly contains some privileged information, the unprivileged portions of the document must be produced during discovery. The proper procedure in such instances is to redact the allegedly privileged communication, and produce the redacted document. The allegedly privileged information then should be described in a properly executed privilege log.

Breon v. Coca-Cola Bottling Co. of New England, 232 F.R.D. 49, __ (D. Conn. 2005).

2. The court here found that most of the documents did not even qualify for privilege in the first place. Because assertions of privilege raise costs and slow down proceedings, attorneys should not raise objections based on privilege without a good faith basis to do so. Abusing the privilege can provide an independent basis for waiver of privileges. In *Novelty, Inc. v. Mountain View Marketing, Inc.,* -—F.R.D.——, 2009 WL 3444591 (S.D. Ind. Oct. 21, 2009), the plaintiff in a copyright action had failed repeatedly to search for and provide non-privileged responsive information, including failing to request employees to search for responsive emails, and instructing employees to identify only helpful documents. In addition, the plaintiff had not timely provided the court with a proper privilege log, even after the court ordered plaintiff to do so. The court sanctioned plaintiff pursuant to FRCP 37, by holding that plaintiff had waived all privileges.

3. Consider the position of the plaintiffs in *Peterson* after the court's decision. The court has read their "privileged documents" (and even described what they are about and opined as to their usefulness or lack thereof). The defendant has surely read all these documents as well. Of what real value is the court's order that some of these documents be returned or destroyed?

4. Look again at the preliminary problem involving Alvin Andrews and his inadvertent email. Are you better able to advise Alvin regarding whether he has waived the privilege with his disclosure?

10.4 Waiver by Placing a Matter in Evidence

Waiver of the attorney-client privilege and work-product protections can occur whenever the client or attorney places the confidential communication at issue in trial (*State ex rel. Chase Resorts, Inc. v. Campbell,* 913 S.W.2d 832 (Mo. App. 1996)), or even, if the client's attorney simply fails to object to the efforts to obtain privileged communications or protected work product. *Hollins v. Powell,* 773 F.2d 191, 197 (8th Cir.1985). In pretrial discovery, this rule can threaten the progress of discovery, as attorneys worry about waiver if they do not continually object. To prevent this disruption, federal and state procedural rules often permit parties to stipulate that privilege is not waived by failure to object during pretrial discovery (*see* Federal Rules of Civil Procedure, Rule 29).

The most common situation in which this waiver occurs is in the context of a defense based on opinion of counsel. For example, in patent practice, a client may ask an attorney to give an opinion on whether a particular use or product would infringe another's patent. If the client is later sued for infringement, the client would ordinarily deny the allegation of "willfulness" (an essential element of infringement) by arguing that she had relied on the attorney's opinion. However, "when an alleged infringer asserts its advice-of-counsel defense regarding willful infringement of a particular patent, it waives its immunity for any document or opinion that embodies or discusses a communication to or from it concerning whether that patent is valid, enforceable, and infringed by the accused." *In re Echostar Commc'ns Corp.*, 448 F.3d 1294, 1304 (Fed. Cir. 2006). Advice of counsel defenses can arise in other types of actions as well.

In the following case, Convolve, Inc., and Massachusetts Institute of Technology had asserted claims of patent infringement and theft of trade secrets against Compaq Computer Corp. and Seagate Technology, Inc. Seagate manufactures disk drives, while Compaq produces and distributes computer systems. Convolve had shared information with Seagate and Compaq about a computer technology. Seagate had incorporated a similar technology in its production. Before doing so, it consulted with patent attorneys regarding the scope of Convolve's rights. Convolve sued, alleging that Seagate had stolen its patented technology and willfully infringed its patent. Seagate raised an "advice of counsel" defense to the willfulness claim.

Convolve then subpoenaed all the communications between Seagate and the attorney who had provided the advice regarding the scope of Convolve's patent (opinion counsel), claiming that Seagate had waived the privilege by raising this defense. However, it claimed that the scope of that waiver applied, not only to all of Seagate's communications with opinion counsel, but also all of its communications with the attorneys it had hired to defend it in the infringement action (trial counsel). Consider how the court resolved the question of whether the waiver of privilege should extent to communications with trial counsel.

In re Seagate Technology, LLC

497 F.3d 1360 (Fed. Cir. 2007),

cert. denied, Convolve, Inc. v. Seagate Tech., LLC, 552 U.S. 1230 (2008)

... "The widely applied standard for determining the scope of a waiver ... is that the waiver applies to all other communications relating to the same subject matter." *Fort James Corp. v. Solo Cup Co.*, 412 F.3d 1340, 1349 (Fed.Cir.2005). This broad scope is grounded in principles of fairness and serves to prevent a party from simultaneously using the privilege as both a sword and a shield; that is, it prevents the inequitable result of a party disclosing favorable communications while asserting the privilege as to less favorable ones. *In re EchoStar Commc'ns. Corp.*, 448 F.3d 1294, 1301 (Fed.Cir.2006); *Fort James*, 412 F.3d at 1349. Ultimately, however, "[t]here is no bright line test for determining what constitutes the subject matter of a waiver, rather courts weigh the circumstances of the disclosure, the nature of the legal advice sought and the prejudice to the parties of permitting or prohibiting further disclosures." *Fort James*, 412 F.3d at 1349-50.

No extension of waiver to trial counsel

Do you agree that opinion counsel is so different from trial counsel?

In considering the scope of waiver resulting from the advice of counsel defense, district courts have reached varying results with respect to trial counsel. Recognizing the value of a common approach ... we conclude that the significantly different functions of trial counsel and opinion counsel advise against extending waiver to trial counsel. Whereas opinion counsel serves to provide an objective assessment for making informed business decisions, trial counsel focuses on litigation strategy and evaluates the most successful manner of presenting a case to a judicial decision maker. And trial counsel is engaged in an adversarial process. Because of the fundamental difference between these types of legal advice, this situation does not present the classic "sword and shield" concerns typically mandating broad subject matter waiver. Therefore, fairness counsels against disclosing trial counsel's communications on an entire subject matter in response to an accused infringer's reliance on opinion counsel's opinion to refute a willfulness allegation.

Moreover, the interests weighing against extending waiver to trial counsel are compelling. The Supreme Court recognized the need to protect trial counsel's thoughts in *Hickman v. Taylor*, 329 U.S. 495, 510-11, 67 S. Ct. 385, 91 L. Ed. 451 (1947):

> [I]t is essential that a lawyer work with a certain degree of privacy, free from unnecessary intrusion by opposing parties and their counsel. Proper preparation of a client's case demands that he assemble information, sift what he considers to be the relevant from the irrelevant facts, prepare his legal theories and plan his strategy without undue and needless interference. That is the historical and the necessary way in which lawyers act within the framework of our system of jurisprudence to promote justice and to protect their clients' interests.

The Court saw that allowing discovery of an attorney's thoughts would result in "[i]nefficiency, unfairness and sharp practices," that "[t]he effect on the legal profession would be demoralizing" and thus "the interests of the clients and the cause of justice would be poorly served." *Id.* at 511. Although *Hickman* concerned work product protection, the attorney-client privilege maintained with trial counsel raises the same concerns in patent litigation. In most cases, the demands of our adversarial system of justice will far outweigh any benefits of extending waiver to trial counsel.

Rule: No waiver for trial counsel

What kind of exceptional circumstances do you think would provide an exception to the rule the court crafts here?

In sum, we hold, as a general proposition, that asserting the advice of counsel defense and disclosing opinions of opinion counsel do not constitute waiver of the attorney-client privilege for communications with trial counsel. An advice of counsel defense asserted to refute a charge of willful infringement may also implicate waiver of work product protection. Again, we are here confronted with whether this waiver extends to trial counsel's work product. We hold that it does not, absent exceptional circumstances.

Question

This particular litigation produced volumes of discovery disputes, of which this was only one. The suit began in 2000 and the parties were still embroiled in disputes at the end of 2011. Events in the suit included an award of sanctions against Convolve for violation of rules of discovery, *Convolve, Inc. v. Compaq Computer Corp.*, 223 F.R.D. 162 (S.D.N.Y. 2004) and a motion to permit late introduction of evidence when a former Seagate engineer provided an affidavit in December 2010 claiming that Seagate had destroyed evidence of its infringement. *Convolve, Inc., Plaintiffs' Memorandum of Law Supporting Their Motion to Supplement the Summary Judgment Record with New Material Evidence and for Other Relief Required in the Interests of Justice* (Nov. 30, 2009), 2009 WL 7450568.

10.5 Attorney Self-Defense Exceptions

In a number of circumstances, you may wish to disclose or use confidential client information to protect yourself or further your own interests. The ABA Model Rules have always provided an attorney "self-defense" exception to confidentiality, as did the ABA Model Code before. That self-defense exception provides that an attorney may disclose confidential client information in three circumstances: in a suit between the lawyer and client (including a fee collection action); in an action against the lawyer by the government or a third party in which the representation of the client is central to the charge; and in an action in which the attorney's conduct in the representation has been called into question (as, for example, when a former criminal defense client brings an ineffective assistance of counsel claim). In many, but not all, instances, these exceptions are grounded in a notion of waiver — the client's conduct waives his right to confidentiality.

The attorney-client privilege and work-product doctrines have similar self-defense exceptions. Restatement (Third) of the Law Governing Lawyers, § 83 (2000) provides:

> The attorney-client privilege does not apply to a communication that is relevant and reasonably necessary for a lawyer to employ in a proceeding:
>
> (1) to resolve a dispute with a client concerning compensation or reimbursement that the lawyer reasonably claims the client owes the lawyer; or
>
> (2) to defend the lawyer or the lawyer's associate or agent against a charge by any person that the lawyer, associate, or agent acted wrongfully during the course of representing a client.

The most common use of this exception is in order to collect fees. Uniform Rule of Evidence 502(d)(3), for example, provides that the attorney-client privilege does not apply "[a]s to a communication relevant to an issue of breach of duty ... by the client to his lawyer." The court in *Clark v. United States*, 289 U.S. 1, 15 (1933) commented that "The privilege takes flight if the relation is abused." Suppose, for example, you have been representing a client in litigation involving a property dispute. The client has not paid your fee for the past three months, despite repeated requests and warnings that you would seek to withdraw if the client did not bring his account up to date. Obviously you can't just quit representing the client until he pays. You have a duty of diligence — to carry through representation until the end or until you have properly withdrawn. Model Rule 1.3. You also have the duty to expedite litigation. Model Rule 3.2. While as a practical matter, you may choose not to undertake "discretionary" tasks for the client, you can't simply stop working on the case. You either represent a client or you withdraw, following the dictates of Model Rule 1.16(d). You don't leave a client in limbo. *See* Model Rule 1.3, Comment 4.

However, you do know from your study of Rule 1.16 that you would be permitted to seek permission to withdraw under these circumstances. Must you disclose that the client has not paid? Comment 3 to Rule 1.16 notes that "the lawyer may be bound to keep confidential the facts that would constitute such an explanation" and suggests that "the lawyer's statement that professional considerations require termination of the representation ordinarily should be accepted as sufficient." Ordinarily you will not need to disclose confidential information in order to withdraw.

Withdrawal won't get the fee paid, however. May the attorney go further in disclosing information in order to collect the fee? For example, may you turn the client's bill over to a collection agency? The exception to Rule 1.6 that permits you to "establish a claim" would allow this action, as long as disclosure of client information is limited. So, for example, you can provide the dates and amounts due but not the services rendered or any other information about the representation. Reporting to credit agencies is not generally favored because it is not necessary to resolve the compensation dispute and is a disclosure that is greater than reasonably necessary to get the fee. Model Rule 1.6 permits you to disclose client information to the limited extent necessary in the course of attempting to collect your fees, not to punish, shame, or retaliate.

May you sue the client to recover the fee? That seems the clearest example of Model Rule 1.6's reference to "establish a claim" and is the first category of exception to the privilege in the Restatement. Even here, remember that the disclosure of information in that suit must be limited to that necessary to collect the fee. You may not use the suit as an excuse to threaten to reveal any of the client's secrets (e.g., a secret love affair) in order to coerce payment of the fee. That is not "necessary" to establish or collect the fee (at least not in the sense that the disclosure is necessary to establish a claim or a defense). In many states, such a threat constitutes the crime of extortion. That doesn't mean you would not be able to use information you have about the client's finances to further your claim to recover your fee, however. In *Nikasian v. Incontrade,* 409 F. Supp. 1220 (S.D.N.Y. 1976), for example, the court permitted an attorney to attach the client's property about which he had learned in the course of representing the client. If the threat to disclose or the disclosure of client information appears to be overreaching or retaliation, severe discipline can follow, so attorneys should err on the side of the least disclosure necessary to achieve the aim of collecting the fee.

The self-defense exception to confidentiality and privilege also applies when the attorney is being sued by the client. One of the most obvious settings in which a client will have waived the attorney-client privilege by placing the communication at issue is when the client sues the attorney for malpractice. *Ryers v. Burleson,* 100 F.R.D. 436 (D.D.C. 1983) (allegation of lawyer malpractice constituted a waiver of confidential communications under the circumstances). However, this exception to both confidentiality and privilege applies even if the person accusing the attorney of wrongdoing is someone other than the client. Attorneys might be subject to civil or criminal actions, along with or separate from their clients, arising out of their representation. In those circumstances, the attorney should advise the client of the claim by the third person and ask the client to respond or to waive confidentiality to permit you to respond. However, even if the client refuses, the attorney may disclose information necessary to vindicate himself. *Meyerhoffer v. Empire Marine & Fire Ins. Co.,* 497 F.2d 1190 (2d Cir.), *cert. denied,* 419 U.S. 998 (1974) (self-defense exception to attorney-client privilege permitted attorney to testify regarding client confidences to defend himself against a 10b-5 claim); *See, e.g., In re National Mtge Equity Corp. Mtge Pool Certif. Secur. Litig,* 120 F.R.D. 687 (D.C. Calif. 1988) (law firm may disclose otherwise confidential attorney-client communications over the client's objections asserting the privilege when the firm has been charged as co-defendant in securities fraud and other violations). As with any other exception, the disclosure should be no greater than necessary and should be made in a manner that limits access to the information to the tribunal and to persons needing to know. For example, the attorney in *In re Huffman,* 983 P.2d 534 (Ore. 1999) was disciplined for making disclosures of confidential information that were not required to assert a viable defense.

[handwritten margin note: *must limit disclosure to min amt req*]

One issue that arises in applying this exception is determining what constitutes a sufficient "accusation" for the exception to apply. Comments to the Model Rules indicate that the right of an attorney to reveal information in a dispute concerning the client's conduct arises when the assertion of complicity is raised. You need not wait until you are sued. For example, a former criminal defense client may raise issues regarding your competent representation in an ineffective assistance of counsel claim. While you must take care in responding to protect the defendant's due process rights, this is the kind of situation in which you are permitted to make limited disclosures necessary to defend yourself.

There is one category of "self-defense" that is an exception to the ethical duty of confidentiality but not an exception to attorney-client privilege: that is, when an attorney seeks advice about his professional duty. Suppose for example you are trying to determine whether you have a conflict of interest in representing a particular client, so you decide to call up your former professional responsibility professor for some advice. You don't ask for your client's consent because you aren't sure that you can tell your client about the information that may have created the conflict. Have you violated your ethical duty? Rule 1.6 provides an express exception for this disclosure to your law professor in order to obtain advice, but there is no parallel exception to the privilege expressly for this purpose. Of course, if your professor is a licensed attorney, the attorney-client privilege applies to your communication with the professor, but that privilege belongs to you and not to the client. Thus, you should take care when asking for advice about your professional responsibilities to avoid disclosing attorney-client communications if at all possible and ask clients for consent to disclose whenever that is feasible.

[handwritten margin note: *Rl. 6 professor privilege exception ok ... but limited*]

Researching Professional Responsibility 10-A: Finding Case Law on Professional Responsibility Issues

Many issues of confidentiality are fact sensitive and often involve doctrines, such as the attorney-client privilege, that have their development in common law doctrines. Thus case law research will be particularly important in researching your state's approach to many of these issues. The methods you have thus far learned in law school to research case law apply to researching cases in this field as well. In addition, other sources that can be helpful for finding cases include:

The ABA/BNA Lawyers Manual on Professional Conduct, in both its practice guides and current reports sections provides case summaries and citations (see Chapter Two for a discussion of this resource).

The ABA's Annotated Model Rules of Professional Conduct (6th ed. 2007) provides commentary on each rule and citations to supporting cases and ethics opinions. This treatise is also available on Westlaw (ABA-AMRPC).

The Restatement (Third) of the Law Governing Lawyers, (discussed in the prior chapter) provides case citations both to support its restatement and to cases citing the restatement.

Both Lexis and Westlaw have databases of cases interpreting ethics rules. In Lexis, the ETHICS library has files for each state and one for all states. In Westlaw, there are individual state databases and databases for all federal (FETH-CS) and all state cases (METH-CS).

Shepard's Professional and Judicial Conduct Citations (1991-) provides citations to authorities interpreting the Model Rules, Model Code, and ABA formal opinions. Citations include cases, ethics opinions, and law review articles. This resource is available in hard copy only — the electronic versions of Shepard's and KeyCite do not cover the model rules.

Always be careful with cases as they may not be interpreting the same standard you are trying to interpret. The language used may look the same (e.g. "confidential") but the meaning may be quite different depending on the context (e.g. discipline, disqualification, or application of the attorney-client privilege, or ineffective assistance of counsel). Accordingly, one should first focus research on the particular context in which an issue arises. Only if this produces no guidance should one look to similar standards from other contexts.

Dates are important too. Court attitudes toward certain conduct have changed in regard to the practice of law just as in any other area of law (the attitude toward attorney advertising is perhaps the best example of significant change).

Practice your case law research skills with the following problem that has increasingly arisen in application of a self-defense exception to privilege and the ethical duty of confidentiality. Suppose you are representing a client and a question arises as to whether your firm's representation of another client raises a conflict of interest with your current client. You consult your firm's internal ethics counsel on the question and receive advice about how to decrease the risks of the conflict. You follow almost all that advice except for the directions to discuss the matter with your client. For reasons entirely unrelated to the conflict, your representation does not go very well and the client fires you. You again consult with ethics counsel about how to respond to the client's dismissal. Soon thereafter, you find yourself facing a malpractice suit. Your former client's attorney demands that you produce all correspondence between you and ethics counsel regarding your representation of the client. How do you respond? Research this issue, first in your state, and if you find no definitive answers in your own state's case law, search for cases from state or federal courts with similar rules of attorney-client privilege and work-product immunity.

Test Your Understanding

Edgar Lim is an immigration attorney. Ganesh and Padma Krishnamurthy hired him to assist them to obtain a work visa and labor certification enabling Mr. Krishnamurthy to work in the United States and a residency permit for Mrs. Krishnamurthy. Mr. Lim requested a flat fee of $4,500 for this work. The Krishnamurthys paid him $1,000. He did not have a written fee agreement but did tell his clients that he charged late charges of $20 per month plus 9% per year. The Krishnamurthys paid Respondent $1,000.

In October, four months after he was retained, the clients had still not paid Mr. Lim any additional part of the fees. Mr. Lim terminated his representation and sent the Krishnamurthys a letter advising them that "once we are paid…, we will release your labor certification which is still our property until you pay for it." In November, he sued the Krishnamurthys for unpaid fees. In December, he instructed his daughter and law partner to send a letter, on Lim & Lim letterhead, to the Krishnamurthys, threatening to report them to the United States Immigration and Naturalization Service (INS) if they failed to pay immediately. In February of the following year, Mr. Lim sent a letter to the INS reporting that the Krishnamurthys "lack the good moral character needed to obtain immigration benefits" because they had "lied and deceived our office" and had an outstanding balance of "over $7,000." Respondent asked the INS to place the letter in the Krishnamurthys' file "to prevent them from obtaining any further immigration benefits."

The Krishnamurthys have hired you to represent them in the collection action Mr. Lim has brought against them. Are you required to report Mr. Lim to disciplinary authorities for having written this letter to the INS or is this disclosure authorized by the rules and so not a violation? *In re Edgar E. Lim,* 210 S.W.3d 199 (Mo. banc 2007).

To Learn More

To read more about counseling clients and confidentiality, see Stephen Ellmann, *Truth and Consequences*, 69 FORDHAM L. REV. 895 (2000)

For more examples and explanation of waiver and consent issues addressed in this chapter, read the following sections of Chapter Five (Confidential Client Information) of the Restatement (Third) of the Law Governing Lawyers:

Topic 1 — Confidentiality Responsibilities of Lawyers

    Title B — Using or Disclosing Confidential Client Information

        § 61 Using or Disclosing Information to Advance Client Interests

        § 62 Using or Disclosing Information with Client Consent

        § 64 Using or Disclosing Information in a Lawyer's Self-Defense

        § 65 Using or Disclosing Information in a Compensation Dispute

Topic 2 — The Attorney-client privilege

    Title C — Duration of the Attorney-client privilege; Waivers and Exceptions

        § 78 Agreement, Disclaimer, or Failure to Object

        § 79 Subsequent Disclosure

        § 80 Putting Assistance or a Communication in Issue

        § 81 A Dispute Concerning a Decedent's Disposition of Property

        § 83 Lawyer Self-Protection

        § 84 Fiduciary-Lawyer Communications

        § 85 Communications Involving a Fiduciary Within an Organization

Chapter Eleven

Exceptions to Confidentiality Designed to Protect Third Persons

Learning Objectives

After you have read this chapter and completed the assignments, you should be able to:

- Identify three common categories of exceptions to confidentiality designed to protect third persons and express a well-informed opinion regarding the policy wisdom of each of these categories.

- Define key concepts of exceptions to confidentiality to protect third persons including "fraud," "knowledge," and "informed consent," and be able to apply these terms to determine whether an exception to confidentiality exists in a given circumstance.

- Identify laws other than the rules of conduct that may require an attorney to disclose confidential client information.

- Identify how you think you would react when you have the discretion, but are not required, to disclose client information.

Rules to Study

This chapter focuses on the exceptions to confidentiality found in Rule 1.6 and Rule 1.13 and the parallel exceptions to the attorney-client privilege.

Preliminary Problem

Reconsider once more the Alton Logan case introduced in Chapter Ten. Look carefully at Rule 1.6. Could you find an exception to the duty of confidentiality that would permit you to disclose your client's admission that he had committed the crime for which another person has been convicted? Would it matter what sentence the innocent person was facing?

The exceptions to confidentiality are some of the most controversial aspects of attorney regulation. States differ significantly in the exceptions they permit and the rules have evolved in this area over time. There are two reasons that it is important for you to know about these variations over time and across jurisdictions. First, you want to be able to determine which of these exceptions applies in your jurisdiction and familiarity with the patterns allows you to understand where your jurisdiction fits in the larger scheme of exceptions. That understanding provides important insights into how any given issue might be resolved in your jurisdiction. Second, if you are researching case law or ethics opinions on this topic, it is critical for you to know what version of the rules applied at the time the decision was made; since a different outcome may have resulted under the current version of the rules you are applying.

In this chapter we will examine a number of these exceptions and their intersection with exceptions to the attorney-client privilege. We will then practice counseling a client regarding intended wrongdoing or the need to disclose in order to prevent harm.

11.1 Variations on Exceptions to Confidentiality to Protect Third Persons

Over time and across the nation, there are more variations to the exceptions to the duty of confidentiality than nearly any other rule of professional conduct. In 1983, the ABA Model Code provided that an attorney could reveal "the intention of his client to commit a crime and the information necessary to prevent the crime." ABA Model Code of Professional Responsibility, DR 4-101(C)(3) (1983). Likewise, that code provided that lawyers had a mandatory duty to disclose any client fraud to the victims of the fraud. DR 7-102(B)(1) of the Code required a lawyer, upon learning that a client "in the course of the representation [had] perpetrated a fraud upon a person or tribunal" to "reveal the fraud to the affected person or tribunal" if the client failed to rectify it. However, these exceptions to confidentiality seemed at once both too broad and too narrow. In representing a client, an attorney might become aware of information, not necessarily involving the client's intended action, that would threaten another's life. Remember the attorneys in the Logan case from Chapter Ten who knew that their client had committed a murder for which Logan was being wrongfully imprisoned. Since their client's refusal to confess to that murder was not a future crime or a fraud, they could not reveal this information. On the other hand, attorneys were free to disclose information regarding other intended crimes and were required to disclose frauds, no matter how insignificant the harm resulting from that behavior. Despite this problem of under- and over-inclusiveness, a few states retained these versions of the exception to confidentiality.

With the adoption of the Model Rules of Professional Conduct in 1984, an attorney's discretion to disclose information to protect third parties was narrowed considerably. Now attorneys could reveal only information that would "prevent the client from committing a criminal act that the lawyer believes is likely to result in imminent death or substantial bodily harm." ABA Model Rule of Professional Conduct, Rule 1.6(b)(1) (2001). The concern that attorneys could still find themselves in situations in which they acquire confidential information that could save someone's life caused the ABA to disconnect the discretion to disclose information entirely from the client's proposed criminal conduct and broaden the scope of discretion for attorneys to reveal confidential information "to the extent the lawyer reasonably believes necessary ... to prevent reasonably certain death or substantial bodily harm." ABA Model Rule of Professional Conduct, Rule 1.6(b)(1) (2001).

Throughout all of these rule changes since 1984, there had been continual suggestions to include provisions for the discretion to disclose client crimes or fraud that could result in other harms besides death or bodily injury. In 2003, in the wake of Enron and Congressional passage of the Sarbanes-Oxley Act, the ABA again amended Rule 1.6 to provide these exceptions for discretionary disclosure to protect financial and property interests.

With the variations on the ABA Model Rules over time, we also find variations on the states' versions of these rules. Nearly every one of the prior versions of the ABA Models can be found in one or more states. In addition, many states have slightly different standards for these exceptions and a few make the disclosures mandatory in some circumstances.

With all of this instability and variation across jurisdictions, you absolutely must be aware of your own state's rule and you must regularly check for changes to that rule.

11.2 Exceptions to Confidentiality for Death or Substantial Bodily Injury

Perhaps the most fearful situation in which an attorney might choose to disclose client confidences are those situations in which the attorney becomes aware of a threat to kill someone. All state's rules would provide an attorney the discretion to reveal a client's threat to kill, because it is an intent to commit a crime, or because it would result in death or substantial bodily harm, or both. In some jurisdictions, a threat to kill may be so clear that you may even have an obligation to disclose that information. In a number of states, the disciplinary rules require an attorney to disclose information that he reasonably believes necessary to prevent his client's crime that would result in death or substantial bodily harm. Consider these examples:

Illinois Rule of Professional Conduct Rule 1.6

(b) A lawyer shall reveal information about a client to the extent it appears necessary to prevent the client from committing an act that would result in death or serious bodily harm.

Iowa Rule of Professional Conduct Rule 32:1:6

(c) A lawyer shall reveal information relating to the representation of a client to the extent the lawyer reasonably believes necessary to prevent imminent death or substantial bodily harm.

Texas Disciplinary Rules of Professional Conduct Rule 1.05

(e) When a lawyer has confidential information clearly establishing that a client is likely to commit a criminal or fraudulent act that is likely to result in death or substantial bodily harm to a person, the lawyer shall reveal confidential information to the extent revelation reasonably appears necessary to prevent the client from committing the criminal or fraudulent act.

One of the most difficult aspects of this rule is deciding whether you have sufficient information to conclude that there is a risk of death or substantial bodily harm and that your disclosure could prevent that harm.

Consider the situation attorney Christopher Mecca faced when defending an individual charged with murder and the disappearance of two children.

McClure v. Thompson

323 F.3d 1233 (9th Cir. 2003)

[handwritten margin note: Had attorney thinks client on drugs committed crime]

[Attorney Mecca had been retained to represent Robert McClure, who had been arrested in the murder of Carol Jones and the disappearance of her two children, Michael, age 14, and Tanya, age 10. McClure's fingerprints were found in the home where Jones was shot.

Mecca went to the jail on Saturday and met his client and then, over the course of the next two days, spoke to him over the phone several times. At first, McClure claimed he was "being framed" for the murder, but told Mecca that he was nervous about his fingerprints being in the house. McClure's sister met with Mecca and McClure at the jail, frantic because she believed that her brother did indeed murder Jones but she also believed that the children were alive and perhaps tied up or bound someplace. She confronted her brother and begged him to divulge information about the whereabouts of the kids. McClure and his sister discussed how McClure sometimes did "crazy things" when he was using drugs, but McClure strongly maintained his innocence as to Carol Jones' murder and the children's disappearance.

When Mecca met with McClure again on Monday morning, McClure began to tell him of his sexual hallucinations and fantasies involving young girls and about other situations that happened in the past involving things he would do while under the influence of drugs. Mecca felt nearly certain that McClure did indeed murder Jones. He became extremely anxious, thinking that perhaps the children were still alive. He went to visit the crime scene and returned to visit with McClure that afternoon. Here is how Mecca described that meeting:]

As you read these facts, think about whether and when you would decide you could reveal a client's information.

"Each time as I would try to leave," Mecca recalled in his notes, "[McClure] would spew out other information, bits about the children, and he would do it in the form of a fantasy." Mecca wrote that he, "wanted to learn from him what happened to those children." He told McClure "that we all have hiding places, that we all know when we go hiking or driving or something, we all remember certain back roads and remote places," and that McClure "related to me ... one place where a body might be" and then "described [where] the other body would be located." Mecca wrote that he "wasn't going to push him for anything more," but "when I tried to leave, he said, and he said it tentatively, 'would you like me to draw you a map and just give you an idea?' and I said 'Yes' and he did[.]" Mecca recorded that "at that time, I felt in my own mind the children were dead, but, of course, I wasn't sure."

[Late that evening, McClure called Mecca and said "I know who did it." When Mecca asked him who that was, McClure said that "Satan killed Carol." When he asked, "What about the kids?" McClure replied, "Jesus saved the kids." Mecca visited McClure at the jail the next morning and told him that, if there was any possibility the children were alive, he would have to disclose that information to the police. Mecca then arranged to have a photocopy of the map McClure drew delivered to the Sheriff's department. Following the map, they located both the Jones children, who had been shot and were dead. McClure was arrested for their murder as well.

McClure was convicted of the murder of Carol Jones and her two children. In an action for post-conviction relief, McClure raised the ineffective assistance of counsel claim. The court concluded that Mecca had not obtained McClure's informed consent to disclose the map to authorities, so that this exception to confidentiality did not apply. The court then went on to analyze the exception to confidentiality to prevent a crime.] ...

2. Prevention of Further Criminal Acts

The State contends that, even if Mecca did not have informed consent, his revelation of client confidences did not amount to ineffective assistance of counsel because he reasonably believed that disclosing the location of the children was necessary in order to prevent further criminal acts. That is, Mecca reasonably believed that revealing the children's locations could have prevented the escalation of kidnapping to murder. This is not a traditional "prevention of further criminal acts" case, because all of the affirmative criminal acts performed by McClure had been completed at the time Mecca made his disclosure. Mecca was thus acting to prevent an earlier criminal act from being transformed by the passage of time into a more serious criminal offense. Nonetheless, we believe that where an attorney's or a client's omission to act could result in "imminent death or substantial bodily harm" constituting a separate and more severe crime from the one already committed, the exception to the duty of confidentiality may be triggered. ABA Model Rule 1.6(b)(1).

This exception, however, requires that an attorney reveal confidences only to the extent that he "reasonably believes necessary to prevent" those criminal acts and imminent harms. *Id.* In assessing the effectiveness of McClure's counsel in light of this standard, the first step is to determine what a constitutionally effective counsel should be required to do before making a disclosure. That is, we must determine what basis the attorney had for believing that the precondition to disclosure was present, and how much investigation he or she must have undertaken before it was "reasonabl[e]" to "believ[e][it] necessary" to make the disclosure to prevent the harm. The second step is to apply that standard to the facts surrounding Mecca's decision to disclose.

There is remarkably little case law addressing the first analytical step. Citing cases dealing with a separate confidentiality exception allowing attorneys to reveal intended perjury on the part of their clients, McClure argues that a lawyer must have a "firm factual basis" before adopting a belief of impending criminal conduct. *See, e.g., United States v. Omene,* 143 F.3d 1167, 1171 (9th Cir.1998); *United States v. Scott,* 909 F.2d 488, 493-94 & n. 10 (11th Cir.1990); *United States v. Long,* 857 F.2d 436, 444-45 (8th Cir.1988). However, we are not persuaded that the perjury cases provide the proper standard.

McClure is correct that our inquiry must acknowledge the importance of the confidential attorney-client relationship and the gravity of the harm that results from an unwarranted breach of that duty. However, the standard applied in the professional responsibility code asks only if the attorney "*reasonably believes*" disclosure is necessary to prevent the crime. ABA Model Rule

Note that at the time this case was decided, Model Rule 1.6(b)(1) permitted disclosure only to prevent the client's crime that would result in "imminent death or substantial bodily harm." Compare that exception to the current exception in Model Rule 1.6.

The exception referenced here is Rule 3.3, which provides that an attorney who knows that a client has submitted false testimony must take reasonable remedial measures, including disclosing the client's perjury to the court. This disclosure is mandatory.

1.6(b)(1) (emphasis added). Further, the *Strickland* standard likewise focuses on "whether counsel's assistance was *reasonable* considering all the circumstances." 466 U.S. at 688, 104 S. Ct. 2052 (emphasis added). Accordingly, we hold that the guiding rule for purposes of the exception for preventing criminal acts is objective reasonableness in light of the surrounding circumstances.

Reasonableness of belief may be strongly connected to adequacy of investigation or sufficiency of inquiry in the face of uncertainty. Significantly, as indicated above, *Strickland* explicitly imposes a duty on counsel "to make reasonable investigations or to make a reasonable decision that makes particular investigations unnecessary." 466 U.S. at 691, 104 S. Ct. 2052. In any ineffectiveness of counsel case, "a particular decision not to investigate must be directly assessed for reasonableness in all the circumstances, applying a heavy measure of deference to counsel's judgments." *Id.* Thus, in determining whether Mecca's disclosure of confidential client information constituted ineffective assistance of counsel, we must examine whether Mecca "reasonably believed" that the precondition for disclosure existed and whether, in coming to that belief, Mecca conducted a reasonable investigation and inquiry.

The parties vigorously debate both the reasonableness of Mecca's belief that the children were alive and the reasonableness of his level of investigation and inquiry on that point. McClure argues that any conclusion that Mecca had a reasonable belief is unsupported because Mecca himself indicated that he harbored doubts as to the children's state, and yet failed to inquire further. He points to evidence in the record that Mecca, at least at some stages of his representation of McClure, did not believe the children were alive—or that he, at the least, suspected that they were dead. It is indisputable that this evidence exists, and that most of this evidence is contained in statements by Mecca himself, whom the district court found "highly credible." Mecca's notes state that, after McClure drew the map, Mecca "felt in my own mind that the children were dead, but, of course, I wasn't sure." He testified in the district court evidentiary hearing that the conclusion he came to was that, "without telling me, [McClure had] told me he had killed three people." And he stated in this same testimony that, at the time he had his secretary place the anonymous call, he thought there was a "possibility," but not a "strong possibility," that the children were alive.

McClure argues that the statement Mecca says abruptly changed his mind about the status of the children—McClure's comment that "Jesus saved the kids"—was so vague and ambiguous that it was not a sufficient basis for a "reasonable belief" that disclosure was necessary. Despite Mecca's acknowledgment that this comment led him only to "assume" that McClure was saying the children were alive, Mecca never directly asked a question that could have confirmed or refuted that assumption. Mecca repeatedly testified that he never squarely asked about the condition of the children or whether McClure had killed them. Accordingly, McClure argues, any finding that Mecca believed the children were alive is not sufficient to establish effective assistance of counsel, because Mecca's failure to engage in a reasonable level of investigation and inquiry rendered that belief unreasonable.

Given the implicit factual findings of the state court, and the explicit factual findings of the district court, which are at least plausible in light of the record viewed in its entirety, we disagree. The ultimate question of the reasonableness of Mecca's belief is a question of law, which we review de novo.

In answering that question, however, we look to the facts and circumstances of the case, and as to these facts, we give great deference to the findings of the state court and the district court.

The district court made a number of specific findings regarding the factual basis for Mecca's belief that the children were alive. It found that only Mc-Clure knew the true facts and that he deliberately withheld them, leading Mecca to believe the children were alive. It found that McClure controlled the flow of information, and that when Mecca informed McClure that he had an obligation to disclose the children's whereabouts if there were a chance they were alive, McClure did not tell him they were dead. It specifically rejected McClure's assertion that Mecca in fact believed that the children were dead or that he lacked information that they were alive, noting that at the time there was no evidence, other than their disappearance and the passage of time, that they had been injured or killed.

The district court also made specific factual findings regarding the nature of Mecca's investigation and inquiry. It found that "Mecca attempted to discern whether the children were alive" and "that Mecca investigated to the best of his ability under extremely difficult circumstances." McClure argues that these findings are clearly erroneous, and that "arguments that Mr. McClure was manipulative and difficult are essentially irrelevant to the lawyer's obligations." But *Strickland* holds otherwise. The *Strickland* Court emphasized that "[t]he reasonableness of counsel's actions may be determined or substantially influenced by the defendant's own statements or actions." *Strickland*, 466 U.S. at 691, 104 S. Ct. 2052. More specifically, it held that "what investigation decisions are reasonable depends critically" on the "information supplied by the defendant." *Id.*

This is a close case, even after we give the required deference to the state and district courts. The choices made by McClure's counsel give us significant pause, and, were we deciding this case as an original matter, we might decide it differently. But we take as true the district court's specific factual findings as to what transpired—including what McClure said and did, and what actions Mecca took and why he took them—and we conclude that Mecca made the disclosure "reasonably believ[ing] [it was] necessary to prevent the client from committing a criminal act that [Mecca] believe[d] [was] likely to result in imminent death or substantial bodily harm[.]" ABA Model Rule 1.6(b)(1). Mecca therefore did not violate the duty of confidentiality in a manner that rendered his assistance constitutionally ineffective.

Conclusion

For the foregoing reasons, we conclude that McClure did not receive constitutionally ineffective assistance of counsel. Accordingly, the district court's denial of McClure's petition for writ of habeas corpus is AFFIRMED.

Questions

1. If Mecca had gone to the area where the children were located and had found the bodies of the children there, he would no longer have any grounds for disclosing his client's information, because it would not prevent a death or

The dissent concluded that, "Mecca's behavior was unreasonable because he did not possess sufficient information to make his belief that the children were alive reasonable and it was unreasonable for him to rely on the little information he had." Do you agree?

The dissent argues that Mecca should have gone to the location McClure had provided to see for himself whether the children were alive. Do you agree?

future crime. Would there be any other basis on which he might be required to reveal the location of the bodies? In *People v. Belge*, 359 N.E.2d 377 (N.Y. 1976), a client arrested for murder told his attorney where the bodies of the children could be found. The attorney visited the location, confirmed that the children were indeed dead, and kept the information confidential until trial, when he disclosed the information with his client's consent in order to establish an insanity defense. He was then charged with violation of the public health laws that required disclosure of the location of dead bodies. The court, in quashing the indictment, held that the attorney-client privilege and duty of confidentiality excused the attorney from the public health reporting duty.

2. What could the attorney do when visiting the location of the bodies? Could he take photos? Soil or blood samples? Move the bodies? At some point, an attorney would be destroying or altering physical evidence. Model Rule 3.4(a) says that a lawyer shall not "unlawfully obstruct another party's access to evidence or unlawfully alter, destroy, or conceal a document or other material having potential evidentiary value. A lawyer shall not counsel or assist another person to do any such act."

Suppose, for example, that McClure came to Mecca before he was arrested and gave Mecca his gun, indicating that he was afraid he might do more harm with it. If Mecca took the gun, he would have a duty to turn it over to police. Any time an attorney comes into possession of contraband, instrumentalities, or fruits of a crime, the attorney must turn those over to authorities in a way that minimizes the adverse impact on the client and at the same time preserves the evidentiary value. For example, in *Wemark v. State*, 602 N.W.2d 810 (Iowa 1999), attorneys defending a man accused of stabbing his wife to death turned over the location of the murder weapon. The court held that this did not constitute ineffective assistance of counsel because concealing evidence of a client's crime "has no reasonable relationship to the attorney-client privilege and constitutes an abuse of a lawyer's professional responsibilities." Likewise, the court in *Alhambra Police Officers Ass'n v. Alhambra Police Dep't*, 7 Cal. Rptr. 3d 432 (Cal. Ct. App. 2004), held that the "attorney-client privilege does not permit attorneys to disturb evidence without disclosing its original location and condition, nor may they turn over physical evidence to their clients rather than to the police or prosecution."

If a client simply tells the attorney about the evidence, but the attorney never possessed or disturbed the evidence in any way, that information alone would be protected by confidentiality and privilege. Likewise, if the client has given the attorney something that was not an instrumentality or contraband, but simply implicated criminal conduct, such as a copy of his or her journal describing illegal activities, or credit card receipts showing expenditures that might be evidence of criminal conduct, the situation would be easier. In these circumstances, as with general information about criminal conduct, the attorney need not disclose the evidence to law enforcement unless required to do so by a subpoena or court order. However, even here, the attorney should think twice about altering or destroying anything with potential evidentiary value in a criminal case.

The best way to avoid this dilemma is to avoid having these materials come into your possession in the first place. Warn your clients that if they provide evidence that is illegal for you to possess, you will be required to give it to law enforcement. Depending on the type of representation, you may wish to include this warning to clients in a description of your representation or even in your representation agreement. Of course, giving your clients a "Miranda" warning about the limits of your duty of confidentiality will often mean your clients will be reluctant to disclose information. You will want to help clients understand the distinction between telling you about possibly criminal activity in the past (which you can generally keep confidential) and giving you physical evidence of that activity. Finally, document your choices and conversations regarding these matters.

11.3 Reading the Rules: Disclosure of Client Frauds

Even before the Model Rules were amended to allow disclosure of a client's frauds, many states contained this exception to confidentiality, in large part because they had retained the future crime and fraud exception from the older Model Code of Professional Conduct. Today, all states except Alabama, California, Kentucky, Missouri, and Rhode Island have a financial fraud exception to confidentiality. In these states that have rejected the rule, an attorney is permitted to disclose a client's wrongdoing only if it would prevent death or substantial bodily injury.

Iowa is one of the states that adopted the ABA's version of this exception to confidentiality. Read these two provisions carefully to learn the scope of these exceptions.

Iowa Supreme Court, Rules of Professional Conduct Rule 32:1:6

(b) A lawyer may reveal information relating to the representation of a client to the extent the lawyer reasonably believes necessary ...

(2) to prevent the client from committing a crime or fraud that is reasonably certain to result in substantial injury to the financial interests or property of another and in furtherance of which the client has used or is using the lawyer's services;

(3) to prevent, mitigate, or rectify substantial injury to the financial interests or property another that is reasonably certain to result or has resulted from the client's commission of a crime or fraud in furtherance of which the client has used the lawyer's services.

Context

Notice that these exceptions to confidentiality are both tied to the use of the attorney's services. Knowing that a client will commit a crime or fraud alone is not sufficient basis for disclosure.

Relationships

In all the rules, knowing how to define key terms is critical, but perhaps nowhere as critical as in interpreting these exceptions to confidentiality. Look up the definitions of the following terms from the rule that appear in the definitions section of the Model Rule: fraud, informed consent, reasonably, reasonably believes, and substantial.

b2 → prevention
b3 → after crime occurred

Structure

The exceptions to Rule 1.6 for fraud have multiple requirements. The main difference between the exceptions is that (b)(2) is forward looking—it permits disclosures that can prevent crimes or frauds—and (b)(3) applies when those crimes or frauds have already occurred.

Reasons

Policy reasons for Rule 1.6

① dissuade wrong doing

② protect 3rd persons

③ reasonableness protects attorney

These exceptions serve multiple purposes. First, to the extent the attorney can use the threat of disclosure to dissuade clients from wrongdoing, the exceptions provide an important tool for the attorney to balance his multiple roles as representative of a client, officer of the court, and public citizen. The rule of law takes effect not only in the courtroom but in the offices of attorneys counseling their clients. The client can, of course, prevent disclosure by agreeing to abandon plans for wrongdoing. Second, if clients cannot be dissuaded, or if client crimes or frauds using the attorney's services have already occurred, the exceptions to disclosure allow an attorney to take action to protect third persons. Third, by making the disclosures discretionary, attorneys are able to make the difficult judgment calls inherent in a rule calling for action when those attorneys "reasonably believe" their actions will prevent "reasonably certain" harm. Attorneys are not placed at increased risk of liability for failure to make a mandatory disclosure (unless other law might require that disclosure). On the other hand, attorneys do have the leeway to report in order to reduce the risk that they will feel or be seen as complicit with their clients' wrongdoing.

Visualize

There are a number of ways you could visualize this rule. Constructing a flow chart or decision tree would be an excellent way to understand the rule. Another way to visualize the rule is as an intersection of the actions and interest of three parties: the client, the lawyer, and the victim. This may be an especially useful conception because the portion of the rule most students overlook in reading the rule is that part which requires that the lawyer's services have been or are being used to further the client's crime or fraud.

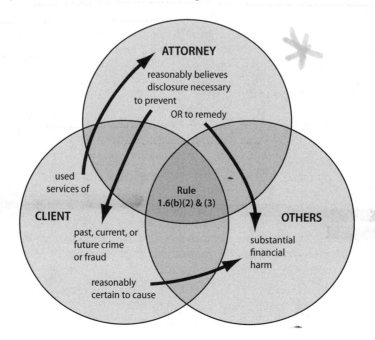

Imagine

Unfortunately, it takes very little imagination to think about how this exception might arise in practice. Some exceedingly notorious fraud scandals have involved attorneys' services over the years. The O.P.M. scandal in 1981 was one such affair. *In re O.P.M. Leasing Services, Inc.*, 13 B.R. 64 (Bankr. S.D.N.Y. 1981), *aff'd*, 670 F.2d 383 (2d Cir. 1982). In that case, the firm of Singer Hutner assisted OPM with a series of fraudulent leasing transactions. The firm discovered the fraud, but continued to represent OPM (which was its largest client) in additional leasing transactions based on OPM's representation that those transactions did not involve fraud. OPM lied, however, and Singer Hutner quietly withdrew from its representation. OPM then turned to its in-house lawyers and the firm of Kaye Scholer to assist unknowingly with further fraudulent deals before the fraud was uncovered.

To read a summary of nine more recent scandals, including Enron, Worldcom, and Quest, and an analysis of the role attorneys may have played in each, see The New York City Bar Association, Report of the Task Force on the Lawyer's Role in Corporate Governance, Appendix D (2006) at www.abcny.org/pdf/report/CORPORATE_GOVERNANCE06.pdf.

11.4 The Crime-Fraud Exception to Privilege

As you will recall from Chapter Nine, the attorney-client privilege applies to communications between an attorney and client for the purpose of securing legal advice or representation. If an attorney-client communication is for other purposes or in other capacities, it does not secure the protections of the privilege. *In re Grand Jury Subpoenas Dated March 9, 2001*, 179 F. Supp. 2d 270, 285 (S.D.N.Y. 2001) (lobbyists); *In re Lindsey (Grand Jury Testimony)*, 158 F.3d 1263, 1272 (D.C. Cir. 1998) (political advisor).

In a parallel concept, even when the protections of the privilege attach to a communication, those protections can be lost if the communication was sought or used to further a crime or fraud and the client then carries out that crime or fraud. Like the attorney-client privilege itself, the crime-fraud exception developed in the common law of evidence and applies in both criminal and civil settings. Different jurisdictions have variations in the standard for the exception and the procedure for its application. The Restatement summarizes this exception as follows:

[handwritten margin note: exception to attorney-client comm. if crime/fraud]

Restatement (Third) of the Law Governing Lawyers
§ 82 Client Crime or Fraud

The attorney-client privilege does not apply to a communication occurring when a client:

(a) consults a lawyer for the purpose, later accomplished, of obtaining assistance to engage in a crime or fraud or aiding a third person to do so, or

(b) regardless of the client's purpose at the time of consultation, uses the lawyer's advice or other services to engage in or assist a crime or fraud.

Notice that both these exceptions require that the client actually have carried out the crime or fraud. Suppose a client comes to you with an elaborate tax evasion scheme he and several friends have come up with. You review the client's proposal and, consistent with Rule 1.2, advise him on the criminal consequences of his plan. You do not suggest ways to avoid getting caught or otherwise break the law, but you do provide him with legal suggestions for reducing his taxes. Persuaded by your counsel, he chooses not to pursue the original plan. His friends do not abandon their plan, however, and the IRS begins to investigate them and your client for tax fraud. Your client is subpoenaed to testify and is asked what advice he had received about the tax scheme. The court would uphold an objection to attorney-client privilege. The crime-fraud exception would not apply because the client was dissuaded from the criminal activity.

Now suppose that this same client had not come to you ahead of time to discuss his tax plan, but instead went ahead with his plan without any legal advice. After the IRS began an investigation, the client hires you to defend him. He discusses with you the details of his tax scheme. Once again, the privilege protects this communication and the crime fraud exception does not apply. This is a communication about a crime already completed and the client is not asking for advice to further this or any other crime. Rather, the client is disclosing information to aid in his defense.

But suppose the client asks you for help in generating false documents that would cover up his illegal tax scheme. Would the communication then fall under the exception? The answer is yes if the client actually carries out the plan to generate the false evidence. What if the client does not reveal the reason behind his request for assistance in creating documents regarding his business transactions and, as far as the attorney can tell, the client is asking for bona fide assistance to create business documents in compliance with the law? Would the crime fraud exception still apply if the client in fact used the documents or the attorney's advice to cover up his tax fraud? Yes, it is irrelevant whether the attorney knows that the client's intent is criminal or fraudulent.

Court must find *prima facie* evidence of crime or fraud before allowing this exception to privilege. *Zolin v. United States*, 491 U.S. 554 (1989). Once the party moving for production has made a threshold showing "of a factual basis adequate to support a good faith belief by a reasonable person" that the crime-fraud exception applies, the court may then conduct an *in camera* inspection of the privileged communication to determine whether the crime fraud exception does indeed apply. A similar exception exists for work-product immunity, though there a protection for the attorney's opinions and impressions is retained. *In re Green Grand Jury Proceedings*, 492 F.3d 976, 980 (8th Cir. 2007).

These differences, and the procedural complications that arise in invoking the crime-fraud exception to privilege, are explored in the following case in which a public defender was willing to go to jail in order to protect her client's confidentiality. The excerpts from this case provides an opportunity for you to review many of the concepts you have learned in this unit and also to consider the special rules governing prosecutors (Rule 3.8) in issuing subpoenas against attorneys. (You may even wish to read the case in its entirety, as there are many other sources cited and points addressed that are not excerpted here.)

State v. Gonzalez

290 Kan. 747, 234 P.3d 1 (Kan. 2010)

BEIER, J.

Sarah Sweet-McKinnon, the Chief Public Defender for the Reno County Public Defender's office, appeals a judgment finding her guilty of direct civil contempt and imposing a $ 1,000 per day coercive sanction. The contempt judgment and sanction arose out of McKinnon's refusal to testify under sub-poena by the State concerning a statement made by a former client, who ex-pressed an intent to commit perjury in the prosecution of defendant Valerie Gonzalez.

FACTUAL AND PROCEDURAL BACKGROUND

In early 2007, McKinnon was appointed to represent defendant Gonzalez on a charge of first-degree murder. McKinnon or one of the attorneys she su-pervised in the Reno County Public Defender's Office represented another defendant on an unrelated case who was in custody at the Reno County Jail at the same time as Gonzalez. At some point, the other client informed her counsel that she intended to commit perjury in Gonzalez' case. The public defender's office filed a motion to withdraw from the other client's case. The case against Gonzalez was dismissed in June 2007.

In January 2009, the State refiled the case against Gonzalez, and McKinnon was again appointed to represent her. The new complaint listed several endorsed witnesses who had not been listed on the 2007 complaint, seven of which were former clients of the public defender's office who had been housed at the Reno County Jail at the same time as Gonzalez in 2007. Among them was the former client who had expressed the intent to commit perjury in Gonzalez' case.

Given the seven newly endorsed witnesses, McKinnon filed a motion to withdraw as Gonzalez' attorney. The motion included the following statements:

> 3. In all of the prior representations of the seven prior Public De-fender clients, the movant has actual information by virtue of the prior representation that would severely restrict the scope of cross-examination of these prosecution witnesses to avoid possible viola-tion of the attorney client privileges of the state's witnesses, including, but not limited to:
>
> > 'a. A statement by a former client of the Public Defender's office that was made during representation that the prior client intended to commit perjury in Ms. [Gonzalez'] case, who is now a prose-cution witness.'

The district judge granted McKinnon's motion to withdraw and appointed new counsel for Gonzalez.

The State then filed a motion to issue a subpoena for McKinnon to appear and testify at Gonzalez' preliminary hearing. The motion was based on Kansas Rule of Professional Conduct (KRPC) Rule 3.8(e) (2009 Kan. Ct. R. Annot. 565), which prohibits a prosecutor from subpoenaing a lawyer in a criminal proceeding "to present evidence about a past or present client unless the pros-ecutor reasonably believes" the evidence is not protected by privilege, is essential to the successful completion of the prosecution, and "there is no other feasi-ble alternative to obtain the information[.]" In its motion, the State requested that the district judge make findings on each of the KRPC 3.8(e) factors. The State explained it was using this unusual procedure out of an "abundance of caution and in light of the serious nature of causing a subpoena [to issue] for a criminal defense attorney[.]"

At the hearing on the motion, the State called Reno County Police Detec-tive John Moore. Moore had conducted the investigation to determine which

What would be the basis for this withdrawal under Rule 1.16?

In a later part of this opin-ion, the case holds this procedure will be manda-tory for these subpoenas.

of the State's endorsed witnesses might have made the statement referenced in McKinnon's motion to withdraw. The district judge granted the State's motion to issue the subpoena, ruling that each of the three KRPC 3.8(e) factors had been established.

... The State then issued and served McKinnon with a subpoena to appear and testify. The prosecutor informed McKinnon that he intended to ask her the following questions concerning the former client's expressed intent to commit perjury in Gonzalez' case: Who made the statement? When was it made? What words were used? What were the circumstances? In what form did she receive that communication?

McKinnon filed a motion to quash the subpoena, arguing that answering the prosecutor's questions would violate her duty of client confidentiality under KRPC 1.6 (2009 Kan. Ct. R. Annot. 468) and KRPC 1.9 (2009 Kan. Ct. R. Annot. 490), exposing her to disciplinary action.

The district judge denied McKinnon's motion to quash. The judge again held that KRPC 3.8(e) supported the subpoena, *i.e.,* that no privilege existed under the first factor and that McKinnon had failed to offer sufficient evidence or argument to rebut the second and third factors. Further, the district judge rejected McKinnon's arguments about her ethical duty of confidentiality, concluding that the rules did not prohibit McKinnon from revealing the information. Specifically, the judge noted that KRPC 1.6(b)(1) allows an attorney to reveal client confidences to prevent a client from committing a crime, and KRPC 1.6(b)(2) protects an attorney from disciplinary action for revealing confidential client information in compliance with a court order.

Immediately after the district judge's ruling, the prosecutor called McKinnon to the witness stand. After a few preliminary questions, the prosecutor asked McKinnon who had made the statement set out in paragraph 3.a of her motion to withdraw. McKinnon refused to answer the question. The judge then ordered McKinnon to answer the question. She again refused. The judge found McKinnon in direct civil contempt of court and imposed a fine of $ 1,000 per day until the contempt was purged by McKinnon's agreement to answer the question.

McKinnon posted an appeal bond to stay execution of the contempt order pending this appeal....

ANALYSIS

... An appellate court reviews a determination that conduct is contemptuous under a de novo standard; contempt sanctions are reviewed for abuse of discretion....

A district court judge's decision on a motion to quash a subpoena calling for disclosure of privileged information is governed generally by K.S.A. 2009 Supp. 60-245(c)(3)(A)(iii), which provides: "On timely motion, the court by which a subpoena was issued shall quash or modify the subpoena if it ... requires disclosure of privileged or other protected matter and no exception or waiver applies." Another subsection of the statute provides that a court shall quash or modify a subpoena that "subjects a person to undue burden." K.S.A. 2009 Supp. 60-245(c)(3)(A)(iv). A further subsection, K.S.A. 2009 Supp. 60-245(c)(3)(B)(iii), is worded more permissively, saying the court "may" quash

---

Margin notes:

The court quotes Moore's testimony which established that he had not been able to locate any witness who admitted discussing the Gonzales case with the public defender and that he had no other way to investigate whether one of them was going to commit perjury.

Notice that Kansas has this older, very broad exception to confidentiality.

She would not have been subject to discipline if she had answered, so why did she refuse?

or modify a subpoena under certain circumstances not present here, or "may" order appearance "only upon specified conditions" if "the party in whose behalf the subpoena is issued shows a substantial need for the testimony or material that cannot be otherwise met without undue hardship and assures that the person to whom the subpoena is addressed will be reasonably compensated." ...

General Distinction Between Privilege Law and Attorney Ethics Rules on Client Confidences

The parties have argued both the attorney-client privilege and the various disciplinary rules concerning an attorney's ethical duties with respect to client confidences and, at times, appear to confuse the two. Because there are fundamental and significant differences between these lines of authority and their applicability, it is necessary that we first clarify that we face one and not the other here.

A privilege is a rule of evidence that allows a person "to shield [a] confidential communication or information from compelled disclosure during litigation." Imwinkelried, The New Wigmore: Evidentiary Privileges § 1.1, p. 2 (2d ed. 2009). In Kansas, the attorney-client privilege is statutory. It is found in the code of evidence at K.S.A. 60-426, which reads in pertinent part:

> "(a) ... [E]xcept as otherwise provided by subsection (b) of this section communications found by the judge to have between lawyer and his or her client in the course of that relationship and in professional confidence, are privileged, and a client has a privilege ... (2) to prevent his or her lawyer from disclosing it.... The privilege may be claimed by the client in person or by his or her lawyer....

> "(b).... Such privileges shall not extend (1) to a communication if the judge finds that sufficient evidence, aside from the communication, has been introduced to warrant a finding that the legal service was sought or obtained in order to enable or aid the commission or planning of a crime or a tort...." K.S.A. 60-426.

This statute protects from compelled disclosure certain confidential communications made between an attorney and client in the course of their professional relationship. The privilege applies narrowly because, like all privileges, it operates to deprive the factfinder of otherwise relevant information.

In contrast, an attorney's ethical duty of client confidentiality arises under the Kansas Rules of Professional Conduct and is part of a system of professional ethical standards designed to "provide guidance to lawyers and ... a structure for regulating conduct through disciplinary agencies." Supreme Court Rule 226, Scope [20] (2009 Kan. Ct. R. Annot. 405). A violation of an ethical rule "should not itself give rise to a cause of action against a lawyer" or "necessarily warrant any other nondisciplinary remedy, such as disqualification of a lawyer in pending litigation." Supreme Court Rule 226, Scope [20].... In contrast to the attorney-client privilege, which is a rule of evidence and applies only when the attorney "may be called as a witness or otherwise required to produce evidence concerning a client[,]" the attorney's ethical duty of confidentiality under the disciplinary rules "applies in all situations *other than those where evidence is sought from the lawyer through com-*

pulsion of law." (Emphasis added.) Comment [5] to KRPC 1.6 (2009 Kan. Ct. R. Annot. 469). Further, in contrast to the narrow scope of the attorney-client privilege, the ethical duty of client confidentiality applies broadly to *all* information related to representation of a client. KRPC 1.6(a); Comment [5] (2009 Kan. Ct. R. Annot. 468-69). It is expansive because the cloak of confidentiality is intended to "facilitate the full development of facts essential to proper representation of the client[.]" Comments [2] and [4] to KRPC 1.6 (2009 Kan. Ct. R. Annot. 469).

There is some overlap between the ethical duty of confidentiality and the attorney-client privilege. By definition, all communications protected by the attorney-client privilege will be confidential and covered by the ethical duty. K.S.A. 60-426(a) (communication must have been made in professional confidence). That overlap is the reason why the ethical duty of confidentiality requires an attorney to invoke the attorney-client privilege when it is applicable. Comment [13] to KRPC 1.6 (2009 Kan. Ct. R. Annot. 470). But not all client confidences inevitably must be protected through invocation of attorney-client privilege.

This is, at base, a privilege case.... The attorney ethics rules on client confidences provide important context to our analysis of the contours of K.S.A. 60-426 attorney-client privilege when a prosecutor attempts to compel a criminal defense attorney to speak, but they do not control it. As the following subsections of our analysis illustrate, another attorney ethical rule, KRPC 3.8(e) (2009 Kan. Ct. R. Annot. 564), does provide an essential overlay to the privilege statute and K.S.A. 2009 Supp. 60-245(c)(3) on motions to quash in situations of this type. It requires certain procedures and proof when a prosecutor seeks a subpoena directed to criminal defense counsel and when the subject of the subpoena seeks to quash such a subpoena.

K.S.A. 60-426 Attorney-Client Privilege and KRPC 3.8(e)

Having addressed the general distinction between privilege law and attorney ethics rules on client confidences, we now turn to the extraordinary nature of the situation in this case and the applicable attorney ethics rule, *i.e.,* a prosecutor's issuance of a subpoena to compel testimony about a former client from a defense lawyer in a criminal proceeding and KRPC 3.8(e). The prosecutor invoked KRPC 3.8(e) to obtain issuance of the subpoena to McKinnon. He did so with good reason. KRPC 3.8(e) speaks directly to the prosecutor's ethical obligation in such a mercifully rare scenario, and it prohibits a prosecutor from subpoenaing a defense lawyer in a

> criminal proceeding to present evidence about a past or present client unless the prosecutor reasonably believes:
>
> (1) the information sought is not protected from disclosure by any applicable privilege;
>
> (2) the evidence sought is essential to the successful completion of an ongoing investigation or prosecution; and
>
> (3) there is no other feasible alternative to obtain the information.

2009 Kan. Ct. R. Annot. at 565.

At least three underlying principles are evident in the language of this rule. First, the prosecutor's role in our criminal justice system is unique, and it carries concomitant responsibilities. The prosecutor is a representative of the government in an adversary criminal proceeding, which means he or she must be held to a standard not expected of attorneys who represent "ordinary" parties to litigation. *Berger v. United States,* 295 U.S. 78, 88, 79 L. Ed. 1314, 55 S. Ct. 629 (1935). As we stated in *State v. Pabst,* 268 Kan. 501, 996 P.2d 321 (2000):

> A prosecutor is a servant of the law and a representative of the people of Kansas.... Sixty-five years ago the United States Supreme Court said that the prosecutor represents 'a sovereignty whose obligation to govern impartially is as compelling as its obligation to govern at all; and whose interest, therefore, in a criminal prosecution is not that it shall win a case, but that justice shall be done.' *Berger v. United States,* 295 U.S. [at] 88." 268 Kan. at 510.

The comments to KRPC 3.8, Comment [1] (2009 Kan. Ct. R. Annot. 565) make this explicit: "A prosecutor has the responsibility of a minister of justice and not simply that of an advocate."

Second, Rule 3.8(e)(1)'s near-total prohibition on subpoenas directed to an attorney to obtain evidence protected by privilege reinforces the indispensability of attorney-client privilege in the effective and efficient functioning of the administration of justice. The attorney-client privilege is the oldest of the common-law privileges and exists "to encourage full and frank communication between attorneys and their clients" in order to "promote broader public interests in the observance of law and administration of justice." *Upjohn Co. v. United States,* 449 U.S. 383, 389, 66 L. Ed. 2d 584, 101 S. Ct. 677 (1981).

Third, the limitations that KRPC 3.8(e)(2) and (3) place on the power to compel an attorney to provide nonprivileged evidence about a client "to those situations in which there is a genuine need to intrude in the client-lawyer relationship" communicate a general unwillingness to intrude. *See* Comment [4] to KRPC 3.8 (2009 Kan. Ct. R. Annot. 566). These limitations are based on "the generally accepted principle that the attorney-client relationship should not be disturbed without cause." *United States v. Colorado Supreme Court,* 189 F.3d 1281, 1288 (10th Cir. 1999) (construing Colorado's equivalent to KRPC 3.8[e])....

In view of the role and importance of a trustworthy and confidential attorney-client relationship, particularly in our adversary system of criminal justice, and of the potential for damage to that system if the relationship is too cavalierly invaded or compromised, we hereby adopt the procedure followed here as a requirement. Moreover, we approve KRPC 3.8(e) as the analytical rubric for a district court judge considering a prosecutor's motion for issuance of a subpoena to compel criminal defense counsel to testify about a current or former client's confidential information....

Critically evaluate this procedure. Do you agree with the balance it strikes?

The first of the factors, the existence of a privilege under K.S.A. 60-426, acts as a threshold consideration, as a privilege generally cannot be overcome by a showing of need. *See Admiral Ins. v. United States Dist. Court for Dist. of Ariz.,* 881 F.2d 1486, 1494-95 (9th Cir. 1989) (privilege takes precedence over need for information); *The St. Luke Hospitals, Inc. v. Kopowski,* 160 S.W.3d 771, 776-77 (Ky. 2005) ("when a communication is protected by the attorney-client privilege it may not be overcome by a showing of need by an opposing party to obtain the information contained in the privileged communication"); *compare* K.S.A. 2009 Supp. 60-245(c)(3)(A)(iii) (subpoena *shall* be quashed if information sought protected by privilege) and K.S.A. 2009 Supp. 60-245(c)(3)(B)(i) (in considering a motion to quash or modify subpoena for confidential trade secrets or commercial information, if issuing party shows substantial need for the information, court *may* impose protective conditions on attendance/production); *see also Wesley Medical Center v. Clark,* 234 Kan. 13, 20-27, 669 P.2d 209 (1983) (recognizing difference between absolute privilege, qualified privilege; absolute privilege makes need irrelevant; qualified privilege allows court to control discovery of nonprivileged confidential information based on considerations that include need).

Accordingly, if the evidence the prosecutor seeks is protected from disclosure by the statutory attorney-client privilege, the KRPC 3.8(e) criteria cannot be met and the subpoena cannot issue, regardless of whether the information is essential to the prosecution and there is no other feasible alternative to obtain the information. If, however, the prosecutor establishes that the information is not protected by the privilege, then the last two factors must also be established in order to approve the issuance of the subpoena.

Evaluation of This Case Under the KRPC 3.8(e) Rubric

Now that we have established the legal rules and procedures governing the situation before us, we turn to our evaluation of the district judge's assessment of the evidence before him and his legal rulings based on that assessment. The facts of the information already disclosed by McKinnon are undisputed, as are the facts of the detective's investigation, the wording of the question the prosecution asked, and her refusal to answer.

First Factor Under KRPC 3.8(e)

In her brief, McKinnon challenges the district judge's determination on the first KRPC 3.8(e) factor—that the attorney-client privilege did not apply because of the crime-fraud exception. In her view, there was nothing other than the former client's communication itself to demonstrate the client's intention to obtain legal advice to enable or assist in the planned perjury. This, she argues, is inadequate to qualify under K.S.A. 60-426(b)(1), which requires "sufficient evidence, *aside from the communication* ... to warrant a finding that the legal service was sought or obtained in order *to enable or aid* the commission or planning of a crime." (Emphases added.) If, as a threshold matter, the attorney-client privilege applies, the three KRPC 3.8(e) factors cannot be met.

... The judge's determination on the first KRPC 3.8(e) factor necessarily depended on his factual finding that evidence beyond the former client's communication itself existed and that it supported an inference that the former client sought legal advice to further a crime or planned crime. This was error. On the undisputed record as developed so far and before us, there is no such evidence. McKinnon's summary of the former client's expression of an intention to commit perjury in Gonzalez' case is the only evidence, and merely reed-thin circumstantial evidence, that the former client sought legal services from the public defender's office "in order to enable or aid the commission or planning of a crime or a tort." K.S.A. 60-426(b)(1). No other evidence of a desire to advance such facilitation exists. K.S.A. 60-426(b)(1) requires additional evidence before the crime-fraud exception to attorney-client privilege will arise, given the threat of serious damage to the essential confidential relationship the privilege ordinarily protects. The attorney-client privilege protecting the communications of the former client to McKinnon or her subordinate was and is intact in this case, absent waiver or a contractual agreement not to claim the privilege. *See* K.S.A. 60-437(a), (b) (privilege may be waived by contract, previous disclosure).

As noted, the State nevertheless argues that McKinnon cannot effectively invoke the privilege because the prosecution merely seeks the client's name or identity, which is not confidential. Although this rule of law may generally be correct, *see In re Grand Jury Subpoenas*, 906 F.2d 1485, 1488 (10th Cir. 1990) (client's identity is not normally protected by the attorney-client privilege); *Bank v. McDowell*, 7 Kan. App. 568, Syl. P 2, 52 Pac. 56 (1898) (client identity not protected by attorney-client privilege), it is not correct in the specific circumstances before us here. McKinnon admits that she had no authorization from the former client to include the substance of the former client's statement in the motion to withdraw and that she did so in violation of the attorney ethics rules governing client confidentiality. *See* KRPC 1.6(a) (2009 Kan. Ct. R. Annot. 468) (attorney shall not reveal client confidences); *State v. Maxwell*, 10 Kan. App. 2d 62, 64, 691 P.2d 1316 (1984), *rev. denied* 236 Kan. 876 (1985) (attorney's unauthorized disclosure of client confidence not equivalent to client waiver).

In this unusual situation, when the content of the confidential communication has already been revealed without the former client's permission, providing the name or identity of the former client would effectively disclose confidential client information; thus, in this case, the name or identity of the former client must be kept confidential to achieve the purpose of the privilege and the attorney ethics rules that provide its context. *See United States v. BDO Seidman*, 337 F.3d 802, 811 (7th Cir. 2003) (limited exception to the general rule that client identity is not privileged applies where "so much of an actual confidential communication has been disclosed already that merely identifying the client will effectively disclose that communication"); *Vingelli v. United States, Drug Enforcement Agency*, 992 F.2d 449, 453 (2d Cir. 1993) ("substantial disclosure" exception to general rule that client identity not privileged communication extends privilege to identity "where the substance of a confidential communication has already been revealed, but not its source, [such that] identifying the client constitutes a prejudicial disclosure of a confidential communication").

Because the continuing existence of the attorney-client privilege makes it impossible for the State to meet its burden to establish all of the three KRPC 3.8(e) factors, the contempt judgment and sanctions order must be vacated and this case remanded for further proceedings. Further discussion of the KRPC 3.8(e) factors is technically unnecessary to the inevitable outcome of this appeal....

The judgment of the district court is reversed and vacated, and the case is remanded to the district court for further proceedings.

Notes

1. Replay and evaluate each of the public defender's choices in this case. Would you have:

   - Withdrawn when you learned that a client intended to commit perjury? Would you do anything else at that point?

   - Withdrawn from the representation of Gonzales when you learned that one of the witnesses was this former client who had planned to perjure himself?

   - Stated the reasons for your withdrawal the same way the attorney did here?

   - Moved to quash the subpoena?

   - Refused to answer the questions after the court overruled your objections, even to the point of contempt?

2. Here the court notes that the attorney concedes that her statement in the withdrawal violated the duty of confidentiality. But why didn't it waive the privilege? Remember that it is only disclosure of a communication that waives the privilege — so if you had not disclosed the communication but only given a warning based on that communication, you would have preserved the privileged communication. In the few cases in which this has arisen, courts have held that the attorney's disclosure under his ethical discretion did not operate to destroy the attorney-client privilege. *Kleinfeld v. State,* 568 So. 2d 937, 939 (Fla. 1990); Newman v. State, 863 A.2d 321 (Md. 2004); *Henderson v. State,* 962 S.W.2d 544 (Tex. Crim. App. 1997).

Reflective Practice: Disclosing Client Wrongdoing

Reflect on the cases and materials you have read in this chapter. Knowing that a client is planning wrongdoing presents one of the most difficult dilemmas an attorney can face. As you can see, states cannot agree on where the lines should be drawn in the balance between a client's confidentiality and an attorney's discretion (or even duty) to reveal a client's intended wrongdoing. What do you do if your personal moral code and personal values as a professional conflict with what the rules require or prohibit? Reflect on a situation in which your personal values have conflicted with rules or even with just the dominant cultural norms in your group. How have you addressed that conflict?

11.5 Required by Law

All states have an exception to confidentiality that allows an attorney to reveal confidential information in order to comply with other law. In the next unit, we examine the tensions created by rules of professional conduct that give priority to protecting tribunals and third-parties over protecting confidentiality of the client and turn some of the discretionary exceptions to 1.6 into mandatory duties to disclose. These are "rules of law" that create exceptions to the duty of confidentiality.

In this section, we will explore some of the "other law" outside the rules of professional conduct that might create duties to disclose confidential client information. For example, an attorney may have a duty to warn under tort law. The duty to warn in tort law, established by *Tarasoff v. Regents of University of California*, 551 P.2d 334 (Cal. 1976) established for psychologists a very limited duty to warn when they have special knowledge of a patient's clear threat to kill a foreseeable victim. *Tarasoff*'s application to attorneys is unclear. The court in *Hawkins v. King County*, 602 P.2d 361 (Wash. App. 1979) held that an attorney did not have a duty to warn his client's mother of his client's signs of mental illness when she was as aware of those signs as was the attorney. In contrast, the court in *Washington v. Hansen*, 862 P.2d 117, 122 (Wash. 1993) held that an attorney who was aware of a threat against a judge had a duty to disclose that threat: "attorneys, as officers of the court, have a duty to warn of true threats to harm a judge made by a client or a third party when the attorney has a reasonable belief that such threats are real." The court distinguished *Hawkins* on the grounds that the mother knew about the threat her son might pose whereas the judge in this case was unaware of the threat.

Given that both disciplinary rules and tort law allow, and may require, disclosing a client's fatal threats, why would an attorney hesitate? Think about what happens if you are in a situation in which your client has made a threat to kill a third person. The first problem you face is in determining the probability that the client will actually carry out the threat. Individuals under stress may make some fairly outrageous threats that serve only to express the depth of their emotions. How can you separate the bluff from the true threat? If you reveal your client's threat to the person threatened, you may be protecting that person or you may simply be escalating the emotional stakes and making the crisis worse rather than better. If you reveal your client's threat to the police or the judge, you have substantially prejudiced your client and will be required to withdraw from the representation. Because revealing a client's threat requires such difficult judgments, most state disciplinary rules leave that decision to the discretion of the attorney. This decision requires consideration of the nature of the relationship with the client and those who might be injured, the lawyer's own involvement in the conduct, and any other extenuating factors that may exist. Generally, an attorney should seek to persuade the client to take suitable action and, if the attorney does decide to disclose, the disclosure should be no greater than the attorney reasonably believes necessary to prevent the crime.

In recent years, there have been efforts to create federal law requiring attorneys to disclose to agencies their clients' financial wrongs. Early versions of the SEC regulations implementing the Sarbanes-Oxley Act, for example, appeared to require attorneys to report client frauds to the SEC. Other laws may impose a duty to report wrongdoing on the general public and the question presents itself regarding whether attorneys are exempt from these requirements. Consider once again the IRS regulation that requires reporting of cash transactions in excess of $10,000. In the future, one might expect increasing pressure on attorneys to police and report their clients. Exceptions to the ethical duty of confidentiality that permit disclosure when required by law keep attorneys from finding themselves in the dilemma of choosing liability or discipline.

Researching Professional Responsibility 11-A: Finding Disclosure Requirements

You represent Matilda in a custody modification action against her ex-husband Frank, the father of her 12-year-old daughter Janine. Janine currently lives with Matilda and Matilda's paramour Paul. You conduct your usual thorough internet searches (assume you break no laws in doing so). What you find disturbs you — Frank has no incriminating material on the web, but Matilda's daughter Janine has posted several photographs in a publicly available photosharing site. The photos show her partially nude and in sexually suggestive poses with Paul. When you confront Matilda with this evidence of her paramours' activities, she is shocked. She insists that she doesn't know anything about the photos or Paul's activities. Yet she also pleads with you to keep this information secret, lest it jeopardize her custody action. You suggest that, as a condition of your continued representation, she should have nothing more to do with Paul, but she seems reluctant, suggesting that she can simply protect her daughter, short of breaking off her relationship. On this basis, you request to withdraw from the case. But what do you do with the information about the child abuse and possible child pornography? Must you report this information to anyone?

Research your state's laws regarding your duty to disclose this information. Remember to start with state statutes, and keep in mind that the duty to disclose may not be one that is imposed only upon attorneys, but may be a duty shared by many professionals or even the general public.

Test Your Understanding

1. Your client has refused to pay you. May you:
   a. Report her to a credit reporting bureau?
   b. Turn the bill over to a collection agency?
   c. Sue and attach the client's secret bank account to collect the fee?

2. Barbara Broker, your client, is under investigation by the SEC regarding securities fraud. In the course of the investigation, the SEC investigator asks you a number of questions about how the prospectus for Barbara's securities was prepared. You refuse to cooperate. The SEC then sends you a letter saying "There appears to be evidence that you have assisted in this fraud. We will be exploring your role in preparing this prospectus."
   a. May you immediately write back and divulge client confidences as necessary to defend yourself?
   b. Must you wait until you are actually charged with fraud and then introduce the client confidences that support your defense?
   c. Regardless of the timing, must you ask your client if she is willing to consent to your disclosure before you respond?

3. You represented a notorious leader of organized crime who recently passed away. You would like to write a novel about your experiences representing him. His wife is the executor of his estate. You obtain her permission to do so. Upon publication of the novel, you are subpoenaed to testify before a grand jury regarding some of the individuals who worked with your client. Do you have a basis for asserting the attorney-client privilege?

To Learn More

To review the materials covered in this chapter complete the CALI lesson on Exceptions to the Ethical Duty of Confidentiality Designed to Protect Third Persons from Harm at http://www.cali.org/lesson/1280.

For further reading on the role of these exceptions in the attorney-client relationship, try For further reading see Clark D. Cunningham, *How to Explain Confidentiality?*, 9 CLINICAL L. REV. 579 (2003) and Fred C. Zacharias, *Rethinking Confidentiality,* 74 IOWA L. REV. 351 (1989).

Unit Three Review

Outline Review

In this unit we have examined the scope of the various doctrines that protect client information and some of the exceptions to those doctrines. Complete the following chart to review those doctrines:

	Confidentiality	Privilege
Purpose	To protect the client from an attorney's disclosure.	To protect the attorney-client communication from compelled disclosure.
In what legal context does this doctrine come up?		Compelled disclosure in trial, discovery, government investigations, or other situations in which third persons seek access through the subpoena power.
What information is protected?	All information related to the representation.	
Who can consent and how?		Only the client has the authority to waive the privilege; however, the attorney as the client's agent has the power to do so.
When does the protection begin and end?	Begins when an attorney receives information relating to a representation. Does not end.	
What disclosures destroy the protection?	None.	
What is the exception for dangerous clients?	Attorney has discretion to disclose information that could prevent death or substantial bodily harm.	

	Confidentiality	Privilege
What is the exception for fraudulent clients?		Attorney may be compelled to disclose communications concerning the client's future crime or fraud, which the client actually carried out (with or without the attorney's help).
What is the self-defense exception?	Attorney has discretion to disclose information to establish a claim or defense on behalf of the lawyer in a controversy between the lawyer and the client, to establish a defense to a criminal charge or civil claim against the lawyer based upon conduct in which the client was involved, or to respond to allegations in any proceeding concerning the lawyer's representation of the client.	

Multiple Choice Review

1. You represent Dan Dollar in a tax fraud matter. You requested that he gather all the relevant records currently in his possession. Dan emailed you copies of all his computerized financial records for the year 2010 (the tax year in dispute) and marked the email "private—attorney-client communications." The IRS has issued a subpoena requesting "all accounting records for the tax year 2010." Assuming you object to the subpoena on the grounds of attorney-client privilege, what is the likely outcome and why?

   A. You will not be required to produce the documents because they are information relating to the representation.

   B. You will not be required to produce the documents because you received the documents in the course of communicating with a client in order to provide legal advice, and the communication was private.

   C. Your objection will not be upheld because the documents were not a communication for the purposes of obtaining legal advice.

   D. Your objection will not be upheld because the attorney-client privilege does not apply to IRS subpoenas.

2. Suppose you took the client's financial records and organized them into a single spreadsheet, without any commentary or analysis, and sent that spreadsheet back to the client to review for errors. The IRS prosecutes the client for tax fraud and subpoenas you asking for "all financial records concerning the taxpayer for tax year 2010." Would you be able to withhold the spreadsheet under the work-product doctrine?

   A. Your objection will not be upheld because the work-product doctrine does not apply in criminal actions.

   B. Your objection will not be upheld because the spreadsheet was not prepared in anticipation of litigation.

⌐   C. Your objection will be upheld because you created the spreadsheet to pre-
        pare for litigation and alternate sources of the information are available
        through discovery without substantial hardship.

     D. Your objection will be upheld because you used the spreadsheet as a means of
        communicating with your client for the purposes of providing legal advice.

3.   Assume that you have been ordered to produce witness statements in a products
     liability case. A client in another pending case would benefit significantly (with-
     out any direct harm to your client) by having access to those same witness state-
     ments. You disclose the statements to the second client without the knowledge
     or consent of the first client. Are you subject to discipline?

     A. No, because the court has overruled your claim of privilege, so the docu-
        ments are no longer confidential.

     B. No, because you are impliedly authorized to disclose confidential informa-
        tion in order to further the representation.

⌐   C. Yes, the documents are confidential and there is no exception to the duty
        that applies here.

     D. Yes, because the witness statements are not admissible evidence in another case.

4.   Your client comes to you for advice regarding his wife's talk of a divorce. He
     wants to prevent the divorce if possible. In the interview, you learn that he has
     contracted Human papillomaviruses (genital warts) from an affair that he has since
     ended. He is still living with his spouse, who is not aware of the affair or the in-
     fection. He has indicated that he will not reveal his infection to her, as this would
     make certain a divorce, and that he "can't promise" that he will refrain from sex-
     ual relations with his wife, as he believes if they can conceive a child, she will
     revisit their marriage. You are trying to determine whether you can disclose this
     information to the wife and you tell a friend who is an OB/GYN about the sit-
     uation. She tells you that there is no cure for HPV but that the infection some-
     times clears on its own. She also tells you that some varieties of HPV are the
     main cause of cervical cancer. Unfortunately, you are not very discreet and the
     doctor realizes that the wife is her patient and tells her about husband's infection.
     Are you subject to discipline?

     A. No, because an attorney may secure advice about the lawyer's compliance
        with the Rules.

     B. No, because an attorney may reveal information to prevent substantial bod-
        ily harm.

⌐   C. Yes, because the attorney revealed confidential information to the doctor.

     D. Yes, because the doctor told the wife about husband's infection.

5.   You agree to represent a number of landowners in a nuisance suit against a neigh-
     boring factory. Your engagement letter contains the following clause:

         "Clients agree that attorney may freely share information obtained dur-
         ing the representation among all co-clients."

     You provide no further information to the clients regarding this clause. In the
     course of your representation, you learn that Client A intends to purchase a
     number of houses in the next block and pursue a commercial development. You
     share this information with the other clients, who organize a protest to the zon-

ing board, effectively blocking Client A's intended development. Are you subject to discipline?

a. Yes, because clients cannot prospectively waive confidentiality.

b. Yes, because the waiver of confidentiality was not informed.

c. No, because the attorney-client privilege does not apply between co-clients.

d. No, because the information was not related to the nuisance action for which you were representing these clients.

Answers and Analysis

1. Answer A is incorrect because the standard quoted is the Rule 1.6 standard for the ethical duty of confidentiality and the question is about privilege. Answer D is incorrect because the attorney-client privilege can be raised in objection to a subpoena. Answers B and C are the mirror opposite of one another (which, on standardized tests, can be a clue that one or the other is the correct answer). Here the correct answer is C—"gathering and sending" documents already in the client's possession is not the same thing as communicating.

2. The correct answer is C. This is work product because even the process of compiling and organizing materials requires analysis and work that the adversary should not be able to take advantage of. A is incorrect as a matter of law. B is incorrect as a matter of fact—whether the timing test or the purpose test is used for work-product analysis, the reason the client sought your representation was in anticipation of a possible tax fraud action. D is incorrect because the standard cited is that of attorney-client privilege and the question is asking about work-product protections.

3. D is just silly. Whether something is admissible has nothing to do with confidentiality. A is not correct because a waiver of privilege objections by a court does not abolish the ethical duty of confidentiality. B is tricky and wrong. You are indeed impliedly authorized to disclose confidential information in order to further the representation, but here, the representation you are furthering is not that of the client whose information you are disclosing. So, C is correct.

4. A is not correct. The rule provides that an attorney may secure legal advice about the lawyer's compliance with these rules. Talking to the doctor was not securing legal advice. Even if it was, it could have been accomplished without revealing the identity of the client and so violated the principle that authorized disclosures may only be "to the extent the lawyer reasonably believes necessary." Whether this is substantial bodily harm is a very close question, and so answer B is tempting, but the attorney's purpose was not to prevent substantial bodily harm but to determine whether the wife was at risk of substantial bodily harm, so the justification—even if it applies—does not fit the facts. Answer C is correct. Answer D is simply the result of the breach of confidentiality by the attorney and so is not the best answer.

5   The correct answer is B. A client's signature on an engagement letter with a clause waiving confidentiality is not evidence of informed consent. Without having actually discussed the waiver with your clients, you do not have consent to disclose this information. Moreover, because clients can always withdraw their consent, you would be ill advised to rely on a prospective waiver of confidentiality regarding information neither you nor the client could have anticipated. Answer D is tempting, but remember that Rule 1.6 provides a standard of "related to the

representation" not "related to the subject matter of the representation." You would have been unlikely to have learned from Client A about his intent to purchase this property were you not representing him. It is information you learned because of the representation and so is information related to the representation. Answer A is also tempting, but like absolute answers, it is difficult to say that a prospective waiver of confidentiality is always prohibited. Difficult? Yes. Impossible? No. Finally, answer C is not correct even though it is true that the attorney-client privilege is waived between co-clients. This is not a question for which the privilege is relevant. Your disclosure was not pursuant to a subpoena or court order.

Unit Four

Candor, Confidentiality, and Compliance

In this unit we will look more closely at the tensions created by duties to the public, the courts, and to third persons, which sometimes may conflict with the duty of confidentiality to a client.

Goals of Unit Four

The major goals of this unit are to gain a more sophisticated understanding of your duty to counsel clients regarding compliance with the law and the limits of confidentiality when faced with a client for whom that counseling has failed. This unit asks you to address some of the major tensions found in the attorney's role—the duty to advocate for the client, to act as an officer of the court, and to act with fairness toward third parties and concern for the public. The adversarial ethic is deeply rooted in American law and lawyer ethics. The 1968 American Bar Association Model Code of Professional Responsibility stated a primary value of adversarial representation in Canon 7: "A lawyer shall represent a client zealously within the bounds of the law." This ethic required an attorney to make the client's interests primary, over any other interest save the law itself. Thus, the required zealousness is described as that which is "within the bounds of the law." Certainly the consideration of the interests of third parties was minimally expressed in the Code. The Code warned that a lawyer must not "intentionally fail to seek the lawful objectives of his client … through reasonably available means permitted by law." Model Code of Prof'l Responsibility DR 7-101(A)(1) (1980).

The more current ABA Model Rules of Professional Conduct retained much of this commitment to the role of attorney as partisan advocate. However, other values, such as candor to tribunals and fairness to third persons, took on greater weight. In this unit you will explore the balance among these values.

259

Pre-Test

1. Which of the following statements most accurately describes the duty of an attorney to police his or her client's conduct for compliance with the law?

    A. A lawyer may not permit clients to violate the law and must report them if they persist in doing so.

    B. A lawyer may not provide a client any information about the law if he reasonably believes the client will use that information to violate the law.

    C. A lawyer may not counsel a client regarding the legal consequences of criminal or fraudulent activity if the lawyer reasonably believes the client intends to engage in that activity.

    D. A lawyer may not counsel a client to violate the law, but may help the client understand the legal consequences if the client should choose to violate the law.

2. Which of the following statements most accurately describes the duty of a lawyer to aid the court in correctly deciding cases before it?

    A. A lawyer may not permit a client to take the stand if the lawyer believes the client may lie.

    B. A lawyer must reveal eyewitnesses discovered during investigation of the client's case.

    C. A lawyer may not retain possession of the fruits or instrumentalities of crimes committed by a client, even if recovered from the client in confidence.

    D. A criminal defense lawyer cannot allow a client to plead not guilty to a criminal charge when the defense lawyer knows that the client has committed the crime.

    E. A lawyer must reveal all legal authority that would support the opponent's case and that the opponent has failed to discover.

3. Which of the following statements most accurately describes the duty of a lawyer to an opposing party in a negotiation?

    A. A lawyer has no duty to an opponent in negotiations other than the duty to act lawfully.

    B. A lawyer has a duty to reveal all relevant information to an opponent in negotiations.

    C. A lawyer shall not seek to obtain waivers of important rights of opposing parties in negotiations.

    D. A lawyer shall not knowingly make a false statement of material fact or law to a third person in negotiations.

    E. A lawyer shall not fail to disclose a material fact to a third person if that disclosure is necessary to avoid assisting in a crime or fraudulent act by the client.

Chapter Twelve

Confidentiality and the Duty of Candor to the Court

Learning Objectives

After you have read this chapter and completed the assignments, you should be able to:

- Define perjury, false, tribunal, knowing, and reasonable belief.
- Apply the duty to be truthful to the court in pleadings and evidence under both the rules of conduct and the rules of procedure.
- Identify the circumstances in which an attorney has a duty to disclose confidential client information in order to comply with the duty of candor.
- Demonstrate methods of persuading clients to be truthful.
- Describe reasonable remedial measures when you or your client have submitted false evidence.

Rules to Study

A number of rules relate to the attorney's duty of candor. While we will reexamine some of these again in the chapter on litigation ethics, for this chapter you should read and study Model Rules 1.2(d), 1.6, 3.1, 3.3, 3.4(b), 4.1, and 8.4. We will also compare these rules to the criminal standards for perjury and civil law standards for fraud and misrepresentation.

Preliminary Problem

Hopefully, you will not have to face a representation in which you must decide whether to reveal confidential information in order to save a life or rectify a substantial fraud. However, unless you are extremely fortunate, you are very likely to face a situation in which your client lies or withholds information. When do you have a duty to dissuade a client from these misrepresentations? If you discover the lie or deception after it has already occurred, what are your options and obligations? In this chapter we will examine the duty of candor (whether to a tribunal or to a third person) and the extent to which that duty is an exception to the duty of confidentiality. Consider how the tension between candor and confidentiality might arise in practice:

You represent Paul Parent in an action for modification of his child support obligation. You are assisting Paul in filling out the form for calculating child support. Paul believes a modification is appropriate because his income has dropped, expenses have increased, and the earnings of his children's mother have increased substantially (or at least your client believes that to be the case). Previously, Paul worked during the week at a local company. He has been laid off from that job and now works for a temporary agency. He often must work on weekends, which is also when he has parenting time with the children. Paul has relatives care for the children while he works and pays those relatives $10 an hour. You have asked Paul for verification of his income and expenses. If Paul explains that he works on a cash basis only and has no independent verification, how do you respond? Pick up the conversation at that point. Can you simply accept your client's statement of income and expenses? What if your client's lifestyle seems to indicate that he is earning substantially more than he is representing?

Suppose you learn that your client has indeed hidden earnings. You confront your client and the client confirms your suspicions. Now what do you do? Suppose you learned this after you have already submitted a draft statement of income and expenses to the opposing party and the couple will be entering mediation based on these numbers? Suppose you learned this after you had already filed a statement of income and expenses with the court? What if you had not learned the truth of your client's income until after the court had ruled on the modification motion?

12.1 Reading the Rules: Rule 3.3 Candor to the Tribunal

When the attorney's role as representative of a client comes into conflict with the attorney's role as officer of the court, which role should take priority? The answer has differed over time and across jurisdictions. Prior to the Model Rules, the prevailing view was that an attorney could not participate in the presentation of false evidence but at the same time the attorney could not breach client confidences in order to prevent it. Thus, if an attorney discovered that a client intended to commit perjury, he or she was required to remonstrate with the client in an attempt to persuade the client to testify truthfully. If that effort failed, the attorney was to attempt to withdraw. Only if all else failed did some jurisdictions allow disclosure to the court. In some cases, particularly those involving criminal defendants, a middle ground was suggested: allowing the client to testify in a free narrative, without questions from counsel, and prohibiting counsel from arguing the false testimony in summation. These proposed solutions — withdrawal and free narrative — removed the *attorney's* involvement in the perjury but did little to effectively solve the underlying problem. These attempted solutions likewise reflected an ambivalence about which competing values should take priority: candor to the tribunal or loyalty (confidentiality) to the client.

A similar inability to reconcile these competing values was reflected in the solution to the problem of past perjury or fraud. In a 1953 ABA Opinion, the committee took the position that an attorney who discovered that a client had perpetrated a fraud during the attorney's representation of the client should remonstrate with the client and if unsuccessful, should sever the relationship but not disclose. ABA Comm. on Ethics and Prof'l Responsibility, Formal Op. 287 (1953). When the Code was adopted, D.R. 7-102(A)(4) and (B)(1) appeared to override Opinion 287 and mandate disclosure, but an amendment to 7-102(B)(1), adopted by the ABA and many jurisdictions, excepted situations in which the attorney knew of the perjury or fraud by means of a "privileged communication." When the ABA later interpreted "privileged communication" to include both confidences and secrets, the disclosure obligation was effectively negated. ABA Comm. on Ethics and Prof'l Responsibility, Formal Op. 341 (1975). Many jurisdictions returned to the mandatory withdrawal coupled with non-disclosure required by Opinion 287. Arguably, in this context, loyalty won out over candor.

Where are we today? Read Ohio's version of Rule 3.3, which is identical to the Model Rules except for the italicized portions.

Ohio Supreme Court Rules of Professional Conduct
Rule 3.3: Candor toward the Tribunal

(a) A lawyer shall not knowingly *do any of the following*:

(1) make a false statement of fact or law to a tribunal or fail to correct a false statement of material fact or law previously made to the tribunal by the lawyer;

(2) fail to disclose to the tribunal legal authority in the controlling jurisdiction known to the lawyer to be directly adverse to the position of the client and not disclosed by opposing counsel;

(3) offer evidence that the lawyer knows to be false. If a lawyer, the lawyer's client, or a witness called by the lawyer has offered material evidence and the lawyer comes to know of its falsity, the lawyer shall take reasonable measures to remedy the situation, including, if necessary, disclosure to the tribunal. A lawyer may refuse to offer evidence, other than the testimony of a defendant in a criminal matter that the lawyer reasonably believes is false.

(b) A lawyer who represents a client in an adjudicative proceeding and who knows that a person, *including the client,* intends to engage, is engaging, or has engaged in criminal or fraudulent conduct related to the proceeding shall take reasonable measures to remedy the situation, including, if necessary, disclosure to the tribunal.

(c) The duties stated in divisions (a) and (b) of this rule continue until *the issue to which the duty relates is determined by the highest tribunal that may consider the issue, or the time has expired for such determination,* and apply even if compliance requires disclosure of information otherwise protected by Rule 1.6.

(d) In an ex parte proceeding, a lawyer shall inform the tribunal of all material facts known to the lawyer that will enable the tribunal to make an informed decision, whether or not the facts are adverse.

Context

Rule 3.3 is the first rule we look at in the section of the rules governing the attorney's role as an advocate. In this chapter we will focus on the ways in which this rule is in tension with confidentiality. We will examine generally the balance between litigation advocacy and competing duties to the court and opponents in Unit Six on fairness and the adversary ethic.

Relationships

As with other rules we have studied, this rule presents a number of ambiguous key terms. For example, what is a "tribunal?" Where would you look for a definition of that term? Remember that some definitions can be found in comments, others in Rule 1.0, and still others require reference to case law. One of the most difficult questions of terminology is the requirement that a lawyer "know" that evidence is false. Can a lawyer avoid knowing? Can he or she do so consistent with good lawyering and one's obligations of competence under Rule 1.1? How certain must a lawyer be that a client is lying before taking action? Try to fashion a line for yourself that makes sense on this question, then read the definition of "know" in Rule 1.0 and the further materials in this chapter. How does your definition of knowledge compare?

Ohio Rule 1.2(d), like the ABA Model Rule, provides that "A lawyer shall not counsel a client to engage, or assist a client, in conduct that the lawyer knows is criminal or fraudulent, but a lawyer may discuss the legal consequences of any proposed course of conduct with a client and may counsel or assist a client to make a good faith effort to determine the validity, scope, meaning or application of the law." Obviously perjury is both a crime and a fraud on the court, so that Rule 1.2(d) would prohibit assisting a client in testifying falsely. However is all "false evidence" perjury?

Compare the federal perjury statute to Rule 3.3.

18 U.S.C. § 1621 (2011)

Whoever—

(1) having taken an oath before a competent tribunal, officer, or person, in any case in which a law of the United States authorizes an oath to be administered, that he will testify, declare, depose, or certify truly, or that any written testimony, declaration, deposition, or certificate by him subscribed, is true, willfully and contrary to such oath states or subscribes any material matter which he does not believe to be true; or

(2) in any declaration, certificate, verification, or statement under penalty of perjury as permitted under section 1746 of title 28, United States Code [unsworn statements subject to perjury], willfully subscribes as true any material matter which he does not believe to be true;

is guilty of perjury and shall, except as otherwise expressly provided by law, be fined under this title or imprisoned not more than five years, or both. This section is applicable whether the statement or subscription is made within or without the United States.

What is the key element required for perjury that does not appear to be required for a violation of Rule 3.3?

If the attorney is aware a witness has lied on the stand, Rule 3.3 requires "remedial measures" that include revealing the lie to the court. But what if the witness is the attorney's client? Wouldn't this violate the duty of confidentiality? Remember that in most states Rule 1.6(b)(6) provides an exception to confidentiality to comply with "other law." Rule 3.3 could certainly be considered "other law" couldn't it? What if your state is one of the eleven states that does not include this "other law" exception in its version of Rule 1.6 but does include 3.3's mandatory duty to take remedial measures? How would you reconcile the two rules?

We will examine more closely the relationship between Rule 3.3 and 4.1, which governs candor to third persons, in the next chapter.

Structure

One useful way to examine the structure of Rule 3.3 is to divide the rule into a list of dos and don'ts. A second examination necessary to understanding the rule is to look carefully at the lines drawn around the rule. In what setting do they apply? The rule's title is "candor toward the tribunal." What is a tribunal? If an attorney knows his client has lied in a deposition, does 3.3 require the attorney to take action? Some states include in the text of the rule the language found in many other state's comments, providing that the rule applies "in an ancillary proceeding conducted pursuant to the tribunal's adjudicative authority, such as a deposition." What about lying in mediation? What if the mediation is court ordered? What if the mediation is required by law as a prerequisite to filing suit? What if the mediation is conducted as part of an attempt to settle before suit is filed? Comment 5 to Rule 2.4 indicates that Rule 3.3 governs only when "dispute-resolution process takes place before a tribunal, as in binding arbitration." Otherwise, Rule 4.1, which we will address in the next chapter, applies. Finally consider misrepresentations made before a legislature, council, or agency that acts in a rule-making or policy-making capacity. Model Rule 3.9 provides a similar duty of candor as that provided by Rule 3.3(a)(1) if the proceeding involves the presentation of argument or evidence.

Notice that part (d) of the rule provides an important qualifier on all the other duties. Why are *ex parte* proceedings treated differently?

A very important aspect of this rule's structure is the timing of each of the duties. When is each duty in the rule most likely to arise? When do the duties of Rule 3.3 end? Ohio provides a fairly clear endpoint in its rule. Most jurisdictions adopt the Model Rule endpoint, "the conclusion of the proceeding," which the comments explain means until the case has been resolved on appeal or the time for appeal has passed. How does that differ from the Ohio endpoint?

Reasons

As you have seen, the balance between loyalty and candor has been weighted differently over time. Which do you think is the best balance? Why?

Visualize

The classic movie depiction of the line between assisting a client with preparing evidence and suborning perjury has been from the 1959 movie *Anatomy of Murder* starring Jimmy Stewart as a criminal defense attorney. The movie is well worth watching to help you visualize the choices an attorney might make in balancing the duty to court and client.

Two important variables to consider in Rule 3.3 are what you know and how well you know it. Think about your duties with each of these combinations:

	Type of falsity			
Attorney's level of knowledge of falsity	*Perjury*	*False Material Evidence*	*Misleading Material Evidence*	*False Immaterial Evidence*
Know				
Believe				
Suspect				

Notice that how you complete these boxes will depend in part on when the attorney becomes aware of false evidence having been submitted.

Imagine

Think about how this rule comes into play at various stages of the representation. What will you say or do to comply with this rule at each of these points?

The initial client interview

The investigation of a client's matter

The formal discovery process

The negotiation process

Pre-trial motions

Trial

Questions

1. Prosecutor has filed a case involving a robbery at a convenience store. The police statement of the store clerk was that an unarmed robber shoved a bag at her and said "Fill it with cash." This is consistent with the testimony of three eyewitnesses (customers in the store) who all insist that the robber did not have a gun. In preparing the clerk for testimony, prosecutor asks the clerk if she is sure that the robber did not have a gun. She then insists that she saw a gun, and describes it as "a big handgun." The clerk is consistent thereafter in her recollection of the event, even after the store's video surveillance camera seems to show that there was no gun.

   Two years later, when the case goes to trial, the clerk testifies that she saw a gun. Does the prosecutor have a duty to take remedial measures? If the defense counsel impeaches her testimony with her prior inconsistent statement, is the clerk guilty of perjury? *Montano v. City of Chicago*, 535 F.3d 558, 564-66 (7th Cir. 2008) ("There is a marked difference between a witness who knowingly lies about a material matter and a witness who is impeached with a prior inconsistent account of a sudden and chaotic event that happened years ago. The former is almost always perjury; the latter may be the product of confusion, mistake, or faulty memory.").

2. Suppose the clerk in the store robbery had shot a customer, thinking he was a robber, and is now being charged with assault with a deadly weapon. The clerk told police that the victim had come into the store minutes before closing time, was "looking nervous," and "hanging around." When the other customer in the store left, the victim came up to the counter and stuck his hand in his pocket. According to the police statement, the clerk feared he was pulling a gun, and she moved to defend herself. When the defense attorney questions the client at the jail, she says she never did actually see a gun. After the clerk learns that the police actually recovered a gun from the victim at the hospital, she says that she thinks, after all, that she did see the victim pull a gun from his pocket before she reacted. May the defense attorney allow the clerk to testify that she saw a gun? That she thinks she saw a gun?

3. Suppose the clerk had been consistent all along in claiming that the victim pulled a gun. Suppose that no gun is found at the scene and that the victim took himself to the hospital. The case proceeds to trial and the client wins, based largely on self-defense. Client joins attorney for a drink after the trial and says

"Boy, that story about the customer pulling a gun really worked. I was pretty convincing huh? I even had you believing it. I'm sorry about having to pull one over on you, but all's well that ends well, eh?"

[handwritten: under the rules, you have no duty to rectify because the case is over; can't appeal an acquittal.]

12.2 Refusing to Offer False Evidence

One way to avoid having to reveal a client's confidential information in order to remedy a false statement is simply to prevent the false testimony in the first place. Rule 3.3(a)(3) provides that an attorney may refuse to offer testimony or evidence "that the lawyer reasonably believes is false." Ordinarily, your client will defer to your professional judgment on the matter. Recall from our study of Rule 1.2 that, while tactics are within the decision making authority of attorneys, if a client disagrees with those tactics—especially witnesses to be called—the rules defer to other law to sort out the impasse. States disagree on the answer. Some courts hold that an attorney's refusal to call a particular witness is the attorney's decision alone and cannot form the basis for ineffective assistance of counsel claims. For example, the court in *Clayton v. State*, 63 S.W.3d 201, 209 (Mo. 2001), commented that "the selection of particular witnesses in general is a matter of trial strategy and is virtually unchangeable on an ineffective assistance claim." Other states apply general agency law and hold that that it is only "when counsel and a fully informed criminal defendant client reach an absolute impasse as to ... tactical decisions ... the client's wishes must control." *State v. Ali*, 407 S.E.2d 183, 189 (N.C. 1991). Obviously, if you decide to cede to your client's insistence that you call a particular witness, despite your reasonable belief that the witness will lie, you may find yourself in the situation of having to reveal that lie to the court if it materializes.

[handwritten: courts are split on when someone can testify in disagreement]

Unfortunately, this issue becomes much more delicate when the witness is your client in a criminal case. When a criminal defendant wishes to testify, in most states Rule 1.2 provides that this is absolutely a decision within the client's authority. The right is grounded in the defendant's Sixth Amendment rights: "[I]t cannot be doubted that a defendant in a criminal case has the right to take the witness stand and to testify in his or her own defense." *Rock v. Arkansas*, 483 U.S. 44 (1987). Moreover, Rule 3.3(a)(3) does not permit an attorney to refuse the client's demand to testify, even if the attorney reasonably believes the testimony will be false, if the client is a criminal defendant. However, the rule does not permit an attorney to knowingly submit false evidence, even in a criminal case. If an attorney knows that his criminal defense client will testify falsely, do the client's Sixth Amendment rights trump Rule 3.3 and require the attorney to assist the client in that testimony?

[handwritten: 6th Amendment right]

The United States Supreme Court addressed this issue in the following landmark case:

[handwritten: lawyer knows of perjury]

Nix v. Whiteside
475 U.S. 157 (1986)

Chief Justice BURGER delivered the opinion of the Court.

We granted certiorari to decide whether the Sixth Amendment right of a criminal defendant to assistance of counsel is violated when an attorney refuses to cooperate with the defendant in presenting perjured testimony at his trial.

[handwritten: issue]

Whiteside was convicted of second-degree murder by a jury verdict which was affirmed by the Iowa courts. The killing took place on February 8, 1977, in Cedar Rapids, Iowa. Whiteside and two others went to one Calvin Love's apartment late that night, seeking marihuana. Love was in bed when Whiteside and his companions arrived; an argument between Whiteside and Love over the marihuana ensued. At one point, Love directed his girlfriend to get his "piece," and at another point got up, then returned to his bed. According to Whiteside's testimony, Love then started to reach under his pillow and moved toward Whiteside. Whiteside stabbed Love in the chest, inflicting a fatal wound.

Whiteside was charged with murder, and when counsel was appointed he objected to the lawyer initially appointed, claiming that he felt uncomfortable with a lawyer who had formerly been a prosecutor. Gary L. Robinson was then appointed and immediately began an investigation. Whiteside gave him a statement that he had stabbed Love as the latter "was pulling a pistol from underneath the pillow on the bed." Upon questioning by Robinson, however, Whiteside indicated that he had not actually seen a gun, but that he was convinced that Love had a gun. No pistol was found on the premises; shortly after the police search following the stabbing, which had revealed no weapon, the victim's family had removed all of the victim's possessions from the apartment. Robinson interviewed Whiteside's companions who were present during the stabbing, and none had seen a gun during the incident. Robinson advised Whiteside that the existence of a gun was not necessary to establish the claim of self-defense, and that only a reasonable belief that the victim had a gun nearby was necessary even though no gun was actually present.

Until shortly before trial, Whiteside consistently stated to Robinson that he had not actually seen a gun, but that he was convinced that Love had a gun in his hand. About a week before trial, during preparation for direct examination, Whiteside for the first time told Robinson and his associate Donna Paulsen that he had seen something "metallic" in Love's hand. When asked about this, Whiteside responded: "[I]n Howard Cook's case there was a gun. If I don't say I saw a gun, I'm dead." Robinson told Whiteside that such testimony would be perjury and repeated that it was not necessary to prove that a gun was available but only that Whiteside reasonably believed that he was in danger. On Whiteside's insisting that he would testify that he saw "something metallic" Robinson told him, according to Robinson's testimony:

> [W]e could not allow him to [testify falsely] because that would be perjury, and as officers of the court we would be suborning perjury if we allowed him to do it; ... I advised him that if he did do that it would be my duty to advise the Court of what he was doing and that I felt he was committing perjury; also, that I probably would be allowed to attempt to impeach that particular testimony.

Robinson also indicated he would seek to withdraw from the representation if Whiteside insisted on committing perjury.

Whiteside testified in his own defense at trial and stated that he "knew" that Love had a gun and that he believed Love was reaching for a gun and he had acted swiftly in self-defense. On cross-examination, he admitted that he had not actually seen a gun in Love's hand. Robinson presented evidence that Love had been seen with a sawed-off shotgun on other occasions, that the

[margin notes:]

Stabbing over drugs

If Whiteside had not said this, would Robinson "know" that he was lying about seeing a gun?

attorney tells client he may be compelled to tell it. about perjury

Why didn't Robinson refuse to call his client to testify?

police search of the apartment may have been careless, and that the victim's family had removed everything from the apartment shortly after the crime. Robinson presented this evidence to show a basis for Whiteside's asserted fear that Love had a gun.

The jury returned a verdict of second-degree murder, and Whiteside moved for a new trial, claiming that he had been deprived of a fair trial by Robinson's admonitions not to state that he saw a gun or "something metallic." The trial court held a hearing, heard testimony by Whiteside and Robinson, and denied the motion. The trial court made specific findings that the facts were as related by Robinson.

lower ct. holding

The Supreme Court of Iowa affirmed respondent's conviction ...

Whiteside then petitioned for a writ of habeas corpus in the United States District Court for the Southern District of Iowa. In that petition Whiteside alleged that he had been denied effective assistance of counsel and of his right to present a defense by Robinson's refusal to allow him to testify as he had proposed. The District Court denied the writ. ...

The United States Court of Appeals for the Eighth Circuit reversed and directed that the writ of habeas corpus be granted. The Court of Appeals accepted the findings of the trial judge, affirmed by the Iowa Supreme Court, that trial counsel believed with good cause that Whiteside would testify falsely and acknowledged that under *Harris v. New York*, 401 U. S. 222 (1971), a criminal defendant's privilege to testify in his own behalf does not include a right to commit perjury. Nevertheless, the court reasoned that an intent to commit perjury, communicated to counsel, does not alter a defendant's right to effective assistance of counsel and that Robinson's admonition to Whiteside that he would inform the court of Whiteside's perjury constituted a threat to violate the attorney's duty to preserve client confidences. According to the Court of Appeals, this threatened violation of client confidences breached the standards of effective representation set down in *Strickland v. Washington*, 466 U. S. 668 (1984). The court also concluded that Strickland 's prejudice requirement was satisfied by an implication of prejudice from the conflict between Robinson's duty of loyalty to his client and his ethical duties. A petition for rehearing en banc was denied, with Judges Gibson, Ross, Fagg, and Bowman dissenting. We granted certiorari and we reverse.

threat?

ct. of appeals categorizes perjury stmt by attorney as a threat

II

* * *

B

In *Strickland v. Washington*, 466 U. S. 668 (1984), we held that to obtain relief by way of federal habeas corpus on a claim of a deprivation of effective assistance of counsel under the Sixth Amendment, the movant must establish both serious attorney error and prejudice. To show such error, it must be established that the assistance rendered by counsel was constitutionally deficient in that "counsel made errors so serious that counsel was not functioning as 'counsel' guaranteed the defendant by the Sixth Amendment." Id. at 687. To show prejudice, it must be established that the claimed lapses in counsel's performance rendered the trial unfair so as to "undermine confidence in the outcome" of the trial. *Id.* at 694.

In *Strickland*, we acknowledged that the Sixth Amendment does not require any particular response by counsel to a problem that may arise. Rather, the Sixth Amendment inquiry is into whether the attorney's conduct was "reasonably effective." To counteract the natural tendency to fault an unsuccessful defense, a court reviewing a claim of ineffective assistance must "indulge a strong presumption that counsel's conduct falls within the wide range of reasonable professional assistance." *Id.* at 689. In giving shape to the perimeters of this range of reasonable professional assistance, *Strickland* mandates that "[p]revailing norms of practice as reflected in American Bar Association Standards and the like, … are guides to determining what is reasonable, but they are only guides." *Id.* at 688.

Under the *Strickland* standard, breach of an ethical standard does not necessarily make out a denial of the Sixth Amendment guarantee of assistance of counsel. When examining attorney conduct, a court must be careful not to narrow the wide range of conduct acceptable under the Sixth Amendment so restrictively as to constitutionalize particular standards of professional conduct and thereby intrude into the state's proper authority to define and apply the standards of professional conduct applicable to those it admits to practice in its courts. In some future case challenging attorney conduct in the course of a state-court trial, we may need to define with greater precision the weight to be given to recognized canons of ethics, the standards established by the state in statutes or professional codes, and the Sixth Amendment in defining the proper scope and limits on that conduct. Here we need not face that question, since virtually all of the sources speak with one voice.

We turn next to the question presented: the definition of the range of "reasonable professional" responses to a criminal defendant client who informs counsel that he will perjure himself on the stand. We must determine whether, in this setting, Robinson's conduct fell within the wide range of professional responses to threatened client perjury acceptable under the Sixth Amendment.

In *Strickland*, we recognized counsel's duty of loyalty and his "overarching duty to advocate the defendant's cause." Plainly, that duty is limited to legitimate, lawful conduct compatible with the very nature of a trial as a search for truth. Although counsel must take all reasonable lawful means to attain the objectives of the client, counsel is precluded from taking steps or in any way assisting the client in presenting false evidence or otherwise violating the law.… [The Court reviews standards of the ABA Canons, the Code of Professional Responsibility, and the Rules of Professional Conduct, especially Rules 1.2 and 3.3.]

These standards confirm that the legal profession has accepted that an attorney's ethical duty to advance the interests of his client is limited by an equally solemn duty to comply with the law and standards of professional conduct; it specifically ensures that the client may not use false evidence. This special duty of an attorney to prevent and disclose frauds upon the court derives from the recognition that perjury is as much a crime as tampering with witnesses or jurors by way of promises and threats, and undermines the administration of justice.

* * *

It is universally agreed that at a minimum the attorney's first duty when confronted with a proposal for perjurious testimony is to attempt to dissuade the client from the unlawful course of conduct. Model Rules of Professional Conduct, Rule 3.3, Comment; Wolfram, *Client Perjury*, 50 S. Cal. L. Rev. 809, 846 (1977). A statement directly in point is found in the commentary to the Model Rules of Professional Conduct under the heading "False Evidence":

> When false evidence is offered by the client, however, a conflict may arise between the lawyer's duty to keep the client's revelations confidential and the duty of candor to the court. Upon ascertaining that material evidence is false, the lawyer should seek to persuade the client that the evidence should not be offered or, if it has been offered, that its false character should immediately be disclosed.

Model Rules of Professional Conduct, Rule 3.3, Comment (1983) (emphasis added).

The commentary thus also suggests that an attorney's revelation of his client's perjury to the court is a professionally responsible and acceptable response to the conduct of a client who has actually given perjured testimony. Similarly, the Model Rules and the commentary, as well as the Code of Professional Responsibility adopted in Iowa, expressly permit withdrawal from representation as an appropriate response of an attorney when the client threatens to commit perjury. Model Rules of Professional Conduct, Rule 1.16(a)(1), Rule 1.6, Comment (1983); Code of Professional Responsibility, DR 2-110(B), (C) (1980). Withdrawal of counsel when this situation arises at trial gives rise to many difficult questions including possible mistrial and claims of double jeopardy.[6]

The essence of the brief amicus of the American Bar Association reviewing practices long accepted by ethical lawyers is that under no circumstance may a lawyer either advocate or passively tolerate a client's giving false testimony. This, of course, is consistent with the governance of trial conduct in what we have long called "a search for truth." The suggestion sometimes made that "a lawyer must believe his client, not judge him" in no sense means a lawyer can honorably be a party to or in any way give aid to presenting known perjury.

D

Considering Robinson's representation of respondent in light of these accepted norms of professional conduct, we discern no failure to adhere to reasonable professional standards that would in any sense make out a deprivation of the Sixth Amendment right to counsel. Whether Robinson's conduct is seen as a successful attempt to dissuade his client from committing the crime

---

6. Instead, counsel would stand mute while the defendant undertook to present the false version in narrative form in his own words unaided by any direct examination. This conduct was thought to be a signal at least to the presiding judge that the attorney considered the testimony to be false and was seeking to disassociate himself from that course. Additionally, counsel would not be permitted to discuss the known false testimony in closing arguments. *See* ABA Standards for Criminal Justice, Proposed Standard 4-7.7 (2d ed. 1980). Most courts treating the subject rejected this approach and insisted on a more rigorous standard. The Eighth Circuit in this case and the Ninth Circuit have expressed approval of the "free narrative" standards. The Rule finally promulgated in the current Model Rules of Professional Conduct rejects any participation or passive role whatever by counsel in allowing perjury to be presented without challenge.

of perjury, or whether seen as a "threat" to withdraw from representation and disclose the illegal scheme, Robinson's representation of Whiteside falls well within accepted standards of professional conduct and the range of reasonable professional conduct acceptable under *Strickland*.

* * *

Robinson's admonitions to his client can in no sense be said to have forced respondent into an *impermissible* choice between his right to counsel and his right to testify as he proposed for there was no *permissible* choice to testify falsely. For defense counsel to take steps to persuade a criminal defendant to testify truthfully, or to withdraw, deprives the defendant of neither his right to counsel nor the right to testify truthfully. In *United States v. Havens*, 446 U. S. 620 (1980) we made clear that "when defendants testify, they must testify truthfully or suffer the consequences." *Id.* at 626. When an accused proposes to resort to perjury or to produce false evidence, one consequence is the risk of withdrawal of counsel.

On this record, the accused enjoyed continued representation within the bounds of reasonable professional conduct and did in fact exercise his right to testify; at most he was denied the right to have the assistance of counsel in the presentation of false testimony. Similarly, we can discern no breach of professional duty in Robinson's admonition to respondent that he would disclose respondent's perjury to the court. The crime of perjury in this setting is indistinguishable in substance from the crime of threatening or tampering with a witness or a juror. A defendant who informed his counsel that he was arranging to bribe or threaten witnesses or members of the jury would have no "right" to insist on counsel's assistance or silence. Counsel would not be limited to advising against that conduct. An attorney's duty of confidentiality, which totally covers the client's admission of guilt, does not extend to a client's announced plans to engage in future criminal conduct. In short, the responsibility of an ethical lawyer, as an officer of the court and a key component of a system of justice, dedicated to a search for truth, is essentially the same whether the client announces an intention to bribe or threaten witnesses or jurors or to commit or procure perjury. No system of justice worthy of the name can tolerate a lesser standard.

The rule adopted by the Court of Appeals, which seemingly would require an attorney to remain silent while his client committed perjury, is wholly incompatible with the established standards of ethical conduct and the laws of Iowa and contrary to professional standards promulgated by that State. The position advocated by petitioner, on the contrary, is wholly consistent with the Iowa standards of professional conduct and law, with the overwhelming majority of courts, and with codes of professional ethics. Since there has been no breach of any recognized professional duty, it follows that there can be no deprivation of the right to assistance of counsel under the *Strickland* standard.

E

We hold that, as a matter of law, counsel's conduct complained of here cannot establish the prejudice required for relief under the second strand of the *Strickland* inquiry.... The *Strickland* Court noted that the "benchmark" of an ineffective-assistance claim is the fairness of the adversary proceeding.

and that in judging prejudice and the likelihood of a different outcome, "[a] defendant has no entitlement to the luck of a lawless decisionmaker." *Strickland,* 466 U. S. at 695.

Whether he was persuaded or compelled to desist from perjury, Whiteside has no valid claim that confidence in the result of his trial has been diminished by his desisting from the contemplated perjury. Even if we were to assume that the jury might have believed his perjury, it does not follow that Whiteside was prejudiced

[handwritten margin note: even if jury believed perjury, no prejudice occurred]

In his attempt to evade the prejudice requirement of *Strickland,* Whiteside relies on cases involving conflicting loyalties of counsel. In *Cuyler v. Sullivan,* 446 U.S. 335 (1980),we held that a defendant could obtain relief without pointing to a specific prejudicial default on the part of his counsel, provided it is established that the attorney was "actively represent[ing] conflicting interests." *Id.* at 350.

Here, there was indeed a "conflict," but of a quite different kind; it was one imposed on the attorney by the client's proposal to commit the crime of fabricating testimony without which, as he put it, "I'm dead." This is not remotely the kind of conflict of interests dealt with in *Cuyler v. Sullivan.* Even in that case we did not suggest that all multiple representations necessarily resulted in an active conflict rendering the representation constitutionally infirm. If a "conflict" between a client's proposal and counsel's ethical obligation gives rise to a presumption that counsel's assistance was prejudicially ineffective, every guilty criminal's conviction would be suspect if the defendant had sought to obtain an acquittal by illegal means. Can anyone doubt what practices and problems would be spawned by such a rule and what volumes of litigation it would generate?

[handwritten margin note: ★ slippery slope argument]

Whiteside's attorney treated Whiteside's proposed perjury in accord with professional standards, and since Whiteside's truthful testimony could not have prejudiced the result of his trial, the Court of Appeals was in error to direct the issuance of a writ of habeas corpus and must be reversed.

Reversed.

Justice BRENNAN, concurring in the judgment.

This Court has no constitutional authority to establish rules of ethical conduct for lawyers practicing in the state courts. Nor does the Court enjoy any statutory grant of jurisdiction over legal ethics.

Accordingly, it is not surprising that the Court emphasizes that it "must be careful not to narrow the wide range of conduct acceptable under the Sixth Amendment so restrictively as to constitutionalize particular standards of professional conduct and thereby intrude into the state's proper authority to define and apply the standards of professional conduct applicable to those it admits to practice in its courts." I read this as saying in another way that the Court cannot tell the States or the lawyers in the States how to behave in their courts, unless and until federal rights are violated.

Unfortunately, the Court seems unable to resist the temptation of sharing with the legal community its vision of ethical conduct. But let there be no mistake: the Court's essay regarding what constitutes the correct response to a criminal client's suggestion that he will perjure himself is pure discourse without force of law.… [T]hat issue is a thorny one, but it is not an issue presented by this case. Lawyers, judges, bar associations, students, and others should understand that the problem has not now been "decided."

Justice STEVENS, concurring in the judgment.

Justice Holmes taught us that a word is but the skin of a living thought. A "fact" may also have a life of its own. From the perspective of an appellate judge, after a case has been tried and the evidence has been sifted by another judge, a particular fact may be as clear and certain as a piece of crystal or a small diamond. A trial lawyer, however, must often deal with mixtures of sand and clay. Even a pebble that seems clear enough at first glance may take on a different hue in a handful of gravel.

As we view this case, it appears perfectly clear that respondent intended to commit perjury, that his lawyer knew it, and that the lawyer had a duty—both to the court and to his client, for perjured testimony can ruin an otherwise meritorious case—to take extreme measures to prevent the perjury from occurring. The lawyer was successful and, from our unanimous and remote perspective, it is now pellucidly clear that the client suffered no "legally cognizable prejudice."

Nevertheless, beneath the surface of this case there are areas of uncertainty that cannot be resolved today. A lawyer's certainty that a change in his client's recollection is a harbinger of intended perjury—as well as judicial review of such apparent certainty—should be tempered by the realization that, after reflection, the most honest witness may recall (or sincerely believe he recalls) details that he previously overlooked. Similarly, the post-trial review of a lawyer's pretrial threat to expose perjury that had not yet been committed—and, indeed, may have been prevented by the threat—is by no means the same as review of the way in which such a threat may actually have been carried out. Thus, one can be convinced—as I am—that this lawyer's actions were a proper way to provide his client with effective representation without confronting the much more difficult questions of what a lawyer must, should, or may do after his client has given testimony that the lawyer does not believe. The answer to such questions may well be colored by the particular circumstances attending the actual event and its aftermath.

Because Justice BLACKMUN has preserved such questions for another day, and because I do not understand him to imply any adverse criticism of this lawyer's representation of his client, I join his opinion concurring in the judgment.

Note

Nix v. Whiteside presented a relatively straightforward case. The attorney *knew* that his client would testify falsely because he announced his intention to do so. The attorney was able to dissuade his client from perjury and, thus, was able to call him to testify. But what if you are not as sure that the client will perjure themselves? What if you are unable to dissuade the client from that perjury? When can you be sure that it is appropriate to refuse to permit a client to testify in a criminal case? These issues were addressed by the Court in the excerpt from the following case:

United States v. Long

857 F.2d 436, 444-47 (8th Cir. 1988), *cert. denied*, 502 U.S. 828 (1991)

* * *

In the instant case, Jackson's lawyer asked to approach the bench after the government had presented its case. The lawyer told the trial judge that Jackson wanted to testify and that he was concerned about his testimony. The lawyer said he advised Jackson not to take the stand. The judge excused the jury and everyone else in the courtroom, except a United States Marshal, Jackson, and his lawyer. At that point, the lawyer said, "I'm not sure if it wouldn't be appropriate for me to move for a withdrawal from this case based upon what I think may be elicited on the stand.... I'm concerned about the testimony that may come out and I'm concerned about my obligation to the Court." The trial judge informed Jackson he had a right under the law to testify on his own behalf, which Jackson said he understood. The court also informed Jackson that his counsel was bound by his professional obligation not to place evidence before the court which he believed to be untrue. Jackson also said he understood this. The judge stated that Jackson could take the stand and give a narrative statement without questioning from his lawyer. The judge noted that if Jackson's attorney found "things which he believes to be not true ... he may have other obligations at that point." The lawyer responded that he had again discussed the matter with Jackson and that Jackson had decided, on his own, not to testify. Upon questioning by the judge, Jackson again stated that he understood his right to testify and his attorney's obligations. Jackson thereupon informed the court that he did not wish to testify.

> If the attorney had simply moved to withdraw at this point, without alerting the court to the reasons why, wouldn't that have solved the attorney's dilemma?

This case differs from *Whiteside* in three respects. Each difference raises important questions which can only be answered after an evidentiary hearing.

First, in *Whiteside*, a finding was made that Whiteside would have testified falsely had he given the testimony he initially wanted to give.... Such a finding has not been made here. In terms of a possible violation of Jackson's rights, this is crucial. If, for example, Jackson's lawyer had no basis for believing Jackson would testify falsely and Jackson, in fact, wanted to testify truthfully, a violation of his rights would occur.

> If the judge permits the defendant to testify in the narrative — without his attorney asking any questions — how is the attorney "presenting" the evidence?

We do not know what measures Jackson's attorney took to determine whether Jackson would lie on the stand. He was required to take such measures as would give him "a firm factual basis" for believing Jackson would testify falsely. As we stated in our opinion in *Whiteside v. Scurr*, 744 F.2d at 1323, rev'd on other grounds, *sub nom Nix v. Whiteside*, 475 U.S. at 157:

> Counsel must act if, but only if, he or she has "a firm factual basis" for believing that the defendant intends to testify falsely or has testified falsely.... It will be a rare case in which this factual requirement is met. Counsel must remember that they are not triers of fact,

but advocates. In most cases a client's credibility will be a question for the jury.

The Supreme Court's majority opinion in *Whiteside* emphasizes the necessity of such caution on the part of defense counsel in determining whether a client has or will commit perjury. In discussing the attorney's duty to report possible client perjury, the majority states that it extends to "a client's announced plans to engage in future criminal conduct." Thus, a clear expression of intent to commit perjury is required before an attorney can reveal client confidences....

The tensions between the rights of the accused and the obligations of her attorney are considerable in the context of potential client perjury. Justice Stevens points to the potential inaccuracy of a lawyer's perception. For many reasons, a lawyer's perception may be incorrect. Ideally, a client will tell her lawyer "everything." But "everything" may not be one consistent explanation of an event. Not only may a client overlook and later recall certain details, but she may also change intended testimony in an effort to be more truthful. Moreover, even a statement of an intention to lie on the stand does not necessarily mean the client will indeed lie once on the stand. Once a client hears the testimony of other witnesses, takes an oath, faces a judge and jury, and contemplates the prospect of cross-examination by opposing counsel, she may well change her mind and decide to testify truthfully.

... A lawyer who judges a client's truthfulness does so without the many safeguards inherent in our adversary system. He likely makes his decision alone, without the assistance of fellow fact finders. He may consider too much evidence, including that which is untrustworthy. Moreover, a jury's determination on credibility is always tempered by the requirement of proof beyond a reasonable doubt. A lawyer, finding facts on his own, is not necessarily guided by such a high standard. Finally, by taking a position contrary to his client's interest, the lawyer may irrevocably destroy the trust the attorney-client relationship is designed to foster. That lack of trust cannot easily be confined to the area of intended perjury. It may well carry over into other aspects of the lawyer's representation, including areas where the client needs and deserves zealous and loyal representation. For these reasons and others, it is absolutely essential that a lawyer have a firm factual basis before adopting a belief of impending perjury.

The record before us does not disclose whether Jackson's lawyer had a firm factual basis for believing his client would testify falsely. This can only be adequately determined after an evidentiary hearing.

Second, in *Whiteside*, the defendant did testify and was "'restricted' or restrained only from testifying falsely." Here, Jackson did not testify at all. It simply is impossible to determine from the record before us whether Jackson was "restrained" by his lawyer from giving truthful testimony. Again, this can only be determined after an evidentiary hearing.

Third, in *Whiteside*, the defense attorney did not reveal his belief about his client's anticipated testimony to the trial court. In contrast, the disclosure to the trial court here was quite explicit. The attorney said to the judge that he might have to withdraw because of what might be elicited on the stand. Such a disclosure cannot be taken lightly. Even in a jury trial, where the judge does not sit as the finder of fact, the judge will sentence the defendant, and such a disclosure creates "significant risks of unfair prejudice" to the defendant.

[handwritten margin note: ★ risk of unfair prejudice to disclose]

We note that, once the possibility of client perjury is disclosed to the trial court, the trial court should reduce the resulting prejudice. It should limit further disclosures of client confidences, inform the attorney of his other duties to his client, inform the defendant of her rights, and determine whether the defendant desires to waive any of those rights. The trial judge here acted primarily with these concerns in mind. The judge discussed the conflict with only the attorney and his client present. He prevented further disclosures of client confidences. He advised Jackson of his right to testify and determined that Jackson understood his rights and his attorney's ethical obligation not to place false testimony before the court. He advised Jackson that if he took the stand, his lawyer would be required to refrain from questioning Jackson on issues which the lawyer believed Jackson would perjure himself and that Jackson would have to testify in narrative form. He then directly asked Jackson if he wished to testify. We add that a trial court should also impress upon defense counsel and the defendant that counsel must have a firm factual basis before further desisting in the presentation of the testimony in question.

[handwritten margin note: trial ct. had good procedure]

Under such a procedure, the chance for violations of the defendant's constitutional rights will be reduced, the revelation of further client confidences will be prevented, and the defendant can make a knowing waiver of her constitutional right to testify and to counsel. It will also be necessary to establish that the waiver was voluntary and that the defendant's rights were not violated prior to the waiver. Such inquiries, however, are best made at an evidentiary hearing.

CONCLUSION

The most weighty decision in a case of possible client perjury is made by the lawyer who decides to inform the court, and perhaps incidentally his adversary and the jury, of his client's possible perjury. This occurs when the lawyer makes a motion for withdrawal (usually for unstated reasons) or allows his client to testify in narrative form without questioning from counsel. Once this has been done, the die is cast. The prejudice will have occurred. At a minimum, the trial court will know of the defendant's potential perjury. For this reason, defense counsel must use extreme caution before revealing a belief of impending perjury. It is, as Justice Blackmun noted, "the rarest of cases" where an attorney should take such action. Once the disclosure of the potential client perjury has occurred, the trial judge can limit the resulting prejudice by preventing further disclosures of client confidences, by informing the attorney of the obligation to his client, and by informing the client of her rights and determining whether she desires to waive any of them. The determination whether the prejudice was undue must occur at an evidentiary hearing....

[handwritten margin note: RARE ★ counsel must take extreme caution before revealing — Extreme caution req'd before ruling perjury by client b/c of possible prejudice — prejudice finding at evidentiary hearing]

Notes

1. The "firm factual basis" standard is only one of many used by different courts to determine when an attorney "knows" that the client will lie. Not unex-

pectedly, courts have adopted differing standards to determine what an attorney must "know" before concluding that his client's testimony is perjury. *Commonwealth v. Mitchell*, 781 N.E.2d 1237, 1246, 1250-51 (Mass.) (discussing various standards including "good cause," "compelling support," "knowledge beyond a reasonable doubt," and "actual knowledge" or "firm factual basis" and adopting a "firm basis in objective fact" standard), *cert. denied*, 539 U.S. 907 (2003). Some standards, like the "firm factual basis" standard are very difficult to satisfy short of an outright confession. For example, the Wisconsin court in *State v. McDowell*, 681 N.W.2d 500, 514 (Wis. 2004), in commenting on the level of knowledge needed to justify permitting a client to testify in the narrative, stated, "Absent the most extraordinary circumstances, such knowledge must be based on the client's expressed admission of intent to testify untruthfully. While we recognize that the defendant's admission need not be phrased in 'magic words,' it must be unambiguous and directly made to the attorney." Other tests are more lenient, coming closer to a reasonable belief standard, such as "good cause to believe the defendant's proposed testimony would be deliberately untruthful," *State v. Hischke*, 639 N.W.2d 6, 10 (Iowa 2002). Which standard do you believe provides the better balance between candor and confidentiality?

2. The court in this case allowed the client to testify in "narrative form"—in other words, the client would take the stand and simply "tell his story" without any direct examination from his attorney. This procedure was recommended by the American Bar Association in its Standards for Criminal Justice, Proposed Standard 4-7.7 (2d ed. 1980) but the American Bar Association House of Delegates failed to approve it. As a footnote in the *Long* opinion commented, this procedure "has been criticized because it would indicate to the judge and sophisticated jurors that the lawyer does not believe his client, *see, e.g.,* J. McCall, *Nix v. Whiteside: The Lawyer's Role in Response to Perjury*, 13 HASTINGS CONST. L.Q. 443, 469, and because the lawyer would continue to play a passive role in the perjury." *Long*, 857 F.2d at 446, ft. 7. What do you think of this alternative?

3. The court here defers many of the actual findings of prejudice to an evidentiary hearing. Consider what such a hearing would look like. Given all the court's reservations, what would be sufficient evidence for an attorney to prove that he had a "firm factual basis" for refusing to call the defendant? What evidence would be elicited regarding the question of whether the attorney had dissuaded the client from giving truthful testimony? What might the evidence be other than the defendant's own testimony? Suppose that, in the evidentiary hearing, the client testifies that he told his attorney about a range of truthful testimony he intended to provide. Suppose that isn't true. What may the Attorney do in response?

4. Does the duty of candor to a court require an attorney to report the client's violation of a court order? For example, suppose you are representing a client charged with a criminal offense who is released on bond. In the week before the trial date approaches, you are unable to contact your client. His wife tells you that he packed several bags and left and she also is unable to contact him. May you ask for a continuance saying that you need additional time "to secure necessary witnesses and evidence" or that you have a scheduling conflict? In *United States v. Del Carpio-Cotrina*, 733 F. Supp. 95 (S.D. Fla. 1990), the court held that the attorney had an obligation to inform the court as soon as he had a firm factual basis for believing his client was going to jump bond.

However, the court was applying Florida's version of Rule 1.6 which, at that time, required an attorney to disclose information to prevent a client from committing a crime. What result would you predict under your state's rules of conduct?

5. How does Rule 3.3 apply to prosecutors? Obviously, prosecutors are subject to the rules just as any other attorney. However, prosecutors have a special role to insure justice. Consider the additional duties a prosecutor might have when she discovers that false evidence has been presented to the court. For example, Rule 3.8(a) of the Model Rules of Professional Conduct directs prosecutors to prosecute charges only if they are supported by probable cause and 3.8(d) incorporates the prosecutor's obligations under the *Brady* rule to disclose exculpatory evidence to the defense as well as mitigating evidence in sentencing. *Brady v. Maryland*, 373 U.S. 83 (1963) (holding due process violated when the prosecution withheld information requested by the defense that was material to the issue of guilt or to sentencing). Finally Rule 3.8(g) provides that, if the prosecutor knows of "new, credible and material evidence" establishing a reasonable likelihood of a wrongful conviction, the prosecutor has certain affirmative duties to disclose and, if in her jurisdiction, remedy the situation. To read more about it, see Bennett L. Gershman, *The Prosecutor's Duty to Truth*, 14 Geo. J. Legal Ethics 309 (2001).

6. Does Rule 3.3's prohibition on submitting false evidence apply to devices that, while not testimony or evidence, are designed to mislead? For example, suppose you are representing a criminal defendant. May you have your client's brother sit at counsel table, have the witness identify the "defendant" and then use that false identification to impeach the witness's credibility, or to establish the state's failure to prove every element of its case? Courts consider tactics such as this as frauds on the court and will hold attorneys in contempt. *People v. Simac*, 603 N.E.2d 97 (Ill. Ct. App. 1992) (affirming criminal contempt order), aff'd, 641 N.E.2d 416 (Ill. 1994); *United States v. Thoreen*, 653 F.2d 1332 (9th Cir. 1981); *United States v. Sabater*, 830 F.2d 7 (2d Cir. 1987). The court in *Miskovsky v. State ex rel. Jones*, 586 P.2d 1104 (Okla. Crim. App. 1978) suggested that an attorney should seek permission of the court before attempting this "credibility testing" and that in nearly all circumstances courts would not approve the tactic.

12.3 Interviewing to Establish Trust and Encourage Candor

As you can see from these cases, if in the course of preparing your witness, you suspect that he or she is lying, you must have a good deal of confidence that the evidence is indeed false before you refuse to permit evidence to be submitted or disclose a client's confidential information in order to correct false evidence. Consider the following discussion by Professors Jean R. Sternlight & Jennifer Robbennolt as they advise a hypothetical attorney "Jack" on how to distinguish truth from lies in interviewing.

Jean R. Sternlight & Jennifer Robbennolt,
Good Lawyers Should Be Good Psychologists: Insights for Interviewing and Counseling Clients
23 Ohio St. J. on Disp. Resol. 437, 487-491, 499-504 (2008)

D. Identifying Liars and Truth Tellers

While there is a lot of folklore regarding how to distinguish liars from truth tellers, it turns out that identifying liars is extremely difficult, even for experts. Although Jack feels comfortable in his own lie-detection abilities, there is no particular cue or set of cues that can reliably be used to identify a lie. Many of the cues that could be associated with deception can also be associated with other states likely common to legal clients, such as stress. Indeed, across a variety of studies, psychological research has found that people are not adept at distinguishing those who are lying from those who are telling the truth — performing at levels that are little or no better than chance. Moreover, there is little correlation between our degree of certainty that we have identified a liar and our accuracy. Apparent experts do not tend to perform any better than lay people, though they do tend to be more confident in their determinations. Thus, whereas Jack may believe that he is quite good at figuring out whether clients are lying based on whether they blink, look away, or tap their fingers, he is probably wrong as often as he is right.

A primary reason why people are unable to reliably distinguish lies and truths is that we pay attention to the wrong things. Psychological research has identified a number of cues that people believe are related to deception. In particular, people strongly believe that liars avert their gaze, engage in lots of movement (e.g., shifting position, hand movements, foot movements, gestures of illustration), smile, and have more disturbed speech (e.g., hesitation, pauses, slower speech). Many of these anticipated cues are thought to be associated with nervousness. However, many of these believed indicators do not in fact prove reliable in distinguishing liars and truth tellers. Accordingly, it is important that Jack not rely on stereotypes about lying that do not discriminate between liars and truth tellers.

On the other hand, Jack can learn even more from psychology regarding the detection of liars than simply to be careful about his intuitions. There are some dimensions on which liars do tend to differ from those who are telling the truth. Liars tend to offer fewer details, give accounts that are less plausible and coherent, and speak with more vocal tension and higher pitch though the size of these effects can be quite small. Unfortunately, these cues, too, can also be present for other reasons — for example, a high pitch could be a sign of lying or a sign that the person is upset or nervous for some other reason (such as the stress of being questioned or talking about personal information). Similarly, lack of detail or coherency can reflect poor memory rather than lying. Thus, cues such as these ought to be seen as signals that are worth pursuing further in order to get more information.

In addition, particular attention can be paid to changes in the behavior of the particular speaker. While one individual's speech and behavior may simply differ from another person's even when they are telling the truth, making distinctions difficult to draw, changes in an individual's behavior may be more predictive and worth following up. Thus, just as within-person confidence is more useful in assessing memory than are cross-person comparisons, within-person behavior is more useful in identifying lying.

Additional guidance can be provided by examining the handful of people who tend to be better than most at distinguishing liars and truth tellers. These lie detection "wizards" have been shown to perform better than others at identifying liars, although they do not perform better than others at identifying truthfulness. Such wizards' success may be attributable in part to the fact that they are more likely than others to keep an open mind as to whether someone is lying, and avoid committing to a conclusion until they have processed all the information. In considering all the available information, the wizards have been found to pay closer and more sophisticated attention to nonverbal cues and to focus closely on nuances of language. Relatedly, good lie-detection has been shown to be related to the ability to identify brief expressions of emotion on people's faces.

All of this is complicated by the fact that much of the time people are not dealing with others who are blatantly lying but instead who hold varying versions of reality.

Telling the whole truth and nothing but the truth is rarely possible or desirable. All self-presentations are edited. The question is one of whether the editing crosses the line from the honest highlighting of aspects of identity that are most relevant in the ongoing situation to a dishonest attempt to mislead.

Probably the most common way in which clients lie to their attorneys is that they fail to inform the attorney of particular details. Such omissions may be deliberate. Notwithstanding attorneys' incantation of the attorney- client privilege and urging their clients to be forthright, some clients may believe that their attorneys will represent them more effectively if they are not aware of certain skeletons in the clients' closets. Clients may also fear that if they disclose damaging information to the attorney, the attorney will feel compelled to disclose it to the opposing side or to a finder of fact. In other instances, such omissions may simply be a function of misconstrual or a need to be viewed positively. If outright lies are difficult to discern, surely it is even more difficult to discern nuances of shading, positive spin, or editing.

Thus, Jack should be aware that clients may lie, recognize his own limitations in detecting lies, keep an open mind, and be prepared to try to check clients' veracity. A few helpful measures can include using documents to confirm or contradict clients' accounts, interviewing multiple or married clients-such as the Kiddos-separately, and interviewing other witnesses who might be in a position to serve as a check on the clients' stories.

* * *

4. Trust and Rapport

Trust is central to the attorney-client relationship. To trust is to "accept vulnerability based on positive expectations of the intentions or behavior of another." Clients, who are often in a vulnerable position, trust their attorney when they rely on the attorney to act in ways that are consistent with the clients' well-being-expecting both that the attorney will act with fidelity to their interests and will act competently in doing so.

Trust can further the attorney-client relationship by improving communication between attorney and client-promoting disclosure of important information by the client and facilitating the counseling process. Clients want to believe that their lawyer is their ally and advocate—and may hesitate to provide full information if they don't feel supported. In contrast, people tend to be more willing to share more information (particularly sensitive or personal information) with those whom they trust. In addition, if clients trust their attorneys, discussions regarding settlement and other options will be far more successful. Clients who trust their attorneys may be more willing to consider and follow the attorneys' advice. It is natural that when an attorney begins to discuss settlement, the client may feel let down or even abandoned. The lawyer who the client had seen as her knight in shining armor is now urging that the client's position may not be so strong after all. Is the lawyer perhaps looking out for her own interests rather than those of the client? However, if the client has real trust in her attorney, she is less likely to feel that the attorney misled her at any point.

Trust can be facilitated in a variety of ways. As an initial matter, existing reputations and institutional structures-such as the requirements and norms of professional responsibility—can lay a foundation for a relationship of trust. While lawyers often inform their clients that their communications are covered by the attorney-client privilege, urging clients to be forthcoming on this basis, merely informing clients of the existence of such a privilege may not be enough to create real trust. Beyond this, however, trust is influenced by patterns of communication and interpersonal interaction. Moreover, people can build trust through the ways in which they communicate openness and concern for the other's needs. Through his words, conduct, eye contact, and body language, Jack needs to try to communicate a genuine concern for his clients. Communicating in such a way as to provide information that is accurate and to provide explanations for actions also contributes to a sense of trust. In particular, advisor explanation of and elaboration on the information provided has been shown to be associated with trust. In addition to communication, trust is influenced by the degree to which a person acts consistently and predictably, competently, and with integrity and honesty. Moreover, shared control and participation in decisionmaking tends to foster a sense of trust. In particular, psychological research has found that criminal defendants whose actual participation in their cases was congruent with their level of desired participation were more trusting of their attorneys. In short, Jack can build his clients' trust in him by spending ample time on the initial interview, responding promptly to subsequent client queries, sharing with his clients some of his thinking about the pros and cons of various courses of action, and allowing clients to participate in decisions regarding their case.

Rapport in a relationship or interaction is closely related to trust and has been conceptualized as having three interrelated characteristics: 1) mutual attentiveness—where both participants attend to and are involved with each other; 2) "positivity"—a reciprocal sense of consideration for each other; and 3) "coordination"—a sense of responsiveness to each other or of being "in sync." Some have argued that "[b]uilding rapport is considered so important that it is listed as a discrete training phase in most prominent investigative interview protocols." Indeed, psychological research has found that rapport can result in increased trust and more cooperative interactions. More generally, people tend to remember and disclose greater amounts of information when they feel comfortable and at ease. People may also be more forthcoming as a sense of rapport contributes to feeling "less constrained to present [them]selves continuously in a favorable or pleasant light." Finally, people may be more willing to consider and comply with professional advice when they have a trusting and comfortable relationship with their advisor.

A number of nonverbal behaviors have been found to contribute to a sense of rapport. In particular, a variety of behaviors related to posture and orientation—such as directly facing the other person, leaning forward, and not crossing one's arms—are associated with assessments of rapport in interpersonal interactions. Similarly, other non-verbal behaviors that signal attentiveness and coordination—such as smiling and nodding—are also related to the development of rapport. Studies have also found that feelings of rapport are facilitated when people spend some time getting to know each other—engaging in small talk, "schmoozing," or discussing personal or shared interests can provide the opportunity to develop a connection.

Notes

1. This excerpt suggests a number of ways in which attorneys can improve their ability to obtain reliable information and judge the veracity of the information they have. Summarize some of these techniques.

2. While an attorney always wants to establish her client's trust, does she always want to obtain the client's story? Some criminal defense attorneys report that they do not ask for and do not want their client's story, but want only to know what evidence others will have against the client. By carefully avoiding "knowing" whether the client actually committed the acts charged, the defense attorney avoids the dilemmas presented by Rule 3.3. What do you think of this approach?

Professional Responsibility Skills 12-A: Counseling a Client for Candor

As a practical matter, the balance of duty to client and court takes place in the lawyer's office, working with a client. Work with a partner. One of you should take the role of the client and the other the attorney. Practice how you might draw the lines you believe are appropriate. Trade roles and try again. Compare your approaches.

You represent an elderly woman who has been working with you to set up her estate. She has directed you to draft several documents, including a power of attorney for her son in case she becomes incapacitated. Your client is to meet you tomorrow to execute the documents, when she has a debilitating stroke. Your client's son comes to you to discuss his options. You explain that, because the power of attorney wasn't signed, you will have to bring a guardianship proceeding, and you explain the time and expenses involved in that proceeding. The son asks whether, if he had his mother's signature on the power of attorney, you could backdate it in order to avoid the expense of a guardianship proceeding. He says, "It's what Mother wanted, right? What would be the harm?" How do you respond? *See, Office of Disciplinary Counsel v. Shaffer*, 785 N.E.2d 429, 429-30 (Ohio 2003). Suppose the mother had indeed signed the power of attorney, but you had lost the only copy. Would "re-creating" the original be so wrong? *Atty. Griev. Comm'n of Md. v. Gordon*, 991 A.2d 51 (Md. Ct. App.2010) (attorney suspended in reciprocal discipline action for submitting original signature page in breach of contract action that had been signed the night before summary judgment motion but dated five years earlier).

12.4 False or Frivolous?

Part of the mythology of the adversary system is that litigating lawyers may file any claim and assert any position, so long as it is advantageous to a client. The reality is that rules of professional conduct, rules of procedure and the law of malicious prosecution and abuse of process have always prohibited a lawyer from asserting frivolous claims. In addition to imposing sanctions under Rule 11 of the Federal Rules of Civil Procedure and 28 U.S.C. § 1927 ... federal district court judges (as well as most state trial judges) have inherent power to take action against attorneys appearing before them who litigate in bad faith.

2 Geoffrey C. Hazard, W. William Hodes & Peter R. Jarvis, The Law of Lawyering § 27.2 (3d ed. Supp. 2007).

Far more common than the problem of presenting affirmatively false evidence is presenting an assertion or claim when there is no evidence to support the claim at all. Must an attorney investigate his client's factual assertions? What is the difference between making an "allegation of fact" and a "statement of fact"? Rule 3.3 requires an attorney to disclose adverse controlling authority if the opposing side has not done so, but what if the situation is that there is neither adverse nor supporting controlling authority? What if the lawyer makes assertions of law without any authority other than logic and policy to support those assertions? An attorney who lies to the court about the law or facts would obviously violate Rule 3.3. But even ignorance of the rules and facts can lead to sanction, discipline, and liability. Rule 3.1 directs that an attorney shall not submit frivolous claims, defenses, assertions, or denials. However, as the quote above notes, this is an area is that is controlled by a range of procedural and substantive rules in addition to discipline. As you know, Rule 11 of the Federal Rules of Civil Procedure (and the state counterparts) regulate pleadings, papers, and the advocating of assertions or denials contained in these papers. Rule 26 of those same rules extends the requirements of good faith assertions to discovery and Fed. R. Civ. P. 37 provides sanctions for violations of these discovery standards.

Recently, the legislatures have enacted various statutes directed at reducing lawsuits seen as exploitative or frivolous. For example, tort reform measures in some states have required pre-trial screening panels or imposed certificate-of-merit prerequisites for medical malpractice actions. States also have adopted anti-SLAPP statutes ("strategic litigation against public participation"). The New Jersey court, in surveying the history of these statutes, noted that they are designed to deal with the phenomenon of:

> large commercial interests [who use] litigation to intimidate citizens who otherwise would exercise their constitutionally protected right to speak in protest against those interests.... [T]he goal of such litigation was not to prevail, but to silence or intimidate the target, or to cause the target sufficient expense so that he or she would cease speaking out.... [However] what appears to one party to be a SLAPP suit may, to the other party, be a good faith effort to protect one's own reputation or business either through a suit for defamation or for tortious interference with a contract or a prospective business opportunity. Defining the line that divides one from the other is neither simple nor straightforward.

LoBiondo v. Schwartz, 970 A.2d 1007 (N.J. 2009).

In commenting on the difficulty of identifying whether a suit is motivated by a desire to shut down public criticism or by a sincere need to defend one's rights, the *LoBiondo* court identified what is a key difficulty in interpreting any of these laws prohibiting frivolous actions. Should a cause of action that is arguably valid from an objective standpoint be considered frivolous if it is brought for improper purposes? What about a cause of action that is baseless from an objective standpoint but is brought with a sincere belief that the law could be changed or the facts developed so that the claim could prevail?

Whether considering sanctions under Rule 11, liability for malicious prosecution or abuse of process, or discipline under Rule 3.1, this preliminary issue of whether a subjective or objective test should apply is one that courts have answered differently over time and in different types of proceedings. Original formulations of state and federal rules of procedure and state disciplinary standards largely applied a subjective "good faith" test to pleadings. That is, an attorney could not be sanctioned if he subjectively believed he had a good faith factual and legal basis for claims and defenses, even if that belief was objectively unreasonable. Most states' torts for abuse of process or malicious prosecution require this type of proof of subjective bad faith. Today, Fed. R. Civ. P. 11 applies a standard of "objective reasonableness under the circumstances." *Business Guides, Inc. v. Chromatic Commc'ns Enters., Inc.*, 498 U.S. 533, 549, 111 S. Ct. 922, 112 L. Ed. 2d 1140 (1991). Likewise, recent amendments to Rule 3.1 of the Model Rules of Professional Conduct have implemented an objective standard and many states have amended their disciplinary rules accordingly. However, quite a few have kept the prior standard for subjective bad faith.

Among all of these various standards for good faith in court papers, the most significant in impact and risk is Fed. R. Civ. P. 11 and its state counterparts. Perhaps you have already studied Rule 11 as part of a civil procedure or pre-trial practice course. The chart on the next page compares the standards of Rule 11 to those of the states that have adopted the most recent version of Rule 3.1 of the rules of professional conduct.

As you can see, the standards for Rule 11 and the rules of conduct are very similar. So much so that in disciplinary actions courts will consider an attorney's previous sanction under rules of procedure or a court's inherent power. At a minimum, most courts will consider the sanction as evidence in the disciplinary proceeding. *People v. Fitzgibbons*, 909 P.2d 1098 (Colo. 1996); *Florida Bar v. Richardson*, 591 So. 2d 908 (Fla. 1991); *Attorney Grievance Comm'n v. Alison*, 709 A.2d 1212 (Md. 1998); *In re Caldwell*, 491 N.W.2d 482 (Wis. 1992). Susan L. Thomas, Annotation, *Bringing of Frivolous Civil Claim as Ground for Discipline of Attorney*, 85 A.L.R. 4th 544 (1991, 2010 Supp.). A few courts go so far as to hold that the doctrine of issue preclusion applies so that an attorney who has been sanc-

F.R.C.P. 11 Compared to Rules of Professional Conduct 3.1

	Fed. R. Civ. P. 11	Rules of Discipline* *R3.1*
Applies	"presenting to the court a pleading, written motion, or other paper — whether by signing, filing, submitting, or later advocating it" *Rule 11* [Rule 26 extends very similar standards to "every disclosure under Rule 26(a)(1) or (a)(3) and every discovery request, response, or objection." *Rule 26(g)*]	"bring or defend a proceeding, or assert or controvert an issue therein" *Rule 3.1* "in pretrial procedure" *Rule 3.4(d)* "In representing a client" *Rule 4.4(a)*
Duty: No improper purposes	"improper purpose, such as to harass, cause unnecessary delay, or needlessly increase the cost of litigation" *Rule 11(b)(1)* and *Rule 26(g)(1)(b)(ii)*	"no substantial purpose other than to embarrass, delay, or burden a third person" *Rule 4.4(a)*
Duty: Investigation and research	"after an inquiry reasonable under the circumstances" *Rule 11(b)*	"inform themselves about the facts of their clients' cases and the applicable law" *Rule 3.1, cmt. 2*
Duty: Grounded in fact	"factual contentions have evidentiary support or, if specifically so identified, will likely have evidentiary support after a reasonable opportunity for further investigation or discovery" and "denials of factual contentions are warranted on the evidence or, if specifically so identified, are reasonably based on belief or a lack of information." *Rule 11(b)(3)&(4)*	"not frivolous" *Rule 3.1*
Duty: Grounded in law	"claims, defenses, and other legal contentions are warranted by existing law or by a nonfrivolous argument for extending, modifying, or reversing existing law or for establishing new law;" *Rule 11(b)(2)*	"not frivolous, which includes a good faith argument for an extension, modification or reversal of existing law" *Rule 3.1*
Persons Responsible	"any attorney, law firm, or party that violated the rule or is responsible for the violation. Absent exceptional circumstances, a law firm must be held jointly responsible for a violation committed by its partner, associate, or employee." *Rule 11(c)(1)*	Attorney who violated the rule; Attorney who attempted to violate, assisted or induced another to violate, or violated through another; *Rule 8.4* Supervising attorneys in some circumstances; *Rule 5.1* Subordinate attorneys unless acting at direction of a supervising attorney's reasonable resolution of an arguable question of professional duty; *Rule 5.2*

* Rules of Professional Conduct in this section are quoted from Missouri Supreme Court Rule 4, Rules of Professional Conduct. Missouri has adopted the most recent versions of the ABA Model Rules on the rules quoted.

tioned by a court for violation of frivolous pleading or discovery will be precluded from arguing that his actions were not frivolous under disciplinary standards. E.g., *In re Caranchini*, 956 S.W.2d 910 (Mo. 1997). Other courts disagree and permit the attorney to relitigate the question of frivolousness. E.g., *In re Levine*, 847 P.2d 1093 (Ariz. 1993); *Neely v. Comm'n for Lawyer Disciplinelain*, 976 S.W.2d 824 (Tex. App. 1998). In either approach, of course, the court must still determine what discipline is appropriate.

In the criminal setting, these rules are overshadowed by the accused's constitutional rights to a privilege against self-incrimination, a presumption of innocence, and right to assistance of counsel. Accordingly, Rule 3.1 reminds attorneys that "A lawyer for the defendant in a criminal proceeding, or the respondent in a proceeding that could result in incarceration, may nevertheless so defend the proceeding as to require that every element of the case be established." This doesn't mean that a criminal defense attorney has no duty to avoid truly frivolous affirmative assertions. "Current professional standards do not require a defense counsel to assert every potential defense, regardless how farfetched or implausible. To the contrary, attorneys are routinely cautioned against advancing frivolous positions." *United States v. Rico*, 51 F.3d 495, 511 (5th Cir. 1995). In the words of the Supreme Court: "It is the obligation of any lawyer—whether privately retained or publicly appointed—not to clog the courts with frivolous motions or appeals." Thus, if a criminal defense client is convicted and wishes to file an appeal, the attorney must withdraw if there is no non-frivolous basis for that appeal. Some states require that the attorney first file a "no-merit" or "Anders" brief, combing the record for anything that might arguably support an appeal. *Anders v. California*, 386 U.S. 738 (1967). In 2000, the United States Supreme Court held that this procedure was only one of many that would permit a defense counsel to withdraw without violating his client's constitutional right to counsel. *Smith v. Robbins*, 528 U.S. 259 (2000). Accordingly, some states have liberalized their procedures for attorneys to withdraw from frivolous appeals in criminal cases.

On the prosecutor's side of the equation, Rule 3.8(a) requires prosecutors to "refrain from bringing or continuing a charge that the prosecutor knows is not supported by probable cause." At least one court has interpreted this provision to require proof that a prosecutor had actual knowledge that a case lacked probable cause, rather than the more objective "should have known" standard. *In re Lucareli*, 611 N.W.2d 754 (Wis. 2000). In that case, a prosecutor had filed a baseless criminal charge against an attorney defending an individual accused of sexual assault. The Wisconsin Court of Appeals, in upholding the trial court's decision to grant the accused a new trial, referred to the prosecutor's action as a "truly evil scheme … to either get an adjournment or to put a cloud over the defense in the form of impairing defense." *State v. Lettice*, 221 Wis. 2d 69, 76, 585 N.W.2d 171 (1998). However, the Wisconsin Supreme Court in the subsequent disciplinary action declined to apply issue preclusion to these findings and affirmed the disciplinary referee's findings that there was not clear and convincing evidence that the prosecutor had known that his charge against the defense attorney was specious. The court did not address the question of whether this conduct violated Rule 3.1, however, because the issue had not been briefed.

Whether in a criminal or civil setting, the impact of sanctions, discipline, and liability threats should give you significant pause before bringing or defending an action without adequate research and factual investigation. In light of the uncertainty of these overlapping standards, a cautious approach is your best defense. That doesn't mean you must distrust your clients or double-check everything they say. It does mean, however, that you may not ignore signals that would give an objective attorney reason to doubt. Just how far you go in researching an action, will depend largely on the circumstances, timing, and your relationship with your client.

Problem

Read the following problem and decide how far you would go in investigation before filing. Compare your reactions to your colleagues.

> Your client is Bob Borrower. He borrowed $50,000 from Linda Lender and has not repaid the amount. Linda has threatened to sue him. He says that it's true that he borrowed the money from Linda but that she took his 1968 Mustang convertible, worth $50,000, as security and has refused to return it. He thinks she might have sold the car to Oscar Other. He's not sure, but he has seen Oscar driving a car that looks like his. Linda says she still has the car in storage. Bob thinks that if Linda has sold the car, he shouldn't have to pay back the money and she should pay him any extra money she made on the sale. You have analyzed the party's agreement and the governing law and have concluded that, regardless of whether he owes her the money, she has no right to the car. If she has the car, she must give it back. If she sold the car, she owes him the fair market value of the car. Under Rule 11, may you file a complaint against Linda at this point? If not, what else do you need to do first? Suppose you check the Department of Motor Vehicles and it lists the title to Bob's car in Linda's name. Suppose you also talk to Oscar and he says that he did purchase the car. May you properly sue both Oscar and Linda and plead in the alternative for the return of the car from Linda or the recovery from her of the price paid by Oscar?

Researching Professional Responsibility 12-A: Researching Pleading Sanctions

Try researching the Bob Borrower problem under your state's rules of civil procedure and its disciplinary rules. To research your state's civil procedure rules governing frivolous pleadings, you might begin with the state rule of procedure. (See Researching Professional Responsibility 9-A for additional guidance on researching rules of procedure.) Because state rules of civil procedure are often similar to the federal rules, you may look to federal cases when trying to research a civil procedure issue for state court. This is especially true for pretrial issues such as Rule 11 motions, because there are more written federal court opinions at the trial court level. Two treatises specifically address court sanctions for frivolous pleadings and other litigation abuse:

GEORGENE M. VAIRO, RULE 11 SANCTIONS: CASE LAW PERSPECTIVES AND PREVENTIVE MEASURES (3d ed. 2003).

GREGORY JOSEPH, SANCTIONS: THE FEDERAL LAW OF LITIGATION ABUSE (4th ed. 2008).

Test Your Understanding

1. *The Alibi*

Dennis Defend is awaiting trial on a charge of armed robbery. You have been appointed to represent him in this action. In your initial interview with Defend, you ask how he would like to plead. He says he wants to strike a deal with the prosecutor—he will confess and plead guilty in exchange for a lighter sentence. You ask if he would be willing to give any information to assist the prosecutor in apprehending the others involved in the robbery. Defend tells you that he can't do that because he didn't rob the bank. Defend insists, however, that he wants to confess and plead guilty. He refuses to consider a *nolo contendere* or Alford plea (in which defendant maintains his innocence but pleads guilty). When you press him for a reason, he provides you with a vivid description of his activities on the afternoon of the robbery—that he was in a nearby small town where he murdered three people. The robbery conviction is the perfect alibi to that crime. After speaking with him further and some discrete investigation, you are confident he is telling you the truth about his motivations. You are equally confident that you will not be allowed to withdraw from this case.

You ask two colleagues in the office for their advice. Alfred Attorney advises that you enter a not guilty plea on your client's behalf. He insists that this is the only ethical step you can take since you can't assist Dennis to lie to the court and entering the plea is a procedural legal step that is within your scope of authority as the attorney. Della Defender reminds you that Dennis has constitutional rights and that he should be able to plead anything he wants. She argues that you can enter a plea of guilty on Dennis's behalf because a plea is not evidence and that, so long as you remain silent and don't actively assist Dennis when the judge asks questions in order to establish the factual basis for the plea, you are doing the right thing.

Of course you will want to research the issue under your state's law. Having done so, and considering the rules of professional conduct and the rights of your client under that law, what are your options? Which of those options are available to you at this point? Which is the best?

Analysis

The communication between you and your client would be confidential of course, and it would also be covered by the attorney-client privilege, because it was a communication made for the purposes of obtaining legal advice. No exception permits you to disclose a client's past crime in which you were uninvolved.

You should recognize that Della's advice that a plea of guilty is not "false evidence" under Rule 3.3 has some merit. A plea is, after all, not a statement of fact or law, which is what Rule 3.3 regulates. Moreover, Model Rule 1.2(a) requires a lawyer to abide by the client's decision as to whether to plead guilty and whether to testify in a criminal case. Moreover, there is no question that an attorney may enter a plea of "not guilty" even when the attorney knows that the client in fact committed the crime charged. (See the second sentence of rule 3.1, which emphasizes this point.) One could argue that the same leeway should be given to a client who wants to plead guilty to a crime irrespective of actual innocence. Consider the number of prosecutors and defense attorneys who regularly secure agreements that defendants can plead guilty to "defective equipment" in order to avoid speeding convictions.[2] The only thing that makes this situation different is the se-

---

2. Compare *Iowa Supreme Court Disciplinary Bd. v. Howe*, 706 N.W.2d 360 (Iowa 2005) (city prosecutor's agreements for some offenders to plead down to violation of traffic statute he knew to be obsolete violated Iowa's version of rule 3.8 that requires prosecutors to have probable cause in charging crimes).

riousness of the crime and the fact that the prosecutor isn't aware of the deception. Is this significantly different enough to make a difference?

However, you should also recognize the practical limit of Della's approach. While the plea isn't a statement of fact or law, the court will likely ask the defendant a series of questions about the plea, which is likely then to elicit false testimony. In a typical plea, questions come from the Court, but the lawyer is still participating in presenting false testimony. In several jurisdictions, the lawyer is required to communicate to the Court his non-participation in his client's answers to the Court's questions. A lawyer must also refuse to sign a statement acknowledging the truth of facts that are known to be false, such as a factual statement incident to a plea that contains false statements. *See* ACTL Code of Trial Conduct Rules 18(b), 22(l). In other jurisdictions, an attorney must disclose false statement here as well. Compare, for example, *In re Cardwell*, 50 P.3d 897 (Colo. 2002) where a defendant denied that he had prior alcohol-related convictions in entering a guilty plea. The court held that the defense attorney was required to correct his client's misstatement. Particularly when *nolo contendere* pleas are available as an alternative, there is little justification for saying the client has a right to perjure himself in order to secure a guilty plea.

So, in part, the resolution of this dilemma will depend a great deal on what state law provides regarding pleas and the local court's procedures in accepting pleas.

Regardless of the room available to permit the client to submit a false plea, you would need to communicate (Rule 1.4) with your client. As a matter of competence, you would need to advise him on the legal consequences of his intended action (which would be unlikely to be the unbreakable alibi he thinks it would be). You should attempt to change his mind about using a false guilty plea as an alibi. You can bring to bear not only legal, but practical and moral factors in this discussion (Rule 2.1). You should explain to him your obligations regarding candor and the likelihood that you will be required to reveal his deception to the court.

While this problem takes withdrawal off the table as an option, there would certainly be good cause for withdrawal if one believed the court would grant the motion.

2. *"It's in the Mail"*

When the attorney, rather than a client, is the one who makes false statements to a court, a long list of ethical violations follow. Read the following chronology of one attorney in his failure to respond to interrogatories and requests for documents and spot the rules violations:

April 17	Judge granted a motion to compel and directed Attorney to respond, but Attorney filed no response;
May 9	Defendant filed a motion to dismiss;
May 31	Defendant filed a motion for summary judgment;
June 5	Judge denied the motion to dismiss without prejudice, giving Attorney until June 14 to respond to the motion to dismiss, and to timely respond to a motion for summary judgment;
June 17	Attorney told Judge's secretary he had been ill and would file that day asking for more time to respond;
July 1	Judge's law clerk telephoned Attorney, who assured her he would file something by July 2.
July 8	Judge's law clerk called and left a message for Attorney;

July 9	Attorney returned the phone call, and again, promised to file something;
July 16	A show cause order was entered, giving Attorney ten (10) days to explain why he should not be removed as counsel;
July 19	Attorney signed for the certified mail containing the show cause order.
July 31	Judge removed Attorney from the case and directed him to immediately provide his client with a copy of the order, continued the trial to an unstated date, and stayed any action on the summary judgment motion until his client had obtained another attorney;
September 24	Judge responded to an undated letter from Attorney's client, indicating Attorney had telephoned him on September 19 informing him of the order;
December	Judge received a letter from Attorney's Client requesting his case be dismissed because he did not have the money to hire another attorney; and,
December 19	Judge entered a voluntary dismissal without prejudice.

See, Ligon v. Price, 200 S.W.3d 417 (Ark. 2004) (The rule violations charged included Rules 1.1, 1.16(d), 3.2, 3.3(a), 3.4(c), 8.4(c), and 8.4(d). The Rule 3.3 violation was based on the fact that the attorney "talked with a secretary in chambers and with Judge Wright's law clerk by telephone, giving repeated excuses for delay and promising that pleadings would be forthcoming, but he failed to file any.") Do you agree that overpromising is the same as making a false statement of material fact?

To Learn More

To learn more about the law of perjury, see Daniel J. McGinn-Shapiro, *Perjury*, 48 Am. Crim. L. Rev. 997 (2011).

To read more about the scholarly debate over the proper balance between candor and confidentiality, see one of the following articles:

W. William Hodes, *Seeking the Truth versus Telling the Truth at the Boundaries of the Law: Misdirection, Lying, and "Lying with an Explanation"*, 44 S. Tex. L. Rev. 53 (Winter 2002).

Monroe Freedman, *Getting Honest About Client Perjury*, 21 Geo. J. Legal Ethics 133 (2008).

Richard C. Wydick, *The Ethics of Witness Coaching*, 17 Cardozo L. Rev. 1 (1995).

To learn more about client interviewing and counseling, see David A. Binder, Paul Bergman, Susan C. Price & Paul R. Tremblay, Lawyers as Counselors: A Client-Centered Approach (2nd ed. 2004).

Chapter Thirteen

Confidentiality and Misrepresentations in Negotiations

Learning Objectives

After you have read this chapter and completed the assignments, you should be able to:

- Define fraud and misrepresentation.
- Recognize the duty to be truthful in negotiations and be able to identify the limited circumstances in which affirmative misstatements are permitted.
- Identify the circumstances in which an attorney has a duty to disclose confidential client information in order to comply with the duty of candor in negotiations.
- Demonstrate the ways in which attorneys may persuade their clients to be truthful in negotiations, and counsel a client regarding the consequences of misrepresentations in negotiations.
- Describe the ethical dilemmas caused by the opportunity to capitalize on an opponent's error, identify steps you can take to avoid this dilemma, and clarify your own personal ethical perspectives on this issue.

Rules to Study

We will study Rule 4.1 and revisit exceptions to Rule 1.6. We will also examine the common law doctrines of fraud and misrepresentation.

Preliminary Problem

As you saw in the prior chapter, the duty of candor to the tribunal can often outweigh the attorney's duty of confidentiality. But what about the duty of candor when dealing with third persons? Here, the balance seems to favor client confidentiality. It is an uneasy balance, however, with much pressure for attorneys to police their clients to avoid fraud.

Practice Context Review

Dear Ethics Expert,

Thank you for agreeing to help me in this matter. Here is a summary of my situation that you requested.

One year ago, I represented Curtis Client in a personal injury and wrongful death action arising out of an accident that killed Curtis's wife and left Curtis totally and permanently disabled. Pursuant to a settlement agreement approved by the court, the defendant insurance company has since been sending me compensation checks once a month. In accordance with my agreement with Curtis, I deduct 25% from each check as my legal fee, and remit the remainder to Curtis.

Recently I had to hire a new accountant to handle my books, as my previous accountant had made one too many errors. I hired Susan Sharp. Today, after receiving the monthly check from the insurance company, Susan came into my office and pointed out that the insurance company's check was for $1,500 more than it should have been. I looked at the check, said, "No, that's the same amount as always," and asked why she thought the insurance company must have made a mistake. She showed me the original agreement and provided the calculations for what the monthly amount under that agreement should be.

Unable to believe what I was seeing, I spent the next two hours poring over the files, the account records, and the numbers. She was right. The insurance company had been overpaying on the settlement by $1,500 a month for the past 12 months. I determined that the original error was clearly caused by the insurance company's miscalculation, as I never sent a billing statement or any other calculations to the company that would have resulted in this overpayment. At the same time, I realize that my accountant (or I) could have also caught the error at any time if I had ever simply done a routine check against the original file.

I immediately called Curtis and told him of the overpayments. Curtis said: "Well I knew something must be wrong, but with medical expenses and all, I can barely make ends meet as it is. Double check the numbers, but whatever you do, don't rock the boat. If they're stupid enough to send the money, it's sure not up to me to wise them up." I told him that I would double check my figures and get back with him at the end of the week. I've checked my calculations and the agreement and have verified that there is indeed an overpayment of $18,000. I have also concluded that the amount I have received thus far does not exceed the total amount I would be due under the settlement, nor has Curtis gotten more than he was due under the total settlement—he's just gotten it earlier. However, if we continue to receive these checks in this amount, and I continue to take 25% of the current payments, we both will soon be overpaid.

I need to know what my options are for dealing with this situation. I am fairly confident that Curtis will not agree to my disclosing the error to the insurance company, but if you have any advice on how I might convince him to do so, that is the route I would prefer. Assuming I can't convince him to disclose, I need to know whether I have the discretion to do so without his consent. If there is any other way out of this mess, I'd be pleased to hear it! I understand I may already be in hot water for not having caught the mistake in the first place; you don't need to remind me of

that. I am licensed to practice only in our state and this representation all took place in our state, so I need to know how this will be treated here.

Thank you again for your help. If you include a billing statement with your advice, I will be happy to immediately remit your fee.

Sincerely,

Barb Fines

Barb Fines
Attorney at Law
OurState Bar #57353

13.1 Reading the Rules: Rule 4.1 and the Role of Comments to the Rules

Rule 4.1 is an example of a rule in which the comments substantially modify the meaning of the rule itself. Read Oklahoma's version of Rule 4.1, identical to the Model Rules in both rule and comments. First read carefully the text of the rule. Then read the comments to the rule. How do the comments change your understanding?

Oklahoma Rules of Professional Conduct
Rule 4.1. Truthfulness in Statements to Others

In the course of representing a client a lawyer shall not knowingly:

(a) make a false statement of material fact or law to a third person; or

(b) fail to disclose a material fact to a third person when disclosure is necessary to avoid assisting a criminal or fraudulent act by a client, unless disclosure is prohibited by Rule 1.6.

Comment

Misrepresentation

[1] A lawyer is required to be truthful when dealing with others on a client's behalf, but generally has no affirmative duty to inform an opposing party of relevant facts. A misrepresentation can occur if the lawyer incorporates or affirms a statement of another person that the lawyer knows is false. Misrepresentations can also occur by partially true but misleading statements or omissions that are the equivalent of affirmative false statements. For dishonest conduct that does not amount to a false statement or for misrepresentations by a lawyer other than in the course of representing a client, see Rule 8.4.

Statements of Fact

[2] This Rule refers to statements of fact. Whether a particular statement should be regarded as one of fact can depend on the circumstances. Under generally accepted conventions in negotiation, certain types of statements ordinarily are not taken as statements of material fact. Estimates of price or value placed on the subject of a transaction and a party's intentions as to an acceptable settlement of a claim are ordinarily in this category, and so is the existence of an undis-

perhaps more relevant than rule

closed principal except where nondisclosure of the principal would constitute fraud. Lawyers should be mindful of their obligations under applicable law to avoid criminal and tortious misrepresentation.

Crime or Fraud by Client

[3] Under Rule 1.2(d), a lawyer is prohibited from counseling or assisting a client in conduct that the lawyer knows is criminal or fraudulent. Paragraph (b) states a specific application of the principle set forth in Rule 1.2(d) and addresses the situation where a client's crime or fraud takes the form of a lie or misrepresentation. Ordinarily, a lawyer can avoid assisting a client's crime or fraud by withdrawing from the representation. Sometimes it may be necessary for the lawyer to give notice of the fact of withdrawal and to disaffirm an opinion, document, affirmation or the like. In extreme cases, substantive law may require a lawyer to disclose information relating to the representation to avoid being deemed to have assisted the client's crime or fraud. If the lawyer can avoid assisting a client's crime or fraud only by disclosing the information, then under paragraph (b) the lawyer is required to do, unless the disclosure is prohibited by Rule 1.6.

Context

According to the Scope section of the Model Rules, the comments to the rules of professional conduct "are intended as guides to interpretation, but the text of each Rule is authoritative." The Scope points out several roles of the comments:

- Provide "should" statements to indicate aspirational standards.

- Provide guidance for practicing in compliance with the Rules.

- Explain relationships to other law.

Look again at each of the comments to Rule 4.1. Which of these roles does each comment appear to play? Do you agree that the comments do not impose additional obligations? In adopting their versions of the model rules, the states vary in their adoption of the comments. Most states, like Oklahoma, adopt the rules and the comments with some variations. Some of these states emphasize more forcefully the limited role of the comments. For example, the preamble to the Texas Rules of Professional Conduct states, "no disciplinary action may be taken for failure to conform to the Comment." Six states (Louisiana, Montana, Nevada, New Jersey, New York, and Oregon) have adopted a variation of the rules only, without adopting the comments, while four states (Maine, Michigan, Minnesota, and New Hampshire) have adopted variations on the rules and authorized the publication (but not adopted) the comments.

Relationships.

Each comment suggests a relationship to other law. Comment one reminds us that Rule 8.4 prohibits conduct involving "dishonesty, fraud, deceit or misrepresentation" and conduct "prejudicial to the administration of justice." An ABA formal opinion addressing the "Lawyer's Obligation of Truthfulness When Representing a Client in Negotiation: Application to Caucused Mediation" suggested that "Rule 8.4(c) … does not require a greater degree of truthfulness on the part of lawyers representing parties to a negotiation than does Rule 4.1." ABA Comm. on Ethics and Prof'l Responsibility, Formal Op. 06-439 (2006). However, not all courts agree. Some conduct that might not technically violate Rule 4.1 might still subject an attorney to discipline under these broader standards. For example, in *Cincinnati Bar Ass'n v. Wallace*, 700 N.E.2d 1238 (Ohio 1998), an attorney assisted the client in fashioning a real estate transfer to his current spouse in order to avoid child support, and then assisted the client in answering "none" in response to an interrogatory regarding real estate ownership. While the answer to the interrogatory was technically true, the attorney was nonetheless reprimanded for acting in an unprofessional manner.

Comment two incorporates "generally accepted conventions" of negotiations to create what appears to be an exception to the rule. The comment then hands off the fine points of the distinction to the law of "criminal and tortious misrepresentation." Dean Irma Russell reminds us of the significance of this relationship.

> Some lawyers interpret the Rule to allow statements to third parties that are not entirely accurate as long as they are "subjective" and "non-verifiable." It makes sense that lawyers reading this Rule might conceptualize the exceptions as safe harbors. Such a reading undervalues the indeterminacy of the categories incorporated from the common law, however. The comment ultimately serves the interest of lawyers by reminding them of the continuing application of positive law to lawyers. Indeed, the common law (with its messy complexity) would continue to apply to lawyers in civil suits, even if the rules expressly claimed to displace application of the law to lawyers. It would create an anomalous result to believe that even without this reference, a legal ethics rule could obviate the otherwise applicable rules of tort law. Creating a rule of ethics that actually displaced the law of misrepresentation would have startling and unsupportable consequences; creating a disjuncture between ethics duties and legal duties.... Considering the law of misrepresentation, lawyers should be wary of seeking a safe harbor in the exceptions to Model Rule 4.1 and should realize that what counts as meeting the exception will be based on the court's judgment of the reasonableness of the other party's reliance not on the lawyer's own subjective view.... Lawyers may be disciplined and, additionally, held liable for misrepresentations and for rescinded contracts and other damages to their clients. Indeed, a misrepresentation that is based on a subjective belief or non-verifiable fact may, nevertheless, provide a basis for the remedies of rescission and damages. Ethics rules do not toll or neutralize tort law as it applies to lawyers. There is no precedent for the idea that the lawyer gets a "free card" based on his status as a lawyer.

Irma S. Russell, *The Evolving Regulation of the Legal Profession: The Costs of Indeterminacy and Certainty,* 2008 ABA Prof. Law. 137.

Comment three to the Rule connects the dots between Rules 1.2(d), 1.6, and 4.1. Depending on the nature of your client's misrepresentation, its timing and effect, and the degree to which your services are involved, your duties could range along a spectrum from informing your client of the consequences of the misrepresentation, or persuading the client to avoid or rectify the misrepresentation; through quiet or "noisy" withdrawals; all the way to disclosures of the misrepresentation.

Structure

Consider the structure of part (b) of the rule. First, notice the double negative "a lawyer shall not knowingly fail to disclose." In other words, "the lawyer must disclose." The next part of the sentence tells us what disclosure is necessary, to whom, and under what circumstances. Here, too, the phrasing is somewhat backward: "avoid assisting." Finally, there is the exception clause "unless disclosure is prohibited by Rule 1.6" which could swallow the entire rule given the breadth of Rule 1.6. However, Rule 1.6 has many exceptions, all of which in the Model Rules are exceptions permitting but not requiring disclosure. The effect of Rule 4.1 is to turn some of those discretionary exceptions into mandatory exceptions. Can you blend Rule 1.6 and 4.1 together to create an affirmative statement of your duty to disclose? Complete this sentence: "An attorney must disclose a client's misrepresentation to a third person if …".

Reasons

Why doesn't the rule simply prohibit lying altogether? The justifications for not doing so include the primacy of client loyalty, the centrality of lying to negotiation practice, and the reluctance to impose higher duties of candor on attorneys than on the general public. Despite these assumptions about the need to lie, empirical evidence indicates that a reputation for honesty makes one a more effective negotiator. Andrea Schneider, *Shattering Negotiation Myths: Empirical Evidence on the Effectiveness of Negotiation Style*, 7 HARV. NEG. L. REV. 143 (2002).

Visualize

Rule 4.1(b) is particularly challenging simply because it is written as a double negative and refers to the exceptions to another rule. Try re-writing the rule in positive fashion. This is the type of rule for which a visual representation of the elements and their relationships to one another may be especially helpful. Try filling in the blanks on this summary of Rule 4.1(b):

You MUST disclose	A Material Fact	
IF		You Know
	AND	*It is necessary to avoid*
	AND	Your silence will assist the crime or fraud
AND	You reasonably believe it is necessary to reveal	
BECAUSE	OR	It's reasonably certain that someone will die or be hurt badly if you don't reveal
	OR	*Your services are being engaged in fraud*
	OR	
	OR	The court or another law requires you to reveal
	OR	Client gives informed consent

Imagine

Professor Reily provides the following examples of lies in negotiations. For each category, think of an example and consider whether it would violate Rule 4.1:

1. the current or future value (including long-term performance claims) of whatever is being discussed in the negotiation (whether it be goods, services, or something else);

2. one's goals, priorities or interests in the negotiation;

3. one's reservation point;

4. one's best alternative option if a deal is not agreed upon;

5. one's willingness, ability, or authority to negotiate or to reduce the deal terms to contract form;

6. the existence of objective standards and how they might inform the negotiation;

7. one's own opinions or the opinions of clients, outside experts, or others;

8. the existence of other offers or competing bidders;

9. one's willingness or ability to go to trial;

10. promises (including commitments to future actions) or threats made during the negotiation to entice (or coerce) the other party into agreement; and

11. the substantive strengths of one's lawsuit, or weaknesses of the other side's lawsuit.

Peter Reilly, *Was Machiavelli Right? Lying in Negotiation and the Art of Defensive Self-Help*, 24 Ohio St. J. on Disp. Resol. 481, 491 (2008).

One reason that understanding Rule 4.1 is so challenging is that the meaning of fraud or misrepresentation is left for "other law" to define. Even the definition of fraud in the terminology section of the rules refers the reader to "the substantive or procedural law of the applicable jurisdiction" clarifying only that fraud requires "a purpose to deceive." Rule 1.0(d). However, the other law to which the rules defer is itself unclear and complex.

> No learned inquiry into the history of fraud is necessary to establish that it is not limited to misrepresentations and misleading omissions. Fraud is a generic term, which embraces all the multifarious means which human ingenuity can devise and which are resorted to by one individual to gain an advantage over another by false suggestions or by the suppression of truth. No definite and invariable rule can be laid down as a general proposition defining fraud, and it includes all surprise, trick, cunning, dissembling, and any unfair way by which another is cheated.

McClellan v. Cantrell, 217 F.3d 890, 893 (7th Cir. 2000).

One of the reasons for this broad and shifting definition is that the concept of misrepresentation or fraud can be found in many areas of law. In the criminal law, there are not only general crimes that have their basis in fraud, such as theft by deception, but numerous criminal statutes prohibiting deceits or misrepresentation in specific areas (e.g., securities fraud, mail fraud, healthcare fraud). In tort law, torts based on fraud include intentional and negligent misrepresentation. For example, the Restatement (Second) of Torts defines the tort of "fraudulent misrepresentation" in this way: "one who fraudulently makes a misrepresentation of fact, opinion, intention or law for the purpose of inducing another to act or to refrain from action in reliance upon it, is subject to liability to the other in deceit for pecuniary loss caused to him by his justifiable reliance upon the misrepresentation." Restatement (Second) of Torts, § 25 (1977). Compare that definition to that of the Restatement (Second) of Contracts: "A misrepresentation is an assertion that is not in accord with the facts." Restatement (Second) of Contracts § 159 (1981). Depending on the type of misrepresentation, the resulting contract may be void, voidable, or subject to reformation.

It is little wonder, then, that Rule 4.1 simply defers to common law rather than defining fraud. Where the comments to the rule do attempt to clarify, they do so only by explaining that certain statements are *not* fraud. Here we find the concept of "puffery" or "opinion" that attorneys so easily read more broadly than the law actually provides. The Restatement explains that the line between actionable misrepresentations and mere puffery is one that must be drawn on a case-by-case basis:

> Whether a misstatement should be so characterized depends on whether it is reasonably apparent that the person to whom the statement is addressed would regard the statement as one of fact or based on the speaker's knowledge of facts reasonably implied by the statement or as merely an expression of the speaker's state of mind. Assessment depends on the circumstances in which the statement is made, including the past relationship of the negotiating persons, their apparent sophistication, the plausibility of the statement on its face, the phrasing of the statement, related communication between the persons involved, the known negotiating practices of the community in which both are negotiating, and similar circumstances.

RESTATEMENT (THIRD) OF THE LAW GOVERNING LAWYERS § 98, cmt c (2000).

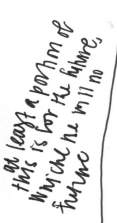

Test Your Understanding

You represent a nine-year-old boy who was the victim of a gruesome amusement park accident, which severed his left arm. Surgeons were able to reattach the arm, but he will never regain full use of the arm, even with extensive physical therapy, and he will always have residual pain. Your fee agreement provides you a 30% contingent fee. As the trial date nears, your negotiations with the defendant's insurer are coming very near to settlement. The company's last settlement offer was for half a million dollars, which included $100,000 for past pain and suffering and medical expenses and the remainder for lost earning capacity, future medical expenses, and future pain and suffering. Your client's mother has authorized you to settle for this amount. However, today your client's mother calls, distraught. Her son was playing with friends, ran out into the street, and was hit by a bus and killed. You are to meet this afternoon with the defendant insurer to finalize the settlement.

Despite decades of cases in which attorneys have failed to disclose the fact that their client has died and have had settlements voided and discipline imposed, these cases are still surprisingly frequent. What are these attorneys thinking? Why are they wrong? *Virzi v. Grand Trunk Warehouse & Cold Storage Co.*, 571 F. Supp. 507, 509-12 (E.D. Mich. 1983); *Yoh v. Hoffman*, 27 P.3d 927, 931 (Kan. Ct. App. 2001); *Harris v. Jackson*, 192 S.W.3d 297, 305-07 (Ky. 2006); *Kingsdorf v. Kingsdorf*, 797 A.2d 206, 211-15 (N.J. Super. Ct. App. Div. 2002); *In re Becker*, 804 N.Y.S.2d 4, 5-6 (N.Y. App. Div. 2005); *In re Edison*, 724 N.W.2d 579, 584 (N.D. 2006).

13.2 Consequences of Misrepresentations

As you can see from the following case, misrepresentation can have a number of repercussions.

Roth v. La Societe Anonyme Turbomeca France

120 S.W.3d 764 (Mo. App. W.D. 2003).

The Roths sued originally for injuries sustained by Sheila Roth in a 1993 helicopter crash in which she was permanently crippled. She was working as a nurse on the flight. The helicopter's engine failed because of a defective engine part manufactured by La Societe Anonyme Turbomeca and distributed by Turbomeca Engine. The pilot and a medical patient being transported in the helicopter died in the crash. A respiratory therapist on board also suffered serious injuries.

The Roths, the therapist and relatives of the two decedents sued Turbomeca and others. Because of the multiplicity of lawsuits with identical issues, the circuit court ordered that all of the plaintiffs share discovery.... One of the plaintiffs asked in interrogatories submitted to Turbomeca whether or not the firms had insurance to cover any judgment arising from the helicopter crash. Turbomeca responded that the maximum insurance coverage was approximately $50 million. The Roths later learned that, in fact, the firms had a maximum insurance coverage of approximately $1 billion.

Why do attorneys believe that lying about insurance limits would not be considered a material misrepresentation?

The circuit court scheduled the Roths' suit for trial after the suits of the other plaintiffs. Before learning of the actual amount of insurance coverage, the Roths feared that $50 million in insurance coverage would not be sufficient to satisfy all of the plaintiffs' judgments, so they decided to settle. On April 14, 1995, they executed a release and settlement agreement with Turbomeca. The following week, the defendants established and funded annuities to fulfill the settlement agreement.

On May 3, 1995, the Roths discovered the actual amount of insurance coverage. The Roths, however, decided against asking the circuit court to set aside the settlement agreement in favor of suing on an independent action for fraud. One reason, they explained at oral argument, was that the settlement moneys had been dispersed and expended, making its return highly impracticable. Pursuant to their release, the Roths voluntarily dismissed their lawsuit with prejudice, and later filed this action naming multiple defendants, including Turbomeca, various primary and excess insurers, and the attorneys providing legal representation for the defendants in the underlying personal injury action, Mendes and Mount, Kevin Cook, and Douglas N. Ghertner.

The suit sounded in four counts and sought recovery for the harm caused by alleged misrepresentations regarding insurance coverage. Count I alleged fraud and named as defendants all of the defendants except for the attorneys. Count II alleged negligent misrepresentation and named only the attorneys as defendants. Counts III and IV alleged fraudulent concealment and civil conspiracy and named all of the defendants as defendants. [The circuit court dismissed all claims in response to defendants' motion to dismiss.] The Roths appeal.

* * *

[The court addressed previous precedent holding that fraud in inducing a release or settlement agreement does not permit the victim the choice of rescinding the contract or enforcing it and also suing independently for the damages resulting from the fraud.] We first disagree with the underlying assumption that the releasor would be reneging on the bargain. He would not be reneging because he would not be pursuing the released tort claim, but an independent claim created by the fraud. Second, damages for the fraud are not "inextricably bound" to the nature and extent of the injuries involved in the underlying tort. They are conceptually different. The measure of damages for the fraud is not the nature and extent of the injuries arising from the underlying tort claim, but the nature and extent of the damages caused by fraudulently inducing the plaintiff to enter the release. Thus, the underlying injuries are relevant to the independent fraud claim only to the extent of their effect on the settlement value in light of the true insurance coverage available.... Moreover, difficulty in assessing damages is not uncommon and should not be a sufficient basis for refusing to recognize a valid cause of action.

... [T]he Roth's release was voidable at their election because of the nature of Turbomeca's alleged fraud. They could enforce their settlement agreement with Turbomeca and still maintain an independent tort claim for fraud.... [T]he Roths pleaded facts that, if proven, satisfied the nine elements for establishing fraud: (1) a representation; (2) its falsity; (3) its materiality; (4) the speaker's knowledge of its falsity; (5) the speaker's intent that it be acted on by the hearer in the manner reasonably contemplated; (6) the hearer's ignorance of the falsity of the representation; (7) the hearer's reliance on the representation being true; (8) the hearer's right to rely on the representation; and (9) the hearer's consequent and proximate injury. That the Roths sustained injuries—not whether they could have done something about those injuries after the fact—is what satisfies the damage element of a fraud claim. In other words, the cause of action was complete when the Roths sustained the damage.

Turbomeca next argues ... that an independent action for fraud cannot arise from misrepresentations made during a lawsuit's discovery stage. We agree that, as a general proposition, if a party to a lawsuit discovers that a fraud was perpetrated against him during discovery and the action is still pending, he should request relief at that time rather than bringing a second action. The rule ... is sound and serves a valid function. Its rationale, however, does not warrant its application to the Roths' case.

When discovery misconduct comes to light while a case is pending, the rules of civil procedure provide complete and adequate relief. A plaintiff, however, who does not discover the fraud until after the parties have executed the settlement agreement does not have an opportunity to consider whether or not the rules provide adequate relief.... [T]he Roths are not suing because they endured the inconvenience or aggravation of a discovery violation, but because that violation resulted in their executing a settlement agreement that they would not have executed had they known the truth. This is a distinction of major significance.

Turbomeca argues that, had the Roths informed the circuit court of the alleged misrepresentation rather than dismissing their lawsuit, the circuit court could have employed appropriate sanctions pursuant to Rule 61.01 and could have allowed the Roths to take their underlying tort claims to trial. But at what cost to the Roths? Were they to proceed to trial, they would risk recovering nothing, even if the case went to trial on the issues of damages only.[4] Rule 61.01 makes sanctions a matter of the circuit court's discretion, and we are very doubtful that the circuit court would have been willing to impose sanctions equal to the amount that the Roths had obtained in their settlement agreement. Moreover, whether or not Rule 61.01(b)(1), with its specific provision for striking pleadings, dismissal, or judgment by default authorizes entry of monetary sanctions for improper interrogatory answers is in some doubt.

Because the Roths had secured some recovery, they should not be forced to forfeit it at the risk of recovering nothing. Rule 61.01 surely was not intended to punish a party who has already suffered prejudice while potentially rewarding the non-compliant party's fraud.

policy reason against adopting Δ arg 2

A federal court considered an analogous situation in *Cresswell v. Sullivan and Cromwell*, 668 F.Supp. 166 (S.D.N.Y.1987). In that case, the court considered whether or not a party alleging fraud during discovery should be required to seek to set aside a judgment, tender back a settlement's proceeds, and go to trial on the underlying claim. The court declared:

analogous case

> If this were the rule, few plaintiffs would choose to enforce their claims of fraud in connection with a settlement, no matter how valid their cause of action. A plaintiff who must give up any benefit he has gained and risk receiving nothing in return will be reluctant to enforce his rights as a victim of fraud. Of course, he may ultimately gain more than he received in settlement the first time, either by going to trial this time around or settling for more[.] ... But this chance of receiving more does not justify the deterrent effect of requiring a plaintiff to give up the settlement he received[.] [E]ven plaintiffs who have settled should not have to run still more risks in recovering their damages[.]

Id. at 172.

Whether or not the Roths can establish the elements of their fraud claim is wholly another matter. What we determine here is only that they have stated a claim upon which relief may be granted against Turbomeca and the respondent insurance companies. We do not disturb the circuit court's dismissal of those insurers not named as respondents to this appeal.

Count II

The Roths contend that the circuit court erred in dismissing Count II of their petition in which they alleged negligent misrepresentation by Mendes and Mount, Cook, and Ghertner. The circuit court dismissed the count on the ground that, except in a few situations involving intentional torts, an attorney is not liable for an injury to a non-client arising from his representation of his client.

---

4. Rule 61.01(b)(1) authorizes the circuit court to enter a default judgment against the defendants, and to submit the case for trial on the issue of damages.... A default judgment is a serious and drastic remedy usually reserved for those cases where a party has shown a "contumacious and deliberate disregard for the court's authority." ... Even assuming such a sanction would withstand judicial scrutiny under the facts of this case, it would also have subjected the Roths to the same risk that we conclude is unjust.

Generally, an attorney is not liable to a third party who is not his or her client because the attorney is not in privity of contract—or in an attorney-client relationship—with the third party.... Courts have found privity between an attorney and a third party in cases in which a client specifically intended for the attorney's services to benefit the third-party. *Donahue v. Shughart, Thomson and Kilroy, P.C.*, 900 S.W.2d 624, 626-29 (Mo. banc 1995). An attorney also may be liable to a third party in exceptional cases, such as cases involving fraud, collusion, or malicious or tortious acts by the attorney. The "exceptional circumstances" rule, as it has come to be called, has been limited to intentional torts.

[margin note: exceptional circumstances rule]

Because the intended benefit rule requires specific intent to benefit the third party, the courts have held that an attorney is not liable to the third party for malpractice alleged to have occurred during adversarial proceedings on the rationale that adversaries would never desire to benefit one another. The Roths argue that this rule should not be analogized to their case because they are suing the attorneys for negligent misrepresentation and not malpractice.

We need not determine this issue because, even if we were to agree with the distinction that the Roths make, it would not aid the Roths. The negligent misrepresentation of which they complain occurred in answers to interrogatories. As assumed by Rule 57.01, a party, not his or her attorney, is to answer interrogatories under oath. Indeed, the Roths pleaded that Turbomeca provided the interrogatory answers of which they complain. Thus, Turbomeca made the representations, and the circuit court properly refused to impute the representations to the attorneys. Although an attorney is an agent of his or her client and acts as the client's alter ego, the converse is not true.

[margin note: misrepresentation by client, not attorneys]

The Roths also pleaded, however, that the attorneys learned of the true limits of insurance coverage and did not convey this information to them until it was too late. They seem to be claiming negligent misrepresentation by silence, but we need not address the claim because an attorney does not have a duty to disclose his client's misrepresentations to his or her client's adversary.

[margin note: The clients sign the interrogatories, but don't most attorneys assist their clients in preparing interrogatories? Would the defendant-attorneys in this action be liable in malpractice to their clients? How does this statement compare to Rule 4.1?]

[margin note: no duty for attorney to disclose clients misrepresentation]

The attorney-client privilege protects confidential communications between an attorney and client concerning matters regarding the representation. The rule is not absolute, but an attorney does not have a duty to disclose privileged communications in anticipation that his or her client might commit a civil offense. An attorney's duty is to serve his or her client. Although an attorney should endeavor to avoid causing needless pain to opposing parties in litigation, the law does not impose a duty to do so.

The Roths point to Rules 4-4.1 and 4-8.4 as imposing a duty on attorneys to disclose to third parties. Rule 4-4.1 prohibits an attorney from knowingly failing to disclose a material fact when necessary to avoid fraud, but it makes an exception for those cases in which Rule 4-1.6 would prohibit disclosure. Rule 4-4.1(b). Rule 4-1.6 did not provide an exception permitting the attorneys to disclose what they knew, and although Rule 4-8.4 prohibits an attorney from engaging in dishonest, fraudulent, or deceitful conduct, it also declares that an attorney cannot disclose information protected by Rule 4-1.6. Rule 4-8.4(a) and (c).

[margin note: R 1.6 provides no exception to disclose, ∴ R 8.4 and R 4.1 not violated]

[margin note: This case was decided before Rule 1.6 contained financial injury exceptions. Would those exceptions change the court's analysis here?]

An attorney who knows that his or her client is making a misrepresentation is in a precarious situation. An attorney should not allow himself or herself to be used to perpetrate civil offenses, but what an attorney must do to avoid running afoul of his ethical obligations is another matter. The Rules of Professional Conduct do not form the basis for a civil cause of action. While they provide standards and violation of them result in disciplinary action, they do not augment an attorney's substantive legal duty or the extra-disciplinary consequences of violating such a duty.[5]

We affirm the circuit court's dismissal of Count II of the Roths' petition for failure to state a claim.

* * *

Count IV

In their final point, the Roths argue that the circuit court erred in dismissing Count IV of their petition. That count alleged a civil conspiracy among the defendants. They appeal, however, only as to the attorneys. The circuit court determined that a civil conspiracy between an attorney and client is not legally possible because, as agent and principal, they are not legally distinct and cannot conspire with one another. The circuit court also determined that the exceptional circumstances rule did not apply to allow the claim.

A civil conspiracy is an agreement or understanding between at least two persons to do an unlawful act, or to use unlawful means to do an act that would otherwise be lawful. A conspiracy is not actionable in its own right because it does not exist apart from the statement of an underlying claim. The unlawful acts done in pursuit of a conspiracy give rise to the action. Proving the conspiracy concerns only the co-conspirators' liability as joint tortfeasors.

Because an attorney is an alter ego of his or her client, a conspiracy between the attorney and client usually is not possible. If, however, an attorney, serving his or her own interest, acts outside the scope of an agency relationship, or if he or she, rather than the client, commits fraud or another intentional tort during the course of his or her representation, the attorney may be liable for conspiracy.

Neither exception applies in this case. The Roths did not allege that the attorneys acted out of self-interest. Furthermore, the Roths did not appeal the circuit court's dismissal of Count III, which alleged fraudulent concealment by the attorneys; therefore, the Roths do not allege an underlying claim that the attorneys committed fraud or any other intentional tort. Although the Roths claim that Turbomeca committed fraud, that claim is not sufficient to support a civil conspiracy claim against the attorneys. The Roths do not allege that the attorneys committed fraud. That they allege that their clients did is insufficient. A client's misconduct cannot be imputed to his attorney, and, to the extent that it is attributed to the attorney as the client's agent, it does not support a conspiracy.

The Roths argue that we must also consider their allegation that the attorney's negligent misrepresentation supported a claim of conspiracy. The argument fails because the Roths did not make an underlying claim for negligent misrepresentation against the attorneys. Furthermore, negligent mis-

---

Do you think it is likely that the defendant attorneys in this action did indeed violate 4.1? What facts would make that more or less likely to be true?

[handwritten margin note:] 2 exceptions where conspiracy b/w attorney-client
① acts outside scope
② commits fraud / intentional tort during representation

---

5. We do not suggest that the attorneys are guilty of violating any rules of professional conduct. We note only that the accusation they have done so is an insufficient basis to argue the existence of a duty that, if breached, would support a civil cause of action for negligent misrepresentation.

representation is not an intentional tort and does not fit within the exceptional circumstances rule.

We affirm the circuit court's dismissal of Count IV of the Roth's petition for failure to state a claim.

Questions

1. If this misrepresentation was made during discovery, wouldn't it also be considered a false statement of material fact to a tribunal and thus violate Rule 3.3 as well? *See Mississippi Bar v. Land*, 653 So. 2d 899 (Miss. 1994) (lawyer suspended from practice for one year for assisting client in providing deceptive and untruthful answers to interrogatories in order to conceal evidence); *United States v. Shaffer Equipment Co.*, 11 F.3d 450 (4th Cir. 1993) (In a CERCLA action for recovery of costs of a cleanup directed by an administrative coordinator, the EPA attorneys discovered that the administrator had lied about his credentials, thus putting the records on the cleanup into question. The administrator continued to lie about his credentials during depositions and the attorneys did not dissuade him or otherwise correct his misstatements. Court held that attorneys had violated Rule 3.3 and remanded for imposition of sanctions.).

2. One of the most potent consequences of misrepresentations is the reputational cost of such sharp practices. What do you think the Roth's attorneys will do the next time they face the defendant-attorneys?

Professional Responsibility Skills 13-A: Protecting Your Client from Misrepresentations

Rule 4.1 counsels attorneys to be honest in dealing with others. It provides little guidance for how to deal with attorneys who would skirt its boundaries. Reconsider the attorneys in the *Roth* case, who were apparently willing to permit their client to sign an interrogatory misstating the amount of insurance coverage. How could the attorneys for the Roth's have prevented or discovered this misrepresentation? They might have simply done a more thorough job of research. Rather than relying on the interrogatory answer, they could have requested a copy of the insurance policy, for example.

Sometimes attorneys are victimized by deception, not because other attorneys lie in their answers to questions but because they avoid answering the questions at all. In his article, *Was Machiavelli Right? Lying in Negotiation and the Art of Defensive Self-Help*, 24 Ohio St. J. on Disp. Resol. 481 (2008), Professor Peter Reilly offers a number of suggestions for defensive lawyering, including "Recognize and thwart tactics of evasion." He illustrates these tactics of evasion as "ignoring the question, offering to return to the question later; answering only part of the question; answering a related but less intrusive, specific or direct question; or calling the question unfair or inappropriate and therefore not entitled to a response." These tactics should alert a perceptive attorney to the presence of sensitive information and the risk of misrepresentation. However, calm persistence in the face of these tactics can often reveal the information being hidden.

Second, as you saw in the prior chapter, relationships reduce misrepresentation. Establishing rapport with opposing attorneys and getting to know them well enough to have a "baseline" against which to measure their communications will both reduce the risk that they will lie and increase your ability to spot the lies they do tell. Civility and respect toward one's opponents will have the practical effect of increasing their reliability toward you. With a basis of respect, one can even ask "Is there anything else I need to know?" and sometimes be rewarded with information that would not have otherwise been disclosed. Of course, sometimes you cannot establish rapport with an opposing attorney because the attorney is unprofessional and willing to engage in unethical tactics in an effort to gain an advantage. The only reasonable relationship to maintain with these individuals is one of formality and strict adherence to the rules. We will explore further how to deal with unethical opponents in chapter 21.5.

13.3 Exploiting an Opponent's Error and Hardball Negotiation

Sometimes the most difficult ethical issues involving the tension between fairness to opponents and confidentiality are presented by an incompetent opposing counsel. If an opponent makes a mistake in negotiations, may you capitalize on the opponent's error? May you bring the error to the attention of the opposing party? This problem presents a key tension in legal representation: The attorney owes the client a duty to competently and diligently pursue the client's lawful objectives, to preserve the client's information, and to respect the client's decision-making autonomy; yet the attorney also owes the opposing party a duty of honesty and fair dealing. When those duties are in conflict, the attorney has three choices: defer to the client's resolution even if it places the client and attorney at risk of liability; act without the client's authorization to resolve the dilemma; or counsel the client and agree with the client on a resolution or withdraw if that consensus cannot be achieved. Because most of these dilemmas are resolved in one of these three ways without subsequent legal challenge, there are few clear rules or definitive case law to guide the attorney's choice. Which of these choices is best depends largely on the factual and legal context and the attorney's default standard for the allocation of authority in the attorney-client relationship.

Suppose you represent the borrower who has fallen behind on a very large loan. You are in the process of negotiating a work-out agreement by which your client will only have to pay on an annual basis for several years a negotiated percentage of what the project makes, which in this context is intended to be the gross income of the project less certain specified, actual, hard dollar expenses.

In the draft of the document, the lender's counsel has included depreciation as one of the deducts. You're no math whiz or business major, but you can see that including depreciation, particularly on an unlimited basis, will probably mean that your client will never have to pay anything. It's an obvious mistake and one that is inconsistent with the "deal."

What do you do? You mention this to your client, and his clear, specific instructions are to make no mention of it. His attitude is that the lender, and particularly the lawyer who drafted the document, have been jerks. He insists, "Let them do their own checking. They get what they deserve."

May the attorney counsel the client to simply accept the agreement without investigating whether there is an error in the offer?

The attorney has duties to third persons under the rules, but their boundaries depend largely on substantive law. Both Rule 1.2(d) and Rule 4.1(b) incorporate the standards of fraud in constraining an attorney's representation. The question here is whether capitalizing on the opponent's error is assisting in a crime or fraud. Under Oklahoma Rule 1.0, "'Fraud' or 'fraudulent' denotes conduct that is fraudulent under the substantive or procedural law of the applicable jurisdiction and has a purpose to deceive." Capitalizing on the unilateral mistake of opposing counsel is unlikely to rise to the level of fraud as defined in the rules. This is especially so in those situations in which there is a decent argument that the opposing party's offer was the result of a change in negotiation position rather than a transposition error.

While the failure to inquire about the possible error and taking advantage of this error may not be fraudulent, it may rise to the level of dishonesty or deceit under the Rule 8.4 definitions of misconduct. That rule is much broader in scope than Rule 1.2. Accordingly there remains some risk to the attorney in proceeding with the settlement without checking for error. Cases can be found on either side of the issue: The traditional view is that a party need not point out an opponent's errors in settlement negotiations. *See, e.g., Brown v. Genessee County,* 872 F.2d 169 (6th Cir. 1989) (defense lawyer in discrimination case not obligated to correct other side's miscalculation of amount of pay the plaintiff would have received if hired); *Swinton v. Whitinsville Savings Bank,* 42 N.E.2d 808 (Mass. 1942) (seller of home had no duty to inform buyer that house was infested with termites, absent a request for that information). More recent cases and commentary have taken the other position. *In re Conduct of Gallagher,* 26 P.3d 131, 132, 135-36 (Or. 2001) (lawyer had duty to correct known error in settlement checks made by opposing counsel, rather than "duping" opposing counsel); *Stare v. Tate,* 98 Cal. Rptr. 264 (Ct. App. 1971) (settlement overturned after attorney used other side's mathematical mistake in the settlement offer to procure an advantageous counter-offer). *See generally,* Nathan M. Crystal, *The Lawyer's Duty to Disclose Material Facts in Contract or Settlement Negotiations,* 87 Ky. L. J. 1055, 1078-79 (1998) (improper to capitalize on opponent's mathematical errors).

For the client as well, there is a risk in agreeing to the offer. At a minimum, the attorney should counsel the client regarding that risk. The risk depends largely on the facts and the practice setting. There is little risk to a criminal defendant who has been offered a plea agreement that it too good to be true. Criminal defendants have a constitutional presumption of innocence. U.S. Constit. Amend V & VI. Under Rule 3.8, the prosecutor has the duty to meet the high burden of proof necessary to overcome this presumption and the prosecutor has a duty to protect the defendant's interests as well as the public. Consistent with the protection of that presumption of innocence, the rules do not permit a lawyer to refuse to offer the testimony of a criminal defendant even when the lawyer "reasonably believes but does not know that the testimony will be false." Rule 3.3 comment 9. Likewise, the rule on meritorious claims and contentions provides that "A lawyer for the defendant in a criminal proceeding, or the respondent in a proceeding that could result in incarceration, may nevertheless so defend the proceeding as to require that every element of the case be established." Rule 3.1. Accordingly, there is little basis for concluding that a defense attorney has any kind of duty to correct a prosecutor's error when the defense counsel did nothing to induce or further that error. Of course, the attorney should counsel the client that the prosecutor's decision not to prosecute criminally does not mean the client would be free of civil liability (or even conceivably other criminal liability, such as contempt).

In a negotiation context, the risks of the client accepting the offer are much more significant. Where the error so clearly appears to be a transposition of numbers, the failure to point out the error would likely provide a basis for rescission of the agreement for unilateral mistake. If one of the parties, through mistake, names a consideration that is out of all proportion to the value of the subject of negotiation, and the other party, realizing that a mistake must have been committed, takes advantage of it, and refuses to let the mistake be corrected when it is discovered, he cannot, under these conditions, claim an enforceable contract. For example, the court in *Sheinbein v. First Boston Corp.*, 670 S.W.2d 872, 877 (Mo. Ct. App. 1984), held that when there is a mistake that on its face is so palpable as to place a person of reasonable intelligence upon his guard, there is not a meeting of the minds of the parties, and consequently there can be no contract.

Moreover, when negotiations occur in the context of an ongoing relationship that must continue after this particular negotiation has concluded, good faith and fair dealing are even more important principles. Ongoing relationships create plenty of opportunities for "paybacks" for perceived sharp practices. The reputational values at stake for both parties and the attorneys all counsel scrupulous fair dealing, even at the risk of further prolonging the negotiations.

Thus, the attorney may counsel the client to simply accept the agreement without disclosure of the error, but there is some risk to the attorney that this would be considered dishonesty and even greater risk to the client that capitalizing on the error now would place the client in worse position overall in the long run. So, may the attorney contact opposing counsel and investigate whether there is an error without first consulting with the client? The ABA Committee on Ethics and Professional Responsibility suggests that a lawyer should give an opposing party notice of an inadvertent omission from a contract in order to prevent unfair advantage to the attorney's client because of the error. However, the opinion leaves open the question of what the attorney must do if the client insists on capitalizing on the error. ABA Comm. on Ethics and Prof'l Responsibility, Informal Op. 86-1518 (1986). That raises the question of whether the attorney must ask the client at all before contacting opposing counsel. The answer is not crystal clear in the rules and may depend on the attorney's agreed-upon relationship with the client from the beginning.

The client has the right to accept or reject the settlement or plea and the attorney may not do so on behalf of the client without prior authorization. Rule 1.2(a). So the attorney must bring a settlement offer to the client's attention unless the client has already clearly allocated to the attorney the authority to accept or reject certain offers. The question is whether this same principle determines whether an attorney can check with the opposing attorney regarding the accuracy of an offer before conveying the offer to the client.

As you will recall, attorneys must "promptly inform" clients of any "decision or circumstance" with respect to which their informed consent is necessary. The comments to Rule 4.1 specifically indicate that "If these Rules require that a particular decision about the representation be made by the client, paragraph (a)(1) requires that the lawyer promptly consult with and secure the client's consent prior to taking action…" Since checking with opposing counsel to clarify the offer before bringing it to the client's attention could jeopardize the offer, this option would seem to fall within the definition of "taking action" in the comment.

Moreover, the suspicion that the offer contains an error would be information relating to the representation and so would be confidential. While checking with the opposing attorney would not necessarily be a *disclosure* of that information, it would surely be a *use* of client information to the disadvantage of the client, and so would violate the duty of loyalty to the client. Two exceptions to confidentiality might permit disclosure here: the exception allowing disclosure to prevent substantial financial harm resulting from the client's fraud when the attorney's services were used to further that fraud and the exception allowing disclosure to comply with other law. Whether either of these exceptions applies depends largely on whether capitalizing on the error would be considered a "fraud." Given the prior analysis indicating that failing to disclose the error might provide defenses of unilateral mistake or misrepresentation in some circumstances but would not easily fit within definitions of fraud, the attorney would want to think twice about relying on these exceptions to the duty of confidentiality to disclose his or her suspicion of error to the opposing attorney without the client's consent.

In other circumstances, attorneys clearly have the discretion to correct opposing counsel's errors even at a cost to the client. The rules provide a number of instances in which attorneys are permitted or even required to temper their zeal:

> A lawyer is not bound ... to press for every advantage that might be realized for a client. For example, a lawyer may have authority to exercise professional discretion in determining the means by which a matter should be pursued. Rule 1.2. The lawyer's duty to act with reasonable diligence does not require the use of offensive tactics or preclude the treating of all persons involved in the legal process with courtesy and respect.

Oklahoma Rules of Prof'l Conduct R. 1.3, cmt. 1 (2005). For example, Rule 3.3 requires revealing controlling contrary authority overlooked by opposing counsel. Rule 4.4 requires that an attorney who receives a document that was inadvertently transmitted should notify the sender. While not an inadvertent transmittal, this is a closely analogous situation, so that it seems the attorney should have some discretion, if not duty, permitting him or her to contact the opposing counsel and ask them to check their figures.

Suppose the attorney does check with the opposing attorney and there is a mistake and the attorney then withdraws the offer. The client might be angry and upset, but it is unlikely the client will sue the attorney for malpractice. Given the lack of clarity of the rules regarding the standard of care here and the uncertainty of any damage or prejudice (after all, the client would be arguing that he lost the opportunity to get a settlement that could have been rescinded later), the cost of proving the case would be prohibitive. Disciplinary counsel may also be unlikely to pursue the case given the uncertainty of the law. So one might imagine that there are a number of attorneys who, believing this falls more within the "means" end of the allocation of authority with the client and valuing their reputation for fair dealing and honesty, would simply talk to the other side before checking with the client.

If the attorney does check with the client first, what is the attorney's right and obligation if the client refuses to allow the attorney to check the settlement? At this point, the attorney would be free to withdraw because the client insists upon taking action with which the lawyer has a fundamental disagreement. Even with a withdrawal, the attorney may also have the discretion to put opposing counsel on notice regarding the offer as well. Just as Comment 10 to Rule 1.2 allows an attorney to disclaim documents upon withdrawal even when the attorney does not have the discretion to disclose the fraudulent nature of those documents; likewise, a request that opposing attorney confirm the terms of the offer would be a "hint" but not a disclosure. Oklahoma Rules of Prof'l Conduct R. 1.2, cmt. 10 (2005). Having this discretion to withdraw and give notice may be sufficient pressure to convince the client that checking the settlement is the right thing to do practically, legally, economically, and ethically.

One of the objections attorneys raise to notifying an opponent of an error is that hardball tactics are necessary to effective negotiation. Empirical research raises some questions about this assumption. Consider this summary of the research on the styles used by successful negotiators:

> Most successful negotiators are able to combine the most salient traits associated with the cooperative/problem-solving and the competitive/adversarial styles. They endeavor to maximize client returns, but attempt to accomplish this objective in a congenial and seemingly ingenuous manner. They look for shared values in recognition of the fact that by maximizing joint returns, they are more likely to obtain the best settlements for their own clients. Although successful negotiators try to manipulate opponent perceptions, they rarely resort to truly deceitful tactics. They know that a loss of credibility will undermine their ability to achieve beneficial results. Despite the fact successful negotiators want as much as possible for their own clients, they are not "win-lose" negotiators who judge their results, not by how well they have done, but by how poorly they think their opponents have done. They realize that the imposition of poor terms on opponents does not necessarily benefit their own clients. All factors being equal, they want to maximize opponent satisfaction. So long as it does not require significant concessions on their part, they acknowledge the benefits to be derived from this approach. The more satisfied opponents are, the more likely those parties will accept proposed terms and honor the resulting agreements.
>
> These eclectic negotiators employ a composite style. They may be characterized as competitive/problem-solvers. They seek competitive goals (maximum client returns), but endeavor to accomplish these objectives through problem-solving strategies. They exude a cooperative approach and follow the courtesies of the legal profession. They avoid rude or inconsiderate behavior, recognizing that such openly adversarial conduct is likely to generate competitive/adversarial responses from their opponents. They appreciate the fact that individuals who employ wholly inappropriate tactics almost always induce opposing counsel to work harder to avoid exploitation by these openly opportunistic bargainers. Legal negotiators who are contemplating the use of offensive techniques should simply ask themselves how they would react if similar tactics were employed against them.

Charles B. Craver, *Ethics: How to Be Deceptive Without Being Dishonest/How to Be Assertive Without Being Offensive*, 38 S. Tex. L. Rev. 713, 729-30 (1997).

In negotiations in particular, tactics can easily step over the line. In addition to the problem of misrepresentation, another common tactic is the use of threats. To a certain extent, threats — even more than deception — are a necessary part of settling any legal dispute. The threat of going to trial to resolve a dispute is often the prime inducement to settle. When is a threat over the line? The only express direction regarding threats in the rules of professional conduct was that found in the 1968 Model Code of Professional Responsibility, DR 7-105(A). That rule prohibited a lawyer from bringing or threatening criminal charges if the sole purpose was to gain an advantage in a civil matter. The rule was not incorporated into the Model Rules of Professional Conduct because it was considered overbroad and vague. Nonetheless, half of the states retained the provision when they adopted the Model Rules. Even without the rule, other provisions of the rule have been applied in various circumstances of threats: most commonly, Rule 3.4 (Fairness to Opposing Party and Counsel), Rule 4.1 (Truthfulness in Statements to Others), Rule 4.4 (Respect for Rights of Third Persons), and Rules 8.4(b), (d), and (e) (Misconduct — especially "conduct prejudicial to the administration of justice").

How do you negotiate the line between legitimate pressure tactics in a settlement and unlawful or unethical threats? Courts may consider a number of factors in evaluating an attorney's threats. Threatening the possibility of criminal action is more likely to be proper if the criminal matter and the civil claim relate to one another. Thus threatening to refer a child support case to the prosecutor for criminal nonsupport or criminal contempt as a way of pressuring settlement of a civil action to recover past due child support is more likely to be considered acceptable pressure than making the same threat in order to induce settlement of a debt entirely unrelated to child support.

The risk of discipline increases significantly whenever a threat is combined with misrepresentation or a frivolous claim. Threatening criminal action to induce settlement is not appropriate where the facts do not support either the criminal charge or the civil claim. An attorney is far more likely to incur discipline or liability if the threats are baseless. *State ex rel. Oklahoma Bar Ass'n v. Worsham*, 957 P.2d 549 (Okla. 1998) (lawyer's threat of criminal prosecution without basis in fact or law is violation of disciplinary rule that prohibits assertion of frivolous claims and rule regarding truthfulness). Moreover, even if there is a strong basis for suggesting that a criminal charge might arise, the lawyer should not attempt to exert improper influence over the criminal process, or suggest that she has such influence. An especially important consideration in weighing the legitimacy of the threat is the fairness of the demand the threat is pressuring. If the demand is for a sum that exceeds the clients actual financial losses (perhaps with no allocation for less quantifiable types of damage such as emotional distress) the threat is more likely to be considered excessive. If any part of the sum demanded appears to include a price simply for keeping quiet, the threat to pursue criminal charges would most certainly be extortion.

The directness of the threat appears also to be a factor. Merely raising the criminal implications of conduct is not as likely to be considered improper as is making an actual threat. For example, the Oregon court declined to discipline an attorney who sent a letter to a hit-and-run driver in which he contrasted his client's generous offer to settle with the driver's own criminal behavior. The court was influenced by the attorney's statement, "I am not telling you this to threaten you." *In re McCurdy*, 681 P.2d 131 (Or. 1984).

You should never threaten to report something that you have a legal duty to report (e.g., reporting another attorney's violation of the rules that raises your duty to report under your state's version Model Rule 8.3) or make promises that would otherwise violate the law (e.g., destruction of evidence, suborning perjury). These statements violate the rules of professional conduct because by merely threatening, you imply that you will not follow through on your legal duty to report if you obtain the result you desire.

Reflective Practice: Fair Game?

What is your personal reaction to the problem of exploiting an opponent's error in negotiations? In your everyday life you've likely had many opportunities to consider the broader question of the morality of taking advantage of another's error. Do you let your opponent in a game have a "do-over" when he's made a foolish error? Is it wrong to keep the money when the cashier at the checkout stand gives you too much change? Would you point out to a fellow student that she made a mistake in preparing an assignment? The answer may depend on what "the rules" provide—but what are you inclined to feel about those rules?

When we step into the attorney's role, the adversary ethic provides a powerful vision that can discourage a cooperative attitude toward opponents. When rules shift the balance toward increased obligations to third parties and to the courts, they are often subject to considerable criticism as threatening fundamental aspects of the attorney-client relationship. Theodore Schneyer, *Professionalism as Politics: The Making of a Modern Legal Ethics Code,* in LAWYERS' IDEALS/LAWYERS' PRACTICES: TRANSFORMATIONS IN THE AMERICAN LEGAL PROFESSION, 95, 113-17, 122-23, 127-30 (Robert L. Nelson et al. eds., 1992).

Write about your personal views on the ethics of capitalizing on an opponent's errors.

Test Your Understanding

You represent "Backbreak Acres, LLP." The partners are David Brown, his son Joe, and grandson Matthew. The Brown Family has owned the same parcel of land for generations. Recently, the family has been watching with anticipation as the nearby city has slowly crept closer to their homestead. After much deliberation, the partners have made a difficult (yet potentially very profitable) decision. They would like you to arrange a sale of a portion of some of the land they own and assistance in a development plan for the remaining property. The potential purchaser is Dan Developer, who wants to use the land to build yet another Super Target-strip mall combination. Dan has requested an environmental audit of the land.

You select an auditor and receive the completed report. The audit indicates that the property subject to sale itself has no environmental problems. However, in the auditor's cover letter, the auditor indicates that the neighboring parcel of land, which also belongs to your clients, is the habitat of a voracious rodent. The rodent is protected under The Endangered Species Act of 1973.

When you discuss the audit with the partners, Matthew commented that they knew about the rodents, but they have been trapping and poisoning them for years.

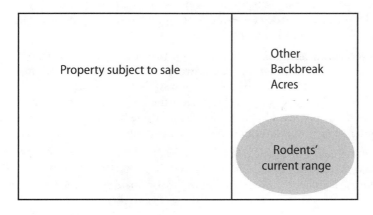

Your research tells you that this is not a solution. (16 U.S.C. § 1538(a)(1)(G) : [I]t is unlawful for any person to violate any regulation pertaining to any threatened species of fish or wildlife listed pursuant to section 1533 of this title. 50 CFR 17.21, ¶ (c)(1): "[i]t is unlawful to take endangered wildlife within the United States." Under 16 U.S.C. § 1532(19), "[t]he term 'take' means to harass, harm, pursue, hunt, shoot, wound, kill, trap, capture, or collect, or to attempt to engage in any such conduct." Both civil and criminal penalties attach to violations.)

Your clients, based on your advice, quit trapping the rodents. The bad news is that the rodents look as though they will extend their range onto the subject property by the close of the year. You have concluded that your clients face some risk of misrepresentation if they do not disclose the rodent problem. However, your presentation should focus not on what your client must disclose but on your duties to disclose or respond.

Dan Developer has asked for the results of the audit. How will you respond? Specifically: Can you tell him no? Can you give him the audit? Can you give him the audit report without the cover letter? Suppose Dan's attorney, in negotiating the deal, says "Your client has indicated that the audit came back without problems." Can you agree? Can you summarize the audit for him, stating "the property subject to the sale is free of any environmental problems"?

Analysis

You should have concluded that you must first consult with your clients before responding to the opposing counsel's request for the results of the audit since the audit is confidential client information. You should have also concluded that your response to the request for the audit report would be either yes or no. You could refuse to release the report, though that would undoubtedly signal a problem to the buyers. You could release the report and try to negotiate a mutually acceptable solution to the problem it presents. However releasing the audit without the cover letter presents a significant risk of misrepresentation and fraud. Summarizing the audit results with a "problem free" statement could be viewed as an even worse choice. You should counsel your clients of these risks and refuse to assist them if they are determined to deceive the buyers.

Likewise in terms of affirming any statements the clients have made to the buyers. If your clients had affirmatively represented that Backbreak Acres had "no problems," you would be well advised to convince your clients to retract that statement. While the statement may be technically true concerning the subject property, the cover letter contains what would likely be found as a materially adverse fact.

If Backbreak Acres still insists on deception, you could withdraw. Upon termination, you could not disclose any confidences, however comments to Rule 1.6 suggest that you might wish to notify all parties of your withdrawal and disaffirm documents prepared on the client's behalf but this would likely alert the buyers that a problem exists. Should your services have been used in any way to defraud the buyers, you might be required to disclose under the combination of Rules 4.1(b) and 1.6(b)(3) or (4).

To read more about this issue, see J. William Futrell, *Environmental Ethics, Legal Ethics and Codes of Professional Responsibility*, 27 Loy. L.A. Rev. 825 (1995), Patrick E. Donovan, *Serving Multiple Masters: Confronting the Conflicting Interests That Arise in Superfund Dis-*

putes, 17 B.C. ENVTL. AFF. L. REV. 371, 372 (1990); or—J.B. Ruhl, *Malpractice and Environmental law: Should Environmental law "Specialists" be Worried?* 33 HOUS. L. REV. 173 (1996).

To Learn More

There are many fine books on negotiation skills and ethics that are well worth your time to read and study.

ROGER FISHER, WILLIAM URY & BRUCE PATTON, GETTING TO YES (2d ed. 1991).

> The classic text on negotiation, this is essential reading for understanding the basics of dispute resolution that ground not only principled negotiation, but also mediation and collaborative law processes. The book is concise and straightforward. The authors have produced many fine books since then that you may want to explore (for example, Fisher, *Beyond Reason: Using Emotions as You Negotiate*; Ury, *Getting Past No;* or Stone, Patton, Heen & Fisher, *Difficult Conversations: How to Discuss what Matters Most*).

CARRIE MENKEL-MEADOW AND MICHAEL WHEELER, WHAT'S FAIR: ETHICS FOR NE-
GOTIATORS (2004).

> A very readable collection of readings all directed toward the ethical issues arising in negotiations.

In addition, the following articles are helpful to understanding the attorney's duty of candor to third persons:

Gerald B. Wetlaufer, *The Ethics of Lying in Negotiation*, 76 Iowa L. Rev. 1219 (1990). (An excellent starting point for considering the duty of candor in negotiations, the article explores various forms of lies and deceptions used in negotiation and argues that while some of these may at times be effective, they are nevertheless unethical.)

Lisa Lerman, *Lying to Clients*, 138 U. Pa. L. Rev. 659 (1990). (As the title implies, the article explores the situations in which attorneys lie to their clients. Based on the author's interviews with attorneys, the article examines lawyers' deception of their clients, both directly and through a third party. The article discusses the ethics and costs of this deception and makes suggestions for reforms in legal practice.)

Douglas R. Richmond, *Lawyers' Professional Responsibilities and Liabilities in Negotiations*, 22 Geo. J. Legal Ethics 249 (2009). (A primer on the attorney's duties of communication and candor with clients, opponents, and the courts.)

Art Hinshaw and Jess K. Alberts, *Doing the Right Thing: An Empirical Study of Attorney Negotiation Ethics*, 16 HARV. NEGOTIATION L. REV. 95 (2011). (Reporting results of a study of attorney negotiation ethics in which most attorneys refused to assist a client in fraudulent conduct and exploring the reasons for the substantial minority of attorneys who agreed to assist the client. Reasons included misunderstandings of the prohibitions of Rule 4.1 and common law misrepresentation and misunderstandings of the scope of the duty of confidentiality.)

Chapter Fourteen

Confidentiality and Counseling Compliance

Learning Objectives

After you have read this chapter and completed the assignments, you should be able to:

- Distinguish between informing a client of the law and assisting a client in evading or breaking law.
- Recognize that regulations other than rules of professional conduct may control the attorney's relationship with a client, especially in practice before federal agencies, and be able to locate and analyze those regulations.
- Analyze the attorney's duty to counsel the client to comply with the law, whether an individual or an entity.
- Assess your own comfort with the attorney's role as a counselor and gatekeeper.

Rules to Study

We will look at a number of rules that address the attorney's role as a counselor, primarily Rules 1.2, 2.1, and 1.13, and we will look back again at Rules 1.6 and 1.16 as it relates to this role. We will also consider some federal regulations that govern the attorney-client relationship: in particular, the bankruptcy code provision regarding advice to an individual client and the Sarbanes-Oxley regulations regarding duties to counsel compliance in certain corporations.

Introductory Problem

You work in the legal department of Big Oil Company, which is a large petroleum company. One of your fellow attorneys is Will Dane. Will has stepped into your office for some advice. As part of his duties, the general counsel has asked him to prepare a report on the Company's compliance with environmental laws. In the course of his investigation, he discovers a number of egregious environmental violations that, if discovered, are likely to lead to stiff fines as well as the potential for private litigation. He prepares a report that includes a very straightfor-

317

ward and painfully honest assessment of the subsidiary's failure to comply with environmental law. To give the head of the environmental division, MaryAnn Bridges, advance notice of the impact that the report's findings might have, he sent her the attached memorandum. A rather incensed Ms. Bridges demanded a copy of the incomplete report. After reviewing it, she cornered Mr. Dane and declared the report "inaccurate" and "inflammatory." She then insisted that he revise the report to cover up the company's breaches of environmental law. He says that in light of recent financial problems the company has experienced, it cannot afford the cleanup, fines, or potential judgments. He explained that the information in the report was accurate, and that the company was violating environmental laws and had a number of steps to take to bring itself into compliance with the law. Mary Ann suggests that he should follow her advice to "tone down" the report if he wants to keep his job. What should he do now?

INTER-OFFICE MEMORANDUM

To: MaryAnn Bridges,
From: Will Dane, In-House Environmental Counsel, Big Oil Company
Re: Environmental Law Compliance Report

The legal department is currently putting the finishing touches on the environmental compliance report for Big Oil Company you requested. In the course of our investigation, information that is likely to have damaging effects on the corporation came to light. Because the company is bound to disclose this information to the appropriate governmental authorities, I thought it appropriate to give you advance notice for planning purposes.

In our investigation, we brought in independent scientists to analyze water and soil specimens collected from around Big Oil's Refinery. Their tests revealed that waste from the refinery is spilling into nearby water sources as well as seeping into the soil. Thankfully, the area around the refinery is industrial, and it appears as there is no immediate threat to human life. However, according to our scientists, the effects of the leak are being felt in a nearby nature preserve which is 15 miles away from our refinery.

We need to meet to discuss action that must be taken in light of this recently discovered information. We are legally required to disclose this information about the leak to authorities. Big Oil will likely be required to pay for the cleanup, additionally stiff monetary penalties are likely to be imposed, and there is the possibility of private litigation.

Please contact me as soon as possible to formulate our course of action for disclosure.

How would you advise Will about what his next steps should be?

14.1   The Lawyer as Gatekeeper

As you have read, one of the primary purposes of confidentiality is to promote trust and communication between attorney and client so that the attorney can represent the client effectively. One of the most important components of that representation is counseling the client. However, that counseling looks quite different in different practice settings. In particular, counseling a client who is facing allegations of wrongdoing for past conduct is quite different from counseling a client who is planning or in the midst of activities that may violate the law. The exceptions to confidentiality make this difference quite clear—if a client comes to an attorney after having killed or injured someone or having caused irreparable financial or property harm, the attorney may not disclose the client's confidential information. The attorney's duty is to defend the client. However, the many variations on Rule 1.6 all either give the attorney direction or discretion to reveal confidential information to *prevent* certain client wrongdoing.

When acting as a partisan advocate, an attorney may assist a client in avoiding the legal consequences of his or her action (or, more accurately stated, to require an opponent to hold the client accountable by proper legal process and proof). But when the attorney is counseling a client in a forward-looking manner, it is less clear what the balance is between the attorney's duty to the client and the attorney's duty to the system and the public. You know that you cannot counsel a client to evade the law but can you counsel a client how to avoid the law? Is counseling an individual client to comply with the law a different process than counseling an entity client regarding compliance? Does the type of law about which you are counseling a client affect the advice you may or must give?

The fact that an attorney's counseling occurs in private, without the testing of the adversarial system, suggests that attorneys should counsel their clients from the perspective of an agent of the legal system, as well as an advocate for the client. Attorneys counseling governmental agencies and large corporations are less likely to have the influence over their client's decision as might an attorney counseling an individual. Federal laws in particular have increasingly attempted to influence the counseling relationship, requiring attorneys to exert more direct influence over their clients to comply with the law.

In this chapter, we examine more closely the conversations an attorney might have with a client (whether an individual or an entity) when the client is planning or in the midst of activity that violates the law or causes harm. We have already studied many rules that make it clear that an attorney may not assist a client in wrongdoing. We know that under Rule 1.4 the attorney has the duty to counsel the client about the limits of her role if she knows that the client expects her to step over the bounds of the rules or law. We also know that Rule 1.16 requires an attorney to withdraw from representation if the attorney knows the client has or will be using the attorney's services to further a crime or fraud. Likewise, the discretionary withdrawal rules of 1.16(b) give attorneys the discretion to withdraw whenever they reasonably believe their services are being used to further crime or fraud or when the client insists on pursuing an objective with which the attorney fundamentally disagrees. So we know attorneys have a right and duty to disassociate themselves from client wrongdoing, but does an attorney have a duty to try to dissuade the client from that wrongdoing?

This question has been raised increasingly in recent years, as corporate and financial scandals have left the public and regulators asking, "Where were the attorneys?" Of course this question is relevant to the representation of all clients, not just entities. Yet, the very fact that an entity client is composed of many individual decision makers, as well as individuals who can cause the entity to violate the law, makes counseling in this setting especially difficult and subject to complex regulation outside the basic criminal law standards of aiding and abetting or the structures of disciplinary rules.

Let's begin with the disciplinary rules that require attorneys to counsel their clients to obey the law. Rule 1.2(d) is the main rule on this issue. The Iowa Rules, for example, provide:

> A lawyer shall not counsel a client to engage, or assist a client, in conduct that the lawyer knows is criminal or fraudulent, but a lawyer may discuss the legal consequences of any proposed course of conduct with a client and may counsel or

assist a client to make a good faith effort to determine the validity, scope, meaning or application of the law.

Iowa Supreme Court, Rules of Professional Conduct, Rule 32:1.2(d) (2007)(based on ABA Model Rule 1.2).

The rule prohibits what would seem self-evident: attorneys may not assist their clients in committing crimes or frauds. The prohibition on assisting in client crimes or frauds is read broadly. ABA Comm. on Ethics and Prof'l Responsibility, Formal Op. 87-353 (1987) (interpreting the term "assisting" to include more than "criminal law concepts of aiding and abetting or subornation"); *see also* ABA Comm. on Ethics and Prof'l Responsibility, Formal Op. 93-376 (1993) (reaffirming Formal Op. 87-353). As to the counseling portion of the rule, notice that the command here is negative — the attorney shall not counsel a client to engage … in conduct…. This leaves open the question, "If you know that a client intends to engage in behavior that is harmful to himself or others, but the client does not ask for your advice or assistance, do you have a duty to dissuade the client?" Notice also that the categories of wrongdoing are limited to criminal or fraudulent behavior. So if a client asks for your assistance in wrongdoing that is not criminal or fraudulent but appears to violate an administrative regulation or to be a basis for civil liability, what is your role? The rule that speaks most directly to an attorney's counseling obligations is Rule 2.1.

> In representing a client, a lawyer shall exercise independent professional judgment and render candid advice. In rendering advice, a lawyer may refer not only to law but to other considerations such as moral, economic, social and political factors, that may be relevant to the client's situation.

Iowa Supreme Court, Rules of Professional Conduct, Rule 32:2.1 (2007).

Notice the difference between the "shall" part of the rule and the "may." Independent professional judgment requires that the attorney base her advice on an objective, reasonable analysis of the client's situation. Sometimes an attorney so identifies with the client and the client's goals that it is difficult to step back and evaluate the client's situation objectively and independently. Cassandra Burke Robertson, *Judgment, Identity, and Independence*, 42 Conn. L. Rev. 1 (2009) (discussing identity theory and its relationship to cognitive biases). Attorneys acting as counselors must recognize that their role is distinct from that of advocate.

A series of memoranda from the Department of Justice's Office of Legal Counsel (OLC) regarding legal limits on torture of prisoners highlighted the importance of this distinction in stark terms. The memos concluded that the CIA and Department of Defense would not violate international or domestic laws prohibiting torture when engaged in interrogation tactics such as waterboarding and sleep deprivation. In testimony to Congress on these memos, Professor David Luban explained why these memos violated the attorney's role as a counselor:

> When a lawyer advises a client about what the law requires, there is one basic ethical obligation: to tell it straight, without slanting or skewing. That can be a hard thing to do, if the legal answer isn't the one the client wants. Very few lawyers ever enjoy saying "no" to a client who was hoping for "yes." But the profession's ethical standard is clear: a legal adviser must use independent judgment and give candid, unvarnished advice. In the words of the American Bar Association, "a lawyer should not be deterred from giving candid advice by the prospect that the advice will be unpalatable to the client."

> That is the governing standard for all lawyers, in public practice or private. But it's doubly important for lawyers in the Office of Legal Counsel. The mission of OLC is to give the President advice to guide him in fulfilling an awesome con-

stitutional obligation: to take care that the laws are faithfully executed. Faithful execution means interpreting the law without stretching it and without looking for loopholes. OLC's job is not to rubber-stamp administration policies, and it is not to provide legal cover for illegal actions.

No lawyer's advice should do that. The rules of professional ethics forbid lawyers from counseling or assisting clients in illegal conduct; they require competence; and they demand that lawyers explain enough that the client can make an informed decision, which surely means explaining the law as it is. These are standards that the entire legal profession recognizes.

Unfortunately, the torture memos fall far short of professional standards of candid advice and independent judgment. They involve a selective and in places deeply eccentric reading of the law. The memos cherry-pick sources of law that back their conclusions, and leave out sources of law that do not. They read as if they were reverse engineered to reach a pre-determined outcome: approval of waterboarding and the other CIA techniques.

My written statement goes through the memos in detail, Mr. Chairman. Let me give just one example here of what I am talking about. Twenty-six years ago, President Reagan's Justice Department prosecuted law enforcement officers for waterboarding prisoners to make them confess. The case is called *United States v. Lee*. Four men were convicted and drew hefty sentences that the Court of Appeals upheld.

The Court of Appeals repeatedly referred to the technique as "torture." This is perhaps the single most relevant case in American law to the legality of waterboarding. Any lawyer can find the *Lee* case in a few seconds on a computer just by typing the words "water torture" into a database. But the authors of the torture memos never mentioned it. They had no trouble finding cases where courts didn't call harsh interrogation techniques "torture." It's hard to avoid the conclusion that Mr. Yoo, Judge Bybee, and Mr. Bradbury chose not to mention the Lee case because it casts doubt on their conclusion that waterboarding is legal....

Testimony of David Luban, Senate Judiciary Committee, Subcommittee on Administrative Oversight and the Courts Hearing: "What Went Wrong: Torture and the Office of Legal Counsel in the Bush Administration" (May 13, 2009).

While controversies regarding the legality or ethics of the attorneys involved in writing these memos continue, for new attorneys the lessons are clear nonetheless. When counseling a client, the attorney should first conduct an objective and disinterested analysis of the client's facts and the application of the law to those facts and provide that independent professional judgment to the client, regardless of whether it is the judgment the client might want. When an attorney's independent judgment leads to the conclusion that the client should be dissuaded from plans, the attorney's duty to convey that perspective to the client is part of the basic duty of the attorney-counselor.

Legal advice often involves unpleasant facts and alternatives that a client may be disinclined to confront. In presenting advice, a lawyer endeavors to sustain the client's morale and may put advice in as acceptable a form as honesty permits. However, a lawyer should not be deterred from giving candid advice by the prospect that the advice will be unpalatable to the client.

Iowa Supreme Court, Rules of Professional Conduct, Rule 32:2.1, cmt. 1 (2007). Comment 5 provides even more guidance on the scope of the attorney's counseling function:

In general, a lawyer is not expected to give advice until asked by the client. However, when a lawyer knows that a client proposes a course of action that is likely to result in substantial adverse legal consequences to the client, the lawyer's duty to the client under rule 32:1.4 may require that the lawyer offer advice if the client's course of action is related to the representation.... A lawyer ordinarily has no duty to initiate investigation of a client's affairs or to give advice that the client has indicated is unwanted, but a lawyer may initiate advice to a client when doing so appears to be in the client's interest.

Iowa Supreme Court, Rules of Professional Conduct, Rule 32:2.1, cmt. 5 (2007).

Still, notice that the focus in the counseling function is on the client's interests. One can presume that most wrongdoing a client might propose would result in adverse legal consequences to the client, but that presumes clear wrongdoing. How do you counsel a client who seeks to take advantage of a "loophole"—a technicality, ambiguity, or uncertain application of the law? In recent years, legislatures have moved to direct the advice of attorneys and other professionals in more specific terms than those provided by these rules and in part to foreclose assisting clients in avoiding the spirit if not the letter of the law. Under these regulations, "the lawyer increasingly becomes not just an advocate and advisor but a gatekeeper as well, so that not just the details of legal representation but its rationale and function are changing." John Leubsdorf, *Legal Ethics Falls Apart*, 57 BUFFALO L. REV. 959, 960 (2009).

To learn more about how these laws are interpreted, we will revisit the Supreme Court's decision in *Milavetz, Gallop & Milavetz, P.A. v. United States*, which we first read in Chapter Two. You may remember that that case involved the Bankruptcy Act. The Supreme Court concluded that the Act's regulation of "debt relief agencies" extended to attorneys. We now will look at that part of the opinion that examined the Bankruptcy Act's requirement that attorneys may not advise clients to take on more debt "in contemplation of bankruptcy." Before you read the court's interpretation, think about what it means to do something "in contemplation of bankruptcy."

Milavetz, Gallop & Milavetz, P.A. v. United States

130 S.Ct. 1324, 176 L. Ed. 2d 79; 2010 U.S. LEXIS 2206 (2010)

Having concluded that attorneys are debt relief agencies when they provide qualifying services, we next address the scope and validity of §526(a)(4). Characterizing the statute as a broad, content-based restriction on attorney-client communications that is not adequately tailored to constrain only speech the Government has a substantial interest in restricting, the Eighth Circuit found the rule substantially overbroad. For the reasons that follow, we reject that conclusion.

Section 526(a)(4) prohibits a debt relief agency from "advis[ing] an assisted person" ... "to incur more debt in contemplation of" filing for bankruptcy."... The Court of Appeals concluded that "§526(a)(4) broadly prohibits a debt relief agency from advising an assisted person ... to incur any additional debt when the assisted person is contemplating bankruptcy." *Id.*, at 793. Under that reading, an attorney is prohibited from providing all manner of "beneficial advice—even if the advice could help the assisted person avoid filing for bankruptcy altogether." *Ibid.*

Agreeing with the Court of Appeals, Milavetz contends that §526(a)(4) prohibits a debt relief agency from advising a client to incur any new debt while considering whether to file for bankruptcy. Construing the provision more broadly still, Milavetz contends that §526(a)(4) forbids not only affirmative advice but also any discussion of the advantages, disadvantages, or legality of incurring more debt. Like the panel majority's, Milavetz's reading rests primarily on its view that the ordinary meaning of the phrase "in contemplation of bankruptcy encompasses any advice given to a debtor with the awareness that he might soon file for bankruptcy, even if the advice seeks to obviate the need to file." Milavetz also maintains that if §526(a)(4) were construed more narrowly, as urged by the Government and the dissent below, it would be so vague as to inevitably chill some protected speech.

The Government continues to advocate a narrower construction of the statute, urging that Milavetz's reading is untenable and that its vagueness concerns are misplaced. The Government contends that §526(a)(4)'s restriction on advice to incur more debt "in contemplation of" bankruptcy is most naturally read to forbid only advice to undertake actions to abuse the bankruptcy system. Focusing first on the provision's text, the Government points to sources indicating that the phrase "in contemplation of" bankruptcy has long been, and continues to be, associated with abusive conduct. For instance, Black's Law Dictionary 336 (8th ed. 2004) (hereinafter Black's) defines "contemplation of bankruptcy" as "[t]he thought of declaring bankruptcy because of the inability to continue current financial operations, often coupled with action designed to thwart the distribution of assets in a bankruptcy proceeding." Use of the phrase by Members of Congress illustrates that traditional coupling. See, e.g., S. Rep. No. 98-65, p. 9 (1983) (discussing the practice of " 'loading up' [on debt] in contemplation of bankruptcy"); Report of the Commission on the Bankruptcy Laws of the United States, H. R. Doc. No. 93-137, pt. I, p. 11 (1973) ("[T]he most serious abuse of consumer bankruptcy is the number of instances in which individuals have purchased a sizable quantity of goods and services on credit on the eve of bankruptcy in contemplation of obtaining a discharge"). The Government also points to early American and English judicial decisions to corroborate its contention that "in contemplation of" bankruptcy signifies abusive conduct. *See, e.g., In re Pearce,* 19 F. Cas. 50, 53, F. Cas. No. 10873, 21 Vt. 611 (No. 10,873) (D. Vt. 1843); *Morgan v. Brundrett,* 5 B. Ad. 288, 296-297, 110 Eng. Rep. 798, 801 (K. B. 1833) (Parke, J.).

To bolster its textual claim, the Government relies on §526(a)(4)'s immediate context. According to the Government, the other three subsections of §526(a) are designed to protect debtors from abusive practices by debt relief agencies: §526(a)(1) requires debt relief agencies to perform all promised services; §526(a)(2) prohibits them from making or advising debtors to make false or misleading statements in bankruptcy; and §526(a)(3) prohibits them from misleading debtors regarding the costs or benefits of bankruptcy. When §526(a)(4) is read in context of these debtor-protective provisions, the Government argues, construing it to prevent debt relief agencies from giving advice that is beneficial to both debtors and their creditors seems particularly nonsensical.

*Do any ①
BAPCPA remo*

Given these remedies, does the concern that the section might be read broadly seem so "nonsensical"?

Are you convinced by this reasoning?

Finally, the Government contends that the BAPCPA's remedies for violations of § 526(a)(4) similarly corroborate its narrow reading. Section 526(c) provides remedies for a debt relief agency's violation of § 526, § 527, or § 528. Among the actions authorized, a debtor may sue the attorney for remittal of fees, actual damages, and reasonable attorney's fees and costs; a state attorney general may sue for a resident's actual damages; and a court finding intentional abuse may impose an appropriate civil penalty. § 526(c). The Government also relies on the Fifth Circuit's decision in *Hersh v. United States ex rel. Mukasey*, 553 F.3d 743 (2008), and Judge Colloton's dissent below for the observation that "Congress's emphasis on actual damages for violations of section 526(a)(4) strongly suggests that Congress viewed that section as aimed at advice to debtors which if followed would have a significant risk of harming the debtor." *Id.*, at 760; *see* 541 F.3d at 800 (opinion concurring in part and dissenting in part). By contrast, "legal and appropriate advice that would be protected by the First Amendment, yet prohibited by a broad reading of § 526(a)(4), should cause no damage at all." *Ibid.*; *see Hersh*, 541 F.3d at 760.

Milavetz contends that the Government's sources actually undermine its claim that the phrase "in contemplation of" bankruptcy necessarily refers to abusive conduct. Specifically, Milavetz argues that these authorities illustrate that "in contemplation of" bankruptcy is a neutral phrase that only implies abusive conduct when attached to an additional, proscriptive term. As Black's states, the phrase is "often coupled with action designed to thwart the distribution of assets" in bankruptcy, Black's 336 (emphasis added), but it carries no independent connotation of abuse. In support of that conclusion, Milavetz relies on our decision in *Pender*, 289 U.S. 472, 53 S. Ct. 703, 77 L. Ed. 1327, contending that we construed "in contemplation of" bankruptcy in that case to describe "conduct with a view to a probable bankruptcy filing and nothing more." Brief for Milavetz 61.

After reviewing these competing claims, we are persuaded that a narrower reading of § 526(a)(4) is sounder, although we do not adopt precisely the view the Government advocates. The Government's sources show that the phrase "in contemplation of" bankruptcy has so commonly been associated with abusive conduct that it may readily be understood to prefigure abuse. As used in § 526(a)(4), however, we think the phrase refers to a specific type of misconduct designed to manipulate the protections of the bankruptcy system. In light of our decision in *Pender*, and in context of other sections of the Code, we conclude that [7] § 526(a)(4) prohibits a debt relief agency only from advising a debtor to incur more debt because the debtor is filing for bankruptcy, rather than for a valid purpose.

Pender addressed the meaning of former § 96(d), which authorized reexamination of a debtor's payment of attorney's fees "in contemplation of the filing of a petition." Recognizing "'the temptation of a failing debtor to deal too liberally with his property in enabling counsel to protect him,'" 289 U.S., at 478, 53 S. Ct. 703, 77 L. Ed. 1327 (quoting *In re Wood & Henderson*, 210 U.S. 246, 253, 28 S. Ct. 621, 52 L. Ed. 1046 (1908)), we read "in contemplation of ... filing" in that context to require that the portended bankruptcy have "induce[d]" the transfer at issue, 289 U.S., at 477, 53 S. Ct. 703, 77 L. Ed. 1327, understanding inducement to engender suspicion of abuse. In so construing the statute, we identified the "controlling question" as "whether the thought of bankruptcy was the impelling cause of the transaction." *Ibid.* Given the substantial similarities between §§ 96(d) and 526(a)(4), we think the controlling question under the latter provision is likewise whether the impelling reason for "advis[ing] an assisted person … to incur more debt" was the prospect of filing for bankruptcy.

To be sure, there are relevant differences between the provision at issue in *Pender* and the one now under review. Most notably, the inquiry in *Pender* was as to payments made on the eve of bankruptcy, whereas § 526(a)(4) regards advice to incur additional debts. Consistent with that difference, under § 96(d) a finding that a payment was made "in contemplation of" filing resolved only a threshold inquiry triggering further review of the reasonableness of the payment; the finding thus supported an inference of abuse but did not conclusively establish it. By contrast, advice to incur more debt because of bankruptcy, as prohibited by § 526(a)(4), will generally consist of advice to "load up" on debt with the expectation of obtaining its discharge—i.e., conduct that is abusive per se.…

That "[n]o other solution yields as sensible a" result further persuades us of the correctness of this narrow reading. *United States v. Granderson*, 511 U.S. 39, 55, 114 S. Ct. 1259, 127 L. Ed. 2d 611 (1994). It would make scant sense to prevent attorneys and other debt relief agencies from advising individuals thinking of filing for bankruptcy about options that would be beneficial to both those individuals and their creditors. That construction serves none of the purposes of the Bankruptcy Code or the amendments enacted through the BAPCPA. Milavetz itself acknowledges that its expansive view of § 526(a)(4) would produce absurd results; that is one of its bases for arguing that "debt relief agency" should be construed to exclude attorneys. Because the language and context of § 526(a)(4) evidence a more targeted purpose, we can avoid the absurdity of which Milavetz complains without reaching the result it advocates.

For the same reason, we reject Milavetz's suggestion that § 526(a)(4) broadly prohibits debt relief agencies from discussing covered subjects instead of merely proscribing affirmative advice to undertake a particular action. Section 526(a)(4) by its terms prevents debt relief agencies only from "advis[ing]" assisted persons "to incur" more debt. Covered professionals remain free to "tal[k] fully and candidly about the incurrence of debt in contemplation of filing a bankruptcy case." Brief for Milavetz 73. Section 526(a)(4) requires professionals only to avoid instructing or encouraging assisted persons to take on more debt in that circumstance. Cf. ABA Model Rule of Professional Conduct 1.2(d) (2009) ("A lawyer shall not counsel a client to engage, or assist a client, in conduct that the lawyer knows is criminal or fraudulent, but a lawyer may discuss the legal consequences of any proposed course of conduct with a client and may counsel or assist a client to make a good faith effort to determine the validity, scope, meaning or application of the law"). Even if the statute were not clear in this regard, we would reach the same conclusion about its scope because the inhibition of frank discussion serves no conceivable purpose within the statutory scheme. Cf. *Johnson v. United States*, 529 U.S. 694, 706, n. 9, 120 S. Ct. 1795, 146 L. Ed. 2d 727 (2000).[5]

---

5. If read as Milavetz advocates, § 526(a)(4) would seriously undermine the attorney-client relationship. Earlier this Term, we acknowledged the importance of the attorney-client

As the foregoing shows, the language of the statute, together with other evidence of its purpose, makes this narrow reading of § 526(a)(4) not merely a plausible interpretation but the more natural one. Accordingly, we reject the Eighth Circuit's conclusion and hold that a debt relief agency violates § 526(a)(4) only when the impetus of the advice to incur more debt is the expectation of filing for bankruptcy and obtaining the attendant relief. Because our reading of the statute supplies a sufficient ground for reversing the Court of Appeals' decision, and because Milavetz challenges the constitutionality of the statute, as narrowed, only on vagueness grounds, we need not further consider whether the statute so construed withstands First Amendment scrutiny.

---

privilege as a means of protecting that relationship and fostering robust discussion. *See Mohawk Industries, Inc. v. Carpenter,* 558 U.S. ___, ___, 130 S. Ct. 599, 175 L. Ed. 2d 458, 467 (2009). Reiterating the significance of such dialogue, we note that § 526(a)(4), as narrowly construed, presents no impediment to "'full and frank'" discussions. *Ibid.* (quoting *Upjohn Co. v. United States,* 449 U.S. 383, 389, 101 S. Ct. 677, 66 L. Ed. 2d 584 (1981)).

Notes

1. The 8th Circuit Opinion provided examples of the types of situations in which advising a bankruptcy client to incur debt would be wise advice:

   > For instance, it may be in the assisted person's best interest to refinance a home mortgage in contemplation of bankruptcy to lower the mortgage payments. This could free up additional funds to pay off other debts and avoid the need for filing bankruptcy all together. Hersh, 347 B.R. at 24. Moreover, it may be in the client's best interest to incur additional debt to purchase a reliable automobile before filing for bankruptcy, so that the debtor will have dependable transportation to travel to and from work, which will likely be necessary to maintain the debtor's payments in bankruptcy. Id. Incurring these types of additional secured debt, which would often survive or could be reaffirmed by the debtor, may be in the debtor's best interest without harming the creditors.

   Milavetz, Gallop & Milavetz, P.A. v. United States, 541 F.3d 785, 793 (8th Cir. 2008).

   The Supreme Court addressed this issue in a footnote:

   > The hypothetical questions Milavetz posits regarding the permissibility of advice to incur debt in certain circumstances, *see* Brief for Milavetz 48-51, are easily answered by reference to whether the expectation of filing for bankruptcy (and obtaining a discharge) impelled the advice. We emphasize that awareness of the possibility of bankruptcy is insufficient to trigger § 526(a)(4)'s prohibition. Instead, that provision proscribes only advice to incur more debt that is principally motivated by that likelihood. Thus, advice to refinance

a mortgage or purchase a reliable car prior to filing because doing so will reduce the debtor's interest rates or improve his ability to repay is not prohibited, as the promise of enhanced financial prospects, rather than the anticipated filing, is the impelling cause. Advice to incur additional debt to buy groceries, pay medical bills, or make other purchases "reasonably necessary for the support or maintenance of the debtor or a dependent of the debtor," §523(a)(2)(C)(ii)(II), is similarly permissible.

Milavetz, Gallop & Milavetz, P.A. v. United States, 130 S. Ct. 1324, 1339 ftnt. 6 (2010).

Where does this leave an attorney advising a client in bankruptcy? If an attorney did not provide the advice to incur additional debt to reduce interest rates or improve the ability to pay, would the attorney have violated Rules 1.1 and 1.4 of the Rules of Professional Conduct? Would the attorney be liable for malpractice? What if an attorney is unsure of the effect of a proposed additional debt? If the attorney simply "discussed" and did not "advise" the client regarding debt, would the attorney escape liability under the Bankruptcy code? Would this be competent representation?

2. If the problem is client behavior (i.e., debtors incurring additional debt in bad faith before filing for bankruptcy), why is regulating attorney advice the solution? Consider a similar attempt to deter individuals from "spending down" their assets in order to qualify for Medicaid. Congress first made it a crime for a person to transfer assets to qualify for Medicaid. There was such protest over the "Granny Goes to Jail" law that Congress repealed the law and, instead, passed legislation making it a crime to "advise, for a fee, a person to transfer assets" (even though it was at that point entirely legal for the person to do so in order to qualify for Medicaid). 42 U.S.C.A. §1320a-7b(a)(6)(1997). The New York District Court enjoined the "Granny's Lawyer Goes to Jail" law as an unconstitutional infringement on attorney free speech rights. *New York State Bar Ass'n v. Reno,* 999 F. Supp. 710, 716 (N.D.N.Y. 1998). *See also, Magee v. United States,* 93 F. Supp. 2d 161, 162 (D.R.I. 2000) (recognizing unconstitutionality of Medicaid statute prohibiting certain legal advice).

3. The Bankruptcy Code is not the only federal regulation that regulates attorney advice to clients. Professor Leubsdorf has identified a number of areas of regulation that restrict an attorney's advice and action. He identified five trends that characterize this regulation:

> First, the innovations [in regulation] have tended on the whole to restrain the freedom of lawyers to pursue their clients' interests at the expense of others. No doubt they reflect the view—common outside the profession and among academics—that lawyers are too adversarial. Often, the interests to be protected are those of the government itself, and the innovation can be seen as restricting the independence of the bar. Sometimes they are those of opposing parties or the public. In either case, the lawyer increasingly becomes not just an advocate and advisor but a gatekeeper as well, so that not just the details of legal representation but its rationale and function are changing. And even when the new regulations appear to leave intact the substance of previous rules balancing the interests of clients and those

of nonclients, they often impose more stringent penalties that will sway lawyers to pay more attention to the latter.

Second, the innovations tend to enact requirements that are relatively particularized in their content and in their addressees compared to the generalities addressed to all lawyers that prevail in the lawyer codes. As the functions of lawyers have multiplied, as their numbers have increased, and as faith in their high mindedness has declined, lawmakers have turned to narrower and more specific provisions. These provisions in turn foster specialization by making it harder for lawyers to venture into new fields of practice.

Third, despite being narrow, the new requirements have often included nonlawyers as well as lawyers within their scope. The regulators may not even mention lawyers specifically, and may not have considered how lawyers might differ from others doing the same sort of thing. Likewise, they may not have addressed existing regulation by the bench and bar—though in other instances, it has been the real or perceived inadequacy of that regulation that opened the way for new interventions. That lawyers, like everyone else, are forbidden to break their contracts or engage in fraud is nothing new; but they are now subject to a web of additional and particularized requirements. Ultimately, we might often find it more convenient to think of some practitioners as tax or bankruptcy professionals or the like rather than as lawyers.

Fourth, more and more regulators have sought to regulate the bar. If once the American Bar Association's codes dominated the field, now courts have become increasingly unwilling to defer to them, and legislators and administrators have become increasingly unwilling to defer to either bar associations or courts. We are witnessing the decline of the ideal of professional self-regulation at the same time that the ideal has been almost entirely demolished in England.

Fifth, the new regulators—whether legislative, administrative, or judicial—tend to be federal ones. Although state supreme courts continue to promulgate professional rules and state legislatures occasionally seek to regulate lawyers, the more important and striking initiatives during recent decades have come from the federal government. In this respect, innovation has been centripetal rather than centrifugal. Considering the growth of multijurisdictional practice and the tendency toward federalization of many bodies of law, one can expect this trend to continue. We seem to be moving from a system of rules that are uniform for all lawyers but vary from state to state to one of nationwide rules that vary by specialty.

The fragmentation of the law of the legal profession has begun to bring about a number of more general consequences. It complicates the lives of lawyers, and increases the need for them to obtain advice about their own obligations, as well as the need for law firms to provide internal mechanisms to promote compliance. It means that, more than in the past, changes in the law governing lawyers will result from a political process involving trade offs among various interested groups inside and outside the profession, worked out in a variety of judicial, administrative, and legislative bodies, and often including competition among those bodies.

John Leubsdorf, *Legal Ethics Falls Apart*, 57 BUFFALO L. REV. 959, 959-62 (2009). Among the areas of practice Professor Leubsdorf addresses in his article are banking law, tax law, criminal defense practice, legal aid practice, debt collection work, securities law, bankruptcy law, class action representations, and corporate law.

Researching Professional Responsibility 14-A: Finding Federal Regulations

How do you go about discovering whether there are regulations that affect your area of practice and your interactions with clients? When you develop a specialization in an area of law, you will soon learn about these specialized regulations as you become a content expert in that particular field. At this stage in your career however, discovering whether there are regulations that restrict the advice you can give to a client is the kind of research problem that requires you to start with the big picture. Starting with a secondary source—whether a scholarly article such as Professor Leubsdorf's or a CLE outline or a practice handbook—is often a sensible place to begin. Online, some useful directory of practice area research guides includes:

- Legal Subjects Index (FindLaw)—http://www.findlaw.com/01topics/index.html
- Practice Areas Index (LexisOne) http://www.lexisone.com/legalresearch/legal-guide/practice_areas/practice_areas_index.htm
- Legal Research Guide—http://www.lexisnexis.com/infopro/zimmerman/

If you are generally aware of the regulations you are looking for, you may want to simply locate the regulation. For federal regulations, you would search the Code of Federal Regulations. For state regulation, often the best approach is to go to that state agency's website. You can search United States government websites from the federal government's official search engine at usa.gov website (http://www.usa.gov/), or from the Library of Congress "Thomas" website (http://thomas.loc.gov/home/thomas.php), or the GPO's search tool (http://www.gpo.gov/fdsys/). Alternately, you might use a specialized search engine, such as www.unclesamsearch.com/ or a Google search limited to .gov sites.

To search federal regulations, you would search The Code of Federal Regulations *(CFR)*. Regulations are grouped by departments and agencies into 50 titles (e.g., title 11 contains Federal Election Commission regulations), which are further divided into parts and sections. The code includes a *CFR Index and Finding Aids* volume which indexes regulations by departments, agencies, and topics. This volume also contains a "Parallel Table of Authorities and Rules" listing sources of federal law under which current regulations have been issued. Another useful index is the *Index to the Code of Federal Regulations* published by the Congressional Information Service. All *CFR* titles are on the Internet in the GPO Access database at http://www.gpoaccess.gov/index.html.

To check to see if your regulation has been updated or amended recently, check the Federal Register, which is published daily and publishes proposed and final departmental regulations, executive orders, and other federal agency information. The last few volumes are on the Internet in the GPO Access database at http://www.gpoaccess.gov/index.html, which you can search using a keyword approach.

Practice your skills in searching federal regulation of attorney practice with the following problem. You have been developing a practice advising small businesses in their property and employment matters. You would like to expand your practice to include business formation and tax advising. To get started, you have agreed to prepare tax returns for one of your small business clients. Your client is being very aggressive in his position on certain deductions. You have begun to feel very uncomfortable in advising him on this matter. A friend who is a tax attorney says to you, "Watch out—you're subject to federal law when you start advising clients on tax matters." Is that true? When do treasury department regulations apply to an attorney?

14.2 Reading the Rules: Counseling the Entity Client

When wrongdoing occurs within a corporate entity that is your client, what is your responsibility? Rule 1.13 provides the basic outline of duties for the attorney representing an entity. Under that rule, a certain set of circumstance trigger the attorney's duty to take further action. Read the Iowa court's adoption of that rule carefully now.

Iowa Supreme Court Rules of Professional Conduct
Rule 32:1.13

(a) A lawyer employed or retained by an organization represents the organization acting through its duly authorized constituents.

(b) If a lawyer for an organization knows that an officer, employee, or other person associated with the organization is engaged in action, intends to act, or refuses to act in a matter related to the representation that is a violation of a legal obligation to the organization, or a violation of law that reasonably might be imputed to the organization, and that is likely to result in substantial injury to the organization, then the lawyer shall proceed as is reasonably necessary in the best interest of the organization. Unless the lawyer reasonably believes that it is not necessary in the best interest of the organization to do so, the lawyer shall refer the matter to higher authority in the organization, including, if warranted by the circumstances to the highest authority that can act on behalf of the organization as determined by applicable law.

(c) Except as provided in paragraph (d), if

(1) despite the lawyer's efforts in accordance with paragraph (b) the highest authority that can act on behalf of the organization insists upon or fails to address in a timely and appropriate manner an action, or a refusal to act, that is clearly a violation of law, and

(2) the lawyer reasonably believes that the violation is reasonably certain to result in substantial injury to the organization, then the lawyer may reveal

information relating to the representation whether or not rule 32:1.6 permits such disclosure, but only if and to the extent the lawyer reasonably believes necessary to prevent substantial injury to the organization.

(d) Paragraph (c) shall not apply with respect to information relating to a lawyer's representation of an organization to investigate an alleged violation of law, or to defend the organization or an officer, employee, or other constituent associated with the organization against a claim arising out of an alleged violation of law.

(e) A lawyer who reasonably believes that the lawyer has been discharged because of the lawyer's actions taken pursuant to paragraphs (b) or (c), or who withdraws under circumstances that require or permit the lawyer to take action under either of those paragraphs, shall proceed as the lawyer reasonably believes necessary to ensure that the organization's highest authority is informed of the lawyer's discharge or withdrawal.

(f) In dealing with an organization's directors, officers, employees, members, shareholders, or other constituents, a lawyer shall explain the identity of the client when the lawyer knows or reasonably should know that the organization's interests are adverse to those of the constituents with whom the lawyer is dealing.

(g) A lawyer representing an organization may also represent any of its directors, officers, employees, members, shareholders, or other constituents, subject to the provisions of rule 32:1.7. If the organization's consent to the dual representation is required by rule 32:1.7, the consent shall be given by an appropriate official of the organization other than the individual who is to be represented, or by the shareholders.

Context

The current Rule 1.13 provisions are some of the most recent amendments to the Model Rules, adopted in the wake of Enron and similar scandals. The rules requirements for "reporting up and reporting out" wrongdoing within the corporation, along with Rule 1.6 exceptions for client crime and fraud, were part of a package of reforms suggested by an ABA task force on Corporate Responsibility. You can read the report at http://www.abanet .org/buslaw/corporateresponsibility/final_report.pdf.

Relationships

The corporate scandals of the last decade have resulted in a series of federal statutes and regulations that affect the attorney's duties in responding to corporate wrongdoing. After Enron, Global Crossing, and World Com, Congress adopted Section 307 of the Sarbanes-Oxley Act of 2002, requiring the Securities and Exchange Commission (SEC) to promulgate rules of professional conduct for lawyers appearing and practicing before the SEC. 15 USC § 7245. These rules are at 17 C.F.R. §§ 205.1-205.7. These standards define "appearing and practicing before the Commission" as "providing advice in respect of the United States securities laws or the Commission's rules or regulations thereunder regarding any document that the attorney has notice will be filed with or submitted to, or incorporated into any document that will be filed with or submitted to, the Commission, including the provision of such advice in the context of preparing, or participating in the preparation of any such document." 17 CFR 205.2 (2007). In short, any attorney who represents a company that is required to file periodic reports with the SEC should be familiar with the provisions of these regulations.

Likewise, after the 2008 collapse of the financial and housing markets and the Bernard Madoff matter, to date the largest Ponzi scheme in U.S. history, President Barack Obama signed the Dodd-Frank Wall Street Reform and Consumer Protection Act ("Dodd-Frank") into law on July 21, 2010. Dodd-Frank Wall Street Reform and Consumer Protection Act, Pub. L. No. 111-203, §§ 922-4, 124 Stat. 1376, 1841-50 (2010). The Act provides significantly increased oversight and regulation of banks and other financial institutions.

Of special importance to attorneys in dealing with corporate wrongdoing are the Federal sentencing guidelines, which are used for sentencing of corporate defendants. Sentencing Reform Act of 1984, Pub. L. No. 98-473, 98 Stat. 1987 (codified as amended at 18 U.S.C. §§ 3551-3742 (1994) and 28 U.S.C. §§ 991-998 (1994)). However, as with most matters before the courts, settlement, rather than sentencing, resolves these disputes. Federal prosecutors investigating corporate criminal activity increasingly use deferred and non-prosecution agreements that either delay or decline indictment in exchange for the payment of significant fines, structural and personnel changes, and governance reforms.

Structure PMS 1.13 in layman's terms

Rule 1.13 outlines a chronological series of steps corporate attorneys must take when they become aware of wrongdoing within the corporation. An attorney need not necessarily take the next steps if the situation is resolved by the prior step.

1. Attorney learns of activity or inaction by a constituent. Rule 1.13(b)— What level of knowledge is required?

2. Attorney analyzes the legality and impact of the activity or inaction. Rule 1.13(b)— What standard applies for this analysis?

3. The attorney plans a response. Rule 1.13(b)— What is the standard for this response? Note that comment 4 to the rule identifies a number of factors relevant to this plan: the seriousness of the conduct and consequences, the motives and responsibility of the constituent and company policies.

4. The attorney must decide whether to report up. Rule 1.13(b) To whom? When may an attorney NOT report?

5. The attorney must decide whether to "report out." Rule 1.13(c)— To whom? When?

6. The attorney must decide whether to withdraw or, if fired, how to follow up. Rule 1.16 and Rule 1.13(e).

Notice that Rule 1.13 makes explicit for corporate clients issues that are not spelled out as clearly when representing individuals (e.g., who is the client, what are the steps an attorney must take if she is aware of her client's wrongdoing, how do the rules differ when the attorney is acting as an advisor versus an advocate?). Notice as well that Rule 1.13(d) provides that the discretion to report an entity client's failure to rectify a violation that would cause the organization substantial injury does not apply "with respect to information relating to a lawyer's representation of an organization to investigate an alleged violation of law, or to defend the organization or an officer, employee, or other constituent associated with the organization against a claim arising out of an alleged violation of law."

When an attorney is conducting an investigation for an entity client, he must make his role very clear to all constituents with whom he speaks. Of course these *Upjohn* warnings, as they are sometimes called, can discourage individuals from speaking, knowing that what they say will not be held in confidence should the entity decide to reveal it. Because of this, attorneys sometimes do not provide sufficient disclaimers and put themselves in a position in which they are representing both an employee (who may be a target of an investigation) and the entity. For an example of what can happen when inadequate warnings are given, see *United States v. Nicholas,* 2009 U.S. Dist. LEXIS 29810.

Reasons

The ABA Task Force on Corporate Responsibility described the reasoning behind the changes in Rule 1.13 and other reforms as necessary to insure that attorneys "are and should be important participants in corporate governance and important contributors to corporate responsibility ... In their role of promoting their organizational clients' compliance with law, a key function of lawyers is to bring issues of legal compliance to the attention of appropriate authorities within the organization." ABA Task Force on Corporate Responsibility, 11-12 (March 31, 2003). Why does Rule 1.13(d) exempt attorneys who are called in to investigate a wrongdoing or to defend a company accused of wrongdoing? The role of the attorney changes in those instances to a role more like a criminal defense attorney.

Policy person

Visualize

Comparative charts can often help bring greater clarity to both sets of rules being compared. Using Sarbanes-Oxley as an example, fill in the chart on the nexe page describing the parallel duties in Rule 1.13.

Imagine

Revisit the preliminary problem in this chapter. Imagine you are Will Dane and are having a conversation with MaryAnn Bridges about your environmental report. How would Rule 1.13 come into that discussion?

Reflective Practice: Thinking about the Attorney's Public Role

Read Professor Robert Gordon's analysis of the corporate attorney's role and consider whether you agree that the changes to Rule 1.13 are consistent with a lawyer's role as an agent of the legal system.

Robert W. Gordon, *A New Role for Lawyers?:*
The Corporate Counselor after Enron
35 Conn. L. Rev. 1185, 1206-07 (2003)

Corporate lawyers could actually learn something useful from the role of the criminal defense lawyer. And that is that the adversary-advocate's role — like that of all lawyers — is in large part a public role, designed to fulfill public purposes: The ascertainment of truth and the doing of justice; the protection of the autonomy, dignity and rights of witnesses and especially of the accused; and the monitoring and disciplining of police and prosecutorial conduct. The defense lawyer is not merely or even mostly a private agent of his client, whose function is to zealously further the client's interest (which is usually to evade just punishment for his past conduct, or continue to engage in it in the future). He is assigned a specialized role in a public process in which his zealous advocacy is instrumental to the service of various public objectives. He is encouraged to make the best possible arguments for suppressing unlawfully seized evidence, not for the purpose of furthering his

Sarbanes-Oxley	Rule 1.13
Attorney who becomes aware of evidence of activity by an issuer or by any officer, director, employee, or agent of the issuer, 205.3(b)(1),	
that indicates a material violation of securities law or breach of fiduciary duty has occurred, is ongoing, or is about to occur, 205.2(e),	
shall report such evidence to the issuer's chief legal officer (or the equivalent thereof) or to both the issuer's chief legal officer and its chief executive officer (or the equivalents thereof) forthwith. 205.3(b)(1)	
If the lawyer reasonably believes the CLO or CEO has not made an "appropriate response" within a reasonable time, the attorney shall report shall report the evidence of a material violation to the audit committee or equivalent independent committee of the issuer's board of directors, to a qualified legal compliance committee (QLCC) or, if no committee, directly to the board. 205.3 (b)(3)	
If attorney has reported to anyone other than a QLCC and still sees no appropriate response within a reasonable time, the attorney shall explain to the CLO, CEO, and directors and may disclose to the SEC. 205.3(b)(3)	
Reporting out is limited to situations in which the attorney reasonably believes this report is necessary to prevent a material violation that is likely to cause substantial injury to the financial interest or property of the issuer or investors; or to prevent perjury or otherwise defraud the SEC, or to rectify substantial financial or property injury to the issuer or investors caused by a material violation if the attorney's services were used. 205.3(d)(2)	
An attorney who reasonably believes he was fired for reporting evidence of a material violation may notify the board of directors. 205.3(b)(10)	

client's interest in freedom or getting away with crimes, but to protect third parties who are not his clients, i.e., other citizens whose freedom and security will be put at risk unless police misconduct is deterred. He is allowed to present a very one-sided, partial, and selective version of the evidence favoring the defense, in part because resourceful adversaries can poke holes in his story and present a counter-story, but even more to fulfill a public purpose — that of keeping prosecutors up to the mark, making sure they know that they have to put together a defense-proof case, deterring them from indicting where they do not have the evidence. Defense counsel's zeal is restricted precisely at the points where it might help the client at the risk of damage to the performance of his public functions and the integrity of the procedural framework that those functions are designed to serve. He may not, for example, lie to judges, suppress or manufacture real evidence, pose questions on cross-examination that he has no basis in fact for asking, or suborn or knowingly put on perjured testimony.

If you extend this analysis of the public functions of the defense bar to the corporate bar, what might you conclude? That, like the defense lawyer's, the corporate lawyer's role has to be constructed so that it serves and does not disserve its public functions as well as its private ones. I have explained the public benefits of allowing defense lawyers to suppress unlawfully seized evidence, or to refrain from volunteering inconvenient facts pointing to their clients' guilt. But what are the benefits of allowing lawyers to conceal — or hide in a maze of fine print — facts from regulators and investors that would be highly relevant to determining what the companies' real earnings were, or whether its tax shelters had some economic purpose beyond avoidance, or that managers were setting up side deals paying themselves and their cronies huge bonuses? What is the virtue of allowing lawyers to pull the wool over the eyes of the understaffed bureaucrats who monitor their transactions and try to enforce the laws? Even if all of these schemes should turn out to be (at least arguably) technically legal, what values of overall human happiness, individual self-fulfillment, or economic efficiency are served by helping clients promote them? The autonomy of clients generally is a good thing, to be sure; but there is no virtue per se in action, any old action, that is freely chosen, if it is likely to bring destruction in its wake — including, in these examples, harm to the real clients themselves, not their incumbent managements but the long-term corporate entities and their constituent stake-holders.

The real lesson from the defense lawyer's or advocate's role is simply that the lawyer is, in addition to being a private agent of his clients, a public agent of the legal system, whose job is to help clients steer their way through the maze of the law, to bring clients' conduct and behavior into conformity with the law — to get the client as much as possible of what the client wants without damaging the framework of the law. He may not act in furtherance of his client's interest in ways that ultimately frustrate, sabotage, or nullify the public purposes of the laws — or that injure the interests of clients, which are hypothetically constructed, as all public corporations should be, as good citizens who internalize legal norms and wish to act in furtherance of the public values they express.

Do you agree with Professor Gordon's analysis? Write a short reflection reacting to Professor Gordon's analysis.

Test Your Understanding

Lawyer is general counsel for LMN Corporation, which manufactures computers. He has been asked to conduct an internal investigation after a production manager raised concerns regarding possible employee theft of components. Lawyer interviews several managers and line employees. He discovers during this investigation that there was significant theft. In addition, one of the consequences of the theft is that an entire line of computers now contains a serious defect, which will cause significant data loss over time. He advises a Vice President of Production that the corporation would reduce the risk of potential negligence liability by issuing a recall. The Vice President listens to the argument but concludes that, in his best business judgment, a recall would be too costly and the chances that the consumers would trace their data loss to the product defect are low enough that the risk of increased negligence liability is—even at the level postulated by Lawyer—acceptable. The Vice President's obligations include having the responsibility to determine when to enhance product design or issue product recalls to decrease the risk of products liability. Lawyer knows that the potential financial liability is significant but not substantial. Evaluate the following statements as True or False:

1. If the Vice President fires Lawyer because of Lawyer's insistence that he pursue the matter further in the corporation, Lawyer has no further obligations to report anything to anyone within the corporation.

2. Lawyer may not ask for an outside legal opinion regarding his own ethical responsibilities because to do so would violate confidentiality.

3. Lawyer must report this matter to the President of the Division and ask for a reconsideration of the matter.

4. Lawyer may refer this matter as high as the board of directors if need be.

5. If Lawyer comes to believe that the corporation's refusal to act is a clear violation of the law which is reasonably certain to result in substantial injury to the organization, he may not report outside the corporation to prevent that injury unless his services were used to commit or further the violation.

6. Even if Lawyer had authorization for reporting under Rule 1.13(c), he could not report outside the corporation in these circumstances because his knowledge of a violation came because he was asked to investigate possible thefts.

To Learn More

Understanding the role of the attorney as counselor, especially in the challenging contexts of entity representation, is—like most topics in this text—something to which one could devote an entire course. An important part of learning about counseling clients is understanding the client's world. If you intend to become a patent attorney, you should know how inventors work and think. A divorce attorney should understand basic principles of child development, family systems, and the dynamics of divorce. If you want to represent businesses in real estate development, you need to know a lot about real estate. To learn more about the kinds of challenges you are likely to face in counseling clients in your field of practice, return to the organizations, websites, and publications you identified in Chapter Two and read about how those attorneys view developments in regulation of their practice and its impact on their relationships with clients. If you can join an email discussion list or social networking group for your field of practice, you will be able to listen in on many interesting conversations about relationships with clients.

In recognition of the recent growth of regulation that places attorneys in a gatekeeping role, Judge Veasey, former chief justice of Delaware (where more than 60% of Fortune 500 companies are chartered) and his law partner have published the following manual for chief legal officers. E. NORMAN VEASEY & CHRISTINE T. DI GUGLIELMO, INDISPENSABLE COUNSEL (OXFORD 2012).

Unit Four Review

The following diagrams may help you to understanding the interrelationship between the duty of confidentiality, the exceptions to that duty in Rule 1.6, the duty of candor to the tribunal, and the duty of candor to third persons in negotiations.

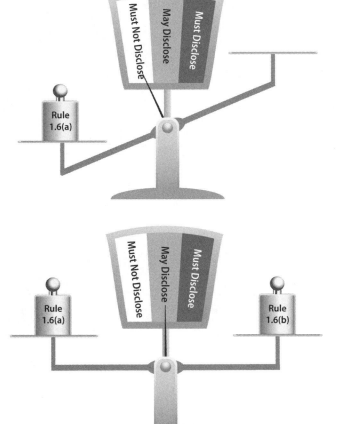

Rule 1.6(a)
Shall not reveal information relating to the representation

Rule 1.6(b) exceptions:
May disclose if:

- Informed consent, OR
- Death or substantial injury, OR
- Client crime/fraud + attorney used = substantial financial or property harm, OR
- Attorney self defense, OR
- Compliance with law or court order

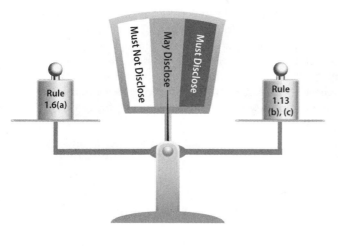

Rule 1.13(b), (c)
exceptions:

May disclose if:
Attorney for an organization
• knows of clear violation
• related to the representation
• likely to substantially injure the
  organization
• highest authority refuses to take
  timely and appropriate action

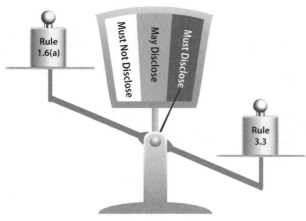

Rule 3.3 exception:

• Attorney **must** disclose if evidence
  submitted by or through her
  known to be false
• Attorney must take reasonable
  remedial measures, including,
  if necessary, disclosure, if:
  she knows of criminal or fraudulent
  conduct relating to the proceeding

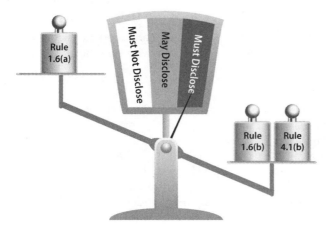

Disclosures that become mandatory
in combination with Rule 1.6(b)
discretionary exceptions:

Rule 1.6(b) permits but does not
require disclosure. However, other
rules may require disclosure if 1.6(b)
permits the disclosure.

These rules turn the "may" of Rule
1.6(b) into a "must" and include
Rules 1.2(d), 4.1(b), 8.1, 8.3, and
other law external to the rules.

Practice Review: Communicating about Confidentiality

Given the exceptions to confidentiality and privilege, what should you say to your clients about your duty of confidentiality? In the corporate context, counsel for corporations are often urged to provide the individuals within the corporation an "Upjohn warning" (so called because of *Upjohn Co. v. United States*, 449 U.S. 383 (1981), which you will recall was the case that clarified the scope of the corporate attorney-client privilege). The American Bar Association's White Collar Crime Committee Working Group suggests the following script for attorneys conducting internal investigations:

> I am a lawyer for Corporation A. I represent only Corporation A, and I do not represent you personally.

> I am conducting this interview to gather facts in order to provide legal advice for Corporation A. This interview is part of an investigation to determine the facts and circumstances of X in order to advise Corporation A how best to proceed.

> Your communications with me are protected by the attorney-client privilege. But the attorney-client privilege belongs solely to Corporation A, not you. That means Corporation A alone may elect to waive the attorney-client privilege and reveal our discussion to third parties. Corporation A alone may decide to waive the privilege and disclose this discussion to such third parties as federal or state agencies, at its sole discretion, and without notifying you.

> In order for this discussion to be subject to the privilege, it must be kept in confidence. In other words, with the exception of your own attorney, you may not disclose the substance of this interview to any third party, including other employees or anyone outside of the company. You may discuss the facts of what happened but you may not discuss this discussion.

> Do you have any questions?

> Are you willing to proceed?

ABA WCCC Working Group, *Upjohn Warnings: Recommended Best Practices When Corporate Counsel Interacts with Corporate Employees* 3 (July 17, 2009).

What should be your "script" when you are discussing confidentiality with someone who is your client? Consider these two contrasting views on the question and think about your clients.

Compare:

> [A] study showed that many lawyers rarely fully advise their client of these rules [about exceptions to confidentiality] and that many clients significantly misunderstand [them].... Lawyers owe it to the public to do a better job explaining confidentiality in light of the study's findings of widespread public misunderstanding. The best place to do this is where the lawyer meets the public, i.e. during the initial interview. Because a proper client understanding of fees and confidentiality are important to establishing and maintaining trust and competence, we suggest that lawyers carefully plan how to explain them to their clients. It may be useful to distribute a written explanation of the rules on

confidentiality and the lawyer's fee structure before the initial interview. A written explanation of confidentiality allows the lawyer to
cover both the ethical rule on confidentiality and the attorney-client
privilege rule in that jurisdiction. This allows the lawyer to provide a
full explanation to the client in a more efficient manner than a mini-
lecture at the beginning of the interview, when the client may not be
listening intently.

ROBERT COCHRAN, JOHN DePIPPA & MARTHA PETERS, COUNSELOR-AT-LAW: A
COLLABORATIVE APPROACH TO CLIENT INTERVIEWING AND COUNSELING 70-71
(Second ed. 2006).

with:

[S]uch a warning is going to impede, if not wholly frustrate, the already difficult task of establishing a relationship of trust and confidence with the client.... The question in the client's mind is "Can I
really trust you?" And the client will not be reassured by a lawyer who
invites full disclosure and at the same time cautions the client about the
possible betrayal of his confidences.... The lawyer who gives a Miranda warning is not the client's champion against a hostile world; on
the contrary, she presents herself at the outset as an agent of that hostile world.... [I]t is important to recognize that the frightened and
confused client who is given a lawyer-client Miranda warning may well
be innocent. As Professor Stephen A. Saltzburg has observed, "Good
persons (or persons with good claims) may shrink from the attorney
who gives Miranda warnings as quickly as bad persons (or persons with
bad claims)." Note too that the lawyer-client Miranda warning must
be given before any serious lawyer-client discussions can begin—that
is, before the lawyer can possibly make an informed judgment about
the client's guilt or innocence.

MONROE H. FREEDMAN & ABBE SMITH, UNDERSTANDING LAWYERS' ETHICS 155
(2nd ed. 2002).

Reflect in writing on when and what you will say to clients about your duty
of confidentiality and the limits of that duty.

Multiple Choice Review

1. Arthur Attorney is preparing for trial in a complex products liability action. He
contacts an expert engineer to conduct independent tests and possibly testify
regarding the results of those tests. The expert completes the testing in two
days (which is unusual but, as far as the attorney knows, not impossible) and
prepares an opinion that is extremely favorable to the client. After speaking
with the expert, Arthur suspects that the expert may not have really tested the
product very carefully and was simply trying to find the results that would
support Arthur's case. He tells his client about the testing and his suspicions
about the expert, but the client tells him that he does not want to pay for any
further testing or evaluation of this expert's tests or incur the necessary delay.
Arthur calls the witness and asks him a number of questions about the testing he conducted.

Is Arthur subject to discipline?

A. Yes, because the attorney submitted evidence he reasonably believed was false.

B. Yes, because the attorney did not adequately investigate the accuracy of the expert's testing.

C. No, because the attorney followed the client's directions.

D. No, because the attorney did not know that the expert's testimony was false.

2. Patrick Prosecutor prosecuted Darren Defendant for burglary. After the conviction, but before sentencing, Patrick receives evidence that would favorably affect the defendant's sentencing. It would not, however, have any impact on the conviction. Patrick Prosecutor does not disclose this information before or during sentencing.

Is Patrick subject to discipline?

A. Yes, because the Prosecutor has a duty to disclose to the defense and to the tribunal all unprivileged mitigating information known to the prosecutor before sentencing.

B. Yes, because the Prosecutor has a continuing duty to provide the court with all evidence relating to a defendant's sentencing.

C. No, because Prosecutors are not required to disclose evidence unless a formal request is made during discovery or by the court.

D. No, because Prosecutors are not required to disclose evidence unless there was a reasonable likelihood that the defendant did not commit the burglary for which he was convicted.

3. You represent a criminal defendant. He was convicted, and at the sentencing hearing the judge stated: "The pre-sentence report states there are no prior convictions. Is that correct, counselor?" In fact, the prosecutor's office inadvertently omitted reference to your client's conviction for armed robbery which occurred 3 years ago. You know the pre-sentence report is erroneous. Which of the following responses best satisfies your conflicting ethical obligations?

A. "That's right, your honor."

B. "In all candor, your honor, I must tell you there was a prior conviction three years ago."

C. "With all due respect, your honor, I cannot say, ask my client."

D. "With all due respect, that is not a proper question for me, I will defer to the prosecutor."

4. You represent the defendant in an order of protection case. You appear at the hearing for the order of protection. The petitioner (appearing pro se) asks whether the order of protection statute can include an order for your client to pay her rent. The judge says that the statute does not permit this remedy. You know that the state legislature has just amended the statute permitting this remedy. Which must you do:

A. Remain silent on the issue.

B. Tell the judge about the amendment.

C. Consult with your client before the hearing, and tell the judge about the amendment only if your client consents.

D. Provide the petitioner a copy of the statute immediately before the hearing.

5. Barbara Barrister represented a seller in negotiating the sale of 100 wooded acres. Client told Barbara that he wanted to sell the property as soon as possible because most of the trees on the property were ash trees and the ash

borer, a voracious insect that had been decimating ash trees across the United States, was projected to arrive in the state within two years. The forest would be unlikely to survive and the value of the land would plummet. The information about the ash borer infestation is readily available in news and on the internet and is something about which any forester would be fully aware. However, the buyer is not aware and has said that he wants to purchase the property to develop as a hunting range. However, as the negotiations proceeded, the buyer appeared to be losing interest in the deal. Hoping to restore the buyer's interest, Barbara says, "You won't find many beautiful forests like this for the price. Think about it. Wouldn't you like to be out there right now hunting and camping without any competition?" The buyer bought the forest land, the ash borer arrived the next year, and the forest is now a field of dead and dying trees, with buyer having to pay the price to have the land cleared.

Is Barbara subject to discipline?

A. Yes, because the attorney made a false statement of fact to the buyer.

B. Yes, because the attorney did not disclose the threat of ash borers to the buyer.

C. No, because the attorney represented the seller, not the buyer.

D. No, because the attorney's statement constituted an acceptable statement in negotiation.

Analysis & Answers:

1. C is rarely the correct answer when it comes to truthfulness. An attorney may not excuse using false evidence because "the client told me to." B sounds enticing. The attorney had suspicions that the experts' testing was inadequate. While the attorney may have wanted to consult another expert simply as a matter of improving the evidence available for the client or determining whether the expert's testing would withstand cross examination, the attorney was not required to do so. This leaves A or D, which present a choice about the standard of knowledge required for an attorney to be subject to discipline for submitting false evidence. (This is an example of a situation in which two answers are the opposite of each other—often a clue that one or the other is the correct answer.) The standard under Rule 3.3 is "knowing" and, thus, A is incorrect. While an attorney *may* refuse to submit evidence he reasonably believes is false, he is not required to refuse to use this evidence. Thus D is the correct answer.

2. Answer A is correct. Rule 3.8(d). Answer B is nearly correct, except it does not provide a time limit on this duty. While Rule 3.8(g) and (f) indicate that prosecutors have a duty even after sentencing when they learn information that creates a reasonable likelihood of a wrongful conviction, this duty does not extend to wrongful sentencing. D reads those requirements as the only requirements to disclose evidence and so is far too narrow a summary of the prosecutor's obligations. C is simply wrong. The prosecutor's obligations under *Brady v. Maryland*, 373 U.S. 83 (1963) do not depend on the defense attorney's request for exculpatory information. *Brady v. Maryland*, 373 U.S. 83 (1963).

3. D is the best resolution. A violates Rule 3.3. B is not required and harms your client. C just creates an opportunity for your client to lie or harm himself.

4. The correct answer is B. Under Rule 3.3 you must inform the judge of the amendment because it is controlling law directly adverse to your client and not dis-

closed by opposing counsel. This duty is not subject to your client's permission or veto (as answer C would suggest) nor is it satisfied by informing the opposing party if that party does not raise the authority to the court (as answer D would suggest).

5. While Barbara will likely have acquired a reputation as an attorney who engages in sharp negotiation practices, she will not be subject to discipline. She did not make an affirmative false statement and had no duty to disclose the ash borer infestation because it was not a latent defect. C is generally correct but D is more specifically correct and so is the correct choice.

UNIT FIVE

Conflicts of Interest

Goals of Unit Five

Conflicts of interest are some of the most complicated rules regulating attorneys. The goal of this unit is for you to be able to understand and apply the legal standards for various types of conflicts of interest. Equally important, you should also understand the reasons that we tolerate risks of conflicting interests more or less depending on the nature of the conflict and the reasons that attorneys have difficulty in applying conflict of interests rules to their own practice.

Pre-Test

Applying the ABA Model Rules of Professional Conduct, are the following statements True or False?

1. An attorney must avoid the appearance of impropriety.

2. An attorney always has the burden to prove that her business transaction with a client is fair and was the product of the client's free and informed consent.

3. An attorney forming a business for a client may not take a percentage interest in the business because a lawyer shall not acquire a proprietary interest in the cause of action or subject matter of a representation.

4. An attorney may not represent a client in asserting a particular legal position if the attorney has argued a contrary legal position on behalf of another client in a different case before that same court.

5. Attorney makes a mistake in representing client. He discloses the error to the client. Client files a disciplinary complaint against Attorney but does not fire Attorney and wishes attorney to continue in the representation. Attorney must withdraw.

6. Client, an adult of sound mind, is a long-time client of Attorney. They are not related but they have developed a fairly close social relationship in addition to their professional relationship. Client asks that Attorney draw up a will and asks that the will leave a significant portion of the estate to Attorney. Attorney may not draw up the will, but Attorney's partner may.

7. An attorney may never sue a current client.

8. An attorney may not represent a client in preparing a will that would disinherit one of the client's children if, at the same time, the attorney is also representing the child to be disinherited, even if that representation is totally unrelated to the will, because the two clients would be directly adverse.

9. An attorney may represent a husband and wife in a divorce if it is a friendly divorce and the couple does not disagree about child custody or financial issues.

10. An attorney may never represent a client in a situation in which the attorney would be a material witness in the client's case.

11. A conflict of interest will not arise merely from a prospective client's initial interview with an attorney if the attorney declines the representation.

12. An attorney may accept payment from a third person for representing a client as long as the attorney's independent judgment and the client's confidentiality are protected.

13. Because parties proposing to form a business are legally adverse, one attorney may not represent all those parties in setting up the business.

14. Attorneys may never defend both an employer and employee in a suit arising out of the employee's actions because of the possibility of a cross claim.

15. Attorneys may sue former clients so long as the attorney does not have any confidential information from the former representation that could be used against the former client.

16. Conflicts of interest are evaluated by a subjective standard: if an attorney does not remember that he had previously represented an opposing party in a similar matter, there is not a conflict of interest.

17. An attorney who worked as a district attorney and now works in a private law firm may represent a private client in a civil suit against an individual the attorney had prosecuted in a criminal action because the matters are compatible.

18. Attorneys A and B are married. Attorney A may not ordinarily represent a client who is adverse to a client represented by Attorney B, and this disqualification is imputed to Attorney A's partners.

19. Attorneys may cure the imputation of conflicts of interest that arise in their firms by screening the disqualified attorney from participating in and from sharing fees from the case, and by giving the clients written notice of that screen.

20. If an attorney's representation of a client in a case violates the state court's version of ABA Model Rule 1.9 (former client conflicts), the trial court in which that action has been brought must grant a motion to disqualify that attorney from the case.

Chapter Fifteen

Overview of Conflicts of Interest

Learning Objectives

After you have read this chapter and completed the assignments, you should be able to:

- Articulate the several different policies that drive conflicts of interest analysis in different settings.
- Recognize that the disciplinary rules tolerate risks of some actual betrayals of trust and loyalty more than other betrayals.
- Explain the basic structure of conflicts analysis.

Rules to Study

In this chapter we will look briefly at all the rules governing conflicts of interest and focus especially on Rules 1.7 and 1.10.

15.1 Interests and Risks

Conflict of interest is a difficult concept for both law students and attorneys. There are several reasons for this difficulty. The rules are full of terms that are both open-textured and fact sensitive. When are the interests of persons "adverse"? What would cause a "material limitation" of an attorney's representation? When are matters "substantially related"? To complicate matters further, there are several underlying policies that drive interpretation of these rules—some of which courts find more compelling in some circumstances than others.

The concern for confidentiality is at the heart of much of conflicts analysis. Rule 1.9(c) for example makes clear that an attorney's duty of confidentiality to former clients prevents revealing that client's information or using the information to the former client's detriment unless the information is generally known. If we consider this the core of conflicts of interest, we would create a rule that defines conflicts as those situations in which confidential information will be used against a client. The shape of conflicts would then look like this:

Attorney has a reason to use or disclose a client's confidential information, without the client's consent, in order to advantage himself or another.

However, if this rule were the only way a client could prove a conflict of interest, the client would be forced to reveal the very information that he or she is trying to protect in order to invoke the rule. So instead, we draw the lines a little more broadly and provide that a former client can establish that his representation is the "same or substantially related matter" as the attorney's current representation. This then raises a presumption about what information the attorney *was likely to* have received in that type of case rather than asking what information the attorney actually *did* receive. Confidentiality is protected without having to reveal confidential information.

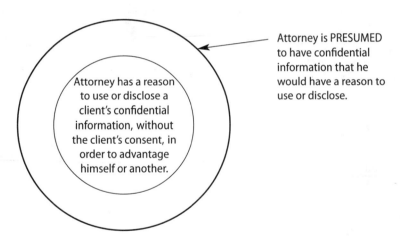

Attorney has a reason to use or disclose a client's confidential information, without the client's consent, in order to advantage himself or another.

Attorney is PRESUMED to have confidential information that he would have a reason to use or disclose.

The concept of loyalty to the client is also a central policy in conflicts analysis, as it is in general agency law. Indeed the root of the term "fiduciary" is "fides" (loyal). But what exactly is loyalty? Think about how and when you talk about loyalty in your everyday life. You might talk about a husband or wife being loyal or faithful to one another. But different couples may have different understandings of what faithfulness means. We talk about our dog being loyal to us. But certainly we aren't required to obey our client's commands in the same way our dogs give us unwavering loyalty.

Loyalty is a virtue directed less toward particular circumstances or information than it is about a relationship. Loyalty means putting the interests of clients before those of oneself or another. In legal ethics, loyalty is closely connected to the concept of independent professional judgment. Certainly, loyalty is implicated if an attorney's own interests or the interests of a third person are at risk of harming the attorney's representation of a client. Many of the prohibitions of Rule 1.8 aim to prevent circumstances in which a client's interests may be negatively affected by an attorney's own financial or personal interests.

If loyalty is central to conflicts of interest, conflicts rules must reach further than if confidentiality is the only concern. An attorney may hurt a client in more ways than by simply using confidential information against them. For example, an attorney might represent a client in one suit and, at the same time, sue them in an entirely unrelated suit in which any confidential information the attorney may have received would be irrelevant. Nonetheless, the client might rightfully object to having his attorney as an adversary, fearing that the attorney's judgment will be negatively affected by their allegiance to the opposing party.

Attorney is
or will be acting
adversely to the client's
interests, even if no
confidential
information is
threatened.

Loyalty may demand an even higher standard than avoiding actual harm to the attorney's judgment. If the client's trust or the public's trust in the legal system is harmed, that too can be a breach of loyalty. In this sense, one sometimes sees expressions of conflicts of interest that harken back to the Canon of Ethics urging attorneys to "avoid even the appearance of impropriety." Today, the appearance of impropriety standard is no longer used in most state's definitions of attorney conflicts of interest; however, one can still find this concept in the code of judicial conduct.

As with confidentiality protection, the rules broaden the scope of conflicts to prevent the *risk* of disloyalty rather than prohibiting only *actual* disloyalty. The best example of this broadening of the scope of conflicts is seen in the principle of imputed conflicts. Model Rule 1.10 provides that if one attorney in a firm has a conflict of interest, all the attorneys in that firm have the same conflict — even if those other attorneys practice in an entirely different geographic or practice area. In this sense, rule 1.10 broadens the conflict of interest scope dramatically.

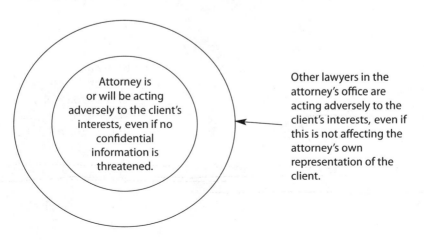

Attorney is
or will be acting
adversely to the client's
interests, even if no
confidential
information is
threatened.

Other lawyers in the attorney's office are acting adversely to the client's interests, even if this is not affecting the attorney's own representation of the client.

operational policies ①

Juxtaposed against these policy concerns of confidentiality, loyalty, and trust are operational policies that arise in the enforcement of these standards. First there is simply the question of enforceability. Many conflicts of interest are known only to the attorney involved and are extremely difficult to prove. Particularly if the question goes to professional judgment, how are we to know for sure whether an attorney's choices are motivated by pursuit of the client's interests or by a self-serving interest of the attorney? The costs of a system that enforces only actual conflicts of interest — that is, situations in which confidentiality and independent judgment are in fact compromised — would be enormous and would likely leave many, many instances of conflicts undetectable or unrestrained. Thus, we draw lines that are clearer and easier to enforce and that target behaviors or circumstances that are easier to see.

However drawing conflicts lines too broadly has costs as well. Conflicts rules can deny clients their choice of attorneys, raise the costs of legal services, and interfere with the ability of attorneys to pursue their careers, particularly with respect to moving from firm to firm.

When studying conflicts, it is helpful to understand that conflicts of interest analysis is about the degree of risk we are willing to tolerate in our system. In the judicial system, where the public's trust in the system of justice is at risk, we draw the line very broadly — prohibiting judges from a range of behaviors and circumstances that create the "appearance of impropriety." For attorneys we draw the lines closer to the core of actual conflicts. For some kinds of risks, we draw lines more broadly — especially those circumstances in which the risk is that an attorney's self-interest will interfere with the representation. For other conflicts, we create very narrow conflicts rules — such as in addressing the risks of a lateral hire bringing confidential information regarding a representation from his former firm into a new firm.

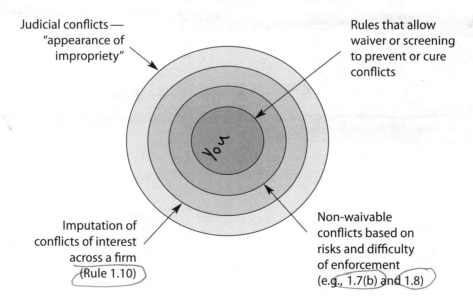

Thus, conflicts of interest rules have multiple layers, reflecting differing degrees of risk and the ability to detect or regulate those risks.

We will divide our study of conflicts of interest among the various rules that define conflicts of interests in different settings. In each of these settings, consider carefully the reasons why the lines are drawn where they are and the pressures on attorneys to disregard those lines.

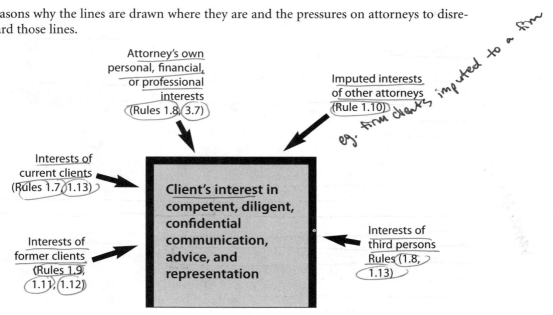

15.2 Reading the Rules: The General Principles of Conflicts

While many rules regulate some aspect of conflicts, the basic rule that provides the general mode of analysis for conflicts is Rule 1.7.

Illinois Rule 1.7: Conflict of Interest: Current Clients

(a) Except as provided in paragraph (b), a lawyer shall not represent a client if the representation involves a concurrent conflict of interest. A concurrent conflict of interest exists if:

(1) the representation of one client will be directly adverse to another client; or

(2) there is a significant risk that the representation of one or more clients will be materially limited by the lawyer's responsibilities to another client, a former client or a third person or by a personal interest of the lawyer.

(b) Notwithstanding the existence of a concurrent conflict of interest under paragraph (a), a lawyer may represent a client if:

(1) the lawyer reasonably believes that the lawyer will be able to provide competent and diligent representation to each affected client;

(2) the representation is not prohibited by law;

(3) the representation does not involve the assertion of a claim by one client against another client represented by the lawyer in the same litigation or other proceeding before a tribunal; and

(4) each affected client gives informed consent.

Context

The rules of professional conduct regarding conflicts are designed to be applied in disciplinary settings. However, these issues are far more likely to be raised in motions to disqualify, in malpractice cases, and in appeal of criminal convictions alleging ineffective assistance of counsel. In each of these settings, courts may look at disciplinary rules for general indications of standards, but other policies may affect the interpretation of these standards, making it more or less likely that a conflict of interest will be found.

A complex system such as conflicts of interest is put into practice through a system of individual standards of practice and local professional norms. For example, even though there is a risk of conflict of interest when representing an employer and employee, we might be more likely to accept a waiver of that conflict from certain employers and employees than others, depending on the sophistication of the clients, the risks involved, and the culture of practice in that area of law. We may be more willing to accept an attorney's representation of both buyer and seller in a real estate transaction than we would the representation of husband and wife in a divorce, even though both circumstances may require that the attorney act as a mere scrivener. Conflicts of interest for the small town attorney or legal aid attorney might look quite different than for the firm that represents large organizations simply because of the availability of legal services for those clients. Attorneys may decline representations, not because the conflicts of interest rules demand that they do, but because an important client would be unhappy to know of the representation. As Susan Shapiero, who conducted an extensive empirical study of conflicts of interest, reports: "the demands from or fear of antagonizing, alienating, or losing important clients often trumped ethics rules—commanding usually higher standards— in how law firms responded to potential conflicts of interest. The impact of malpractice insurers on a firm's self-regulatory system was so high that I was often able to guess a firm's professional liability insurer ... from what respondents had told me about how their firm deals with conflicts of interest." Susan Shapiero, *If it Ain't Broke ... An Empirical Perspective On Ethics 2000, Screening, and the Conflict of Interest Rules,* 2003 ILL. L. REV. 1299, 1307 (2003).

What this means for your study of conflicts of interest is that you must be careful not to over-generalize from any one case or experience with the application of the rules. You must develop sensitivity to the relevant policies and interests behind any given rule or decision. Finally, you must be tolerant of the ambiguity that necessarily surrounds many parts of conflicts analysis and know how to make decisions about conflicts in the face of this ambiguity.

Relationships

Even if there were no rules of professional conduct governing conflicts of interest, general agency law would mandate an attorney's loyalty to a client. However, the rules of professional conduct do address conflict of interests. Rule 1.7 is the basic conflict of interest rule. In any situation, you should apply its mode of analysis. However, there are many other rules of professional conduct that provide more specific, and often more restrictive rules that must also be applied. However, even if your analysis of these more specialized rules indicates that no conflict exists, you should still analyze the situation by applying the standards of Rule 1.7.

Rule 1.2(b)	Reminds us that an attorney's professional loyalty to the client's interest is different than personally identifying with that interest.
Rule 1.6	While this rule is not about conflicts, conflicts is often about confidentiality, so understanding conflicts requires understanding confidentiality.

Rule 1.8	This rule provides a number of very specific limitations and prohibitions that are, for the most part, examples of conflicts between the attorney's personal interest and that of the client.
Rule 1.9	This rule provides the specific rules governing situations in which a former client's interest can present a conflict with a current client.
Rule 1.10	This rule provides that some of an individual attorney's conflicts may be imputed to other attorneys and the ways that imputation might be avoided.
Rule 1.11	This is a specialized conflict rule for attorneys who are working or have worked in a government position.
Rule 1.12	The parallel rule to Rule 1.11 for individuals who have previously served as a decision maker or neutral in a matter.
Rule 1.13	Part (g) of this rule gives guidelines for concurrent representation of an entity and an entity person (e.g., a corporation and an employee).
Rule 1.18	Parts (c) & (d) of this rule identify the conflicts that can arise from a prospective client.
Rule 2.3	This rule clarifies the attorney's duties of loyalty and confidentiality when evaluating a matter for a third person on behalf of a client.
Rule 3.7	This prohibition on attorneys acting as witnesses in a client's case can be viewed as a more specific identification of a potential conflict of interest between attorney and client.
Rule 5.4	This rule is designed to prevent a structural and role conflict implicit in all these arrangements.
Rule 5.6	This rule eliminates the source of a potential conflict of interest when your client's settlement depends on your willingness to curtail future representations.
Rule 5.7	Identifies when conflicts rules (and other duties) attach even to clients who are being provided services besides legal services (e.g., the tax client who is provided accounting and legal services).
Rule 6.3	Limits conflicts of interest in order to encourage membership in organizations that provide access to the legal system.
Rule 6.4	Limits conflicts of interest in order to encourage attorneys to work to improve the law.
Rule 6.5	Limits conflicts of interest in order to encourage participation in these programs that provide access to the legal system.

Structure

The structure of Rule 1.7 gives us a series of questions we must ask in evaluating any representation:

Is there a conflict?

Is it a conflict to which the client can give consent?

Some attorneys conflate the entire rule to the notion of consent. But look at part (b) carefully. You will see that there are three additional hurdles before the consent step: Is it unreasonable to ask for consent? Does the law prohibit consent? Is this a situation of

non consentable or
nonwaivable conflicts

354 *rts*

clients suing one another? If the answer to any of these questions is yes, the attorney may not ask for client consent. These situations are often referred to as "nonconsentable" or "nonwaivable" conflicts.

Reasons

R1.7
policy
reasons

As you read in the opening discussion in this chapter, there are many policies underlying conflicts analysis. Rule 1.7 reflects all of these: confidentiality, loyalty, integrity of the legal system, enforceability, and access to attorneys.

Visualize

Conflicts analysis lends itself well to a decision-tree or flow chart approach. The rule is structured to facilitate this type of analysis. Another way to visualize the rule, however, is to think of the rule as creating three different outcome categories: no conflicts, conflicts that are consentable, and conflicts that are not consentable. Try describing each of these categories.

No Conflict of Interest	Conflict of Interest to Which Affected Clients Can Consent	Conflict of Interest That Cannot Be Waived

Imagine

Developing sensitivity to conflicts is an important part of your professional development. To do so, you must be aware of the many situations in which client interests can be influenced or harmed by other interests. Much of conflicts analysis requires a "what if" analysis. You are representing an entity and an officer or employee of the entity comes to you for advice. What if you learn the employee has been harming the company? You are representing several individuals in putting together a business. What if they disagree about the strategies for business formation? You are asked to represent a debtor in an action against the bank. What if the bank later wants you to represent it in other debt matters? You are working as a clerk at the bankruptcy court. What if you later want a job at a local bankruptcy firm? In each situation you must imagine the ways in which your current interests might conflict with future interests.

Conflicts analysis is very fact intensive. The best way to master the analysis is to work through many examples — whether in reading cases or simply imagining and then analyzing the many situations in which conflicts might arise.

15.3 Imputed Conflicts

In addition to the basic conflicts analysis reflected in Rule 1.7, there is a second foundational concept in conflicts analysis you must master: the concept of imputed conflicts. The concept is fairly straightforward to describe but difficult to apply. We will examine the basic concept here. Where the rule becomes complicated is when attorneys move from one firm to another. We will return to examine these complications in a subsequent chapter.

The basic concept is this: if one attorney in a law firm has a conflict of interest, that conflict will be imputed to all other attorneys in the firm. For example, if an attorney in a firm represents a bank in various collection matters, another attorney in the firm cannot knowingly represent one of the debtors in defending an action by the bank. If an attorney has confidential information regarding a client's business development plan, another attorney cannot represent a second client in a transaction for which having access to that confidential information would permit that client to undermine the first client's plan.

Why is this so? The rule is grounded in the basic policies of loyalty and confidentiality that drive all of conflicts analysis. Loyalty is one consideration in the rule. Why might a client prefer an attorney in a firm over a solo attorney? One reason is that when a client hires an attorney who is a part of a law firm, the client expects that she has the advantage of an entire firm's resources that can, if necessary, contribute to her representation. In a sense, many clients hire a firm, not a lawyer. If one part of that firm is representing an interest that conflicts with the client, the client may justifiably be concerned that her attorney's loyalty will be compromised. Confidentiality is an even more profound justification for imputing conflicts among attorneys in a firm. The rule assumes that attorneys in the same firm can, and often do, share information. In many firms, there is unrestricted access to client files, and in some firms, regular meetings are held at which progress on cases is discussed. Thus, in many cases, it is reasonable to presume that, when an attorney in a firm represents a client, the attorney's partners and associates have access to, and in fact have, protected information about that client. Imputation protects the confidentiality of that information.

Of course, the complexity of modern law firms provides some challenge to these policies. If a firm has hundreds of lawyers spread across the globe, do the assumptions of shared information and shared identity really hold? If a "firm" includes attorneys tangentially connected to the firm through outsourcing to independent contractors, of counsel arrangements, and joint representation agreements, how practically can imputed conflicts be identified and managed? If public attorneys, such as prosecutors, public defenders, or agency attorneys, are all part of the same firm, how can the government provide adequate representation for the inevitable imputed conflicts that arise? Despite these challenges, courts generally do not make exceptions to the imputation rules based on the size of the firm. If an association of attorneys is considered a single business entity under general law, it will be considered a firm for the purposes of imputation, and all attorneys who are owners or employees of that entity will share conflicts.

Even less formal arrangements can create imputed conflicts. In general, in situations of office sharing, of counsel arrangements, or different government agencies, the courts will look to the degree to which information is freely available and the clients' expectations of these attorneys. So for example, in *State v. Bryan*, 2000 Ten. Crim. App. LEXIS 605, two attorneys who owned separate practices took out a shared one page ad. The ad did not identify the separate practices nor identify the attorneys as members of separate firms. They only listed one phone number on the advertisement. The defendant's attorney was disqualified because it appeared that the charging attorney was in practice with the defense attorney even though they just shared space. Likewise in *Kansallis Fin. V. Fern*, 40 F.3d 476 (1st Cir. 1994), attorneys shared offices and advertised as a firm in phone book and in the Martindale-Hubbel directory, so they were found to be acting as a firm.

Nearly all types of conflicts of interest are shared among members of a firm. One of the few exceptions is a personal conflict of interest such as one that arises from intimate or family relationships or from the attorney's own personal views or values. Rule 1.10(a)(1) and Rule 1.8(k). Another exception is the conflict created when an attorney would be a necessary witness in a trial. Rule 3.7. In some circumstances, the courts will permit firms to create "screens" to isolate a conflict so that it does not impute to other attorneys in the firm. We examine the practice of screening more fully in a subsequent chapter.

For now, the important concept for you to keep in mind is the basic principle that if one attorney cannot represent a client because he has a conflict of interest, neither can any other attorney associated with that attorney in the firm. Without understanding this basic principle, some of the circumstances in which conflicts of interest arise would simply not make any sense at all.

15.4 Common Misconceptions About Conflicts of Interest

Conflicts of interest is an area that in which law students often have some common misconceptions that can be quite stubborn. Before we begin to examine the conflicts rules in particular, let's see if we can wipe the slate clean of these preconceptions that can interfere with your understanding of conflicts of interest.

If I don't know about a client in the firm or a former client whose interest is directly adverse to my personal client, I don't have a conflict of interest.

This is a recipe for disaster. It is no excuse for an attorney to say "I didn't know" when engaged in conflicted representation. Attorneys have a responsibility to know whom they, and members of their firms, represent, and to monitor for possible conflicts of interest. Conflict-checking systems are a critical component of effective law practice management. Even solo practice attorneys need to have conflict-checking systems. It is foolish to assume that you will remember that you represented another client in the past in a substantially related matter as your current representation. The only instance in which the rules permit an attorney to rely on actual knowledge of conflicts is in Model Rule 6.5. Many states have adopted this rule, which provides that attorneys acting in certain legal services program are subject to Rule 1.7 only if the lawyer knows that the representation presents a conflict. The rule applies to attorneys participating in nonprofit, short-term, limited legal services programs such as hotlines or on-site clinics at shelters.

Once I have determined that I do not have a conflict of interest with a potential client, I don't have to worry about conflicts any more in that representation.

If only it were that easy. Conflicts can arise at any time during a representation. New facts emerge, new parties become involved, interests and positions of clients and other parties shift, sometimes the very identity of a client changes (as when a corporate client merges or is acquired by another corporation). An attorney must keep an eye out for conflicts throughout a representation, not just at the beginning.

If my client has signed a waiver of conflicts, I do not need to worry about disqualification or discipline.

A signature on a representation agreement that contains a prospective waiver of conflicts of interests is very little protection against conflicts. First, you should recognize that under Rule 1.7(b) there are several categories of conflicts that are simply non-consentable. Second, keep in mind that a client's waiver of conflicts requires informed consent, which is more than a signature but is a process of counseling the client. In many cases, an attorney cannot foresee the facts that would give rise to a conflict in order to be able to even counsel the client about the advantages and disadvantages of waiving future conflicts. Third, recall that clients can always withdraw their consent. That is not to say that waivers of conflicts cannot cure some conflicts situations, but it is to say that waivers are not a cure-all.

If I have a conflict of interest that would prevent me from representing a particular client, other attorneys in my firm may represent that client if I am screened from participation in that case.

Screening is a process in which an attorney is shielded from participation in a case or from receiving any of the fees from the case. The idea behind a screen is that the attorney who has a conflict of interest with a firm's client will be shielded in such a way that he will not have access to confidential information nor will he be able to share any confidential information he has from the conflicted source (usually a former client). The rules of professional conduct in most states provide that screens may be used to prevent the imputation of conflicts only in limited circumstances (e.g., conflicts arising from a former government lawyers work or when an attorney moves from firm to firm). Even in these settings, screens may not cure conflicts. Sometimes conflicts arise in such a way that it is too late to erect any effective screen. Some practice settings are simply too small for screening. And some conflicts cannot be cured by screening.

Yet you may hear attorneys talk about screening much more than would be expected given the limited provisions for screening in the rules. Firms sometimes obtain a client's consent to a conflict of interest, and one of the reassurances they provide to a client, as a condition for securing the waiver of conflicts, is that they will screen the conflicted attorney from the client's representation. This consent with screening is much different than a screen that can cure a conflict without the client's consent or even without the client knowledge. However, just because the rules do or do not permit screening doesn't mean that courts in disqualification motions will agree. Many courts do not consider their discretion to disqualify an attorney from a representation to be controlled by the rules of professional conduct. So don't be misled into thinking that all conflicts can be easily solved with ethical screens.

If a client would be upset if he knew I was representing another client, I have a conflict of interest that would permit that client to disqualify me from representing the other client.

While many attorneys will not take cases for fear that other important and well-paying clients will be unhappy, that is a business decision, not one required by the rules of professional conduct. Even representing two different clients who are economic competitors with one another does not necessarily raise a conflict, though it may raise eyebrows of a client if not handled carefully. Comment 6 to Rule 1.7 indicates that "simultaneous representation in unrelated matters of clients whose interests are only economically adverse, such as representation of competing economic enterprises in unrelated litigation, does not ordinarily constitute a conflict of interest and thus may not require consent of the respective clients."

If a conflict rule prohibits a representation, I cannot form an attorney-client relationship with the conflicted client.

This misunderstanding is a logical fallacy that students sometimes adopt. For example, if an attorney represents an entity, and she gives legal advice to an employee of the entity whose interests are adverse to the entity, sometimes students will say that, even though the attorney acted like an attorney for the employee and provided legal advice that the employee relied upon, the attorney could not have formed an attorney-client relationship with that employee because that would have been a conflict of interest. The student is confusing "shall not" with "cannot"—just because the rules prohibit entering into conflicted representations, doesn't mean an attorney can't form the prohibited attorney-client relationship. She can. She shouldn't. She will be in big trouble if she does. She may find herself in a situation in which no matter what she does, she is violating a rule. But attorneys can and do put themselves in these positions because they do not know the rules or recognize the risks.

Review Problems

No matter how many conflicts of interest rules there are, attorneys are almost sure to face a conflicts situation that the rules do not directly address. This is when Rule 1.7's general analysis is especially helpful. Try using 1.7's analysis to resolve the following problems:

Husband and Wife are involved in a support and custody suit involving their infant son. Husband's father is an attorney and would like to represent his son in the action. May he? *Kennedy v. Eldridge*, 2011 Cal. App. LEXIS 1561 (Cal. App. Dec. 13, 2011). May the grandfather's partner represent the son?

Attorney is also a medical doctor. The state's medical malpractice statute requires a doctor's affidavit that a malpractice claim is not frivolous as a condition for filing suit. May attorney provide this affidavit for his own client? *Fuller v. Crabtree*, 2009 Tenn. App. 137 (Tenn. App. April 16, 2009).

Imogene Injured wants to hire Robert Representative to sue a company involved in producing a very dangerous product that has caused Imogene significant injuries. Robert has heard through the grapevine that the company has settled most of the previous cases on the condition that the plaintiffs agree to refrain from disclosing or authorizing the disclosure of any information relating to their suits. Robert wants to help Imogene but he also wants to be able to use the information he gains in her representation to assist other victims in their suits. He is outraged by the company's practice — believing it to be just this side of extortion. He wonders whether he could ask Imogene to agree to authorize his use of information to assist other clients as a condition of his representation.

To Learn More

An excellent source for reading about conflicts of interest is the website Freivogel on Conflicts, http://www.freivogelonconflicts.com/. Mr. Frievogal is an attorney/scholar who specializes in ethics issues. He collects conflicts cases at his website and provides summaries and occasional commentary. The website is organized into categories of conflicts. You can learn a lot about the landscape of conflicts by simply scanning the categories and reading a few case summaries. A major treatise on conflicts is RICHARD E. FLAMM, LAWYER DISQUALIFICATION: CONFLICTS OF INTEREST AND OTHER BASES (2003) (annual updates).

A second source to help you see the big picture of conflicts of interest is SUSAN P. SHAPIRO, TANGLED LOYALTIES: CONFLICT OF INTEREST IN LEGAL PRACTICE (2002). Dr. Shapiro is a Senior Research Fellow at the American Bar Foundation. In this book, she travels across the state of Illinois, interviewing attorneys in many different practice settings, to understand the practitioner perspective on conflicts. For a law review article summarizing some of her work, see Susan P. Shapiro, *Everests of the Mundane: Conflict of Interest in Real-World Legal Practice*, 69 FORDHAM L. REV. 1139 (2000).

Chapter Sixteen

An Attorney's Own Interests in Conflict with the Client's

Learning Objectives

After you have read this chapter and completed the assignments:

- You should be able to identify the inherent risks of conflicts of interest that exist in the attorney-client relationship in the area of law in which you intend to practice and should be able to reflect upon and articulate how you can achieve a reasonable balance of your own personal interests and those of your clients.

- In evaluating your personal interests, you should be able to articulate the circumstances in which those interests would materially limit your willingness or ability to protect your client's interest.

- In evaluating a proposed fee agreement or other business relationship with a client, you should be able to determine whether that arrangement is prohibited and, if not prohibited, how to structure the relationship in a way to reduce the risks of discipline and liability.

Rules to Study

In this chapter we will examine Rules 1.7 and 1.8.

Preliminary Problem

   You received the following email message today from a friend you have known since college:

From: Francisco Amand [famand@smail.net]
Sent: Wednesday, February 22, 2012 5:17 PM
To: You
Subject: A Proposal for you

Hey You! How's it been? Say, I've got a proposition for you. I need some legal assistance putting together a microbrewery business my friend Mary and I have been cooking up (no pun intended) over the past six months. I don't know if you remember my friend

Mary, but she's got a great business and marketing sense. She tried some of my home brewed beer a while back and said she thought I'd gotten good enough to sell my beer. We've been working on different recipes (well I have — she's been taste-testing) and researching the business (well, she has anyway) and I think we've got a great business plan put together. Trouble is, we need some legal help. Apparently there are all kinds of licenses and regulations involved in commercial brewing. I remembered that you do a lot of business advising and wondered if you would be interested in helping us out. We can't afford your rates, for sure, but if you'd be willing to help us get the business going during the first year — incorporate, get the licenses, advise us on the regulations, and that sort of thing — we'd give you a 10% cut of the business. Microbrewery businesses are really hot right now and I think we could make a nice chunk of change on this. Do you want in?

What kinds of ethical issues does this proposal raise?

16.1 Reading the Rules: Attorney-Client Conflicts

When representing a client, you must always guard against allowing outside influences to dilute your loyalty to your client. However, the greatest threats to that loyalty sometimes come from within — with your own personal interests. An attorney's financial property and business interests can conflict with a client's interests, as can the attorney's non-economic professional and personal interests. On a day-to-day level, there is a constant balance between professional and personal priorities that can present significant conflicts of interest if not carefully monitored.

Rule 1.8 provides detailed regulation of a variety of situations in which an attorney's self interest can create conflicts with the client or the legal system. Read Tennessee's version of Rule 1.8 (variations from the ABA Model Rules are itacilized).

Tennessee Rules of Professional Conduct
Rule 1.8: Conflict Of Interest: Current Clients: Specific Rules

(a) A lawyer shall not enter into a business transaction with a client or knowingly acquire an ownership, possessory, security or other pecuniary interest adverse to a client unless:

(1) the transaction and terms on which the lawyer acquires the interest are fair and reasonable to the client and are fully disclosed and transmitted in writing in a manner that can be reasonably understood by the client;

(2) the client is advised in writing of the desirability of seeking and is given a reasonable opportunity to seek the advice of independent legal counsel on the transaction; and

(3) the client gives informed consent, in a writing signed by the client, to the essential terms of the transaction and the lawyer's role in the transaction, including whether the lawyer is representing the client in the transaction.

(b) A lawyer shall not use information relating to representation of a client to the disadvantage of the client, unless the client gives informed consent, except as permitted or required by these Rules.

(c) A lawyer shall not solicit any substantial gift from a client *to the lawyer or a person related to the lawyer*, including a testamentary gift, or prepare on behalf of a client an instrument giving the lawyer or a person related to the lawyer any substantial gift, unless the lawyer or other recipient of the gift is related to the client. For purposes of this paragraph, related persons include a spouse, child, grandchild, parent, grandparent or other relative or individual with whom the lawyer or the client maintains a close, familial relationship.

(d) Prior to the conclusion of the representation of a client, a lawyer shall not make or negotiate an agreement giving the lawyer literary or media rights to a portrayal or account based in substantial part on information relating to the representation.

(e) A lawyer shall not provide financial assistance to a client in connection with pending or contemplated litigation, except that:

(1) a lawyer may advance court costs and expenses of litigation, the repayment of which may be contingent on the outcome of the matter; and

(2) a lawyer representing an indigent client may pay court costs and expenses of litigation on behalf of the client.

(f) A lawyer shall not accept compensation *or direction in connection with the representation of* a client from one other than the client unless:

(1) the client gives informed consent;

(2) there is no interference with the lawyer's independence of professional judgment or with the client-lawyer relationship; and

(3) information relating to representation of a client is protected as required by RPC 1.6.

(g) A lawyer who represents two or more clients shall not participate in making an aggregate settlement of the claims of or against the clients, or in a criminal case an aggregated agreement as to guilty or nolo contendere pleas, unless:

(1) *each client is given a reasonable opportunity to seek the advice of independent legal counsel in the transaction; and*

(2) each client gives informed consent, in a writing signed by the client. The lawyer's disclosure shall include the existence and nature of all the claims or pleas involved and of the participation of each person in the settlement.

(h) A lawyer shall not:

(1) make an agreement prospectively limiting the lawyer's liability to a client *or prospective client* for malpractice; or

(2) settle a claim or potential claim for such liability with an unrepresented client or former client unless *the lawyer fully discloses all the terms of the agreement to the client in a manner* that *can reasonably be understood by the client and advises the client* in writing of the desirability of seeking and *gives the client* a reasonable opportunity to seek the advice of independent legal counsel in connection therewith.

(i) A lawyer shall not acquire a proprietary interest in the cause of action or subject matter of litigation the lawyer is conducting for a client, except that the lawyer may:

(1) acquire a lien authorized by law to secure the lawyer's fee or expenses; and

(2) contract with a client for a reasonable contingent fee in a civil case.

(j) [Reserved][Tennessee declined to adopt the ABA Model Rule prohibiting beginning a sexual relationship with a client.]

(k) While lawyers are associated in a firm, a prohibition in the foregoing paragraphs (a) through (i) that applies to any one of them shall apply to all of them.

Context

To some extent, a conflict of interest is almost inherent in the relationship of attorney and client. Consider the private practice attorney. Those attorneys have a personal interest to set and collect fees in a way that insures that their own financial and professional goals are met. Their clients' interest is to have their representation provided with high quality and low cost. Most of the ethical problems attorneys face in fee setting and collection are, at their heart, examples of conflicts of interest. Will one more deposition really advance the client's case or will it simply advance the billing statement? Will settling the case now really resolve the dispute on the best terms or will it simply help the attorney close the books at the end of the month? Will traveling to a beautiful locale to work out a deal rather than working on the phone really insure a better negotiation or simply facilitate a better vacation? Attorneys who do not charge their clients a fee, but who work on a salaried basis representing a government or private entity, have similar professional and personal interests that may conflict with the interests of the entity they represent. Do the personal relationships with powerful individuals within that entity count more than the interests of the entity itself? Will a particular action or approach truly advance the interests of the entity or does it merely raise the visibility and standing of the attorney in a way that will advantage the attorney's career?

An attorney's personal values may conflict with those of the client. As we discussed in Chapter Eight, whether those values conflict with your representation will depend in part on the model of the attorney-client relationship you adopt. If you believe that you are morally responsible for your client's objectives, you may be more likely to be limited in representing your client if you disagree with her objectives than if you maintain a more instrumental view of your role and relationship with your client.

Even without Rule 1.8, these situations of conflict between an attorney and client would be regulated by the general rule on conflicts (1.7) and by agency principles.

Relationships

Some of the rules, such as 1.8(a), are simply restatements of general agency law; others, such as 1.8(e), have historical roots in common law restrictions on attorneys. Each section of Rule 1.8 is an independent rule. The Rule 1.8 provisions are in addition to Rule 1.7. An attorney's interests may present a conflict of interest, even if there is not a specific prohibition on the relationship. If the attorney's interest would limit his advice, judgment, or representation of a client, the attorney has a conflict of interest. A client may be able to consent to this conflict if a reasonable attorney would conclude that the attorney can provide competent and diligent representation.

Structure

Rule 1.8 is a collection of rules. There are two different types of rules in 1.8. First, there are some transactions and relationships that are prohibited. If those prohibitions apply, your client may not waive the prohibition. Second, some rules regulate but do not prohibit conduct. These rules apply when an attorney has a financial, property, or business interest in a transaction with a client. In those circumstances, the attorney bears the burden of proving that the transaction was fair and that the client freely gave informed consent. As the court in *Mayhew v. Benninghoff*, 62 Cal. Rptr. 2d 27 (Cal. App. 1997) stated, "Attorneys wear different hats when they perform legal services on behalf of their clients and when they conduct business with them. As to the latter, the law presumes the hat they wear is a black one."

Reasons

The situations prohibited and regulated by Rule 1.8 may not pose a "real" conflict of interest in the sense that an attorney's loyalty may not be compromised in fact. Nonetheless, the rule's prohibitions apply. Rule 1.8 is an example of a conflict rule that is drawn broadly to provide clear lines and enforceable standards that guard against the risk of conflicts. Some of the conflicts that the rule identifies are conflicts between attorney and client. Some are directed as much toward concerns of integrity of the legal system. We will consider each of the subsections of 1.8 more carefully in this chapter to determine the underlying rationale for the rule.

Visualize

Because Rule 1.8 is a collection of rules, some of which are prohibitions and others regulation, one of the most helpful steps you can take to master this rule is to simply divide up the list into these two categories.

Imagine

Each of these rules provides a fairly specific circumstance of conflicts. Try to identify the types of practice in which each rule would most likely arise.

16.2 Prohibited Transactions

Rule 1.8 provides a number of specific prohibitions on attorney's interests in their representations. Some of these rules are designed to protect attorneys from having too great an interest in their clients' matters in ways that threaten the integrity of the legal system or present significant risks of overreaching.

For example, Rule 1.8(d) prohibits an attorney from negotiating for or acquiring literary or media rights concerning the representation until after the representation has ended. The rule bars not just agreements, but even the negotiation of an agreement. The rule is concerned with the effect on an attorney's representation if he has an interest in exploiting the representation for "a good story." A good story may require drama, surprise, and conflict; a good representation would likely seek to minimize these. Even if both the attorney and client desire drama, the legal system prefers peaceful and efficient resolutions of disputes.

If Rule 1.8 did not exist, an attorney would still have to assess whether negotiating for media rights would constitute a conflict of interest, but the analysis would be whether the negotiation for media rights would pose a significant risk of materially limiting the attorney's competent and diligent pursuit of the client's legal interests and protection of the client's confidentiality. The decision as to whether an agreement for media rights would present a conflict would be individualized, subject to the "reasonable attorney" standard. Not every single negotiation for literary or media rights would necessarily present a conflict. Both the attorney and the client may be interested in the potential value of the client's story in the media in much the same way. The story behind a representation may be a significant source of value, without which clients may not have the resources to vindicate their rights. Having media rights might not influence in even a negligible way the attorney's advice or representation. Yet, with 1.8(d)'s prohibition, it does not matter if an attorney's independent professional judgment would not be threatened and it does not matter if the client agrees to the arrangement. These agreements are prohibited because the courts have concluded that, more often than not, these agreements threaten the integrity of the legal system and pose a high probability of an actual conflict between the attorney's interest and that of the client.

Notice that this rule is not necessarily concerned that an attorney's interests would always be adverse to the client's interest. Sometimes, both the attorney and the client's interests may be aligned in a way that would undermine the system of justice. Just as an attorney can have a conflict of interest because his interests are adverse to the client, so an attorney's interests can become too closely aligned with the client's.

Yet another policy consideration in examining these prohibitions is the effect on access to justice. The more broadly a conflicts rule reaches, the more it reduces the client's ability to choose an attorney. In the criminal defense context, the prohibition against negotiating for media rights can raise constitutional issues if it interferes with a defendant's ability to engage counsel of his choosing. If the client is a criminal defendant and this arrangement is a way for him to get a good attorney, doesn't this prohibition interfere with Sixth Amendment rights? In *Maxwell v. Superior Court*, 639 P.2d 248 (Cal. 1982 *en banc*), in the context of an ineffective assistance of counsel claim, the California Supreme Court allowed a defendant faced with a capital crime to retain an attorney in exchange for an agreement that the attorney could publish the client's life story. The court concluded that the defendant's interest in having his preferred counsel outweighed the state's interest in protecting against potential conflicts.

A number of rules are designed to protect the attorney's independent professional judgment by prohibiting relationships with clients that could impair that judgment. For example, Rule 1.8(c) prevents a lawyer from soliciting a substantial gift or preparing an instrument transferring a substantial gift for himself or for a person closely related to the lawyer unless the client is related to the donee. As you can imagine, the term "substantial gift" provides some room for interpretation. Some attorneys might attempt to work their way around the rule by having another attorney draft the instrument, which could work so long as the attorney who is to receive the gift does not play any role in arranging for that other attorney. Recall that Rule 8.4 provides that an attorney may not violate the rules indirectly by inducing others to do what the rules prohibit the attorney from doing directly.

Likewise, an attorney might believe that she could avoid the operation of the rule by structuring this bequest as a "deferred payment of fees." Or an attorney may convince himself that he did not solicit the gift and $15,000 is not "substantial" under the circumstances. Depending on the circumstances, these attorneys may be right. The problem with this approach to the rules, however, is that attorneys can all too readily convince themselves that their view of the rules and the facts is reasonable. An attorney's special skills include the ability to find a multitude of interpretations of a given opinion or rule and to generate arguments for the interpretation that best fits the client's desired outcome. However, when it comes to assessing their own conduct for disciplinary risks or defending their conduct when charged with disciplinary violations, this skill can actually be a detriment to attorneys. Accordingly, before interpreting the "reasonableness" of a transaction with a client, or whether a gift is substantial, ask for a reality check from a disinterested person, preferably a non-lawyer, since those are the people who will be on the jury when your conduct is being questioned later in court.

In addition to too readily interpreting rules in their favor, attorneys may underestimate the harm resulting from creating a transaction that is subject to challenge, even if they would ultimately prevail in that challenge. Thus, the attorney who agrees to a testamentary transfer faces the considerable risk that the disposition will be challenged as being the product of undue influence. In most circumstances, a court will presume undue influence when an attorney prepares a contract or instrument in favor of the attorney. The effect of this presumption is to shift the burden to the attorney to produce or prove by credible evidence that the transaction was fair and just and was not the result of the attorney's undue influence. *Klaskin v. Klepak*, 534 N.E. 2d 971 (Ill. 1989); *Krischbaum v. Dillon*, 567 N.E.2d 1291 (Ohio 1991). In many states, the lawyer's testimony alone will not be sufficient to overcome the presumption.

There are several similar prohibitions in the rules of professional conduct that, like Rule 1.8(c), are not subject to client waiver. Rule 1.8(e) prohibits providing financial assistance to clients, with limited exceptions. Rule 1.8(i) prohibits attorneys from taking an ownership interest in a cause of action or subject matter of litigation with very limited exceptions. Finally, Rule 3.7 prohibits attorneys from representing clients at trial when the attorney is likely to be a necessary witness, with limited exceptions. What policy is driving each of these? Are the rules protecting clients from attorneys? The integrity of the legal system? Enforceability of the rules?

Researching Professional Responsibility 15-A: Finding Policies and Purpose

As you have seen in reading the rules of professional conduct, understanding the reasons behind a rule is critical to understanding its operation. Where do you find the underlying rationale behind a particular rule? There are several sources you can look to.

First, there is the rule itself and your own independent analysis. The placement of the rule within a particular section and the title of that section can give you some guidance. The rationale behind other sections of the same rule might be clearer and might give you a clue regarding the rationale behind the rule you are examining. Finally, comments to the rules often explain the reasons for rules.

Second, as with any other enacted law, you can search for "legislative history." With rules of professional conduct being adopted by courts rather than legislatures, you may find that history in the court orders adopting a rule, in the statements and drafts from the committee appointed by the court to recommend the rules, and in bar publication explanations of the rules upon their adoption. Comparing the current rule to prior versions of the rule can often be instructive.

Third, since the American Bar Association plays a key leadership role in the development of rules of professional conduct, the ABA House of Delegates debates and committee reports in the development of a model rule are important sources. The ABA publishes A LEGISLATIVE HISTORY: THE DEVELOPMENT OF THE ABA MODEL RULES OF PROFESSIONAL CONDUCT, which provides a history of each rule, including amendments. It also includes the arguments made for, and against, a rule's adoption.

Fourth, court decisions applying the rules often examine the policies driving a particular rule. Often it will be helpful to search for decisions outside your own jurisdiction that explain the scope and purpose of a rule. Of course, you need to know whether the rule the court in another state is applying is the same as the rule in your own jurisdiction; however, for understanding the underlying policies that drive a particular rule, even a court's analysis of analogous rules can be helpful.

Fifth, scholarly commentary often provides the most comprehensive analysis of the policy tensions present in any given rule. Do keep in mind, however, that each commentator may be advancing his or her own particular interpretation of the rules, which may not represent the approach of the courts. You can search for commentary in the ABA/BNA Lawyers Manual on Professional Conduct, as well as in law reviews and journals. Several journals focus on professional responsibility articles, such as the *Georgetown Journal of Legal Ethics* and the ABA's *The Professional Lawyer*. Comprehensive commentaries on the rules include: Geoffrey C. Hazard, Jr. & W. William Hodes, *The Law of Lawyering: A Handbook on the Model Rules of Professional Conduct* (3rd ed. 2010) and Ronald D. Rotunda and John S. Dzienkowski, *Legal Ethics: The Lawyer's Deskbook on Professional Responsibility* (2009-2010 ed.).

Test your ability to assess the policies underlying a rule of professional conduct. Re-read Rule 1.8(e), which addresses financial assistance to clients. As you can see, the rule prohibits an attorney from advancing or guaranteeing financial assistance to a client unless the items involve costs of litigation. Such costs and expenses may be advanced with repayment contingent on the outcome of the case, and, if the client is indigent, the attorney may pay costs and litigation expenses for the client. Expenses beyond these, however, are still prohibited.

Suppose you have been appointed to represent a juvenile in a delinquency matter. Your client is a 15-year-old boy who has been charged with car theft. He lives with his grandmother in poverty. He has been attending a private school but, due to a change in the school's tuition and scholarship policy, he will not be able to continue without some financial assistance. He has been doing well in the school and a transfer to the public school system will only make his situation worse and will put him in a much worse position for the dispositional phase of the delinquency hearing. May you pay your client's tuition?

Analyze Rule 1.8(e) and do some research to determine whether the court would be likely to apply the rule to your circumstances.

16.3 Discouraged Transactions

What rules apply when an attorney does business with a client? Rule 1.8(i) prohibits attorneys from owning an interest in a client's cause of action or the subject matter of litigation. Thus an attorney may not acquire an interest in his client's property or patent or business when the attorney is representing the client in litigation regarding that property. The client can pay an attorney with property of course, but only after the representation is concluded.

This rule applies only to litigation, however, and not to business transactions or other non-litigation matters. Rule 1.8(a) governs transactions with client if in a non-litigation setting. In these other settings, an attorney is not prohibited from having "a piece of the action." Why might attorneys enter into business transactions with a client? A common reason is that clients offer these opportunities as a means of paying the lawyer's fee. Most initial fee agreements are governed by Rule 1.5 and not considered strictly a business transaction with a client. However, any interests in a client's business negotiated as part of the fee agreement and any renegotiation of a fee agreement during the representation should be treated as a business transaction. It is not uncommon for attorneys who form small businesses to be paid with a percentage interest in the business. The client may even ask the attorney to serve as an officer or director of the business.

While these types of business transactions with clients are not *per se* prohibited, in many circumstances they fail the "reasonable attorney" test of Rule 1.7 and are generally discouraged even if they do not present nonwaivable conflicts of interest. For example, comment 35 to ABA Model Rule 1.7 advises that if there is a "material risk" that a conflict will develop from the dual role of attorney and officer or director, the attorney should decline the position.

Why are these transactions so risky? Going into business with a client is a recipe for a malpractice claim if the attorney is also providing any advice or representation to the business. If the business suffers losses, the attorney may be seen as a likely source for compensation. It is more difficult to tell whether advice is legal or business advice in these circumstances. Most importantly, it can be difficult for an attorney to keep his own financial interests in the business from influencing or limiting his independent professional judgment on behalf of the client. Because of these increased risks, malpractice liability insurers often exclude from coverage an attorney's services to a client business entity in which the attorney has an ownership interest. At the same time, an attorney serving as a director or officer might be excluded from the company's directors and officers coverage as well. Additionally, other law may prohibit or regulate the attorney's business transactions with a client, particularly when ongoing investments or securities are concerned. In even a simple loan or sale between attorney and client, contract law presumes that these arrangements are the product of undue influence, so that an attorney has the burden to prove their substantive and procedural fairness in any action seeking to enforce the agreements.

Rule 1.8(a) outlines the high standards of fair dealing required of fiduciaries when entering into transactions with their principals. The Restatement prohibits these business or financial transactions, except a standard commercial transaction in which the lawyer does not render legal services, unless (1) the client has adequate information about the terms of the transaction and the risks presented by the lawyer's involvement, (2) the terms and circumstances of the transaction are fair and reasonable to the client, and (3) the client consents after being encouraged to seek, and given a reasonable opportunity to obtain, independent legal advice. RESTATEMENT (THIRD) OF THE LAW GOVERNING LAWYERS § 128 (2000).

Neither Rule 1.8(i) nor (a) applies unless there is an actual attorney-client relationship between the lawyer and the client at the time the business transaction is entered into. Thus, in a case in which an attorney borrowed a substantial sum from a former client, and gave no indication he was giving legal advice to the former client regarding the current transaction, the Missouri court held that Rule 1.8(a) did not apply. *In re Disney*, 922 S.W.2d 12, 14-15 (Mo. banc 1996). Likewise, in a recent California case in which an attorney purchased a duplex from her long-time friend, for whom she had provided several legal representations over the years, the court dismissed disciplinary charges based on its business transaction rule. The court rejected the state bar counsel's argument that the rule should apply because "once a client, always a client." It also refused to find that the longstanding friendship and attorney-client relationship in the past created an "ongoing aura of inherent influence." *In re Marie Darlene Allen*, 06-O-13329 (Review Dept. State Bar Court, Nov. 19, 2010). Of course, even in these purely private transactions, attorneys must avoid "dishonesty, fraud, deceit or misrepresentation." Rule 8.4(c).

Professional Responsibility Skills 16-A: Documenting Transactions with Clients

Your client Phillip Terrence is a real estate developer. You have represented him in a number of development transactions and you have become friends and fishing buddies over the years. Recently, Phillip came to you with a request that you assist him in obtaining the necessary financing, permits, and licenses for a resort development on some river frontage property that he has recently purchased. Because he knows that you would enjoy owning some of the property in the resort when it is developed, he offers to pay for your legal services with a percentage interest in the proposed development.

Outline the elements required by Rule 1.8 and decide whether the following document would adequately demonstrate your compliance with that rule.

Mr. Phillip Terrence
200 Resort Lane
Anycity, Anystate
Re: Development of Troutland Resorts

Dear Mr. Terrence:

I am pleased you have entrusted your legal interests in the development of Troutland Resorts to my firm. You have asked whether I would be interested in investing in this development as a means of paying your legal fees for this representation.

As we have discussed, my ethical obligations under the laws of this state require that we discuss several matters relating to your proposal. I have summarized our discussion of those matters in this letter.

First, we have discussed the terms and conditions of your offer. Since you proposed this transaction, you do know the basic terms; however for clarity, I will summarize those terms here:

[plain language summary of terms]

Since you have proposed this arrangement as a means of paying for my legal services, we have discussed a number of alternative ways in which you could finance the legal services. These include my willingness to accept a reasonable payment plan and your obtaining financing from third persons to finance this legal work. We have specifically discussed the disadvantages of your proposal, including the possible impact on the value of the property you propose to pledge to secure my legal fees and the possible influence on my advice and representation of you in this development.

You understand that while I am representing you in the Troutland Resorts development matter, I do not represent you in this transaction regarding this property. Of course, you clearly have the right to hire independent counsel to advise you regarding this proposed transaction and I would strongly encourage you to do so. I would be glad to recommend to you any one of several attorneys. I feel so strongly that you should consult independent counsel on this proposal that I will take no steps to accept this proposal for the next thirty days to provide you ample opportunity to consult with an attorney.

When you have consulted with an attorney, please enter his or her name below and then sign and return the copy of this letter to signify your consent for me to have an interest in the property described in this letter.

Sincerely,

Lee Lawyer

I have consulted with _____ and having been advised on this transaction. I agree to Lee Lawyer's acquisition of an interest in my property on the terms outlined in this letter. I believe those terms are fair and reasonable.

_____

Phillip Terrence

16.4 Professional and Personal Interests

An attorney's financial interests are not the only sources of conflicts that can limit an attorney's ability to adequately represent her clients. Personal interests in one's own moral, political, or aesthetic choices can interfere with representation as powerfully as an investment in the client's business. For example, Tennessee rejected the ABA Model Rule 1.8(j), which expressly prohibits initiating sexual relationships with clients. However, even without this rule, courts have recognized that commencing a sexual relationship with a client can impair independent professional judgment and constitute a conflict of interest.

Professional interests such as job stability, prestige, reputation, and advancement can also interfere with an attorney's independent professional judgment. Perhaps the clearest example of a professional conflict between attorney and client is an actual dispute between an attorney and his or her client. As you read in Chapter Six, not every mistake by an attorney means that an attorney has a conflict of interest requiring withdrawal. A conflict exists only if a mistake has actually interfered with the attorney-client relationships to the degree that the client cannot trust the attorney or so that the attorney cannot provide adequate representation. For example, suppose that Lawyer represents Client in a contract dispute. After Lawyer had filed an answer to the complaint against Client and discovery had begun, Lawyer discovered that his legal research failed to turn up an important defense that might reduce client's liability by several thousand dollars. Lawyer tells client of his negligent error and immediately files an amended answer, but the court denies permission to amend. Because Lawyer and Client each have an interest in making sure the representation succeeds from here on, Lawyer need not withdraw from the representation because Lawyer and Client are not yet directly opposed and Lawyer's interests are not materially adverse to the client.

However, once a client has filed a complaint against an attorney or even indicated the intent to do so, the attorney should withdraw without attempting to change the client's mind. Rule 1.8(h) permits the attorney to then negotiate for a release of a malpractice claim but only if the client is advised in writing of the advisability of independent counsel. Tennessee makes the standards for this writing even more clear and strict than the language of the ABA Model Rule. Attorneys may not settle a potential malpractice claim with an unrepresented (Tennessee clarifies that this would usually be a prospective client) or former client unless the client is advised to obtain an attorney and given an opportunity to do so. Even then, the attorney must take great care that the settlement is procedurally and substantively fair. For example, the court in *Marshall v. Higginson*, 813 P.2d 1275 (Wash.Ct. App.1991) set aside a release of malpractice, despite the attorney's compliance with Rule 1.8(h), because he obtained the release by saying he would not testify on behalf of his former client without it.

One of the personal conflicts of interest you may face even before you graduate is the conflict that can arise during employment searches. You may be clerking for a judge or an attorney during law school. Can this impact your job search? Could you place your employer in a conflict of interest situation? Keep in mind that even non-lawyer personnel can cause conflicts of interest because they may have confidential information that could be threatened by conflicts. The ABA Commission on Ethics and Professional Responsibility has concluded that an attorney's negotiation for employment with a law firm could implicate Rule 1.7(b) when there is sufficient likelihood that a conflict will eventuate and could materially interfere with the lawyer's independent professional judgment. ABA Comm. on Ethics and Prof'l Responsibility, Formal Op. 96-400 (1996). Thus, a lawyer who has an active and material role in representing a client in ligation must consult with and obtain the consent of that client, ordinarily before he participates in a substantive discussion of his experience, clients, or business potential or the terms of an association with an opposing firm. So too, you should be aware of conflicts that you can cause in a firm. Protect the confidentiality of the clients of your current or former employers when interviewing and be sure to alert new employers if you become aware of situations in which you may be involved in representing a client who is adverse to one of your former employer's clients. In the August 2012 amendments to the ABA Model Rules of Professional Conduct, the ABA house of delegates added an additional exception to Rule 1.6 permitting attorneys to disclose confidential information to the extent reasonably necessary "to detect and resolve conflicts of interest arising from the lawyer's change of employment or from changes in the composition or ownership of a firm, but only if the revealed information would not compromise the attorney-client privilege or otherwise prejudice the client." As you will see in later chapters, when conflicts arise from non-lawyer employees, steps can be taken short of withdrawal or disqualification to eliminate those conflicts.

Perhaps one of the most common and difficult personal conflicts arises from your disagreement with your client regarding the objectives of representation. You can avoid some of these conflicts by carefully screening your clients; however, early in your career, your ability to conduct this kind of screening may be limited. Nonetheless, you still have a duty to be aware of situations in which your personal views and relationships would materially limit your ability to provide adequate representation of your clients.

Problem for Discussion

Ashley has been employed as the city attorney for a large city for the past six years. Ashley loves her job, but recent events in the office have her troubled. For the past year, Ashley has defended and lost several major race discrimination suits against the city. She has now designed a training program for all city management employees designed to reduce the risk of future discrimination actions. However, the mayor has come to her and asked her to suspend the program because it is generating a good deal of controversy from the police chief, who has been speaking out in the local media against the program. Furthermore, the mayor has asked the city attorney to file an action against certain employees who had assisted the plaintiffs in the discrimination lawsuits, charging them with illegal use of city property because of their use of city phones and computers to communicate about the cases.

Ashley feels that the suits would be fruitless at best and more probably frivolous. However, she does know that they would cause enough concern among employees that they would be more cautious about their complaints. Mostly she is concerned that the mayor's motivation in these directives is to gain political advantage in an election that is highly racially charged. She believes the mayor's directives are designed to be a "litmus test" of her loyalty. She is absolutely mortified at the idea of bringing a suit in order to squelch complaints.

Considering Ashley's views, may or must she refuse to bring these cases? If she is fired for refusing to do so, does she have any recourse?

Consider the following case:

Mendoza Toro v. Gil

110 F. Supp. 2d 28 (D.P.R. 2000)

Plaintiff Lilliam Mendoza Toro, an Assistant United States Attorney, brings this action to enjoin Defendant Guillermo Gil, the interim United States Attorney, from assigning her to prosecute persons charged with trespassing on the United States Navy base in Vieques. She claims that such an assignment would violate her First Amendment rights. She asserts jurisdiction pursuant to 28 U.S.C. § 1331. In an order issued July 11, 2000, the Court ordered Plaintiff to show cause why this claim should not be dismissed on the grounds that this Court lacked jurisdiction to hear it and on the grounds that she failed to state a claim for which relief could be granted. Plaintiff has responded to the order to show cause, and the Government has filed a reply. Additionally both sides have filed sealed motions. The Court has considered all of these documents, and it is now ready to rule.

> Bringing a lawsuit against an employer is a drastic step. Why do you suppose Ms. Toro thought this was necessary or prudent?

* * *

2. Failure to state a claim

… Plaintiff claims that her work assignment violates her First Amendment rights. The Supreme Court has developed two lines of cases to address the First Amendment rights of public employees. One line of cases involves the extent to which the government can take adverse action against an employee because of her political affiliation. *See Rutan v. Republican Party of Illinois,* 497 U.S. 62, 110 S. Ct. 2729, 111 L. Ed. 2d 52 (1990); *Branti v. Finkel,* 445 U.S. 507, 100 S. Ct. 1287, 63 L. Ed. 2d 574 (1980); *Elrod v. Burns,* 427 U.S. 347, 96 S. Ct. 2673, 49 L. Ed. 2d 547 (1976). The second line involves government employees who claim to be victims of retaliation taken against them as reprisals for their having spoken out on matters of public concern. *See Rankin v. McPherson,* 483 U.S. 378, 107 S. Ct. 2891, 97 L. Ed. 2d 315 (1987);

Connick v. Myers, 461 U.S. 138, 103 S. Ct. 1684, 75 L. Ed. 2d 708 (1983); *Pickering v. Board of Education*, 391 U.S. 563, 88 S. Ct. 1731, 20 L. Ed. 2d 811 (1968).

The problem with Plaintiff's claim is that it does not fit under either of these two lines of cases. She does not claim to have suffered an adverse employment action because of her political affiliation. Nor does she claim to have been retaliated against for having spoken out on a matter of public concern. Rather, she claims that she has a First Amendment right to choose not to do a legitimate work assignment. However, she cites to no case law that affords government workers such a right, and the Court is unaware of any jurisprudence that makes such a holding.

Plaintiff does invoke part of the three-pronged *Pickering* balancing test to support her cause of action. Under this test, when the government is acting as an employer, it has broader powers to limit speech than it does when it is acting as the sovereign. The government should be given wide discretion and control to manage its own internal affairs and personnel. A public agency need not be run as a roundtable to hear and consider every employee complaint regarding the agency's internal affairs.

At the first prong of the *Pickering* test, a court must determine whether the employee was speaking "as a citizen upon matters of public concern," or "as an employee upon matters only of personal interest." If the topic is merely a personal matter and not one of public concern, the employment decision will generally not be subject to challenge in federal court. A court should not presume that all matters dealt with in a government office are of public concern. To do so would be to make every government employee's remark or criticism the grounds for a constitutional case. An employee's complaints or grievances regarding personal working conditions are not protected.

In the present case, Plaintiff claims that she told her supervisors that she had a moral conflict with prosecuting Vieques cases. Her expression that her personal beliefs prevent her from working on Vieques cases is not a matter of public concern. It is a purely personal matter regarding her attitude towards a particular work assignment. In her response to the order to show cause, Plaintiff misconstrues the illustration utilized by the Court to distinguish between expressions on the Vieques issue and Plaintiff's expressions on her personal feelings on the issue.

The Court did not hold in its order to show cause that the Vieques issue is not a matter of public concern. Certainly, it is. However, Plaintiff's speech is not about the merits of the argument over whether the United States Navy should leave Vieques. Rather, her speech is to the effect that she is morally opposed to prosecuting trespassers on Navy property. Her statements or personal feelings vis-a-vis her work assignment are not an issue of public concern. Rather, they are complaints about her work duties.

To the extent that Plaintiff is arguing that her being forced to work on Vieques cases is itself an infringement of her right to free expression, she is mistaken. Her work as an Assistant U.S. Attorney is not expression protected by the First Amendment. Her personal beliefs do not relieve her of her professional obligation to complete legitimate work assignments. *Cf. Hennessy v. City of Melrose*, 194 F.3d 237, 244 n.1 (1st Cir. 1999) (Public school teacher's

If this is the standard for government employers, how much more do you suppose a private employer has the right to set the terms of employment and limit employee speech?

religious beliefs did not excuse him from implementing school's legitimate curriculum). Plaintiff's First Amendment rights are not absolute. She does not have a First Amendment right to pick and choose work assignments that suit her moral beliefs. A government lawyer's work on a particular case is not a forum for her to express her personal beliefs. *Cf. Gentile v. State Bar of Nevada*, 501 U.S. 1030, 1071-74, 111 S. Ct. 2720, 2743-44, 115 L. Ed. 2d 888 (1991) (In the context of courtroom litigation, an attorney's free expression rights are subject to limitations to which an average citizen would not be); *Berner*, 129 F.3d at 26-28 (Courtroom is a nonpublic forum and therefore prohibitions of political expressions within it are justified). Plaintiff's legitimate work assignments are duties which she must complete. They are not a means by which she may express her views on political or social issues. Quite simply, Plaintiff does not have a First Amendment right to choose her work assignments.

In her response to the order to show cause, Plaintiff argues that the second prong of the *Pickering* test favors her position because there would be "minimal potential disruption" if other Assistant U.S. Attorneys instead of her were to be assigned to work on Vieques cases.

At this second prong, a court must balance the employee's First Amendment rights, as well as any public interest in the information about which the employee was speaking, against the government's interest in promoting the efficient performance of the service the government agency seeks to provide through its employees. *Pickering*, 391 U.S. at 568, 88 S. Ct. at 1734-35. The court should consider the significance of the interests of the employee's speech against the government employer's interests of avoiding unneeded disruptions to its mission of serving the public. It is the government's dual role of a public employer and the sovereign operating under the First Amendment's constraints which makes this balancing necessary. When an agency requires close working relationships to enable it to fulfill its public duties, the public employer's judgment should be afforded a wide degree of deference. This balancing is a legal question.

The Court disagrees with Plaintiff's application of this second prong of the test. To begin with, a public employee has an obligation to complete legitimate work assignments. As discussed above, her speech regarding her moral conflict is not a matter of public concern, and her work itself does not constitute protectable expression. Additionally, the Court must consider Defendant's interest in ensuring the efficient performance of the U.S. Attorney's Office. The balancing of these factors weighs heavily against Plaintiff. She has a professional obligation to do the work assigned her. Her arguments that the Vieques cases can be reassigned to other lawyers is unavailing. First Amendment jurisprudence does not authorize the Court to analyze the case assignments within the U.S. Attorney's Office and determine which attorney should be assigned what cases. Defendant is entitled to wide discretion and control to manage the internal affairs and personnel of his office. To hold otherwise would allow any disgruntled Assistant U.S. Attorney who is not satisfied with his or her work duties to seek this Court's intervention and involvement in the management and assignment of cases. The Court is unaware of any case law which would support such judicial oversight, and Plaintiff has cited to none. In the context of political patronage, the Supreme Court held, "if an employee's private political beliefs would interfere with the discharge of his public duties, his First Amendment rights may be required to yield to the State's vital interest in maintaining governmental effectiveness and efficiency." *Branti*, 445 U.S. at 517, 100 S. Ct. at 1294. This holding has a resonance here. Plaintiff's private beliefs on Vieques must give way to the Government's legitimate interest in effectively and efficiently carrying out its functions.

Plaintiff makes a number of other arguments, none of which are persuasive. She asserts that she must conform her conduct with the Canons of Ethics and that she is thus precluded from working on Vieques cases because she has a conflict of interest. The Court disagrees. The conduct of practitioners in the U.S. District Court for the District of Puerto Rico is governed by the ABA Model Rules of Professional Conduct. Local Rule 211(4)(B). The Model Rules state, "A lawyer's representation of a client ... does not constitute an endorsement of the client's political, economic, social or moral views or activities." Model Rules of Professional Conduct 1.2(b). Thus, Plaintiff's work on Vieques cases does not necessarily constitute an endorsement by her of the United States Government's position on this issue.

The Model Rules do prohibit a lawyer from representing a client when the client's and lawyer's interests conflict. Rule 1.7(b). However, the commentators on this rule indicate that it is intended to address conflicts of pecuniary or professional interests, not a conflict between the attorney's personal beliefs and the client's legal position. *See* Model Rules of Professional Conduct Rule 1.7 comment [6] (1999); 1 Geoffrey C. Hazard, Jr. & W. William Hodes, *The Law of Lawyering: A Handbook on the Model Rules of Professional Conduct* § 1.7:301-1, at 256.2-256.4 (1998). Thus, there is no impediment in the Model Rules which would prohibit Plaintiff from complying with the work assignments she has been given.[3]

Plaintiff also argues that she is not objecting to the prosecution of other federal laws or other trespassing cases, but that she only wants to avoid having to prosecute Vieques trespassing cases. As discussed above, she does not have a constitutional right to choose to work on some cases and decline to work on others. She further argues that at the time she applied to be an Assistant U.S. Attorney it was not foreseeable that she would be called upon to work on such cases. Plaintiff again fails to cite to any case law to support her argument. The expectations she had of her job at the time she applied for it in no way delineate the scope of her responsibilities. The fact that the Vieques controversy was not foreseeable at the time she applied for her position has no bearing whatsoever on her duty now to fulfill her professional obligations. There is no right to refuse to work on a case merely because it is novel or unusual.

... Lastly, in its order to show cause, the Court noted that attorneys in both the private and public sectors are often "called upon to represent clients

---

3. Attorneys for the federal government are also subject to local laws governing the conduct of attorneys. 28 U.S.C.A. § 530B(a) (West Supp. 2000). Thus, Plaintiff is also subject to the Canons of Ethics which apply to attorneys in Puerto Rico's local court system. However, the Canons do not define "conflict of interest" in the way that Plaintiff attempts to do so here. *See* 4 L.P.R.A. App. IX, C. 21 (1998); *see generally Liquilux Gas Corp. v. Berrios, Zaragoza*, 138 D.P.R. 850, 857-61 (1995); *In re Orlando Roura*, 1987 PR Sup. LEXIS 131, 119 D.P.R. 1, 5-7 (1987); *In re Pizzaro Santiago*, 1986 PR Sup. LEXIS 118, 117 D.P.R. 197, 202-03 (1986).]

[Margin annotations: "Policy supports Δ"; "R 1.7 (b)"; "Note that the court later changed this statement in the opinion. Can you see why?"]

and argue positions which may not square with their own personal beliefs." Docket no. 4, at 8. Plaintiff contests this point and argues that while a private attorney may choose not to represent clients with disagreeable positions, a government employee such as herself is denied this "fundamental right." Docket no. 5, at 19. Again, the Court disagrees. If Plaintiff finds that the United States Government policy on the Vieques issue is too opprobrious or onerous for her moral beliefs, she has available the same option as a private attorney: she may choose to cease representing the Government and resign her position. She may not, however, utilize the Constitution and the federal courts to avoid her position's legitimate responsibilities or tailor the duties of her position to make them more palatable to her.

WHEREFORE, the Court finds that Plaintiff's complaint fails to state a claim for which relief could be granted. Accordingly, this case is hereby dismissed. Judgment shall be entered accordingly.

Notes

1. Interestingly, this same court in a subsequent opinion on a motion to amend the judgment retreated some from its assertion that personal interests cannot constitute conflicts:

   > It is true that a conflict may also include a non-pecuniary interest such as close family ties, see, e.g., In re Grand Jury Proceedings, 700 F. Supp. 626, 629-30 (D.P.R. 1988). There is not, however, a conflict merely because an attorney does not believe in her client's position.

   Mendoza Toro v. Gil, 110 F. Supp. 2d 28, 2000 U.S. Dist. LEXIS 12198 (D.P.R. 2000).

   Do you agree with the court's conclusion? Why couldn't a personal opinion about the justness of your client's position constitute a conflict? Does the answer depend on your model of the attorney-client relationship? If your personal beliefs can't limit your representation, why does Rule 1.16(b)(4) permit withdrawal under circumstances in which "the client insists upon taking action that the lawyer considers repugnant or with which the lawyer has a fundamental disagreement"? Can you see how this rule could support rather than undermine the court's position?

2. How might you approach an employer if you felt that your personal beliefs would limit your ability to represent a particular client?

Reflective Practice: Personal and Professional Identity Conflicts

At some point in your professional career, you might find yourself in a situation in which your personal identity and your professional identity come into conflict. It may be as simple a matter as the clothing you wear or as complex as the attorney in the proceeding case for whom prosecuting a set of cases may have raised profound questions of religious, cultural, and political identity.

Reflect in writing on the dilemma Lilliam Mendoza Toro faced and on the ways in which you anticipate your personal identity might clash with your professional obligations in different legal practice settings. What type of case or client would you feel compelled to avoid? How difficult would it be for you to raise that concern? Why?

Problems for Review

1. Last year your uncle passed away. You were very close to your uncle and his wife Juliet, who had no children of their own. You even lived with them for three years when you were in college. Recently Aunt Juliet spoke to you at her 65th birthday party, asking if you would help her with a living will and some estate planning. You have drafted some wills and simple trusts in your practice, so you agree to do so. You are surprised when Aunt Juliet indicates that she wants to leave the majority her estate (with a value of about $70,000) to you. Juliet has an older sister in her seventies who would be her heir under the intestacy statute. You suggest that perhaps her sister should be the beneficiary of her estate, but Juliet insists that her sister doesn't need the money and doesn't deserve it. You could certainly use $70,000 (or whatever her estate might be when she passes on) but are loathe to risk your license for that amount. Are you subject to discipline if you draft the will? *Cooner v. Alabama State Bar*, 59 So. 3d 29 (Ala. 2010).

2. Valerie is a well-known portrait artist. Valerie hired Dolores to help recover some of Valerie's paintings that had "disappeared" and Valerie was having trouble recovering them. For example, one person had taken some of Valerie's paintings to sell for her and had not returned the unsold works. In another case, a museum claimed that Valerie had agreed to a "permanent loan" of the painting, but had no documentation to back up that claim. Dolores and Valerie entered into a contract regarding recovery of the paintings. Valerie agreed in writing to pay Dolores $200 an hour for the time Dolores spent on recovery of the paintings. In addition, Valerie also agreed that Dolores could keep one of every three paintings she recovered. Dolores recovered seventeen of Valerie's paintings and chose five paintings to keep. Is Dolores subject to discipline? If Valerie refused to give Dolores any of the paintings, could Dolores enforce their agreement?

3. Last year, when Wendy Wife was thinking about divorcing Harold Husband, she hired Sal Solicitor. Sal was a wonderful attorney, she thought. He helped Wendy in explaining the divorce to her children. He didn't talk down to her, as some people do to housewives. He was strong, smart, and a very good listener. One evening, after Sal had just concluded negotiating the terms of Wendy and Harold's settlement, Sal asked Wendy if she would be his guest for dinner. At dinner, he suggested that Wendy and he had become good friends and that he would not charge her for the representation if she would agree to go out with him some more. Wendy was flattered and agreed. Sal showed up at Wendy's apartment the next night with champagne and his toothbrush, and they maintained a sexual relationship throughout the next two months. If the state court in Sal's jurisdiction has not adopted a specific rule prohibiting attorneys from initiating and maintaining a sexual relationship with a client, may attorney's conduct nonetheless be subject to sanction as a conflict of interest?

4. You represent an inventor who has come to you asking that you file a patent application for his new invention. In your judgment, the inventor's enthusi-

asm for the product is well founded and he will likely earn hundreds of thousands of dollars once the patent is issued. The problem is that he cannot afford your representation. He has proposed that you be paid by a 5% interest in the patent. Obviously, if you are unsuccessful in obtaining the patent, your interest will be worthless. Can you agree to this arrangement?

5. Attorney represented Client in a matter that attracted widespread publicity because of claimed violations of Client's civil rights. Client cannot afford Attorney but has agreed to sign over his "made for TV movie" rights to Attorney to pay for the representation. May Attorney accept this deal? Suppose instead, Attorney represented client pro bono. Client lost in the trial court but was vindicated on appeal. The case is now over. Attorney has now been asked to serve as consultant on the preparation of a documentary film for immediate release on television. The film will be based on Client's case. May Attorney take the deal?

To Learn More

To read more about some of the specific prohibitions of Rule 1.8:

John S. Dzienkowski & Robert J. Peroni, *The Decline in Lawyer Independence: Lawyer Equity Investments in Clients,* 81 Tex. L. Rev. 405 (Dec. 2002).

Douglas R. Richmond, *Other People's Money: The Ethics of Litigation Funding,* 56 Mercer L. Rev. 649 (Winter 2005).

Nancy J. Moore, *Ethical Issues in Third-Party Payment: Beyond the Insurance Defense Paradigm,* 16 Rev. Litig. 585 (Summer 1997).

Chapter Seventeen

Conflicts of Interest and the Problem of Client Identity

Learning Objectives

After you have read this unit and completed the assignments, you should be able to:

- Identify and reduce the risks of having a conflict of interest arise from common situations of client ambiguity.
- Recognize and manage the risks of conflicts of interest arising from prospective clients.
- Describe the reasons that attorneys find it difficult to limit the influence of third parties who pay for representation.

Rules to Study

Rules governing the identity of the client are mostly found in common law, as we studied in the chapter on forming the attorney-client relationship. However, in this chapter we will examine three specific situations in which conflicts and client identity become particularly problematic: the prospective client (Rule 1.18); the entity client (Rule 1.13); and third-party payors (Rule 1.8).

Prospective entity Third party

Preliminary Problems

One of the first steps in conflicts of interest analysis is identifying the client. As we have seen, the rules of professional conduct do not answer the question of whether someone is a client and the answer may depend on the reason you are asking the question. Sometimes it is not entirely clear whether an individual is someone to whom you owe a duty of loyalty at all.

Assume you are representing Albert Allwell in a disqualification motion. Albert represents the Green family in an action brought by Martin Brown. That action alleges that the Greens defrauded Brown and breached the terms of a contract they had entered into with Brown for the sale of Brown's business. A portion of Martin Brown's affidavit follows.

UNITED STATES DISTRICT COURT
FOR THE CENTRAL DISTRICT OF NEW STATE

Martin Brown,
 	
                            Plaintiff,
 	
-against-
 	
James Green, Mary Green, and the
Green Family Holding Company,
                          Defendants.
	11-cv-0000
	
	Affidavit in Support of Motion to
	Disqualify Defendant's Counsel

STATE OF NEW STATE)
: SS
CITY OF SPRINGFIELD)
Martin Brown, being duly sworn, deposes and says:

1. I am an individual and Plaintiff in the captioned action, I have personal knowledge of the facts and circumstances stated in this Affidavit, which I submit in support of Plaintiffs' Motion to Disqualify Arnold Allwell, Esq. ("Allwell") from providing legal representation in this action on behalf of Defendants, pursuant to the authority and responsibility of this Court to supervise attorneys admitted to practice before it, and to uphold the applicable ethical precepts of the district in which it sits.*

2. Prior to the commencement of this Action for fraud and breach of contract, Allwell was a long time personal friend and confident. Allwell has lived across the street from me for fifteen years.

3. In fact, so close was that relationship that when, in or about 2007, Allwell advised me that he was suffering from substantial cash flow short falls and could not pay his bills, and when he asked for a loan to bail him out, I complied without reservation. In response to that request I loaned Allwell $10,000.00, unsecured, without requesting interest, and without even asking for a promissory note to evidence that loan. Not long after that loan was made, it was repaid without any offer to pay interest.

4. In many instances in the course of our social relationship, which included fairly regular golf games, Allwell suggested that he would do whatever I would like to help me or my business. I frequently perceived him to be soliciting business in that connection.

5. Allwell was also a long-time friend and/or acquaintance of members of the Green Family, the defendants herein; and the Greens were aware that Allwell and I were long time and close personal friends, and that we played golf together frequently.

6. Allwell is, as I was until recently, a member of the Greenway Golf & Country Club ("Greenway"), which is the venue where most of our golf games took place.

7. The Greens are also members of Greenway.

8. In respect of the claims of the Complaint, I had many discussions with Allwell over the period extending from October, 2005 through late April and into early May, 2009, concerning my contract negotiations with Defendants. Subsequently, I had discussions with Allwell relating to ensuing business and office problems that I was experiencing with Defendants, which matured into breaches of Defendants' covenants and representations made in connection with the agreements that underlie the Complaint in this action.

9. In these discussions and exchanges I revealed to Allwell many of my motivations for agreeing to various provisions in the underlying operative agreements between Plaintiffs and Defendants, and why I would or would not want to take certain actions.

10. It readily appears that Allwell is now using and employing against me many of those disclosures made in confidence.

11. At no time in the course of those meetings and discussions did Allwell ever say to me that he was discussing these matters with me exclusively as my friend, and not as an attorney; and at no time did he ever directly or indirectly advise me that I could not or should not expect that he would not keep our discussions confidential, or that I should not expect that he would not trade on any information I discussed with or disclosed to him.

12. WHEREFORE, I respectfully pray that this Court grant the application and motion of Plaintiffs for an Order disqualifying Allwell from serving and acting as counsel for the Defendants in this Action, and for such other relief as to this Court may seem fair and just, including an award of all legal fees, costs and expenses incurred by Plaintiffs in making and prosecuting this motion.

Martin Brown

Subscribed and sworn before me this 23 day of October, 2011

Nancy Notary

---

* This motion presents the incongruous situation and circumstance in which I am relegated to detail certain conversations with Allwell that were intended to be confidential attorney-client communications, as the means by which to demonstrate that Allwell has engaged in unethical conduct, proscribed by New York Rules of Professional Conduct, Rule 1.18. requiring Allwell's disqualification from serving as counsel in this action, while at the same time attempting to preserve the confidentiality of the more sensitive and material of my conversations with Allwell. Accordingly, I have attempted to recount in this Affidavit only those matters that were previously disclosed in the Complaint in this action; and nothing herein is intended to be a waiver of the attorney-client privilege. In that vein, certain further conversations had with and disclosures made to Allwell are withheld from recitation herein, but will be presented to the Court in a separate Affidavit which Plaintiffs deliver to Chambers under seal, with the request that it be reviewed exclusively in camera.

[margin handwritten note: Is he talking or a friend or a lawyer? a friend or talking as a lawyer?]

Assume you are representing Albert Allwell in this disqualification motion. He says that Martin and he were friends before this lawsuit, but that he had never represented Brown and that, in fact, Brown was represented by another attorney in all his negotiations with the Greens. He admits that Brown did discuss his business and the negotiations for its sale with him, but can't believe his "let me know if there is anything I can do" friendship statements turned those country club breakfasts into solicitations of employment. How will you defend Albert? How likely do you think it is that the court will grant the disqualification motion?[1]

17.1 Reading the Rules — Rule 1.18: Prospective Clients

For many years, the rules of professional conduct did not address whether an attorney had any duties to an individual who came to you seeking representation but whom you did not subsequently represent. Rule 1.18 is helpful in understanding conflicts of interest because its development and enforcement demonstrate some key principles in conflicts of interest analysis:

- First, conflicts of interest rules are designed to protect confidential information;
- Second, unless otherwise excepted, an individual attorney's conflicts of interest are imputed to all of the other attorneys in the same firm;
- Third, regardless of what the rules of professional conduct provide, courts have other interests to consider when deciding whether to disqualify an attorney for conflicts of interest.

Read Minnesota Rule 1.18, which was adopted recently without variation from the ABA Model Rules.

Minnesota Rules of Professional Conduct
Rule 1.18: Duties to Prospective Clients

(a) A person who discusses with a lawyer the possibility of forming a client-lawyer relationship with respect to a matter is a prospective client.

(b) Even when no client-lawyer relationship ensues, a lawyer who has had discussions with a prospective client shall not use or reveal information learned in the consultation, except as Rule 1.9 would permit with respect to information of a former client.

(c) A lawyer subject to paragraph (b) shall not represent a client with interests materially adverse to those of a prospective client in the same or a substantially related matter if the lawyer received information from the prospective client that could be significantly harmful to that person in the matter, except as provided

---

1. This problem is modeled on *Miness v. Ahuja*, 762 F.Supp.2d 465 (E.D.N.Y. 2010) and some of the language in the affidavit is quoted from the actual plaintiff's motion, though with some changes in the facts. The motion, affidavits of plaintiff and defendant, memoranda in support and opposition to the motion, and the decision of the court are available on LEXIS and WESTLAW. They are, of course, much more complicated than this simplified affidavit, but the issue is very similar. An important difference between this problem and the actual case is that the attorney defended his own disqualification motion.

in paragraph (d). If a lawyer is disqualified from representation under this paragraph, no lawyer in a firm with which that lawyer is associated may knowingly undertake or continue representation in such a matter, except as provided in paragraph (d).

(d) When the lawyer has received disqualifying information as defined in paragraph (c), representation is permissible if:

(1) both the affected client and the prospective client have given informed consent, confirmed in writing; or

(2) the lawyer who received the information took reasonable measures to avoid exposure to more disqualifying information than was reasonably necessary to determine whether to represent the prospective client, and

(i) the disqualified lawyer is timely screened from any participation in the matter and is apportioned no part of the fee therefrom; and

(ii) written notice is promptly given to the prospective client.

Context

Rule 1.18 is a new addition to the Model Rules, adopted in 2002. This was the first time that the rules had directly addressed the issue of duties to prospective clients. Before that time, this issue existed in an "ethics limbo." Margaret C. Love, *Duties to Prospective Clients*, 87 A.B.A.J. 59 (2001). Before this rule existed, courts developed similar standards to resolve many of the issues of relationships with prospective clients in disqualification motions. *Dana Corp. v. Blue Cross & Blue Shield Mut. of N. Ohio*, 900 F.2d 882 (6th Cir. 1990) (three part test for determining whether an interview with a prospective client creates a conflict of interest). 2012 amendments to the rule have provided more explanation in comments regarding whether communicating information creates a relationship.

Relationships

Conflict of interest issues arise most often in the context of motions to disqualify counsel rather than in disciplinary cases. The power to disqualify attorneys is part of a court's inherent power to control the conduct of litigation. Disqualification decisions are reviewed on an abuse of discretion standard and are not necessarily controlled by the rules of professional conduct. "Although disqualification ordinarily is the result of a finding that a disciplinary rule prohibits an attorney's appearance in a case, disqualification never is automatic.... [T]he court should disqualify an attorney only when it determines, on the facts of the particular case, that disqualification is an appropriate means of enforcing the applicable disciplinary rule." *U.S. v. Miller*, 624 F.2d 1198, 1201 (3d Cir. 1980). In ruling on disqualification motions, courts should "consider the ends that the disciplinary rule is designed to serve and any countervailing policies, such as permitting a litigant to retain the counsel of his choice and enabling attorneys to practice without excessive restrictions." *Id.* This relationship between disqualification and disciplinary rules is critical to your understanding of all rules regarding conflicts of interest. When researching conflicts, remember that just because a court denies a disqualification motion does not mean that a conflict of interest did not exist.

Structure

Notice that the rule provides definitions, explains duties of both confidentiality and conflicts, and outlines the circumstances in which those duties are imputed to others in the firm. In this sense, Rule 1.18 is a microcosm of conflicts analysis.

Reasons

Comment 1 to the rule explains the purpose behind the rule, to provide "some but not all of the protection afforded clients."

Visualize

As you have likely learned, the little words in rules are often the most critical to understanding the rule. Almost any rule can be structured as an IF—THEN—UNLESS that looks much like a mathematical formula. Sometimes visually structuring the rule so that these relationship words are emphasized can help to make clear the structure of a rule in a way that simply reading the rule cannot. Fill in this structural chart for Rule 1.18

IF		An individual speaks with the attorney about the possibility of the attorney representing him or her
	AND	
THEN		The attorney may not represent a client with interests materially adverse to those of the prospective client in the same or a substantially related matter
UNLESS	EITHER		OR	
	AND	
	AND	

Imagine

Obviously, a key factor in applying Rule 1.18 is the information an attorney gains in an initial interview and the expectations the prospective client has. It is difficult to balance your need to get enough information to know whether you can and will represent a prospective client with your need to limit information so that you will not be setting yourself up for a conflict of interest. Think about how you might talk to a potential client about how much information to give you.

Practice Problem

You are an attorney in one of several large firms who have commercial litigation departments. Complete Construction, Inc., one of the largest construction companies in town, is interested in bringing major litigation against 2020 Futures, a major developer whose project went from one disaster to another and now has left the project in limbo. Complete Construction is shopping for a law firm to handle the litigation. Complete sends you a solicitation, in which it invites proposals from your firm and several others and invites them each to make a presentation regarding their firm's expertise, experience, and resources and how they could bring that to bear on their legal problems. The winner of this "beauty contest" will have netted a very lucrative client with a high-profile litigation that is likely to bring in additional business.

You meet with the CEO and General Counsel of Complete Construction for about 90 minutes, during which time Complete provides you details of their dispute with 2020 and asks you for your opinion on how your firm would handle several legal issues and strategic aspects of the dispute. You discuss some of the financial aspects of the litigation and Complete asks you what type of representation you could supply given their insurance and other financial resources for the litigation. You are quite confident that your presentation has landed you the representation. However, by the time you get back to the office, you have a phone message from the CEO of Complete indicating that they will give the representation to the firm that is your major competitor.

The next day, one of the partners in the firm calls you to ask about your meeting with Complete. It seems that General Counsel of 2020 has called him, asking if he would be willing to meet with 2020 to discuss the possibility of our representing them in connection with its failed development project, including the dispute with Complete. The partner wants to know whether your meeting would present a conflict of interest that would prohibit his representing 2020. If it does, he wants to know how the firm can prevent these beauty contests from creating conflicts of interest in the future.

Recall that the first part of Rule 1.18 is actually a definition. Not every interview with an attorney creates a conflict under this rule—the interview must be for the purposes of establishing an attorney-client relationship. Some questions to ask yourself in making this determination:

a. Was the communication unilateral? (comment 2) Unsolicited emails, letters, or phone calls are unlikely to fall within this rule, especially if an attorney takes no further steps to communicate with the author of those communications.

b. Is there evidence that the client may be "taint shopping"—seeking to disqualify rather than engage your representation in the matter? Does the very rapid response of the prospective client in this situation suggest that perhaps the client may not have ever actually intended to hire the firm?

c. Is there evidence that the individual speaking with the attorney knew that the attorney could not or would not represent him or her?

If the client in this problem was a prospective client, is there a conflict of interest? Complete your analysis of this problem, applying Rule 1.18 and considering how this issue might actually arise.

Professional Responsibility Skill 17-A: Disclaimers and Electronic Communication

Individuals increasingly look to the internet to find answers to their problems. Legal problems are no exception. Look at one of the following online fora that provide legal advice.

http://www.justanswer.com/law/
http://law.freeadvice.com/

http://www.worldlawdirect.com/asklawyer/

Most of these websites have disclaimers and exclusions of liability. For example, the JustAnswer terms of service have the following statement:

> 7. Information Not Advice; No Client-Professional Relationship
>
> Answers of Experts on the Site are provided by Experts and are to be used by Customers for general information purposes only, not as a substitute for in-person evaluation or specific professional (medical, legal, veterinary, tax, financial, etc.) advice. For example, Experts in the Legal category will provide only general information about the law, and will not provide legal advice nor propose a specific course of action for a Customer; by answering questions, Experts do not form attorney-client or doctor-patient relationships with Users of the Site. The laws, regulations, other governing authorities, standards, practices and procedures that apply to your particular question may differ depending on your location and information typically discovered through in-person evaluations or visits. Experts in some categories may be licensed, certified, educated, employed by or have experience in only particular jurisdictions.
>
> No professional-client relationships shall be formed on the Site.
>
> Communications on this Site are not confidential and shall not be the subject of any associated privileges. Communications on this Site are limited, as described above, do not involve in-person evaluations or visits, and do not include safeguards and procedures typical of in-person evaluations and visits.
>
> Before you can interact with an Expert, you will be required to agree to a Disclaimer reminding you of these and other important provisions of the Terms.

Suppose you would like to expand your practice to include some on-line advising. How can you design a website that will attract clients without turning everyone who happens to send you something into a prospective client under Rule 1.18 (or even worse, a real client)? Try designing a website interface that could accomplish this.

17.2 The Entity Person

As you have read in Rule 1.13, when you represent an entity, you represent the entity itself, not the persons in that entity: officers or employees, for example. But what exactly is the "entity" an attorney represents? We ordinarily think of the entity this rule contemplates as a corporation, but it can be any organization: a partnership, union, or government agency, for example. There are two particularly difficult problems with the identity of the client when applying conflict of interest rules. At one end of the spectrum are those entities that are so small—a close corporation, partnership, or sole proprietorship, for example—that it is very difficult to practically distinguish the entity from the individuals who own or direct that entity. At the other end of the spectrum are those organizations that are so large, and have multiple forms and allied entities that the contours of the client are not clear.

An organizational constituent or a corporate subsidiary may claim that an attorney for the entity represents the constituent or the subsidiary in three different settings: a malpractice action, a disqualification motion, or an invocation of the attorney-client privilege. Predicting the outcome of these actions can be difficult because these are fact-intensive determinations.

For small organizations, the confusion that arises is one that can arise in any entity representation: that is, an individual in the entity (an officer, director, shareholder, or employee) believes that the attorney represents the individual in addition to or instead of representing the entity. But in order to represent the entity effectively, the attorney must be able to obtain information from these individuals. If the organization's policies provide, Rule 1.13(d) does permit attorneys to provide individual advice if it does not conflict with the organization. Organizational attorneys work with organizational constituents daily and develop relationships of trust. Thus, it is not hard to see why these persons, these organizational constituents, often believe that the entity's lawyer represents them individually.

The dilemma for the organizational attorney is to treat these persons fairly while also being able to obtain critical information needed by the organization. Rule 4.3 requires that attorneys who know that individuals are confused about the attorney's role must take steps to clarify their role. For the organizational attorney, this means informing the constituent that communications with the attorney are privileged but that the organization, rather than the individual, owns that privilege. In many circumstances, an officer or employee's interests are aligned with the entity and the individual will want to communicate fully and frankly with the attorney. In other circumstances, however, the entity's interests may conflict with the individual's.

Where the constituent's interests do conflict, and the entity counsel has not made her role clear, the attorney may find herself in a situation of representing conflicting interests. Recall that an attorney-client relationship can be implied when an individual reasonably believes an attorney is representing him and relies on the attorney's advice. Whether an attorney represents the partner in a partnership, or the shareholder in a close corporation, or an officer in a corporation, is a question of fact in most states. Professor Simon suggests that judicial responses to these issues have been " incoherent and implausible" due to the lack of a satisfactory theory to explain entity representation. William Simon, *Whom (or What) Does the Organization's Lawyer Represent?: An Anatomy of Intraclient Conflict*, 91 CALIF. L. REV. 57, 60 (2003). Most courts do not readily imply an attorney-client relationship between an entity attorney and a constituent; however, some circumstances are more likely to raise these inferences than others. Some factors that might lead a court to imply a relationship with the individual constituent include:

- The entity is relatively small or did not operate as an entity clearly separate from the individual.
- The attorney represented an individual in forming the entity.
- The attorney had an ongoing personal or representational relationship with the individual.
- The attorney represented the individual in legal matters separate from the entity's representation.
- The attorney did not clarify the relationship with the individual, either by disclaiming an attorney-client relationship or clarifying the scope of a representation the attorney did agree to provide.
- The individual had an interest separate from the entity that should have been apparent to the attorney.
- The attorney provided advice to the individual.

- The attorney obtained confidential information from the individual that could now be used adversely.
- The attorney collected a fee or other benefit from the individual.

How do you avoid this confusion?

The confusion can be just as profound when the question of client identity arises among large complex corporate or governmental entities. Does representation of a corporation automatically include representation of the corporation's subsidiaries, sisters, or other affiliates? Comment 35 to Rule 1.7, which incorporates the analysis of ABA Comm. on Ethics and Prof'l Responsibility, Formal Op. 95-390 (1995), indicates that there is no *per se* rule that an attorney who represents a corporation also represents other affiliates. While there is some early case law that applies a *per se* rule, the majority of jurisdictions follow the approach of the Model Rules. Rather, Comment 35 and the cases addressing disqualification motions suggest a number of circumstances in which an attorney is more likely to be considered to represent a corporate affiliate. In a recent case, the Second Circuit explained this approach to conflicts analysis in the corporate family context.

GSI Commerce Solutions, Inc. v. BabyCenter, L.L.C.

618 F.3d 204, 210-12 (2d Cir. N.Y. 2010)

Try diagramming this relationship.

[This case involved attorneys in the Blank Rome law firm, who represented Johnson & Johnson Companies (J&J) in compliance matters involving J&J and J&J affiliates in connection with the European Union Data Protection Directive and potential certification to the U.S. Safe Harbor. Blank Rome began representing GSI in a suit against Baby Center. BabyCenter is a limited liability company that operates websites with information about babies and some sales of baby items. Its sole member is BC Acquisition group, which is itself a wholly-owned subsidiary of J&J. The suit involved GSI and BabyCenter's E-Commerce Agreement, under which GSI agreed to run the day-to-day operations of BabyCenter's online store. BabyCenter brought a motion to disqualify the Blank Rome attorneys representing GSI in that suit, based on Blank Rome's representation of J&J.]

We agree that representation adverse to a client's affiliate can, in certain circumstances, conflict with the lawyer's duty of loyalty owed to a client, a situation that we shall refer to as "a corporate affiliate conflict."

The factors relevant to whether a corporate affiliate conflict exists are of a general nature. Courts have generally focused on: (i) the degree of operational commonality between affiliated entities, and (ii) the extent to which one depends financially on the other. As to operational commonality, courts have considered the extent to which entities rely on a common infrastructure. *See, e.g., Discotrade Ltd. v. Wyeth-Ayerst Int'l, Inc.*, 200 F. Supp. 2d 355, 359 (S.D.N.Y. 2002) (corporate affiliates deemed single entity where each used the same computer network, e-mail system, travel department, and health benefit plan); *Eastman Kodak Co. v. Sony Corp.*, Nos. 04-CV-6095, 04-CV-6098, 2004 U.S. Dist. LEXIS 29883, 2004 WL 2984297, at 3-4 (W.D.N.Y. Dec. 27, 2004) (corporate affiliates deemed single entity based on, inter alia, integration of technology systems). Courts have also focused on the extent to which the affiliated entities rely on or otherwise share common personnel such as managers, officers, and directors. *See, e.g., Certain Underwriters at Lloyd's, London,* 264 F. Supp. 2d at 923 (substantial overlap in management); *Eastman Kodak,* 2004 U.S. Dist. LEXIS 29883, 2004 WL 2984297, at *4 (shared directors, officers and legal department); *Discotrade Ltd.,* 200 F. Supp. 2d at 359 (same board, directors and President). In this respect, courts have emphasized the extent to which affiliated entities share responsibility for both the provision and management of legal services. *See Eastman Kodak,* 2004 U.S. Dist. LEXIS 29883, 2004 WL 2984297, at *4; *Certain Underwriters at Lloyd's, London v. Argonaut Ins. Co.,* 264 F. Supp. 2d 914, 923-24 (N.D. Cal. 2003); *Discotrade Ltd.,* 200 F. Supp. 2d at 357; *Hartford Accident & Indem. Co. v. RJR Nabisco, Inc.,* 721 F. Supp. 534, 540 (S.D.N.Y. 1989; *Morrison Knudsen Corp. v. Hancock, Rothert & Bunshoft,* 69 Cal. App. 4th 223, 231, 81 Cal. Rptr. 2d 425 (Cal. App. 1st Dist. 1999). This focus on shared or dependent control over legal and management issues reflects the view that neither management nor in-house legal counsel should, without their consent, have to place their trust in outside counsel in one matter while opposing the same counsel in another.

As to financial interdependence, several courts have considered the extent to which an adverse outcome in the matter at issue would result in substantial and measurable loss to the client or its affiliate. *See Hartford Accident and Indem. Co.,* 721 F. Supp. at 540; "entity theory" of representation. *See* Charles W. Wolfram, *Legal Ethics: Corporate-Family Conflicts,* 2 J. INST. STUDY LEGAL ETHICS 295, 357-58 (1999). Courts have also inquired into the entities' ownership structure. *See Discotrade Ltd.,* 200 F. Supp. 2d at 358-59. Some have even suggested that an affiliate's status as a wholly-owned subsidiary of the client may suffice to establish a corporate affiliate conflict. *Carlyle Towers Condo. Ass'n, Inc. v. Crossland Sav., FSB,* 944 F. Supp. 341, 346 (D.N.J. 1996) ("[T]here is sufficient case law which supports the proposition that, for conflict purposes, representation of a subsidiary corporation is equivalent to representation of its parent, and vice-versa...."); *Stratagem Dev. Corp. v. Heron Int'l N.V.,* 756 F. Supp. 789, 792 (S.D.N.Y. 1991) (treating the entities as one client because "the liabilities of a [wholly-owned] subsidiary corporation directly affect the bottom line of the corporate parent"). However, we agree with the ABA that affiliates should not be considered a single entity for conflicts purposes based solely on the fact that one entity is a wholly-owned subsidiary of the other, at least when the subsidiary is not otherwise operationally integrated with the parent company. *See* American Bar Ass'n Comm. on Prof'l. Ethics, Formal Opinion 95-390 (1995).

> Why are financial relationships relevant?

However, the record here establishes such substantial operational commonalty between BabyCenter and J&J that the district court's decision to treat the two entities as one client was easily within its ample discretion. First, Babycenter substantially relies on J&J for accounting, audit, cash management, employee benefits, finance, human resources, information technology, insurance, payroll, and travel services and systems. Second, both entities rely on the same in-house legal department to handle their legal affairs. The member of J&J's in-house legal department who serves as "board lawyer" for Baby-Center helped to negotiate the E-Commerce Agreement between BabyCenter and GSI that is the subject of the present dispute. Moreover, J&J's legal department has been involved in the dispute between GSI and BabyCenter since it first arose, participating in mediation efforts and securing outside counsel for BabyCenter. Finally, BabyCenter is a wholly-owned subsidiary of J&J, and there is at least some overlap in management control.

When considered together, these factors show that the relationship between the two entities is exceedingly close. That showing in turn substantiates the view that Blank Rome, by representing GSI in this matter, "reasonably diminishes the level of confidence and trust in counsel held by" J&J. *Certain Underwriters at Lloyd's, London*, 264 F. Supp. 2d at 922 (internal quotation marks omitted).

Notes

1. One of the issues also addressed by the court in this case was whether J&J had consented to this conflict. In its initial engagement letter with J&J, Blank Rome had included several waivers of specific conflicts involving its representation of Kimberly Clark in patent matters. As Blank Rome's patent litigation practice grew, it had updated its engagement letter thereafter to include additional conflicts in these waivers. An addendum to the engagement letter also contained the following clause: "Unless otherwise agreed to in writing or we specifically undertake such additional representation at your request, we represent only the client named in the engagement letter and not its affiliates, subsidiaries, partners, joint venturers, employees, directors, officers, shareholders, members, owners, agencies, departments, or divisions." *GSI Commerce Solutions, Inc.*, 618 F.3d at 213. The court held that this broad waiver language did not provide consent to the conflict in this case. It pointed out that "construed as a waiver of all corporate affiliate conflicts involving the entities listed therein, this clause would raise a serious ethical problem. Specifically, Blank Rome cannot, consistent with its duty of loyalty to J&J, sue unincorporated departments or divisions of J&J." *Id.* at 214. Why do you think Blank Rome had not secured J&J's consent to this particular conflict when it had done so for the patent conflicts?

2. The court pointed out that the legal staff of J&J helped BabyCenter to negotiate its agreement with GSI. Why wasn't it a conflict of interest for the in-house attorneys to represent the subsidiary? When would it be? If in-house counsel becomes aware that it has a conflict in representing both the parent and subsidiary or affiliate company, what does he or she do to resolve that conflict?

3. Identifying the client among entities is an issue for attorneys representing government agencies as well. Does an attorney who represents a government agency have a conflict if that attorney brings an action against some other agency of that same government? ABA Comm. on Ethics and Prof'l Responsibility, Formal Op. 97-405 (1997) addressed this issue and concluded that the question is resolved by looking first to the representation agreement and second, by reference to the reasonable expectations of the clients, "taking into account such functional considerations as how the government client presented to the lawyer is legally defined and funded, whether it has independent legal authority with respect to the matter for which the lawyer has been retained — e.g., contracting, litigating, or settling a claim — and the extent to which the matter involved in the proposed representation has general importance for other government components in the jurisdiction."

4. In a footnote, the court explained that this was a close case:

> These factors are not clearly outweighed by those that would support a different conclusion. It is true that the dispute between GSI and BabyCenter is unrelated to the matters upon which Blank Rome represents J&J. Also, J&J and BabyCenter do not publicly present themselves as a single legal entity; in fact, the E-Commerce Agreement at issue here expressly forbids GSI from representing that J&J is one of its strategic partners. GSI also claims that the court should have given more weight to the fact that J&J is not financially dependent on Baby-Center. BabyCenter is only one of many J&J affiliates and does not account for much of J&J's revenue. But, given the extent of J&J's and BabyCenter's operational commonality, the district court did not abuse its discretion in giving these counter factors little weight.

Which side do you find more persuasive? Why?

17.3 Third-Party Payors

Often, the person paying for your representation is not your client, but an insurer, a pre-paid legal plan, the government, or an employer or friend. Rules 1.7(b), 1.8(f) and 5.4 (c) all counsel caution in these circumstances. Suppose that Frank calls you about his nephew, Jonny, a 21-year-old accused of possession and sale of cocaine. Jonny has been arrested and released after Frank paid his bail. Now Frank wants to hire you to represent Jonny. They both arrive at your office. What do you do to insure that you comply with the rules?

First, you need to consider whether this arrangement will present a conflict of interest. Rule 1.8(f) and 5.4(c) also emphasize that the arrangement not interfere with the attorney's independent professional judgment. How might that happen? Isn't Frank's payment bound to influence you in some ways, even if it is just because the amount of money available for your representation will surely influence your discretionary decisions about tactics, evidence, and the like. THE RESTATEMENT (THIRD) OF THE LAW GOVERNING LAWYERS § 215(2) (2000) remarks that "if the influence is reasonable in scope and character and the client expressly consents to the possible influence" a lawyer may undertake a representation paid for by a third party.

Because this is a criminal matter, you would want to be especially careful and consider whether Frank is involved in Jonny's activities in any way. If Frank were not only Jonny's uncle, but were also involved in drug activities, there would be an inherent danger that Frank would be directing the representation to protect his own interests rather than Jonny's. *Wood v. Georgia*, 450 U.S. 261, 268-69 (1981). Even if Frank did not try to control the representation directly, he might do so by increasing, delaying, or stopping payments or by controlling Frank's decisions. The court in *Quintero v. U.S.*, 33 F. 3d 1133 (9th Cir. Ct. App. 1994), warned "trial judges, particularly in drug cases, to determine whether or not third parties are paying the fees of retained counsel when the defendant is indigent and, if so, whether the defendant understands the potential conflict of interest that may exist in such an arrangement and voluntarily waives the conflict."

Second, you need Jonny's informed consent to the arrangement. What would be the advantages, disadvantages, and alternatives you might discuss with Jonny? Two extremely important considerations are confidentiality and conflicts. Just because Jonny consents to having Frank pay, does not automatically mean that he has consented to your disclosing confidential information to Frank. Re-read Tennessee Rule 1.8(f) in Chapter 16.1. You will note that it requires that, among other considerations in arranging for third party payment, confidential information be "protected as required by RPC 1.6." Does that mean that you could not share information about the representation with Frank, even if Jonny wanted you to? Could you permit Frank to be present during your meetings with Jonny? Recall that, unless Frank's presence was necessary to facilitate the representation, the attorney-client privilege would be waived if he attended your meetings with Jonny.

Third, you must make the nature of your relationship clear to not only the client but the third party payor. In some circumstances, when the payor has a legal interest in the subject matter of the representation, the payor may be a co-client rather than a third party. How do you know whether an individual who is paying for your representation is a client or simply a third-party payor? The answer may depend on the nature of the legal rights and obligations between the "client" and the "payor"—for example in the insurance context, the agreement between the insurer and insured and state law will affect whether you represent the insurer or the insured. If there was an assignment of claim or a direct-action statute, you may represent the insurance company. Otherwise, most courts would find that you represent the insured only. Some jurisdictions hold that an insurer who reserves its right to deny coverage must pay the reasonable costs of hiring independent counsel for the insured. Other jurisdictions have held that an enhanced obligation of good faith is imposed on the insurer in a reservation of rights context.

In recent years, insurance companies, like many other corporations, have begun to use their own in-house counsel for more matters, rather than referring matters to outside counsel. May an insurance company use these "captive counsel" to represent an insured? Jurisdictions are split on their approach to the question, which involves not only questions of conflicts of interest but also the practice of law by a corporation. ABA Comm. on Ethics and Prof'l Responsibility, Formal Op. 03-430 (2003) concluded that "insurance staff counsel may ethically undertake the representations as long as the lawyers inform all insured whom they represent that the lawyers are employees of the insurance company and exercise independent professional judgment in advising or otherwise representing the insured." Compare the approach by the Arkansas court in the following case:

Brown v. Kelton

2011 Ark. 93 (Ark 2011)

A diagram of the parties can help you to follow the court's analysis.

[This case involved a car accident in which Brian Kelton's vehicle was struck by a vehicle owned by Mid-Central Plumbing Company, Inc. Kelton sued Mid-Central and its sole shareholder John Rogers alleging damages from the collision. Mid-Central and Rogers were insured by Truck Insurance Exchange ("TEI") for $1,000,000, and TEI was reinsured by Farmer's Insurance Exchange ("FIE"). Stephen Brown is an attorney who works for FIE. About three months into the case, the attorney for Mid-Central and Rogers filed a motion for substitution, seeking to name Stephen Brown as the new attorney on the case. Kelton objected. The trial court disqualified Brown on the basis that his representation would have constituted the unauthorized practice of law by the insurance company and that he had a nonwaivable conflict of interest. This interlocutory appeal followed. The court addressed several arguments. Italicized headings, in the form of questions, are added to help you to focus on each of these in turn.]

[*1. By assigning its own staff attorney to represent Mid-Central and Rogers, was FIE practicing law in violation of Arkansas statutes that prohibit corporations from practicing law?*]

Appellants first argue that Ark.Code Ann. § 16-22-211 does not prohibit an insurance carrier from assigning the defense of an insured's lawsuit to in-house counsel and that such is true in a majority of other jurisdictions as well. Kelton responds that the circuit court's application of section 16-22-211 was correct and that using in-house counsel to represent an insured equates to the insurance company unlawfully practicing law.

We review statutory interpretation de novo, as it is for this court to determine the meaning of a statute. *See Dachs v. Hendrix*, 2009 Ark. 542, ___ S.W.3d ___. Our rules of statutory construction are well settled:

> The basic rule of statutory construction is to give effect to the intent of the legislature. Where the language of a statute is plain and unambiguous, we determine legislative intent from the ordinary meaning of the language used. In considering the meaning of a statute, we construe it just as it reads, giving the words their ordinary and usually accepted meaning in common language. We construe the statute so that no word is left void, superfluous or insignificant, and we give meaning and effect to every word in the statute, if possible.

Dachs, 2009 Ark. 542, at 7-8, ___ S.W.3d ___, at ___ (quoting *City of Little Rock v. Rhee*, 375 Ark. 491, 495, 292 S.W .3d 292, 294 (2009)).

Section 16-22-211 states, in relevant part:

> (a) It shall be unlawful for any corporation or voluntary association to practice or appear as an attorney at law for any person in any court in this state ...
>
> ... (d) This section shall not apply to a corporation or voluntary association lawfully engaged in the examination and insuring of titles to real property, nor shall it prohibit a corporation or a voluntary association from employing an attorney or attorneys in and about its own immediate affairs or in any litigation to which it is or may become a party.

Ark.Code Ann. § 16-22-211(a),(d) (Supp.2009).

Appellants argue that FIE falls into the exception created by subsection (d) because the insured's lawsuit is a matter that is "in and about its own immediate affairs." However, they attempt to de-emphasize the language that follows. The exception created is two-fold. The plain language of the statute allows a corporation to employ an attorney in two scenarios: (1) for matters "in and about its own immediate affairs"; or (2) in any litigation to which it is or may become a party." *Id.* (emphasis and numeral added).

Appellants argue that the language of section 16-22-211 should not be interpreted as creating disjunctive alternatives. However, "[i]n its ordinary sense, the word 'or' is a disjunctive particle that marks an alternative, generally corresponding to 'either,' as 'either this or that'; it is a connective that marks an alternative." *McCoy v. Walker*, 317 Ark. 86, 89, 876 S.W.2d 252, 254 (1994) (quoting *Beasley v. Parnell*, 177 Ark. 912, 918, 9 S.W.2d 10, 12 (1928)). Additionally, were we to hold that "in and about its own immediate affairs" includes litigation to which it is not a party, but to which it is closely connected or has an interest in the outcome, the language following would be superfluous. Obviously, litigation to which it is a party or could become a party would then be included in the first exception. As noted, "[w]e construe the statute so that no word is left void, superfluous or insignificant, and we give meaning and effect to every word in the statute, if possible." *Dachs, supra.*

> Some states do allow insurance companies to be sued directly. In these "direct action" states, the insurance company itself would be the defendant.

In the instant case, it is undisputed that FIE is not a party and will not become a party to the underlying lawsuit. Therefore, it was prohibited by Ark.Code Ann. § 16-22-211 from assigning appellant Brown, one of its in-house counsel, to defend the insureds in the litigation.

[2. Is a statute prohibiting corporations from practicing law an unconstitutional infringement on the judiciary's power to regulate the practice of law?]

Appellants next argue that Ark.Code Ann. § 16-22-211 is unconstitutional because the statute conflicts with the exclusive power to regulate the practice of law vested on this court by Amendment 28 of the Arkansas Constitution. Kelton avers that this statute, much like others upheld by this court, is simply an aid in regulating the practice of law and is not in derogation of it.

> Recall that Arkansas is one of the few states with express constitutional delegation of this power. Most states however consider it an inherent part of the power of the judiciary.

Amendment 28 of the Arkansas Constitution provides that "[t]he Supreme Court shall make rules regulating the practice of law and the professional conduct of attorneys at law," and this court has recognized that Amendment 28 "put to rest for all time any possible question about the power of the courts to regulate the practice of law in the state." *McKenzie v. Burris*, 255 Ark. 330, 341, 500 S .W.2d 357, 364 (1973). However, as even the appellants recognize, this court considered and rejected the idea of a possible conflict between Amendment 28 and the legislative act prohibiting corporations from practicing law. *See Arkansas Bar Ass'n v. Union Nat'l Bank of Little Rock*, 224 Ark. 48, 273 S.W.2d 408 (1954). While facts of that case differed, this court observed:

> In many jurisdictions, as in this state, the judiciary has on occasions apparently given approval to certain enactments by the legislative body, but these enactments are considered to be in aid of the judicial prerogative to regulate the practice of law and not to be in derogation thereof.

Id. at 54, 273 S.W.2d at 412.

The approach taken by this court in the Union National Bank case has since been utilized. *See McKenzie, supra.* We have recognized that "[s]tatutes which provide a penalty for unauthorized practice of law by a nonresident of the forum state have been held to be cumulative to the powers of the courts to punish." *McKenzie*, 255 Ark. at 342, 500 S.W.2d at 365. Statutes relating to the practice of law are merely in aid of, but do not supersede or detract from the power of the judicial department to define, regulate, and control the practice of law. *See id.* The legislative branch may not, in any way, hinder, interfere with, restrict, or frustrate the powers of the court. *See id.* Moreover, we have "chosen to recognize and apply certain statutes which are not necessarily inconsistent with, or repugnant to, court rules, and do not hinder, interfere with, frustrate, pre-empt or usurp judicial powers, at least when the statutes were, at the time of enactment, clearly within the province of the legislative branch, and when the courts have not acted in the particular matter covered by the statute." *Id.* at 343, 500 S.W .2d at 365.

While there is no question that we hold the power to define, regulate, and control the practice of law, section 16-22-211 reflects the consensus of this court as found in prior case law and implied by our court rules. We have observed that "[c]orporations shall not practice law." *Union National Bank,* 224 Ark. at 53, 273 S.W.2d at 411 (1954) (*quoting People ex rel. Committee on Grievances of Colorado Bar Ass'n v. Denver Clearing House Banks*, 99 Colo. 50, 54, 59 P.2d 468, 470 (1936)). Additionally, Rule 1.7 of the Arkansas Rules of Professional Conduct sets forth the general principle that an attorney may not represent a client if the representation involves a concurrent conflict of interest. Upon consideration of public policy and recognizing the inability of any person to faithfully serve two masters, we hold that the statute, which prohibits corporations, including insurance companies, from practicing law on behalf of a third party, is constitutional.

… While Mid-Central and Rogers allege that they gave the proper informed consent to be represented by Brown, even had they given such consent, a lawyer may not represent the client if that representation is prohibited by law. *See* Ark. R. Prof'l Conduct 1.7(b)(2) (2010).

Because we hold that Ark. Code Ann. § 16-22-211 prohibited Brown from representing Mid-Central and Rogers, and in light of our decision to hold the statute constitutional, any decision on the remaining arguments presented on appeal—that there was not an inappropriate conflict and that no breach of duty to preserve Mid-Central and Roger's confidences had occurred— would be purely advisory. It is well-settled that we will not issue an advisory opinion. *See Jewell v. Fletcher,* 2010 Ark. 195, ___ S.W.3d ___.

Affirmed.

JIM HANNAH, Chief Justice, concurring.

I concur in the result reached by the majority, but I write separately to set out the analysis by which I reach that same result. Brown correctly argues that Arkansas Code Annotated section 16-22-211 (Supp. 2009) "cannot control the outcome of this case because the statute intrudes on this court's exclusive power." A statute, being an enactment of the legislative branch, may not control what is within the exclusive authority of the judicial branch. As the highest court in the judicial branch of government, this court holds exclusive authority over the regulation of the practice of law.[1]…

The circuit court decided this case largely on an analysis of section 16-22-211, and while this was in error, the circuit court nonetheless reached the right result. …

Are you satisfied with this analysis of the consent issue?

---

1. It is true that this court has occasionally referred to section 16-22-211 (formerly Arkansas Statutes Annotated section 25-205) in cases discussing the regulation of the practice of law. However, in such cases we have noted that despite our reference to the statute, it is solely within the judicial prerogative to regulate the practice of law. *See Ark Bar Ass'n v. Union Bank*, 224 Ark. 48, 54, 273 S.W.2d 408, 412 (1954). We are not bound by section 16-22-211 because section 16-22-211 violates the separation-of-powers doctrine. The law would be clarified if this court distances itself from any perceived reliance on section 16-22-211. The statute should be declared unconstitutional.

An attorney may not serve two masters. If an attorney is an employee of the insurance carrier responsible for paying the legal fees, costs, and any settlement or judgment of an insured in a lawsuit, then that attorney may not represent the insured in that lawsuit. The reason is simple. Such an attorney's loyalties are divided between the insured, who does not pay the attorney, and the insurance carrier employer, which does. This conflict is inherent in every case where a company lawyer attempts to represent the legal interests of his or her employer's clients or customers. The attorney-client relationship "cannot exist between an attorney employed by a corporation to practice law for it, and a client of the corporation, for he would be subject to the directions of the corporation and not to the directions of the client." *See Rhode Island Bar Ass'n v. Auto Servs. Ass'n*, 179 A. 139, 145 (R.I.1935). Further, an insurance carrier, for example, is a business and is naturally concerned with profits and retaining as much of the insurance premiums as possible, which translates in a lawsuit into a desire to pay as little in fees, costs, and judgments as possible. The insured's interests are not the same as the insurance company's, and those interests may vary greatly. For example, an insured may be concerned about the effect a settlement may have on his or her business reputation, and may wish to proceed to trial, whereas an insurance carrier may determine it is in its best interest to settle the case and cut the costs.

In *Arkansas Bar Ass'n v. Block*, 230 Ark. 430, 435, 434 S.W.2d 912, 914 (1959) (modified by *Creekmore v. Izard*, 236 Ark. 558, 565, 367 S.W.2d 419, 423 (1963) (*Block* modified to provide that a real estate broker may be permitted to fill in blanks in simple standardized real estate forms)), this court stated that a corporation may not practice law, which would be the case if its attorneys were representing the corporation's clients in legal matters. According to the analysis in *Block*, "[a]rtificial creations," such as corporations cannot provide the confidential and undivided allegiance due a client by an attorney. Id., 434 S.W.2d at 915.

> The relation of an attorney to his client is pre-eminently confidential. It demands on the part of the attorney undivided allegiance, a conspicuous degree of faithfulness and disinterestedness, absolute integrity and utter renunciation of every personal advantage conflicting in any way directly or indirectly with the interest of his client.

Id. at 435, 434 S.W.2d at 915 (quoting *State Bar Ass'n of Connecticut v. Connecticut Bank & Trust Co.*, 140 A.2d 863, 870 (Conn.1958)). If an attorney is called on to represent the clients of his or her employer, a conflict of interest arises between the duty owed by the attorney to his or her employer and the duty that attorney owes to the client. The conflict is not resolved by consent of the client because the attorney in that setting cannot provide the required undivided allegiance to his or her employer's clients. Based on our precedent and our authority to regulate the practice of law, I believe that the circuit court correctly disqualified Brown.

Why do you suppose the dissent's opinion did not carry the day?

Notes

1. Why can't corporations practice law? Professor Giesel argues that the rationale for this rule is illogical and based on outdated reasoning regarding corporations:

The case law generally abides by the following reasoning. First, courts note that only those with a license may practice law. Second, the courts note that a corporation can never be licensed to practice law because it cannot attain the educational and character requirements necessary for a license. Thus, a corporation cannot practice law.... The courts then state that even if the employee of the corporation rendering the legal service is a licensed attorney, that attorney-employee is an agent of the corporation such that the corporation is practicing law. The corporation is not given the benefit of the employee's license, however, so the corporation is practicing law without a license, and the attorney-employee is aiding the unauthorized practice of law.

Grace M. Giesel, *Corporations Practicing Law Through Lawyers: Why the Unauthorized Practice of Law Doctrine Should Not Apply,* 65 Mo. L. Rev. 151, 174-75 (2000) (citations omitted). Do you agree with her conclusion that this reasoning is "bothersome at best"?

2. Why is it more problematic for the insurance company to employ its own staff attorney to defend insureds than for the company to hire outside attorneys? Do you agree with the Kentucky Supreme Court in *American Insurance Ass'n v. Kentucky Bar Ass'n,* 917 S.W.2d 568, 571 (Ky. 1996) that permitting insurance staff attorneys to represent insureds is based on a "Pollyanna postulate that house counsel will continue to provide undivided loyalty to the insured"? Or do you find more persuasive the opinion of the New Jersey Supreme Court in *In re Weiss, Healey & Rea,* 536 A.2d 266, 269 (N.J. 1988) that "These are not second class lawyers; these are first class lawyers who are delivering legal services in an evolving format"?

3. What are the values at stake in the choice to permit insurance company attorneys to represent insureds?

4. Insurance companies often have "billing guidelines" that they use when hiring counsel to represent insureds. These litigation controls may limit hiring experts, conducting certain investigations, taking depositions, using computerized research (such as Lexis or Westlaw), or employing multiple attorneys. If an attorney determines that these controls are materially limiting the representation of the client, she must notify the insurance company and either secure their consent to removing the limitations or prepare to withdraw.

5. So common are the issues involved when attorneys are hired by insurance companies that some states have begun to provide more detailed regulation of this issue in their rules. For example, the Rule 1.8 of the Ohio Rules of Professional Conduct provides the following additional provisions to govern this issue:

Ohio Rules of Professional Conduct

Rule 1.8 (f) A lawyer shall not accept compensation for representing a client from someone other than the client unless divisions (f)(1) to (3) and, if applicable, division (f)(4) apply:

(1) the client gives *informed consent*;

(2) there is no interference with the lawyer's independence of professional judgment or with the client-lawyer relationship;

(3) information relating to representation of a client is protected as required by Rule 1.6;

(4) if the lawyer is compensated by an insurer to represent an insured, the lawyer delivers a copy of the following Statement of Insured Client's Rights to the client in person at the first meeting or by mail within ten days after the lawyer receives notice of retention by the insurer:

STATEMENT OF INSURED CLIENT'S RIGHTS

An insurance company has retained a lawyer to defend a lawsuit or claim against you. This Statement of Insured Client's Rights is being given to you to assure that you are aware of your rights regarding your legal representation.

1. Your Lawyer: Your lawyer has been retained by the insurance company under the terms of your policy. If you have questions about the selection of the lawyer, you should discuss the matter with the insurance company or the lawyer.

2. Directing the Lawyer: Your policy may provide that the insurance company can reasonably control the defense of the lawsuit. In addition, your insurance company may establish guidelines governing how lawyers are to proceed in defending you — guidelines that you are entitled to know. However, the lawyer cannot act on the insurance company's instructions when they are contrary to your interest.

3. Communications: Your lawyer should keep you informed about your case and respond to your reasonable requests for information.

4. Confidentiality: Lawyers have a duty to keep secret the confidential information a client provides, subject to limited exceptions. However, the lawyer chosen to represent you also may have duty to share with the insurance company information relating to the defense or settlement of the claim. Whenever a waiver of lawyer-client confidentiality is needed, your lawyer has a duty to consult with you and obtain your informed consent.

5. Release of Information for Audits: Some insurance companies retain auditing companies to review the billing and files of the lawyers they hire to represent policyholders. If the lawyer believes an audit, bill review, or other action initiated by the insurance company may release confidential information in a manner that may be contrary to your interest, the lawyer must advise you regarding the matter and provide an explanation of the purpose of the audit and the procedure involved. Your written consent must be given in order for an audit to be conducted. If you withhold your consent, the audit shall not be conducted.

6. Conflicts of Interest: The lawyer is responsible for identifying conflicts of interest and advising you of them. If at any time you have a concern about a conflict of interest in your case, you should discuss your concern with the lawyer. If a conflict of interest exists that cannot be resolved, the insurance company may be required to provide you with another lawyer.

7. Settlement: Many insurance policies state that the insurance company alone may make a decision regarding settlement of a claim. Some policies, however, require your consent. You should discuss with your lawyer your rights under the policy regarding settlement. No settlement requiring you to pay money in excess of your policy limits can be reached without your agreement.

8. Fees and Costs: As provided in your insurance policy, the insurance company usually pays all of the fees and costs of defending the claim. If you are responsible for paying the lawyer any fees and costs, your lawyer must promptly inform you of that.

9. Hiring your own Lawyer: The lawyer hired by the insurance company is only representing you in defending the claim brought against you. If you desire to pursue a claim against someone, you will need to hire your own lawyer. You may also wish to hire your own lawyer if there is a risk that there might be a judgment entered against you for more than the amount of your insurance. Your lawyer has a duty to inform you of this risk and other reasonably foreseeable adverse results.

Do you think this regulation helps to address some of the confusion involved in representation of insureds? Could you use portions of this statement to help inform clients of the scope of your representation even in states other than Ohio?

Researching Professional Responsibility 17-A: Research Problem

What is your state's approach to the question of the insurer's relationship to an attorney retained to defend an insured? Be sure to research both statutes and case law to answer this question. You may start with your own state's sources or you may wish to begin with a secondary source and see if your state's laws are discussed or cited. For example, the issue is addressed by THE RESTATEMENT (THIRD) OF THE LAW GOVERNING LAWYERS § 134 cmt. f (2000); Thomas Morgan, *Whose Lawyer Are You Anyway?*, 23 WM. MITCHELL L. REV. 11 (1997).

Test Your Understanding

As you can see from the three examples we have focused on in this chapter, determining whether someone is your client (or, even if not a client in a technical sense, is someone to whom you owe a duty of confidentiality and loyalty) is a difficult task. The prospective client, entity client, and third-party payor are but three of many difficult client identity issues. What do all of these problems have in common? Could you use the analysis from one of these problem types to analyze problems of client identity in another context?

Suppose you have been hired by your state's child support enforcement agency. As an attorney in the agency, you are required by federal law to provide paternity establishment and child support services to individuals who seek your services. The most common circumstance in which people would seek your services is because they are receiving government benefits for their children (such as food stamps or cash assistance) and are therefore required to cooperate in establishing child support and to assign their child support benefits to the state. A portion of any child support you collect in these cases will be paid to the state, but some goes directly to the recipient parent. You also are required to represent parents who are paying child support and wish to have that child support modified. The legislature in your state has passed a law providing that attorneys paid by the state do not represent the clients on whose behalf they are appearing in court, but are rather representing the state in delivering legal services to those recipients.

One year ago, you represented a mother in establishing paternity and collecting child support from the father of her child. You obtained a broad range of confidential information from her to facilitate this representation. Now the father seeks to have that support order modified to reflect his reduced income. May you represent father?

To Learn More

Different client identity problems arise in different areas of practice, though few areas of practice escape the problem. To read summaries other client identity/conflict situations, see the following topics in Frievogel on Conflicts (http://www.freivogeloncon-flicts.com/): Banks/Trust Departments; Class Actions; Client Mergers/Asset Sales; Corporate Families; Derivative Actions; Expert Witness; Government Entities; Initial Interview; Insurance Defense; Partnerships; and Trade Associations.

Chapter Eighteen

Conflicts Among Current Clients

Learning Objectives

After you have read this chapter and completed the assignments:

- You should be able to identify the limits of client consent to conflicts and draft enforceable consents.

- In evaluating a particular proposed representation or relationship, you should be able to determine whether the interests of two clients are adverse and if the interests of one client would materially limit your representation of another client and draft an agreement where appropriate.

- You should be able to describe your own personal conception of loyalty.

Rules to Study

The primary rules we will examine in this chapter are Rules 1.7 and portions of Rule 1.13. We will also examine the relationship between these rules and judicial disqualification orders.

Preliminary Problem

How would you resolve this inquiry brought to a state ethics committee?

Company hires Attorney to help its employees with immigration matters. In a particular matter, the attorney filed an immigration visa petition on behalf of the company, as well as an immigration visa application on behalf of the worker. At the same time, the attorney filed a temporary employment authorization request on behalf of the worker. The government issued a temporary employment authorization that on its face is still in effect. However, the government denied the visa application because the worker did not meet certain conditions, and it notified the worker and the attorney — but not the employer — that the worker's temporary authorization was being revoked.

The worker does not have any viable visa options and needs to leave the United States or face serious immigration consequences. Although Attorney told the worker to inform Company about the revocation, the worker has not done so and has asked the attorney not to do so. The employer does not know that the worker's employment authorization has been revoked, and is under the impression that it is authorized to continue the worker's employment until the employment authorization expires in a year. Attorney believes that because the employer badly needs foreign workers to help run its business, the employer would prefer to remain ignorant of the revocation.

What must Attorney do? If Attorney had not secured each client's waiver of confidentiality ahead of time, which duty trumps: the duty of confidentiality to the worker or the duty of communication to Company?

Compare your analysis to that in Massachusetts Bar Ass'n Comm. on Professional Ethics, Op. 09-03 (Jan. 15, 2009), available at http://www.massbar.org/publications/ethics-opinions/2000-2009/2009/opinion-09-03.

18.1 An Overview of Concurrent Conflicts

Perhaps no other aspect of the rules depends upon practice setting more than the analysis of conflicts between current clients. For example, an attorney should think very carefully before agreeing to jointly represent criminal co-defendants. Representation of co-parties in civil litigation is more common, though the risks vary considerably. Representing the driver and passenger as co-plaintiffs in an automobile accident generally will be more difficult than representing a doctor and a hospital as co-defendants in a malpractice action. Representation of multiple clients is even more common in transactional settings, though here too, one can find areas in which this joint representation is more common than others. Compare for example the issues that are posed by joint representation of persons seeking to form a business together to the joint representation of a couple in drafting a prenuptial agreement. To complicate matters further, the communities in which one practices will influence how these potential conflicts are evaluated. As a practical matter, solo attorneys in smaller communities and rural practice face different challenges in applying the conflicts rules than do attorneys practicing in large corporate law firms in metropolitan areas.

In understanding the conflicts of interest rules as they apply to current clients in these many different settings, the comments to Rule 1.7 are very helpful, giving numerous examples of concurrent conflicts and indicating the likelihood that these conflicts would be ones a client could waive. The comments describe the purpose for the rules and refer to other law where relevant to understanding the rule. Excerpts from the Tennessee Supreme Court's adoption of the comments to Rule 1.7 are quoted in this chapter.

This chapter will examine the situations in which current clients can present a conflict of interest. First we will examine the notion of "adversity"—those clients whose interests diverge in such a way that an attorney cannot competently represent or cannot preserve the confidences of one or the other. Perhaps the most obvious example of adverse representations are those situations in which an attorney is representing a client in one matter while at the same time, the attorney or a member of his firm is suing that same client in another matter. We will consider the limits of waiver as a solution to these conflicts.

A second category of concurrent conflicts arises when an attorney represents two parties at the same time in a litigation setting. While the parties may not be directly adverse because they are on the same side of the courtroom, the attorney's representation of one may materially limit the representation of the other. The attorney may simply be representing common clients: for example, an attorney may represent several different employers in very similar types of cases. Or the attorney may be representing joint clients — co-plaintiffs or co-defendants in the same litigation. The distinction is critical because, as you will recall from Chapter Ten, there is no attorney-client privilege among clients in a joint representation.

A third category of concurrent conflicts are those that arise in transactional settings. Here the situations in which an attorney's representation of one client might materially limit the representation of another are more subtle and a representation that may begin with clients whose interests align perfectly may become one of direct adversity. Planning for potential future conflicts is a critical part of any joint representation, but is especially important in transactional practice.

Before we begin to examine each of these problems of concurrent conflicts, take a moment to recall what you learned about the policies underlying conflicts of interest law. In concurrent conflicts of interest, loyalty plays a very important role. Even if confidentiality is not at risk, an attorney should consider carefully whether a concurrent representation would be viewed as a betrayal. It is easy to keep this in mind if you have a client who is a source of substantial business for you. These powerful clients can impose their own restraints by requiring you to avoid clients or cases even if the rules would not necessarily prohibit those representations. Even those clients for whom your representation is limited or free can be the source of a conflict, however.

Confidentiality is also a key consideration in concurrent conflicts, especially in securing client consent to conflicts. Sometimes, obtaining that consent requires disclosing confidential information. Securing the consent to disclose that information in order to obtain consent to the conflict can be tricky. In other circumstances, the conflict is not present but only potential. Perhaps the worst conflict in which to find yourself is a situation in which you owe one client a duty to communicate information that you obtained from another client in confidence. To avoid this dilemma, in any joint representation, clients should agree that any information one shares with the attorney may be communicated to the other clients.

18.2 Representing Opposing Parties

When are clients directly adverse? Obviously if you are asked to represent opposing parties in the same litigation, the parties are directly adverse. Rule 1.7 prohibits this representation even if different lawyers from the same firm work on the opposite sides and even if the parties request this representation. Clients cannot waive the conflict. In most states, for example, an attorney may not represent both a husband and wife in a divorce. The same rule applies when one attorney in a firm represents a defendant in a civil case arising out of an assault and another attorney in the firm works as a part-time prosecutor in the office prosecuting the defendant for criminal assault arising out of the same incident.

Clients can be directly adverse in less obvious ways, however. Suppose you represent Imogene Injured in a small auto accident case. You have just received the opponent's answer to your demand letter and it looks as though you may be able to settle the matter on terms quite favorable to Imogene. Suppose further that a local bank approaches you and asks you to represent them in some debt collection work. This could be a very lucrative opportunity for you, with the possibility of steady work from the bank. When you get the list of the debtors, however, you notice Imogene's name on one of the files.

Could you bring a collection action against Imogene at the same time that you are representing her in the tort action? If so, how would you go about getting informed consent from each client? Note that the analysis in this case does not differ if, rather than you being asked to represent the bank, another attorney in your firm has been approached to take on the bank's work.

As you read the following case, think about the policies the court is emphasizing in its conflicts analysis. Consider the approach these attorneys took to this problem.

In re Dresser Industries, Inc.

972 F.2d 540 (5th Cir. 1992)

In this petition for a writ of mandamus, we determine whether a law firm may sue its own client, which it concurrently represents in other matters. In a word, no; and most certainly not here, where the motivation appears only to be the law firm's self-interest.[1] We therefore grant the writ, directing the district judge to disqualify counsel.

The material facts are undisputed. This petition arises from a consolidated class action antitrust suit brought against manufacturers of oil well drill bits. *Red Eagle Resources et al. v. Baker Hughes* ("Drill Bits").

Dresser Industries, Inc., ("Dresser") is now a defendant in Drill Bits, charged — by its own lawyers — with conspiring to fix the prices of drill bits and with fraudulently concealing its conduct. Stephen D. Susman, with his firm, Susman Godfrey, is lead counsel for the plaintiff's committee. As lead counsel, Susman signed the amended complaint that levied these charges against Dresser, his firm's own client.

What is a plaintiff's committee? Does this arrangement present conflicts issues as well?

Susman Godfrey concurrently represents Dresser in two pending lawsuits. *CPS International, Inc. v. Dresser Industries, Inc.*, No. H-85-653 (S.D.Tex.) ("CPS"), is the third suit brought by CPS International, a company that claims Dresser forced it out of the compressor market in Saudi Arabia. CPS International initially sued Dresser for antitrust violations and tortious interference with a contract. The antitrust claim has been dismissed, but the tort claim is scheduled for trial. Susman Godfrey has represented Dresser throughout these actions, which commenced in 1985. During its defense of Dresser, Susman Godfrey lawyers have had relatively unfettered access to data concerning Dresser's management, organization, finances, and accounting practices. Susman Godfrey's lawyers have engaged in privileged

---

1. "Drill Bits was going to be a case that was going to be active, big, protracted, the first price fixing case that's come along in Houston in a long time. I had made somewhat of a reputation in that area, and I guess it's kind of painful not to be able to play in the game anymore, ..." Deposition of Stephen D. Susman.

communications with Dresser's in-house counsel and officers in choosing antitrust defenses and other litigation strategies. Susman Godfrey has also, since 1990, represented Dresser in Cullen Center, Inc., et al. v. W.R. Gray Co., et al., a case involving asbestos in a Dresser building, which is now set for trial in Texas state court.*

On October 24 and November 24, 1991, Susman Godfrey lawyers wrote Dresser informing it that Stephen Susman chaired the plaintiffs' committee in Drill Bits, that Dresser might be made a Drill Bits defendant, and that, if Dresser replaced Susman Godfrey, the firm would assist in the transition to new counsel. Dresser chose not to dismiss Susman Godfrey in CPS and Cullen Center.

Dresser was joined as a defendant in Drill Bits on December 2, 1991. Dresser moved to disqualify Susman as plaintiffs' counsel on December 13. Both Dresser and Susman Godfrey submitted affidavits and depositions to the district court, which, after a hearing, issued a detailed opinion denying the motion.

[The District Court, in ruling on the motion, looked to the Texas Disciplinary Rules.]

The district court described the Drill Bits complaint as a civil antitrust case, thus somewhat softening Dresser's description of it as an action for fraud or criminal conduct. The court held, "as a matter of law, that there exists no relationship, legal or factual, between the Cullen Center case and the Drill Bits litigation," and that no similarity between Drill Bits and the CPS suits was material. The court concluded that "Godfrey's representation of the plaintiffs in the Drill Bits litigation does not reasonably appear to be or become adversely limited by Susman Godfrey's responsibilities to Dresser in the CPS and Cullen Center cases," and accordingly denied the motion to disqualify....

[The court determined that mandamus was appropriate to review the denial of a motion to disqualify counsel where the "petitioner can show its right to the writ is clear and undisputable." It then focused on what rules it should apply in determining whether disqualification was required. It concluded that it must "consider the motion governed by the ethical rules announced by the national profession in the light of the public interest and the litigants' rights." It then continued:]

Our most far-reaching application of the national standards of attorney conduct to an attorney's obligation to avoid conflicts of interest is *Woods v. Covington County Bank,* 537 F.2d 804, 810 (5th Cir. 1976). We held in *Woods* that standards such as the ABA canons are useful guides but are not controlling in adjudicating such motions. The considerations we relied upon in *Woods* were whether a conflict has (1) the appearance of impropriety in general, or (2) a possibility that a specific impropriety will occur, and (3) the likelihood of

> Why do you think Dresser didn't dismiss Susman right away?

> Compare these 1976 standards to the standards for a conflict today

---

* [It is very helpful in conflicts analysis to chart the relationships among the attorneys and clients. So, for example, the suits and attorneys here are:

CPS v. **Dresser (Susman)**
Cullen Center/**Dresser (Susman)** v. Gray
Red Eagle **(Susman)** v. **Dresser**/Drill Bits.]

public suspicion from the impropriety outweighs any social interests which will be served by the lawyer's continued participation in the case....

In *Woods* [and subsequent cases], we applied national norms of attorney conduct to a conflict arising after the attorney's prior representation had been concluded. Now, however, we are confronted with our first case arising out of concurrent representation, in which the attorney sues a client whom he represents on another pending matter. We thus consider the problem of concurrent representation under our framework in *Woods* as tailored to apply to the facts arising from concurrent representation.

[margin: new issue]

We turn, then, to the current national standards of legal ethics to first consider whether this dual representation amounts to impropriety. Neither the ABA Model Rules of Professional Conduct [1.7] nor the Code of Professional Responsibility allows an attorney to bring a suit against a client without its consent. This position is also taken by the American Law Institute in its drafts of the Restatement of the Law Governing Lawyers. Unquestionably, the national standards of attorney conduct forbid a lawyer from bringing a suit against a current client without the consent of both clients. Susman's conduct violates all of these standards—unless excused or justified under exceptional circumstances not present here.

[margin: Why national standards? This case actually arose out of Texas, where the state rules on concurrent conflicts are unique — permitting representations many other states would prohibit.]

Exceptional circumstances may sometimes mean that what is ordinarily a clear impropriety will not, always and inevitably, determine a conflicts case. Within the framework we announced in *Woods*, Susman, for example, might have been able to continue his dual representation if he could have shown some social interest to be served by his representation that would outweigh the public perception of his impropriety.[4] Susman, however, can present no such reason. There is no suggestion that other lawyers could not ably perform his offices for the plaintiffs, nor is there any basis for a suggestion of any societal or professional interest to be served. This fact suggests a rule of thumb for use in future motions for disqualification based on concurrent representation: However a lawyer's motives may be clothed, if the sole reason for suing his own client is the lawyer's self-interest, disqualification should be granted.[5]

[margin: Several Reasons could have allowed continued representation]

---

4. [The Texas rule would allow some concurrent adverse representation, for example where] necessary either to prevent a large company, such as Dresser, from monopolizing the lawyers of an area or to assure that certain classes of unpopular clients receive representation. Although we do not now reach the matter, our consideration of social benefit to offset the appearance of impropriety might allow such a representation if the balance clearly and unequivocally favored allowing such representation to further the ends of justice. We believe, moreover, that the Texas rules are drawn to allow concurrent representation as the exception and not the rule. Even if the Texas rules had applied, no special circumstances being present here, Texas rule 1.06's prohibition of representation of potentially adverse interests would have barred the representation.

5. This result accords with the approach of other circuits, which have similarly found concurrent representation to be grossly disfavored. *See, e.g., International Business Machines Corp. v. Levin*, 579 F.2d 271 (3d Cir.1978) (antitrust plaintiff firm disqualified from suing company for which it was on retainer); *Cinema 5, Ltd. v. Cinerama, Inc.*, 528 F.2d 1384 (2d Cir.1976) (antitrust plaintiff counsel's representation while firm was counsel in an unrelated antitrust case was prima facie improper); *EEOC v. Orson H. Gygi Co., Inc.*, 749 F.2d 620 (10th Cir.1984) (attorney disqualified from defending employer in sex discrimination suit by employee represented in state annulment proceeding).

V

We find, therefore, that Dresser's right to the grant of its motion to disqualify counsel is clear and indisputable. We further find that the district court clearly and indisputably abused its discretion in failing to grant the motion. We have thus granted the petition and have issued the writ of mandamus, directing the [District Court] to enter an order disqualifying Stephen D. Susman and Susman Godfrey from continuing as counsel to the plaintiffs in Red Eagle Resources et al. v. Baker Hughes.

Notes

1. Many courts in disqualification cases do not feel constrained by the rules of professional conduct. Courts increasingly are permitting representations that the rules would appear to prohibit and prohibiting others that would appear permissible under the rules. Accordingly, while the *Dresser* case appears to adopt a strict rule prohibiting attorneys from representing directly adverse clients, more recently some courts have begun to take a less strict approach, particularly when the conflict involves very large firms and sophisticated clients. Consider the opinion of Judge Pisano in a recent case in which two large pharmaceutical companies were suing one another.

Wyeth v. Abbott Laboratories
2010 U.S. Dist. LEXIS 11032 (D. N.J. 2010)

[In this case, Wyeth sued Boston Scientific Corp. and Abbott Laboratories in the United States District Court for the District of New Jersey for patent infringement. Boston Scientific hired the Howrey law firm to represent them in the case. Wyeth moved to disqualify Howrey because the firm was also representing a Wyeth entity in Europe in a patent opposition against another company in the European Patent Office. The magistrate judge granted the disqualification motion and the district court reversed.]

The Court of Appeals for the Third Circuit has noted that "[a]lthough disqualification ordinarily is the result of a finding that a disciplinary rule prohibits an attorney's appearance in a case, disqualification never is automatic." *U.S. v. Miller*, 624 F.2d 1198, 1201 (3d Cir. 1980). The question of whether disqualification is appropriate is committed to the sound discretion of the district court, which "means that the court should disqualify an attorney only when it determines, on the facts of the particular case, that disqualification is an appropriate means of enforcing the applicable disciplinary rule." *Id.* Indeed, as other courts in this district have stated, "[m]otions to disqualify are viewed with 'disfavor' and disqualification is considered a 'drastic measure which courts should hesitate to impose except when absolutely necessary.'" *Carlyle Towers Condo. Ass'n v. Crossman Sav.*, 944 F.Supp. 341, 345 (D.N.J. 1996).

"Disqualification questions are intensely fact-specific, and it is essential to approach such problems with a keen sense of practicality as well as a precise picture of the underlying facts." *Carlyle Towers*, 944 F.

Policy reasons to consider before disqualifying Counsel

Supp. at 345. "Because disqualification during pending litigation is an extreme measure, courts must closely scrutinize the facts of each case to avoid injustice." *In re Cendant Corp. Securities Litigation*, 124 F. Supp 2d 235, 249 (D.N.J. 2000). In ruling on such a motion, courts should "consider the ends that the disciplinary rule is designed to serve and any countervailing policies, such as permitting a litigant to retain the counsel of his choice and enabling attorneys to practice without excessive restrictions." *U.S. v. Miller*, 624 F.2d 1198, 1201 (3d Cir. 1980). Notably, "ethical rules should not be blindly applied without consideration of the relative hardships." *Carlyle Towers*, 944 F. Supp. at 345.

modern factors to consider

Although some courts have advocated a mandatory disqualification rule, *see Manoir-Electroalloys Corp. v. Amalloy Corp*, 711 F. Supp. 188, 195 (D.N.J. 1989) (disqualification should be mandatory for violation of RPC 1.7), a more modern approach is for courts, when faced with a conflict problem, to carefully examine the totality of the circumstances, taking a balanced approach that includes evaluating the impact, nature and degree of a conflict, see, e.g., *Elonex I.P. Holdings, Ltd. v. Apple Computer*, 142 F. Supp. 2d 579, 583-584 (D. Del. 2001) (balancing factors to find disqualification unwarranted); *University of Rochester v. G.D. Searle & Co., Inc.*, 2000 U.S. Dist. LEXIS 19030, 2000 WL 1922271 (W.D.N.Y. Dec. 11, 2000) (requiring moving party to "come forward with facts tending to show that [the concurrent representation] has tainted the trial by affecting counsel's presentation of the case, by placing counsel in a position to use privileged information, or by otherwise allowing counsel to gain an unfair advantage"). Modern litigation, like the instant patent case, often involves multinational companies and multinational law firms among whom conflicts occasionally arise due to the broad reach of their respective businesses. Further, patent cases are more likely to involve intensely complex, specialized issues that require experienced, knowledgeable counsel, and mandatory disqualification may work prejudice to a party by depriving it of its counsel of choice. As such, mandatory disqualification may serve to encourage the use of disqualification motions solely for tactical reasons — a use courts have repeatedly expressed concerns about. *See, e.g., In re Congoleum Corp.*, 426 F.3d 675, 686 (3d Cir. 2005) (noting the existence of "concerns about the tactical use of disqualification motions to harass opposing counsel.") (citing *Richardson-Merrell, Inc. v. Koller*, 472 U.S. 424, 436, 105 S.Ct. 2757, 86 L.Ed.2d 340 (1985)) (expressing the same concern and referring to this practice as a "dangerous game."). Moving away from a mandatory disqualification rule is in no way intended undermine the purposes of the Rules of Professional Conduct (and in this case RPC 1.7), but rather, it allows courts to fashion more equitable solutions to a conflict problem while still maintaining the high ethical standards of the profession.

technical field of patents requires some degree of rotating counsel of choice / adverse effect of mandatory disqualification

* * *

When presented with a motion to disqualify counsel, a court must strike a "delicate balance" between the competing considerations. On the one hand, the Court must examine the potential hardships that one party will experience if his lawyer is disqualified. On the other, the Court must weigh the potential hardships to the adversary if counsel is permitted to proceed. Further, while weighing these considerations, a Court must also be mindful of the ends served by the ethics rules and the need "to maintain the highest standards of the [legal] profession." *In re Cendant Corp. Securities Litigation*, 124 F. Supp. 2d at 249. Courts have an obligation to maintain these professional standards, "promot[e] public confidence in the integrity of the bar and the judicial system," *Manoir-Electroalloys Corp. v. Amalloy Corp*, 711 F. Supp. 188, 196 (D.N.J. 1989), and ensure that trial of every case be "free from taint," *Carlyle Towers*, 944 F. Supp. at 345. However, a court must "exercise extreme caution not to act under the misguided belief that disqualification raises the standard of legal ethics and the public's respect; the opposition effect is just as likely—encouragement of vexatious tactics, which increase public cynicism about the administration of justice." *Id.*

Factors that this Court should consider in determining whether disqualification is warranted include: (1) prejudice to Wyeth; (2) prejudice to BSC; (3) whether Howrey's representation of Wyeth in the Lonza matter has allowed BSC access to any confidential information relevant to this case; (4) the cost—in terms of both time and money—for BSC to retain new counsel; (5) the complexity of the issues in the case and the time it would take new counsel to acquaint themselves with the facts and issues; (6) which party, if either, was responsible for creating the conflict.

Apply these factors to the Dresser facts.

Also, with the goal of approaching the issue "with a keen sense of practicality," *id.*, the Court finds it relevant in this case to address the nature and degree of the actual conflict created by Howrey's concurrent representation. To this end, the Court finds the following additional factors to be relevant to the disqualification analysis: (a) whether the two matters at issue are related in substance; (b) whether both matters are presently active; (c) whether any attorneys from the firm have been involved in both matters; (d) whether the matters are each being handled from offices in different geographic locations; (e) whether the attorneys from the law firm work with different client representative for each matter; and (f) the relative time billed by the law firm to each matter.

Weighing all of the above considerations, the Court finds that the disqualification of Howrey is not warranted here. The interest protected by RPC 1.7 is that of loyalty, and while fully appreciating the duty of loyalty Howrey owes to Wyeth arising from the representation undertaken in the Lonza matter, the Court is hard-pressed to see how this duty will be compromised under the facts of this case.

2. Remember that, for purposes of disqualification (and discipline under Rule 1.7), courts treat an entire law firm as one unit. Rule 1.10. This prohibition may prevent representation where a lawyer in one office of a "mega-firm" on one coast represents a client, and another attorney in the same firm, a continent away on the other coast (who the first attorney has never even heard of or met), sues that client for something totally unrelated. Should this make a difference to applicability of the rule? Or is this merely a price the firm pays for the benefits of large-scale, multi-office practice?

3. Why can't the firm just withdraw from client #1 and turn the situation into a "former client, subsequent representation" case? When former clients are involved, no disqualification is required unless the matters are substantially related (as you will see in the next chapter). In *Dresser*, the client refused to discharge the attorney. Could the firm withdraw in any event? See Rule 1.16. Would this resolve the problem? Most courts say no. They are unwilling to "allow a law firm to drop a client 'like a hot potato' in order to shift resolution of the conflict question from Rule 1.7 to Rule 1.9." LAW. MAN. ON PROF. CONDUCT (ABA/BNA) Practice Manual § 51:213. The situation is different if the original client agrees to the firm's withdrawal. In such a situation, the concerns of "unceremoniously dumping" the client are not involved. *In re Sandahl*, 980 F.2d 1118, 1121 (7th Cir. 1992).

4. When are clients directly adverse in transactional matters? A common example is when you are asked to represent both the buyer and seller in a transaction. Real estate brokers have to grapple with this potential conflict regularly. Is this a conflict that can be cured by the informed consent of both parties? How would you go about obtaining that consent? What about representing two buyers in two different transactions that will result in the buyers being competitors? For example, suppose you have two clients, each of whom wants to open a fast food restaurant along a new highway expansion. May you represent them both? Recall that mere "economic adversity" does not constitute a conflict. What would be the harm in asking for the consent of each client even if the law would not consider these representations to present a conflict of interest?

5. An area that has caused some confusion is issue, or positional, conflict. Under what circumstances should an attorney be prohibited from advancing arguments for one client that potentially may be harmful to another client? Can an attorney take inconsistent positions in different courts, for different clients, at the same time? In the same court? If the rules are too strict in this regard, won't this substantially limit the lawyer's ability to practice, perhaps restricting lawyers to only one side of any given area of law? Won't this also limit client access to competent lawyers, especially in specialized areas?

Comment 24 to Tennessee Rule 1.7 provides this guidance on positional conflicts:

> Ordinarily a lawyer may take inconsistent legal positions in different tribunals at different times on behalf of different clients. The mere fact that advocating a legal position on behalf of one client might create precedent adverse to the interests of a client represented by the lawyer in an unrelated matter does not create a conflict of interest. A conflict of interest exists, however, if there is a significant risk that a lawyer's action on behalf of one client will materially limit the lawyer's effectiveness in representing another client in a different case, for example, when a decision favoring one client will create a precedent likely to seriously weaken the position taken on behalf of the other client. Factors relevant in determining whether the clients need to be advised of the risk include: where the cases are pending; whether the issue is substantive or procedural; the temporal relationship between the matters; the significance of the issue to the im-

mediate and long-term interests of the clients involved; and the clients' reasonable expectations in retaining the lawyer. If there is significant risk of material limitation, then, absent informed consent of the affected clients, the lawyer must refuse one of the representations or withdraw from one or both matters.

As a practical matter, why are positional conflicts fairly uncommon in most practices?

Reflective Practice: Loyalty to a Client

In her book *Tangled Loyalties*, Susan Shapiero describes the influence that clients have in shaping an attorney's choice of other clients. How you react to a client's suggestions regarding your other representations depends in part on your personal conception of loyalty to the client. What if a current client asks you to refrain from representing any other clients in the same business as the client? What if that client asks you to refrain from joining organizations with particular political or social agendas with which the client disagrees? Reflect on these questions and decide where your personal boundaries are within which your concept of loyalty operates.

18.3 Representing Co-Parties in Litigation

Much of a litigation attorney's practice will involve representation of many different clients in similar types of cases. For example, an employment attorney may have several clients who are bringing or defending discrimination actions and a tort attorney may represent many accident victims or manufacturers. Suppose, for example, you are an education law attorney and have developed a specialty in representing students and parents in their claims against schools and school districts. You may represent several parents in different actions against the same school, perhaps even involving the same type of issue—perhaps under special education or privacy laws for example. In these common representations, one client does not know about another client, even though their cases have some common legal issues. There is ordinarily no risk of conflict of interest in these common, but unconnected cases.

Sometimes, however, you may wish to represent two or more clients in the same case. This is joint representation and it may involve co-plaintiffs or co-defendants. Joint representation in litigation is not prohibited, but requires consent and a high degree of caution. Initially, if undertaking joint representation, it is necessary to insure that, although nominally aligned on the same side, the parties are not in fact adverse. If the representation is truly adverse, the prohibition against adverse representation applies.

If the parties appear to have similar interests, you may represent all the parties if they each consent and if you believe you can adequately serve all the clients' interests. Rule 1.7(a) and (b). Watch for signs of actual conflict that may appear later, however. You may be required to secure further consents or withdraw if these conflicts do arise. Additionally, lawyers must make clear to jointly represented clients the scope of confidentiality as between co-clients and the limits that joint representation entails.

Why would multiple parties desire the same attorney? Certainly there are advantages to sharing representation. One attorney may be less expensive and parties having a consistency of theory and evidence can strengthen their action. However, there are risks as well. Clients may be required to waive some claims or forego some theories in order to make the joint representation work well. Remember that joint clients do not have the protections of the attorney-client privilege among themselves. For attorneys, representation of co-clients constitutes a prime source of malpractice claims and a frequent source of discipline. Finally, if conflicts arise later that require withdrawal, the clients, the court, and the attorneys are all worse off than if the clients had begun with separate counsel or *pro se* representation. In what circumstances are the risks likely to outweigh the benefits? What precautions must be taken to avoid problems when representing multiple parties? Should attorneys avoid these representations altogether? Note that joint representation is frequently discouraged and many attorneys have strict policies against it.

Are there special problems or issues in some areas of practice? For example, what about representation of multiple co-defendants in a criminal case? Joint representation is not *per se* impermissible. However, there are so many potential conflicts of interest in criminal defense and the consequences so severe, the practice is discouraged. Strategic conflicts include the very common tactic of blame shifting in criminal defense. Often the most likely person to whom one criminal defendant can shift blame is another defendant. Evidence that works well for one defendant may not be as strong for the other. One client's testimony or credibility may undermine the credibility of the joint defense. One defendant may be willing to accept a plea agreement when the other does not.

Only when the defendants' interests are truly the same and they stand more to gain from a united front than either does individually alone might joint representation be permissible. Both courts and prosecutors will police these joint representations carefully. Most Public Defender offices will not engage in joint representation of multiple co-defendants. In order to fully protect a defendant's Sixth Amendment right to counsel, an attorney representing joint defendants should notify the court immediately when a real conflict becomes apparent. If a defense attorney objects to being appointed to a joint representation, and the court orders that the attorney must continue, the conviction is readily overturned. *Holloway v. Arkansas*, 435 U.S. 475 (1978). Even if no one objects to a joint representation, if later a conviction is challenged on the basis of ineffective assistance of counsel, the convicted individual need only show that the joint representation significantly affected the representation, rather than the more difficult *Strickland* standard of actual prejudice. *Cuyler v. Sullivan*, 466 U.S. 920 (1980).

In civil litigation, joint representation is more common. However, the risks are still substantial. If you are representing co-defendants in a civil action, there are similar concerns as one finds in criminal defense. The differences, however, permit joint representation more often. For example, because the most common outcome of civil litigation is damages, co-defendants can agree ahead of time to how they might share any potential liability or their interests in settlement. With adequate information to permit informed consent, cross-claims between parties in civil actions can be waived from the beginning of representation. With any joint representation, whether of co-plaintiffs or co-defendants, you must take great care that the parties have a commonality of objectives and roughly equal power lest you find yourself representing one party at the expense of another. A joint defense or joint representation agreement must be airtight: with informed consent regarding alternatives to the joint representation, the effect on privilege, and a clear agreement that information will be freely shared among all co-clients. The agreement should spell out what would happen in the case of a conflict. Finally, while the rules only require consents to conflicts to be "confirmed in writing" the wise attorney has joint representation agreements in writing signed by the client.

Some co-representations simply are not ones to which clients can consent. Family law attorneys often have requests for joint representation. Married couples sometimes will ask one lawyer to represent both of them in "their" divorce. Joint representation is appealing to a couple in a relatively amicable divorce, as it substantially reduces the costs and may reduce the animosity that might otherwise develop in an adversarial setting. However, Rule 1.7(b)(3) prohibits representation in which the representation involves "the assertion of a claim by one client against another client represented by the lawyer in the same litigation or other proceeding before a tribunal." This rule would appear to prohibit joint representation of spouses in a divorce, because no matter how amicable or settled the issues are, the divorce is still an adversary proceeding. *See, e.g., Holmes v. Holmes*, 248 N.E.2d 564, 570-71 (Ind. App. 1969) (joint representation of husband and wife impermissible in both negotiating agreements and in representing parties before the court); *Lawyer Disciplinary Bd. v. Frame*, 479 S.E. 2d 676 (W. Va. 1996) (attorney reprimanded for representing husband in divorce and also preparing answer for unrepresented wife to sign). The American Academy of Matrimonial Lawyers also suggests that this dual representation is never appropriate. *See* AAML BOUNDS OF ADVOCACY, Goal 3.1 (2000). An attorney who represents a husband and wife in a situation of conflict may not only be subject to discipline but may face subsequent liability to one of the clients as well. In *Vinson v. Vinson*, 588 S.E.2d 392 (Va. Ct. App. 2003), the trial court found that an attorney's retainer agreement in which the attorney identified both husband and wife as his clients in a divorce "on its face" was a "gross conflict of interest." The appellate court affirmed the court's finding of liability in the husband's suit against the attorney.

In a few states, courts permit an attorney to represent husband and wife in uncontested divorces where there is no disagreement regarding the terms of the divorce. California case law, for example, permits attorneys to act as "scriveners"—drafting divorce settlements but giving no advice and resolving no disputes between the parties. *Klemm v. Superior Court*, 142 Cal. Rptr. 509 (Cal. Ct. App. 1979) (court held that the same counsel may represent both husband and wife in an uncontested dissolution proceeding if the conflict of interest is potential, not actual, and the parties give an informed, intelligent consent in writing after full disclosure). *See also, In re Eltzroth*, 679 P.2d 1369 (Or. Ct. App.1984) (lawyer may represent both parties in amicable divorce, but when property settlement they reach is obviously inequitable and based on inaccurate information, lawyer must withdraw from representing either of them and advise clients to retain separate lawyers). However, even in these states, attorneys who choose to represent both husband and wife are presenting themselves and their clients with considerable risk. *See, e.g., In re Gamino*, 753 N.W.2d 521 (Wisc. 2008) (Attorney suspended for two years for dual representation of husband and wife in acting as "scrivener" for divorce and property settlement without informed consent and then appearing in court on behalf of husband only). In terms of any settlement reached, "the validity of any agreement negotiated without independent representation of each of the parties is vulnerable to easy attack as having been procured by misrepresentation, fraud, and overreaching." *Klem,* 142 Cal. Rptr. at 514.

Another special circumstance of joint representation is the class action. Attorneys representing a class need only report to and take direction from the named class representative. The rules for class certification mediate some of the conflicts issues—because they insure commonality and representativeness. To evaluate whether a conflict exists when disagreement arises among co-clients who are generally aligned on one side of complex or multiparty litigation, the Restatement suggests evaluating whether issues common to the clients' interests predominate, whether circumstances such as the size of each client's interest make separate representation impracticable, and the extent of active judicial supervision of the representation.

In litigation settings in which an attorney represents multiple parties, special rules govern the settlement of multiple claims. Where aggregate settlements are involved, each client must consent after consultation that must include disclosure of the existence and nature of all claims involved and the participation of each person in the settlement. Re-read Tennessee Rule 1.8(g) in Chpater 16.1. Failure to obtain proper consent may be grounds to void a settlement. *Hayes v. Eagle-Pilcher Indust., Inc.*, 513 F.2d 892 (10th Cir. 1975).

18.4 Representing Multiple Parties in Transactions

In non-adversarial settings, such as estates or business planning, multiple clients often request simultaneous representation. For example, what if a couple asks you to draft wills for them? The American College of Trusts and Estate Counsel (ACTEC) Commentaries argues that: "In some instances the clients may actually be better served by such a representation, which can result in more economical and better coordinated estate plans prepared by counsel who has a better overall understanding of all of the relevant family and property considerations." American College of Trusts and Estate Counsel, Commentaries on the Model Rules of Professional Conduct, Third Edition: *Commentary to Rule 1.7* (1999). However, these economies can be at the cost of significant conflict if those risks are not addressed early in the representation.

If you do decide to represent more than one family member at the same time, you must make sure that the clients understand whether this will be a separate or a joint representation. In a separate representation, even though you are representing the family members at the same time, each representation is separate, and neither client will have a right to receive information about the other client's matter. In a joint or common representation, you are representing the family members on the same matter. In joint representations, the clients waive the attorney-client privilege among themselves. They should understand and consent to freely share information among themselves.

Thus, in representing husband and wife in drafting their wills, you may determine that a joint representation is more appropriate; whereas if you are drafting estate plans for two adult clients who happen to be parent and child and do not have shared assets or businesses, separate representation may be appropriate. As the National Academy of Elder Law Attorneys emphasizes, "The attorney should take reasonable steps to ensure that all the clients understand how different types of representation impose different duties on the attorney and different consequences for the clients. The more complex the situation, the more important a well-drafted engagement agreement becomes." Professionalism and Ethics Committee of the National Academy of Elder Law Attorneys, Aspirational Standards for The Practice of Elder Law With Commentaries 11 (2006). Available at http://www.naela.org/pdffiles/Aspirational-Standards.pdf. That engagement agreement should explain the benefits and risks of the multiple representation, the effects on confidentiality duties and privilege, and the risks that, should conflicts arise among the clients, you will be required to withdraw from the representation.

Failure to clarify the respective roles and obligations in a multiple representation can place you in a no-win ethical situation. For example, in *A v. B*, 726 A.2d 924 (N.J. 1999), a law firm had drafted wills for Husband and Wife, each naming the other as sole heir. Soon thereafter, the firm was retained by a woman to bring a paternity suit against Husband for the child he had fathered while married to Wife. Because of a clerical error in entering Husband's name in the firm's records, the firm did not recognize the conflict. When it was discovered, the firm withdrew from the paternity action and told Husband that he should reveal the existence of this child to Wife, as the child could inherit her property if she predeceased her husband. However, Husband refused.

Consider the position the firm was in at this point. On the one hand, what they had learned about the child was confidential information that could not be disclosed. On the other hand, without this information, Wife's estate plan was based on information that was incomplete at best and fraudulent at worst. Withdrawal couldn't cure the dilemma as the wills had already been drafted. The firm's agreement with this couple contained an express waiver of conflicts and an explanation that "information provided by one spouse could become available to the other" but did not contain an express waiver of confidentiality. *A v. B*, 726 A.2d at 925. How would you resolve this dilemma?

In this case, the firm told Husband that if he did not tell Wife about the child, they would. Husband obtained an injunction to prevent the firm from revealing the information. On appeal, the New Jersey Supreme Court concluded that the husband had "used the law firm's services to defraud his wife in the preparation of her estate" and permitted the disclosure. New Jersey's Rules of Professional Conduct allows attorneys to reveal information relating to the representation to rectify a fraud resulting in substantial financial harm to another if the lawyer's services were used to perpetrate that fraud. Not all states have such an exception, however. The court emphasized that the attorney could have avoided this dilemma in the first place: "an attorney, on commencing joint representation of co-clients, should agree explicitly with the clients on the sharing of confidential information.... Such a prior agreement will clarify the expectations of the clients and the lawyer and diminish the need for future litigation."

Professional Responsibility Skill 18-A: Agreements Concerning Joint Representation

In general you should consider that any waiver of conflicts must do the following:

- identify the nature of the conflict (or risk of conflict)
- identify the harms that could result from the conflict and the steps you have taken to reduce those risks
- identify the reasons the client wants to waive the conflict (the benefits of the representation)
- advise the client that he can seek other representation
- expressly waive the conflict
- identify any circumstances in which you would seek to withdraw even given the client's consent
- address any confidentiality waivers that might be a part of this consent to conflict

You try it. Suppose that you represent General Widgets in its employment matters. The CFO Frank Lee has been accused of sexually harassing a finance manager. General Widgets is sued for sexual harassment, negligent supervision, and retaliation. The CFO is sued for battery, intentional infliction of emotional distress, and false imprisonment. You are confident the CFO is telling you the truth when he says that he did nothing to harass the employee. General Widgets's board has agreed that you can represent both the company and the CFO. Edit the following letter:

Dear Frank Lee and General Widgets General Counsel:

Our law firm will be representing both General Widgets and Frank Lee in the action by Elma Employee for sexual harassment. We have discussed the potential for a conflict of interest to arise between you. Neither you nor we have as yet detected a basis for a conflict. You both wish this firm to represent General Widgets and Mr. Lee in order to present a united front and keep expenses down. General Widgets will pay all legal fees and expenses. We do not believe that will in any way compromise our ability to represent Mr. Lee fairly and effectively.

[handwritten margin note: Lee must give informed consent]

During this joint representation we will share with both of you all information that we gather from either of you and from third parties. If we learn something from one of you that we think the other needs to know, we will disclose the information to the other. If we discover evidence that Mr. Lee did engage in the acts complained of, we would have a conflict of interest.

If a conflict does develop, this law firm will have the right to terminate its representation of Mr. Lee and continue on behalf of General Widgets. We will have the right to take positions adverse to Mr. Lee and use information that we obtained from Mr. Lee during our representation of him. There may be circumstances in which this would not be appropriate, and a court might not permit it.

This is further to confirm that we have urged Mr. Lee to retain other counsel to review this letter and the arrangement proposed above.

Sincerely,
Barbara Glesner Fines

For other examples of letters consenting to conflicts, see Frievogal on Conflicts at http://www.freivogelonconflicts.com/ (click on consents/waivers).

Test Your Understanding

After graduating from law school, you became licensed to practice law in your state and spent two years working as an attorney in a small real estate law firm focusing on real estate closings, land use, and environmental issues. The firm only had four attorneys including you and you learned a great deal. Nevertheless, you leave to start your own firm. In your second week in your own solo practice, your best friend from childhood Pandora Plaintiff seeks your advice.

First, she wants your advice about possible dissolution of her partnership with Denny and her winding up of the business (a restaurant). Denny agrees with her that it's time for them to dissolve the business and would like you to represent him in this matter as well. The partnership is an at-will partnership, which gives both partners the legal right to dissolve and wind up the business. There is no buy-sell or continuation agreement between them. What Denny doesn't know is that Pandora wants to use the proceeds of the partnership break-up to purchase some partnership assets and open up a different restaurant.

Question One: May you represent both Pandora and Denny? What additional information do you need to decide this question?

After the dissolution of the partnership, Pandora tells you that she's decided she's had it with the restaurant business after all. Instead, she's decided she wants to open an event planning business. She brings her friend Newton to your office. Pandora and Newton would like you to assist them in forming their new event planning business. They have already worked out most of the terms of their arrangement and have written a memorandum of understanding detailing their agreements. You look it over and it looks like a reasonable arrangement. They want to you form a partnership for them and then continue as the attorney for the business on an ongoing basis.

Question Two: May you help Pandora and Newton form their business entity and agree to represent the resulting business? What additional facts would you need to decide whether to accept this representation?

Pandora next comes to you about her parents. Her parents are in an assisted living facility and are physically extremely feeble but mentally appear to be aware and competent. Pandora tells you that they have signed a document that she prepared for them indicating that she can handle their financial affairs for them. She wants to hire you to draft a living will and health care power of attorney for both of her parents, and a will for each of them dividing their property 50% to the other surviving spouse and the other 50% divided equally among the children. She also wants you to be the executor for the will. She will be paying for your services.

Question Three: May you prepare these documents for Pandora's parents under Pandora's direction?

To Learn More

THE RESTATEMENT (THIRD) OF THE LAW GOVERNING LAWYERS (2000) is an excellent source for more additional detail about concurrent conflicts of interest. § 121 provides the basic conflicts rule and concurrent representation is discussed in four sections: § 128 (civil litigation), § 129 (criminal cases), § 130 (non-litigated matters), and § 131 (representing organizations).

Chapter Nineteen

The Current Client and a Former Client

Learning Objectives

After you have read this chapter and completed the assignments:

- You should appreciate the importance of clarifying when a representation has ended and be able to draft closing letters that provide that clarity.

- In evaluating a particular proposed representation or relationship, you should be able to determine whether the proposed representation is the same or substantially related to a matter for which you have provided a prior representation to a client adverse to the current client.

- You should recognize the limits of waiver and withdrawal as tools to eliminate conflicts.

- You should be able to describe and use a system of analyzing a problem for research.

- You should be able to describe how and why conflicts rules differ when the former client is a government.

Rules to Study

The primary rules we will examine in this chapter are Rules 1.7, 1.9, and portions of Rule 1.13. We will also examine the relationship between these rules and judicial disqualification orders.

Preliminary Problem

Maggie Morrison was a registered nurse for many years before she went to law school. Ten years ago, after she graduated from law school and was admitted to practice in the state, she went to work for the firm of Strifer, Duke, and Vail (SD&V) in their health law department. The health care department of SD&V was roughly divided between the attorneys who provided transactional and risk management counseling and the attorneys who defended health care providers in litigation. Maggie worked exclusively on the risk management side of the department.

One of the department's biggest clients is Johnson Hospital in Central City, Mokan. Maggie's risk management work for Johnson Hospital (and other clients) focused on providing annual "risk audits" in which she would identify problems that could give rise to potential liability for clients, their employees, physicians, and other health care providers. She would then counsel the client on ways to correct these problems. Her work also included counseling clients after an event or incident occurred that could create potential liability.

For the last four years she worked at the firm, Maggie billed 1,314 hours to Johnson Hospitals. She provided four risk audits for the hospital and assisted Johnson Hospital in responding to a number of doctor and nurse errors that raised potential liability concerns. She also helped develop a number of important risk management policies for Johnson Hospital.

One of the most significant policies Maggie developed was the "apology calculus." The "apology calculus" identified those cases and patients to whom an apology would reduce the risk of a lawsuit while not increasing the risk of liability if a lawsuit were filed in spite of the apology. In general, patients who suffered only financial injury or temporary or minor physical risk or injury, who had long-term relationships with their medical provider, and who were the victim in isolated errors would receive notice of the error and an apology. No apologies were issued to patients who did not have a long-standing relationship with a provider (generally younger or poorer patients), or whose injuries or risks were permanent or severe, or who were victims of errors that resulted from more routine or widespread errors. Rather the response in these cases was to deny error and attempt to shift blame—implicitly or explicitly—either to the patients themselves or to other professionals whose actions could not be attributable to the hospital and to turn the case over to the litigation defense team.

Two years ago in March, Maggie provided Johnson Hospital with her usual risk audit, which she completed in April. In May, Maggie was at a CLE meeting of the local health care attorneys association. After the presentation, while standing in line to speak to the presenter (a local ethics professor), she overheard Harold Inhouse, an attorney employed in the Office of Legal Counsel of Johnson Hospital, quietly asking the professor about a "hypothetical"—what if, he asked, a hospital attorney learned that the hospital pharmacy was regularly substituting generic drugs for the brand-name drugs prescribed to patients, even if the prescription specifically indicated "no substitutions allowed"? What if the hospital were then billing (and seeking Medicare/Medicaid or insurance company reimbursements) for the much more costly brand-name drug? What obligation would the attorney have to respond? Maggie stepped out of line and left the room as quickly as possible with a sinking feeling in her stomach.

Even though she did not currently have any pending work for Johnson Hospital, Maggie felt that her on-going responsibility to Johnson Hospital was to update her risk audit whenever she thought a significant liability issue arose. For example, in the past, Maggie had sent unsolicited letters to Harold Inhouse about recent changes in health care law that would impact the hospital's practices. This time, Maggie undertook some brief investigation and discovered that the "hypothetical" was in fact the practice that was occurring at Johnson Hospital. Maggie then approached Harold with her concerns. Harold said "Don't worry. This isn't your job, it's mine. I know how to nip this in the bud in no time. Leave this to me." Maggie was worried by the response. She had been looking for another job for some time and so she decided to put more serious effort into her job search.

Six weeks later, Maggie joined a small plaintiff's personal injury firm in order to try her hand at litigation. That was August of two years ago. She swiftly grew to love her new practice, and developed an excellent medical malpractice practice. Four months ago, Watson Widower came to Maggie seeking legal representation. Watson's wife Darla had died a few months earlier at Johnson Hospital of anaphylactic shock (a severe allergic reaction). The hospital had never admitted error in Darla's death, insisting that the reaction must have been to something she ingested before she entered the hospital and that she had the responsibility to inform the hospital if she was allergic to any medication and she had not done so. Watson's wife was not, in fact, allergic to any medication. Darla's only allergy as far as he knew was to red wine, which she had given up years previously. Watson suspected that the hospital was somehow at fault for his wife's death and wanted Maggie to investigate and bring a malpractice claim if necessary.

Maggie consulted Rule 1.9 and concluded that because she had never worked on any actual malpractice cases against Johnson Hospital (if suit was filed, the cases were always transferred to the litigation department) and because any of the malpractice risk counseling she had done had been for doctors and nurses, not pharmacists, she was not prohibited from representing Maggie. She agreed to represent Watson.

Was Maggie's analysis correct?

Maggie began by asking a pharmacist friend whether the generic drug substitution for Darla's medication contained any different ingredients than the brand-name drug and learned that the generic drug used bisulfite, which the brand name drug did not. When she asked the pharmacist what bisulfite was, the pharmacist answered, "Oh it's a preservative — mostly used in wines." This was enough to convince Maggie that it was the hospital's substitution of generics that caused his wife's death. Maggie wrote a demand letter to the hospital, which responded by insisting that Maggie could not represent Watson and could not reveal any information she had about Johnson Hospital's drug policies. Harold Inhouse personally filed a complaint against Maggie with the Mokan chief disciplinary counsel.

How much trouble is Maggie in?

19.1 Reading the Rules: Former Client Conflicts

While Rule 1.7 provides a standard for assessing conflicts of interest generally, when the question is whether there is a conflict between the interests of a current client and that of a former client, the more specific Rule 1.9 also applies. Study Rule 1.9. Here is Utah's adoption of the Model Rule:

Utah Supreme Court Rules of Professional Practice
Chapter 13 Rules of Professional Conduct
Rule 1.9 Duties to Former Clients

(a) A lawyer who has formerly represented a client in a matter shall not thereafter represent another person in the same or a substantially related matter in which that person's interests are materially adverse to the interests of the former client unless the former client gives informed consent, confirmed in writing.

(b) A lawyer shall not knowingly represent a person in the same or a substantially related matter in which a firm with which the lawyer formerly was associated had previously represented a client

(1) whose interests are materially adverse to that person; and

(2) about whom the lawyer had acquired information protected by Rules 1.6 and 1.9(c) that is material to the matter;

unless the former client gives informed consent, confirmed in writing.

(c) A lawyer who has formerly represented a client in a matter or whose present or former firm has formerly represented a client in a matter shall not thereafter:

(1) use information relating to the representation to the disadvantage of the former client except as these Rules would permit or require with respect to a client or when the information has become generally known; or

(2) reveal information relating to the representation except as these Rules would permit or require with respect to a client.

Context

In addition to discipline, representations that present a conflict with a former client may result in disqualifications, malpractice or breach of fiduciary duty claims, or forfeiture of fees. Of these, disqualification motions are the most common setting in which former client conflict issues arise, and the rules of professional responsibility have drawn from that case law as much as influenced it. In disqualification motions, important policies may outweigh the need to protect against risks of conflicts. One of the most significant is the price of applying conflicts rules broadly. In any given case, disqualification of an attorney for conflicts will likely cause a delay and impose additional costs on the client whose attorney is disqualified. Because of these consequences, courts are sensitive to the risk of abuse of disqualification motions. In areas of law in which access to justice remains an ongoing struggle, courts may be especially reluctant to disqualify attorneys for conflicts when there are few attorneys available to take their place. In comparison, a court considering the question of professional discipline might look at that same conduct quite differently. Thus, when researching and analyzing these issues, one must always be sensitive to the context in which a conflicts question arises.

Relationships

Rule 1.7 is designed to protect the interests of current clients against other interests that would threaten confidentiality and loyalty. Rule 1.9 is designed to protect the confidential information of (and to a lesser extent the loyalty to) former clients. In a conflict between a current client and a former client, both rules are relevant. If your loyalty to a former client or your inability to use information from that prior representation would materially limit your representation of a current client, you have a conflict under Rule 1.7. If the representation of a former client would threaten the confidentiality of a former client's information, there is a conflict under Rule 1.9. Compare the two rules. Which elements are the same? What additional element is necessary for a conflict to exist with a former client that is not an element of concurrent conflicts of interest? Compare Rule 1.9(c) to Rule 1.6. How is the duty of confidentiality to a former client different from the duty of confidentiality to a current client?

Structure

Rule 1.9 has three separate parts: (a) is the general rule; (b) addresses those conflicts an attorney takes with him from a former firm; and (c) is simply a reiteration that an attorney owes a continuing duty of confidentiality to former clients. We will focus in this chapter on parts (a) and (c) and discuss the applications of conflicts when attorneys change firms in the Chapter 20.1.

The ABA/BNA Lawyers Manual suggests that former client conflicts can be analyzed through the application of seven basic questions:

1. Was there ever an attorney-client relationship between the lawyer and a person or entity that may object to the representation?

2. Is the client truly a former client of the lawyer's?

3. Are the interests of the current and former clients adverse?

4. Is there a substantial relationship between the two representations?

5. Has the former client consented to the current representation, or waived objections to it?

6. Is the presumption that the lawyer gained confidential information from the former client rebuttable in this jurisdiction?

7. Has the presumption been rebutted?

LAW. MAN. ON PROF. CONDUCT (ABA/BNA), Practice Manual § 51:201(2002). For each of these questions, think of a fact situation in which the answer is clearly no or yes and one that presents an arguable question. Discuss your hypotheticals with one another.

Reasons

While loyalty remains a concern with former client conflicts, confidentiality is the primary concern. In general, courts are more willing to permit waivers of former client conflicts than concurrent client conflicts. However, remember the general principle from Rule 1.7 still applies here. That is, a reasonable attorney must believe he can represent the client both competently and diligently before he can even ask for a waiver.

Visualize

One of the key phrases in understanding Rule 1.9 is "same or substantially related matter." Often, being able to diagram prior representations and current representations and the contours of the representation can help you to recognize these situations. As you read the cases in this chapter, try diagramming these conflicts. Sometimes just a table describing the two representations can be enough to make the conflicts clear. Using the preliminary problem as an example, here is one diagram of the conflicts:

Case #1	Case #2
[2009-12 MoKan]	[2012 MoKan]
Attorney [Maggie Morrison]	Attorney [Maggie Morrison]
Represents [Johnson Hospitals]	Represents [Watson Widower]
Against [None — risk management]	Against [Johnson Hospital & Pharmacists]
In [General risk management and response to error]	In [Malpractice involving substitution of generic drug]

Imagine

An attorney's representation of a client in the past might present a conflict of interest with a current client in two ways. First, the representation of the current client might threaten the confidentiality that the attorney owes to the former client (Rule 1.9 conflict), or the attorney's interest in the former client (in confidentiality or in loyalty to that former client) might materially limit the representation of the current client (Rule 1.7 conflict). Imagine circumstances in which one or the other of these risks might materialize.

19.2 When Is a Client a "Former Client"?

When does a representation end so that a current client becomes a former client? The answer may not be as obvious at it at first appears. Suppose your client fires you, for example. Surely the representation has ended then, right? Not necessarily. Comment 9 to Rule 1.16 reminds us that "[e]ven if the lawyer has been unfairly discharged by the client, a lawyer must take all reasonable steps to mitigate the consequences to the client." Thus, the attorney must at least give notice or seek permission to withdraw (if required), return papers and unearned fees, and perhaps take other steps to protect the client's interest. An attorney may not, of course, act on the client's behalf beyond that which is necessary to the withdrawal, but preserving the status quo and assisting in the transition to other counsel are often required.

Short of a required withdrawal, your representation generally ends when you have completed the work you agreed to do in the initial engagement. However, like the creation of the attorney-client relationship, the termination of that relationship is not a simple matter of contract law but depends in part on the reasonable expectations of the client. If an attorney has a long-term relationship with a client, has communicated with the client regularly (even if informally), and has not clearly and unambiguously terminated the relationship, the attorney may be deemed to currently represent that client, even after the passage of some time.

Even if a court rules in your favor on a disqualification motion, the expense and delay caused by that dispute is one you want to avoid by eliminating as much as possible any ambiguity about the status of your relationship with a client. For example, in *Revise Clothing, Inc. v. Joe's Jeans, Inc.*, 687 F. Supp. 2d 381 (S.D.N.Y. 2010), a trademark infringement case concerning stitching on denim jeans, the defendant Joe's Jeans had claimed that Revise Clothing Inc. infringed Joe's Jeans' trademark back pocket design. In response, Revise sued, asking for a declaratory judgment that it has not infringed the trademark.

Joe's Jeans was represented by the law firm of Pryor Cashman LLP. Revise moved to disqualify Pryor Cashman under a theory that it currently represented Revise.

Pryor Cashman had represented Revise in trademark litigation against another company the prior year. The firm represented Revise through a settlement of that claim, but did not send a disengagement letter thereafter. The settlement agreement designated Pryor Cashman as Revise's agent for notice of breach of the settlement. The law firm archived its Revise file but continued to send promotional emails to Revise in the hopes of developing future business from the company. The court held that Revise was a former rather than current client of Pryor Cashman, and that the prior representation was not the same or substantially related to the current suit with Joe's Jeans. The court relied on the narrow and specific language in the initial retainer agreement and the limited nature of the attorney's representation of Revise in the single lawsuit. The court was also influenced by the fact that Revise had ordinarily used a different attorney's services to handle its trademark work and that it had only hired Revise on that attorney's recommendation because he was too busy to handle this particular lawsuit.

While successful in the motion, the firm (and presumably its client Joe's Jeans) had to bear the time and expense of numerous affidavits and briefs and two separate hearings on the motion. Compare the result in *The Gerffert Co., Inc. v. Dean*, 2011 U.S. Dist. LEXIS 15530 (E.D.N.Y. Feb. 16, 2011). In that case, Attorney Horowitz had represented the plaintiff Gerffert as its counsel for twenty years and had also represented the defendant Bonella Family over a period of years as well. In 2003, Horowitz agreed to represent both of the parties in negotiating an agreement between the two regarding sales of the Bonellas' assets to Gerffert. The joint representation agreement the clients signed at that time contained a clause in which Horowitz confirmed that "in the event that a dispute should arise between or among any of [the parties], I will not represent any party in any litigation arising therefrom." After the dispute arose between Gerffert and the Bonellas, Horowitz had been continuing to submit bills to the Bonellas for intellectual property work and had offered to mediate between the two sides, but only under a revised conflict waiver. The court found that the Bonellas were current clients of Horowitz and disqualified him from representing Gerffert in the suit. Among the factors the court considered was "absence of an expressed cessation" of the prior representation.

As you can see from these cases, documentation is key to preventing problems with conflicts. Clearly defining the scope of representation in the initial agreement with the client, thinking through the future effects of current representations and the scope of waivers, and sending an unambiguous termination letter all can prevent a former client's perception that you continue represent them. Why don't attorneys take these steps more often? In part, they may have not yet come to realize the value of the time and attention that this documentation demands. In part, clearly terminating an attorney-client relationship can be bad for business.

Even after they have completed their representation, savvy attorneys recognize that continuing a relationship with former clients can pay off in referrals and return business. Therefore, some attorneys use their termination letters to remind the client of additional practice areas and other services available from the firm. Some attorneys keep in touch with former clients by providing them legal updates newsletters, arranging personal meetings, or sending holiday greetings. There is nothing wrong with these efforts to keep your name on the radar screen of former clients. But there is a risk is that you will "sell too well" — that is, that your contacts with a client after the close of representation will create the impression that you are continuing to represent the client. This can make the client a "current client" for purposes of malpractice liability or disqualification.

Professional Responsibility Skill 19-A: Disengagement Letters

Disengagement letters serve several purposes besides simply avoiding future conflicts. These letters provide a clear date upon which the statute of limitations begins to run for any malpractice claims arising out of the representation. But most importantly, the letters clearly communicate to your clients that the representation has concluded, providing an opportunity to moderate any unreasonable expectations they may have regarding continuing representation. The letter can summarize any final advice you have for your clients to follow up the representation. The letter can include a final billing statement, if there are unpaid fees, as well as any files you will return to the client or a description of your file retention policy. If you intend to contact the client with newsletters or other future contacts, your letter can make it clear that this is simply a general service you provide to former clients and others, and give the client an opportunity to opt out ("unless we hear otherwise" would be sufficient). If you want to include in this letter some cross-selling information, keep that information separate. Be sure your language describes any future representation as a possibility not a guarantee.

Try drafting a disengagement letter that serves these purposes without creating ambiguity. Suppose you have drafted a will for Mr. Oliver Old. Oliver has executed the will and you have no further work that you have agreed to provide for him. In the future, you would like Mr. Old to hire you if he decides to change his estate plan or if he has other legal needs. Draft a disengagement letter for Mr. Old.

19.2 Substantial Relationships and Confidential Information

Rule 1.9 describes two types of former client conflicts. 1.9(a) applies when a current matter is the "same or substantially related" to a former representation. 1.9(c) provides that an attorney must protect confidential information from the former representation, even if the two representations are not substantially related. Both are concerned with confidentiality. Under 1.9(a), the same or substantial relationship test compares what information an attorney *would have been likely to gain* in that type of matter and predicts whether that type of information would be useful against the former client in the current matter. Under 1.9(c), the court asks whether the attorney *actually gained* information that could be used against the former client.

In the following case, the court found that the attorneys violated both of these rules.

In re Carey
89 S.W.3d 477 (Mo. banc 2002)

It is a fair characterization of the lawyer's responsibility in our society that he stands "as a shield," to quote Devlin, J., in defense of right and to ward off wrong. From a profession charged with such responsibilities there must be exacted those qualities of truth-speaking, of a high sense of honor, of granite discretion, of the strictest observance of fiduciary responsibility, that have, throughout the centuries been compendiously described as "moral character." *Schware v. Bd. of Bar Exam'rs,* 353 U.S. 232 (1956) (Frankfurter, J., concurring).

The Chief Disciplinary Counsel (CDC) filed a three count information against attorneys John J. Carey and Joseph P. Danis based upon their alleged professional misconduct in prosecuting product liability class action suits against a former client, the Chrysler Corporation, and in making misrepresentations in discovery in the subsequent lawsuit for breach of fiduciary duty brought by Chrysler against them. We find that both John Carey and Joseph Danis engaged in professional misconduct by representing another person in a substantially related matter adverse to the interest of a former client in violation of Rule 4-1.9(a), Rule 4-8.4(a), and by making false discovery responses in violation of Rule 4-3.3(a)(1), Rule 4-8.4(c)], Rule 4-8.4(d), Rule 4-3.4(a) and Rule 4-3.4(d). John J. Carey and Joseph P. Danis are indefinitely suspended from the practice of law, with leave to apply for reinstatement not sooner than one year from the date of this opinion.

I. Factual Background....

A. Representation of Chrysler by John Carey and Joseph Danis

John Carey joined Thompson & Mitchell in 1987, after being admitted to practice law in Missouri. While at Thompson & Mitchell, Carey worked under Charles Newman as part of a "team" of partners and associates that defended Chrysler against product liability and consumer class action cases brought against it nationwide. From January 1992 through December 1995, Carey billed 1,314.6 hours to Chrysler. As part of the Chrysler team, Carey was privy to all aspects of the Chrysler representation and directly participated in nearly all aspects of the Chrysler litigation. In addition, Carey assessed Chrysler's potential liability in pending litigation and helped draft a "blueprint" for Chrysler to follow in defending class action product defect suits pending concurrently with a National Highway Traffic Safety Administration ("NHTSA") investigation.

Joseph Danis was licensed to practice law in Missouri in 1993 and began work as an associate for Thompson & Mitchell that year. Carey acted as Danis' mentor while Danis was a summer associate and again when Danis was a new associate. Danis joined Carey as a member of Charles Newman's Chrysler team. As a new associate, Danis' involvement with the Chrysler class action litigation was less extensive than Carey's. However, as a member of the team, Danis was privy to all aspects of the Chrysler representation. Danis billed 513.5 hours to Chrysler from January 1992 through December 1995.

Newman would circulate information on the widest possible basis to every member of the Thompson & Mitchell team involved in representation of Chrysler. Carey was the primary associate on four different Chrysler class action cases. Charles Newman testified:

> John [Carey] was totally immersed in that case [Osley], along with me, and played the same role that I played in many respects. And

Margin notes:

Conflicts ordinarily arise in disqualification motions. This is one of a few cases in which attorneys were disciplined for violating Rule 1.9.

As you read, try diagramming the facts so you can follow the conflicts that emerge.

Assuming an average of 2,000 billable hours a year, this means Chrysler represented about 15% of Carey's work.

What if it had been only 15 hours?

Think about this practice of sharing information. Why do firms share so widely?

that obviously involved ... determining the legal issues that the case presented. It also involved analyzing the jurisdiction....

He was also involved with me and others in massing the facts relevant to the claims that were asserted, and that involved contacting and principally working with the personnel in the office of the general counsel at Chrysler Corporation.

Newman further testified that in the other three cases, Carey had "a similar role with a few additional aspects."

Danis was not involved in Osley, but did participate in the other three cases. Danis was involved in the lower level associate functions, but worked extensively with both Newman and Carey. Danis worked principally on drafting discovery responses and obtaining information from Chrysler to respond to discovery requests.

Notice that these tasks involve confidential information more so than, for example, research.

The component parts involved in the class action lawsuits Carey and Danis defended while with Thompson & Mitchell were Renault heater coils and Chrysler minivan door latches. Charles Newman and other Chrysler attorneys, William McLellan and Lewis Goldfarb, each stressed, however, that the actual defective component was not materially important in this type of class action lawsuit. Goldfarb testified:

The products at issue in class actions are almost irrelevant to how we go about defending class actions. There's almost an identity of process in terms of how we defend class actions, regardless of the nature of the component involved....

Product-related class action[s], particularly those that follow on the heels of a government investigation, are virtually identical in the way the company handles them. The nature of the component involved is almost irrelevant to these cases because they never go to trial. We're always dealing with the government, that investigation relates to the ongoing class action case. And the class action strategy is almost independent in some respects of the nature of the component involved.

Isn't every defense attorney privy to a client's strategy?

These three Chrysler attorneys also testified that respondents Carey and Danis were privy to a wealth of information that would be useful to them in prosecuting a product-related class action against Chrysler. Newman testified that Carey and Danis learned Chrysler's strategy in defending minivan product liability class action suits:

Respondents [were] present during meetings with in-house Chrysler counsel when there was a discussion of the strengths and weaknesses of various Chrysler employees ... [and] with non-lawyer Chrysler employees; for example, expert witnesses....

We would talk with the client about other pending litigation alleging a similar product or defect.... So we would talk to the attorneys at Chrysler about their defense of those cases, what factual defenses were being developed and implemented, what expert witnesses, if any, they were working with there. The legal strategies in those cases, the legal defenses in those cases. Determine their applicability, determine their usefulness, determine whether they could be implemented in the class action....

Newman also said that Carey and Danis knew that Chrysler was very hesitant to interplead or sue a critical supplier because of the way its supply lines were managed.

> [I]f somebody was thinking of suing Chrysler and knew ... that Chrysler had a predisposition against bringing in third parties, you would know in contemplating a suit against Chrysler that it would be relatively efficient in that Chrysler wouldn't bring in everybody else in the world that might be involved or had a bearing with that particular component or product and that you could tailor your claims accordingly to focus just on Chrysler and not have to worry about suppliers and the like.

Newman testified that, although the component parts differed, there were many similarities in available defenses, such as statute of limitations, improper certification of the class, improper class representatives, and improper assertion of claims. Finally, Newman indicated that many expert witnesses overlap: economists, automotive repair experts and human factor engineers. Newman testified that "[t]he Respondents ... learn[ed] which experts Chrysler chose to use and not use." He stressed that Carey and Danis helped formulate Chrysler's defense strategy in class action product liability cases involving Chrysler minivans.

William McClelland confirmed that Carey and Danis were "made aware about the types of information Chrysler kept, the sources of information within Chrysler relevant to the defense of a product liability class action lawsuit involving the minivan." McClelland testified that respondents' specific knowledge of the minivan would be extraordinarily helpful.

> [T]he minivan was incredibly important to Chrysler. It still is today. I'm not sure the public fully understands its importance to our profitability. They know Chrysler makes solid minivans, but not I think the importance that we attach to it internally. We were just coming out with a brand-new minivan at the time. We had put over a billion dollars investment into that minivan and were very concerned from a marketing and public relations perspective.

> One of the strategies of the plaintiffs' bar would be to muddy our name. We noticed during that time Ford was coming out with ads touting its safety record. Carey's and Danis' first-hand knowledge of the minivan's importance would allow them to "know what hot buttons to push."

Lewis Goldfarb also discussed respondents' work for Chrysler. Goldfarb testified that Carey and Danis had access to "detailed, internal information and analysis done by the in-house legal department, as well as [Chrysler] engineers and other personnel, regarding the status of a confidential government investigation...." He emphasized that Carey and Danis had a "road map as to how we [Chrysler] look at and analyze alleged defects concerning our products."

The "road map" Goldfarb spoke of referred to a "matrix" or "blueprint" that the Chrysler team—including John Carey and Joseph Danis—developed to formulate Chrysler's defense to class action product liability cases involving Chrysler minivans. The team prepared a matrix of all considerations that Chrysler should consider in deciding whether or not to settle the minivan

How important is the size and scope of this prior litigation to the conflicts analysis?

latch cases. This matrix listed relevant criteria and matched those criteria with a factual scenario. For each scenario, the team gave thoughts about the applicability of the criteria and its impact on the company. The matrix also included a form of a decision tree. The decision tree visually described the different scenarios and their implication on important areas of the company like marketing, public and consumer relations, dealer relations, and the recall itself.

This information was very important to Chrysler. Charles Newman summed up Chrysler's position on the matrix in saying:

> [T]his is highly confidential information and it was shared with us by our client in confidence. We had a discussion, extensive discussions with the client that resulted in the creation of this document, this matrix or template. And to have a plaintiff's lawyer know, for instance, of the very considerations themselves what Chrysler's thought process deemed important and deemed material and how I in representing them analyzed each of those aspects would be very sensitive, confidential information that neither the company nor I would want to share with anyone.

B. Carey & Danis, L.L.C.—The Chrysler ABS Class Action

In January 1995, Carey and Danis left Thompson & Mitchell and formed their own firm, Carey & Danis, L.L.C. Carey & Danis shared office space with the firm of David Danis—Joseph Danis' father—Danis, Cooper, Cavanagh & Hartweger, L.L.C. The two firms shared staff, a bookkeeper, a fax machine, and unlocked (but separate) filing cabinets.

In August 1995, a Thompson & Mitchell secretary referred her brother-in-law, Dennis Beam, to Carey & Danis after he experienced problems with the anti-lock brake system on his Chrysler minivan. Carey discussed the potential case with Beam. Carey, obviously aware that he and Danis had represented Chrysler, and researched Rule 1.9 of the Model Rules of Professional Conduct for an hour or two to determine if a conflict existed. Carey testified that he "made the determination that since Joey [Danis] and I had no knowledge or information at all concerning anti-lock brakes ... that those were not substantially related under my review of the case law and reading those rules." Carey determined there was not a conflict. However, Carey & Danis did not file suit because Thompson & Mitchell had been referring business to them and they did not want to embarrass their former firm by filing suit against a former client.

Carey & Danis arranged for the Danis, Cooper firm to represent Beam and a class of plaintiffs against Chrysler. Danis, Cooper was to get help on the case from another St. Louis law firm, Blumenfeld, Kaplan & Sandweiss. Carey and Danis met with attorneys from Danis, Cooper and the Blumenfeld firm to discuss the Beam class action suit over lunch at a restaurant. According to Evan Buxner, who was working for Blumenfeld at the time, the "purpose of the meeting was to discuss generally if Blumenfeld, Kaplan & Sandweiss participated in the litigation what our role was and what we might expect representing a plaintiff in a proposed class in a plaintiffs' class action case." Carey & Danis was the only firm with any significant class action litigation experi-

Why can he discuss this confidential information here?

Do you see why these are relevant facts?

What went wrong with Carey's research and analysis?

Shouldn't this reluctance have raised a red flag?

ence among the three firms. The firms discussed a number of topics relating to the class action against Chrysler: attorney time and cost, the fact that NHTSA was conducting an investigation into the brake system, that a proposed class action could ride the government coattails and let the government agency do most of the work, the effect of a recall on a potential class action, the necessity (or lack thereof) of hiring experts, and that they could expect a barrage of motions from Chrysler.

Shortly after their involvement began, Blumenfeld was informed that Carey & Danis' involvement in Beam was being investigated for conflict of interest. Blumenfeld then withdrew from the Beam litigation. Carey explained:

> Once they withdrew David [Danis] and Richard [Cooper] approached Joey [Danis] and I and asked us if we would be interested in getting involved in the case, we knew that there was no conflict of interest, and they needed help because ... there was a motion to transfer that was pending in St. Louis City. They needed help. There wasn't time to try and go out and find another co-counsel.

Carey & Danis entered their appearance on behalf of the Beam plaintiffs. However, neither Carey nor Danis sought or received Chrysler's consent to act as plaintiffs' counsel against Chrysler.

In December 1995, Joseph and David Danis met in New York with Stanley Grossman, an attorney who had a similar ABS class action suit against Chrysler in New Jersey. At the meeting they discussed joining—and later did join—the two class actions as well as a third group of plaintiffs from Mississippi represented by John Deakle. Following the meeting, Joseph Danis wrote Grossman to confirm the discussion regarding the ABS cases. Danis also inquired as to allocation of attorneys' fees if the cases were consolidated, saying there was "plenty of money for all.... Consequently, we will all be better served working together against Chrysler...." This correspondence has been termed "the Grossman letter."

While Danis and his father were in New York meeting with Grossman, Carey received a letter from Charles Newman accusing Carey & Danis of having a conflict of interest in the Beam case. Carey was "very upset" upon reading Newman's letter and immediately called Newman to tell him that he believed "in the strongest terms that [Carey & Danis] did not have a conflict of interest," but that he did not want to cause any trouble with Newman, Thompson & Mitchell, or Chrysler. Carey inquired if they could put an end to "all this ugliness and nastiness" if he and Danis withdrew from the Beam case. Newman did not make any promises, but thought that might appease Chrysler.

Thereafter, the Beam case was voluntarily dismissed and then joined with Grossman's case in New Jersey. Carey & Danis withdrew from Beam, but the Danis, Cooper firm and John Deakle were among the attorneys listed for the plaintiffs. Carey & Danis associated with a group of class action attorneys— David Danis and John Deakle, among others, that often worked together on cases and shared information. A number of these attorneys were involved in Chrysler ABS litigation. Members of this group would forward correspondence regarding the ABS litigation to each other and many of these communications would find their way to Carey & Danis.

C. Chrysler v. Carey & Danis—False and Misleading Statements

Why sue? Why wasn't disqualification a sufficient remedy?

Respondents Carey and Danis notified their malpractice insurer of a potential lawsuit by Chrysler and gave the insurer copies of documents that could be relevant—including the Grossman letter. The insurer later met with Lou Basso, the attorney Carey and Danis had chosen to represent them. The insurer gave the documents respondents had compiled to Mr. Basso. Basso made copies and then returned the documents to the insurer. Carey and Danis had also given the original Grossman letter to Basso, along with some other documents, when Basso was originally retained.

On March 26, 1996, Chrysler sued Carey & Danis for breach of fiduciary duty and respondents were served with process. Chrysler alleged that Carey & Danis, though not attorneys of record, assisted a group of lawyers in prosecuting ABS class action claims against Chrysler. Chrysler served interrogatories and requests for production upon both Carey and Danis, individually. [The Court discussed requests for production of documents related to this litigation and the attorney's failure to produce documents pursuant to those requests. The Court found that both attorneys made misrepresentations regarding the existence and production of those documents. Based on this failure to produce and misrepresentation, the judge in the civil case brought by Chrysler struck the attorneys' response and entered a default judgment against them.]

II. Discussion

A. Count I: Conflict of Interest

Count I alleges professional misconduct by violating Rule 4-1.9(a), which governs conflict of interest with former clients. Rule 4-1.9(a) states:

> A lawyer who has formerly represented a client in a matter shall not thereafter: (a) represent another person in the same or a substantially related matter in which that person's interests are materially adverse to the interests of the former client unless the former client consents after consultation....

It is not disputed that respondents Carey and Danis formerly represented the Chrysler Corporation, nor is it disputed that respondents' representation of the plaintiffs against Chrysler in Beam was materially adverse to Chrysler. The only issue presented is whether the Beam case was "substantially related" to Carey's and Danis' previous defense work for Chrysler.

"Gallons of ink" have been consumed by those trying to articulate or explain the test for deciding whether a substantial relationship exists between two representations. ABA/BNA Lawyer's Manual on Professional Conduct, 51:215. *See also Chrispens v. Coastal Ref. & Mktg., Inc.,* 257 Kan. 745, 897 P.2d 104, 111 (1995). The "substantially related" test was first announced in *T.C. Theatre Corp. v. Warner Brothers Pictures, Inc.,* 113 F. Supp. 265 (S.D.N.Y. 1953). In announcing the rule, the court was primarily concerned with preserving client confidences and avoiding conflicts of interest The court said:

> It would defeat an important purpose of the rule of secrecy—to encourage clients fully and freely to make known to their attorneys all

facts pertinent to their cause. Considerations of public policy, no less than the client's private interest, require rigid enforcement of the rule against disclosure. No client should ever be concerned with the possible use against him in future litigation of what he may have revealed to his attorney. Matters disclosed by clients under the protective seal of the attorney-client relationship and intended in their defense should not be used as weapons of offense. The rule prevents a lawyer from placing himself in an anomalous position. Were he permitted to represent a client whose cause is related and adverse to that of his former client he would be called upon to decide what is confidential and what is not, and, perhaps, unintentionally to make use of confidential information received from the former client while espousing his cause. Lawyers should not put themselves in the position "where, even unconsciously, they might take, in the interests of a new client, an advantage derived or traceable to, confidences reposed under the cloak of a prior, privileged relationship." In cases of this sort the Court must ask whether it can reasonably be said that in the course of the former representation the attorney might have acquired information related to the subject of his subsequent representation. If so, then the relationship between the two matters is sufficiently close to bring the later representation within the prohibition....

Id. at 269 (citation omitted).

Important policies behind the rule include the promotion of "fundamental fairness ... by prohibiting an attorney from using an informational advantage gained in the course of a former representation, the desire to promote client disclosure of all pertinent information ..., and the desire to promote confidence in the integrity of the judicial system." *Columbus Credit Co. v. Evans*, 82 Ohio App. 3d 798, 613 N.E.2d 671, 676 (1992).

There are three primary tests for substantial relationship used throughout the country. *Chrispens*, 897 P.2d at 111. The first approach compares the facts of the former and current representations. *Id.* The second approach, which has not been widely adopted, insists that the issues involved in the two representations be identical or essentially the same. *Id.* The third approach, developed by the Seventh Circuit Court of Appeals, blends the fact and issue comparisons into a three-step test. *Id.* The Seventh Circuit test states:

> [D]isqualification questions require three levels of inquiry. Initially, the trial judge must make a factual reconstruction of the scope of the prior legal representation. Second, it must be determined whether it is reasonable to infer that the confidential information allegedly given would have been given to a lawyer representing a client in those matters. Finally, it must be determined whether that information is relevant to the issues raised in the litigation pending against the former client.

Westinghouse Elec. Corp. v. Gulf Oil Corp., 588 F.2d 221, 225 (7th Cir.1978).

The test "does not require the former client to show that actual confidences were disclosed. That inquiry would be improper as requiring the very disclosure that [MRPC 1.9(a)] is intended to protect." *Chrispens*, 897 P.2d at 112.

Missouri addressed substantial relationship in *State v. Smith*, 32 S.W.3d 532 (Mo. banc 2000). Our approach is consistent with that set out in *Westinghouse* and *Chrispens*, combining an analysis of both the facts and issues in determining substantial relationship. In *Smith* we said that the court "employs a focused approach, where the court examines the relevant facts of the case in order to determine whether the various matters are substantially related." *Smith*, 32 S.W.3d at 543. "[W]hether there is a 'substantial relationship' involves a full consideration of the facts and circumstances in each case." *Id.* at 542 (citations omitted). "The underlying question is whether the lawyer was so involved in the matter that the subsequent representation can be justly regarded as a changing of sides in the matter in question." Rule 4-1.9 cmt. The key to the analysis is whether there was a central issue common to both representations. *Smith*, 32 S.W.3d at 542-43.

The fact that a lawyer has previously represented a client does not automatically preclude the lawyer from opposing that client in a later representation. The court must determine whether confidential information acquired in the course of representing the former client is relevant to the issues raised in the current litigation. *Chrispens*, 897 P.2d at 111.... The court's conclusion must be based on a close and careful analysis of the record. Id. Without such an analysis, the test serves "as a substitute for analysis rather than a guide to it. It is easier to find 'doubt' than to resolve difficult questions of law and ethics." *Id.*

Chrispens offers a short, non-exclusive list of six factors that courts following the Seventh Circuit approach have considered in determining whether a substantial relationship exists. See *Chrispens*, 897 P.2d at 112. The factors include:

(1) the case involved the same client and the matters or transactions in question are relatively interconnected or reveal the client's pattern of conduct;

(2) the lawyer had interviewed a witness who was key in both cases;

(3) the lawyer's knowledge of a former client's negotiation strategies was relevant;

(4) the commonality of witnesses, legal theories, business practices of the client, and location of the client were significant;

(5) a common subject matter, issues and causes of action existed; and

(6) information existed on the former client's ability to satisfy debts and its possible defense and negotiation strategies.

Id. (citations omitted). In some cases, one factor, if significant enough, can establish that the subsequent case is substantially related. *Id.* Careful review of the facts at hand in relation to these six factors provides a specific framework for resolution of this case.

First, when compared to the prior representation, the ABS cases involve the same client, Chrysler. Because the cases all involve the Chrysler minivan in the same "type" of case, Chrysler's pattern of conduct is applicable despite the different specific component parts involved. It is undisputed that Carey and Danis defended the Chrysler Corporation on product liability class action lawsuits involving Chrysler minivan components and then later prosecuted a

---

Notice this is a test that is concerned as much with loyalty as with confidentiality.

Notice how similar this test is to the "same transaction or occurrence" test for claim preclusion and joinder of parties in civil procedure.

product liability class action lawsuit involving another minivan component against Chrysler. The subject matter of the lawsuits was components of Chrysler's minivan. Carey and Danis also knew how important the minivan was to Chrysler and had access to "detailed, internal information and analysis done by the in-house legal department...." In fact, both Carey and Danis helped formulate the "blueprint" Chrysler used when defending a product liability class action suit involving the minivan.

Second, respondents interviewed or deposed a number of expert witnesses while working for Chrysler that could have been called to testify in the Beam lawsuit. Carey and Danis were present during meetings with in-house Chrysler counsel when there was a discussion of the strengths and weaknesses of various Chrysler employees and expert witnesses. Carey and Danis had personal contact with a number of expert witnesses that could be used in both cases and had learned which experts Chrysler chose to use and not use. Specifically, Charles Newman stated that "... I contacted some of the same experts for possible use in the defense of the ABS case that we had contacted in the defense of the Osley case." Two witnesses, Mr. Pat Gross, an auto mechanic, and Dr. Mather, an economist, were mentioned by name and the general nature of their testimony common to these cases was briefly discussed.

Third, Carey's and Danis' knowledge of Chrysler's negotiation strategies were particularly relevant. Respondents helped formulate the decision matrix used by Chrysler when defending suits precisely like Beam. The matrix listed criteria Chrysler deemed relevant and matched those criteria with a factual scenario. For each scenario, the team gave thoughts about the applicability of the criteria and the impact on the company.

Fourth and Fifth, the commonality of witnesses, legal theories, and business practices of the client were significant, and there was a common subject matter as well as common issues and causes of action. This case involved the Chrysler minivan. Although the particular minivan parts at issue may have been different, in this case, testimony indicated that the actual components at issue in this type of product liability class action suit are almost irrelevant to how Chrysler defended the case. Lewis Goldfarb testified:

> Product-related class action[s], particularly those that follow on the heels of a government investigation, are virtually identical in the way the company handles them. The nature of the component involved is almost irrelevant to these cases because they never go to trial. We're always dealing with the government, that investigation relates to the ongoing class action case. And the class action strategy is almost independent in some respects of the nature of the component involved.

Finally, information existed on Chrysler's possible defense and negotiation strategies. As previously discussed, Carey and Danis knew of and actually helped formulate Chrysler's defense and negotiation strategies.

Respondents' justification for prosecuting a consumer class action lawsuit involving Chrysler minivans, within one year after having represented Chrysler, was that the component parts were different. Carey and Danis defended Chrysler on Chrysler minivan door latch cases while Beam involved Chrysler minivan anti-lock brake systems.

Certainly, a client does not own a lawyer for all time. In appropriate circumstances our rules allow lawyers to take positions adverse to former clients and even to bring suit against them. *See* Rule 4-1.9. The similarity of each case and its facts and issues is the determinative factor. Rule 4-1.9, however, simply does not allow respondents to cut such a sharp corner here. This is why the rule is not limited to "the same" matter but also extends to "a substantially related" matter.

Upon a close examination of the facts and issues surrounding the respondents' representation of Chrysler, the fact that Carey and Danis defended Chrysler in product liability class action claims involving Chrysler's minivan overshadows the fact that different automotive parts were at issue. Respondents' work at Thompson & Mitchell allowed them access to information and strategy considerations that could not be turned fairly against their former client after changing employment. Although these lawsuits concerned different parts, the issues in the lawsuits and Chrysler's defense strategies were shown to be unavoidably linked. The expertise that Carey and Danis developed at Chrysler's expense and the confidences shared with them by Chrysler cannot be used by respondents to harm their former client.

"No client should ever be concerned with the possible use against him in future litigation of what he may have revealed to his attorney. Matters disclosed by clients under the protective seal of the attorney-client relationship and intended in their defense should not be used as weapons of offense." The public must have confidence in the integrity of the Bar and every "client has a right to expect the loyalty of his attorney in the matter for which he is retained." "Every lawyer owes a solemn duty ... to strive to avoid not only professional impropriety but also the appearance of impropriety."

It is this Court's duty to not only dispense justice, but equally important, to maintain the integrity of the judicial system. The public's trust and confidence in the system is essential to the ability of the system to function efficiently and justly. As this Court has previously noted "even an appearance of impropriety may, under the appropriate circumstances, require prompt remedial action...."

> The "appearance of impropriety" standard is no longer part of the rules, but you can see here it still carries weight.

By representing Dennis Beam in a products liability class action lawsuit against Chrysler, respondents Carey and Danis represented another person in a substantially related matter that was materially adverse to their former client in violation of Rule 4-1.9.

B. Count II: Client Confidentiality

Count II alleges that Carey and Danis violated Rule 4-8.4 by using confidential information obtained while representing Chrysler to later prosecute the ABS class action claim against Chrysler. The Disciplinary Hearing Panel found that respondents did not violate Rule 4-8.4. We agree.

The Chief Disciplinary Counsel's contention is based in large part on the fact that respondents took over 800 pages of documents from Thompson & Mitchell when they left. The CDC argues that many of these documents were confidential and that Carey and Danis violated their duty of loyalty by using some of these documents as templates for the pleadings filed in the Beam case. The only specific document identified was a Chrysler petition used by

Carey and Danis as a form for the Beam petition. The Chrysler petition had been filed and was thus a public record. It was not confidential.

W. David Wells, the head of litigation at Thompson & Mitchell when respondents left that firm, testified that he had reviewed the documents Carey and Danis had taken and did not find them to be confidential. Wells testified that most of the documents were either a matter of public record or were generic memos that could apply to a variety of clients. Wells further testified that he believed that it was not uncommon for lawyers to take copies of such documents when they leave one law firm for another.

Count II alleges specifically that respondents used confidential documents against Chrysler, and this must be proved specifically. Given the testimony of those involved, the preponderance of the evidence supports a finding that respondents did not take confidential documents from Thompson & Mitchell and use them against Chrysler. We hold that respondents Carey and Danis did not violate Rule 4-8.4.

Note that Missouri is among a small minority of states that have a public record exception to Rule 1.6.

III. Discipline

The purpose of discipline is not to punish the attorney, but to protect the public and maintain the integrity of the legal profession. Those twin purposes may be achieved both directly, by removing a person from the practice of law, and indirectly, by imposing a sanction which serves to deter other members of the Bar from engaging in similar conduct....

Assessing discipline in cases such as this is always difficult. Here, two talented young lawyers, full of promise, lost their way among the economic temptations of modern practice and then again lost their way while struggling to defend themselves. In doing so, they violated two of the most fundamental principles of our profession, loyalty to the client and honesty to the bench. Significant discipline must follow to maintain the public's trust and confidence in our ability to police ourselves. A "slap on the wrist" will not suffice.

While disbarment would ordinarily be expected in a case such as this, the mitigating factors warrant some degree of leniency and offer hope that respondents can return to the responsible practice of law having learned a very hard lesson.

What besides the fact they are "talented young lawyers" is a mitigating factor?

John J. Carey and Joseph P. Danis are indefinitely suspended from the practice of law, with leave to apply for reinstatement not sooner than one year from the date of this opinion.

Notes

1. The *Carey* case involves a number of factors that independently have been held to constitute conflict of interests. First, under a liberal reading of the "same or substantial relationship" test, even without Chrysler's testimony about specific information the attorneys gained from prior class action litigation, the fact that both the former and current litigation involved minivan parts failures could be enough to infer that confidential information would have been gained in the first representation that would be used against the former client.

Second, the specific types of information that had been gained and would be used against Chrysler, according to their testimony, involved what is often called "playbook" information — that is, information about a client's approach to litigation and settlement based on recurring types of litigation or information about the client's financial condition and decision-making processes. Courts are divided on the question of whether knowledge of a company's policies and practices is sufficient to create a conflict. Though Comment 3 to Rule 1.9 and comments to the *Restatement (Third) of the Law Governing Lawyers* § 132 cmt. d(iii) (2000) both discourage this basis for finding a conflict, there are still many cases in which an attorney's insight into the client's litigation policies has provided a basis for disqualification.

Third, in this case, the attorneys not only knew about Chrysler's litigation policies, they had helped to develop those policies (the matrix and decision tree mentioned in the opinion). That makes their subsequent suits against Chrysler reminiscent of cases in which attorneys attack their own work product. If an attorney's subsequent representation questions the efficacy of legal work the attorney performed for the former client (such as challenging the enforceability of a contract, deed, patent, business structure, or testamentary document), most courts will find a conflict even if confidential information is not at risk. Moreover, the attorney is these cases may find herself in the position of becoming a necessary witness in the case, in which instance, the attorney would be prohibited from representing the client at trial under Rule 3.7. Finally, even if there were no rules prohibiting attorneys from arguing the invalidity or ambiguity of their own work product, attorneys who do so and lose are likely to face malpractice claims by their clients who will argue that the attorney soft-pedaled the attack in order to protect his own reputation.

2. The attorneys in this case researched and analyzed the conflicts of interest issue and concluded that their prior work for Chrysler did not involve the same or substantially related matters as the current lawsuits. While the opinion paints their analysis as influenced by greed rather than ignorance, you should not underestimate the difficulty in determining from prior cases whether a matter is substantially related to a former representation. Summarizing the state of the law on this issue, William Freivogel comments:

> Hundreds, if not thousands, of cases have turned on this question. Yet not much as changed since Judge Edward Weinfeld introduced the term in 1953 in *T.C. Theatre Corp. v. Warner Bros. Pictures, Inc.*, 113 F. Supp. 265 (S.D.N.Y. 1953). The cases have consistently over the years remained fact-intensive, and there appear to be no trends in applying the basic test. Some recent examples: several courts have found that work involving a piece of property was not substantially related to another matter involving the same piece of property. *Quicken Loans v. Jolly*, No. 2:07-CV-13143, 2008 U.S. Dist. LEXIS 48266 (E.D. Mich. June 24, 2008); *Henery v. 9th St. Apt., L.L.C.*, No. A-00-968, 2001 Neb. App. LEXIS 117 (Neb. Ct. App. June 5, 2001) (adjoining property); *Adams Creek Assocs. v. Davis*, 652 S.E.2d 677 (N.C. Ct. App. 2007). A Florida court held that a lawyer who defended a nursing home in pressure ulcer and fall matters could take on a case against the nursing involving pressure ulcers and falls, but which involved a different patient. *Health Care & Retirement Corp. of Am., Inc. v Bradley*, 961

So. 2d 1071 (Fla. Dist. Ct. App. 2007). In another case a court refused to disqualify a law firm that was handling a trademark case involving words on clothing although earlier the firm had represented the current opponent in a trademark matter involving the pattern of stitching on clothing. *Revise Clothing, Inc. v. Joe's Jeans, Inc.*, 687 F. Supp. 2d 381, (S.D.N.Y. 2010). The beat goes on, but the analysis has not changed.

William Freivogel, *A Short History of Conflicts of Interest. The Future?*, 20 ABA PROF. LAW. 3 (2010).

3. Should the test for "substantial relationship" be a strict one, or should it be fairly liberal? Which approach does the *Carey* court appear to take? As noted, some courts require that the relationship be "patently clear," while other courts appear to require merely that there be an opportunity for "greater insight" into the affairs of the client. The courts using a strict approach are usually concerned primarily, if not exclusively, with protecting confidential information. Those courts using broader tests are frequently also concerned about appearance of impropriety. How would it *look* to the public to allow the attorney to sue his or her former client in this situation? Is this an appropriate consideration? Canon 9 of the ABA Code of Professional Responsibility provided that a lawyer should avoid the appearance of impropriety. The Model Rules contain no such provision. Is appearance of impropriety an appropriate basis for disqualification if there is little or no real risk to confidential information? Most courts do not apply this standard absent a particular statute or rule that requires that standard for special practice areas (such as prosecutors). *Harker v. Commissioner of Internal Revenue*, 82 F.3d 806. 808-809 (8th Cir. 1996) (not appropriate); *President Lincoln Hotel Venture v. Bank One*, 271 Ill. App. 3d 1048, 649 N.E.2d 432, 441 (1994) (appearance of impropriety "too slender a reed" on which to base disqualification even under the Code). Nonetheless, courts may still speak in terms of appearance of impropriety in their analysis. Predicting a disqualification motion requires knowing what policies a court believes are at the core of former client conflicts rules.

4. The *Carey* case was a disciplinary case, but most conflict of interest cases involve disqualification motions. The burden of proof is upon the party alleging conflict and moving for disqualification. When a court finds a substantial relationship, it will presume that the attorney has access to confidential information that would be helpful in the current litigation. Most courts hold this presumption to be irrebuttable and require disqualification. However, an increasing number of courts are permitting an attorney who has switched firms to rebut the presumption that she has confidential information from a representation in her prior firm.

    If no substantial relationship is found, the party seeking disqualification may still be permitted to demonstrate that there is a substantial risk that confidential information may be used improperly. RESTATEMENT (THIRD) OF THE LAW GOVERNING LAWYERS § 213 (2000). If such a risk exists, disqualification is appropriate. Does the availability of disqualification even in the absence of a finding of substantial relationship indicate that the test ought to be a narrow one? After all, the test only addresses when *automatic* disqualification is required. If no such relationship exists, the party seeking disqualification still can prove that specific information is at risk. But doesn't the need to do so put the information even more at risk?

5. When an attorney has been disqualified, most courts will permit that attorney to turn over work product to new counsel unless actual confidential information is included or other improper advantage is likely. *See, e.g., First Wisconsin Mortgage Trust v. First Wisconsin Corp.*, 584 F.2d 201 (7th Cir. 1978) and *Canadian Gulf Lines, Inc. v. Triton International Carriers, Ltd.*, 434 F. Supp. 691 (D. Conn. 1976); *see also EZ Painter Corp. v. Padco, Inc.*, 746 F.2d 1459, 1463 (Fed. Cir. 1984) (work product created after new lawyers who possessed information came to firm not turned over; previous work product could be given to new counsel).

Researching Professional Responsibility: Working the Problem

You have learned a number of sources and approaches to researching issues of professional responsibility. Test those skills with the following problem that combines issues of confidentiality, conflicts, and contracts. Remember that it is critical for you to decide first, before you begin to research, if you understand what the problem requires by way of research.

Suppose your supervising attorney comes to you asking whether you can find any authority to resolve the following problem: Last year, the attorney had represented an individual in a suit against a pharmaceutical company and the case settled. As a term of the settlement, the client agreed to keep all information relating to the suit confidential, with a substantial liquidated damages provision for breach. Of course, the attorney wasn't a party to that agreement because he believed that doing so would violate Rule 5.6 (prohibiting agreements that restrict practice).

Now the attorney has another client who has a claim against this same company involving the same drug. Attorney's knowledge from the prior case will make the overall preparation of the case much more efficient and effective. He will know who to ask for what documents in discovery. He already has experts that have prepared to testify regarding this drug. He has a pleading he can recycle to begin the suit.

The attorney doesn't see how the current client's interests would be adverse to the former client. The former client's settlement has been paid and the former client would not have any involvement in this case at all. However, the attorney is concerned about whether the former client's confidentiality agreement creates a conflict of interest. He wants an answer today so he can secure the representation of this new client, if possible.

Before you begin to research, be sure you understand the problem. Review the following outline of questions[1] you should answer before you begin your research.

1. Who are the parties involved?

2. What descriptive words will provide research terms for the facts involved? What descriptive words provide the research terms for the legal issues involved?

---

1. This outline of questions is built on Professor Paul Callister's materials in his advanced research class, available at http://www1.law.umkc.edu/faculty/callister/bootcamp/survival/tab1.html. *See also,* Paul Callister, *Working the Problem*, 91 ILL. B.J. 43-44 (Jan. 2003).

3. What sources should I consult? What law governs this problem? For example, is the attorney concerned about discipline, tort liability, fee forfeiture, disqualification or all of these? Is this a matter for which I need to learn more about the law in general before I can identify the relevant legal issues, so that a secondary source might be the best place to begin? Or is this a problem in which I am aware of the relevant rule or doctrine and need only locate interpretations (such as cases or ethics opinions)?

4. Where does this problem arise? What are the jurisdictions in which I should be researching?

5. What time periods do you need to research? Is this an area in which the law has changed significantly so that older research will be irrelevant or inaccurate?

6. When does the attorney need the answer? Does he want a quick answer or exhaustive research?

7. In what form does the attorney want the research? A memo? A copy of a case? An oral report?

8. Which is more important: precision or recall? Does the attorney want all the possible sources on the topic or only the best or most on point?

9. How much time should I spend on the project? May I use a research source that will incur additional costs, such as LEXIS and/or Westlaw?

10. Has anyone in the firm ever done similar research on a related topic that I should know about?

Discuss these questions and develop a plan for researching this topic.

19.3 Consents and Waivers of Conflicts

When you determine that you have a conflict between a current and former client, you may be able to address the conflict by obtaining consent. For example, in *Carey,* the court noted that the attorneys had not sought the consent of Chrysler to their participation in a class action against them. However, consent is rarely a solution when a conflict has arisen. First, keep in mind that you must obtain consent from both the current client (Rule 1.7) and the former client (Rule 1.9). Notice that Rule 1.7 requires that, before you can even ask for this consent, you must conclude that a reasonable attorney would believe that she could provide competent and diligent representation. Moreover, the very process of informed consent invites a reasonableness test—if there is no rational reason for a client to agree to waive confidentiality and conflicts, how can we say his consent was truly informed? Thus, before an attorney assumes that consent is the answer to a conflict, she must conclude that it is reasonable to ask for that consent.

One way that firms make consent to a conflict more reasonable is by screening off the former client's attorney from the firm's attorneys that are engaged in the current, adverse representation. While these screens do not prevent or "cure" a conflict by themselves, combined with client consent, they may permit a firm to take on a new client without generating a disqualification motion. Particularly for sophisticated entity clients, working with large national law firms, a consent conditioned on such a screening mechanism allows clients to engage attorneys with expertise without a significant risk to confidentiality. Increasingly, the rules of professional conduct provide for circumstances in which these screens actually prevent the imputation of a conflict of interest, even without client consent. We will examine those screening mechanisms in more detail in the next chapter.

While advance consent to conflicts is permissible, it is difficult to enforce because of the requirement of informed consent. See ABA Comm. on Ethics and Prof'l Responsibility, Formal Op. 93-372 (1993) and the RESTATEMENT (THIRD) OF THE LAW GOVERNING LAWYERS § 202, cmt d (2000), both of which permit waiver of future conflicts with informed consent in most circumstances. There is always a likelihood that the client will revoke consent, that the court will consider the waiver uninformed given the subsequent developments, or that the conflict that has arisen is nonconsentable.

Consider the preliminary problem in this chapter in which Maggie Morrison worked for a law firm with a health law specialization. Suppose the firm decides that it would like to develop a personal injury practice alongside its compliance practice. Could Maggie's firm ask for an advance waiver of conflicts from its hospital and medical care providers that would permit it to later bring medical malpractice actions against these former clients? *See generally,* Richard Painter, *Advance Waiver of Conflicts,* 13 GEO. J. LEGAL ETHICS 289 (2000).

A second way in which a client may be held to have consented to a conflict is by failing to raise the conflict in a timely fashion. That is not to say that clients will be deemed to have consented to a conflicting representation based simply on their silence upon learning that an attorney is representing a new adverse client in a substantially related matter. Rather, the waiver of a conflict generally occurs when that silence appears to be a tactical choice in order to unfairly raise the costs of a disqualification motion by waiting until it will have the most negative impact. *See generally, Rohm & Haas Co. v. American Cyanamid Co.,* 187 F. Supp. 2d 221 (D.N.J. 2001) (collecting cases).

19.4 Reading the Rules: Conflicts and the Former Government Employee

When an attorney's former client is the government, special conflicts rules apply. While Rule 1.9(c) applies to these attorneys, a special rule provides additional guidance. Read the provisions of this rule and pay particular attention to the additional restrictions placed on an attorney who is moving from government service to private practice.

Utah Supreme Court Rules of Professional Practice, Chapter 13
Rules of Professional Conduct
Rule 1.11. *Special Conflicts of Interest for Former and Current Government Employees*

(a) Except as law may otherwise expressly permit, a lawyer who has formerly served as a public officer or employee of the government:

(1) is subject to Rule 1.9(c); and

(2) shall not otherwise represent a client in connection with a matter in which the lawyer participated personally and substantially as a public officer or em-

ployee, unless the appropriate government agency gives its informed consent, confirmed in writing, to the representation.

(b) When a lawyer is disqualified from representation under paragraph (a), no lawyer in a firm with which that lawyer is associated may knowingly undertake or continue representation in such a matter unless:

(1) the disqualified lawyer is timely screened from any participation in the matter and is apportioned no part of the fee therefrom; and

(2) written notice is promptly given to the appropriate government agency to enable it to ascertain compliance with the provisions of this Rule.

(c) Except as law may otherwise expressly permit, a lawyer having information that the lawyer knows is confidential government information about a person acquired when the lawyer was a public officer or employee may not represent a private client whose interests are adverse to that person in a matter in which the information could be used to the material disadvantage of that person. As used in this Rule, the term "confidential government information" means information that has been obtained under governmental authority and which at the time the Rule is applied, the government is prohibited by law from disclosing to the public or has a legal privilege not to disclose and which is not otherwise available to the public. A firm with which that lawyer is associated may undertake or continue representation in the matter only if the disqualified lawyer is screened from any participation in the matter and is apportioned no part of the fee therefrom.

(d) Except as law may otherwise expressly permit, a lawyer serving as a public officer or employee:

(1) is subject to Rules 1.7 and 1.9; and

(2) shall not:

(i) participate in a matter in which the lawyer participated personally and substantially while in private practice or nongovernmental employment, unless the appropriate government agency gives its informed consent, confirmed in writing; or

(ii) negotiate for private employment with any person who is involved as a party or as lawyer for a party in a matter in which the lawyer is participating personally and substantially, except that a lawyer serving as a law clerk to a judge, other adjudicative officer or arbitrator may negotiate for private employment as permitted by Rule 1.12(b) and subject to the conditions stated in Rule 1.12(b).

(e) As used in this Rule, the term "matter" includes:

(1) any judicial or other proceeding, application, request for a ruling or other determination, contract, claim, controversy, investigation, charge, accusation, arrest or other particular matter involving a specific party or parties; and

(2) any other matter covered by the conflict of interest rules of the appropriate government agency.

Context

According to the U.S. Bureau of Labor Statistics, about 16% of attorneys in the United States work for the government, roughly split one-third each for federal, state, and local.

At the federal level, the United States Departments of Justice, Treasury, and Defense employ the majority of federal government lawyers. Starting salaries for government attorneys were lower than any other job sector except academia or judicial clerkships, but jobs for attorneys in government are expected to grow as government, like industry, is increasingly using staff attorneys to meet legal needs rather than employing outside counsel.

Why do attorneys work in the government sector? Obviously, there are a variety of motivations. Government practice may present an opportunity to do significant work, gain early courtroom experience, have a varied and interesting practice, or be assured of an acceptable work/life balance. Some might consider work within a government office to be a stepping-stone to better opportunities in private sector practice. Rule 1.11 is primarily designed to blunt the desire to exploit a government position for private gain.

Relationships

As you can see, Rule 1.11 modifies many of the rules of conflicts of interest and imputation of conflicts. Thus, attorneys who are currently working in government as a public officer or employee must follow not only Rules 1.7 and 1.9(a) and (b), but also the more specific restrictions of Rule 1.11(d)(2). Much of the early law on screening of conflicts of interest developed from former government attorneys, since the screening provisions of this rule pre-dated more recent provisions allowing for screening in Rules 1.10 and 1.18.

Rule 1.11 operates in a larger context of governmental ethics rules. Nearly all levels of government have special ethical rules for their officials and employees, whether or not they are attorneys. These rules cover issues of conflicts of interest, private use of government property, outside employment, gifts, and nepotism, to name a few. These rules apply to all government employees, not just attorneys. At the federal level, the most important of these is the Ethics in Government Act, 18 U.S.C. § 207, which criminalizes certain activities by former government official and employees. In addition, on March 22, 2012, Congress passed the Stop Trading on Congressional Knowledge Act of 2012 (STOCK Act) (S. 2038), which prohibits members and employees of Congress from using "any nonpublic information derived from the individual's position ... or gained from performance of the individual's duties, for personal benefit." These laws do not exempt attorneys from their coverage and Rule 1.11 does not trump these federal laws.

Structure

Use one of the methods we have learned in prior rule reading exercises to analyze the relationship between the parts of this rule.

Reasons

The key purpose of the additional protections in this rule is to prevent corruption, "to prevent a lawyer from exploiting public office for the advantage of another client." (Comment 3, Utah R. Prof. Conduct 1.11). How might that happen? Obviously, an attorney who has worked for the government has a wealth of specialized knowledge of people, processes, and politics that others do not and that knowledge is very valuable to private clients. While some criminal defendants may not want to have a former prosecutor represent them, others may believe that the attorney's prior position with government will allow him to make deals another criminal defense attorney could not. General governmental ethics rules prohibit "revolving door" uses of contacts and information to private advantage when leaving government office. Rule 1.11 is simply another example of this kind of rule. However, the rule must strike a balance. If the concerns for protecting against the exploitation of government service so restrict the job opportunities for a former government attorney in the private sector, many highly qualified attorneys may avoid government service entirely.

Visualize

Complete the following comparative chart regarding the conflicts consequences of moving from one firm to another versus leaving government service and going to a private firm.

	Rule 1.9 & 1.10	Rule 1.11
What policies do the rules serve?	Protecting confidentiality of former client information (and perhaps protecting loyalty to those clients)	Protecting the public from misuse of public office by attorneys.
What conflicts does an attorney take with him when he moves?	Any matters in which the attorney has information about a former firm's clients. 1.9(b)	Any matters where a gov't lawyer participated personally and substantially in the matter
When can the moving attorney be screened to prevent imputation of his conflicts of interest?		
What is the definition of "matter"?		
When can the attorney use information from the prior employment setting in representing a new client?		

Professional Responsibility Skills 19-B: Assessing a Career Path

Interview an attorney who works in a government office about how he views his role and whom he sees as his client. What kinds of work does he do? How often do attorneys in his field leave for private practice? How does he see their work as compared to private practice? Share your insights with others in the class. Jennifer Anne Adair, *To Be or Not to Be a "Government Attorney,"* Better Lawyer (Columbus Ohio Bar Association) (Fall 2009) available at http://www.cbalaw.org/articles/publications/better-lawyer/2009/.

Test Your Understanding

Suppose you work in the U.S. Attorney's Office. Recently, your office has been assigned an incredibly complex white collar crime case against BigBad Company.

Veronica Victim is one of the victims of the corporate fraud perpetrated by Big-Bad. She has asked if you would be able to file a civil action against the defendants as well, so that she may obtain compensation. You are confident, given what you have already seen of the case, that Victim has a very good case and would likely recover a multi-million dollar verdict. You are also aware that there are other, similarly situated victims of BigBad as well as a number of other companies and individuals against whom the prosecutor's office has not yet initiated investigations or actions.

You would love to move into the civil litigation area, but right now you still like the job security (even if the pay isn't great) of the prosecutor's office. This seems like a one-time opportunity to make a career shift. What can you do?

1. May you represent Victim in a civil action against BigBad while you are working as a prosecutor?

2. If not, may you quit your job at the U.S. Attorney's Office to take the case?

3. You have a friend who has a solo practice specializing in fraud litigation — he would be happy to have you join him and bring these civil cases with you. If you couldn't handle these particular cases yourself, could you at least join his firm and refer the clients to him, screening yourself from participation in this particular case, but building a practice based on civil actions arising out of corporate criminal activities?

4. How would you answer these questions if, instead of working for the U.S. Attorney's Office, you were representing the shareholders in a derivative suit against BigBad?

To Learn More

A classic article on former client conflicts is Charles Wolfram, *Former-Client Conflicts*, 10 Geo. J. Legal Ethics 677 (1997). The practice manual of the ABA/BNA Lawyers Manual provides a comprehensive analysis of former client conflicts as well.

Chapter Twenty

Conflicts of Interest and Imputed Disqualification

Learning Objectives

After you have read this chapter and completed the assignments, you should be able to:

- Identify which of the conflicts that are imputed to an attorney while in a firm the attorney takes with her when she moves to a new firm.

- Identify which of an attorney's own conflicts continue to be imputed to that attorney's firm after she has left the firm.

- Identify the types of conflicts for which screening the disqualified attorney will prevent the imputation of that attorney's conflicts and describe the elements of an effective ethical screen.

Rules to Study

The primary rules we will examine in this chapter are 1.9(b) and 1.10 and the disqualification cases related to these rules. We will also revisit Rule 1.18 to learn about ethical walls or "screening" to prevent conflicts.

Preliminary Problem

When she graduated from law school, Ashley worked in the ABC law firm as an associate. Following a practice that has gone out of style for most law firms, the ABC firm has all new associates spend their first 18 months rotating through various departments in the law firm so they can have an overall sense of the firm's practice and be evaluated by a number of partners. Ashley worked hard and received glowing reviews by her supervising attorneys. At the end of the 18 months, Ashley settled in the products liability department of the firm. At the end of her third year with the firm, she was approached by an attorney (Paul Partner) of the PQR law firm to join them. Ashley agreed.

In the process of making the move, PQR had to consider whether any of Ashley's prior work at ABC would create a conflict of interest and, if so, how it could be addressed. A preliminary comparison of the client and matter lists revealed only one potential conflict. Ashley worked on three cases at ABC in which the firm represented Big Business Inc. in employment discrimination matters. PQR has just begun representing Francis Former, an employee of BBI who was denied a promotion, in an employment discrimination action against BBI. How would PQR assess this conflict? What questions would it need to ask? What steps could it take to eliminate the conflict?

20.1 Imputed Conflicts and Traveling Attorneys

As you have learned, attorneys in a firm may not knowingly represent a client if any one of them, practicing alone, would be prohibited from doing so. Imputed disqualifications are most difficult to apply in situations in which attorneys move from one firm to another. If you think of conflicts of interest as a nasty virus that "infects" fellow attorneys, when does an attorney take the "taint" of his former partner's conflicts with him if he moves and how much of his own disqualification does he leave behind?

Rule 1.9(b) addresses the first question. An attorney who leaves a firm takes all his imputed disqualifications with him. But in most courts today, if the attorney did not work on a case, he can rebut the presumption that he acquired confidential information and thus purge his conflict. One of the first cases to recognize this principal was *Silver Chrysler Plymouth Inc. v. Chrysler Motors Corp.*, 518 F.2d 751 (2d Cir. 1975) which, like the *Carey* case in the prior chapter, involved a conflict arising out of representation of Chrysler Motors Corporation. Chrysler sought to disqualify opposing counsel because a member of their firm had previously worked at a firm that had represented Chrysler. The court denied the motion because the individual lawyer had only a "peripheral involvement" in any Chrysler work at the former firm. Of course, proving a negative is difficult. How would you go about proving that you never worked on a particular case and didn't receive confidential information about it?

For the firm that is left behind, how much of the departing attorney's disqualification stays with his former firm? Rule 1.10(b) says that any of the conflicts that arose because of the departing attorney's representation leave with him unless the former firm's attorneys have material confidential information that could raise a conflict.

As you recall, imputation rules are premised on a presumption of shared information. However, should that presumption be irrebuttable? New attorneys in a firm might be asked to research a discrete issue in a case and receive few, if any facts, about the case. The attorney may have no access to the client file and little opportunity to discuss the case with others. Is it reasonable to presume that this attorney has confidential information of the client that would be at risk if the attorney were on the other side?

These questions are critical to the courts' attempts to resolve the issue of imputed disqualification. Under what circumstances should the courts presume that an attorney who did not actually represent a client has protected information? Under what circumstances should the courts allow an attorney who actually worked on a case to deny that he or she has such information? While these matters are difficult enough, they are further complicated by the fact that it may not be the lawyer himself, but rather the lawyer's new firm, that is undertaking the subsequent representation.

When disqualification is sought against a lawyer whose firm previously represented a client against whom the lawyer now is adverse, the courts have generally used two levels of presumptions to determine whether disqualification is required. The first presumption is that the attorney who represented the client in fact had confidential information that could be used against the client (if the matters are substantially related, and the subsequent representation is materially adverse). This presumption is routinely viewed as irrebuttable. But when the attorney whose disqualification is sought did not actually work on the matter, most courts will apply a rebuttable presumption on the issue of whether that attorney has protected information. If the attorney can rebut that presumption, by showing, for example, that he or she had no access to files and spoke to no one about the case, disqualification will not be ordered unless the other side comes back with information to the contrary. In that case, the courts, not wanting a "swearing contest," will generally allow the presumption to carry the day and will disqualify the attorney.

If, however, the attorney actually worked on the matter, most courts will not allow the presumption of access to confidential information to be rebutted. In these situations, disqualification will be mandatory. Some courts, however, are concerned about the limited access problem. In order to facilitate mobility among lawyers and choice of counsel by clients, these courts will allow rebuttal where the attorney was only "peripherally involved" in the previous matter. "... [T]here is a reason to differentiate for disqualification purposes between lawyers who become heavily involved in the facts of a particular matter and those who enter briefly on the periphery.... Under the latter circumstances the attorney's role cannot be considered 'representation.'" *Silver Chrysler Plymouth Inc. v. Chrysler Motors Corp.*, 518 F.2d 751, 756-57 (2d Cir. 1975).

In order for the automatic disqualification to take place under Rule 1.9(a), there must be a showing that the attorney whose disqualification is sought actually represented the former client, not just that his or her law firm did so. This allows attorneys on the periphery of issues to avoid being cast as having represented a client when, in fact, they merely belonged to the firm. This also corresponds to the comment to Rule 1.9, which states: "The lawyer's involvement in the matter can also be a question of degree." Although the court in *Silver Chrysler* refused to draw a controlling distinction between partners and associates in addressing this question, it seems clear that this doctrine is designed to protect those with limited access to information, most likely younger associates. For the most part, it is only when the scope and degree of representation by their nature rebut the presumption of shared confidences that the *Silver Chrysler* peripheral involvement approach has been accepted.

While the use of these presumptions to resolve issues of disqualifications has been generally accepted for some time, the advent of the Model Rules has begun to cause a change in focus. Under the Model Rules, a lawyer should not represent a person in the same or a substantially related matter in which that lawyer's prior firm previously represented a client whose interests are materially adverse and about whom the lawyer has acquired protected information. Rule 1.9(b). The disciplinary rule allows for discipline only if the lawyer in fact possesses such information, although proof of such fact may be aided by "inferences, deductions or working presumptions." Comment 6.

Courts in a number of jurisdictions that have adopted the Model Rules increasingly use the language of the rules, rather than the presumptions, to resolve disqualification issues. Thus, in *Parker v. Volkswagenwerk Aktiengesellschaft*, 781 P.2d 1099 (Kan. 1989), the court focused not on whether it should presume access to information, but rather on whether there had been a showing that the attorney "had knowledge of material and confidential information." *See also Graham v. Wyeth Labs*, 906 F.2d 1419 (10th Cir. 1990) (applying Kansas law). Does this provide sufficient protection to the former client's information? Does it adequately address appearances? Is use of the Model Rules appropriate in this context? Why or why not?

20.2 Ethical Screens

If it is not the attorney, but the attorney's new firm, that is currently representing a client adverse to the attorney's former client, can the attorney be screened from the current representation so that the firm can continue in the representation? Note that the rules permit screening to prevent imputation of conflicts in several discrete situations. In the prospective client context, Rule 1.18 permits screening as a means of limiting imputed disqualification. Likewise in the situation of government attorneys and judges, where conflicts arise rather easily given the breadth of the rule, the rules allow screening to prevent disqualification. Rules 1.11(b) & (c) and 1.12(c). Comment 4 to Rule 1.10 indicates that screening is appropriate to prevent imputation of conflicts arising from non-lawyers. Finally, in the most recent amendment to the Model Rules, screening has been permitted to prevent conflicts from being imputed when lawyers move from one firm to another.

Courts have been reluctant to expand the use of screening because the relative informality of information exchange within most law firms makes it difficult to truly "screen" an attorney from information. Moreover, there are powerful economic incentives to use information to win cases and no one outside the firm can ever really be sure what has transpired inside the firm. Note that an ethical screen would not allow a client to consent to a conflict that is, under the rules, nonconsentable. *Westinghouse Corp. v. Kerr-McGee Corp.*, 580 F.2d 1311 (7th Cir. 1978). For cases in which client can waive conflicts, a growing minority of courts have begun to recognize screening as a legitimate means of curing imputed conflicts based on the new realities of law practice, which require a balancing of interests. *Manning v. Waring, Cox, James, Sklar & Allen*, 849 F.2d 222, 225 (6th Cir. 1988); *Schiessle v. Stephens*, 717 F.2d 417, 421 (7th Cir. 1983).

Where screening is permitted, it generally requires that the screened attorney be denied access to files, not discuss the matter with others in the firm, and not share in profits or fees derived from the representation. The most recent amendment to the Model Rules now allows screening in limited situations of attorneys switching firms. That rule sets up fairly strict screening standards. How should a court (or a client for that matter) evaluate the effectiveness of a screen? The Ohio court in *Kala v. Aluminum Smelting & Ref. Co.*, 688 N.E.2d 258 (Ohio 1998) suggested the following factors:

> Factors to be considered in deciding whether an effective screen has been created are whether the law firm is sufficiently large and whether the structural divisions of the firm are sufficiently separate so as to minimize contact between the quarantined attorney and the others, the likelihood of contact between the quarantined attorney and the specific attorneys responsible for the current representation, the existence of safeguards or procedures which prevent the quarantined attorney from access to relevant files or other information relevant to the present litigation, prohibited access to files and other information on the case, locked case files with keys distributed to a select few, secret codes necessary to access pertinent information on electronic hardware, instructions given to all members of a new firm regarding the ban on exchange of information, and the prohibition of the sharing of fees derived from such litigation.

Some courts have held that unrebutted affidavits attesting to an [ethical wall][1] are sufficient to prevent disqualification. However, we reject such a bright-line test, as the court should maintain discretion to weigh issues of credibility. The court should be free to assess the reputation of an attorney and law firm for integrity and honesty.

Professional Responsibility Skill 20-A: Designing a Screen

Ethical screens first were recognized in the rules of professional conduct to prevent conflicts that former government attorneys had because of their personal and substantial involvement in matters while they worked for the government. Screening the former government attorney prevented her conflicts from being imputed to other attorneys in the firm that she had now joined.

Suppose you work in an 18-person firm that does land use planning and environmental law. You wish to hire an attorney from the Environmental Protection Agency. However, that attorney worked on an investigation of one of your current clients, Polluticorp Company, while he was at the EPA. Describe how you would screen that attorney so that the firm could continue to represent Polluticorp.

20.3 Identifying Conflicts

Every attorney should have a system to identify conflicts of interest. Conflicts systems are built upon a list of names, dates, attorneys, and matters. Remember that Rule 1.7(a)(2) provides that a conflict can arise from the interests of "third parties," so the names must include not only clients but adverse parties, witnesses, and any other person who has any significant involvement in a representation. Names of the client's employer or any businesses closely owned by the client should also be included. Dates are important because a conflict that involves a current client will be judged differently than one judges a conflict that involves a former client. Although conflicts are imputed among attorneys, when attorneys leave a law firm, there are many conflicts that they take with them, without leaving the imputation behind. Thus, a conflicts checking system should include the names of the attorneys involved in a matter. Finally, the system should allow you to access the scope of the representation and types of information collected in that representation.

---

1. The court actually used the older term "Chinese Wall." The term was developed in the 1920s and borrowed from the practice of erecting walls between workers in Chinese porcelain studios that separated workers who each would know only one step of the production process and would pass their pieces through a small window to the next worker, thus protecting the secret of porcelain production. The term has been discarded in favor of "ethical wall" or "ethical screen" to avoid the insensitivity of the ethnic reference. *See Peat, Marwick, Mitchell & Co. v. Superior Court,* 200 Cal. App. 3d 272, 293–294, 245 *Cal.Rptr.* 873, 887–888 (1988) (referring to the term as "a subtle form of linguistic discrimination"). In researching issues of ethical screens, however, it is useful to know that this term was used in earlier opinions.

A conflicts system can be built on a billing system, but simply relying on billing records alone can allow some critical conflicts to slip through the cracks; especially where the person being billed and the person being represented are not the same. For some attorneys, who keep all their representation information in computerized form, a desktop search engine might provide a sufficient system to be able to identify potential conflicts. For larger firms, a more specialized system is likely to be necessary, with a separate database created—often out of the firm's case management and calendaring system—for purposes of checking for conflicts of interest. Of course all these systems can do is unearth names and matters. Someone must still analyze the information provided to determine whether an actual conflict exists.

As with any system, the key is to use the system religiously. At the first contact by a potential client, and before obtaining any confidential information about the matter, you should obtain the same "who" information from the potential client that you have in your conflicts database. You may wish to explain to the potential client that a list of all the persons who might be involved in the matter allows you to check for disqualifying conflicts of interest before the client invests her time, money, and private information. These names can then be checked against the conflicts database. If that check reveals a conflict, you then can consider whether the conflict is one for which consent may be obtained or whether the conflict precludes representation. If you must decline the representation because of a conflict, you should send the client a "non-acceptance letter." Since the fact that a conflict exists might itself require revealing confidential information, a non-acceptance letter need not say that that the reason you are declining the representation is a conflict of interest. Instead, you may simply indicate that, while you would ordinarily be pleased to take on the representation, you are simply not in a position to do so at this time.

Even if your screening process does not identify a conflict, or your clients have consented to proceed in the face of a conflict, you should continually monitor your representations for changes that may create new conflicts.

As you saw in the preliminary problem, one of the most difficult areas in which to identify conflicts is when attorneys join a new firm or when law firms merge. Since the rules in most states permit attorneys moving from one firm to another to be screened in order to prevent imputation of conflicts to other members of the firm, how does an attorney inform the new firm of the conflicts that will now be imputed to the firm? Wouldn't the necessary disclosures violate Rule 1.6 or could you argue that these disclosures fall under the exception "to secure legal advice" about the lawyer's ethical duties? Ordinarily, all that would need to be disclosed is the name of the client, a general description of the matter, and some dates. However, even this information could be extremely sensitive for a client who, for example, is seeking a divorce, considering an investment, or has been investigated or charged with a crime. Recognizing this difficulty in discovering conflicts presented when attorneys move from firm to firm, the American Bar Association in August 2012, amended Rule 1.6 to include an additional exception. Model Rule 1.6(b)(7) permits attorneys to reveal confidential information to the extent reasonably believed necessary "to detect and resolve conflicts of interest arising from the lawyer's change of employment or from changes in the composition or ownership of a firm, but only if the revealed information would not compromise the attorney-client privilege or otherwise prejudice the client." New comment 13 to the rule suggests that, if the privilege would be involved or disclosure would prejudice the client, the attorney must obtain the client's informed consent to disclosure. But if a disclosure would prejudice a client, how could one reasonably ask the client to consent to that disclosure?

Test Your Understanding

1. Revisit the preliminary problem. You should now recognize the analysis the firm would need to undertake to decide whether a conflict exists:

   Some questions the firm would want to ask to determine whether the two cases are the same or substantially related:

   What departments or personnel were involved in the ABC cases?

   What was the nature of the discrimination alleged in the ABC cases?

   How long had the ABC firm represented BBI?

   What is the nature of the discrimination alleged in the current suit against BBI?

   Some questions the firm would want to ask to determine whether Ashley acquired confidential information or if the presumption of shared information could be rebutted:

   What kind of involvement did Ashley have in the ABC cases?

   What were ABC's patterns of sharing client information?

   Some questions the firm would want to ask to determine if steps to avoid the conflict are prudent and efficient:

   Can Ashley be screened from the Francis Former case?

   Would Francis and BBI waive the potential conflict?

To Learn More

The following articles are helpful for learning more about some of the issues that will continue to create tensions in imputed disqualification rules:

John Sahl, *Thinking of Leaving? The Ethics of Departing One Firm for Another*, 19:1 PROF'L LAW. 2 (2008).

Eli Wald, *Lawyer Mobility and Legal Ethics: Resolving the Tension between Confidentiality Requirements and Contemporary Lawyers' Career Paths*, 31 J. LEGAL PROF. 199 (2007).

Paul R. Tremblay, *Migrating Lawyers and the Ethics of Conflict Checking*, 19 GEO. J. LEGAL ETHICS 489 (2006).

Susan P. Shapiro, *If It Ain't Broke ... An Empirical Perspective on Ethics 2000, Screening, and the Conflict-of-Interest Rules*, 2003 U. ILL. L. REV. 1299 (2003).

Unit Five Review

Revisit the pre-test at the beginning of this unit. You should now recognize that all the statements are false except statements #2,4,5, and 12.

While you have seen that conflicts is a very fact-sensitive inquiry that can make management and prediction of conflicts very difficult, you must at least be able to start your analysis in the right place. Be sure you understand which rules apply to which types of conflicts of potential conflicts:

Interests	Potential Conflicts
Your own and the client's	1.8 rules may prohibit the action or representation. Conflict may be imputed to other attorneys, depending on the nature of the conflict. Attorney has burden to prove that client consent is informed and reasonable.
Current client and former prospective client	1.18 Conflict No imputation to firm if attorney limited information received and is timely screened.
Current client and another client (current or former) Not adverse Not related	No conflicts.
Current client and former government matter On which you worked personally and substantially	1.11 Conflict Consent possible but unlikely. No imputation to firm if timely screened and notice given to government.
Current clients Directly adverse Substantially related matters	1.7 Conflict Imputed to firm unless personal interest. Nonconsentable if the same matter in litigation; Generally nonconsentable in many jurisdictions; Unlikely to be able to secure consent in most situations.
Current and former client Adverse Substantially related matters	1.9 Conflict Imputed to firm unless personal interest. May be able to secure consent.

Interests	Potential Conflicts
Current clients Directly adverse Unrelated matters	Probably 1.7 Conflict Unlikely to be able to secure consent. Nonconsentable in most jurisdictions; Unlikely to be able to secure consent in most situations. Imputed to firm unless personal interest.
Current and former client Adverse Unrelated matters	Not a 1.9 conflict unless confidential information was obtained that could be used adversely to former client. If so, imputed to firm, unless personal interest.
Current clients Not adverse Substantially related matters	Not a 1.9 conflict. Possibly a 1.7 conflict: Is your representation materially limited by the common representation? If so, can you take protective action? Can clients provide informed consent?
Current and former client Not adverse Substantially related matters	Not a 1.9 conflict, unless confidentiality would be breached. If so, imputed to firm unless personal interest.
Current client and third person	Not a 1.7 conflict unless your own competence & diligence or ability to safeguard client's confidentiality would be materially limited by loyalty to the third person. (See Rule 1.8 also.) If conflict, imputed to firm.
Current client and a client of a former firm Adverse Same or substantially related matter You received confidential information about former client	1.9 conflict Can prevent imputation through timely screening. Consentable.
Current client and a client of a former firm Adverse Same or substantially related matter You did not receive confidential information about former client	No 1.9 conflict if can rebut the presumption of shared information (by showing no or only peripheral involvement and no opportunities for shared information).
Current client and a former client of an attorney who has since left firm Adverse Same or substantially related matter Attorneys in firm received confidential information about former client	1.10 conflict Consentable.
Current client and a former client of an attorney who has since left firm Adverse Same or substantially related matter Attorneys in firm did not receive confidential information about former client	No 1.10 conflict if can rebut the presumption of shared information (very difficult to do in most large law firms unless an entire department left the firm).

Multiple Choice Review

1. As a favor to a friend, Attorney agrees to represent Geraldine in a dispute she has with National Bank regarding credit card fees. He meets with Geraldine for 45 minutes, collects a $50 consultation fee, and has her sign a representation agreement. The next week, before he can do any work on Geraldine's case, the in-house counsel for National Bank calls Attorney and asks if Attorney will take on the bank's foreclosure business. Attorney agrees and receives a list of the bank's customers against whom foreclosures will be commenced. Geraldine's name appears on the list. Attorney decides he is uncomfortable with the situation and sends Geraldine a letter indicating that he must withdraw from her case and returns the file to her and refunds her the $50 consultation fee. Is Attorney subject to discipline?

   A. No, Attorney's conflict required him to withdraw from the representation of Geraldine.
   B. No, Attorney's withdrawal was one reasonable way to resolve the conflict of interest.
   C. Yes, Attorney did not have a conflict of interest because the two representations were not the same or substantially related so withdrawal was not proper.
   D. Yes, Attorney may not withdraw from representing a current client in order to resolve a current client conflict of interest.

2. Attorney has a family law practice. Occasionally he helps out the prosecutor's office with child support enforcement actions when the office has a conflict of interest. Six months ago, Attorney prosecuted a child support action on behalf of the state to collect child support against David Dad. The support action involved David's child Sonny. Sonny's mother Mary had sole custody of Sonny and Dad had child support obligations. Mary had been required to assign Sonny's child support to the state as a condition of receiving welfare benefits. Attorney was successful in recovering $20,000 of back support from Dad.

   Attorney has now been approached by Mary to defend her in an action brought by Dad to change custody. Mary is willing to change their arrangement to a joint custody arrangement, which would likely then lower Dad's child support obligations. May Attorney represent Mary?

   A. Yes, there are no restrictions on an attorney's right to represent a former client in a new action.
   B. Yes, the action to change custody would not attack any of Attorney's prior work.
   C. No, Attorney's representation would be the same or substantially related to his representation of the state in the former action and would be adverse to the state because it would interfere with the state's ability to collect child support from Dad.
   D. No, Attorney's representation of Mary would involve a matter in which Attorney participated personally and substantially as a public employee.

3. Barbara Barrister worked for Remaigne & Mantuvo (R&M), a five-person, boutique employment law firm for five years. During the time at the firm,

she was general labor counsel to the Central School District. She represented the district in employment litigation, including several claims involving discrimination and civil rights. She also handled a number of other key employment law matters, including the preparation of a revised employee manual with provisions that permitted the district to modify retirement benefits at any time. She also provided general employment law advice and participated in confidential meetings, which included employment and personnel matters. The firm had two secretaries and three paralegals that all attorneys shared. All attorneys in the firm worked on employment matters.

Barbara left the law firm and joined a new firm, where she continued to represent the district. Renard Remaigne, her former partner at R&M was approached by Paul Plaintiff, a retired teacher in the Central School District, to bring a civil rights suit on behalf of him and his mother over cancellation of retiree health benefits for dependents of the retirees. Paul knew that Barbara had previously represented the district. Paul alleged that the cancellation of the retiree benefits was in retaliation for Paul's political activity in speaking out about educational issues in the district. Renard agreed to represent Paul. Almost immediately after he entered his appearance, the district filed a motion to disqualify. Will Renard be disqualified from representing Paul?

A. Yes, because Barbara participated personally and substantially in employment matters for the district.
B. Yes, because Paul's matter is substantially related to Barbara's representation of the district and the R&M firm acquired material confidential information.
C. No, because Barbara took the District with her as a client when she left the firm.
D. No, because Paul consented to the conflict.

Answers and Analysis

1. D is the correct answer. Geraldine and First National would both be current clients and would be directly adverse to one another. Even though the matters are not related, this is a conflict, which is why C is incorrect because it applies the former client conflict standard. Withdrawal is not an acceptable method to resolve these conflicts (recall the "hot potato" doctrine), so A and B are incorrect.

2. The key to this problem is recognizing that the state was the client in the first action, so that the correct standard to apply for conflicts is Rule 1.11. D is the correct answer under that rule.

3. The correct answer is B. A is incorrect because, while Barbara represented the district, she was not a "government employee" so Rule 1.11 does not apply. C is not correct because even though Barbara left the firm and the client followed her, the firm would still have information about her prior representation (it is a small firm, all attorneys do employment law, and they share secretaries and paralegals). D is not correct because in a former client conflict situation both the former and current client must give informed consent. Answer B is correct (Rule 1.10(b)). The question is based on *Henry v. Delaware River Joint Toll Bridge Commission*, 2001 WL 1003224 (E.D. Pa. 2001).

Practice Context Review

Test your ability to analyze conflicts overall with the following problem:

Memo

To: You Yourself
From: Alfred Attorney
Re: Your advice please

One of the reasons I was so happy to leave my old firm (Olson, Smith & Wyatt) last year to join you all here at Brown & Green is the fact that our firm has people like you that can help a partner out in a jam. Take a look at the attached motion to disqualify I was just served. The weird thing is, I don't even represent Bee Manufacturing Company anymore and Aye Corporation is still trying to disqualify me! I think the motion makes the situation pretty clear, but just to give it to you in a nutshell: Bee was my client at Olson, Smith & Wyatt. I worked on some IP matters for them, including some patent infringement matters. Bee decided to stay with Olson when I left, but I still had three opinion letters that I needed to wrap up. I finished them about a week after I joined our firm. Unfortunately, the opinion letters concerned possible infringement of the patent held by Aye Corporation.

As I understand it, Aye Corporation is a regular client of John Brown in our firm. Unfortunately, we didn't catch the conflict when I joined the firm. I listed Bee as one of my clients on our conflicts screen, but I could hardly reveal their business plan to manufacture advanced widget designs similar to that of Aye's! That would be inside information that I'm sure Bee would not have authorized me to disclose. When Aye came to John to represent them in this suit, after Bee began manufacturing, our screen flagged my final bill to Bee and he declined the case based on a conflict.

Anyway, that apparently wasn't enough to satisfy Aye, who now wants to disqualify me and require that I withdraw my opinion letters. I sure don't want to have to withdraw my opinions. Bee was a great client and I'd hate to think what kind of reputation I'd have if I sold them out. On the other hand, I know that John really values Aye's business as a long-term client of the firm. And I have to predict the court's reaction to this motion. What do you think I should do?

In the United States District Court
for the District of Kansas

AYE CORPORATION,
    a Delaware corporation, Plaintiff,
 	
v.
 	
BEE MANUFACTURING COMPANY,
    a Kansas corporation, Defendant.
	No. 10-C-0000
	November 8, 2012

MOTION TO DISQUALIFY OPINION COUNSEL AND EXCLUDE EVIDENCE

Plaintiff Aye Corporation moves to disqualify attorney Arnold Attorney from participation in this matter and to exclude any evidence of his opinions regarding the patent
at issue in this case. In support of this motion, movant shows the court the following:

1.   Plaintiff, AYE CORPORATION (hereafter "Aye"), is a corporation organized and existing under the laws of the State of Delaware, with its principal place of business located
at 000 West First in Chicago, Illinois.

2.   Defendant BEE MANUFACTURING COMPANY (hereafter "Bee"), is a corporation
organized and existing under the laws of the State of Kansas, with its principal place of
business located at 000 East Main in Topeka, Kansas.

3.   From January 1, 2009, through June 30, 2011, attorney Arnold Attorney of the firm
of Oldham, Smith, & Wyatt, located at 000 West Avenue, Topeka, Kansas represented
the defendant Bee during which time he prepared several opinion letters advising Bee regarding its manufacturing of advanced widget designs and whether that manufacturing
infringed on patents held by other companies, including the patents held by Aye.

4.   During this same time period and to the present date, John Brown and the Brown
& Green law firm represented Aye in connection with its intellectual property matters,
including prosecuting the patents at issue in this action, in preparing cease and desist
against infringers, and in connection with other related matters.

5.   John Brown performed extensive legal work for Aye on each of the above-described
matters, devoting approximately 250 hours to the continuing representation of Aye.

6.   Arnold Attorney ceased his association with Oldham & Smith and joined the firm of
Brown & Green on June 21, 2011.

7.   Arnold Attorney's representation of Bee terminated on June 30, 2011, when he delivered his opinion letters to Bee.

8.   On January 15, 2012, plaintiff Aye approached John Brown to engage his services in
relation to Bee's infringement of its patent for advanced widgets. John Brown declined the
representation, citing conflict of interests.

9.   On January 20, 2012, plaintiff Aye engaged present counsel to commence this action
for patent infringement against Bee.

10. Bee has produced, and intends to rely upon, non-infringement and invalidity opinions obtained from Arnold Attorney.

11. These opinions concerning Aye's patent were issued in violation of Rule 1.7(a) of the
Kansas Rules of Professional Conduct, and in violation of the fiduciary duty to Andrew.

12. Bee's reliance on these opinion letters in this matter is directly adverse to the interests of Aye Corporation, a continuing client of the law firm of Brown & Green, of which Arnold Attorney is a partner.

13. At no time has either Aye or Bee executed a waiver of its rights to object to conflicting representations.

14. The use of Attorney's opinion letters in this action against Aye is a violation of the duty of fidelity that is imposed on Alfred Attorney as a member of the Kansas Bar and as an attorney admitted to practice before the United States District Court of Kansas pursuant to Code of Professional Conduct of the American Bar Association.

15. Alfred Attorney should therefore be disqualified from participating in this action on behalf of Bee Manufacturing Company and should be required to withdraw the opinion letters issued in violation of the rules of professional conduct and his fiduciary duties to Aye.

Wherefore, movant respectfully requests the following relief:

1. An order temporarily enjoining Alfred Attorney or the firm of Brown & Green from representing or cooperating in the representation of Bee Manufacturing Company in this case until this matter can be determined by the court;

2. An order permanently disqualifying Alfred Attorney or the firm of Brown & Green from representing or cooperating in the representation of Bee Manufacturing Company in this case until this matter can be determined by the court;

3. An order requiring Alfred Attorney to withdraw and disclaim any opinion letters issued to defendant Bee in relation to Aye's patents.

4. Any further relief that the court determines is just and proper.

Sam Solicitor

Sam Solicitor
Attorney for Plaintiffs

This problem is based on *Andrew Corp. v. Beverly Mfg. Co.* 415 F.Supp.2d 919 (N.D. Ill. 2006). In that case, the attorney who issued the opinion letters was barred from testifying on behalf of his client and was required to withdraw the opinion letters, leaving his client without a defense against the claim of willful infringement.

Fairness and the Boundaries of Adversarial Zeal

Goals of Unit

The overall goal of this unit is that you will recognize the tensions inherent in the multiple roles of an attorney as an advocate for a client and as a representative of the legal system. You should recognize that much of litigation practice is regulated by substantive and procedural rules, to which the rules of professional conduct defer. Finally, you should have developed some practical strategies for protecting yourself and your clients from those who are willing to break these rules in order to gain an advantage in litigation.

Pretest

Before you study the materials in this unit, take a moment to consider your own personal views on the proper role of an advocate. Jot down your answers to the following questions.

1. What does it mean to be a zealous advocate?

2. Do you think that most opposing attorneys can agree on guidelines for their discovery in litigation? Why or why not?

3. If an opposing attorney violates the rules, when should you confront the attorney and try to resolve the issue yourself and when should you go to the court for sanctions?

4. Do you think you should have to get the permission of opposing counsel to speak to his or her client? How would you feel about opposing counsel speaking to your client without your knowledge or permission?

5. Do you have an obligation to treat unrepresented opponents differently than whose who are represented by an attorney?

Chapter Twenty-One

Ethics in Litigation Practice

Learning Objectives

After you have read this chapter and completed the assignments, you should be able to:

- Identify limits on methods of obtaining evidence or using evidence others have obtained.
- Identify standards limiting an attorney's use of trial publicity and constitutional standards that apply to that regulation.
- Describe the differences in role and responsibility when representing a client in mediation.
- Locate local rules and practice regarding deposition practice.
- Strategize appropriate responses to attorneys who engage in abusive tactics.

Rules to Study

The primary rules of professional conduct that govern the attorney as an advocate are found in Rules 3.1-3.9. We have already studied Rule 3.3 in Chapter Twelve and its tension with the duty of confidentiality. As we saw there, the rules of procedure and evidence play an important role in defining the attorney's duties as an advocate in litigation, so we will revisit some of those rules here. We will also look at how some tort, contract, and criminal law standards can affect attorneys acting as advocates, whether in the courtroom or at the negotiation table.

Preliminary Problem

Suppose you have agreed to represent Clyde Cycler who was severely injured in a bicycle accident when his brakes failed. You have investigated the claim and bring a products liability action against Thwinn Bicycles, Inc., who manufactured the bicycle and the brake system. A week before the first set of depositions is scheduled, you find a blank envelope slipped under your door. Inside you find what appears to be a printout of an email between two employees at Thwinn, discussing the fact that the company was ignoring the results of routine company inspections that revealed serious brake defects:

To: Jane Ryder, VP Sales
From   Melvin Smith, Plant manager

Dear Jane:

 I just heard about the latest suit against us on the X-837 brakes. I told you there was a problem with the brake production line for the mountain bikes. I've dumped the inspection files but we really do need to get those X-837s off the market!

Mel

Thwinn's attorney is Fred Rambo. He has a reputation for having "scorched earth" tactics and a trigger temper. You consider withdrawing just so you don't have to deal with him, but decide Clyde doesn't deserve being left to Fred's mercy. The discovery conference is fairly routine, but after you file your first set of interrogatories requesting some fairly straightforward information about the number of bikes sold, the manufacturer of the brakes, the number of complaints received and the like, Fred refuses to respond. When you finally file a motion to compel, he files a document objecting to each one of your interrogatories as "Objection. This Request is overly broad, vague, unduly burdensome, and therefore not reasonably calculated to lead to the discovery of admissible evidence but rather intended to harass." A motion to produce documents that pertain to the design and safety record of the brakes results in his providing you with a terabyte hard drive with all the company's products documents in a format that cannot be electronically searched. Fred insists this is how Thwinn archives its records and so he has produced the records "as they are maintained in the course of business."

At the first deposition, Fred appears with Satyam Raju, the senior VP of the manufacturing division of Thwinn. As you begin to question Mr. Raju, Fred continually interrupts with disruptions such as "if you remember" or objections, followed by long explanations designed to signal to Mr. Raju how he should answer the question. When you object to his continual interruptions he calls for a break. He then raises his voice and begins to walk to your side of the table and stands over you, saying "Now about all these frivolous objections. You're such a f—ing rookie! You can shove you f—ing objection! I'll represent my client any way I want. What are you going to do about it?"

How should you deal with the evidence and discovery in this suit?

21.1 Reading the Rules: Tensions in the Role of the Advocate

The rules of professional conduct section labeled "Advocate" speaks primarily to the restrictions on that role. The attorney's duties as an advocate are the same fundamental duties as in any other role: competence, diligence, communication, confidentiality, and loyalty. However, these duties are balanced with duties to the courts and society. Read Connecticut's Rule 3.4, which is identical to the Model Rules except for the italicized additional provision.

Connecticut Rules of Professional Conduct
Rule 3.4 Fairness to Opposing Party and Counsel

A lawyer shall not:

(1) Unlawfully obstruct another party's access to evidence or unlawfully alter, destroy or conceal a document or other material having potential evidentiary value. A lawyer shall not counsel or assist another person to do any such act;

(2) Falsify evidence, counsel or assist a witness to testify falsely, or offer an inducement to a witness that is prohibited by law;

(3) Knowingly disobey an obligation under the rules of a tribunal except for an open refusal based on an assertion that no valid obligation exists;

(4) In pretrial procedure, make a frivolous discovery request or fail to make reasonably diligent effort to comply with a legally proper discovery request by an opposing party;

(5) In trial, allude to any matter that the lawyer does not reasonably believe is relevant or that will not be supported by admissible evidence, assert personal knowledge of facts in issue except when testifying as a witness, or state a personal opinion as to the justness of a cause, the credibility of a witness, the culpability of a civil litigant or the guilt or innocence of an accused; or

(6) Request a person other than a client to refrain from voluntarily giving relevant information to another party unless:

(A) The person is a relative or an employee or other agent of a client; and

(B) The lawyer reasonably believes that the person's interests will not be adversely affected by refraining from giving such information.

(7) Present, participate in presenting, or threaten to present criminal charges solely to obtain an advantage in a civil matter.

Context

The Model Code of Professional Responsibility, predecessor to the current Model Rules of Professional Conduct, provided in Canon 7: "A Lawyer Should Represent a Client Zealously within the Bounds of the Law." That principle of *zealous representation*, while no longer found in the black-letter rules of conduct, still plays a powerful force in most attorneys' conception of their role as an advocate. Judith L. Maute, *Sporting Theory of Justice: Taming Adversary Zeal with a Logical Sanctions Doctrine*, 20 CONN. L. REV. 7, 10 (1987). Passion for your clients, passion for a client's cause, and passion for winning can all blind you to the difference between zeal and zealotry or between the roles of advocate and adversary. Some clients in particular look for attorneys who will "do whatever it takes" to win. An attorney's obligation to counsel the client includes making ethical boundaries clear to these clients. Rule 3.4 is designed to describe some of those limits. We have already examined some of these limits. In Chapter Twelve, we examined the duty of candor and its limits on partisan advocacy before a tribunal. In Chapter Thirteen, we examined the problem of misrepresentation and some of the ways you can protect your client from that particular form of abusive advocacy.

Relationships

Go back and re-read Rule 3.4. Notice how often it refers to law outside the rules. Knowing the rules of conduct without understanding this other law leaves you with very little clear guidance. Thus, in this chapter, we will study criminal and evidentiary rules governing factual investigation and handling of evidence and procedural rules governing discovery and trial practice. Since all of these laws vary considerably across different jurisdictions and even from courtroom to courtroom, keep in mind that you will need to research your own system to clarify your duties.

Structure

This rule provides a hodgepodge of rules governing the attorney as advocate. Rule 3.5 on Impartiality and Decorum goes on to provide an additional list regarding interactions with court personnel and jurors. There is little relationship between each of the subparts of this rule. The rule is labeled "fairness" but does that capture fully the theme of this rule? How else might you describe the overall concern of this rule?

Reasons

Why provide a separate set of rules to govern litigation conduct when most of the rules have an analogue in procedural or substantive law or even defer to that law? Often the most powerful constraints on attorney misconduct in advocacy are rules of procedure, rather than the rules of professional conduct. In fact, all of the rules of procedure are integrated into the rules of professional conduct. (Do you see how? Look again at Rule 3.4(c)). Professor Andrew Perlman argues that the rules of professional conduct governing litigation conduct have achieved "near-obsolescence."

> Despite the pervasive role that pleadings and discovery play in litigators' lives, litigators and judges rarely need to refer to these rules. The reason is simple: Rules 11 and 26 of the Federal Rules of Civil Procedure (or their state equivalents) as well as 28 U.S.C. § 1927 (in federal cases) establish the relevant standards in these areas. Lawyers and judges look to these authorities for guidance rather than to the relevant rules of professional conduct.

> It is surprising that the Model Rules fail to acknowledge this development. For example, Model Rule 3.1 governs frivolous pleadings, and Comment [3] observes that a "lawyer's obligations under this Rule are subordinate to federal or state constitutional law that entitles a defendant in a criminal matter to the assistance of counsel in presenting a claim or contention that otherwise would be prohibited by this Rule." Notably absent from the Comment is any recognition ... that a lawyer's obligation may be different under the federal or state rules of civil procedure or other applicable statutory law. The failure to acknowledge that law other than constitutional law governs this area is a surprising omission given the widespread understanding that other law, such as rules of civil procedure, has effectively taken over this area of regulation.

> Like Model Rule 3.1, Model Rule 3.4(d) fails to acknowledge that most jurisdictions have rules of civil procedure that govern precisely the same topic. Model Rule 3.4(d) states that a lawyer shall not, "in pretrial procedure, make a frivolous discovery request or fail to make reasonably diligent effort to comply with a legally proper discovery request by an opposing party." But Rules 26(g)(3) and 37 of the Federal Rules of Civil Procedure (and their state equivalents) already provide for sanctions under these circumstances.

> Model Rule 3.2 raises similar issues. It states that "[a] lawyer shall make reasonable efforts to expedite litigation consistent with the interests of the client."

In federal court, judges have no need to refer to Model Rule 3.2, because a statute governs this area. It provides that "any attorney ... who so multiplies the proceedings in any case unreasonably and vexatiously may be required by the court to satisfy personally the excess costs, expenses, and attorneys' fees reasonably incurred because of such conduct." 28 U.S.C. § 1927 (2006). And in state courts that have no statutory provision similar to 28 U.S.C. § 1927 (2006), the behavior described in the Model Rule is tacitly accepted by lawyers and the courts. Indeed, a comment to the Model Rule explicitly acknowledges that the bench and bar often condone this behavior. That concession raises a question that cuts across Model Rules 3.1, 3.2, and 3.4(d): if the civil procedure rules and related statutes regulate the conduct in these areas and if any other conduct covered by these Rules is condoned, what purpose do these Model Rules serve?

There are two plausible answers. One possibility is that these Model Rules supply a form of aspirational guidance that is not intended to be enforced. This view, however, is inconsistent with the widespread understanding of the Model Rules as black letter, enforceable norms of conduct. Moreover, such a view would make redundant various efforts to draft professionalism codes that are supposed to supply unenforceable standards of conduct. Finally, the very idea of professionalism codes is controversial, and it would be made even more so if it is done surreptitiously under the cover of the Model Rules.

A second and more plausible answer is that these Rules are supposed to be used for attorney discipline, not court-imposed sanctions. But as is the case in the conflicts context, there is little evidence that lawyers are actually disciplined for violating these provisions in the absence of a corresponding violation of the civil procedure rules. Moreover, it is not clear why separate rules of professional conduct should even be necessary to discipline lawyers who run afoul of—and are sanctioned for—violations of the rules of civil procedure or related statutes. After all, Model Rule 3.4(c) already provides that a lawyer shall not "knowingly disobey an obligation under the rules of a tribunal." Thus, Model Rule 3.4(c) supplies an adequate basis for discipline. Finally, the existence of parallel authority can generate confusion about the relevant standard or, worse, lead lawyers to conclude that they can ignore the rules of professional conduct without consequence. For all of these reasons, the Model Rules in these areas do not appear to serve any useful purpose; if anything, they generate confusion and undermine the law-like status of the Model Rules as a whole.

Andrew Perlman, *Civil Procedure and the Legal Profession: The Parallel Law of Lawyering in Civil Litigation*, 79 FORDHAM L. REV. 1965, 1971-1973 (2011).

What is the lesson to be drawn from Professor Perlman's observations? While it is important for you to understand your obligations under the Rules of Professional Conduct regarding litigation conduct, it is likely far more important that you understand your obligations under the rules of procedure, which will be the more immediate control of your litigation conduct.

Visualize

Because these rules defer to other law, a useful exercise would be to annotate the rules with flags that identify the laws referenced by the rules. For example, here is an annotation of the first subsection of this rule:

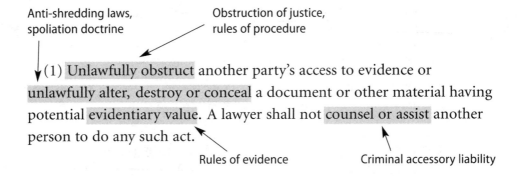

Anti-shredding laws, spoliation doctrine

Obstruction of justice, rules of procedure

(1) Unlawfully obstruct another party's access to evidence or unlawfully alter, destroy or conceal a document or other material having potential evidentiary value. A lawyer shall not counsel or assist another person to do any such act.

Rules of evidence

Criminal accessory liability

Imagine

For individuals with a highly developed sense of fair play, it is sometimes hard to imagine all the ways in which attorneys can play hard ball and exceed the boundaries of the rules. Many recent televisions series have featured attorneys who were walking advertisements for violations of Rule 3.4 and the other Rule 3 restrictions on advocacy. Try watching a few episodes of *Boston Legal* and spot the ethics violations.

Reflective Practice: Your Attitudes Toward Conflict

Before you study the law governing your conduct as an advocate, take a few moments to reflect on your own personal attitudes and values toward disputes. Just as it is important to understand the limits of varying approaches to advocacy, so too it is important to recognize your own personal stance toward what is fair and effective in resolving disputes. Think about different situations in which you have had to deal with conflict—from friendly disagreements in low-stakes decisions to high-tension, high-stakes conflicts. How would you describe your approach to conflict? When is your approach effective? When do you think it is less effective? How else might you approach conflict to improve your ability to resolve conflict?

In addition to reflecting on past experience, there are several tools you might consider to help you become more aware of your responses to conflict. One tool is a conflict style inventory. Two popular inventories are:

Thomas Kilmann Conflict Mode Instrument (http://www.kilmann.com/conflict.html);

Kraybill Conflict Style Inventory (http://www.riverhouseepress.com/Conflict_Style_Inventory.htm).

Using the Myers-Briggs Type Indicator and its four personality preferences (extraverted-introverted, sensing-intuitive, thinking-feeling, and judging-perceiving) may also provide insight for your reflection. *See* Don Peters, *Forever Jung: Psychological Type Theory, The Myers-Briggs Type Indicator and Learning Negotiation*, 42 DRAKE L. REV. 1 (1993). Professor Len Riskin has suggested that mindfulness meditation may be an effective method of developing insights into your own responses to conflict. Leonard L. Riskin, *The Contemplative Lawyer: On the Potential Contributions of Mindfulness Meditation to Law Students, Lawyers and Their Clients*, 7 HARV. NEGOT. L. REV. 1 (2002).

Write a short reflection on your approach to conflict and your role as an attorney in representing clients in disputes.

21.2 Gathering and Preserving Evidence

Fact investigation is a critical step in any representation. When representing clients in transactional matters, informal fact gathering accompanies exchange of information. In litigation matters, informal investigation precedes filing suit and is a low-cost alternative to formal discovery. Sometimes your clients may want to assist in the fact gathering process, and you certainly will want them to do so in many instances. However, you must take care that neither you nor your client violate the law or the rights of others in investigations. Like most of the rules governing the attorney's advocacy roles, the Model Rules defer to other law in this regard. Rule 4.4 prohibits engaging in behaviors with no substantial purpose other than delay or harassment or using methods of gathering evidence that violate the legal rights of a third person. What laws define those legal rights?

A. Legal Limits on Gathering Evidence

Attorneys must understand the legal limits to fact investigation, not only for themselves but also for any person, including their client, who might assist in investigations. There are some obvious outside boundaries of fact investigation—regularly violated by television and movie characters but a sure route to disbarment, sanction, and even jail for attorneys in real life. For example, attorneys who engage in behavior that amounts to breaking and entering or who trespass on private property have no immunity from criminal and civil liability simply because they were investigating their client's case. But what happens if it is your client who has broken the law to obtain evidence? In some cases, the court will exclude the evidence. *Adams v. Shell Oil Co. (In re Shell Oil Refinery),* 143 F.R.D. 105, 108 (E.D. La. 1992), *amended by* 144 F.R.D. 73 (E.D. La. 1992) (holding that the admission of documents obtained through the defendant's employee was error because the plaintiff obtained the documents in violation of the discovery orders).

If the attorney uses this evidence before its source is apparent, the court may enter summary judgment as a sanction. For example, in *Lipin v. Bender,* 644 N.E.2d 1300 (N.Y. Ct. App. 1994) an employee who was suing for employment discrimination had been acting as her attorney's paralegal. During a deposition, she sat at the table next to opposing attorney and in front of a stack of documents he had placed on the table. The deposition was very contentious and while the attorneys were arguing, she began to read the opposing attorney's documents. She noticed that the top document was a memo detailing the opposing attorney's interviews with employees of the defendant. She surreptitiously took the document, copied it, and gave it to her attorney, who attempted to use the document to force a settlement. The trial court dismissed the employee's action as a sanction for the misconduct. Likewise, in *Stephen Slesinger, Inc. v. Walt Disney Co.,* 155 Cal. App. 4th 736 (2007) in contentious litigation over licensing rights to the Winnie the Pooh books, the plaintiff's investigator trespassed on Disney's private properties, not otherwise accessible to the public, and also trespassed onto a document destruction firm's secure facility. He took documents from both these places, altered them to make them appear to be non-privileged, and attempted to use them. The court exercised its inherent authority to dismiss the action as a sanction. One of the defenses raised by the plaintiff was that Disney had earlier been sanctioned for destroying evidence in the case and that the plaintiff's misconduct simply "evened the playing field."

When a client brings evidence to you, do you have an obligation to ask how a client obtained that information? Suppose for example that Wife has retained you to represent her in her divorce action. Throughout the case you ask her to deliver certain information regarding the marital property and other items of interest. One day Wife gives you a flash drive with financial records from her husband's business. Wife does not work at her husband's business. Do you ask how she obtained these records? There is considerable risk in your using this evidence without being aware of how it was obtained.

Introducing or using evidence that has been illegally obtained may result in discipline or liability. If your client has violated the law in obtaining evidence, he may be inclined to suggest that he did so at your direction. Recall that rule 8.4(c) prohibits an attorney from engaging in conduct involving dishonesty, fraud, deceit, or misrepresentation. This rule may be applied to an attorney who uses evidence wrongfully obtained, regardless of whether the law allows that use. At least one state has suggested that an attorney may not advise a client to make a surreptitious recording of a conversation for purposes of generating evidence in a child abuse case. Even if the evidence would be admissible, the conduct would be unethical as involving fraud, deceit, and misrepresentation. Standing Committee on Legal Ethics of Virginia State Bar, Opinion 1448 (1992).

The use of wiretap evidence is especially fraught with risk. Many state laws and federal wiretapping statutes have been held to apply to interspousal wiretaps. The consequences for you if your client produces such evidence are, at best, that the court will exclude the evidence. *Stamme v. Stamme*, 589 S.W.2d 50 (Mo. Ct. App. 1979). At worst, you may find yourself subject to discipline or liability. The Electronic Communications and Privacy Act of 1986, which includes the Wiretap Act, 28 U.S.C. § 2510 et seq. (2000), and the Stored Communication Act, 18 U.S.C. §§ 2701-2711 (2000), was enacted with domestic surveillance in mind. In *United States v. Wuliger*, 981 F.2d 1497 (6th Cir. 1992), *cert denied* 510 U.S. 1191 (1994), an attorney represented a husband in a divorce action. His client installed a wiretap on the family phone and recorded his wife's conversations, including conversations with her priest, her marriage counselor, and her attorney. The client told the attorney that the wife knew that her conversations were being recorded. The attorney had all the conversations transcribed and used some of them during two different depositions and to impeach the wife's testimony during a hearing.

The wiretap act provides criminal liability for "any person who intentionally intercepts [or] endeavors to intercept ... any wire, oral, or electronic communication" and for any person who makes any use or disclosure of the contents of a communication obtained in violation of that section. 18 U.S.C. § 2511(1). The attorney was convicted of violating that provision, fined $5,000 and placed on probation for two years provided that he surrender his license to practice law and serve a thirty-day home detention. The 6th Circuit reversed the conviction and remanded for a new trial, but not before clarifying a number of important standards regarding the applicability of the Act to attorneys:

> The defendant asserts that as an advocate his role is not to pre-judge the merits of his client's factual allegations. [The client] represented to the defendant that the tapes were made with his wife's knowledge, in which case they would not violate Title III. The defendant argues that he should be able to rely on the factual representations of his client regardless of his personal opinion as to the

client's credibility. He points to his professional duty to present any evidence or theory which is arguably viable, subject to standards of good faith and reasonableness. Because he proceeded on the belief his client was telling the truth, the defendant contends he had no "reason to know" [his client's wife] did not in fact consent to the recordings.

There is nothing in the Act which affords attorneys special treatment.... However, an attorney's professional duties may be a factor in determining whether there is reason to know that recorded information, given by the client, was illegally obtained. Although an attorney must not turn a blind eye to the obvious, he should be able to give his clients the benefit of the doubt. This countervailing duty is one the jury may take into account in deciding whether defendant had reason to know.

... Next, the defendant claims that there is a statutory "good faith" defense which authorized his conduct. To support his theory, he cites section 2520(d), which provides in pertinent part that:

> a good faith reliance on ... a court warrant or order, a grand jury subpoena, a legislative authorization, or a statutory authorization ... is a complete defense against any ... criminal action brought under this chapter....

18 U.S.C. § 2520(d). The defendant then asserts that because the Ohio Code of Professional Responsibility is both a court order and a legislative authorization, he is entitled to an acquittal since he "relied on" the Code in deciding whether or not to use the tapes. Nothing in the Code "authorizes" the defendant to violate Title III in carrying out his professional duties. The defendant's reliance on section 2520 is mistaken; it is not applicable to this case. This defense was intended in part to protect telephone companies or others who cooperate under court order with law enforcement officials. *Jacobson v. Rose*, 592 F.2d 515, 522-23 (9th Cir.1978), *cert. denied*, 442 U.S. 930, 99 S. Ct. 2861, 61 L. Ed. 2d 298 (1979)....

The attorney also argued that he should not be liable because he had researched the law regarding interspousal wiretaps and had found cases indicating that courts permitted the use of evidence from these wiretaps at trial. The court found that this was essentially a mistake of law defense, which "has long been recognized as no defense to a criminal prosecution. *Cheek v. United States*, 498 U.S. 192, ___, 111 S. Ct. 604, 609, 112 L. Ed. 2d 617 (1991)."

This case provides a frightening example of the range of risks one faces when using wiretap evidence. While the appellate court reversed the initial conviction in this case and remanded for a new trial, the attorney was nonetheless indefinitely suspended. *In re Wuliger*, 583 N.E.2d 1317 (Ohio 1992). He was reinstated the next year. *In re Wuliger*, 606 N.E.2d 961 (Ohio 1993). In a subsequent civil suit later filed by the wife, the attorney escaped liability because the divorce decree included a broad release of the parties and their lawyers. The court held that the language of the release covered a suit for violation of the Wiretap Act. *Ricupero v. Wuliger, Fadel & Beyer*, 1994 WL 483871 (N.D. Ohio. 1994).

Today, much of the law regarding electronic surveillance has moved on from telephone wiretapping to computer surveillance. While the Electronic Communications Privacy Act (ECPA) does provide an exclusionary rule for intercepted electronic communication, most courts examining this issue have determined that interception under the ECPA must occur contemporaneously with transmission. *Fraser v. Nationwide Mut. Ins. Co.*, 352 F.3d 107, 113 (3d Cir. 2003). For example, in *U.S. v. Szymuszkiewic*, 622 F.3d 701 (2010), an IRS agent who, worried about whether his employer was going to fire him, had put a rule in his boss's Outlook e-mail program that forwarded a copy to him of every e-mail to her. He was convicted of violating the wiretap act. If instead he had accessed her computer and copied these emails from her hard drive, these communications would not have been captured as they were transmitted, so this rule would not apply to exclude using these emails in evidence. *Fraser v. Nationwide Mut. Ins. Co.*, 352 F.3d 107, 113 (3d Cir. 2003).

At this point, however, another federal law may come into play. The Computer Fraud and Abuse Act of 1984 (CFAA) provides liability if a person "intentionally accesses a computer without authorization or exceeds authorized access, and thereby obtains ... information from any protected computer if the conduct involved an interstate or foreign communication." 18 U.S.C. § 1030 (2000). Given the ways in which information is transmitted through the internet, accessing another person's computer to obtain confidential emails or to track website visits, may well fall within the scope of this Act. The most difficult issue in applying the Act to computer surveillance in many states is in determining whether one has "authorization" to access the computer. In *US Bioservices Corp. v. Lugo*, 595 F. Supp. 2d 1189 (D. Kan. 2009), employees of a pharmaceutical company obtained confidential information on their work computers, e-mailed it to their personal e-mails, and later disclosed it to their new employer. The court held that their actions could not constitute access to protected computer "without authorization" under Computer Fraud and Abuse Act (CFAA) because they had access to the computers as part of their job. However, the court did find that the employer stated a claim for the employees having "exceeding authorized access" under CFAA, because they had accessed reports that were outside the scope of their duties and e-mailed confidential information to their personal accounts.

The most recent chapter in the saga of electronic evidence is the use of evidence found on Facebook, Twitter, or other social networking sites. On the one hand, investigating these sites for evidence is part of a thorough investigation of the client's case. The court in *Griffin v. Maryland*, 192 Md. App. 518, 535 (2010), suggested that, "[i]t should now be a matter of professional competence for attorneys to take the time to investigate social networking sites." Electronic evidence can be useful in a variety of litigation settings: divorce attorneys may find evidence of marital fault; employment attorneys, evidence of employer discrimination or employee misconduct; prosecutors, proof of criminal activities; and intellectual property attorneys, proof of infringement.

However, just as in any other investigations, searching for electronic evidence can go out of bounds when it involves deception or invasion of privacy. For example, can an attorney "friend" an opponent in order to gain access to her Facebook page? Does it matter if the attorney simply sends a friend request without a message? What if he asks his secretary to "friend" the targeted individual? New York City Bar Association Formal Ethics Opinion 2010-02 analyzed these questions and concluded that: "A lawyer may not attempt to gain access to a social networking website under false pretenses, either directly or through an agent." New York State Bar Ethics Opinion 843 suggested that, "A lawyer who represents a client in a pending litigation, and who has access to the Facebook or MySpace network used by another party in litigation, may access and review the public social network pages of that party to search for potential impeachment material. As long as the lawyer does not 'friend' the other party or direct a third person to do so, accessing the social network pages of the party will not violate Rule 8.4 (prohibiting deceptive or misleading conduct), Rule 4.1 (prohibiting false statements of fact or law), or Rule 5.3(b)(1) (imposing responsibility on lawyers for unethical conduct by nonlawyers acting at their direction)."

B. Destroying or Tampering with Evidence

The opposite of the issue of wrongfully gathering evidence is destroying or tampering with evidence. As you have read, tampering with or obstructing access to evidence is prohibited by Rule 3.4(a). Destruction or alteration of evidence can also trigger sanctions or liabilities. For example, the spoliation doctrine allows the fact finder to draw an adverse evidentiary inference against the party who destroyed evidence when the party had a duty to retain that evidence. Accordingly, an attorney who told his client to remove a photo from his social media site was sanctioned with a fine of $540,000, and the court fined the client $180,000 for spoliation of evidence. *Lester v. Allied Concrete Company*, Nos. CL08-150, CL09-223 (Va. Cir. Ct. Oct. 21, 2011).

Federal and state criminal laws provide liability for destroying evidence also. For many years, the major statute used to prosecute document destruction was 18 U.S.C. § 1512(b)(1) (2012). Technically a witness tampering statute, it has been used to prosecute individuals for document destruction under a theory that those individuals told other persons to destroy the documents. The reach of the statute was narrowed by the United States Supreme Court in *Arthur Andersen, L.L.P. v. United States,* 544 U.S. 696 (2005), where the Court held that the document destruction must be in contemplation of a "foreseeable official proceeding." The Court noted that there had to be a "relationship in time, causation, or logic" between the defendant's conduct and the judicial proceedings.

As part of the Sarbanes-Oxley reforms, Congress sought broader criminal liability for document destruction. Congress adopted the "anti-shredding statute" 18 U.S.C. § 1519 (2010), which provides:

> Whoever knowingly alters, destroys, mutilates, conceals, covers up, falsifies, or makes a false entry in any record, document, or tangible object with the intent to impede, obstruct, or influence the investigation or proper administration of any matter within the jurisdiction of any department or agency of the United States or any case filed under title 11 [Securities Act], or in relation to or contemplation of any such matter or case, shall be fined under this title, imprisoned not more than 20 years, or both.

The statute has been interpreted broadly to apply to a range of behavior beyond document shredding and to require only "the belief that a federal investigation directed at the defendant's conduct might begin at some point in the future" rather than a specific investigation. *United States v. Kernell*, 667 F.3d 746 (6th Cir. 2012). In *Kernell*, the defendant was convicted of violating § 1519 by changing passwords of computer files and defragmenting the disk drive, thus destroying potential evidence, and then posting to 4chan, an internet chat board, that he had done so because he was afraid the FBI would discover the information. *See also, United States v. Gray*, 642 F.3d 371, 374 (2d Cir. 2011) (plain language of § 1519 does not require prosecutors to prove a nexus between a defendant's obstructive conduct and a pending official proceeding).

The statute does require proof of intent to obstruct. In *United States v. Stevens*, 771 F. Supp. 2d 556, 561 (D. Md. 2011), a pharmaceutical company's in-house counsel was indicted under § 1519 in connection with her responses to an FDA inquiry into the promotion of the drug Wellbutrin for weight-loss. The attorney had withheld presentation slides used by speakers at promotional events discussing off-label uses of the drug and had made false written responses to FDA inquiries. The company had secured outside counsel to assist the in-house counsel in preparing these responses. The court dismissed the indictment, holding that the defendant was entitled to an instruction that her reliance on attorney advice regarding the legality of her responses could act as evidence that she acted in good faith, and thus did not fall under the statute's requirement of an intent to obstruct.

But what about the attorneys who had advised her regarding the document production? 18 U.S.C. § 1515(c) (2012) provides that 18 USCS §§ 1501 et seq. "does not prohibit or punish the providing of lawful, bona fide, legal representation services in connection with or anticipation of an official proceeding." In *United States v. Kloess*, 251 F.3d 941 (11th Cir. 2001), one of the rare cases involving this statute, the court concluded that the provision created an affirmative defense to the federal obstruction of justice crimes. "Section 1515(c) provides a complete defense to the statute because one who is performing bona fide legal representation does not have an improper purpose. His purpose—to zealously represent his client—is fully protected by the law. *Id.* at 948. The court explained that a defendant attorney raises the defense by showing that "he was a practicing attorney at the time of the offense" and that "he was retained to provide legal representation in connection with the charged conduct." *Id.* at 946. The burden then shifts to the state to prove beyond a reasonable doubt that the attorney's "conduct did not constitute lawful, bona fide legal representation." *Id.* at 949.

The safe harbor of § 1515 does not provide foolproof protection of an attorney who destroys evidence. In a widely criticized decision, *United States v. Russell*, 639 F. Supp. 2d 226, 231 (D. Conn. 2007), an attorney was indicted for violating the obstruction of justice statue. The attorney, Russell, represented a church. The choirmaster of the church was discovered to have child pornography on his laptop computer, and the church did not want to report him to the police. The laptop was turned over to Russell who believed the laptop was contraband, and thus illegal to possess no matter how acquired. Russell dismantled the computer, thus destroying the evidence. Unknown to Russell, the FBI had already begun an investigation of the employee. Russell was charged with violating § 1519. The case was settled when Russell pled guilty to federal misprision of felony, a statute rarely used except as a lesser-included offense to resolve difficult prosecutions. *See* Stephen Gillers, *Guns, Fruits, Drugs, and Documents: A Criminal Defense Lawyer's Responsibility for Real Evidence*, 63 Stan. L. Rev. 813, 835-36 (2011) (discussing the attorney's options).

The attorney in this case was in a nearly impossible position. He couldn't keep the evidence and he couldn't give it back either. Possessing or transferring child pornography is itself a crime. 18 U.S.C. § 2251-52A, 2256 (2010). Destroying the laptop was a crime as well. Even if the laptop was not something that is in itself illegal to possess (i.e. contraband), an attorney may not simply hold on to the fruits or instrumentalities of a crime if that would hinder investigation. However, his client, the church, had requested that he not turn over the choirmaster to the police.

Most authorities hold that an attorney who comes into possession of the instrumentalities or fruits of a crime is required to turn that evidence over to the police. In *Wemark v. State*, 602 N.W.2d 810 (Iowa 1999), attorneys defending a man accused of stabbing his wife to death turned over the location of the murder weapon. The court held that this did not constitute ineffective assistance of counsel because concealing evidence of a client's crime "has no reasonable relationship to the attorney-client privilege and constitutes an abuse of a lawyer's professional responsibilities." Likewise, the court in *Alhambra Police Officers Ass'n v. Alhambra Police Dep't*, 7 Cal. Rptr. 3d 432 (Cal. Ct. App. 2004) held that the "attorney-client privilege does not permit attorneys to disturb evidence without disclosing its original location and condition, nor may they turn over physical evidence to their clients rather than to the police or prosecution."

Thus, if you come into possession of contraband, instrumentalities, or fruits of a crime, you must turn those over to authorities. You should do so in a way that minimizes the adverse impact on the client. If your client has simply told you about the evidence, but you have never possessed or disturbed the evidence in any way, that information alone would be protected by confidentiality and privilege. Likewise, if your client has given you something that was not an instrumentality or contraband, but simply implicates criminal conduct, such as documents evidencing illegal activities, you need not disclose the evidence to law enforcement unless required to do so by a subpoena, court order, or discover rules.

In summary, there are several steps you can take to protect you from liability, sanction, or discipline for illegally obtained, altered, or destroyed evidence. First, educate your clients and your staff about the boundaries of legal investigation. Second, be careful what you accept. Don't blindly accept evidence that appears to have been obtained in violation of the law. Try to avoid taking possession of the fruits or instrumentalities of crimes. Third, warn your clients that if they provide you evidence that it is illegal for you to possess, you will be required to give it to law enforcement. Depending on the type of representation, you may wish to include this warning to the clients in a description of your representation or even in your representation agreement. Of course, giving your clients a "Miranda" warning about the limits of your duty of confidentiality will often mean your clients will be reluctant to disclose information, and you will want to help clients to understand the distinction between telling you about possibly criminal activity in their past (which you can generally keep confidential) and giving you the products of that activity. Fourth, counsel your clients and staff regarding appropriate approaches to destroying documents or other materials to avoid destruction of items with potential evidentiary value. Fifth, document your choices and conversations regarding these matters. Finally, before you make any decisions to receive, alter, or destroy potential evidence, do your research to determine the approach your jurisdiction takes to your duties. Knowing the substantive law regarding evidence is the only way to insure that you can properly comply with your ethical duties.

21.3 Cooperation in Discovery

Time and money are powerful weapons in litigation and the longer and more burdensome a pretrial process becomes, the more difficult it is for a client with fewer resources to maintain an action. Some attorneys take advantage of this fact and conduct a war of attrition in litigation. Rule 3.2 advises that attorneys must expedite litigation. However, it is often difficult to draw the line between appropriate and unethical delay and disruption. Similarly Rule 3.1 prohibits frivolous pleadings and Rule 3.4 prohibits frivolous discovery. Unlike the rules of conduct, which provide broad prohibitions on unethical litigation conduct, the rules of procedure provide affirmative directions for attorneys to engage in a cooperative approach to discovery.

The cost of discovery is one of the most easily abused aspects of litigation practice. Particularly today, when technology has allowed us to generate and preserve the equivalent of millions of pages of data, requests for documents or information can require the assistance of specialists in electronically stored information (ESI) and cost much more than many lawsuits would generate (or save) in recovery. The rules of civil procedure, drafted before personal computers became the norm, were not designed to address ESI.

Electronic data has unique qualities compared to paper documents. Data can be easily preserved but even more easily and inadvertently destroyed or altered. Even when data is deleted, it may still exist. Finally, data can be impossible to access if one does not have the appropriate software and hardware. All these aspects of ESI make discovery requests and responses subject to extraordinary abuse.

For example, in *S.E.C. v. Collins & Aikman Corp.*, 256 F.R.D. 403 (S.D.N.Y. Jan. 13, 2009), a securities fraud case, the plaintiffs requested that the SEC "produce for inspection and copying the documents and things identified" in fifty-four separate categories. Even though the SEC had already searched through its ESI to determine relevant documents, it responded to the discovery request by producing 1.7 million documents (10.6 million pages) "maintained in thirty-six separate Concordance databases—many of which use different metadata protocols." *Id.* at 406-07. In response to the subsequent discovery dispute, the court rejected the SEC's defense that attorney work-product doctrine protected its methods of searching through the database and that the plaintiffs should be required to search the databases as they were in their raw form. The court concluded, "The first step in responding to any document request is an attorney's assessment of relevance with regard to potentially responsive documents. It would make no sense to then claim that an attorney's determination of relevance shields the selection of responsive documents from production." *Id.* at 410.

The case is but one example of an increasing insistence by courts that they will no longer tolerate overbroad discovery requests, document dumps, and vague and non-responsive objections. Rather, the rules of civil procedure are increasingly being enforced to require attorneys to cooperate in designing discovery together. The growing judicial intolerance for discovery gamesmanship is reflected in the comment by United States District Court Judge Wayne Alley that "If there is a hell to which disputatious, uncivil, vituperative lawyers go, let it be one in which the damned are eternally locked in discovery disputes with other lawyers of equally repugnant attributes." *Krueger v. Pelican Prod. Corp.*, C/A No. 87-2385-A, slip op. (W.D. Okla. Feb. 24, 1989).

An excellent example of the growing attitude from the bench can be found in the following case, in which 39 mostly non-English speaking Latino industrial laundry workers sued Mayflower Textile Services Co. and its labor provider, Argo Enterprises Inc., both of whom were represented by the same attorneys. The suit claimed that the defendant employers violated the Fair Labor Standards Act of 1938 ("FLSA"), 29 U.S.C. §§ 201 *et seq.* and parallel state laws by failing to pay overtime and by illegally deducting wages from the employees' pay. The Plaintiffs filed an extensive set of interrogatories against the Defendants, seeking employment and pay records for all employees over several years, as well as other information. Two examples of the Plaintiffs' requests for production of documents, and Defendant Mayflower's responses, are as follows:

DOCUMENT REQUEST

1. The contract or contracts between each of the Mayflower entities and Lunil Services, Agency, L.L.C. ("Lunil") reflecting Lunil's agreement to provide plant production workers for the Mayflower laundry for all the years in which the agreement or agreements between the Mayflower entities and Lunil were in effect.

RESPONSE: Objection. This request is overly broad and unduly burdensome, and is not reasonably calculated to lead to the discovery of material admissible in evidence at the trial of this matter in that it contains no time limitation whatsoever, and clearly seeks documents outside of the limitations period governing this action. Subject to and without waiving this objection, see attached agreement between Lunil Services Agency, LLC and Mayflower Healthcare Textile Services, LLC.

DOCUMENT REQUEST

4. Any and all correspondence, e-mail, and/or notes of oral conversations, and any other recordings, including documentation of payments that support the formation of a contract between Mayflower and Argo whereby Agro [sic] agreed to provide plant production workers for the Mayflower laundry plant, and any and all records that reflect the terms of that agreement.

RESPONSE: Subject to and without waiving this objection, any responsive non-privileged documents, in [sic] any exist, ill [sic] be produced at a time mutually acceptable to the parties.

After these objections, further discovery disputes arose until the parties appeared before Magistrate Judge Paul W. Grimm to decide the motions to produce and objections. Judge Grimm ordered the parties to meet and confer to work out their discovery disputes and provided the following opinion to guide their discussions. As you read the opinion, think about the discovery process the judge describes. Is this the process that you expect from discovery or what you may have experienced in your community? Do you think the judge's approach will deter misuse of discovery?

Mancia v. Mayflower Textile Servs. Co.

253 F.R.D. 354 (D. Md. 2008)

One of the most important, but apparently least understood or followed, of the discovery rules is Fed. R. Civ. P. 26(g), enacted in 1983. The rule requires that every discovery disclosure, request, response or objection must be signed by at least one attorney of record, or the client, if unrepresented. Fed. R. Civ. P. 26(g)(1). The signature "certifies that to the best of the person's knowledge, information, and belief formed *after a reasonable inquiry*," the disclosure is complete and correct, and that the discovery request, response or objection is:

> (a) consistent with the rules of procedure and warranted by existing law (or by a nonfrivolous argument for extending, modifying, or reversing existing law, or for establishing new law); (b) is not interposed for any improper purpose (such as to harass, cause unnecessary delay, or needlessly increase the cost of litigation); and (c) is neither unreasonable nor unduly burdensome or expensive, (considering the needs of the case, prior discovery in the case, the amount in controversy, and the importance of the issues at stake in the action).

Stop and study this rule carefully.

Fed. R. Civ. P. 26(g)(1)(A), (B)(i)-(iii). If a lawyer or party makes a Rule 26(g) certification that violates the rule, without substantial justification, the court (on motion, or sua sponte) must impose an appropriate sanction, which may include an order to pay reasonable expenses and attorney's fees, caused by the violation. Fed. R. Civ. P. 26(g)(3)....

Rule 26(g) and its commentary provide many important "take away points" that ought to, but unfortunately do not, regulate the way discovery is conducted. First, the rule is intended to impose an "affirmative duty" on counsel to behave responsibly during discovery, and to ensure that it is conducted in a way that is consistent "with the spirit and purposes" of the discovery rules, which are contained in Rules 26 through 37. *Id.* It cannot seriously be disputed that compliance with the "spirit and purposes" of these discovery rules requires cooperation by counsel to identify and fulfill legitimate discovery needs, yet avoid seeking discovery the cost and burden of which is disproportionally large to what is at stake in the litigation. Counsel cannot "behave responsively" during discovery unless they do both, which requires cooperation rather than contrariety, communication rather than confrontation.

Second, the rule is intended to curb discovery abuse by requiring the court to impose sanctions if it is violated, absent "substantial justification," and those sanctions are intended to both penalize the noncompliant lawyer or unrepresented client, and to deter others from noncompliance. Fed. R. Civ. P. 26(g)(3). As the Advisory Committee's Notes state, "Because of the asserted reluctance to impose sanctions on attorneys who abuse the discovery rules, Rule 26(g) makes explicit the authority judges now have to impose appropriate sanctions and requires them to use it. This authority derives from Rule 37, 28 U.S.C. § 1927, and the court's inherent authority." Fed. R. Civ. P. 26(g) advisory committee's notes to the 1983 amendments (internal citations omitted).

Third, the rule aspires to eliminate one of the most prevalent of all discovery abuses: kneejerk discovery requests served without consideration of cost or burden to the responding party. Despite the requirements of the rule, however, the reality appears to be that with respect to certain discovery, principally interrogatories and document production requests, lawyers customarily serve requests that are far broader, more redundant and burdensome than necessary to obtain sufficient facts to enable them to resolve the case through motion, settlement or trial. The rationalization for this behavior is that the party propounding Rule 33 and 34 discovery does not know enough information to more narrowly tailor them, but this would not be so if lawyers approached discovery responsibly, as the rule mandates, and met and conferred before initiating discovery, and simply discussed what the amount in controversy is, and how much, what type, and in what sequence, discovery should be conducted so that its cost—to all parties—is proportional to what is at stake in the litigation. The requirement of discovery being proportional to what is at issue is clearly stated at Rule 26(g)(1)(B)(iii) (lawyer's signature on a discovery request certifies that it is "neither unreasonable nor unduly burdensome or expensive, considering the needs of the case, prior discovery in the case, the amount in controversy, and the importance of the issues at stake in the action"), as well as Rule 26(b)(2)(C)(i)-(iii) (court, on motion or on its own, must limit the scope of discovery if the discovery sought is unreasonably cumulative or duplicative, can be obtained from a more convenient source, could have been previously obtained by the party seeking the discovery or the burden or expense of the proposed discovery outweighs its likely benefit).

Similarly, Rule 26(g) also was enacted over twenty-five years ago to bring an end to the equally abusive practice of objecting to discovery requests reflexively—but not reflectively—and without a factual basis. The rule and its

How do you determine what is disproportionate?

What explains this reluctance?

commentary are starkly clear: an objection to requested discovery may not be made until after a lawyer has "paused and consider[ed]" whether, based on a "reasonable inquiry," there is a "factual basis [for the] ... objection." Fed. R. Civ. P. 26(g) advisory committee's notes to the 1983 amendments. Yet, as in this case, boilerplate objections that a request for discovery is "overbroad and unduly burdensome, and not reasonably calculated to lead to the discovery of material admissible in evidence," ... persist despite a litany of decisions from courts, including this one, that such objections are improper unless based on particularized facts....

boilerplate/ too many obj.

The failure to engage in discovery as required by Rule 26(g) is one reason why the cost of discovery is so widely criticized as being excessive — to the point of pricing litigants out of court. *See, e.g.,* Am. Coll. of Trial Lawyers & Inst. for the Advancement of the Am. Legal Sys., *Interim Report on the Joint Project of the American College of Trial Lawyers Task Force on Discovery and the Institute for the Advancement of the American Legal System* 3 (2008) ("Although the civil justice system is not broken, it is in serious need of repair. The survey shows that the system is not working; it takes too long and costs too much. Deserving cases are not brought because the cost of pursuing them fails a rational cost-benefit test, while meritless cases, especially smaller cases, are being settled rather than being tried because it costs too much to litigate them.") ... The Sedona Conference, *The Sedona Conference Cooperation Proclamation* 1 (2008) [hereinafter *Cooperation Proclamation*], *available at* http://www.thesedonaconference.org/content/miscFiles/cooperation_Proclamation_Press.pdf ("The costs associated with adversarial conduct in pre-trial discovery have become a serious burden to the American judicial system. This burden rises significantly in discovery of electronically stored information ("ESI"). In addition to rising monetary costs, courts have seen escalating motion practice, overreaching, obstruction, and extensive, but unproductive discovery disputes — in some cases precluding adjudication on the merits altogether....."); Kent D. Syverud, *ADR and the Decline of the American Civil Jury*, 44 UCLA L. Rev. 1935, 1942 (1997) ("Our civil process before and during trial, in state and federal courts, is a masterpiece of complexity that dazzles in its details — in discovery, in the use of experts, in the preparation and presentation of evidence, in the selection of the fact finder and the choreography of the trial. But few litigants or courts can afford it.")....

What has caused this increase in cost and complexity?

Rule 26(g) charges those responsible for the success or failure of pretrial discovery — the trial judge and the lawyers for the adverse parties — with approaching the process properly: discovery must be initiated and responded to responsibly, in accordance with the letter and spirit of the discovery rules, to achieve a proper purpose (i.e., not to harass, unnecessarily delay, or impose needless expense), and be proportional to what is at issue in the litigation, and if it is not, the judge is expected to impose appropriate sanctions to punish and deter.

The apparent ineffectiveness of Rule 26(g) in changing the way discovery is in fact practiced often is excused by arguing that the cooperation that judges expect during discovery is unrealistic because it is at odds with the demands of the adversary system, within which the discovery process operates. But this is just not so.... However central the adversary system is to our way of formal dispute resolution, there is nothing inherent in it that precludes cooper-

What exactly are the demands of the adversary system?

ation between the parties and their attorneys during the litigation process to achieve orderly and cost-effective discovery of the competing facts on which the system depends. In fact, no less a proponent of the adversary system than Professor Lon L. Fuller[1] observed:

> Thus, partisan advocacy is a form of public service so long as it aids the process of adjudication; it ceases to be when it hinders that process, when it misleads, distorts and obfuscates, when it renders the task of the deciding tribunal not easier, but more difficult....
>
> The lawyer's highest loyalty is at the same time the most tangible. It is loyalty that runs, not to persons, but to procedures and institutions. The lawyer's role imposes on him a trusteeship for the integrity of those fundamental processes of government and self-government upon which the successful functioning of our society depends.
>
> ... A lawyer recreant to his responsibilities can so disrupt the hearing of a cause as to undermine those rational foundations without which an adversary proceeding loses its meaning and its justification. Everywhere democratic and constitutional government is tragically dependent on voluntary and understanding co-operation in the maintenance of its fundamental processes and forms.
>
> It is the lawyer's duty to preserve and advance this indispensable co-operation by keeping alive the willingness to engage in it and by imparting the understanding necessary to give it direction and effectiveness....
>
> ... It is chiefly for the lawyer that the term "due process" takes on tangible meaning, for whom it indicates what is allowable and what is not, who realizes what a ruinous cost is incurred when its demands are disregarded. For the lawyer the insidious dangers contained in the notion that "the end justifies the means" is not a matter of abstract philosophic conviction, but of direct professional experience.

Lon L. Fuller & John D. Randall, *Professional Responsibility: Report of the Joint Conference*, 44 A.B.A. J. 1159, 1162, 1216 (1958).

How would you explain this to a client?

A lawyer who seeks excessive discovery given what is at stake in the litigation, or who makes boilerplate objections to discovery requests without particularizing their basis, or who is evasive or incomplete in responding to discovery, or pursues discovery in order to make the cost for his or her adversary so great that the case settles to avoid the transaction costs, or who delays the completion of discovery to prolong the litigation in order to achieve a tactical advantage, or who engages in any of the myriad forms of discovery abuse that are so commonplace is, as Professor Fuller observes, hindering the adjudication process, and making the task of the "deciding tribunal not easier,

---

1. Professor Fuller, 1902-1978, was a celebrated professor at Harvard Law School who wrote extensively on jurisprudence, including the importance of the adversary system. His publications include the influential article *The Forms and Limits of Adjudication*, 92 Harv. L. Rev. 353 (1978).

but more difficult," and violating his or her duty of loyalty to the "procedures and institutions" the adversary system is intended to serve.

Thus, rules of procedure,[2] ethics[3] and even statutes[4] make clear that there are limits to how the adversary system may operate during discovery.

Although judges, scholars, commentators and lawyers themselves long have recognized the problems associated with abusive discovery, what has been missing is a thoughtful means to engage all the stakeholders in the litigation process—lawyers, judges and the public at large—and provide them with the encouragement, means and incentive to approach discovery in a different way. The Sedona Conference, a non-profit, educational research institute[5] best known for its *Best Practices Recommendations and Principles for Addressing Electronic Document Production,*[6] recently issued a *Cooperation Proclamation* to announce the launching of "a national drive to promote open and forthright information sharing, dialogue (internal and external), training, and the development of practical tools to facilitate cooperative, collaborative, transparent discovery." *Cooperation Proclamation, supra,* at 1. To accomplish this laudable goal, the Sedona Conference proposes to develop "a detailed understanding and full articulation of the issues and changes needed to obtain cooperative fact-finding," as well as "[d]eveloping and distributing practical 'toolkits' to train and support lawyers, judges, other professionals, and students in techniques of discovery cooperation, collaboration, and transparency." *Id.* at 3. If these goals are achieved, the benefits will be profound.

> Do you think these conversations can solve the problem? If not, what can?

In the meantime, however, the present dispute evidences the need for clearer guidance as to how to comply with the requirements of Rules 26(b)(2)(C) and 26(g) in order to ensure that the Plaintiffs obtain appropriate discovery to support their claims, and the Defendants are not unduly burdened by discovery demands that are disproportionate to the issues in this case.

As previously noted, Plaintiffs served Rule 33 interrogatories and Rule 34 document production requests on each of the Defendants. Initially, there was communication between counsel, as well as some degree of cooperation, as

---

2. *See, e.g.,* Fed. R. Civ. P. 26(f) (requiring parties and their counsel to confer to "consider the nature and basis of their claims and defenses," the possibility of settlement and to develop and agree on a proposed discovery plan to submit to the court); Fed. R. Civ. P. 26(g) (requiring that discovery not be initiated, responded to, or objections made unless there first has been a reasonable inquiry, and the discovery, response or objection is founded in law, not interposed for an improper purpose, and neither unreasonable nor unduly burdensome); Fed. R. Civ. P. 26(c)(1), 37(a)(1) (prohibiting the filing of discovery motions without first certifying that the moving party has conferred in good faith with the adverse party in an effort to resolve the dispute without court action).

3. *See, e.g.,* Model Rules of Prof'l Conduct R. 3.4(d) (2007).

4. *See, e.g.,* 28 U.S.C. § 1927 (2008).

5. The Sedona Conference, http://www.thesedonaconference.org/content/faq (last visited Oct. 8, 2008).

6. The Sedona Conference, *Best Practices Recommendations and Principles for Addressing Electronic Document Production* (rev. 2004), *available at* http://www.thesedonaconference.org/content/miscFiles/SedonaPrinciples200401.pdf.

Plaintiffs agreed to give the Defendants an extension of time to answer this discovery. When they did answer, however, [the Defendants] objected to a number of Plaintiffs' document production requests by making boilerplate, non-particularized objections.... Rule 33(b)(4) requires that "the grounds for objecting to an interrogatory must be stated with specificity" and cautions that "any ground not stated in a timely objection is waived, unless the court, for good cause, excuses the failure;" therefore, the boilerplate objection to Plaintiffs' interrogatory waived any legitimate objection Defendant may have had. The same is true for the boilerplate objections to Plaintiffs' document production requests. The failure to particularize these objections as required leads to one of two conclusions: either the Defendants lacked a factual basis to make the objections that they did, which would violate Rule 26(g), or they complied with Rule 26(g), made a reasonable inquiry before answering and discovered facts that would support a legitimate objection, but they were waived for failure to specify them as required. Neither alternative helps the Defendants' position, and either would justify a ruling requiring that the Defendants provide the requested discovery regardless of cost or burden, because proper grounds for objecting have not been established.

However, Rule 26(b)(2)(C) imposes an obligation on the Court, sua sponte, to:

> [L]imit the frequency or extent of discovery otherwise allowed by [the] rules ... if it determines that:
>
>> (i) the discovery sought is unreasonably cumulative or duplicative, or can be obtained from some other source that is more convenient, less burdensome, or less expensive;
>>
>> (ii) the party seeking discovery has had ample opportunity to obtain the information by discovery in the action; or
>>
>> (iii) the burden or expense of the proposed discovery outweighs its likely benefit, considering the needs of the case, the amount in controversy, the parties' resources, the importance of the issues at stake in the action, and the importance of the discovery in resolving the issues.

Fed. R. Civ. P. 26(b)(2)(C)(i)-(iii). I noted during the hearing that I had concerns that the discovery sought by the Plaintiffs might be excessive or overly burdensome, given the nature of this FLSA and wage and hour case, the few number of named Plaintiffs and the relatively modest amounts of wages claimed for each. Because the record before me lacked facts to enable me to make a determination of overbreadth or burden under Rule 26(b)(2)(C), I ordered counsel to meet and confer in good faith and do the following. First, I asked Plaintiffs and Defendants each to estimate the likely range of provable damages that foreseeably could be awarded if Plaintiffs prevail at trial. In doing so, I suggested that the Plaintiffs assume for purposes of this analysis that their pending motion to certify a FLSA collective action would be granted, because doing so would allow the parties to gauge the "worst case" outcome Defendants could face. I then ordered that counsel for Plaintiffs and Defendants compare these estimates and attempt to identify a foreseeable range of damages, from zero if Plaintiffs do not prevail, to the largest award they likely could prove if they succeed. I also asked Plaintiffs' counsel to estimate their

Don't you think most attorneys conduct this analysis anyway? Do you think this calculation will help control discovery? Why or why not?

attorneys' fees. While admittedly a rough estimate, this range is useful for determining what the "amount in controversy" is in the case, and what is "at stake" for purposes of Rule 26(b)(2)(C)'s proportionality analysis. The goal is to attempt to quantify a workable "discovery budget" that is proportional to what is at issue in the case.

Second, I ordered Plaintiffs' counsel and Defendants' counsel to discuss the amount and type of discovery already provided, and then discuss the additional discovery still sought by Plaintiffs, in order to evaluate the Rule 26(b)(2)(C) factors, to determine whether Plaintiffs' legitimate additional discovery needs could be fulfilled from non-duplicative, more convenient, less burdensome, or less expensive sources than those currently sought by the Plaintiffs. I further instructed Defendants' counsel that during this portion of the discussion, the burden was on the Defendants to provide a particularized factual basis to support any claims of excessive burden or expense.

I then advised counsel that in their discussion they should attempt to reach an agreement, in full or at least partially, about what additional discovery (and from what sources) should be provided by Defendants to Plaintiffs. In doing so, I suggested that they consider "phased discovery," so that the most promising, but least burdensome or expensive sources of information could be produced initially, which would enable Plaintiffs to reevaluate their needs depending on the information already provided.

Finally, I advised counsel that when they had completed their discussion, they were to provide me with a status report identifying any unresolved issues, and if there were any, I gave them a format to use to present them to me in a fashion that would enable me to rule on them expeditiously.

It is apparent that the process outlined above requires that counsel cooperate and communicate, and I note that had these steps been taken by counsel at the start of discovery, most, if not all, of the disputes could have been resolved without involving the court. It also is apparent that there is nothing at all about the cooperation needed to evaluate the discovery outlined above that requires the parties to abandon meritorious arguments they may have, or even to commit to resolving all disagreements on their own. Further, it is in the interests of each of the parties to engage in this process cooperatively. For the Defendants, doing so will almost certainly result in having to produce less discovery, at lower cost. For the Plaintiffs, cooperation will almost certainly result in getting helpful information more quickly, and both Plaintiffs and Defendants are better off if they can avoid the costs associated with the voluminous filings submitted to the court in connection with this dispute. Finally, it is obvious that if undertaken in the spirit required by the discovery rules, particularly Rules 26(b)(2)(C) and 26(g), the adversary system will be fully engaged, as counsel will be able to advocate their clients' positions as relevant to the factors the rules establish, and if unable to reach a full agreement, will be able to bring their dispute back to the court for a prompt resolution. In fact, the cooperation that is necessary for this process to take place enhances the legitimate goals of the adversary system, by facilitating discovery of the facts needed to support the claims and defenses that have been raised, at a lesser cost, and expediting the time when the case may be resolved on its merits, or settled. This clearly is advantageous to both Plaintiffs and Defendants.

Doesn't this entire discussion depend on whether the attorneys and parties are willing to trust to the good faith of the other side?

Notes

1. Nine months later, and despite the court's extensive guidance, the parties in this case continued to dispute discovery, resulting in the court issuing an order to show cause why the defendant labor supplier should not be sanctioned under Rules 37 and 11. *Mancia v. Mayflower Textile Servs. Co.*, 2009 U.S. Dist. LEXIS 65210 (July 2009). Are you surprised? What explains this unwillingness to comply with discovery to the point of incurring sanctions?

2. By November 2009, the parties had reached a settlement after a day-long settlement conference in front of another federal magistrate. The case settled for $300,000. $98,000 of that was in payments to 37 of the 39 plaintiffs and represented about 75% of the maximum recovery expected from the case. The settlement amounts for each individual plaintiff were estimated to range from $12 to more than $12,000. FMLA cases also provide for fee shifting, so the award included $190,000 in attorneys' fees and $12,000 in litigation expenses. The attorneys' fees awarded were less than half the hourly bills for the lawyers. Brendan Kearney, *Mayflower Textile Services Co. and Harford County Industrial Laundry Workers Reach Settlement of $300K in U.S. District Court*, Baltimore Daily Record (November 2, 2009). Given these numbers, do you think the discovery battles were worth it?

3. Despite the resistance to cooperative approaches to discovery, federal courts are increasingly following the *Mayflower* approach and ordering joint discovery plans and proportionality assessments, especially in cases involving ESI. *See, e.g., In re Facebook PPC Adver. Litig.*, No. C09-03043 JF (HRL), 2011 WL 1324516 (N.D. Cal. April 6, 2011); *Am. Fed'n of State County & Mun. Emps. v. Ortho-McNeil-Janssen Pharm. Inc.*, No. 08-CV-5904, 2010 WL 5186088 (E.D. Pa. Dec. 21, 2010); *Dunkin' Donuts Franchised Rests. LLC v. Grand Cent. Donuts Inc.*, No. CV 2007-4027, 2009 WL 1750348 (E.D.N.Y. June 19, 2009).

4. Judge Grimm has produced a number of important opinions on discovery, including *Victor Stanley, Inc. v. Creative Pipe et al.*, No. MJG-06-2662 (D. Md. Sept. 9, 2010), in which he addressed "the single most egregious example of spoliation that I have encountered in any case that I have handled or in any case described in the legion of spoliation cases I have read in nearly 14 years on the bench." So egregious was the defendant's destruction of evidence that Judge Grimm held the defendant in civil contempt, ordering that he be jailed for up to two years "unless and until he pays to Plaintiff the attorney's fees and costs that will be awarded." The opinion details the federal law of spoliation of evidence and includes an appendix with a table providing the sanctions and standards for spoliation in each of the federal circuits.

5. Is the obligation to cooperate in discovery in order to lower costs and facilitate exchange of information part of a larger duty under Rule 3.2 to expedite litigation? Does an attorney have an obligation to suggest to clients some alternatives to litigation for the resolution of their disputes? Counseling clients regarding the availability of alternative dispute resolution mechanisms in general and mediation in particular is an important part of your initial consultation with clients in nearly every dispute. Comment 5 to Rule 2.1 suggests but does not necessarily mandate this advice. However, in some states attorneys must discuss alternatives to litigation with their clients as a matter of

court rule or as part of the disciplinary code. *See, e.g.,* Mo. Sup. Ct. R. 17.02(b) (2009) (requiring attorneys to advise clients of ADR availability); Va. R.P.C. R. 1.4 & cmt 1a (2008) (attorneys must discuss alternatives to litigation that might be more appropriate to the client's goals). *See generally,* Marshall J. Berger, *Should an Attorney be Required to Advise a Client of ADR Options?*, 13 Geo. J. Legal Ethics 427, Appendix I-II (2000) (comprehensive listing of court rules, state statutes, and ethics provisions).

Professional Responsibility Skill 21-A: Cooperating in Planning Discovery

Rewind the *Mayflower* case and, in a group of four, role-play the case, filling in factual gaps with probable scenarios. Two of you should play the roles of the attorneys and two of you play the roles of the clients. First, the attorneys should meet and try to carry out the direction of the court in the opinion. Once you have a discovery plan prepared, meet your client to explain that plan and secure the client's consent and cooperation. What impediments to cooperation existed? What made it easier?

21.4 Deposition Practice

Any one of us can act unprofessionally in the right circumstances. Studies have revealed that "an attorney's willingness to violate legal or professional rules depends heavily on the exposures to temptation, client pressures, and collegial attitudes in his practice setting." Deborah Rhode, *Moral Character as a Professional Credential*, 94 Yale L.J. 491, 559 (1985). Nonetheless, there are those attorneys who regularly cross the line from diligent and loyal representation to overzealous abuse, whether for greed, unbalanced zealousness, or mere orneriness. There are some classic difficult opponents that you will likely have to face in many types of practice. Some attorneys are unethically aggressive on behalf of their clients—using threats and intimidation to gain an advantage. Others engage in more passively aggressive techniques—delay and obfuscation. Still others have no compunction about lying or engaging in deceptive tactics. Finally there are those who are bigots: treating individuals in the legal system badly simply because of who those individuals are.

Some areas of practice seem especially prone to "Rambo" litigation tactics. For example, a recent study of negotiating behaviors among attorneys in various practice areas found that "Family law had the highest percentage of unethical adversarial lawyers .... compared to all other practice areas." Andrea Kupfer Schneider and Nancy Mills, *The Ineffective Family Lawyer*, Innovations in Family Law Practice 13, 19 (Kelly Browe Olson & Nancy Ver Steegh, eds. 2008). The authors of the study suggest that this disproportionate representation of unethical adversarial practice in family law may be explained by a constellation of factors: the emphasis on the adversarial system in legal culture, the wishes of clients who push negative behavior, and the emotional context of family law disputes. The authors also speculate that easy cases are handled *pro se*, leaving only the highest conflict cases for legal representation. Finally, the authors suggest that many family law cases may be handled by generalist attorneys who are unprepared for the unique emotional demands of this practice field.

Regardless of the substantive law area of practice, abusive tactics appear most commonly in discovery practice and in depositions in particular. Why are attorneys tempted to abuse deposition rules? Because most cases are settled, depositions are often the critical step in litigation. They take a great deal of time for both attorney and client to prepare for and conduct, often requiring travel to inconvenient locations, and so are discovery tools that can be a weapon to wear down an opponent with fewer resources. Depositions do not just develop evidence. They permit opportunities to conduct a "practice trial"—observing how witnesses will respond to questioning and sending powerful signals to opposing parties about the strength of their case. Moreover, depositions take place in relative privacy—it is difficult to capture on a transcript the pace and tone of words and the nonverbal behavior that can heat up a deposition to the boiling point. While protective orders and sanctions are available, attorneys know that most judges do not appreciate being called in to mediate discovery disputes.

In a deposition, clients see you interacting with opposing parties and counsel and, if you don't explain ahead of time, may be upset if you are "too friendly with the enemy." Clients may not understand that you can effectively represent them while still extending professional courtesies to the other side. When an opposing attorney engages in unprofessional conduct, it is tempting to "fight fire with fire" returning threats, shouts, or unethical tactics one for one. For example, in *Ross v. Kansas City Power & Light Co.*, 197 F.R.D. 646 (W.D. Mo. 2000) both parties' attorneys were ordered to pay over $33,000 total to the local legal aid organization as sanction for their behavior in depositions. The attorneys were "snide, rude and nasty" to one another, made frivolous threats to report one another to prosecutors or disciplinary counsel for behavior they claimed was criminal or unethical, and instructed their clients not to answer questions. The court suspended the sanction depending on their behavior in the remainder of the case and ordered them to provide a copy of the sanction order to their clients.

In preparing witnesses for depositions and trial, some attorneys walk the tightrope of creating false evidence in violation of Rule 3.4. All authorities agree that it is permissible for you to discuss the kind of questions that will be asked, encourage your client to answer the questions asked, and give him general reactions to his demeanor without specific directions as to what to say. While commentators disagree on whether it is proper to suggest wording or suggest that witnesses review other written evidence when answering questions, there are those attorneys who move well past these uncertain areas to the clearly unethical practice of deliberately scripting witness testimony so that in the deposition or trial, the witness is simply parroting the attorney's coaching rather than testifying about what he actually does or does not know.

Even when their perfectly coached witness appears at the deposition, these attorneys may go further still to manage the witness testimony. These behaviors might include off the record conferences with the deponent, speaking objections, and rephrasing for the record the defending attorney's interpretation of the interrogator's question, all for the purposes of distorting, closing down, or shaping the client's testimony. When these attorneys are conducting depositions, they are just as likely to use questions as an opportunity to distort testimony—rephrasing a client's answer in an inaccurate way and then asking a question based on that distortion; asking rude, irrelevant, or bigoted questions; or using anger or vulgarity to bully a witness.

Study the following case for an explanation of one state's limitations on these behaviors:

In re Anonymous Member of South Carolina Bar
346 S.C. 177, 552 S.E.2d 10 (S.C. 2001)

II. Deposition Conduct

We take this opportunity to alert the bar to the enactment of Rule 30(j), SCRCP and to address attorney conduct in depositions in general so that attorneys in South Carolina will be aware of what actions can result in sanctions both by the trial court under the South Carolina Rules of Civil Procedure and by this Court under the Rules of Professional Conduct.

A. New Rule 30(j), SCRCP

"A lawyer is a representative of clients, an officer of the legal system and a public citizen having special responsibility for the quality of justice." Rule 407, SCACR pmbl. In depositions attorneys may face the greatest conflict between their obligations to the court and opposing counsel under Rule 3.4,[1] and their obligations to their own client under Rule 1.3.[2] Since depositions almost always occur without direct judicial supervision, lawyers must regulate themselves during this highly critical stage of litigation. In the past, this Court has sanctioned attorneys who have failed to properly conduct themselves during depositions. *See Matter of Golden*, 329 S.C. 335, 496 S.E.2d 619 (1998). In addition to subjecting themselves to possible ethical sanctions, attorneys who engage in misconduct during depositions may find themselves sanctioned by the trial court as well. *See* Rule 37, SCRCP.

Rule 30(j), SCRCP is nearly identical to the guidelines used in federal district court in South Carolina. The rule states:

Conduct During Depositions

> Study this rule carefully before reading the remainder of the opinion.

(1) At the beginning of each deposition, deposing counsel shall instruct the witness to ask deposing counsel, rather than the witness' own counsel, for clarifications, definitions, or explanations of any words, questions or documents presented during the course of the deposition. The witness shall abide by these instructions.

(2) All objections, except those which would be waived if not made at the deposition under Rule 32(d)(3), SCRCP, and those necessary to assert a privilege, to enforce a limitation on evidence directed by the Court, or to present a motion pursuant to Rule 30(d), SCRCP, shall be preserved.

(3) Counsel shall not direct or request that a witness not answer a question, unless that counsel has objected to the question on the

---

1. "A lawyer shall not:
(a) Unlawfully obstruct another party's access to evidence … ; …
(d) In pretrial procedure, make a frivolous discovery request or fail to make a reasonably diligent effort to comply with a legally proper discovery request by an opposing party." Rule 3.4, Rule 407, SCACR.

2. "A lawyer shall act with reasonable diligence and promptness in representing a client." Rule 1.3., Rule 407, SCACR. The comment to this rule states "A lawyer should act with commitment and dedication to the interests of the client and with zeal in advocacy upon the client's behalf."

ground that the answer is protected by a privilege[3] or a limitation on evidence directed by the court or unless that counsel intends to present a motion under Rule 30(d), SCRCP. In addition, counsel shall have an affirmative duty to inform a witness that, unless such an objection is made, the question must be answered. Counsel directing that a witness not answer a question on those grounds or allowing a witness to refuse to answer a question on those grounds shall move the court for a protective order under Rule 26(c), SCRCP, or 30(d), SCRCP, within five business days of the suspension or termination of the deposition. Failure to timely file such a motion will constitute waiver of the objection, and the deposition may be reconvened.

(4) Counsel shall not make objections or statements which might suggest an answer to a witness. Counsel's objections shall be stated concisely and in a non-argumentative and non-suggestive manner, stating the basis of the objection and nothing more.

(5) Counsel and a witness shall not engage in private, off-the-record conferences during depositions or during breaks or recesses regarding the substance of the testimony at the deposition, except for the purpose of deciding whether to assert a privilege or to make an objection or to move for a protective order.

(6) Any conferences which occur pursuant to, or in violation of, section (5) of this rule are proper subjects for inquiry by deposing counsel to ascertain whether there has been any witness coaching and, if so, to what extent and nature.

(7) Any conferences which occur pursuant to, or in violation of, section (5) of this rule shall be noted on the record by the counsel who participated in the conference. The purpose and outcome of the conference shall be noted on the record.

(8) Deposing counsel shall provide to opposing counsel a copy of all documents shown to the witness during the deposition, either before the deposition begins or contemporaneously with the showing of each document to the witness. If the documents are provided (or otherwise identified) at least two business days before the deposition, then the witness and the witness' counsel do not have the right to discuss the documents privately before the witness answers questions about them. If the documents have not been so provided or identified, then counsel and the witness may have a reasonable amount of time to discuss the documents before the witness answers questions concerning the document.

(9) Violation of this rule may subject the violator to sanctions under Rule 37, SCRCP.

Our Rule 30(j), SCRCP, is derived from Judge Robert S. Gawthrop's seminal opinion in *Hall Clifton Precision*, 150 F.R.D. 525 (E.D.Pa.1993). Having adopted the *Hall* approach, our Court requires attorneys in South Carolina to oper-

---

3. For purposes of this rule, the term "privilege" includes but is not limited to: attorney-client privilege; work-product protection; trade secret protection and privileges based on the United States Constitution and the South Carolina Constitution.

ate under one of the most sweeping and comprehensive rules on deposition conduct in the nation.

B. Off-the-Record Conferences

Rule 30(j), SCRCP, makes clear that a deposition's beginning signals the end of a witness's preparation. Once a deposition begins, an attorney and a client may have an off-the-record conference only when deciding whether to assert a privilege or to discuss a previously undisclosed document. *See* Rule 30(j)(5), SCRCP; Rule 30(j)(8), SCRCP. Before beginning such a conference, the deponent's attorney should note for the record that a break is needed to discuss the possible assertion of a privilege or a newly produced document. After any such conference, the conferencing attorney should state on the record why the conference occurred and the decision reached. If the party decides to assert a privilege, the basis for the privilege should be clearly stated. Whether or not a privilege is asserted, deposing counsel may inquire on the record into the subject of the conference to determine if there has been any witness coaching. *See* Rule 30(j)(6), SCRCP. Conferences called to assist a client in framing an answer, to calm down a nervous client, or to interrupt the flow of a deposition are improper and warrant sanctions.

Imagine how this would sound.

Off-the-record conferences not specifically permitted by the rule are not allowed whether they are called by the deponent's attorney or the deponent. "There is simply no qualitative distinction between private conferences initiated by a lawyer and those initiated by a witness. Neither should occur." *Hall*, 150 F.R.D. at 528. According to our rule, even during breaks in the deposition such as a lunch or overnight break, witnesses and their counsel cannot talk substantively about prior or future testimony in the deposition. *See* Rule 30(j)(5), SCRCP.

C. Suggestive Objections and Interjections

In order to prevent witness coaching during depositions, the rule prohibits lengthy "speaking" objections and brief suggestive interjections. As noted by Judge Gawthrop in *Hall*, the rules of evidence "contain no provision allowing lawyers to interrupt the trial testimony of a witness to make a statement. Such behavior should likewise be prohibited at depositions, since it tends to obstruct the taking of the witness's testimony." *Hall*, 150 F.R.D. at 530; *see also* Rule 30(c), SCRCP ("Examination and cross-examination of witnesses may proceed as permitted at the trial under the provisions of the South Carolina Rules of Evidence ..."). Therefore, interjections during a deposition by the witness's attorney such as "if you remember" and "don't speculate" are improper because they suggest to the witness how to answer the question. Attorneys can easily make these admonitions to their client before the deposition begins. As summarized by Judge Gawthrop:

> The underlying purpose of a deposition is to find out what a witness saw, heard, or did—what the witness thinks. A deposition is meant to be a question-and-answer conversation between the deposing lawyer and the witness. There is no proper need for the witness's own lawyer to act as an intermediary, interpreting questions, deciding which questions the witness should answer, and helping the witness to formulate answers. The witness comes to the deposition to testify, not to

indulge in a parody of Charlie McCarthy, with lawyers coaching or bending the witness's words to mold a legally convenient record. It is the witness—not the lawyer—who is the witness.

Hall, 150 F.R.D. at 528.

Rule 30(j)(1), SCRCP also directs the deponent to look to the attorney asking the question, not the witness's own counsel, for any clarifications or explanations. A witness's attorney cannot object to a question just because the attorney does not understand the question. *See Hall*, 150 F.R.D. at 530 n. 10. Furthermore, it is improper for counsel to state for the record their interpretations of questions, since such interpretations are completely irrelevant and improperly suggestive to the deponent. *Id.* A witness's attorney must also refrain from rephrasing questions for the witness.

Think about how these rules affect your duty to prepare a witness.

D. Instructions Not to Answer

New Rule 30(j), SCRCP, also limits when an attorney may advise a witness not to answer a question during a deposition. The only circumstances under which an attorney may instruct the witness not to answer a question in a deposition are: (1) when counsel has objected to the question on the ground that the answer is protected by a privilege; (2) when the information sought is protected by a limitation on evidence directed by the court; and (3) when the witness's counsel intends to present a motion under Rule 30(d), SCRCP (witness harassment). *See* Rule 30(j)(3), SCACR. The rule even requires attorneys to affirmatively direct their witnesses to answer a question unless they make one of these objections. *Id.*

On this point, instructing a witness not to respond to a question because it has been "asked and answered" will generally be improper. No rule prevents a deposing attorney from asking the same question more than one time or different variances of the same question. The witness's attorney can question the witness after the opponent's examination is done to clarify any confusion brought about by the witness's answers. An attorney may use the "asked and answered" objection without an instruction not to answer the question to establish a record of abuse where the attorney believes the questioning is approaching the level of harassment. If repetitive questioning reaches the point of harassment, the witness's attorney should make a motion under Rule 30(d), SCRCP.

E. Handling Discovery Abuse in Depositions

"The primary objective of discovery is to ensure that lawsuits are decided by what the facts reveal, not by what facts are concealed." *In re Alford Chevrolet-Geo*, 997 S.W.2d 173, 180 (Tex. 1999). The entire thrust of our discovery rules involves full and fair disclosure, to prevent a trial from becoming a guessing game or one of surprise for either party. *Samples v. Mitchell*, 329 S.C. 105, 495 S.E.2d 213 (Ct. App. 1997). In this respect, the discovery process is designed to "make a trial less a game of blind man's bluff and more a fair contest with the basic issues and facts disclosed to the fullest practicable extent." *See United States v. Procter & Gamble Co.*, 356 U.S. 677, 682, 78 S.Ct. 983, 986-87, 2 L.Ed.2d 1077 (1958).

Contrast this goal with the goal of efficiency and proportionality discussed in the Mancia case above.

Depositions are widely recognized as one of the "most powerful and productive" devices used in discovery. *See* A. Darby Dickerson, *The Law and*

Ethics of Civil Depositions, 57 Md. L. Rev. 273, 277 (1998). Since depositions are so important in litigation, attorneys face great temptation to cross the limits of acceptable behavior in order to win the case at the expense of their ethical responsibilities to the court and their fellow attorneys. Claiming that any such improper behavior was merely "zealous advocacy" will not justify discovery abuse. When attorneys cross the line during a deposition, their actions do not promote the "just, speedy, and inexpensive determination of every action." *See* Rule 1, SCRCP.

Actions taken in a deposition designed to prevent justice, delay the process, or drive up costs are improper and warrant sanctions. In South Carolina, our judges have broad discretion in addressing misbehavior during depositions. *See* Rule 37, SCRCP. In addition to their traditional contempt powers, judges may issue orders as a sanction for improper deposition conduct: (1) specifying that designated facts be taken as established for purposes of the action; (2) precluding the introduction of certain evidence at trial; (3) striking out pleadings or parts thereof; (4) staying further proceedings pending the compliance with an order that has not been followed; (5) dismissing the action in full or in part; (6) entering default judgment on some or all the claims; or (7) an award of reasonable expenses, including attorney fees. *Id.* Among the costs a judge may deem appropriate could be those incurred for future judicial monitoring of depositions or payment for the retaking of depositions. Our judges must use their authority to make sure that abusive deposition tactics and other forms of discovery abuse do not succeed in their ultimate goal: achieving success through abuse of the discovery rules rather than by the rule of law.

Notes

1. Suppose you are facing an opposing attorney who is notorious for abusive deposition practice. Could you negotiate with the attorney to agree to procedures for the deposition that would incorporate these rules? Would asking the court to enter an order similar to these rules help?

2. Not all courts have agreed with the South Carolina court's approach to restrictions on deposition practice. For example, on the question of whether interruptions for conferences are permissible, the court in *In re Stratosphere Corp. Sec. Litig.,* 182 F.R.D. 614, 621 (D. Nev. 1998), stated "To deny a client any right to confer with his or her counsel about anything, once the client has been sworn to testify, and further to subject such a person to unfettered inquiry into anything which may have been discussed with the client's attorney ... is a position this Court declines to take." *See also, McKinley Infuser, Inc. v. Zdeb,* 200 F.R.D. 648 (D. Colo. 2001) (court declined to deny witness right to confer with counsel between sessions of his deposition). Which approach do you agree with?

Researching Professional Responsibility: Deposition Practice

The particular rules governing matters such as how to state an objection in a deposition or whether attorneys may consult with clients once the deposition begins are matters that vary from jurisdiction to jurisdiction. Most of deposition practice is governed by local custom and practice or by local court rules. Knowledge of those rules and customs is very important in defending your client from attorneys who use depositions as opportunities for abuse. Research your local court's rules and practices regarding depositions. Research of local practice is best conducted by simply picking up the phone and asking someone. You can research local court rules online or by calling the court clerk's office. Particularly where a judge has a "standard discovery order" that is not necessarily part of the local court rules, there is no way to find such a guideline without asking. Call attorneys who regularly take depositions in your community and ask about their opinions on some of these deposition behaviors.

Share the results of your research with your classmates. If you came to different conclusions about local practice, try to figure out why.

21.5 Protecting Your Clients from Discovery Abuses

How do you combat unethical deposition tactics and other misbehavior by opposing attorneys?

1. Prepare for the worst and make boundaries clear.

You can anticipate problems and take steps to make rules even clearer. For example, pre-trial discovery conferences can be used to obtain court orders to limit the opportunities for misbehavior. Fed. R. Civ. P. 26(d)(1) provides that discovery may not begin before there has been a discovery conference under Rule 26(f). Prepare for that discovery conference carefully, considering potential problems and realistic limits on depositions and other discovery. To discover if there are likely to be these problems, research your opposing attorney's reputation. If you anticipate problems, request that depositions be held at the courthouse. This will prevent deposition scheduling at inconvenient times or places and will permit access to a magistrate, commissioner, or judge for protective orders if necessary. If you are facing a "coached" witness, you can use your skills in questioning — listening carefully, skillful use of narrow and specific questions, and timing of questions — these can all catch a well-prepared client unawares and still bring out the truth. If you know an attorney is likely to engage in these tactics, request a court order setting out the ground rules for how depositions will be conducted, including whether objections about the form of the questions will be preserved for trial. As a deposition begins, remind the opposing attorney (and the deponent) of the ground rules and seek counsel's agreement.

2. Stay formal and make a record.

If you are facing an abusive opponent, follow court rules and procedures to the letter. Do not grant any favors and do not act informally. Prefer written to oral communication; videotaped recording to transcription; and communication on the record to off the record. Call misbehavior each time you see it and do so in ways that make a record. In depositions, describe behavior that might not be obvious on the record or, if necessary, arrange for video depositions. The cost is often worth the savings in deterred misconduct. Put your objections to opposing counsel's tactics in writing. Avoid name-calling or threats, but simply name the behavior in concrete and objective terms and indicate the behavior you believe is required by the rules instead. Sometimes even just a well-placed question, quietly stated, ("Why would you ask/say/do that?") can slow down a tantrum or tactic.

3. Don't threaten unless you are ready to act.

Sometimes a threat to stop a deposition or file a motion for sanctions can be powerful in bringing a rogue attorney into line. However, beware that your threat is not seen as a tactic to secure anything other than an end to the attorney's misbehavior. In particular, do not threaten to report an attorney to disciplinary counsel. You can point out that you believe the attorney's behavior violates the rules of conduct and how, but if you believe the attorney's behavior requires reporting, do so. You may be motivated to "give them another chance" and say "If you don't…, I will report you." But this can easily make it appear that you are willing to negotiate away your duty to report misconduct.

Threats to report to outside authorities can end up subjecting you to discipline. Re-read Connecticut Rule 3.4(7). This rule was not incorporated into the Model Rules of Professional Conduct because it was considered overbroad and vague. Nonetheless, half of the states retained the provision when they adopted the Model Rules. Even without the rule, other provisions of the rule could apply in various circumstances of threats: most commonly, Rule 3.4 (Fairness to Opposing Party and Counsel), Rule 4.1 (Truthfulness in Statements to Others), Rule 4.4 (Respect for Rights of Third Persons), and Rules 8.4(b), (d) and (e) (Misconduct—especially "conduct prejudicial to the administration of justice"). Threatening sanctions in order to secure an advantageous settlement would raise these same concerns. Instead, simply tell your opponent what behavior must change and, if it does not, let them know that you are going to take additional action to protect your client.

4. Don't respond in kind.

Probably the worst way to respond to rude or aggressive conduct is to permit yourself to be goaded into equally unprofessional conduct. Remember Mark Twain's warning against wrestling with pigs—you will both get muddy but the pig will enjoy it. Act consistently with the rules and your own values. If you are dealing with an opposing attorney who is consistently abusive, don't bother with trying to establish a personal or social relationship—it won't work and will only give the attorney more opportunities and ammunition for abuse. If you find yourself losing your cool, take a time out to cool down. If abusive conduct has become personal to you, bring in another attorney for a fresh perspective.

5. Warn and prepare your client.

Prepare clients for baseless threats, angry outbursts, coarse language, or confusing and inaccurate statements and questions. Explain that these are merely unethical tactics and will work against the attorney in the long run so long as the client does not permit himself to be manipulated by them.

5. Seek the protection of the court if necessary.

Motions to terminate or limit depositions are available when attorneys overschedule. Most rules provide for a variety of sanctions for failure to appear at a hearing or deposition or failure to answer discovery. These can include the payment of reasonable expenses of party and attorney, orders denying a party the right to cross-examine witnesses or present evidence, and the entry of default findings or even judgment.

21.6 Trial Publicity

In a world of reality television and Court TV, it is tempting to assume that attorneys should consider using media as a tool of persuasion. However, in litigation, the right of attorneys to speak to the press is in tension with the right to a fair trial. Courts have had difficulties drawing clear lines between these rights. The United States Supreme Court addressed this balance in *Gentile v. State Bar of Nevada*, 501 U.S. 1030 (1991). There were three opinions in that case. Justice Kennedy announced the judgment of the Court, but the entirety of his opinion was joined only by Justices Marshall, Blackmun, and Stevens. Chief Justice Rehnquist's entire opinion was joined only by Justices White, Scalia, and Souter. Justice O'-Connor joined Justice Kennedy on the issue of the vagueness of the Nevada statute; joined the Chief Justice's opinion regarding the standard to be applied to attorney speech; and also wrote a separate concurring opinion. Justice Kennedy opined that the standard should be "clear and present danger," particularly in a case such as this involving criticism of the government. However, the standard adopted by the majority of the court was expressed by those portions of Chief Justice Rehnquist's opinion, which was joined by Justice O'Connor. The following excerpts from the various opinions reflect the areas in which a majority of the Court (though a shifting majority) agreed. As you read the opinion, outline the rule that you believe should result. When you have completed reading the opinion, compare your suggested rule to that ultimately adopted by the ABA in reaction to the case.

Gentile v. State Bar of Nevada
501 U.S. 1030, 111 S. Ct. 2720, 115 L. Ed. 2d 888 (1991)

[The following portions of Chief Justice Rehnquist's opinion, which were joined by Justice O'Connor to make a majority opinion, addressed the standard by which attorney speech should be judged.]

Petitioner [Gentile] was disciplined for making statements to the press about a pending case in which he represented a criminal defendant [Sanders]. The state bar, and the Supreme Court of Nevada on review, found that petitioner knew or should have known that there was a substantial likelihood that his statements would materially prejudice the trial of his client. Nonetheless, petitioner contends that the First Amendment to the United States Constitution requires a stricter standard to be met before such speech by an attorney may be disciplined: there must be a finding of "actual prejudice or a substantial and imminent threat to fair trial." Brief for Petitioner 15. We conclude that the "substantial likelihood of material prejudice" standard applied by Nevada and most other States satisfies the First Amendment.

I

Petitioner's client was the subject of a highly publicized case, and in response to adverse publicity about his client, Gentile held a press conference on the day after Sanders was indicted. At the press conference, petitioner made, among others, the following statements:

> When this case goes to trial, and as it develops, you're going to see that the evidence will prove not only that Grady Sanders is an innocent person and had nothing to do with any of the charges that are being leveled against him, but that the person that was in the most direct position to have stolen the drugs and the money, the American Express Travelers' checks, is Detective Steve Scholl.

> There is far more evidence that will establish that Detective Scholl took these drugs and took these American Express Travelers' checks than any other living human being..... .

> ... the so-called other victims, as I sit here today I can tell you that one, two — four of them are known drug dealers and convicted money launderers and drug dealers; three of whom didn't say a word about anything until after they were approached by Metro and after they were already in trouble and are trying to work themselves out of something.

> Now, up until the moment, of course, that they started going along with what detectives from Metro wanted them to say, these people were being held out as being incredible and liars by the very same people who are going to say now that you can believe them.

App. to Pet. for Cert. 8a-9a.

The following statements were in response to questions from members of the press:

> ... because of the stigma that attaches to merely being accused — okay — I know I represent an innocent man.... The last time I had a conference with you, was with a client and I let him talk to you and I told you that that case would be dismissed and it was. Okay?

> I don't take cheap shots like this. I represent an innocent guy. All right?..... .

> [The police] were playing very fast and loose.... We've got some video tapes that if you take a look at them, I'll tell you what, [Detective Scholl] either had a hell of a cold or he should have seen a better doctor.

Id., at 12a, 14a.

Articles appeared in the local newspapers describing the press conference and petitioner's statements. The trial took place approximately six months later, and although the trial court succeeded in empaneling a jury that had not been affected by the media coverage and Sanders was acquitted on all charges, the state bar disciplined petitioner for his statements.

The Southern Nevada Disciplinary Board found that petitioner knew the detective he accused of perpetrating the crime and abusing drugs would be a witness for the prosecution. It also found that petitioner believed others whom he characterized as money launderers and drug dealers would be called as prosecution witnesses. Petitioner's admitted purpose for calling the press conference was to counter public opinion which he perceived as adverse to his client, to fight back against the perceived efforts of the prosecution to poison the prospective juror pool, and to publicly present his client's side of the case. The board found that in light of the statements, their timing, and petitioner's purpose, petitioner knew or should have known that there was a substantial likelihood that the statements would materially prejudice the Sanders trial.

The Nevada Supreme Court affirmed the board's decision, finding by clear and convincing evidence that petitioner "knew or reasonably should have known that his comments had a substantial likelihood of materially prejudicing the adjudication of his client's case." 106 Nev. 60, 62, 787 P.2d 386, 387 (1990). The court noted that the case was "highly publicized"; that the press conference, held the day after the indictment and the same day as the arraignment, was "timed to have maximum impact"; and that petitioner's comments "related to the character, credibility, reputation or criminal record of the police detective and other potential witnesses." *Ibid.* The court concluded that the "absence of actual prejudice does not establish that there was no substantial likelihood of material prejudice." *Ibid.*

II

Gentile asserts that the same stringent standard applied in *Nebraska Press Assn. v. Stuart,* 427 U.S. 539, 96 S. Ct. 2791, 49 L.Ed.2d 683 (1976), to restraints on press publication during the pendency of a criminal trial should be applied to speech by a lawyer whose client is a defendant in a criminal proceeding. In that case, we held that in order to suppress press commentary on evidentiary matters, the State would have to show that "further publicity, unchecked, would so distort the views of potential jurors that 12 could not be found who would, under proper instructions, fulfill their sworn duty to render a just verdict exclusively on the evidence presented in open court." *Id.,* at 569, 96 S. Ct., at 2807. Respondent, on the other hand, relies on statements in cases such as *Sheppard v. Maxwell,* 384 U.S. 333, 86 S. Ct. 1507, 16 L.Ed.2d 600 (1966), which sharply distinguished between restraints on the press and restraints on lawyers whose clients are parties to the proceeding: "Collaboration between counsel and the press as to information affecting the fairness of a criminal trial is not only subject to regulation, but is highly censurable and worthy of disciplinary measures." *Id.,* at 363, 86 S. Ct., at 1522.

… Currently, 31 States in addition to Nevada have adopted—either verbatim or with insignificant variations—Rule 3.6 of the ABA's Model Rules. Eleven States have adopted Disciplinary Rule 7-107 of the ABA's Code of Professional Responsibility, which is less protective of lawyer speech than Model Rule 3.6, in that it applies a "reasonable likelihood of prejudice" standard. Only one State, Virginia, has explicitly adopted a clear and present danger standard, while four States and the District of Columbia have adopted standards that arguably approximate "clear and present danger."

Petitioner maintains, however, that the First Amendment to the United States Constitution requires a State, such as Nevada in this case, to demonstrate a "clear and present danger" of "actual prejudice or an imminent threat" before any discipline may be imposed on a lawyer who initiates a press conference such as occurred here. He relies on decisions such as *Nebraska Press Assn. v. Stuart*, 427 U.S. 539, 96 S. Ct. 2791, 49 L.Ed.2d 683 (1976), *Bridges v. California*, 314 U.S. 252, 62 S. Ct. 190, 86 L.Ed. 192 (1941), *Pennekamp v. Florida*, 328 U.S. 331, 66 S. Ct. 1029, 90 L.Ed. 1295 (1946), and *Craig v. Harney*, 331 U.S. 367, 67 S. Ct. 1249, 91 L.Ed. 1546 (1947), to support his position. In those cases we held that trial courts might not constitutionally punish, through use of the contempt power, newspapers and others for publishing editorials, cartoons, and other items critical of judges in particular cases. We held that such punishments could be imposed only if there were a clear and present danger of "some serious substantive evil which they are designed to avert." *Bridges v. California, supra*, 314 U.S., at 270, 62 S. Ct., at 197. Petitioner also relies on *Wood v. Georgia*, 370 U.S. 375, 82 S. Ct. 1364, 8 L.Ed.2d 569 (1962), which held that a court might not punish a sheriff for publicly criticizing a judge's charges to a grand jury.

Respondent State Bar of Nevada points out, on the other hand, that none of these cases involved lawyers who represented parties to a pending proceeding in court. It points to the statement of Holmes, J., in *Patterson v. Colorado ex rel. Attorney General of Colorado*, 205 U.S. 454, 463, 27 S. Ct. 556, 558, 51 L.Ed. 879 (1907), that "[w]hen a case is finished, courts are subject to the same criticism as other people, but the propriety and necessity of preventing interference with the course of justice by premature statement, argument or intimidation hardly can be denied." Respondent also points to a similar statement in *Bridges, supra*, 314 U.S., at 271, 62 S. Ct., at 197:

> "The very word 'trial' connotes decisions on the evidence and arguments properly advanced in open court. Legal trials are not like elections, to be won through the use of the meeting-hall, the radio, and the newspaper."

These opposing positions illustrate one of the many dilemmas which arise in the course of constitutional adjudication. The above quotes from *Patterson* and *Bridges* epitomize the theory upon which our criminal justice system is founded: The outcome of a criminal trial is to be decided by impartial jurors, who know as little as possible of the case, based on material admitted into evidence before them in a court proceeding. Extrajudicial comments on, or discussion of, evidence which might never be admitted at trial and *ex parte* statements by counsel giving their version of the facts obviously threaten to undermine this basic tenet.

At the same time, however, the criminal justice system exists in a larger context of a government ultimately of the people, who wish to be informed about happenings in the criminal justice system, and, if sufficiently informed about those happenings, might wish to make changes in the system. The way most of them acquire information is from the media. The First Amendment protections of speech and press have been held, in the cases cited above, to require a showing of "clear and present danger" that a malfunction in the criminal justice system will be caused before a State may prohibit media speech or publication about a particular pending trial. The question we must answer in this case is whether a lawyer who represents a defendant involved with the criminal justice system may insist on the same standard before he is disciplined for public pronouncements about the case, or whether the State instead may penalize that sort of speech upon a lesser showing.

It is unquestionable that in the courtroom itself, during a judicial proceeding, whatever right to "free speech" an attorney has is extremely circumscribed. An attorney may not, by speech or other conduct, resist a ruling of the trial court beyond the point necessary to preserve a claim for appeal. *Sacher v. United States,* 343 U.S. 1, 8, 72 S. Ct. 451, 454, 96 L.Ed. 717 (1952) (criminal trial); *Fisher v. Pace,* 336 U.S. 155, 69 S. Ct. 425, 93 L.Ed. 569 (1949) (civil trial). Even outside the courtroom, a majority of the Court in two separate opinions in the case of *In re Sawyer,* 360 U.S. 622, 79 S. Ct. 1376, 3 L.Ed.2d 1473 (1959), observed that lawyers in pending cases were subject to ethical restrictions on speech to which an ordinary citizen would not be. There, the Court had before it an order affirming the suspension of an attorney from practice because of her attack on the fairness and impartiality of a judge. The plurality opinion, which found the discipline improper, concluded that the comments had not in fact impugned the judge's integrity. Justice Stewart, who provided the fifth vote for reversal of the sanction, said in his separate opinion that he could not join any possible "intimation that a lawyer can invoke the constitutional right of free speech to immunize himself from even-handed discipline for proven unethical conduct." *Id.,* at 646, 79 S. Ct., at 1388. He said that "[o]bedience to ethical precepts may require abstention from what in other circumstances might be constitutionally protected speech." *Id.,* at 646-647, 79 S. Ct., at 1388-1389.

The four dissenting Justices who would have sustained the discipline said:

> Of course, a lawyer is a person and he too has a constitutional freedom of utterance and may exercise it to castigate courts and their administration of justice. But a lawyer actively participating in a trial, particularly an emotionally charged criminal prosecution, is not merely a person and not even merely a lawyer.... He is an intimate and trusted and essential part of the machinery of justice, an 'officer of the court' in the most compelling sense.

Id., at 666, 668, 79 S. Ct., at 1398, 1399 (Frankfurter, J., dissenting, joined by Clark, Harlan, and Whittaker, JJ.).

Likewise, in *Sheppard v. Maxwell,* where the defendant's conviction was overturned because extensive prejudicial pretrial publicity had denied the defendant a fair trial, we held that a new trial was a remedy for such publicity, but

> we must remember that reversals are but palliatives; the cure lies in those remedial measures that will prevent the prejudice at its inception. The courts must take such steps by rule and regulation that will protect their processes from prejudicial outside interferences. Neither prosecutors, counsel for defense, the accused, witnesses, court staff nor enforcement officers coming under the jurisdiction of the court should be permitted to frustrate its func-

tion. Collaboration between counsel and the press as to information affecting the fairness of a criminal trial is not only subject to regulation, but is highly censurable and worthy of disciplinary measures.

384 U.S., at 363, 86 S. Ct., at 1522....

We think that the quoted statements from our opinions in *In re Sawyer,* 360 U.S. 622, 79 S. Ct. 1376, 3 L.Ed.2d 1473 (1959), and *Sheppard v. Maxwell, supra,* rather plainly indicate that the speech of lawyers representing clients in pending cases may be regulated under a less demanding standard than that established for regulation of the press in *Nebraska Press Assn. v. Stuart,* 427 U.S. 539, 96 S. Ct. 2791, 49 L.Ed.2d 683 (1976), and the cases which preceded it. Lawyers representing clients in pending cases are key participants in the criminal justice system, and the State may demand some adherence to the precepts of that system in regulating their speech as well as their conduct.... Because lawyers have special access to information through discovery and client communications, their extrajudicial statements pose a threat to the fairness of a pending proceeding since lawyers' statements are likely to be received as especially authoritative.... We agree with the majority of the States that the "substantial likelihood of material prejudice" standard constitutes a constitutionally permissible balance between the First Amendment rights of attorneys in pending cases and the State's interest in fair trials.

When a state regulation implicates First Amendment rights, the Court must balance those interests against the State's legitimate interest in regulating the activity in question. The "substantial likelihood" test embodied in Rule 177 is constitutional under this analysis, for it is designed to protect the integrity and fairness of a State's judicial system, and it imposes only narrow and necessary limitations on lawyers' speech. The limitations are aimed at two principal evils: (1) comments that are likely to influence the actual outcome of the trial, and (2) comments that are likely to prejudice the jury venire, even if an untainted panel can ultimately be found. Few, if any, interests under the Constitution are more fundamental than the right to a fair trial by "impartial" jurors, and an outcome affected by extrajudicial statements would violate that fundamental right. Even if a fair trial can ultimately be ensured through voir dire, change of venue, or some other device, these measures entail serious costs to the system. Extensive voir dire may not be able to filter out all of the effects of pretrial publicity, and with increasingly widespread media coverage of criminal trials, a change of venue may not suffice to undo the effects of statements such as those made by petitioner. The State has a substantial interest in preventing officers of the court, such as lawyers, from imposing such costs on the judicial system and on the litigants.

The restraint on speech is narrowly tailored to achieve those objectives. The regulation of attorneys' speech is limited—it applies only to speech that is substantially likely to have a materially prejudicial effect; it is neutral as to points of view, applying equally to all attorneys participating in a pending case; and it merely postpones the attorneys' comments until after the trial. While supported by the substantial state interest in preventing prejudice to an adjudicative proceeding by those who have a duty to protect its integrity, the Rule is limited on its face to preventing only speech having a substantial likelihood of materially prejudicing that proceeding.

* * *

[The following excerpts from Part III of Justice Kennedy's Opinion, concluding that the rule was void for vagueness, were joined by Justice O'Connor to make it a majority opinion on this issue]

III

As interpreted by the Nevada Supreme Court, the Rule is void for vagueness, in any event, for its safe harbor provision, Rule 177(3), misled petitioner into thinking that he could give his press conference without fear of discipline. Rule 177(3)(a) provides that a lawyer "may state without elaboration ... the general nature of the ... defense." Statements under this provision are protected "[n]otwithstanding subsection 1 and 2(a-f)." By necessary operation of the word "notwithstanding," the Rule contemplates that a lawyer describing the "general nature of the ... defense" "without elaboration" need fear no discipline, even if he comments on "[t]he character, credibility, reputation or criminal record of a ... witness," and even if he "knows or reasonably should know that [the statement] will have a substantial likelihood of materially prejudicing an adjudicative proceeding."

Given this grammatical structure, and absent any clarifying interpretation by the state court, the Rule fails to provide "'fair notice to those to whom [it] is directed.'" *Grayned v. City of Rockford*, 408 U.S. 104, 112, 92 S. Ct. 2294, 2301, 33 L.Ed.2d 222 (1972). A lawyer seeking to avail himself of Rule 177(3)'s protection must guess at its contours. The right to explain the "general" nature of the defense without "elaboration" provides insufficient guidance because "general" and "elaboration" are both classic terms of degree. In the context before us, these terms have no settled usage or tradition of interpretation in law. The lawyer has no principle for determining when his remarks pass from the safe harbor of the general to the forbidden sea of the elaborated.

Petitioner testified he thought his statements were protected by Rule 177(3). A review of the press conference supports that claim. He gave only a brief opening statement, and on numerous occasions declined to answer reporters' questions seeking more detailed comments. One illustrative exchange shows petitioner's attempt to obey the rule:

> "QUESTION FROM THE FLOOR: Dominick, you mention you question the credibility of some of the witnesses, some of the people named as victims in the government indictment.
>
> "Can we go through it and elaborate on their backgrounds, interests—
>
> "MR. GENTILE: I can't because ethics prohibit me from doing so.
>
> "Last night before I decided I was going to make a statement, I took a good close look at the rules of professional responsibility. There are things that I can say and there are things that I can't. Okay?
>
> "I can't name which of the people have the drug backgrounds. I'm sure you guys can find that by doing just a little bit of investigative work." App. to Pet. for Cert. 11a (emphasis added).

Other occasions are as follows:

"QUESTION FROM THE FLOOR: Do you believe any other police officers other than Scholl were involved in the disappearance of the dope and-

"MR. GENTILE: Let me say this: What I believe and what the proof is are two different things. Okay? I'm reluctant to discuss what I believe because I don't want to slander somebody, but I can tell you that the proof shows that Scholl is the guy that is most likely to have taken the cocaine and the American Express traveler's checks.

"QUESTION FROM THE FLOOR: What is that? What is that proof?

"MR. GENTILE: It'll come out; it'll come out." App. to Pet. for Cert. 9a.

"QUESTION FROM THE FLOOR: I have seen reports that the FBI seems to think sort of along the lines that you do.

"MR. GENTILE: Well, I couldn't agree with them more.

"QUESTION FROM THE FLOOR: Do you know anything about it?

"MR. GENTILE: Yes, I do; but again, Dan, I'm not in a position to be able to discuss that now.

"All I can tell you is that you're in for a very interesting six months to a year as this case develops." *Id.*, at 10a.

"QUESTION FROM THE FLOOR: Did the cops pass the polygraph?

"MR. GENTILE: Well, I would like to give you a comment on that, except that Ray Slaughter's trial is coming up and I don't want to get in the way of anybody being able to defend themselves.

"QUESTION FROM THE FLOOR: Do you think the Slaughter case— that there's a connection?

"MR. GENTILE: Absolutely. I don't think there is any question about it, and—

"QUESTION FROM THE FLOOR: What is that?

"MR. GENTILE: Well, it's intertwined to a great deal, I think.

"I know that what I think the connection is, again, is something I believe to be true. I can't point to it being true and until I can I'm not going to say anything.

"QUESTION FROM THE FLOOR: Do you think the police involved in this passed legitimate-legitimately passed lie detector tests?

"MR. GENTILE: I don't want to comment on that for two reasons:

"Number one, again, Ray Slaughter is coming up for trial and it wouldn't be right to call him a liar if I didn't think that it were true. But, secondly, I don't have much faith in polygraph tests.

"QUESTION FROM THE FLOOR: Did [Sanders] ever take one?

"MR. GENTILE: The police polygraph?

"QUESTION FROM THE FLOOR: Yes.

"MR. GENTILE: No, he didn't take a police polygraph.

"QUESTION FROM THE FLOOR: Did he take one with you?

"MR. GENTILE: I'm not going to disclose that now." *Id.*, at 12a-13a.

Nevertheless, the disciplinary board said only that petitioner's comments "went beyond the scope of the statements permitted by SCR 177(3)" and the Nevada Supreme Court's rejection of petitioner's defense based on Rule 177(3) was just as terse. The fact that Gentile was found in violation of the Rules after studying them and making a conscious effort at compliance demonstrates that Rule 177 creates a trap for the wary as well as the unwary.

The prohibition against vague regulations of speech is based in part on the need to eliminate the impermissible risk of discriminatory enforcement, for history shows that speech is suppressed when either the speaker or the message is critical of those who enforce the law. The question is not whether discriminatory enforcement occurred here, and we assume it did not, but whether the Rule is so imprecise that discriminatory enforcement is a real possibility. The inquiry is of particular relevance when one of the classes most affected by the regulation is the criminal defense bar, which has the professional mission to challenge actions of the State. Petitioner, for instance, succeeded in preventing the conviction of his client, and the speech in issue involved criticism of the government.

The judgment of the Supreme Court of Nevada is reversed.

Notes

1. After this case, the ABA amended Model Rule 3.6. Nevada followed, adopting the ABA Model Rule without change:

Nevada Supreme Court Rules of Professional Conduct
Rule 3.6. Trial Publicity.

(a) A lawyer who is participating or has participated in the investigation or litigation of a matter shall not make an extrajudicial statement that the lawyer knows or reasonably should know will be disseminated by means of public communication and will have a substantial likelihood of materially prejudicing an adjudicative proceeding in the matter.

(b) Notwithstanding paragraph (a), a lawyer may state:

(1) The claim, offense or defense involved and, except when prohibited by law, the identity of the persons involved;

(2) Information contained in a public record;

(3) That an investigation of a matter is in progress;

(4) The scheduling or result of any step in litigation;

(5) A request for assistance in obtaining evidence and information necessary thereto;

(6) A warning of danger concerning the behavior of a person involved, when there is reason to believe that there exists the likelihood of substantial harm to an individual or to the public interest; and

(7) In a criminal case, in addition to subparagraphs (1) through (6):

(i) The identity, residence, occupation and family status of the accused;

(ii) If the accused has not been apprehended, information necessary to aid in apprehension of that person;

(iii) The fact, time and place of arrest; and

(iv) The identity of investigating and arresting officers or agencies and the length of the investigation.

(c) Notwithstanding paragraph (a), a lawyer may make a statement that a reasonable lawyer would believe is required to protect a client from the substantial undue prejudicial effect of recent publicity not initiated by the lawyer or the lawyer's client. A statement made pursuant to this paragraph shall be limited to such information as is necessary to mitigate the recent adverse publicity.

(d) No lawyer associated in a firm or government agency with a lawyer subject to paragraph (a) shall make a statement prohibited by that paragraph.

> Does this revised version of the rule solve the problems identified by the court in *Gentile*? Does the standard pass the Constitutional balancing test? Does it solve the vagueness problem? Would Gentile's press conference statements violate this rule?

2. While an attorney may not be subject to discipline for publicity statements, might the attorney have a risk of liability under laws of defamation or invasion of privacy? The Restatement (Second) of Torts, § 586 provides a privilege against defamation liability:

> An attorney at law is absolutely privileged to publish defamatory matter concerning another in communications preliminary to a proposed judicial proceeding, or in the institution of, or during the course and as a part of, a judicial proceeding in which he participates as counsel, if it has some relation to the proceeding."

The absolute privilege shields attorneys from liability for statements made in pleadings, briefs, arguments to the jury, and other statements in a judicial proceeding. The absolute privilege has been extended to informal complaints to government agents, interviews of witnesses before trial, and settlement negotiations.

The privilege is not unlimited however. The determination of whether the privilege applies to statements made in connection with a judicial proceeding is made on a case-by-case basis. For example, in *Asay v. Hallmark Cards, Inc.*, 594 F.2d 692 (8th Cir. 1979), an employee of Hallmark Cards had sued the company for wrongful termination of employment. Attorney Asay released a copy of his complaint to news services. The complaint included allegations that Hallmark had violated antitrust laws and was investigated for illegal campaign contributions. Likewise, Asay had sent letters to other Hallmark employees allegedly in connection with the litigation. Hallmark counterclaimed for defamation based on the statements in the complaints and letters. The court of appeals reversed the district court's dismissal of the defamation counterclaim, noting that publication to the press is not sufficiently connected with judicial proceedings to protect those statements from liability, even if the matter published to the press is also contained in a pleading. Likewise, the court commented that "Asay's letters of inquiry to other employees allegedly containing

defamatory statements are suspect as possibly showing champerty in encouraging litigation and a pattern of harassment of Hallmark."

3. Courts are split on the relationship between the ethical rules and the court's
   authority to issue gag orders, restraining attorneys, parties, and witnesses in
   cases from speaking to the press. Courts apply standards that range from "reasonably likely to prejudice" to "clear and present danger." Annotation, Validity, and Construction of State Court's Pretrial Order Precluding Publicity or
   Comment About Pending Case by Counsel, Parties, or Witnesses, 33 A.L.R.
   3d 1041 (1978, 2010 Supp.); Jeffrey F. Ghent, Validity and Construction of Federal Court's Pretrial Order Precluding Publicity or Comment About Pending
   Case by Counsel, Parties, or Witnesses, 5 A.L.R. Fed. 948 (1978, 2010 Supp.).

4. How would these standards apply to an attorney's blog comments about a
   case? How about Facebook postings? Would it matter if the attorney's social
   networking page was not open to the public?

5. How can you best defend your client against an opponent's threat to "take it
   to the press?"

21.7 Representing Clients in Mediation

Increasingly, disputes are being resolved by alternatives to trials. Mediation is an especially important form of alternative dispute resolution. Advocating for a client in mediation is very different than advocacy for a client in trial. Rather than adversarial processes,
mediation advocacy requires, at a minimum, training in interest-based negotiation. However, even with training, interest-based bargaining may be sufficiently foreign to some
attorneys that they may conclude that they simply lack the aptitude or attitude to successfully represent clients participating in mediation processes:

> ... the zealous advocate will likely prove a failure in mediation, where creativ-
> ity, focus on the opposing sides' interests, and a broadening, not narrowing of
> issues, may be more valued skills.... Some have suggested the settlement func-
> tion is sufficiently different from the adversarial function requiring different in-
> dividuals, with different personalities and orientations as well as ethics. Thus, as
> courts struggle with such legal issues as what it means to attend a settlement
> proceeding "in good faith," representatives of parties (which is the term I prefer
> to the term "advocates") have to consider how to become effective in a different
> forum. A different orientation to the client and to the "adversary" may be es-
> sential in the kind of creative option generation and problem-solving that is es-
> sential in a mediation setting.

Carrie Menkel-Meadow, *Ethics in Alternative Dispute Resolution: New Issues, No Answers from
the Adversary Conception of Lawyer's Responsibilities*, 38 S. Tex. L. Rev. 407, 427-28 (1997).

Your duties in representing a client in mediation begin with helping the client to choose
a mediator. Models of mediation vary depending on region, type of practice, and type
of case. A common form of mediation is built on a model of facilitative mediation. Facilitative mediation is process-focused rather than outcome-oriented. The mediator assists individuals to communicate with one another to jointly solve the problems that have

brought them to mediation. Rather than having the mediation revolve around each party's position, mediation communication grounds itself in each person's interests. The key to choosing a mediator is insuring that the mediator is well trained and effective in these key skills. Many states provide certification standards for mediators in various areas of law.

Some mediators try to maintain a strictly neutral stance toward the legal, financial, or emotional wisdom of the party's proposed solutions, offering no expert evaluation of proposals. Of course, if a mediator is to truly facilitate the process, she will have to offer some routes to evaluation, even if they are simply questions designed to help the parties test the practicality or wisdom of their ideas. However, other mediators use a more explicitly evaluative approach in mediation. These mediators may propose their own solutions rather than having the parties generate all solutions. They may evaluate the parties' solutions in light of their expert prediction of how those outcomes compare to the results that might be achieved through judicial resolution. When mediators take this approach, attorneys must carefully consider the qualifications of the mediator to provide substantive expertise and the possibility of bias, as these concerns are significantly magnified in the presence of evaluative mediation.

In addition to these more traditional models of mediation, a variety of other less traditional models may be appropriate for certain clients or problems. Some mediators with mental health expertise may offer therapeutic or "transformative" mediation, in which the goal of the mediation is to improve the relationship skills of the parties, with a settlement of the dispute being an incidental outcome of that improvement. Other mediators may offer hybrids of arbitration and mediation, in which they will serve to recommend outcomes to the parties or the court if the parties are unable to come to agreement in the mediation process. Helping a client to choose the right mediator requires understanding how these models of mediation work and when one model might be preferable to another.

Having chosen a mediator, you must next prepare the client for mediation. Mediation requires that you allocate to the client a greater sharing of decision-making responsibility than is envisioned by the Rule 1.2 means/ends distinction. In some states, attorneys are not allowed to participate in mediation processes or the mediator has the discretion to exclude attorneys. Even when you will be present in the mediation, however, your responsibility is to empower the client to be able to participate effectively in the process.

One of the most difficult aspects of this preparation is helping the client to understand how different the language and demeanor of the attorney and client must be in this setting as compared to an adversarial setting. Clients must understand that respectful listening and collaborative problem solving are essential to this process, as opposed to adversarial posturing and partisan advocacy. You must not only explain your own attitudes and behaviors in mediation but must prepare the client to approach mediation in the same way.

A key to this preparation is helping your client to understand and prepare for dealing with conflict. Conflict can be threatening: situations can be tense and threatening, outcomes are uncertain, and relationships fragile. But conflict can also be productive, when it provides a vehicle for addressing issues, releasing tension, stimulating creative problem solving, and ultimately strengthening relationships and improving outcomes. You will need to help your client understand what he or she is fighting about and how he or she might approach that conflict.

In terms of the subject matter of the conflict, mediator Christopher W. Moore describes five different "spheres of conflict" that may characterize what people fight about: interest, structural, value, relationship, and data conflicts. CHRISTOPHER W. MOORE, THE MEDIATION PROCESS 27 (2nd ed. 1986). Interest conflicts are caused by perceived or actual competitive interests. Those interests might be substantive, procedural, or psychological interests. Being able to identify those interests and recognize when they are the cause of conflict can be a powerful problem solving tool. Structural conflicts are caused by destructive patterns of behavior or interaction, unequal power or resources, time constraints, or other environmental factors that interfere with cooperation. Addressing these structural conflicts is critical to insuring a fair mediation or negotiation process. Value conflicts are caused by belief systems and differing criteria for evaluating ideas or behavior. Realistic problem solving must take these intrinsic values into account. Relationship conflicts are caused by strong emotions (usually negative) or may be the result of poor communication skills. In many instances, relationship conflicts are most productively addressed in mediation, which can provide a structure for dealing constructively with emotions and improving communication. Finally, data conflicts are caused by missing, inaccurate, or conflicting information, or differing interpretations or assessments of the data. Third party decision-makers can be especially helpful in breaking impasses over data conflicts.

Once you have helped your client identify the types of conflict involved in the dispute, you next need to think about how your client might address that conflict. Is your client likely to go into the mediation with a competitive mindset — determined to direct the process and decide the outcome? Would your client be more likely to cooperate and try to find ways to achieve win-win solutions as possible? How likely is your client to compromise and give up some points? Would your client do so simply to avoid having to deal with conflict? Does your client appear to have insight into the perspectives and attitudes of the other parties in the conflict? How is your client likely to express her emotions in the mediation? To prepare your client for mediation, you must not only understand your client's communication style and attitudes toward conflict, you must help your client understand how these aspects of her personality will impact the mediation.

An additional issue to consider in preparing the client for mediation is the protection of confidentiality. If statements made in mediation could later be used in court as evidence, this might create incentives for tactical abuse of the process. Thus, most states provide some form of protection for the confidentiality of mediation statements. Ellen E. Deason, *Secrecy and Transparency in Dispute Resolution: The Need for Trust as a Justification for Confidentiality in Mediation: A Cross-Disciplinary Approach*, 54 Kan. L. Rev. 1387 (2006). Like other communications privileges, these protections extend only to statements made in mediation and not to information otherwise discoverable or admissible. The ability to misuse the mediation process as a tactical tool for adversarial discovery calls for choosing an experienced and well-trained mediator and making sure you have a well-prepared client.

One of the most important roles for attorneys in representing clients in mediation is that of preparing and reviewing an agreement. If you do not participate in the mediation itself, you should caution your clients to refrain from signing any agreements until you have had an opportunity to review those agreements. Even if you are participating in the mediation, the final settlement agreement should be concluded after the mediation has closed, so that the parties can testify regarding the agreement, facilitating its acceptance by the court and later enforcement.

Test Your Understanding

Review the preliminary problem in light of the materials we have read in this chapter. The following are some of the issues you should be able to identify and analyze:

1. Regarding the mysterious document under your door, without some indication of where it came from and how it came to be under your door, the document is of very little use to you. You presumably would have asked for inspection records for the brakes even if you hadn't seen this letter and, if indeed the records have been destroyed, your ability to prove that is not markedly increased by this copy of a letter of uncertain provenance. Better for you to simply proceed as though you had never seen the letter than trying to use it in some way and risk having evidence excluded, pleadings struck, or financial sanctions issued against you or your client because of the manner in which it was acquired.

2. Fred's interrogatory objections call for a meeting with Fred to ask what it is that he does not understand or specifically why he objects. If the overly broad objection was simply the result of laziness, this might be enough to get him to answer the questions. If, however, he is simply being obstreperous, a documented explanation and offer to work on a discovery plan together will provide the court with evidence to fashion an order to compel with some threat of sanction behind it.

3. Fred's response to the document request is not appropriate. Attorneys responding to document discovery requests are required to make a preliminary decision regarding relevance and provide only those documents that are truly responsive. Again, calling Fred on his behavior by providing a clear, well-documented analysis and demand for response would lay the groundwork for the court to take action if Fred continues to resist discovery.

4. For the deposition, Fred's behaviors require a strategic analysis. Are the question and objections so harmful to your case that you need to stop them? If so, document your objections on the record, ask Fred to conform his behavior to the local rules, and if he does not, seek a protective order and arrange for a video recorded deposition.

5. Finally, if Fred's behavior toward you and your client is part of an overall pattern, you should report him to the local disciplinary counsel as this most certainly is a violation that raises a substantial question as to his fitness to practice.

To Learn More

In addition to the articles and web resources cited in this chapter, the following resources are helpful to addressing ethics in litigation practice:

Civility and Professionalism Standards

A number of bar associations and professional organizations have adopted voluntary civility guidelines that you may find useful as guides to practice in representing clients in litigation. Most of these guidelines are available online. A collection links to the various codes can be found at the websites of The National Center for State Courts, http://www.ncsconline.org/wc/courtopics/statelinks.asp?id=45&topic=JudEth and The American Bar Association Center for Professional Responsibility, http://www.abanet.org/cpr/professionalism/profcodes.html. The ABA section on Litigation has a series of free podcasts you can download. Some address issues in this chapter, http://www.american bar.org/groups/litigation/resources/section_audio.html.

Electronic Evidence

The evolving issues in electronic evidence are discussed in several blogs. Two that you might find useful are:

Next Gen eDiscovery Law & Tech Blog, a specialty blog addressing issues of electronic evidence. http://blog.x1discovery.com/

Legalethics.com, a blog that focuses on the ethical issues associated with the use of technology by legal professionals.

Representing Clients in Mediation

HAROLD I. ABRAMSON, MEDIATION REPRESENTATION: ADVOCATING IN A PROBLEM SOLVING PROCESS (NITA 2004). (Designed for attorneys representing clients in mediation, the text explores the attorney's key roles in mediation: advising your clients about the mediation option, negotiating an agreement to mediate with other attorneys, preparing cases and clients for the mediation session, and appearing in the pre-mediation conferences, mediation sessions, and post-sessions. The text has checklists, sample forms, and other helpful guides.)

Chapter Twenty-Two

Communicating with Litigants, Witnesses, and Jurors

Learning Objectives

After you have read this chapter and completed the assignments, you should be able to:

- Identify and apply the standards regarding communication with represented persons and appropriate use of exceptions to these standards.

- Identify risks presented by dealing with a pro se litigant and steps you can take to reduce that risk.

- Identify limitations on contact with witnesses and jurors.

- Locate and analyze your own jurisdiction's laws on contact with third persons.

Rules to Study

In this chapter we study Rules 4.2, 4.3, and 3.5 regarding communication with persons in the legal system. For many students and attorneys, these rules are some of the least intuitive and easiest to unintentionally violate, often with severe consequence. As with many other rules governing litigation conduct, these rules refer to local rules of procedure for standards, and court sanctions and contempt are common methods of enforcing these standards.

Preliminary Problem

You have been hired by ABC Insurance to represent Dan Defendant in a products liability action brought by Paula Plaintiff. Paula is represented by Owen Opposing. You have conveyed several settlement offers to Owen but you strongly suspect that Opposing is not conveying these offers to his client. May you, without the consent of opposing counsel, send Paula copies of letters you have written to Opposing that contain your settlement offers? May the insurance company that has hired you to represent Dan contact Paula and convey this information? May you ask Dan Defendant to contact Paula? What if Paula contacts you directly to ask about settlement? What if she says she would like to fire her attorney?

512   22 · COMMUNICATING WITH LITIGANTS, WITNESSES, AND JURORS

Suppose Paula is not represented at all. What are the limits of your communication with her? May you negotiate a settlement with her? May you explain to her what some of the terms of a proposed settlement agreement mean?

22.1 Reading the Rules: Communication with Represented Persons

Read the following rule regarding communications with persons who have attorneys. The rule is fairly straightforward, but its application has raised sometimes difficult questions:

Washington State Rules of Professional Conduct
Rule 4.2 Communication with Persons Represented by Counsel

In representing a client, a lawyer shall not communicate about the subject of the representation with a person the lawyer knows to be represented by another lawyer in the matter, unless the lawyer has the consent of the other lawyer or is authorized to do so by law or a court order.

Context

Prior versions of this rule prohibited communications with unrepresented "parties" — the rule was amended in 2002 to extend to any "person" represented by counsel. The rule applies in both litigation and transactional contexts. *See, e.g., In re Waldron,* 790 S.W.2d 456, 458-9 (Mo. 1990). Even in a business negotiation, you should not be speaking to other persons in the negotiation who are represented by counsel without the permission of their attorney. Even if communicating with someone represented by counsel would seem innocent or even designed to advance that individual's interest, the rule operates strictly.

What are the consequences of violating this rule? In addition to potential disciplinary sanction, courts have disqualified lawyers from continuing representation in cases where the rule has been violated, *See, e.g., Papanicolaou v. Chase Manhattan Bank,* 720 F. Supp. 1080 (S.D.N.Y. 1989); *Cronin v. Nevada District Court,* 781 P.2d 1150 (Nev. 1989). In other cases, courts have issued sanctions including exclusion of evidence, disclosure of statements, and monetary sanctions. *See, e.g., Holdren v. General Motors Corp.,* 13 F. Supp. 2d 1192 (D. Kan. 1998).

Relationships

Notice that this rule provides another example of how disciplinary rules refer to other law ("authorized to do so by law"). The comments help to explain what that law might be. Comment 5 to the Washington rule provides:

Communications authorized by law may include communications by a lawyer on behalf of a client who is exercising a constitutional or other legal right to communicate with the government. Communications authorized by law may also include investigative activities of lawyers representing governmental entities, directly or through investigative agents, prior to the commencement of criminal or civil enforcement proceedings. When communicating with the accused in a criminal matter, a government lawyer must comply with this Rule in addition to honoring the constitutional rights of the accused. The fact that a communication does not violate a state or federal constitutional right is insufficient to establish that the communication is permissible under this Rule.

One of the key terms in this rule is "knows." Remember that Rule 1.0's definition of knowledge means that the attorney must have actual knowledge of the fact of the representation; but actual knowledge may be inferred from the circumstances. *See* Rule 1.0(f). As comment 8 to Rule 4.2 points out, "the lawyer cannot evade the requirement of obtaining the consent of counsel by closing eyes to the obvious." A second key term in the rule is "communicate." You can communicate in person or in writing, by speaking, and even by listening.

Structure

The rule is one sentence only, but it has three parts. Look again at the rule. Do you see these three parts? As with other rules, the dependent phrase at the beginning of the rule qualifies its meaning significantly. Note that the rule is only triggered "In representing a client." The second part of the sentence is the heart of the rule. Finally, the clause after "unless" provides two important exceptions.

Reasons

Comment 1 to the rule explains that its purpose is to protect "the proper functioning of the legal system by protecting a person who has chosen to be represented by a lawyer in a matter against possible overreaching by other lawyers who are participating in the matter, interference by those lawyers with the client-lawyer relationship and the uncounseled disclosure of information relating to the representation." Think about each of these three purposes. Why is a flat ban on communications with represented persons necessary to protect these three interests? The rule is, like the attorney-client privilege, designed to protect the attorney-client relationship. However, unlike the privilege, the client does not have the power to waive its protections. Comment 3 provides that "The Rule applies even though the represented person initiates or consents to the communication." Why should that be so?

Visualize

One way to visualize the grammatical structure of a sentence is to diagram it. At one time, diagramming sentences was a popular method for teaching grammar. Elaborate rules described how to represent various sentence structure forms. While you do not need to know these rules of "correct" diagramming, you may nonetheless find that visually diagramming a complex one-sentence rule like this can help reveal relationships. Here is a simple diagram of the rule separating its parts:

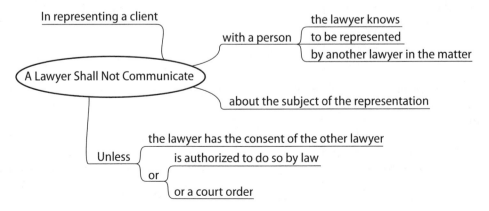

Imagine

Can you imagine circumstances in which you could "accidentally" communicate with someone whom you know is represented by an attorney? Think about email communications, depositions, or social contacts. How can you keep your guard up to insure you don't inadvertently violate this rule?

Applications of the Rule

1. The social contact

What if you simply meet an opposing party in a social setting? Must you avoid speaking with that individual? Look again at the rule—it does not prohibit all communication but only communication regarding "the matter." The danger, of course, is that it may not be clear that you are limiting your communication to only social talk—so most attorneys limit even socializing with individuals represented by counsel in a matter in which they are engaged by another client.

2. The uncommunicated offer

The preliminary problem in this chapter poses the dilemma presented by opposing attorneys who will not present your offers to their clients. Suppose you are representing an individual in negotiating a settlement of a dispute. You have communicated several good faith offers of settlement to the opposing attorney. However, it has become clear to you that the opposing attorney has not and will not pass on those offers to his client. May you send the settlement offers directly to the opposing client? If you cannot convey the settlement offers to the opposing party, may you direct your client to do so? If you can't do either of these things, what can you do to get the settlement offers to the opposing client?

The answers to these questions are found in the language of the rules. There is no exception in the rule for communicating with a represented person about the matter simply because that person's attorney refuses to pass on communications. Moreover, recall that under Rule 8.4, what you cannot do yourself, you cannot do through the acts of another, so asking the client to convey your offer would be over the line as well. But what if the client says, "Can I talk to him?" You may tell the client that he has no restrictions on speaking with the opposing party and you can provide some limited assistance. A recent ABA formal opinion suggests that you may even supply your client with documents for the other person to sign and talking points for discussions with them. The opinion does indicate that attorneys may not "script" the conversation, however, and does suggest that the attorney should tell the client to advise the person with whom he is speaking to consult with her attorney. ABA Standing Comm. on Ethics and Professional Responsibility, Formal Op. 11-461 (2011). Likewise, the opinion directs attorneys to include a warning to seek counsel on any agreement that the attorney has drafted for the client to present to the opponent.

In some circumstances you simply would not want your client to act as a conduit for information or discuss the matter with an opposing client. Opportunities for confusion, misrepresentations, angry confrontations, or simply distress are enough to dissuade your client from discussing matters with opponents. Even in a situation in which it would be unwise for your client to speak to the other person, you are not without recourse. Remember that there are two exceptions to the prohibition on *ex parte* communication in addition to consent of the attorney: court order or other law. So you could certainly ask the court to issue an order permitting you to convey settlement offers directly to the opposing client. Generally the threat to request such an order is sufficient to move opposing counsel to improve her communication.

3. The second opinion

Suppose that an individual who is represented by counsel comes to you seeking a second opinion, concerned about the quality of his attorney's representation or advice. May you speak to that individual without violating Rule 4.2? While the other attorney may not be particularly happy with your consulting with his client about his representation, he cannot prohibit his client from seeking your advice nor are you violating the rules by providing that consultation. Comment 4 to Washington's Rule 4.2 makes this quite clear:

> This Rule does not prohibit communication with a represented person, or an employee or agent of such a person, concerning matters outside the representation. For example, the existence of a controversy between a government agency and a private party, or between two organizations, does not prohibit a lawyer for either from communicating with nonlawyer representatives of the other regarding a separate matter. Nor does this Rule preclude communication with a represented person who is seeking advice from a lawyer who is not otherwise representing a client in the matter. A lawyer may not make a communication prohibited by this Rule through the acts of another. *See* Rule 8.4(a). Parties to a matter may communicate directly with each other, and a lawyer is not prohibited from advising a client concerning a communication that the client is legally entitled to make. Also, a lawyer having independent justification or legal authorization for communicating with a represented person is permitted to do so.

[handwritten margin note: Independent authorization ?]

As a recent Louisiana ethics opinion noted, "despite the beliefs and/or hopes of some lawyers — especially those made uncomfortable by a mistaken belief that their clients are engaging in some imagined form of 'professional adultery' — Rule 4.2 is not an 'anti-poaching' rule and cannot be used to shield clients from their own decisions to consult another lawyer." Louisiana State Bar Ass'n Rules of Professional Conduct Comm., Op. 07-RPCC-014, 10/12/07.

4. The federal investigation

One aspect of this rule that has been very controversial is the extent to which it applies to United States attorneys. The Department of Justice for some time took the position that federal prosecutors were "authorized by law" to speak to persons represented by counsel. They argued that the rule, combined with Rule 8.4's extension of the rule to those who work for an attorney, interfered too much with the investigation powers of U.S. attorneys and the law enforcement personnel under their direction. However, the court in *United States ex rel. O'Keefe v. McDonnell Douglas Corp.*, 132 F.3d 1252 (8th Cir. 1998) held that the Justice Department did not have the power to define the "authorized by law" exception to Rule 4.2 and unilaterally authorize federal prosecutors to communicate with represented persons without going through that individual's attorney. In particular, the question arose as to the extent to which prosecutors would be violating Rule 4.2 by directing undercover or covert operations in which law enforcement officials would be communicating with (and gathering evidence from) suspects who were represented by counsel. The controversy was further fueled when it became a jurisdictional battle over the power of a state court to discipline a federal prosecutor for violation of the rule. The controversy was finally resolved in 1998 when Congress passed the Citizens Protection Act, (the McDade Amendment) which made clear that federal prosecutors are subject to the disciplinary rules of the jurisdictions in which they are licensed to practice law. 28 U.S.C. § 530B (2012). Nonetheless, the rule continues to permit federal prosecutors to direct pre-indictment undercover communications. *See United States v. Grass*, 239 F. Supp.2d 535 (M.D. Pa. 2003).

5. The unbundled client

Washington state provides for limited task or "unbundled" representation. This rule permits attorneys to provide very discrete tasks (such as drafting a pleading) rather than an entire representation. (We examine this rule in more detail in Chapter 24.4). If an attorney has provided this type of limited scope representation for a client, should that client be considered a "represented person" for the purposes of this rule? Washington provides a separate comment to address this issue:

> [11] An otherwise unrepresented person to whom limited representation is being provided or has been provided in accordance with Rule 1.2(c) is considered to be unrepresented for purposes of this Rule unless the opposing lawyer knows of, or has been provided with, a written notice of appearance under which, or a written notice of time period during which, he or she is to communicate only with the limited representation lawyer as to the subject matter within the limited scope of the representation.

6. The represented entity and its employees

Another circumstance in which there has been frequent confusion about this rule is when an attorney is speaking with employees of a corporate party. After considerable litigation to determine the extent to which employees of a represented entity are covered by the rule, most states now provide guidelines regarding that question in comments to their rules. However, there are many variations on this rule across the states. For example, in adopting its rule, Washington State revised its Comment 7 to reflect its approach, which differs from the approach suggested by the ABA Model Rule's comment.

The following case compares these approaches.

Palmer v. Pioneer Inn Associates, Ltd.

118 Nev. 943; 59 P.3d 1237 (Nev. 2002)

[This case involved a federal employment discrimination lawsuit. The attorney for plaintiff Palmer had contacted one of defendant's employees who had a supervisory role (though not someone who was in a position to decide the employment situation of the plaintiff). The trial court sanctioned the plaintiff's attorney for violation of Nevada Supreme Court Rule 182 (SCR 182), which is based on ABA Model Rule 4.2. The court also barred the employee from testifying regarding any of the statements he had made to the plaintiff's attorney in the *ex parte* contact. After judgments for the employers, Palmer appealed. The Ninth Circuit Court of Appeals certified to the Nevada Supreme Court the question of which test the court uses to govern contact with entity employees.]

Discussion

SCR 182 provides:

> In representing a client, a lawyer shall not communicate about the subject of the representation with a party the lawyer knows to be represented by another lawyer in the matter, unless the lawyer has the consent of the other lawyer or is authorized by law to do so.

[handwritten margin note: Managing - speaking agent test]

This rule was adopted verbatim from the original version of ABA Model Rule 4.2, which in turn was copied almost verbatim from Model Code of Professional Responsibility DR 7-104(A)(1). Before that, the same general concept was contained in Canon 9 of the ABA Canons of Professional Ethics.

The primary purpose of the rule is to protect the attorney-client relationship from intrusion by opposing counsel. It protects parties from unprincipled attorneys and safeguards the attorney-client privilege. It also promotes counsel's effective representation of a client by routing communication with the other side through counsel, who can present the information in a way most favorable to the client. Sanctions for violating the rule have included disqualification of counsel, monetary sanctions, exclusion of information obtained by *ex parte* contact, prohibition on the use of such information at trial, and production to the organization's counsel of information obtained by *ex parte* contact, including all or part of the work product connected with the contact....

Various tests for determining which employees are included within the rule's scope

Many competing policies must be considered when deciding how to interpret the no-contact rule as applied to organizational clients: protecting the attorney-client relationship from interference; protecting represented parties from overreaching by opposing lawyers; protecting against the inadvertent disclosure of privileged information; balancing on one hand an organization's need to act through agents and employees, and protecting those employees from overreaching and the organization from the inadvertent disclosure of privileged information, and on the other hand the lack of any such protection afforded an individual, whose friends, relatives, acquaintances and co-workers may generally all be contacted freely; permitting more equitable and affordable access to information pertinent to a legal dispute; promoting the court system's efficiency by allowing investigation before litigation and informal information-gathering during litigation; permitting a plaintiff's attorney sufficient opportunity to adequately investigate a claim before filing a complaint in accordance with Rule 11; and enhancing the court's truth-finding role by permitting contact with potential witnesses in a manner that allows them to speak freely.

Are any of these goals furthered by other rules of conduct in additon to Rule 4.2?

subject matter?

Various courts have formulated several tests for determining who is encompassed within the no-contact rule. At one extreme is the "blanket" test, which prohibits contact with current and former employees of an organizational client; at the other is the "control group" test, which covers only high-level management employees. Several tests fall in the middle, including a party-opponent admission test, a case-by-case balancing test, and a "managing-speaking agent" test.

Decide which of these tests strikes the proper balance.

Blanket test

The blanket test prohibits all contact, and appears to have been adopted in very few published decisions. A federal district court has concluded that a blanket rule prohibiting all contact sets a bright-line rule that is easily followed and enforced. *Public Serv. Elec. & Gas v. Associated Elec. & Gas*, 745 F. Supp. 1037 (D.N.J. 1990), *superseded by rule amendment as recognized in Klier v. Sordoni Skanska Const. Co.*, 337 N.J. Super. 76, 766 A.2d 761 (N.J. Super.

Ct. App. Div. 2001) (incorporating control group test in text of rule as amended).... The primary advantage of this test is its clarity: no employees of a represented organization may be contacted by opposing counsel. It also offers the most protection for the organization. The cost of these advantages, however, is very high. A complete prohibition on informal *ex parte* contact greatly limits, if not eliminates, counsel's opportunity to properly investigate a potential claim before a complaint is filed, as required by Rule 11. Also, the rules of civil procedure, especially the discovery rules, are designed to afford parties broad access to information, and informal interviews are a cost-effective way of gathering facts, as opposed to more expensive depositions, which preserve facts.

Party-opponent admission test

The test based on the hearsay rule appears to encompass almost as many employees as the blanket test.... *See Cole v. Appalachian Power Co.*, 903 F. Supp. 975 (S.D.W. Va. 1995); *Brown v. St. Joseph County*, 148 F.R.D. 246 (N.D. Ind. 1993); *University Patents, Inc. v. Kligman*, 737 F. Supp. 325 (E.D. Pa. 1990).... This test encompasses within the ethical rule any employee whose statement might be admissible as a party-opponent admission under Fed. R. Evid. 801(d)(2)(D) and its state counterparts. According to the evidence rule, an employee's statement is not hearsay, and thus is freely admissible against the employer, if it concerns a matter within the scope of the employee's employment, and is made during the employee's period of employment.

The courts adopting the party-opponent admission test have concluded that the former comment's reference to "admissions" was clearly meant to incorporate the rules of evidence governing admissions.... This test's primary advantage is that it protects the organization from potentially harmful admissions made by its employees to opposing counsel, without the organization's counsel's presence. The organization's interest in this regard is particularly strong because such admissions are generally recognized as a very persuasive form of evidence.

The drawback of this test is that it essentially covers all or almost all employees, since any employee could make statements concerning a matter within the scope of his or her employment, and thus could potentially be included within the rule. Thus, the party-opponent admission test can effectively serve as a blanket test, thus frustrating the search for truth. An attorney attempting to comply with Rule 11's requirements would be faced with two unenviable choices. The first option would be not to contact persons who might be the best, if not the only, source of corroborating information. This option would ensure that the attorney complies with SCR 182's prohibitions, but would result in the attorney's failure to comply with Rule 11. The second option would be for the attorney to second-guess what an employee might say, in an attempt to determine whether contact might be permissible, which would result in the attorney risking an SCR 182 violation.

Isn't there a third choice under Rule 11?

In addition, a party admission may be challenged through impeachment of the witness, by presenting contradictory evidence, or by explaining the admission. Accordingly, it is not clear that this test properly balances the competing policies.

Managing-speaking agent test

The managing-speaking agent test appears to have evolved before the tests discussed above, in response to a United States Supreme Court case discussing the scope of the attorney-client privilege as applied to an organizational client. In *Upjohn Co. v. United States*, 449 U.S. 383, 66 L. Ed. 2d 584, 101 S. Ct. 677 (1981) the Court held that the privilege was not restricted to an organization's "control group." Rather, the Court held that mid- and even low-level employees could have information necessary to defend against a potential claim, and thus communications between such employees and counsel were protected by the privilege. While acknowledging that the *Upjohn* opinion did not expressly apply to the no-contact rule, the courts adopting the managing-speaking agent test in *Upjohn's* wake reasoned that the protection afforded an organization under the no-contact rule should be commensurate with that afforded by the attorney-client privilege. *See Chancellor v. Boeing Co.*, 678 F. Supp. 250 (D. Kan. 1988). At the same time, relying on dicta in *Upjohn* stating that confidential communications, not facts, were entitled to protection, these courts determined that the rule should not be expanded so broadly that informal investigation through *ex parte* interviews was restricted too severely.

> Why should the no-contact rule parallel the privilege?

... No court appears to have adopted precisely the same statement of the test. *Compare*, *Weeks v. Independent School Dist. No. I-89* 230 F.3d 1201 (10th Cir. 2000) (purporting to adopt the managing-speaking test, but applying Fed. R. Evid. 801(d)(2)(D) to determine which employees "speak" for the university), *cert. denied*, 532 U.S. 1020 (2001), *and Chancellor v. Boeing Co.*, 678 F. Supp. 250 (D. Kan. 1988) (implying that evidentiary rules determine which employees have "speaking" authority), *with Wright by Wright v. Group Health Hosp.*, 103 Wn.2d 192, 691 P.2d 564 (Wash. 1984) (emphasizing that only employees who could "bind" the organization are covered), *and Porter v. Arco Metals, Div. of Atlantic Richfield*, 642 F. Supp. 1116 (D. Mont. 1986) (relying on *Wright* but stating the test differently).

In all of its formulations, the managing-speaking agent test restricts contact with those employees who have "speaking" authority for the organization, that is, those with legal authority to bind the organization. *See Chancellor*, 678 F. Supp. at 253; *Porter*, 642 F. Supp. at 1118; *Wright*, 691 P.2d at 569. Which employees have "speaking" authority is determined on a case-by-case basis according to the particular employee's position and duties and the jurisdiction's agency and evidence law. This is the essence of the test as set forth in the most-cited case adopting it, the Washington Supreme Court's opinion in *Wright by Wright v. Group Health Hospital*. 103 Wn.2d 192, 691 P.2d 564....

Courts adopting this test have concluded that it best balances the competing policies of protecting the organizational client from overreaching by opposing counsel through direct contact with its employees and agents, and the adverse attorney's need for information in the organization's exclusive possession that may be too expensive or impractical to obtain through formal discovery. They also note, relying on *Upjohn's* dicta, that the rule's purpose is not to protect an organization from the revelation of prejudicial facts, thus disapproving of the party-opponent admission test.

The test's primary drawback is its lack of predictability. As noted above, several of the courts purporting to adopt the test have stated and applied it very differently. In addition, because the test relies on a particular jurisdiction's agency and evidence law, its application may yield divergent results.

Control group test

The ... "control group" test ... encompasses only those top management level employees who have responsibility for making final decisions, and those employees whose advisory roles to top management indicate that a decision would not normally be made without those employees' advice or opinion. *See Fair Automotive v. Car-X Service Systems*, 128 Ill. App. 3d 763, 471 N.E.2d 554, 560, 84 Ill. Dec. 25 (Ill. App. Ct. 1984).

This test serves the policies of preserving the availability of witnesses, reducing discovery costs by permitting informal interviews of a broad range of employees, and affording the best opportunity for pre-litigation fact investigation. The test has become disfavored following the *Upjohn* decision, because the control group test is narrower than the attorney-client privilege rule approved in that case. Also, it lacks predictability because it is not always clear which employees fall within the "control group."

Case-by-case balancing test

A few courts have adopted a case-by-case balancing approach. Under this test, the particular facts of the case must be examined to determine what informal contacts may be appropriate in light of the parties' specific needs. Factors to be considered are the claims asserted, the employee's position and duties, the employer's interests in protecting itself, and the alternatives available to the party seeking an informal interview. Results under the test have varied. The pertinent cases do not address counsel's difficulty in applying this test before an actual interview, to determine whether the interview might later be found to be a rule violation. Rather, it appears that this test has been applied only when a lawyer seeks prospective guidance from a court, and it has not been used in making an after-the-fact determination of whether an attorney has violated the ethical rule.... [W]hile the balancing approach may be useful in certain limited situations, it cannot feasibly be applied as a universal standard for interpreting SCR 182. *Compare Morrison v. Brandeis University*, 125 F.R.D. 14 (D. Mass. 1989) (permitting *ex parte* contact by counsel for the plaintiff professor, who was denied tenure, with professors sitting on the plaintiff's peer review panel; such contact would appear to be prohibited under every other test), *with Baisley v. Missisquoi Cemetery Ass'n*, 167 Vt. 473, 708 A.2d 924, 933 (1998 (prohibiting *ex parte* contact with a cemetery caretaker in a case seeking damages for injuries suffered by the plaintiffs' child when he fell upon a spiked fence surrounding the cemetery; such contact would appear to be permissible under most of the other tests).

New York test

Finally, an additional test has been formulated by the New York Court of Appeals in *Niesig v. Team I*, 76 N.Y.2d 363, 558 N.E.2d 1030, 559 N.Y.S.2d 493 (N.Y. 1990). The test is often referred to as the "alter ego" test. The court rejected the blanket test as too broad, and the control group test as too narrow. It also expressed dissatisfaction with the existing intermediate tests, because they were too uncertain in application. Instead, while acknowledging that any non-blanket rule engendered some uncertainty, the court formulated its own test:

> The test that best balances the competing interests, and incorporates the most desirable elements of the other approaches, is one that defines "party" to include corporate employees whose acts or omissions in the matter under inquiry are binding on the corporation (in effect, the corporation's "alter egos") or imputed to the corporation for purposes of its liability, or employees implementing the advice of counsel. All other employees may be interviewed informally.

Id. at 1035. In particular, the court noted that its test "would clearly permit direct access to employees who were merely witnesses to an event for which the corporate employer is sued." *Id.* at 1035-36. This test has since been adopted by several courts. *See Strawser v. Exxon Co., U.S.A.,* 843 P.2d 613 (Wyo. 1992); *State v. CIBA-GEIGY Corp.,* 247 N.J. Super. 314, 589 A.2d 180 (N.J. Super. Ct. App. Div. 1991); *Dent v. Kaufman,* 185 W. Va. 171, 406 S.E.2d 68, 72 (W. Va. 1991); *MR & W v. President and Fellows of Harvard,* 436 Mass. 347, 764 N.E.2d 825 (Mass. 2002); *Bouge v. Smith's Management Corp.,* 132 F.R.D. 560 (D. Utah 1990). [The court later notes that *Restatement (Third) of the Law Governing Lawyers* § 100 (2000) also follows this approach.]

One advantage of the New York test is that it balances the protection afforded to the organization with the need for informal investigation, although it may go too far in protecting the organization by including those employees whose conduct may be imputed to the organization. Its disadvantage, as admitted by the *Niesig* court, is that any non-blanket rule has an element of unpredictability, and so in close situations it may be difficult to determine whether a particular employee is within its scope. In particular, as with the managing-speaking agent test on which the New York test is based, it may be difficult to determine which employees have sufficient authority to "bind" the organization.

Analysis

We conclude that the managing-speaking agent test, as set forth below, best balances the policies at stake when considering what contact with an organization's representatives is appropriate. The test protects from overbearance by opposing counsel those representatives who are in a position to speak for and bind the organization during the course of litigation, while still providing ample opportunity for an adequate Rule 11 investigation.

In addition, we conclude that the United States Supreme Court's reasoning in *Upjohn*, while explicitly addressing only the attorney-client privilege, applies with equal force to the no-contact rule, in that the purpose of SCR 182 is to protect the attorney-client relationship, not to protect an organization from the discovery of adverse facts. *See Upjohn,* 449 U.S. 383 at 395-96. The managing-speaking agent test best fulfills this purpose by not being over-inclusive. In particular, the managing-speaking agent test adopted by this court does not protect the organization at the expense of the justice system's truth-finding function by including employees whose conduct could be imputed to the organization based simply on the doctrine of respondeat superior. Finally,

Do you see the difference between this test and the others?

while any non-blanket rule has some uncertainty, we conclude that the test is sufficiently clear to provide significant guidance to counsel.[1]

In embracing the managing-speaking agent test, we do not adopt Model Rule 4.2's ... 2002 comment, which essentially tracks the New York test. Rather, SCR 182 should be interpreted according to the managing-speaking agent test as set forth by the Washington Supreme Court in *Wright by Wright v. Group Health Hospital*, 691 P.2d 564 (Wash. 1984):

> The best interpretation of "party" in litigation involving corporations is only those employees who have the legal authority to "bind" the corporation in a legal evidentiary sense, *i.e.*, those employees who have "speaking authority" for the corporation.... It is not the purpose of the rule to protect a corporate party from the revelation of prejudicial facts. Rather, the rule's function is to preclude the interviewing of those corporate employees who have the authority to *bind* the corporation.... Employees should be considered "parties" for the purposes of the disciplinary rule if, under applicable [state] law, they have managing authority sufficient to give them the right to speak for, and bind, the corporation.

If not evidence law, what law determines who can bind an entity?

Id. at 569 (citations omitted). In applying this test, we specifically note that an employee does not "speak for" the organization simply because his or her statement may be admissible as a party-opponent admission. Rather, the inquiry is whether the employee can bind the organization with his or her statement. Also, an employee for whom counsel has not been retained does not become a "represented party" simply because his or her conduct may be imputed to the organization; while any confidential communications between such an employee and the organization's counsel would be protected by the attorney-client privilege, the facts within that employee's knowledge are generally not protected from revelation through *ex parte* interviews by opposing counsel.[2]

A lawyer must have a reasonable opportunity to conduct an investigation under Rule 11. This investigation would be unduly hampered by an over-inclusive test, such as the party-opponent admission test adopted by the federal district court in this case. Such a test essentially bars contact with all employees, because any employee could make a statement concerning a matter within the scope of his or her employment, which would then be admissible under Fed. R. Evid. Evid. 801(d)(2)(D) or a state equivalent. A lawyer contacting the employee could not know in advance whether the employee might make such a statement, and so would be forced to choose between foregoing

---

1. *See* Thomas W. Biggar, *Discovery and Ethics: Dilemma in Interviewing Corporate Employees*, 1 Nev. L. Rev. 1, 22 (1998) (noting that while ethical rules provide few bright lines, attorneys, who must have a certain level of education, training, and common sense, can survive without them by being aware of when to seek further guidance and what possible consequences may attach to questionable actions).

2. *See Upjohn*, 449 U.S. 383 at 395-96. We note that an attorney who abuses the interview process by inquiring into privileged matters, or even by permitting an employee to refer to confidential communications without immediately warning the employee that such communications are protected and should not be disclosed, is subject to appropriate sanctions.

information that could be useful and even necessary to a proper investigation, or risking sanctions for an SCR 182 violation. Without doubt, an organization is entitled to the protections afforded by SCR 182, but just as for individuals, this protection is not unlimited. The managing-speaking agent test most appropriately balances these competing interests, and so it is the test we adopt.

Notes

1. Which of the approaches to the rule governing contact with represented parties do you prefer? Why?

2. Former employees of an entity can often be important sources of information to an attorney who is opposing that entity in litigation. While former employees are not in a position to bind the entity by their statements, they may be privy to confidential conversations from their former employment. Most states today interpret Rule 4.2 to permit attorneys to conduct *ex parte* interviews of former employees of a corporate opponent, so long as they do not ask about privileged or confidential communications and otherwise conduct their interviews in conformity with the rules of conduct. *ChampionsWorld, LLC v. U.S. Soccer Federation*, 276 F.R.D. 577 (N.D. Ill. 2011).

Researching Professional Responsibility: Who Is a "Represented Person" in an Entity?

As you have seen, the application of Rule 4.1 to situations in which the "represented person" is an entity is one for which there is no uniform answer across the states. Research your own state's approach to this rule. You can look at your state's version of the rule and the comments to see which approach the state appears to take there and when that rule was last amended. You likely will also want to search case law and ethics opinions for interpretations of the rule. This is the type of research for which it is very important that you be aware of the changes in the law over a period of time. Your state court may have taken one approach in case law ten years ago and then it may have adopted a new version of the rules thereafter. Only the more recent interpretations might be found in ethics opinions. How clear is the answer in your state?

22.2 Unrepresented Persons

Rule 4.3 applies when an attorney representing a client finds that a person with whom he or she is dealing is not represented. Under this rule, the attorney may continue the communication, but must not state or imply that the attorney is disinterested. Moreover, if the lawyer knows or should know that the unrepresented person misunderstands the attorney's role, the attorney is required to correct that misunderstanding. Lawyers should document their efforts to clarify their role when dealing with an unrepresented person. For example, the lawyer can write a letter explaining her role as an advocate for the client, or ask the unrepresented person to sign an acknowledgment that he was advised to seek counsel and declined to do so. *E.g., Heutel v. Stumpf*, 783 S.W.2d 421 (Mo. Ct. App. 1989); *Estate of Lutz v. Lutz*, 563 N.W.2d 90 (N.D. 1997). Note that the rule applies to lawyers and, through 8.4(a), to agents of the lawyer. As a practical matter, attorneys who cross the line and give advice to unrepresented persons risk having those persons be considered clients — thus placing the attorney in irreconcilable conflicts and at considerable risk for discipline, disqualification, and liability.

An area in which contact with unrepresented persons can be challenging is when your client is an entity and you are conducting an internal investigation. Recall that Rule 1.13(d) provides that "[i]n dealing with an organization's directors, officers, employees, members, shareholders or other constituents, a lawyer shall explain the identity of the client when it is apparent that the organization's interests are adverse to those of the constituents with whom the lawyer is dealing." To comply with this rule, some lawyers give employees a warning ("I am not your lawyer, I can't give you advice, I represent the company, the company's interests may conflict with yours, our conversation may not be confidential and may be used against you, and you might want to get your own attorney"). However, these warnings can often cause employees to stop communicating with the attorney. Because this can make internal investigations difficult, some attorneys are reluctant to take this important step unless it is clear to them that the individual misunderstands the attorney's role.

In litigation, self representation is increasingly common especially in fields such as family law where some studies have indicated that "eighty percent or more of family law cases involve at least one pro se litigant." Russell Engler, *And Justice for All — Including the Unrepresented Poor: Revisiting the Roles of the Judges, Mediators, and Clerks*, 67 Fordham L. Rev. 1987, 2047 (1999). Increasingly states are providing assistance to pro se litigants in order to address congested court dockets. Thus, you may regularly find yourself facing an unrepresented party and that unrepresented party may look to you for answers to legal questions and for preparation of necessary documents. You must avoid giving legal advice lest you violate the rules.

The one type of advice that you should give an unrepresented person is the advice to seek counsel. Some courts have held that there are instances in which you must give this advice to unrepresented parties. For example, the New York court held in *In re Michelman*, 616 N.Y.S.2d 409, 411-12 (N.Y.App.Div. 1994), that an attorney representing adoptive parents must advise the biological mother of the need for independent counsel. You could also direct an unrepresented party to sources for obtaining help, such as court provided pro se websites or classes. Beyond the advice to obtain counsel, rules in most states prohibit any other advice to unrepresented parties.

The difficulty with this prohibition on advice is that the line between providing information and giving advice is not a clear one. For example, attorneys necessarily tread close to that line whenever they draft a document and then ask a non-client to sign that document. ABA Informal Op. 1140 (1970) concluded that, "As long as these documents are not accompanied by or coupled with the giving of any advice to the defendant, they would constitute only communication ... and ... would be ethical." However, often a non-client will want to ask a question about the document. Would an attorney be "giving advice" by answering questions or describing what that document does? It would depend on the question of course. Answers to innocuous question of fact or procedure such as "Should I sign with my married or maiden name?" "Does this agreement include the XYZ account?" or "How long will it take for the court to hear this?" are likely permissible. However, anything close to the line of "What does this mean?" or "Should I do this?" is going to fall in the category of advice. One way to think about the line between information and advice is to ask whether the question you are answering could only be answered one way, without the exercise of judgment. Another consideration is whether the question relates to the rights or alternatives of the unrepresented person. Any communication with pro se parties should be undertaken with the utmost caution, and especially so in circumstances in which the rules of professional conduct consider joint representation to be a *per se* conflict of interest.

If the opposing party does not secure representation, you have no duty to maintain a position of neutrality. Prior proposed versions of the rules would have gone further than the current rule, prohibiting lawyers from "unfairly exploiting [an unrepresented] party's ignorance of the law or the practices of the tribunal." This broader limitation on advocacy was rejected, however. Of course, attorneys must afford the pro se opponent the same degree of honesty and fairness as a represented opponent. Suppose, for example, you have been asked to file a civil action against an individual on behalf of your client. You are aware that the claim is likely barred by the statute of limitations. May you nonetheless file the claim? An ABA Formal Ethics Opinion 94-387 suggested that you have no duty either to the opposing party or to the court to refrain from filing the action or to raise the issue of the statute of limitations, as that is a defense and may be waived by a defendant. You may not, of course, misrepresent the facts regarding the dates in such a way as to mislead on the issue. Would you feel comfortable filing this action on behalf of your client?

When negotiating agreements with unrepresented parties, helping them to understand why they should have independent counsel is vital to the stability of any agreement you negotiate. Equally important and difficult is educating your own client regarding the need for fairness and balance in furthering his goals in the agreement. Consider the comments of the Washington court regarding dealing with an unrepresented party in drafting a prenuptial agreement:

> An attorney in this situation is presented with a number of choices. He or she may endeavor, if the client consents, to prepare a contract which is designed to meet the [test] of economic fairness for the economically subservient party. Whether or not the client consents to the preparation of a contract which attempts to achieve economic fairness for the economically subservient party, the attorney should explain to that unrepresented party *why* it is so important that he or she seek the advice of independent counsel. That which is obvious to attorneys and judges may not be obvious to the unrepresented and economically subservient party. Every marriage eventually will terminate by one of two means: by marital dissolution or by the death of a spouse during marriage. What is indeed being sought is a divorce settlement and a death settlement. The purpose of independent counsel is more than simply to explain just how unfair a given proposed contract may be; *it is for the primary purpose of assisting the subservient party to negotiate an economically fair contract.* The desire of the economically dominant party to preserve the bulk of his or her wealth, and for some reasonable degree of certainty in the event of divorce, is not necessarily entirely inconsistent with the goal of economic fairness for the disadvantaged party. It is not conducive to marital tranquility to ask a party who comes into the marriage destitute to leave the marriage equally destitute, or

worse, perhaps many years later, and perhaps at a time when age, health and forgone career opportunities dictate that he or she can no longer acquire assets by virtue of employment, to leave the marriage in a far worse position than if the marriage had never taken place. _Both_ parties to a prenuptial contract need to understand the underlying premises which dictate the need for independent counsel.

... In *Friedlander v. Friedlander*, 80 Wn.2d 293, 301, 494 P.2d 208 (1972) the court stated that a prenuptial contract freely and intelligently made is generally regarded as conducive to marital tranquility and the avoidance of disputes about property in the future. To the extent that the parties negotiate an economically fair contract, we fully agree. The same cannot be said of a contract which fails the [economic fairness test]. An attorney who represents either party to a prenuptial contract should seriously consider the implications of RPC 2.1 (In rendering advice, a lawyer may refer not only to law but to other considerations such as moral, economic, social and political factors, that may be relevant to the client's situation.). A client is not well served by an unenforceable contract. Marital tranquility is not achieved by a contract which is economically unfair or achieved by unfair means.

In re Marriage of Foran, 67 Wn. App. 242, 254; 834 P.2d 1081, 1088-89 (Wash. App. 1992).

Helping your client to understand that there is little benefit to be gained in taking advantage of an opponent's lack of representation (or poor representation) is probably some of the hardest counseling you may have to undertake. You may find that the best way to set the tone is to communicate consistently your philosophy of representation in your advertising, your initial interview, your engagement letter or retainer agreement, and, most importantly, in your actions in representation.

You may find yourself in a position in which you find it necessary or useful to draft documents for an unrepresented opposing party to sign. For example, in a divorce action, your client's spouse may be willing to waive service. May you draft the waiver for the spouse to sign? ABA Informal Ethics Opinion 1269 (1973) suggested that this would not be improper so long as you did not advise the spouse. Could you explain what the waiver is? Why the spouse should sign it? Write a letter to accompany this document? The closer to the line of advice you come, the greater the risks that the waiver could be held invalid or you could be subject to discipline.

One special class of unrepresented persons are those individuals you would like to contact as witnesses. The general view is that an attorney may interview witnesses, even those you believe will be testifying against your client, without the presence or consent of opposing counsel. *United States ex rel. O'Keefe v. McDonnell Douglas Corp.*, 961 F. Supp. 1288, 1293 (E.D. Mo. 1997), *aff'd*, 132 F.3d 1252 (8th Cir. 1998). This is permitted as long as the contact is otherwise consistent with the rules.

In terms of the contact, the attorney must insure that the witness knows that the attorney does not represent the witness and should clarify if there is any confusion. The attorney should not give advice in general to the witness and, more particularly, may not ask that the witness keep quiet about what he or she knows. Rule 3.4(f) prohibits requesting that the individual refrain from giving relevant information to another party. The only exception is that an attorney may counsel a client, or the client's relatives, employees, or other agents of the client to refrain from sharing information, but only if the lawyer reasonably believes that the person's interests will not be adversely affected by refraining from communicating.

Of course, some witnesses may choose not to talk to others on their own. Some expert witnesses are constrained by their own professional codes from speaking with an opposing party's counsel. For example, the HIPPA Privacy Rules prohibit health care providers from disclosing patient health information except in very limited circumstances. 45 C.F.R. § 164.502 (2010). Thus the physician of a plaintiff in a personal injury action cannot speak with defense attorneys about the plaintiff's condition.

Obviously, attorneys cannot help witnesses lie or bribe them. Rule 3.4(b) prohibits a lawyer from counseling or assisting a witness to testify falsely or from offering an inducement prohibited by law. An attorney who advises a witness, whether it be the client or someone else, to testify falsely is subject to discipline. *See In re Oberhellman*, 873 S.W.2d 851 (Mo. banc 1994); *In re Storment*, 873 S.W.2d 227 (Mo. banc 1994). This rule also applies to the payment of a fee to a witness that is not permitted by controlling law, such as a contingent fee for witnesses. However, one can pay a witness to cover reasonable and actual expenses: travel, hotel, food expenses, or compensation for loss of wages.

Finally, attorneys must comply with other laws governing tampering with witnesses. For example, 18 U.S.C. § 1512(b)(1) (2012) provides:

> Whoever knowingly uses intimidation, threatens, or corruptly persuades another person, or attempts to do so, or engages in misleading conduct toward another person, with intent to
>
> (1) influence, delay, or prevent the testimony of any person in an official proceeding;
>
> (2) cause or induce any person to
>
>> (A) withhold testimony, or withhold a record, document, or other object, from an official proceeding;
>>
>> (B) alter, destroy, mutilate, or conceal an object with intent to impair the object's integrity or availability for use in an official proceeding;
>>
>> (C) evade legal process summoning that person to appear as a witness, or to produce a record, document, or other object, in an official proceeding; or
>>
>> (D) be absent from an official proceeding to which such person has been summoned by legal process; or
>
> (3) hinder, delay, or prevent the communication to a law enforcement officer or judge of the United States of information relating to the commission or possible commission of a Federal offense or a violation of the conditions of probation, supervised release, parole or release pending judicial proceedings.

Test your understanding of these concepts with the following problem.

Problem for Practice

Memo:

To: Associate

From: Partner

Re: Investigations in Appleton Case

Our client is Diana Appleton. Diana applied for work at Isle of Plenty Resort as a waitress or hostess at one of their restaurants. Diana works days at St. Luke's Cafeteria as a cook and was looking for an evening and weekend job to supplement her income. Diane interviewed with Bob Besluit, Food and Beverage Director. He had told her she was hired but then, when she arrived for work, he told her she had been rejected by one of the general managers because she was pregnant. We wrote the Resort demanding that they reconsider their decision, but received no response. Diana would like to sue and I believe we have a strong case based on the information we have from her and from the EEOC investigation. Now that we are ready to file suit, we need to expand our investigation.

Here is a list of possible witnesses in this case. The resort is represented by Allen Abogado. I know Allen pretty well—he will be circling the wagons pretty tightly, but I'm hopeful some of these folks will be able to give us some good information. I am concerned about Rule 4.2 though. Would any of these witnesses be considered "represented parties" under our state's rule so that we would have to get Allen's permission to speak with them?

- Dave Wagner, Diana's boss at St. Luke's Cafeteria.

- Suzanne Finnegan, who occasionally works for the Resort during busy seasons as an "on-call" bartender. Diana says she might have overhead her interview with Besluit because it took place in the lounge and she was tending bar. Diana says she doesn't think Suzanne is working for the Resort any more.

- Elenora Taylor, who was the previous Food and Beverage Director at the Resort before Besluit. Elenora left after a dispute regarding her eligibility for a bonus.

- Jennifer Walker, a telephone operator, which is a non-supervisory position.

- Diana says that she has been contacted recently by George Apustolu, an executive sous chef at the Resort, who says he would like to speak with us about the case. Apustolu runs the main kitchen at the Resort. He's apparently responsible for interviewing and hiring cooks, dishwashers, and sous chefs, although not waitresses, servers, or restaurant supervisors.

Are there any of these individuals we should avoid? What advice do you have for how we go about interviewing the ones we can speak with?

22.3 Communication with Jurors and Judges

Rule 3.5 deals with communications with judges, jurors, and prospective jurors. For the most part, this rule incorporates the law in the jurisdiction and makes failure to comply with that law a violation of the rules. Thus, the extent of contact with jurors and prospective jurors is governed largely by local law. Generally, these contacts are strictly controlled.

Particularly while a jury is being empaneled or during a trial, contact with jurors can threaten the integrity of the judicial process. This can include efforts to "investigate" jurors. Can you "Google" a jury pool to help you with voir dire? In *Carino v. Muenzen*, No. A-5491-08T1, 2010 WL 3448071(N.J. App. Div. Aug. 30, 2010), *cert. denied,* 205 N.J. 96 (Feb. 3, 2011), the plaintiff's attorney in a medical malpractice case had brought a laptop computer to court and was using it to research potential jurors. The trial judge ordered that the attorney stop using the computer because he had not given advance notice of his intent to research jurors on the internet and the defense counsel (who did not have a laptop computer in the courtroom) was disadvantaged. The appellate court reversed, concluding "There was no suggestion that counsel's use of the computer was in any way disruptive. That he had the foresight to bring his laptop computer to court, and defense counsel did not, simply cannot serve as a basis for judicial intervention in the name of 'fairness' or maintaining 'a level playing field.' The 'playing field' was, in fact, already 'level' because internet access was open to both counsel, even if only one of them chose to utilize it." *Id.*

Not only is researching jurors a good idea, it may be a required part of competent trial preparation. In a Missouri case, after a defense verdict in a medical malpractice case, the plaintiff's attorney checked the state's automated case record service (Case.net) and learned that one of the jurors had been involved in litigation, which the juror had not revealed when asked about prior litigation in voir dire. The attorney brought a motion for a new trial. The Missouri Supreme Court, exasperated that this had not been discovered earlier, held that "a party must use reasonable efforts to examine the litigation history on Case.net of those jurors selected but not empanelled and present to the trial court any relevant information prior to trial." *Johnson v. McCullough*, 306 S.W. 3d 551 (Mo. 2010).

There are limits, of course, to the "research" an attorney can conduct on jurors. Searching a juror's public Facebook page is permitted; friending the juror to be able to access her private account is not. Especially during the course of a trial, when communication with jurors is strictly prohibited, an attorney who takes any active steps to monitor a juror's activity, online or not, risks stepping over the line and having a mistrial declared.

After the jury is discharged, Rule 3.5 permits communication with the former jurors. Most states have adopted Rule 3.5; however, a significant majority limit or even ban this contact. These limitations might be found in the rules of professional conduct, local court rules, statutes, or case law. Those states that restrict contact with jurors are concerned that jurors might find this contact harassing, embarrassing, or even threatening. Thus some courts require court orders in order to speak with jurors. Others provide in the rules express prohibitions on harassment or attempts to influence their future jury service, or requirements that attorneys must cease all contact as soon as a juror expresses a desire to be left alone.

Why might attorneys wish to talk to jurors after a case is over and what concerns do courts have about this contact? One important reason attorneys may want to speak with jurors after a trial is simply to improve their trial skills. Attorneys can do little to develop better trial techniques without speaking to jurors to discover what informed or persuaded them and what they found confusing or prejudicial. A second reason is to discover whether improper influences intruded on jury deliberation. Jurors are unlikely to volunteer this information, in part because they may not be aware that a particular behavior or communication was improper. Of course, some judges may speak with jurors after a case, but jurors might be intimidated about raising concerns in that context. These concerns more often arise in informal interviews with attorneys.

Finally Rule 3.5 prohibits conduct intended to disrupt a tribunal. *See* Rule 3.5(b) and (d). Frequently, this conduct will also subject an attorney to sanctions for direct contempt. (Recall the discussion of the different forms of contempt in Chapter 2.5).

Test Your Understanding

Rebecca White was a plaintiff in a personal injury suit against Denise Jones. Rebecca prevailed at mandatory arbitration and Denise's attorney Barry Welchman filed a timely request for trial de novo. About two weeks later, on November 3, 2010, Denise personally sent an e-mail to Rebecca's attorney, John Williams:

John,

I do not agree to a new trial.

I am not happy with these events, with my lawyers, or with my insurance company pursuing this further. I can not imagine how Ms. White would want more than the existing settlement, and although I do not agree with it, I would rather leave it as is, than open this case back up.

I am consulting with third party attorneys, but feel free to contact me further as I do not wish to represented by Mr. Welchman any longer.

Denise Jones

After receiving this e-mail, Williams obtained from Denise the following signed declaration stating that she did not authorize her attorney to request a trial de novo:

1. I am the named Defendant in the above-captioned case. My current name is Denise Jones.

2. It is my understanding that this case was arbitrated on October 5, 2010, and an award was entered for the Plaintiff Rebecca White.

3. It is now my understanding that my attorney at that time, Philip Welchman, appealed the arbitration award by filing a Request for a Trial De Novo.

4. I did not authorize Mr. Welchman to appeal the arbitration award by filing the Request for a Trial De Novo, nor did I consent to it in any manner.

5. It is my belief that my insurance company told Mr. Welchman to appeal the arbitration award.

6. I was under the impression that I was Mr. Welchman's client, however, it appears that he was really representing my insurance company.

7. I am currently seeking independent counsel, but have not retained an attorney to date.

Denise Jones

Denise's attorney withdrew. Represented by new counsel, Denise moved to strike her own declarations and those of Williams as improperly obtained in violation of the rules of professional conduct. Denise also moved for sanctions against Williams. What result? *See Engstrom v. Goodman*, No. 66557-0-I, 2012 Wash. App. LEXIS 439 (March 5, 2012).

To Learn More

Because of the controversy over the application of Rule 4.2 to United States Attorneys, the department of justice has a chapter of the "Criminal Resource Manual" that addresses this issue: http://www.justice.gov/usao/eousa/foia_reading_room/usam/title9/crm00296.htm. *See also*, Geoffrey C. Hazard, Jr. & Dana Remus Irwin, *Toward a Revised 4.2 No-Contact Rule*, 60 HASTINGS L.J. 797, 831-42 (2009).

For an interesting article examining the application of Rule 4.2's exception for contact with government officials see R. Lisle Baker, *Ethical Limits on Attorney Contact with Represented and Unrepresented Officials: The Example of Municipal Zoning Boards Making Site-Specific Land Use Decisions*, 31 SUFFOLK U. L. REV. 349 (1997).

Chapter Twenty-Three

Judges and the Adversary System

Learning Objectives

After you have read this chapter and completed the assignments, you should be able to:

- Describe the similarities and differences between the core duties of judges and the core duties of attorneys.
- Identify the reasons why attorneys must understand judicial ethics.
- Apply rules governing ex parte communication with judges to a variety of situations.
- Describe methods of protecting clients when dealing with judges who violate their duties.

Rules to Study

In this chapter we will examine selected provisions of the Code of Judicial Conduct and the rules of professional conduct that require attorneys to understand judicial ethics, primarily Rule 8.4(f) and 8.3(b).

Preliminary Problem

Suppose you are representing a teenager in a juvenile delinquency proceeding. The judge before whom you are appearing has one of the highest reversal rates in the state and is notorious for letting his own religious and political views, rather than the law, influence his decisions. To save the costs of court reporters, most proceedings in the juvenile court are audio recorded. Today in the hearing before this judge, you noticed that he reached over and turned off the audio recorder before launching into a tirade against your client, reading to her out of the bible, and threatening her with results that would clearly be outside of the law. He then turned on the recorder and asked your client if she had anything to say. You had no idea what to do, so in order to protect your client, you faked a coughing fit and asked for a recess. The judge said, "Well that's enough for today anyway. You both be back here tomorrow morning at 9:00 a.m."

That evening you went out to dinner and you noticed that at a table in the back of the restaurant the judge was having dinner with the juvenile prosecutor in your case. You walked over to their table and noticed that several papers relating to your case were spread out on the table. When they saw you, they hastily gathered up the papers and began talking about an event that was coming up at the local church they both attend. You greeted them, asked if they enjoyed their meal, and told them you would see them in the morning. You are quite convinced they were discussing your case.

What do you do?

23.1 The Core Duties of Judges

Most law students do not plan on graduating and immediately taking the bench. Nonetheless, all attorneys should be aware of a judge's ethical duties and limits. One of the most straightforward reasons for this is that attorneys can be disciplined for assisting a judge in misconduct or, in certain circumstances, failing to report the misconduct of a judge. Remember the definition of misconduct under Rule 8.4 (from Chapter 2)? Recall that 8.4(f) indicates that it is misconduct for an attorney to "knowingly assist a judge or judicial officer in conduct that is a violation of applicable rules of judicial conduct or other law." Also, remember that an attorney's duty to report professional misconduct includes the responsibility to report judicial misconduct "that raises a substantial question as to the judge's fitness for office." Rule 8.3(b). One reason to know a judge's ethical duties, then, is that you may find yourself in a position in which you are assisting a judge in violating the judicial code or in which you are required to report that misconduct. While both standards include a "knowledge" element, the knowledge is of the action or behavior, not that the behavior violates the rules. Claiming ignorance of the law is unlikely to be a defense for attorneys in any circumstance.

Judges are governed in each state by a code of judicial conduct similar to the code of professional conduct for attorneys. As with regulation of attorney conduct, most states pattern their judicial conduct codes on an ABA model, in this case, the ABA Model Code of Judicial Conduct. These codes govern the activities of full-time judges as well as some activities of part-time judges, magistrates, referees, hearing officers, and the like. Federal judges are regulated by the Code of Conduct for Federal Judges, adopted by the United States Judicial Conference. This code does not apply to the United States Supreme Court.

To understand judicial ethics, you must first understand the overall role of the judge. If the core duties of attorneys are the five C's—competence, communication, confidentiality, conflict-free representation, and candor, one can describe the core duties of a judge as the four I's—independence, integrity, impartiality, and avoiding the appearance of impropriety. The Code of Judicial Conduct defines each of these terms. Read the definitions of these terms, contained in the terminology section of the Wyoming Code of Judicial Conduct[1] and compare these duties to the duties attorneys owe to their clients:

"Impropriety" includes "conduct that violates the law, court rules, or provisions of this Code, and conduct that undermines a judge's independence, integrity, or impartiality." Certainly attorneys are also expected to follow the law, and so in that sense must

---

1. The Wyoming Code of Judicial Conduct definitions are substantially the same as those used in the ABA Model Code of Judicial Conduct.

avoid impropriety. At one time, the ABA Code of Professional Responsibility included a canon that directed attorneys to "avoid even the appearance of impropriety." Today, the ABA rules of conduct for attorneys no longer speak about avoiding "appearances" of impropriety but concentrate more on insuring that attorneys do not engage in actual improprieties (more particularly in conflicts of interest). For judges, however, Canon 1 still speaks of avoiding "impropriety and the appearance of impropriety." Why do appearances matter more for judges than attorneys? Isn't public trust in both attorneys and in judges necessary for the legal system to have legitimacy? Or is it enough that clients trust their own lawyers and the public trusts the judges?

"Integrity" means "probity, fairness, honesty, uprightness, and soundness of character." This definition sounds a great deal like the "good moral character" requirement for admission to practice law and the general definitions of misconduct in Rule 8.4, including the "conduct prejudicial to the administration of justice" category.

"Independence" means "a judge's freedom from influence or controls other than those established by law." We speak of an attorney's "independent professional judgment" as well, meaning that attorneys should be able to provide their clients with objective counseling on the one hand and undiluted loyalty on the other. For judges these qualities of objectivity and undiluted loyalty are part of independence as well, but the loyalty is to the interests of justice and the rule of law, rather than to the interests of a client. A judge's independence can be lost not only if the judge is blinded by personal biases or connections, but it can also be lost if the public does not understand the unique role that judges play in providing a check on majoritarian controls.

"Impartiality" means "absence of bias or prejudice in favor of, or against, particular parties or classes of parties, as well as maintenance of an open mind in considering issues that may come before a judge." Here, of course, is where the roles of attorney and judge diverge. Judges must be neutral and passive, avoiding stepping into the shoes of advocate for one side or another in a case. Attorneys must be partisan and active, exercising advocacy within the bounds of the law on behalf of their clients.

Many of the recent controversies surrounding judicial ethics, whether over campaign contributions to elected judges or over standards and procedures for disqualification, reflect concerns about the judiciary losing its independence or impartiality.

Researching Professional Responsibility: Using a Table of Contents to Guide Research

In today's world of Boolean or "key word" searching, students sometimes overlook the value of a table of contents. When you are researching an area of law with which you are unfamiliar, often the very best tool for you to efficiently and effectively begin your research is a table of contents. By providing an outline of an area of law, a contents list can give you insights into key search terms and relationships between different concepts without having to read through pages of text. Suppose, for example, you are researching an issue in the code of judicial conduct in your state. You could do a key word search in the code and hope you will find the right provisions. However, you can save yourself time and be more effective in researching if you first examine the table of provisions in the code.

State Codes of Judicial Conduct are divided into Canons—generalized statements of principles—under which are organized rules and then comments.

For example, suppose you are concerned about a judge who uses grossly pro-fane language from the bench and are investigating whether this is something for which the judge might be disciplined. Examine carefully the canons and the titles of the rules in the Wyoming Code of Judicial Conduct. Which rules seem likely to address your concern about the judge's language?

Wyoming Code of Judicial Conduct

Canon 1 A judge shall uphold and promote the independence, integrity, and impartiality of the judiciary, and shall avoid impropriety and the appearance of impropriety.

Rule 1.1   Compliance with the Law
Rule 1.2   Promoting Confidence in the Judiciary
Rule 1.3   Avoiding Abuse of the Prestige of Judicial Office

Canon 2 A judge shall perform the duties of judicial office impartially, compe-tently, and diligently.

Rule 2.1   Giving Precedence to the Duties of Judicial Office
Rule 2.2   Impartiality and Fairness
Rule 2.3   Bias, Prejudice, and Harassment
Rule 2.4   External Influences on Judicial Conduct
Rule 2.5   Competence, Diligence, and Cooperation
Rule 2.6   Ensuring the Right to Be Heard
Rule 2.7   Responsibility to Decide
Rule 2.8   Decorum, Demeanor, and Communication with Jurors
Rule 2.9   Ex Parte Communications
Rule 2.10   Judicial Statements on Pending and Impending Cases
Rule 2.11   Disqualification
Rule 2.12   Supervisory Duties
Rule 2.13   Administrative Appointments
Rule 2.14   Disability and Impairment
Rule 2.15   Responding to Judicial and Lawyer Misconduct
Rule 2.16   Cooperation with Disciplinary Authorities

Canon 3 A judge shall conduct the judge's personal and extrajudicial activities to minimize the risk of conflict with the obligations of judicial office.

Rule 3.1   Extrajudicial Activities in General
Rule 3.2   Appearances before Governmental Bodies and Consultation with Government Officials
Rule 3.3   Testifying as a Character Witness
Rule 3.4   Appointments to Governmental Positions
Rule 3.5   Use of Nonpublic Information
Rule 3.6   Affiliation with Discriminatory Organizations
Rule 3.7   Participation in Educational, Religious, Charitable, Fraternal, or Civic Organizations and Activities
Rule 3.8   Appointments to Fiduciary Positions
Rule 3.9   Service as Arbitrator or Mediator
Rule 3.10   Practice of Law
Rule 3.11   Financial, Business, or Remunerative Activities
Rule 3.12   Compensation for Extrajudicial Activities
Rule 3.13   Acceptance and Reporting of Gifts, Loans, Bequests, Benefits, or Other Things of Value

Rule 3.14   Reimbursement of Expenses and Waivers of Fees or Charges
Rule 3.15   Reporting Requirements

Canon 4 A judge or candidate for judicial office shall not engage in political or campaign activity that is inconsistent with the independence, integrity, or impartiality of the judiciary.
Rule 4.1   Political and Campaign Activities of Judges and Judicial Candidates in General
Rule 4.2   Political and Campaign Activities of Judicial Candidates in Public Retention Elections
Rule 4.3[2]   Activities of Candidates for Appointive Judicial Office

23.2 *Ex Parte* Communications — Interactions of Attorney Ethics and Judicial Ethics

An especially important reason for learning a judge's ethical duties is that, for many rules of attorney professional conduct, there are parallel duties imposed on judges. The attorney's duty to avoid improper *ex parte* communications with judges is a perfect example of the interaction of an attorney's ethical duties with judicial ethics.

Rule 3.5 limits *ex parte* communication with the court "unless authorized to do so by law or court order." Compare that requirement with the Wyoming Code of Judicial Conduct provision on *ex parte* communications:

Rule 2.9 Ex Parte Communications

(A) A judge shall not initiate, permit, or consider ex parte communications, or consider other communications made to the judge outside the presence of the parties or their lawyers, concerning a pending or impending matter, except as follows:

(1) When circumstances require it, ex parte communication for scheduling, administrative, or emergency purposes, which does not address substantive matters *or issues on the merits*, is permitted, provided:

(a) the judge reasonably believes that no party will gain a procedural, substantive, or tactical advantage as a result of the ex parte communication; and

(b) the judge makes provision promptly to notify all other parties of the substance of the ex parte communication, and gives the parties an opportunity to respond.

(2) A judge may obtain the written advice of a disinterested expert on the law applicable to a proceeding before the judge, if the judge gives advance notice to the parties of the person to be consulted and the subject matter of the advice to be solicited, and affords the parties a reasonable opportunity to object and respond to the notice and to the advice received.

(3) A judge may consult with court staff and court officials whose functions are to aid the judge in carrying out the judge's adjudicative responsibilities,

---

2. This is the same as ABA Model Code of Judicial Conduct Rule 4.5. The ABA Model contains an additional rule on campaign committees, not included in the Wyoming Code.

or with other judges, provided the judge makes reasonable efforts to avoid receiving factual information that is not part of the record, and does not abrogate the responsibility personally to decide the matter.

(4) A judge may, with the consent of the parties, confer separately with the parties and their lawyers in an effort to settle matters pending before the judge.

(5) A judge may initiate, permit, or consider any ex parte communication when expressly authorized by law to do so.

(B) If a judge receives an *unsolicited*[3] ex parte communication bearing upon the substance of a matter, *which in the interest of justice the court believes is required to be considered,* the judge shall make provision promptly to notify the parties of the substance of the communication and provide the parties with an opportunity to respond.

(C) A judge shall not investigate facts in a matter independently, and shall consider only the evidence presented and any facts that may properly be judicially noticed.

(D) A judge shall make reasonable efforts, including providing appropriate supervision, to ensure that this Rule is not violated by court staff, court officials, and others subject to the judge's direction and control.

Both the attorney's ethics rules and the judicial ethics code expand the restrictions on *ex parte* communications beyond simply the judge and the attorneys appearing before the court. For example, the code restricts a judge's *ex parte* communication about a matter even with attorneys or law professors who are not part of the proceeding, unless the judge follows the procedures of Rule 2.9(A)(2). Notice that the code does permit the court to consult with other judges, court staff, law clerks, and court officials. Rule 2.9(A)(3). Because judges do often confer with other court personnel, attorneys should consider the ban on *ex parte* communications to extend to communication with anyone who is in a position to participate in the decision in the case. This can include commissioners and magistrates, administrative law judges, hearing officers, and even the judge's law clerk or staff attorney. *Mallory v. Hartsfield, Almand & Grisham, LLP,* 86 S.W.3d 863, 867 (Ark. 2002); *Vanzant v. R.L. Products, Inc.,* 139 F.R.D. 435, 438 n.4 (S.D. Fla. 1991).

The code of judicial conduct, like the rules of professional conduct, also defers to other law, providing that judges may communicate *ex parte* when permitted by law. When does the law permit this *ex parte* communication? Comment 4 to the Wyoming rule provides one example: "A judge may initiate, permit, or consider *ex parte* communications expressly authorized by law, such as when serving on therapeutic or 'problem solving' courts, mental health courts, or drug courts. In this capacity, judges may assume a more interactive role with parties, treatment providers, probation officers, social workers, and others." Rules of procedure and statutes may provide for *ex parte* proceedings, such as emergency temporary restraining orders or situations in which an opposing party cannot be located and has been served by publication. Recall that Rule 3.3(d) requires attorneys in these proceedings to inform the court of all material law and facts, whether or not they are adverse, so that the court can make an informed decision.

Other *ex parte* communications are strictly prohibited. "Improper *ex parte* communications undermine our adversarial system, which relies so heavily on fair advocacy and an impartial

---

3. Compared to the ABA Model Code, the Wyoming code deletes the term "inadvertently," and replaces "unauthorized" with "unsolicited" here.

judge. [Such conduct threatens] not only the fairness of the resolution at hand, but the reputation of the judiciary and the bar, and the integrity of our system of justice." *In the Matter of Marek*, 609 N.E.2d 419, 420 (Ind.1993). Accordingly, even if a judge initiates an impermissible *ex parte* communication, the attorney must decline to participate. The way to avoid this improper *ex parte* communication is to include the other attorneys in the case in any communication with the court. If you write a letter to the judge, be sure to send a copy of the letter to opposing counsel. Don't play games with the requirement— if you communicate with the court, share that communication with opposing counsel at the same time and by the same method. Faxing a document to the judge and then sending a copy of the document to opposing counsel through the mail is likely to be considered a violation. *Cormier v. Carty*, 408 N.E.2d 860 (Mass. 1980).

The following case demonstrates the relationships among the rules of professional conduct, the code of judicial conduct, and rules governing *ex parte* communications.

In Re Wilder

764 N.E.2d 617 (Ind. 2002)

The respondent was the town attorney for Utica, Indiana. On August 12, 1998, in his capacity as counsel for the town of Utica, the respondent prepared a declaratory judgment complaint and a request for temporary injunction seeking that the Clark County Commissioners be enjoined from replacing the town of Utica's appointment to a certain local board. The respondent completed the complaint sometime after 4:00 pm. It was prepared for filing in the Clark Superior Court No. 1, where Judge Jerry Jacobi presided. The respondent's appearance indicated that copies of the pleadings had been served either "in person" or by "First Class Mail." At about the same time, the respondent instructed his secretary to take an unfiled copy of the pleadings and unsigned proposed order to the office of the attorney for the Clark County Commissioners, which was located two blocks from the respondent's office. The secretary delivered the papers to a "dark haired" woman in the commissioners' attorney's office.

[handwritten margin note: didn't confirm whether she even worked there!]

[handwritten margin note: Why do you suppose this all took place at the end of the day?]

Meanwhile, sometime after 5:00 pm, the respondent filed the pleadings and met with the judge. The judge signed the temporary injunction order. The next morning, the respondent's secretary delivered copies of the signed order to the commissioners and their attorney.

This Court found that Judge Jacobi violated Canons 1, 2(A), and 3(B)(2) of the Code of Judicial Conduct for his role in this very same incident. *Matter of Jacobi*, 715 N.E.2d 873 (Ind.1999).[2] We suspended him for three days for those violations.

The Commission charged that the respondent violated Prof. Cond. R. 3.5 by communicating *ex parte* with a judge when not permitted by law to do so.

---

2. In Jacobi, we found: The parties agree that Respondent violated Canon 1 of the Code of Judicial Conduct, which generally requires judges to uphold the integrity and independence of the judiciary; Canon 2(A), which generally requires judges to avoid impropriety and the appearance of impropriety, to respect and comply with the law, and to act at all times in a manner which promotes the public's confidence in the integrity and impartiality of the judiciary; and Canon 3(B)(2), which generally requires judges to be faithful to the law. *Matter of Jacobi*, 715 N.E.2d 873, 875.

It also charged that he violated Prof. Cond. R. 8.4(f) by knowingly assisting a judge in conduct that violated the Code of Judicial Conduct. The hearing officer concluded that Ind. Trial Rule 65 (governing notice and hearings for temporary restraining orders) "specifically permits an attorney to secure a temporary restraining order without notice to an adverse party," and, accordingly, found no misconduct.

Trial Rule 65(B) provides, in relevant part:

[a] temporary restraining order may be granted without written or oral notice to the adverse party or his attorney only if:

(1) it clearly appears from specific facts shown by affidavit or by the verified complaint that immediate and irreparable injury, loss, or damage will result to the applicant before the adverse party or his attorney can be heard in opposition; and

(2) the applicant's attorney certifies to the court in writing the efforts, if any, which have been made to give notice and the reasons supporting his claim that notice should not be required.

Stop here and think about how the attorney in this case was reading this rule.

While it is true that T.R. 65(B) permits the granting of a temporary restraining order without notice, it only allows such grant under certain specified circumstances. It is true that the respondent sent his secretary to opposing counsel's office with copies of the pleadings at about the same time that the respondent was meeting with the judge to have the TRO order signed, but that act cannot be said to have been calculated to provide opposing counsel with meaningful notice. It is also clear that the respondent did not accomplish the steps necessary to permit dispensing with notice to the adverse party prior to seeking an *ex parte* TRO. He did not show that immediate and irreparable injury, loss, or damage would result before the commissioners and their attorney could be notified. He also failed to certify to the court in writing the efforts he made to give notice or the reasons supporting any claim that notice should not be required. Accordingly, we find that the respondent violated Prof.Cond.R. 3.5 when he obtained the *ex parte* order of temporary injunction from Judge Jacobi without complying with the provisions of T.R. 65(B). We find further that the respondent violated Prof.Cond.R. 8.4(f) by assisting Judge Jacobi in conduct that violated the Code of Judicial Conduct.

only had an hour to react, if received

Why didn't giving the papers directly to the opposing attorney provide meaningful notice? What would have?

Why didn't the attorney do this?

The respondent would have us believe that by instructing his secretary to personally deliver a copy of the unfiled TRO petition and proposed order to opposing counsel's office at about the same time the respondent was meeting with the judge satisfied the notice requirements contained in T.R. 65(B). However, the hearing officer's findings indicate that opposing counsel did not learn of the respondent's pleading on August 12. On August 16 (the next date opposing counsel was in his office), he was unable to determine whether any of the copies of the pleadings had arrived on August 12. While the pleadings were being walked to opposing counsel's office to be delivered to persons unknown, the respondent was contemporaneously meeting *ex parte* with the judge to obtain relief. This incident is remarkably similar to that in another case where we found an impermissible *ex parte* contact. *See Matter of Anonymous,* 729 N.E.2d 566 (Ind. 2000) (lawyer mailed petition for emergency custody to opposing counsel, then walked to courthouse and met with judge to get relief sought). Because such last-minute delivery of the papers to oppos-

Must have chance to respond, even if opposing side has no reason to object

ing counsel is not adequate notice, the respondent was required to satisfy the conditions for relief with no notice; i.e., claim risk of immediate and irreparable loss and include a certificate regarding notice or lack thereof. He failed to do either.

We must now determine an appropriate sanction for the respondent's misconduct. We suspended Judge Jacobi for three days for this incident. We conclude that the respondent should suffer the same discipline.

Notes

1. Three days' suspension may not seem like a strong sanction, but recall that most states require an attorney who has been suspended to notify all his or her clients of the suspension. Likewise, suspensions will ordinarily be reported in the disciplinary reports published in local bar journals and online. Finally, a suspension of any length is a serious sanction in the sense that the suspension will be considered an aggravating factor in considering sanctions for any future misconduct.

2. Notice that the court does not address the question of whether the attorney *knew* that his application for a TRO violated the procedural rules for these orders. If it had been clear he had simply not known what the procedures were, would that have changed the outcome? Recall the court's analysis of the "mistake of law" defense in the *Wuliger* case involving illegal wiretapping (chapter 21.2). If the knowledge requirement of Rule 3.5 does not speak to knowledge that the *ex parte* communication is prohibited, to what conduct does it apply?

3. What about socializing with judges? Re-read the code of judicial conduct carefully. Can you see that purely social communications are not prohibited by the rule? Nonetheless, attorneys should take great care in socializing with judges before whom there are pending cases, particularly in settings that might raise a question as to whether their communication really is purely social.

23.3 Ethical Duties of Judicial Clerks

The code of judicial conduct permits courts to confer with law clerks and contact with a judge's law clerk is considered to be *ex parte* contact with the judge. "Law clerks are closely connected with the court's decision-making process.... Law clerks are simply extensions of the judges at whose pleasure they serve." *Olivia v. Heller*, 839 F.2d 37, 40 (2d Cir. 1988). What does that suggest to you about a judicial law clerk's responsibilities to the judge? In *Gregorich v. Lund*, 54 F.3d 410 (7th Cir. 1995), a case involving judicial research attorney Gregorich, who was fired after union organizing activities among the staff attorneys, the question for the court was whether the public interest in the special role of judicial clerks outweighed their right to organize. In concluding that the judge was permitted to dismiss the clerk for his organizing activities, the court of appeals made these observations about judicial clerks:

> In *Meeks v. Grimes*, 779 F.2d 417 (7th Cir.1985), we noted in the context of a political patronage firing that a judge's chambers are perhaps "[t]he paradigm example" of an environment in which a close working relationship is essential to perform successfully the public function. *Id.* at 423. Other courts and jurists have recognized that those who work closely with judicial officers must be loyal, cooperative, and responsible.[6]

> Needless to say, confidentiality is essential. As Judge Gewin stated in *Abbott v. Thetford*, "every judge knows the importance of a cooperative and confidential relationship with staff members. The absence of either cooperation or confidentiality is disruptive and inevitably impairs the operation of any court." 529 F.2d 695, 705 (5th Cir.) (Gewin, J., dissenting), *rev'd*, 534 F.2d 1101 (5th Cir.1976) (en banc) (adopting dissent), *cert. denied*, 430 U.S. 954, 97 S.Ct. 1598, 51 L.Ed.2d 804 (1977).[7]

> The record in this case establishes that, like the judicial assistants referenced in the case law cited above, the Illinois Fourth District's research attorneys had a close working relationship with the judges of their court. The research attorneys became privy not only to internal memoranda and draft opinions, but also to the judges' very thought processes. *See* Tr. II at 16-17 (Mr. Gregorich's statement that he prepared research memoranda and either participated in conference discussions following oral argument or received directions on how to draft opinions from the authoring judge); Tr. IV at 26 (Justice Lund's comment that Mr. Gregorich attended conference discussions and suggested how cases should be decided). Therefore, at the time he acted, Justice Lund was entitled to believe that the unionization of the research attorneys would threaten this delicate work-

---

6. *See, e.g., McDaniel v. Woodard*, 886 F.2d 311, 315 (11th Cir.1989) (holding that state trial judge was justified in dismissing confidential secretary for her refusal to obey direct order, and noting that the judge was not required to "'tolerate action which he reasonably believed would disrupt the office, undermine his authority, and destroy close working relationships'") (quoting *Connick*, 461 U.S. at 154, 103 S.Ct. at 1693-94); *Balogh v. Charron*, 855 F.2d 356, 356-57 (6th Cir.1988) ("Judicial aides who work in chambers and are assigned to one judge as court officer ... normally handle sensitive information about cases of a confidential nature, information which is not public information. Judges must be able to rely on the confidentiality of the relationship with such aides, just as they must rely on the confidentiality of their relationship with their private secretaries and law clerks."); *Oliva v. Heller*, 839 F.2d 37, 40 (2d Cir.1988) (noting, in an absolute immunity case, that "a law clerk is probably the one participant in the judicial process whose duties and responsibilities are most intimately connected with the judge's own exercise of the judicial function"); *Hall v. Small Business Admin.*, 695 F.2d 175, 176 (5th Cir.1983) ("Judges' robes must be as spotless as their actual conduct. These expectations extend to those who make up the contemporary judicial family, the judge's law clerks and secretaries."); a199 *Fredonia Broadcasting Corp. v. RCA Corp.*, 569 F.2d 251, 256 (5th Cir.) ("[L]aw clerks may serve as sounding boards for ideas, often affording a different perspective, may perform research, and may aid in drafting memoranda, orders and opinions·A law clerk, by virtue of his position, is privy to his judge's thoughts in a way that the parties cannot be."), *cert. denied*, 439 U.S. 859, 99 S.Ct. 177, 58 L.Ed.2d 167 (1978); *cf. Gerald Gunther,* Learned Hand 141 (1994) (noting that Judge Hand referred to his law clerks as "puny judges").

7. *Cf. B.H. v. McDonald*, 49 F.3d 294, 297-98 (7th Cir.1995) (noting, in case involving question of public access to judicial proceedings, that a judge's chambers is "an area traditionally off-limits to the public eyes and ears").

ing relationship. He was not required to wait for "events to unfold to the extent that the disruption of the office and the destruction of working relationships [was] manifest" before he acted. *Connick,* 461 U.S. at 152, 103 S.Ct. at 1692-93.

Besides being restricted in union organizing activities, how else does the law protect the judge-law clerk relationship? As government employees, judicial clerks are usually governed by the state or federal governmental ethics rules. So for example, in the federal system, law clerks are governed by the Code of Conduct for Judicial Employees. That code is organized in a system parallel to the code of judicial conduct. The Code contains five canons, with rules and comments under each. The canons are:

Canon 1: A judicial employee should uphold the integrity and independence of the judiciary and of the judicial employee's office.

Canon 2: a judicial employee should avoid impropriety and the appearance of impropriety in all activities.

Canon 3: a judicial employee should adhere to appropriate standards in performing the duties of the office.

Canon 4: in engaging in outside activities, a judicial employee should avoid the risk of conflict with official duties, should avoid the appearance of impropriety, and should comply with disclosure requirements.

Canon 5: a judicial employee should refrain from inappropriate political activity.

These codes require that clerks maintain the confidentiality of chambers even after the clerk has left the court. Further guidance is provided by a handbook published by the Federal Judicial Center in cooperation with the Judicial Conference Committee on Codes of Conduct. The handbook, MAINTAINING THE PUBLIC TRUST: ETHICS FOR FEDERAL JUDICIAL LAW CLERKS, is available on-line at http://www.fjc.gov/library/fjc_catalog.nsf.

Finally, judicial law clerks are attorneys as well as government employees and so must comply with the rules of professional conduct. One of the rules that speaks most directly to law clerks is Rule 1.12. Like Rule 1.11, the rule prohibits former judges (and their clerks) from representing any client in a matter on which they participated "personally and substantially" as an adjudicative officer. Rule 1.12(b) provides specific guidance to law clerks who are negotiating for employment while they are employed by the court. That rule permits a law clerk to negotiate for employment with anyone who is a party or an attorney before the court, even if the clerk is working on a matter in which the potential employers are before the court, so long as the clerk first notifies the judge or adjudicative officer.

23.4 Dealing with Unethical Judges

If dealing with an unethical or incompetent opposing attorney poses difficult ethical challenges, dealing with an unethical judge is even more difficult. The following scenarios raise issues of judicial misconduct. Following each scenario are the relevant provisions of the Code of Judicial Conduct that raise questions about the propriety of the judge's conduct. For each scenario, strategize how you would respond.

1. You have matters pending before a judge who seems to be unable to get business done. Hearings are impossible to schedule, motions languish, and orders take months to be completed. In one of your cases, your client is aged and infirm. You are representing her in what seems to you to be a routine quiet title action. However, the judge is sitting on

the final judgment. You have called his clerk several times to ask when you might expect the decision but his clerk has warned you not to push the judge or he might take even longer to decide. Given your client's health and the mess that will be left if this case can't be resolved soon, you are quite desperate.

Wyoming CJC, Rule 2.5 Competence, Diligence, and Cooperation

(A) A judge shall perform judicial and administrative duties competently, *promptly, efficiently*[4] and diligently.

(B) A judge shall cooperate with other judges and court officials in the administration of court business.

Comments:

[1] Competence in the performance of judicial duties requires the legal knowledge, skill, thoroughness, and preparation reasonably necessary to perform a judge's responsibilities of judicial office.

[2] A judge should seek the necessary docket time, court staff, expertise, and resources to discharge all adjudicative and administrative responsibilities.

[3] Prompt disposition of the court's business requires a judge to devote adequate time to judicial duties, to be punctual in attending court and expeditious in determining matters under submission, and to take reasonable measures to ensure that court officials, litigants, and their lawyers cooperate with the judge to that end.

[4] In disposing of matters promptly and efficiently, a judge must demonstrate due regard for the rights of parties to be heard and to have issues resolved without unnecessary cost or delay. A judge should monitor and supervise cases in ways that reduce or eliminate dilatory practices, avoidable delays, and unnecessary costs.

2. You are representing a Mexican-American client in a case involving a breach of an employment contract. You are before a judge who has a reputation of treating Spanish-speaking litigants very badly — refusing interpreters when the law requires them, disparaging them in harsh tones for their accents, and requiring that they prove their immigration status even when it is irrelevant to the issue before the court. In your case, the judge dismisses your petition and says in the hearing, "this isn't the way we do business on this side of the border; maybe you need to move back to where you came from." Your client responded that he was born and raised in Wisconsin. The judge then threatened him with contempt if he ever showed up in his courtroom again.

Wyoming CJC, Rule 2.3: Bias, Prejudice, and Harassment

(A) A judge shall perform the duties of judicial office, including administrative duties, without bias or prejudice.

(B) A judge shall not, in the performance of judicial duties, by words or conduct manifest bias or prejudice, or engage in harassment, including but not limited to bias, prejudice, or harassment based upon race, sex, gender, religion, national origin, ethnicity, disability, age, sexual orientation, marital status, socioeconomic status, or political affiliation, and shall not permit court staff, court officials, or others subject to the judge's direction and control to do so.

(C) A judge shall require lawyers in proceedings before the court to refrain from manifesting bias or prejudice, or engaging in harassment, based upon attributes

---

4. The ABA Model Code does not contain these additional adverbs.

including but not limited to race, sex, gender, religion, national origin, ethnicity, disability, age, sexual orientation, marital status, socioeconomic status, or political affiliation, against parties, witnesses, lawyers, or others.

(D) The restrictions of paragraphs (B) and (C) do not preclude judges or lawyers from making legitimate reference to the listed factors, or similar factors, when they are relevant to an issue in a proceeding.

Comments

[1] A judge who manifests bias or prejudice in a proceeding impairs the fairness of the proceeding and brings the judiciary into disrepute.

[2] Examples of manifestations of bias or prejudice include but are not limited to epithets; slurs; demeaning nicknames; negative stereotyping; attempted humor based upon stereotypes; threatening, intimidating, or hostile acts; suggestions of connections between race, ethnicity, or nationality and crime; and irrelevant references to personal characteristics. Even facial expressions and body language can convey to parties and lawyers in the proceeding, jurors, the media, and others an appearance of bias or prejudice. A judge must avoid conduct that may reasonably be perceived as prejudiced or biased.

[3] Harassment, as referred to in paragraphs (B) and (C), is verbal or physical conduct that denigrates or shows hostility or aversion toward a person on bases such as race, sex, gender, religion, national origin, ethnicity, disability, age, sexual orientation, marital status, socioeconomic status, or political affiliation.

[4] Sexual harassment includes but is not limited to sexual advances, requests for sexual favors, and other verbal or physical conduct of a sexual nature that is unwelcome.

See also, *Gonzalez v Commission on Judicial Performance*, 33 Cal. 3d 359, 188 Cal. Rptr. 880, 657 P.2d 372, *app dism'd* 464 U.S. 1033 (1983) (removing judge from office for, among other violations, interceding in criminal matters on behalf of friends and benefactors, abuse of judicial authority and the conduct of court business in violation of proper procedures, and making comments impugning the character of his judicial colleagues and making ethnic slurs both on and off the bench).

3. You have known a local judge since you were a child, growing up next door to one another. She has been like a big sister to you most of your life and a tremendous mentor during law school and in the transition to law practice. Whenever you appear before her (which is only once every few months) she always treats you exactly like she does any other attorney, but after the case is over, she gives you advice on what you did especially well and how you could improve. Recently, you were having lunch with her and she explained that she was having some financial difficulty. She asked you if you could give her a loan of $5,000. She explained that she would pay standard interest and would give you a promissory note for the loan. You do not have and do not anticipate having a case before her in the near future.

Wyoming CJC, Rule 3.13. Acceptance and Reporting of Gifts, Loans, Bequests, Benefits, or Other Things of Value

(A) A judge shall not accept any gifts, loans, bequests, benefits, or other things of value, if acceptance is prohibited by law or would appear to a reasonable person to undermine the judge's independence, integrity, or impartiality.

(B) Unless otherwise prohibited by law, or by paragraph (A), a judge may accept the following without publicly reporting such acceptance:

(1) items with little intrinsic value, such as plaques, certificates, trophies, and greeting cards;

(2) gifts, loans, bequests, benefits, or other things of value from friends, relatives, or other persons, including lawyers, whose appearance or interest in a proceeding pending or impending before the judge would in any event require disqualification of the judge under Rule 2.11;

(3) ordinary social hospitality;

(4) commercial or financial opportunities and benefits, including special pricing and discounts, and loans from lending institutions in their regular course of business, if the same opportunities and benefits or loans are made available on the same terms to similarly situated persons who are not judges;

(5) rewards and prizes given to competitors or participants in random drawings, contests, or other events that are open to persons who are not judges;

(6) scholarships, fellowships, and similar benefits or awards, if they are available to similarly situated persons who are not judges, based upon the same terms and criteria;

(7) books, magazines, journals, audiovisual materials, and other resource materials supplied by publishers on a complimentary basis for official use; or

(8) gifts, awards, or benefits associated with the business, profession, or other separate activity of a spouse, a domestic partner, or other family member of a judge residing in the judge's household, but that incidentally benefit the judge.

(C) Unless otherwise prohibited by law or by paragraph (A), a judge may accept the following items, and must report such acceptance to the extent required by Rule 3.15:

(1) gifts incident to a public testimonial;

(2) invitations to the judge and the judge's spouse, domestic partner, or guest to attend without charge:

(a) an event associated with a bar-related function or other activity relating to the law, the legal system, or the administration of justice; or

(b) an event associated with any of the judge's educational, religious, charitable, fraternal or civic activities permitted by this Code, if the same invitation is offered to nonjudges who are engaged in similar ways in the activity as is the judge; and

(3) gifts, loans, bequests, benefits, or other things of value, if the source is a party or other person, including a lawyer, who has come or is likely to come before the judge, or whose interests have come or are likely to come before the judge.

Researching Professional Responsibility: Judicial Discipline

Find the code of judicial conduct for your state and use it to answer the preliminary problem in this chapter. Try to find case law against which you can test your interpretation. Since judicial discipline is rare, and reported cases of discipline even more rare, you will probably need to research case law from other ju-

risdictions. Remember that in using case law, from your own or another jurisdiction, it is important to determine whether the rule being applied in that case
is the same as the current rule of conduct in your jurisdiction.

To Learn More

Judicial ethics could be the subject of an entire course; we have only touched the surface of selected issues in this chapter. To learn more, consult one the following resources:

The ABA Joint Commission to Evaluate the Model Code of Judicial Conduct, http://
www.americanbar.org/groups/professional_responsibility/publications/model_code_of_
judicial_conduct.html. From the commission's website, you can find a complete copy
of the latest version of the ABA Model Code of Judicial Conduct, along with tables
showing which states have adopted the code and tables for each state comparing the
state's version to the ABA Model.

Professor Keith Swisher, of the Phoenix School of Law, has a blog on judicial ethics issues, http://judicialethicsforum.com/, which provides news and commentary of developments in the laws of judicial ethics.

In addition to the law clerk handbook described above, the federal judicial center also
publishes a comprehensive reference on judicial disqualification law. CHARLES GARDNER
GEYH, JUDICIAL DISQUALIFICATION: AN ANALYSIS OF FEDERAL LAW (2nd ed. 2010),
http://www .fjc.gov/public/pdf.nsf/lookup/judicialdq.pdf/$file/judicialdq.pdf.

Unit Six Review

Practice Context Review

You are an attorney at Big Apple, a publicly-traded multinational technology corporation that has employees and offices all over the world. The General Counsel Newt is on a safari in Africa so you are the highest ranking in-house lawyer in the company for the time being. Life couldn't be better for you until ten days ago, when you got a call from the CEO, who showed you the following email that his administrative assistant Amanda Assist had just received:

Hey Former Big Apple Saps,

    I'm one of those disgruntled employees who was laid off last month. You're probably next. But don't worry, I have finally figured out how to get back at all of the guys in the C-Suite with their million dollar bonuses. I'm attaching an email that has a list of everyone's salary, including the hourly people. I've just talked to my lawyer and he tells me that I, and many of you, haven't been paid the right way and the scum at the top have violated wage and hour laws all over the place. I've sent a copy of this email to the folks at the Department of Labor, so prepare for the fun!

Signed,

Anonymous

You decided to initiate an immediate investigation. You conducted a search of all company email to determine whether any other employees have received the email yet and to stop delivery where you can. As it turns out, Amanda was the only the staff member who got the email. The IT staff were thus easily able to track the source of the email and discover the true identity of Anonymous. Anonymous was indeed a former employee. You contacted him and indicated that you would immediately file suit to enjoin his distribution of private company information and would refer him for criminal prosecution if he leaked anything. He appeared to be sufficiently cowed and agreed to keep quiet. He returned the originals of the salary data files he had taken.

In addition to monitoring and reviewing emails and voicemails from a number of key employees, you talked to the following employees in person:

Barack, your CFO, cooperated fully but wanted to know how his stock options would be affected if there were a public investigation. He then asked whether he should get a second mortgage on his house just to have some extra money in place. He also asked whether the company would pay his legal fees if there is an investigation. You told him that he should probably prepare for the value of his stock options to fall some, but that he'd have to decide for himself whether to do anything to get some extra cash. You told him that you were pretty sure that the company's O&D insurance would pay for a defense if he got caught up in an investigation or suit.

You flew to Boston and met Mitt from accounting, who told you that he had heard the rumors about the salary leak. You ask Mitt to keep that information confidential. He also revealed that he has had some undocumented landscapers working on his property and wanted to know if you could give him some advice about how to make this right. You told him he could probably apply for a work visa on their behalf and referred him to an immigration attorney.

Then three days ago, Herman, your head of internal audit, informed you that he just got a call from the Wage and Hour Division of the Department of Labor and he wanted to know what information he should give them. You immediately called in outside counsel for advice about how to prepare for that investigation.

Then yesterday, you were served with a complaint from a group of current and former employees, charging violation of the Fair Labor Standards Act and parallel state laws. Today at 4:30, the attorney for the plaintiff calls and leaves a message. You know the attorney—a notoriously nasty litigator who "takes no prisoners." In his message, he asks if you would like to meet to discuss how to conduct discovery in the case. He tells you that he has hired e-discovery experts and that they have already developed a "thorough and extensive search protocol" that they will be using to request your company's documents. He also says that his secretary is dropping off a notice of his intent to seek a temporary restraining order this afternoon. You race to the receptionist who confirms that, yes, she did just receive an envelope from this attorney's office. When you rip open the envelope, you find a request for a restraining order asking the court to prevent you from "altering or destroying any electronic data related to employee pay." If this is granted, your company will be in big trouble because even paying this week's payroll could certainly be considered "altering" the data.

Furious, you close your door and take a few minutes to calm down and take stock. Have you taken any ethical missteps thus far? What should your next steps be?

Multiple Choice Review

1. Your client is one of several individuals who has been sued for nuisance because of a pollution in a nearby lake. Your client lives upstream from the lake and the property owners around the lake claim that sewage from homes upstream are ruining the fishing and boating in the lake. One of the other defendant property owners is represented by Oscar Overman. You prepare a strategy for pursuing settlement in the action and email it to your client, to Oscar, and to his client. Are you subject to discipline for your communication with Oscar's client?
   A. No, because you copied Oscar, this was not *ex parte* communication.
   B. No, because this is not communication with an adverse party.
   C. No, because Oscar's client did not object.
   D. Yes, because you did not ask for permission from the co-defendant's attorney.

2. You have been hired by ABC Insurance Company to defend Dan Defendant in a products liability action brought by Paula Plaintiff. Paula is represented by Abigail Absent. You have conveyed several settlement offers to Abigail but you suspect they have not been conveyed to Paula. You notice Paula for a deposition. During the deposition, Abigail is present but not paying much attention because she is answering email and working on other cases. You ask Paula if she has received your offers of settlement. She asks you, "What offers?" You explain briefly to her what the current settlement offer is. Paula says, "I'll take it." You explain that she will want to discuss the offer with Abigail. Abigail, finally realizing what has been going on, objects. Paula says, "I can't believe you didn't tell me about this offer. You're fired!" Abigail has filed a disciplinary complaint against you for your actions during the deposition. Are you subject to discipline?

   A. No, because Abigail agreed to the deposition and you did not misrepresent or give Paula legal advice.

   B. No, because Paula fired Abigail.

   C. Yes, because you communicated *ex parte* with Paula about the case.

   D. Yes, because you gave Paula legal advice.

3. Attorney represents plaintiff in a trademark infringement case. A principle issue in the case involves the question of whether the defendant was aware of the defendant's trademark. Attorney has found out that Samantha Swenson, a former secretary to the vice president of marketing, may have been present at a key meeting between her boss and one of the sales agents regarding the trademark. Samantha quit the defendant's company over a year ago and is now retired. Attorney calls Samantha, explains who he is, and she agrees to speak with him. She tells Attorney that plaintiff's trademark never came up in the conversation. Attorney thanks her for her information and says, "I'd really appreciate it if you would not speak to anyone else about this." Attorney says nothing to anyone about Samantha. Is Attorney subject to discipline?

   A. Yes, because he spoke with Samantha without getting opposing counsel's permission.

   B. Yes, because he asked her not to speak with anyone else.

   C. No, because Attorney reasonably believed that Samantha's refraining from speaking with others about the case would not adversely affect her.

   D. No, because she was no longer employed by the company and Attorney did not mislead her about his role.

4. Attorney represents Clarence in a criminal trial. During the lunch break, Attorney and Clarence are about to get on the courthouse elevator, when they recognize that the person already in the elevator is a juror in the case. They step onto the elevator and ride the eight floors to the basement, where the courthouse cafeteria is located. They say hello to the juror and ask her if she plans on eating in the cafeteria. They talk briefly about cafeteria food and do not discuss the trial. When they step off the elevator, the prosecutor sees them. Is Attorney subject to discipline?

   A. Yes, because Clarence was with him when they communicated with a juror.

   B. Yes, because he contacted a juror during the course of a trial.

   C. No, because they did not discuss the trial.

   D. No, because he talked to the juror in a public place.

5. Attorney Georgina worked as a law clerk for Judge. During Georgina's one-year clerkship Judge presided over the *Green v. Brown* case. As a clerk to Judge on this case, Georgina wrote jury instructions, prepared legal memoranda, and scheduled motion hearings for this matter. The jury entered a verdict for Brown. Subsequently, Georgina was hired as an associate attorney by the Smith, Westfield law firm. Smith, Westfield is representing Brown on appeal. Georgina has been assigned to assist a partner in writing Brown's appellate brief. Is Georgina subject to discipline?
   A. Yes, because the prior case is concluded and is a matter of public record.
   B. Yes, because she had substantial responsibility for the matter while working as a law clerk.
   C. No, because she is working under the supervision of another attorney.
   D. No, as a law clerk, Georgina is permitted to accept employment even if it involves cases she worked on as a clerk.

6. Judge Jane has a complicated unfair competition case before her. She simply doesn't understand the plaintiff's argument in the motion for summary judgment. She asks her law clerk to research the issue and prepare a memo explaining the confusing issue. The law clerk says, "I'm taking a class from Professor Patenta about that subject right now!" Judge Jane says, "Great. See if she has any suggestions." The clerk takes a copy of the motion to her professor, who gives advice on how to approach the issue and a number of sources of research. Judge Jane denies the motion. Plaintiff learns of the clerk's discussion of the case with the law professor and files a complaint with the judicial disciplinary agency. Is Judge Jane subject to discipline?
   A. No, because a judge is permitted to consult with law clerks about pending matters.
   B. No, because she did not directly communicate with Professor Patenta.
   C. Yes, because she did not give notice to the attorneys that she had told her clerk to contact Patenta.
   D. Yes, because her clerk gave confidential information to Professor Patenta.

Answer and Analysis

1. The correct answer is D. Answer A's assumption that the rule only applies to *ex parte* communications is not correct—the rule does not make any such distinction. B is false because, again, it reads a limiting assumption into the rules that is not there. C is a common misconception about Rule 4.2, but because the rule is to prevent overreaching by attorneys, allowing client consent to be an exception would defeat that protection.

2. The correct answer is A. C is not correct—this was not an *ex parte* communication because Abigail was there. Even if you interpreted her distraction as somehow turning this into an *ex parte* communication, Abigail had given her permission by having Paula appear for the deposition. The fact that Paula fired Abigail (answer B) is irrelevant here, because that happened after the discussion. Answer D is not correct because describing the settlement was not legal advice.

3. This problem asks about two issues—whether it was appropriate for attorney to speak with Samantha without opposing counsel's permission (as suggested by answer A). On that, the answer is yes, because Samantha is a former employee of the defendant. So if that were the only issue in the hypothetical, the correct answer would be D. But there is a second issue—the attorney's request that she

not speak to anyone else. That statement violates Rule 3.4(f) so answer B is correct. Answer C suggests an exception to the rule that only applies to relatives, employees, or other agents of the client.

4.   The correct answer is B. Rule 3.5 prohibits contact with jurors, not only by the litigant but by the attorney as well. It doesn't matter what they talked about or where.

5.   The correct answer is B. Rule 1.12. The conflict rule there applies to law clerks just as it would any other former court official. Answer A ignores the fact that prior cases can create conflicts. Answer C presumes that only one attorney can be subject to discipline at a time, which we know is not true. Rule 5.2. Answer D refers to the law clerk exception to the general rule in 1.12 that prohibits interviewing for employment. That exception applies only to interviewing, not to representation.

6.   The correct answer is C. A is a correct statement of the rule, but doesn't identify the correct issue — the problem was talking with the professor not the clerk. B is not correct because, just as attorneys can violate the rules by acting through another, so too judges cannot circumvent the rules on *ex parte* contact by working through their law clerks. D is simply off base. The clerk gave the professor a motion filed with the court — not confidential information. It was the process of *ex parte* communication regarding the case, not the substance of the conversation, that violated the rules.

Unit Seven

Access to Justice

Goals of Unit

In this unit we will revisit some of the same issues we examined in Unit One regarding the impact of attorney regulation, except here through the lens of how that regulation makes legal services more or less affordable and accessible. We will also review how those regulations impact your own practice.

Pre-Test

Test your assumptions about attorney regulation and the affordability and accessibility of legal services by answering the following questions.

1. When do individuals have a constitutional right to counsel?

2. What are the sources of an attorney's obligation to provide legal assistance to individuals who cannot afford representation?

3. How does the regulation of attorney professional responsibility facilitate or limit access to affordable legal services?

4. What is the definition of the practice of law?

5. Do restrictions on unauthorized practice of law apply when the person who is providing legal services is not charging for them?

6. How do most people find an attorney?

7. What are the governmental interests that justify restrictions on attorney advertising and solicitation of clients?

Chapter Twenty-Four

Making Law Affordable and Accessible

Learning Objectives

After you have read this chapter and completed the assignments, you should be able to:

- Describe the constitutional right to legal representation and the problems present in the current systems used to provide that representation.
- Describe the system of legal services representation in the United States.
- Explain an attorney's obligation to accept court-appointed representation and the bases upon which an attorney may properly avoid such an appointment.
- Locate and analyze local court rules that provide for appointment of attorneys.
- Define unbundled or limited scope representation and describe the risks and benefits of providing this type of representation.
- Describe the ways in which the structure and regulation of the legal profession influences the accessibility of legal services, including the relationship between the professional monopoly and the attorney's duty to provide pro bono and appointed representation; the ways in which standards of competence and diligence become modified in order to encourage attorneys to increase access to representation; and the ways in which conflict of interest standards become modified in order to encourage attorneys to increase access to representation.

Rules to Study

In addition to constitutional standards for the right to counsel, we will review Rules 6.0–6.5 and revisit several rules of conduct we have previously studied including 1.1, 1.2, and 1.3.

Preliminary Problem

In 1956, the Supreme Court observed that "there can be no equal justice where the kind of trial a man gets depends on the amount of money he has." *Griffin v. Illinois*, 351 U.S. 12 (1956).

Suppose you have been approached to become part of the staff of a non-profit corporation that provides a variety of services, including shelter, to homeless individuals and also engages in community outreach to prevent mortgage foreclosures and evictions. Your job would involve providing legal representation for the individuals who receive services from the corporation. You would also supervise a "law day" program in which volunteer attorneys and law students would come to the shelter and provide limited legal services such as help in completing applications for various government assistance programs or advice regarding matters such as child support or misdemeanor warrants.

You would be a salaried employee of the corporation. Your salary would be funded by a separate grant to the corporation from a large charitable entity. The grant is specifically conditioned on its being used to hire a full-time staff attorney to provide legal services. Neither you nor the organization will charge the individual client a fee for the legal services provided. Sometimes, however, the actions you would bring would be under statutes that provide for fee shifting, so that awards might be made to you for the value of your services when actions are successful.

The organization's Board's stated policy is (1) it will not interfere in the attorney-client relationship between you and any individual to whom you provide legal services and (2) it will not in any way impose restrictions on your exercise of professional judgment regarding the handling of a particular case. Each individual whom you would represent will sign an engagement agreement specifying that the organization is not undertaking to give legal advice or represent the individual and that the attorney-client relationship is only between you and the individual. You have agreed to remit all fees recovered under fee-shifting awards to the organization.

What concerns might you have about the effectiveness or ethics of such an arrangement?

24.1 The Need for Legal Services

In 1994, the American Bar Association undertook a large-scale national survey of the legal needs of Americans, examining the kinds of legal needs Americans have and the steps they take (and do not take) to deal with those needs. This Comprehensive Legal Needs Study[1] defined moderate income households as those with yearly incomes ranging from 125 percent above the federal poverty line to $60,000. Low income households, which are eligible for free legal services, were defined as those with yearly incomes less than 125 percent of the poverty line. The report found that about half of both low and moderate income persons reported legal needs during the year of the study.

These legal needs (for both groups) most commonly related to housing and personal finances and to domestic and family law matters. However, of those with legal needs, only 39

---

1. AMERICAN BAR ASSOCIATION, LEGAL NEEDS AND CIVIL JUSTICE—A SURVEY OF AMERICANS (1994), available at http://www.americanbar.org/content/dam/aba/migrated/legalservices/downloads/sclaid/legalneedstudy.authcheckdam.pdf.

percent of moderate income households and 29 percent of low income households looked to attorneys to solve their needs. Those who did use attorneys to solve their problems reported substantially greater satisfaction than those who tried to address their legal needs on their own or through non-lawyers. Many of the legal needs of moderate and low income families are surprisingly similar. Ten percent of moderate income households had legal needs relating to housing or real estate, as did thirteen percent of low income households. Thirteen percent of both types of households had legal needs relating to personal finances.

More recent studies have found that the situation presented in the 1994 study has only worsened. For example, a report commissioned by the Chief Judge of the state of New York made the following findings:

> Each year, more than 2.3 million New Yorkers try to navigate the State's complex civil justice system without a lawyer. The current statistics are staggering, to cite a few:
>
> > 99 percent of tenants are unrepresented in eviction cases in New York City, and 98 percent are unrepresented outside of the City.
> >
> > 99 percent of borrowers are unrepresented in hundreds of thousands of consumer credit cases filed each year in New York City.
> >
> > 97 percent of parents are unrepresented in child support matters in New York City, and 95 percent are unrepresented in the rest of the State; and
> >
> > 44 percent of home owners are unrepresented in foreclosure cases throughout our State.
>
> Seventy percent of civil matters in New York State courts involve family law, consumer credit, landlord-tenant and foreclosure cases. Our courtrooms often are standing room only, with frightened, unrepresented litigants who face the loss of a home, a job, and even a child. Judges report that many valid claims are lost, because the unrepresented often do not present evidence or understand the law.
>
> As a result of the deep recession, which has increased the number of children and adults living in poverty in the Empire State, this crisis of the unrepresented has reached a breaking point. Judges report a substantial increase in the number of unrepresented litigants who have recently become low income. At the same time, funding for civil legal services has declined dramatically, with the Interest on Lawyers Account Fund of New York State ("IOLA") — a critical source of funding — falling with interest rates from close to $32 million annually to less than $8 million (40 cents per person) in a State with nearly 20 million people.
>
> This crisis of the unrepresented adversely impacts everyone in our State, from the strongest financial institution to the most vulnerable child. For those on the other side of the unrepresented — landlords, banks, and other businesses — litigation and other costs are higher, and the opportunity to avoid disputes through mediation and settlement often is lost. Because Judges and court personnel must spend tens of thousands of hours trying to assist the unrepresented in navigating our complex court system, our courts have become less efficient, and the quality of justice has suffered for every New Yorker, including in cases between represented parties.

TASK FORCE TO EXPAND ACCESS TO CIVIL LEGAL SERVICES IN NEW YORK, REPORT TO THE CHIEF JUDGE OF THE STATE OF NEW YORK 1 (November 23, 2010).

How can these legal needs be met? In this chapter we will examine a number of approaches to make legal services accessible and affordable. We will first examine those classes of cases in which legal representation is required as a matter of due process. We will then turn to the attorney's responsibilities and opportunities to accepted appointed representation. Using the example of limited scope representation we will explore how regulation of attorneys can be relaxed to increase availability of legal services. Finally we will examine more broadly other ways in which the structure of the legal profession and its regulation impact the availability of legal services.

24.2 The Right to Counsel

> It is not to be thought of, in a civilized community, for a moment, that any citizen put in jeopardy of life or liberty should be debarred of counsel because he was too poor to employ such aid. No Court could be respected, or respect itself, to sit and hear such a trial. The defence of the poor in such cases is a duty resting somewhere, which will be at once conceded as essential to the accused, to the Court, and to the public.

Webb v. Baird, 6 Ind. 13, 18 (1854).

With this reasoning, the Supreme Court of Indiana first determined that an indigent criminal defendant had a right to publicly financed counsel, a decision well ahead of its time. In the over 150 years since that case, the right to appointed counsel has grown from nascent recognition of the constitutional right in criminal cases to statutory and state constitutional guarantees in a broad range of civil settings. While the Sixth Amendment to the United States Constitution provides that "In all criminal prosecutions, the accused shall enjoy the right ... to have the Assistance of Counsel for his defence," the United States Supreme Court did not address the parameters of this right until the twentieth century. In its first opportunity to do so, in *Powell v. Alabama,* 287 U.S. 45 (1932), the Court held that the Fourteenth Amendment did not incorporate the Sixth Amendment right so as to require states to guarantee counsel to criminal defendants. However, the Court did conclude that as a matter of basic due process, indigent criminal defendants in state capital cases must be appointed counsel. The court explained the importance of counsel to due process:

> The right to be heard would be, in many cases, of little avail if it did not comprehend the right to be heard by counsel. Even the intelligent and educated layman has small and sometimes no skill in the science of law. If charged with crime, he is incapable, generally, of determining for himself whether the indictment is good or bad. He is unfamiliar with the rules of evidence. Left without the aid of counsel he may be put on trial without a proper charge, and convicted upon incompetent evidence, or evidence irrelevant to the issue or otherwise inadmissible. He lacks both the skill and knowledge adequately to prepare his defense, even though he have a perfect one. He requires the guiding hand of counsel at every step in the proceedings against him. Without it, though he be not guilty, he faces the danger of conviction because he does not know how to establish his innocence. If that be true of men of intelligence, how much more true is it of the ignorant and illiterate, or those of feeble intellect. If in any case, civil or criminal, a state or federal court were arbitrarily to refuse to hear a party by counsel, employed by and appearing for him, it reasonably may not be doubted that such a refusal would be a denial of a hearing, and, therefore, of due process in the constitutional sense.... The duty of the trial court to appoint counsel under such circumstances is clear, as it is clear under circumstances such as are disclosed by the record here; and its power to do so, even in the absence

of a statute, can not be questioned. Attorneys are officers of the court, and are bound to render service when required by such an appointment.

Powell, 287 U.S. at 69, 73.

However, ten years later, in *Betts v. Brady*, 316 U.S. 455 (1942), the Court refused to extend this holding to state felony proceedings. It was not until the 1960s that the Court recognized a more general due process right to counsel for criminal defendants in state proceedings. In *Gideon v. Wainwright*, 372 U.S. 335 (1963), the Court overruled *Betts*, and held that the right to be appointed counsel was essential for a fair trial of an indigent criminal defendant accused of serious crimes. The right to counsel was extended to defendants in misdemeanor state proceedings who are faced with a potential loss of liberty in *Argersinger v. Hamlin*, 407 U.S. 25 (1972).

Delinquency proceedings, which are not criminal proceedings per se, often result in juveniles being confined to detention facilities. Accordingly, the Supreme Court in *In re Gault*, 387 U.S. 1 (1967), recognized a right to counsel for these children. Likewise, individuals facing involuntary commitment proceedings clearly face a loss of liberty. However, in *Vitek v. Jones*, 445 U.S. 480 (1980), only four of five justices reaching the merits concluded that a right to counsel exists before being involuntarily committed to a state mental hospital. The fifth justice agreed that some representation was necessary, but indicated that lay counsel may be sufficient.

In civil actions brought by the government, particularly those actions in which the state is exercising its *parens patriae* authority to intervene in a family, the constitutional interests of the parties seem closer to those of the criminal defendant than the civil plaintiff, even though there may be no threat of incarceration. Advocates have had some limited success in establishing a Fourteenth Amendment right to counsel for children and their parents in civil actions based on abuse and neglect and in other family law matters. However, the success has largely been on a case-by-case basis and through legislative efforts.

In *Lassiter v. Department of Social Services*, 452 U.S. 18 (1981), the United States Supreme Court faced the question of whether an indigent parent facing a possible termination of her parental rights had a right to appointed counsel. The Court held that there was no absolute right to counsel in these types of cases. Rather, the Court concluded that due process might, in an individual case, require appointed counsel and that the decision must be made on a case-by-case basis. The right to counsel is determined by applying the three-part due process calculus of *Matthews v. Eldridge*, 424 U.S. 319, 335 (1976), in which the court weighs the state's interest against the private interest implicated and the risk of erroneous decision. The Court in *Lassiter* required that this balance operate in the context of a presumption against the right to counsel absent a threat to physical liberty. *Lassiter*, 452 U.S. at 27. Thus indigent parents and children in the federal courts must establish their right to counsel on a case-by-case basis. *Fowler v. Jones*, 899 F.2d 1088, 1096 (11th Cir. 1990); *United States v. Madden*, 352 F.2d 792, 793 (9th Cir. 1965).

However, most states do recognize the right to counsel for parents in these cases, either in their state constitution, by statute, or through judicial decisions. Some states also require that parents be provided counsel in dependency (abuse and neglect) actions short of termination of parental rights proceedings. Studies have demonstrated dramatically improved outcomes when lawyers are guaranteed to parents in child welfare proceedings. Those outcomes include reunification rates increasing by over 50%, termination of rights decreasing by 45%, foster children aging out of the system decreasing by 50%, and significantly shorter periods of time for children in foster care. Vivek S. Sankaran, *A Hidden Crisis: The Need to Strengthen Representation of Parents in Child Protective Proceeding*, 89 Mich. B. J. 36, 38 (2010).

Similarly, federal law requires that states provide guardian *ad litem* (GAL) representation to children in abuse and neglect actions. Child Abuse Prevention and Treatment Act, 42 U.S.C. §5106a(b)(2)(A)(xiii) (2012). In many states, those guardians must be attorneys, and a few states provide children an attorney to represent them directly, rather than representing their "best interests" as does the GAL. Other areas of family law in which appointed counsel is commonly required include domestic violence, custody, paternity, and even divorces in some circumstances. Laura K. Abel & Max Rettig, *State Statutes Providing for a Right to Counsel in Civil Cases*, 40 CLEARINGHOUSE REV. 245, 246 (July-Aug. 2006) (collecting statutes).

Despite the trend at the state level toward increasing recognition of the right to counsel in civil cases, the United States Supreme Court recently once again rejected a claim for a categorical right to court appointed defense counsel. Read the court's opinion on this issue and try to determine what the court held and what it did not hold. Do you think the opinion is a victory or a defeat for those who advocate for a broader right to counsel in civil cases?

Turner v. Rogers

564 U.S. ___, 131 S. Ct. 2507 (2011).

Justice Breyer delivered the opinion of the Court.

I—A.

South Carolina family courts enforce their child support orders in part through civil contempt proceedings. Each month the family court clerk reviews outstanding child support orders, identifies those in which the supporting parent has fallen more than five days behind, and sends that parent an order to "show cause" why he should not be held in contempt. S.C. Rule Family Ct. 24 (2011). The "show cause" order and attached affidavit refer to the relevant child support order, identify the amount of the arrearage, and set a date for a court hearing. At the hearing that parent may demonstrate that he is not in contempt, say, by showing that he is not able to make the required payments.... If he fails to make the required showing, the court may hold him in civil contempt. And it may require that he be imprisoned unless and until he purges himself of contempt by making the required child support payments (but not for more than one year regardless). *See* S.C. Code Ann. §63–3–620 (Supp. 2010) (imprisonment for up to one year of "adult who wilfully violates" a court order); *Price* v. *Turner*, 387 S.C. 142, 145, 691 S.E.2d 470, 472 (2010) (civil contempt order must permit purging of contempt through compliance).

Consequence of not paying child supp. [handwritten margin note]

This ability to pay and be released is what makes this "civil" contempt rather than "criminal" contempt — though to the person in jail it likely feels the same. [margin note]

B.

[Michael Turner had been ordered to pay $51.73 a week to Rebecca Rogers to help support their child. After repeatedly falling behind, getting caught up, and then falling behind again, Turner was sentenced to six months in a civil contempt judgment. After he was released, he was still in arrears and he was again served with a civil contempt "show cause" order. Neither he nor Rebecca were represented.]

The hearing was brief. The court clerk said that Turner was $5,728.76 behind in his payments. The judge asked Turner if there was "anything you want to say." Turner replied,

> "Well, when I first got out, I got back on dope. I done meth, smoked pot and everything else, and I paid a little bit here and there. And, when I finally did get to working, I broke my back, back in September. I filed for disability and SSI. And, I didn't get straightened out off the dope until I broke my back and laid up for two months. And, now I'm off the dope and everything. I just hope that you give me a chance. I don't know what else to say. I mean, I know I done wrong, and I should have been paying and helping her, and I'm sorry. I mean, dope had a hold to me."

App. to Pet. for Cert. 17a.

The judge then said, "[o]kay," and asked Rogers if she had anything to say. *Ibid.* After a brief discussion of federal benefits, the judge stated,

> "If there's nothing else, this will be the Order of the Court. I find the Defendant in willful contempt. I'm [going to] sentence him to twelve months in the Oconee County Detention Center. He may purge himself of the contempt and avoid the sentence by having a zero balance on or before his release. I've also placed a lien on any SSI or other benefits."

Id. at 18a.

The judge added that Turner would not receive good-time or work credits, but "[i]f you've got a job, I'll make you eligible for work release." *Ibid.* When Turner asked why he could not receive good-time or work credits, the judge said, "[b]ecause that's my ruling." *Ibid.*

The court made no express finding concerning Turner's ability to pay his arrearage (though Turner's wife had voluntarily submitted a copy of Turner's application for disability benefits). Nor did the judge ask any follow up questions or otherwise address the ability-to-pay issue. After the hearing, the judge filled out a prewritten form titled "Order for Contempt of Court," which included the statement: "Defendant (was) (was not) gainfully employed and/or (had) (did not have) the ability to make these support payments when due." *Id.* at 60a, 61a. But the judge left this statement as is without indicating whether Turner was able to make support payments.

C.

While serving his 12-month sentence, Turner, with the help of *pro bono* counsel, appealed. He claimed that the Federal Constitution entitled him to counsel at his contempt hearing. The South Carolina Supreme Court decided Turner's appeal after he had completed his sentence. And it rejected his "right to counsel" claim. The court pointed out that civil contempt differs significantly from criminal contempt. The former does not require all the "constitutional safeguards" applicable in criminal proceedings. 387 S.C., at 145, 691 S.E.2d, at 472. And the right to government-paid counsel, the Supreme Court held, was one of the "safeguards" not required. *Ibid.*

Turner sought certiorari. In light of differences among state courts (and some federal courts) on the applicability of a "right to counsel" in civil contempt proceedings enforcing child support orders, we granted the writ....

III-A

We must decide whether the Due Process Clause grants an indigent defendant, such as Turner, a right to state-appointed counsel at a civil contempt proceeding, which may lead to his incarceration. This Court's precedents provide no definitive answer to that question. [The Court then reviews the cases involving the right to counsel in criminal and civil matters].

B.

Civil contempt proceedings in child support cases constitute one part of a highly complex system designed to assure a noncustodial parent's regular payment of funds typically necessary for the support of his children. Often the family receives welfare support from a state-administered federal program, and the State then seeks reimbursement from the noncustodial parent. *See* 42 U.S.C. §§ 608(a)(3) (2006 ed., Supp. III), 656(a)(1) (2006 ed.); S.C. Code Ann. §§ 43–5–65(a)(1), (2) (2010 Cum. Supp.). Other times the custodial parent (often the mother, but sometimes the father, a grandparent, or another person with custody) does not receive government benefits and is entitled to receive the support payments herself.

The Federal Government has created an elaborate procedural mechanism designed to help both the government and custodial parents to secure the payments to which they are entitled. *See generally, Blessing v. Freestone*, 520 U.S. 329, 333 (1997) (describing the "interlocking set of cooperative federal-state welfare programs" as they relate to child support enforcement); 45 C.F.R. pt. 303 (2010) (prescribing standards for state child support agencies). These systems often rely upon wage withholding, expedited procedures for modifying and enforcing child support orders, and automated data processing. 42 U.S.C. §§ 666(a), (b), 654(24). But sometimes States will use contempt orders to ensure that the custodial parent receives support payments or the government receives reimbursement. Although some experts have criticized this last-mentioned procedure, and the Federal Government believes that "the routine use of contempt for non-payment of child support is likely to be an ineffective strategy," the Government also tells us that "coercive enforcement remedies, such as contempt, have a role to play." Brief for United States as Amicus Curiae 21–22, and n. 8 (citing Dept. of Health and Human Services, National Child Support Enforcement, Strategic Plan: FY 2005–2009, pp. 2, 10). South Carolina, which relies heavily on contempt proceedings, agrees that they are an important tool.

We here consider an indigent's right to paid counsel at such a contempt proceeding. It is a civil proceeding. And we consequently determine the "specific dictates of due process" by examining the "distinct factors" that this Court has previously found useful in deciding what specific safeguards the Constitution's Due Process Clause requires in order to make a civil proceeding fundamentally fair. *Mathews v. Eldridge*, 424 U.S. 319, 335 (1976) (considering fairness of an administrative proceeding). As relevant here those factors include (1) the nature of "the private interest that will be affected," (2) the comparative "risk" of an "erroneous deprivation" of that interest with and without

[Margin note:] Why is this background important to determining whether there is a right to counsel?

[Handwritten margin note:] gov't admits ineffective practice, but still says it has a role to play

[Handwritten margin note:] Rule for Due process

"additional or substitute procedural safeguards," and (3) the nature and magnitude of any countervailing interest in not providing "additional or substitute procedural requirement[s]." *Ibid.*

The "private interest that will be affected" argues strongly for the right to counsel that Turner advocates. That interest consists of an indigent defendant's loss of personal liberty through imprisonment. The interest in securing that freedom, the freedom "from bodily restraint," lies "at the core of the liberty protected by the Due Process Clause." *Foucha v. Louisiana*, 504 U.S. 71, 80 (1992). And we have made clear that its threatened loss through legal proceedings demands "due process protection." *Addington v. Texas*, 441 U.S. 418, 425 (1979).

Given the importance of the interest at stake, it is obviously important to assure accurate decision making in respect to the key "ability to pay" question. Moreover, the fact that ability to comply marks a dividing line between civil and criminal contempt reinforces the need for accuracy. That is because an incorrect decision (wrongly classifying the contempt proceeding as civil) can increase the risk of wrongful incarceration by depriving the defendant of the procedural protections (including counsel) that the Constitution would demand in a criminal proceeding. And since 70% of child support arrears nationwide are owed by parents with either no reported income or income of $10,000 per year or less, the issue of ability to pay may arise fairly often.

On the other hand, the Due Process Clause does not always require the provision of counsel in civil proceedings where incarceration is threatened. *See Gagnon v. Scarpelli*, 411 U.S. 778 (1973)[parole revocation hearings]. And in determining whether the Clause requires a right to counsel here, we must take account of opposing interests, as well as consider the probable value of "additional or substitute procedural safeguards." *Mathews, supra*, at 335.

Doing so, we find three related considerations that, when taken together, argue strongly against the Due Process Clause requiring the State to provide indigents with counsel in every proceeding of the kind before us.

First, the critical question likely at issue in these cases concerns, as we have said, the defendant's ability to pay. That question is often closely related to the question of the defendant's indigence. But when the right procedures are in place, indigence can be a question that in many—but not all—cases is sufficiently straightforward to warrant determination prior to providing a defendant with counsel, even in a criminal case. Federal law, for example, requires a criminal defendant to provide information showing that he is indigent, and therefore entitled to state-funded counsel, before he can receive that assistance. *See* 18 U.S.C. § 3006A(b).

Second, sometimes, as here, the person opposing the defendant at the hearing is not the government represented by counsel but the custodial parent unrepresented by counsel. *See* Dept. of Health and Human Services, Office of Child Support Enforcement, Understanding Child Support Debt: A Guide to Exploring Child Support Debt in Your State 5, 6 (2004) (51% of nationwide arrears, and 58% in South Carolina, are not owed to the government). The custodial parent, perhaps a woman with custody of one or more children, may be relatively poor, unemployed, and unable to afford counsel. Yet she may have encouraged the court to enforce its order through contempt. *Cf.* Tr. Contempt Proceedings (Sept. 14, 2005), App. 44a–45a (Rogers asks court, in light of pattern of nonpayment, to confine Turner). She may be able to provide the court with significant information. *Cf. id.,* at 41a–43a (Rogers describes where Turner lived and worked). And the proceeding is ultimately for her benefit.

A requirement that the State provide counsel to the noncustodial parent in these cases could create an asymmetry of representation that would "alter significantly the nature of the proceeding." *Gagnon, supra,* at 787. Doing so could mean a degree of formality or delay that would unduly slow payment to those immediately in need. And, perhaps more important for present purposes, doing so could make the proceedings less fair overall, increasing the risk of a decision that would erroneously deprive a family of the support it is entitled to receive. The needs of such families play an important role in our analysis. *Cf. post,* at 10–12 (opinion of Thomas, J.).

Third, as the Solicitor General points out, there is available a set of "substitute procedural safeguards," *Mathews,* 424 U.S. at 335, which, if employed together, can significantly reduce the risk of an erroneous deprivation of liberty. They can do so, moreover, without incurring some of the drawbacks inherent in recognizing an automatic right to counsel. Those safeguards include (1) notice to the defendant that his "ability to pay" is a critical issue in the contempt proceeding; (2) the use of a form (or the equivalent) to elicit relevant financial information; (3) an opportunity at the hearing for the defendant to respond to statements and questions about his financial status, (e.g., those triggered by his responses on the form); and (4) an express finding by the court that the defendant has the ability to pay. *See* Tr. of Oral Arg. 26–27; Brief for United States as Amicus Curiae 23–25. In presenting these alternatives, the Government draws upon considerable experience in helping to manage statutorily mandated federal-state efforts to enforce child support orders. *See supra,* at 10. It does not claim that they are the only possible alternatives, and this Court's cases suggest, for example, that sometimes assistance other than purely legal assistance (here, say, that of a neutral social worker) can prove constitutionally sufficient. *Cf. Vitek,* 445 U.S., at 499–500 (Powell, J., concurring in part) (provision of mental health professional). But the Government does claim that these alternatives can assure the "fundamental fairness" of the proceeding even where the State does not pay for counsel for an indigent defendant.

While recognizing the strength of Turner's arguments, we ultimately believe that the three considerations we have just discussed must carry the day. In our view, a categorical right to counsel in proceedings of the kind before us would carry with it disadvantages (in the form of unfairness and delay) that, in terms of ultimate fairness, would deprive it of significant superiority over the alternatives that we have mentioned. We consequently hold that the Due Process Clause does not automatically require the provision of counsel at civil contempt proceedings to an indigent individual who is subject to a child support order, even if that individual faces incarceration (for up to a year). In particular, that Clause does not require the provision of counsel where the opposing parent or other custodian (to whom support funds are owed) is not represented by counsel and the State provides alternative procedural safeguards equivalent to those we have mentioned (adequate notice of the importance of ability to pay, fair opportunity to present, and to dispute, relevant information, and court findings).

We do not address civil contempt proceedings where the underlying child support payment is owed to the State, for example, for reimbursement of welfare funds paid to the parent with custody. *See supra,* at 10. Those proceedings more closely resemble debt-collection proceedings. The government is likely to have counsel or some other competent representative. *Cf. Johnson v. Zerbst,* 304 U.S. 458, 462–463 (1938) ("[T]he average defendant does not have the professional legal skill to protect himself when brought before a tribunal with power to take his life or liberty, wherein the prosecution is presented by experienced and learned counsel" (emphasis added)). And this kind of proceeding is not before us. Neither do we address what due process requires in an unusually complex case where a defendant "can fairly be represented only by a trained advocate." *Gagnon,* 411 U.S. at 788; *see also* Reply Brief for Petitioner 18–20 (not claiming that Turner's case is especially complex).

Can ordinary debt collectors use the threat of jail to enforce their debts?

What would an unusually complex case be?

IV

The record indicates that Turner received neither counsel nor the benefit of alternative procedures like those we have described. He did not receive clear notice that his ability to pay would constitute the critical question in his civil contempt proceeding. No one provided him with a form (or the equivalent) designed to elicit information about his financial circumstances. The court did not find that Turner was able to pay his arrearage, but instead left the relevant "finding" section of the contempt order blank. The court nonetheless found Turner in contempt and ordered him incarcerated. Under these circumstances Turner's incarceration violated the Due Process Clause.

We vacate the judgment of the South Carolina Supreme Court and remand the case for further proceedings not inconsistent with this opinion.

Notes

1. *Turner* was a 5-4 decision. Justices Kennedy, Ginsburg, Sotomayor, and Kagan joined the majority opinion written by Justice Breyer. Justice Thomas, joined by Justice Scalia, agreed with the majority that there was no right to counsel in civil contempt actions because, under their interpretation, "as originally understood, the Sixth Amendment guaranteed only the 'right to employ counsel, or to use volunteered services of counsel'; it did not require the court to appoint counsel in any circumstance." Chief Justice Roberts and Justice Alito joined that portion of Justice Thomas's dissent that took a narrower alternative approach in emphasizing that, even if there is a right to appointed counsel in criminal actions, there is certainly no such right in civil cases. All four dissenting judges agreed that the issue of whether due process required more notice and opportunity to be heard in the contempt proceeding was one that was raised for the first time by amicus on appeal and thus was not properly before the court.

2. Test your understanding of this case by arguing for or against the right to counsel in an action for civil contempt brought by a state child support enforcement agency. Can you use *Turner* to support the position of either side? Given the opinion and the positions of the dissenting judges, along with

the other recent decisions of the court, how would you predict the development of the law in this area? How would your arguments change if you were advocating for or against a legislative proposal to require counsel in these cases?

24.3 Reading the Rules: Pro Bono and Appointed Representation

Historically, when the constitution, courts, or legislature determined that an individual had a right to counsel, that counsel was provided by the court's appointment of an attorney, and the attorney's representation was often without compensation. Today, states provide criminal defense attorneys through state funded public defender systems; however, the need for appointed representation continues in a range of cases. Read Missouri's version of Rule 6.2 which describes the attorney's duty to accept these appointments:

Missouri Supreme Court Rule 4-6.2
Missouri Rules of Professional Conduct.

A lawyer shall not seek to avoid appointment by a tribunal to represent a person except for good cause, such as:

(a) representing the client is likely to result in violation of the Rules of Professional Conduct or other law;

(b) representing the client is likely to result in an unreasonable financial burden on the lawyer; or

(c) the client or the cause is so repugnant to the lawyer as to be likely to impair the client-lawyer relationship or the lawyer's ability to represent the client.

COMMENT

[1] A lawyer ordinarily is not obliged to accept a client whose character or cause the lawyer regards as repugnant. The lawyer's freedom to select clients is, however, qualified. All lawyers have a responsibility to assist in providing pro bono publico service. See Rule 4-6.1. An individual lawyer fulfills this responsibility by accepting a fair share of unpopular matters or indigent or unpopular clients. A lawyer may also be subject to appointment by a court to serve unpopular clients or persons unable to afford legal services.

[2] For good cause a lawyer may seek to decline an appointment to represent a person who cannot afford to retain counsel or whose cause is unpopular. Good cause exists if the lawyer could not handle the matter competently, see Rule 4-1.1, or if undertaking the representation would result in an improper conflict of interest, for example, when the client or the cause is so repugnant to the lawyer as to be likely to impair the client-lawyer relationship or the lawyer's ability to represent the client. A lawyer may also seek to decline an appointment if acceptance would be unreasonably burdensome, for example, when it would impose a financial sacrifice so great as to be unjust.

[3] An appointed lawyer has the same obligations to the client as retained counsel, including the obligations of loyalty and confidentiality, and is subject

to the same limitations on the client-lawyer relationship, such as the obligation to refrain from assisting the client in violation of the Rules.

Context

Most states have adopted some version of the American Bar Association's Model Rule of Professional Conduct 6.1. States have significant variations on the rule, from California and Oregon, which have no counterpart at all, to Florida, which has a mandatory pro bono rule. Judith L. Maute, *Pro Bono Publico in Oklahoma: Time for Change,* 52 Oĸ. L. Rev. 527, 572 (2000). The language is hortatory, directing but not mandating that attorneys provide free or reduced-cost service to persons of limited means. The title of the rule emphasizes that pro bono service is "voluntary" and the operative word throughout is "should," not "shall." The use of this language, and the notes accompanying the rule, confirm that the rule is not meant to be the basis for disciplinary action. If a court appoints an attorney to provide this representation, aspirational goals become enforceable obligations. *Weiner v. Fulton County,* 148 S.E.2d 143 (Ga. Ct. App. 1966), *cert. denied,* 385 U.S. 958 (1966).

[margin handwriting: discipline rare but possible if ct. appoints you to client]

Relationship

The good cause bases for seeking to avoid an appointment parallel the bases for withdrawal under Rule 1.16, but are narrower than that rule. However, Rule 6.2(a) permits withdrawal if an attorney's appointment would cause her to violate the rules. Continuing to represent a client when Rule 1.16(a) requires withdrawal would be one such violation. Of course Rule 1.16 does require an attorney to seek the permission of a court to withdraw if required by court rules. Can a court refuse a withdrawal from an appointment that would otherwise be mandatory under Rule 1.16(a)?

[margin handwriting: R1.16 on withdrawal may apply]

The issue most commonly arises when an attorney seeks to avoid an appointment on the basis that she is not competent to undertake the representation. While your license to practice allows you to practice all areas of law, that does not mean you will be competent to do so. Attorneys can seek to be excused from appointment on the grounds of competence. *Easley v. State,* 334 So. 2d 630 (Fla. Dist. Ct. App. 1976) (counsel cannot be held in contempt for attempting to withdraw as appointed counsel for defendant on grounds of incompetence). Remember, however, that one can become competent in many instances with appropriate preparation and courts will not excuse an attorney simply because he or she is unwilling, rather than unable, to put in the required preparation. *Reese v. Owens-Corning Fiberglass,* 962 F. Supp. 1418 (D. Kan. 1997).

[margin handwriting: withdrawal: incompetence ok]
[margin handwriting: must be unable, not unwilling]

If a court determines that you are competent to continue an appointment, that determination can provide a safe harbor from discipline for incompetence. A further refusal to represent the client can result in contempt of court. *In Re Picerno,* 920 S.W.2d 904 (Mo. App. W.D. 1996). While discipline on the basis of incompetence in these circumstances is unlikely, neglect of the client can be a source of discipline. For example, in *Hawkins v. Walvoord,* 25 S.W.3d 882 (Tex. 2000), an attorney was suspended for one year after neglecting a court-appointed client. The attorney had sought to withdraw on the basis that he was incompetent to handle the representation, but the court denied the withdrawal. The Texas Supreme Court states that a court's order that an attorney continue a representation is a determination that the attorney is competent. *See also, State v. Richardson,* 631 P.2d 221 (Kan. 1981) (lawyer indefinitely suspended for neglecting appointed representation). *But see United States v. Wendy,* 575 F.2d 1025 (2d Cir. 1978) (contempt for refusing to accept appointment on basis of incompetence reversed where attorney without any litigation experience was appointed to defend a felony tax case). As a prac-

[margin handwriting: neglect of client may be disciplined]

duty to accept appt. by ct. enforced through contempt sanctions

tical matter, however, the duty to accept an appointment is enforced by the courts through direct contempt sanctions, rather than through discipline. *State ex rel Picerno v. Mauer*, 920 S.W.2d 904 (Mo. Ct. App. 1996); J.W. Thomey, *Attorney's Refusal To Accept Appointment To Defend Indigent, or To Proceed in Such Defense, as Contempt* , 36 A.L.R. 3d 1221 (1996, 2003 Supp.).

withdrawal ok if fired unless ct. holds necessary

Another basis for mandatory withdrawal would be if a client fires you. May a court refuse an attorney's request to withdraw on this basis? Doesn't a client have a constitutional right to proceed *pro se*? While the United States Supreme Court recognized this right in *Faretta v. California*, 422 U.S. 806 (1975), more recently the Court modified this right, holding that if a defendant is not competent to conduct his own defense, but is competent enough to direct counsel, he may be required to have counsel at trial. *Indiana v. Edwards*, 554 U.S. 164 (2008).

Structure

Why do you suppose the drafters of this rule used the double-negative language of "shall not seek to avoid" rather than "shall accept." The language does suggest that even maneuvers short of outright refusal—such as artificial conflicts of interest or efforts to remove one's name from appointments lists—could violate the rule as well.

Reasons

Policy for pro bono appt.

Notice that the underlying source of the obligation to accept pro bono cases or appointments is not clear from these rules. In cases challenging a court's authority to appoint attorneys, the source of this authority has been found in the inherent authority of courts to control their proceedings, in constitutional guarantees of assistance, or in the unique nature of the attorney's role and professional monopoly. When the appointment is for uncompensated service, attorneys have raised a variety of constitutional challenges. The Supreme Court of the United States has not yet definitively addressed these constitutional issues; resolving the one case in which the issue was presented on the grounds of statutory interpretation rather than constitutional grounds. *Mallard v. U.S. District Court*, 490 U.S. 296 (1989). At the state level, most courts have routinely rejected some arguments, such as involuntary servitude, while other arguments based on due process or takings have been more successful. *See generally, Williamson v. Vardeman*, 674 F.2d 1211, 1214-15 (8th Cir. 1982) (collecting cases). Even within any given state, court opinions on appointment of attorneys are often strongly divided and may turn on the particular context in which the case arises. Judy E. Zelin, Annotation, *Court Appointment of Attorney to Represent, Without Compensation, Indigent in Civil Action*, 52 A.L.R. 4th 1063 (1991, 2012 Supp.).

Constitutional challenges continue to be raised by attorneys appointed without compensation and new arguments under various states' constitutions are possible. However, attorneys are more likely to challenge an appointment on one of the grounds provided in the rules of professional conduct: a good cause basis such as financial hardship or repugnance of the client or a cause that would impair the attorney's ability to represent the client.

Visualize

One way to capture related ideas is through a mind map. A mind map is simply a non-linear diagram of ideas and their relationships. There is no right or wrong way to build a mind map, but it can be useful tool for brainstorming, organizing, and understanding ideas and their relationships. Start with a circle or image in the center of your mind map and print the essential concept you are learning. For example, you might start with "pro bono" in the center. Draw lines from that central image to connect to major related concepts or to show different aspects of the concept. From each of these branches, continue to draw lines out to connect to other ideas. Use different colors and shapes to represent connections and ideas.

Here is one example of an incomplete mind map of the right to counsel. Try building a mind map around the pro bono obligation.

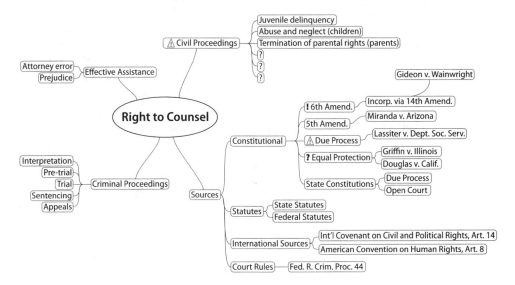

Imagine

Turning down a client is a difficult skill to master, but all the more difficult when the client you are turning down is one appointed by the court. You know from Rule 6.2 of the Model Rules that you have an obligation to accept these appointments unless you have good cause to avoid the appointment. Most appointments of counsel are in criminal law or family law cases, fields of practice that have become increasingly specialized. Yet, unless the criminal defense and family law bar are to bear the entire burden of providing access to justice by being available for appointment, other attorneys must be available to accept these appointments as well. Think about what kinds of appointments you would be willing to accept and those you would feel compelled to avoid.

Researching Professional Responsibility 24-A: Local Court Rules

While a court's authority to appoint attorneys may come from a variety of sources, the more particular procedures courts use for the appointments are often found in court rules, either the state supreme court's rules or the local trial-court-level rules. Local court rules are a sometimes overlooked, but often critical, source of law. Find the rules of the trial level court in your jurisdiction that govern a motion to withdraw. Look in both your state supreme court's rules of procedure and your local court's rules. You can generally find state supreme court rules in a separate paper-bound volume (West publishes court rules volumes for many states) or as an appendix to the state's statues. Most states have their state supreme court's rules published online. The rules of court for the state trial-level courts may be more difficult to locate online, depending on your jurisdiction. You can always try calling the court administrator's office or the court clerk or check with your local academic or county library.

Professional Responsibility Skill 24-A: Motion to Withdraw from Appointed Representation

At what point does your lack of competence constitute "good cause" to reject an appointment? In this problem, you will have an opportunity to practice a withdrawal motion based on competence (note that you could also raise constitutional or procedural objections to the appointment as well, but that is not what we will focus on here).

Suppose that you are an attorney in a firm that has expertise in tax, accounting, and financial transactions. One day you open your mail and discover the following order:

IN THE CIRCUIT COURT OF CENTRAL COUNTY
STATE OF YOURSTATE

State of Yourstate	)		
	)	Case No.	1234
v.	)		
	)	Division No.	7
Criminal Defendant	)		

ORDER

On this day, the consideration of the need for counsel to be appointed to represent Defendant was raised in this case. The court is of the opinion Defendant needs counsel in this case and, after considering Defendant's affidavit regarding indigence, the court is of the opinion Defendant is without sufficient financial means to employ an attorney to represent him in this matter.

IT IS ORDERED that <u>YOU YOURSELF</u>, a practicing attorney in the firm of Aye, Bee, & See, L.L.C., is hereby appointed to represent Defendant in this case and such attorney shall represent Defendant until (1) a judgment of conviction, acquittal, or dismissal is signed; (2) post-trial proceedings are completed; (3) an appeal to the court of appeals is exhausted; (4) the attorney is removed by the court; or (5) the attorney is replaced by other counsel.

SIGNED this 5th day of September, 2012.

Arnold Appointer
Judge Arnold Appointer

Copies to:
DISTRICT ATTORNEY
DEFENDANT
JAIL AND/OR BONDSMAN

You call the court clerk, sure there is some kind of mistake, but the clerk explains that you have been appointed to represent a criminal defendant in a tax fraud case. She explains that the case is not terribly complicated legally but does present some difficulties factually if one does not have much expertise in accounting. Moreover, because the co-defendant in the case has been represented by the public defender's office in similar matters, there is a conflict of interest requiring appointment of counsel outside the public defender's office. The court has turned to your firm, because of your expertise.

Your firm anticipates that this appointment will take at least 150 hours if it does not settle (more hours if the firm does not simply hire a criminal defense attorney to take on the case on their behalf).

You have prepared the following motion to withdraw and will be appearing at a hearing to defend your motion. Consider how delicate it is to bring a motion to withdraw, how unclear the standards are for when one would have good cause to withdraw, and how easily a withdrawal motion in these circumstances could turn into a constitutional case that would take more hours to carry out than would simply defending the action.

IN THE CIRCUIT COURT OF CENTRAL COUNTY
STATE OF YOURSTATE

State of Yourstate	)		
	)	Case No.	1234
v.	)		
	)	Division No.	7
Criminal Defendant	)		

MOTION TO WITHDRAW AS ATTORNEY OF RECORD

Attorney You Yourself requests leave to withdraw as attorney for Defendant. As grounds for this motion, Movant states:

1.   Movant is attorney of record for Defendant by virtue of the court's appointment.

2.   Movant requests leave to withdraw as attorney of record for Defendant because representation of the client is likely to result in the violation of the Yourstate Rules of Professional Conduct. The appointed matter is criminal in nature. Attorney You Yourself and the firm of Aye, Bee & See, L.L.C. specialize in tax, accounting and financial transactions and the firm has no attorneys with any criminal defense experience. Thus, Movant cannot handle the matter competently and representation would result in the violation of Rule 1.1.

3.   Movant requests leave to withdraw as attorney of record for Defendant because representation of the client is likely to result in an unreasonable financial burden on You Yourself and the law firm of Aye, Bee & See, L.L.C. Thus permission to withdraw is authorized by Rule 6.2. Movant anticipates that this appointment will take at least 150 hours if it does not settle, and more hours if the firm is not forced to hire a criminal defense attorney. The time and money is unduly burdensome on You Yourself and the law firm of Aye, Bee & See, L.L.C.

4. Further, Movant requests leave to withdraw as attorney of record for Defendant because representation of the client is likely to result in violation of the Defendant's constitutional right to effective assistance of counsel. Neither You Yourself nor any member of the firm of Aye, Bee & See, L.L.C. has any criminal defense experience; therefore, You Yourself is not equipped to provide the Defendant with his Due Process rights.

5. Movant has advised Defendant of his intention to withdraw as his attorneys by letter dated September 10, 2012, a copy of which is attached to this motion as Exhibit A.

6. This cause is not presently set for trial or hearing.

> Aye, Bee & See, L.L.C.
> You Yourself, Attorney for Defendant
> Bar Number
> 1234 Oak Street
> AnyCity, Yourstate 12345
> (800) 555-0000

A copy of the foregoing served by
mailing same, postage prepaid,
this 10th day of September, 20XX, to:
Prosecutor Office
Address, City, State, Zip Code.

Exhibit A

> You Yourself
> Aye, Bee & See, L.L.C.
> 1234 Oak Street
> AnyCity, Yourstate 12345
> September 1, 20XX

Darren Defendant
AnyCity County Jail
AnyCity, Yourstate

LEGAL MAIL—ATTORNEY-CLIENT PRIVILEGED

Dear Darren,

As you know, I have been appointed by the AnyCity County Court to act as your defense counsel in your case involving the charges of tax fraud. As we discussed in our meeting today, I will be seeking to be excused from representing you. I believe, and you have indicated that you agree, that you would be better served by an attorney with criminal defense experience. Of course, if I am required to continue, I will certainly work diligently to represent you and, with your consent, will engage co-counsel with criminal trial experience. I expect the hearing on our motion will be held tomorrow morning. I will inform you of the outcome of that hearing. In the meantime, please remember my advice to refrain from speaking with anyone about your case until we can resolve this matter of your representation.

Sincerely,
You Yourself

24.4 *Pro Se* Assistance and Limited Scope Representation

One major exception to the rules prohibiting layperson representation is that which allows pro se appearances. This exception allows an individual to act on his or her own behalf in legal proceedings and is justified on the due process requirements that the legal system be accessible to all. In most states, only individuals may act *pro se*; corporations must be represented by attorney. *Osborn v. United States Bank,* 22 U.S. (9 Wheat.) 738, 830, 6 L. Ed. 204 (1824). According to an ABA white paper on *pro se* representation, self representation in the United States has grown exponentially.

> When going to state court, most people proceed *pro se* most of the time. High volume state courts, including traffic, housing and small claims, are dominated by *pro se* litigants. Over the course of the past 20 years, domestic relations courts in many jurisdictions have shifted from those where litigants were predominately represented by lawyers to those where *pro se's* are most common. In these areas of the courts, *pro se* is no longer a matter of growth, but rather a status at a saturated level. Anecdotal evidence suggests that *pro se* representation is increasing in other personal civil matters, as well. In California, Arizona and Florida, independent paralegals (also called Legal Document Assistants) are authorized to help people prepare a range of forms needed to handle certain legal matters pro se. However, in most states, efforts to relax unauthorized practice rules have met with little success.

ABA Standing Committee on the Delivery of Legal Services, An Analysis Of Rules That Enable Lawyers To Serve Pro Se Litigants (2005) at http://www.americanbar.org/content/dam/aba/migrated/legalservices/delivery/downloads/prose_white_paper.authcheckdam.pdf.

In recent years, some states have begun to explore ways in which regulation of lawyers might be relaxed to provide broader access to legal services for *pro se* litigants than is currently available. Limited scope representation may provide a method for reaching clients who would not otherwise hire an attorney. For reasons of financial ability or distrust of the legal system, some clients might prefer this approach to hiring an attorney. Many of these limited scope representations may evolve into a traditional full representation as clients realize the complexity of the legal system and learn to trust and appreciate the services an attorney can provide to them.

About twenty states have amended their rules to expressly provide for limited scope representation, also called "unbundled" or "discrete task" representation. In the rest of the states, a majority have adopted a version of Model Rule 1.2 that allows some limited representation if the limitation is reasonable under the circumstances and the client gives informed consent. The comments to that rule describe, as an example of a permitted limited scope representation, an attorney providing a brief telephone conversation to give general information about the law where that is sufficient to give the client advice upon which they can reasonably rely.

One of the most difficult issues presented by limited task representation is determining when such a limited representation is "reasonable." States vary on the extent to which certain tasks are permitted to be carved out for discrete representations. Suppose a client has asked you to draft an answer to a complaint for breach of contract, with the plan that he would then sign, file, and carry on the case with no further representation on your part.

May you provide this limited representation? Whether this "ghostwriting" would be permitted would depend to a large extent on the court in which the case would be brought and whether the client is an individual or an entity. Ghostwriting has been condemned by a number of federal courts for "a possibly unethical exploitation of *pro se* leniency, violations of Rule 11, violations of local court rules regarding attorney withdrawal, and violations of ethics rules prohibiting misrepresentation to the court." John C. Rothermich, *Ethical And Procedural Implications Of "Ghostwriting" For Pro Se Litigants: Toward Increased Access To Civil Justice*, 67 FORDHAM L. REV. 2687, 2689 (1999). However, state ethics opinions and some state court rules have been more accepting of attorney's preparing pleadings for *pro se* litigants, though some do require that the pleading or other document indicate if attorney assistance was provided.

At the heart of the limited representation is the client's informed consent to that limitation. Before agreeing to undertake a limited scope representation, consider whether your client is able to understand the legal issues and their relationship to the client's goals. For the client's consent to be "informed" you must explain the limitations, and potential risks, of limited service. Thus, you must have sufficient information to decide the appropriate range of services for this particular client so you can provide alternatives to the limited representation. Consider the following suggestions from the Colorado Bar Association:

> A lawyer who limits the scope of the representation must consult with the client about the limited representation and obtain the client's consent to the limitation. Colo. RPC 1.2(c). As noted in the Terminology section of the Colorado Rules of Professional Conduct, "consult or consultation denotes communication of information reasonably sufficient to permit the client to appreciate the significance of the matter in question." A lawyer engaged in unbundled legal services must clearly explain the limitations of the representation, including the types of services which are not being provided and the probable effect of limited representation on the client's rights and interests. Where it is "foreseeable that more extensive services probably will be required" the lawyer may not accept the engagement unless "the situation is adequately explained to the client." Comment, Colo. RPC 1.5.

Colorado Bar Ethics Opinion 101 (2002).

Part of educating clients is warning that matters may become much more complicated than they expect and that, especially in a hearing or trial, there will not later be an opportunity to get help. You should explain to the client, for example, that rules of evidence and procedure can be complicated and raise unexpected legal issues and that rulings or decisions might be made that the client might not understand. As noted in Alaska Ethics Opinion 93-1, in providing unbundled legal services:

> ... the client then proceeds without legal representation into the courtroom for the hearing. The client may then be confronted by more complex matters, such as evidentiary arguments ... to which he is ill-prepared to respond. The client essentially elects to purchase only limited services from the attorney and to pay less in fees. In exchange, he assumes the inevitable risks entailed in not being fully represented in court. In the Committee's view, it is not inappropriate to permit such limitations on the scope of an attorney's assistance.

After you have studied your own state's position on limited scope representation and have screened your client for the advisability of limited scope representation, you will want to be sure to have a clear and complete limited representation agreement. The agreement should detail the counseling you have given the client on the risks and benefits of limited scope representation and should make clear that it is the client's choice to proceed with this form of representation. The agreement must make absolutely clear what legal issues and services will and will not be included in the representation. The agreement should indicate the source or sources of information upon which you will be relying in the representation and advise the client on the need for additional legal advice regarding other matters.

Another issue attorneys must regularly address with limited task representation is the degree of investigation required. Generally, attorneys must investigate a client's facts any time the information supplied by a client is "inconsistent, suspect, or materially incomplete." ABA Comm. on Ethics and Prof'l Responsibility, Formal Op. 335 (1974). However, the comment to Model Rule 1.1 explains that "the required attention and preparation are determined in part by what is at stake; major litigation and complex transactions ordinarily require more elaborate treatment than matters of lesser consequence." Does a lesser standard for factual investigation apply in limited task representation? May you draft a will without examining the client's financial situation? What about a loan agreement? A tax return? A securities offering? Clearly, other law may limit the extent to which limited scope representation is permissible. However, ultimately, the baseline for information gathering may be found in the requirement that a client give "informed consent" to discrete task representation.

Whatever the scope of representation, to what extent does an attorney have the duty to counsel the client on the possibility of remedies or solutions not within the scope of the representation? Comment 5 to Model Rule 2.1 provides that "a lawyer is not expected to give advice until asked by the client" but goes on to suggest that the duty of communication may require an attorney to provide unsolicited advice where to do otherwise would result in "substantial adverse legal consequences." Some courts have held that counseling on other options or remedies is required even in limited representation. For example, in *Nichols v. Keller*, 19 Cal. Rptr. 2d 601, 608 (Cal. Ct. App. 1993), the court held that limited representation of a client in a worker's compensation action required the attorney to counsel the client on other available remedies. Likewise the court in *Keef v. Widuch*, 747 N.E.2d 992 (Ill. App. Ct. 2001), stated that, "Although a representation agreement may limit the scope of representation to a particular legal course of action, the client must be made to understand that the course of action is not the sole potential remedy and that there exist other courses of action that are not being pursued." These cases should warn us that we cannot eliminate the risks of claims for liability for failing to disclose specific risks or options merely by providing a boilerplate caution such as "there are risks to a limited representation and you may have other rights and remedies outside the scope of this representation."

The United States Supreme Court has recently ruled on the constitutional dimensions of this issue when advising a criminal defendant.

Padilla v. Kentucky
130 S. Ct. 1473 (2010)

Justice STEVENS delivered the opinion of the Court.

Petitioner Jose Padilla, a native of Honduras, has been a lawful permanent resident of the United States for more than 40 years. Padilla served this Nation with honor as a member of the U.S. Armed Forces during the Vietnam War. He now faces deportation after pleading guilty to the transportation of a large amount of marijuana in his tractor-trailer in the Commonwealth of Kentucky.

In this postconviction proceeding, Padilla claims that his counsel not only failed to advise him of this consequence prior to his entering the plea, but also told him that he "'did not have to worry about immigration status since he had been in the country so long.'" Padilla relied on his counsel's erroneous advice when he pleaded guilty to the drug charges that made his deportation virtually mandatory. He alleges that he would have insisted on going to trial if he had not received incorrect advice from his attorney.

Assuming the truth of his allegations, the Supreme Court of Kentucky denied Padilla postconviction relief without the benefit of an evidentiary hearing. The court held that the Sixth Amendment's guarantee of effective assistance of counsel does not protect a criminal defendant from erroneous advice about deportation because it is merely a "collateral" consequence of his conviction. In its view, neither counsel's failure to advise petitioner about the possibility of removal, nor counsel's incorrect advice, could provide a basis for relief.

We granted certiorari to decide whether, as a matter of federal law, Padilla's counsel had an obligation to advise him that the offense to which he was pleading guilty would result in his removal from this country. We agree with Padilla that constitutionally competent counsel would have advised him that his conviction for drug distribution made him subject to automatic deportation. Whether he is entitled to relief depends on whether he has been prejudiced, a matter that we do not address.

I

The landscape of federal immigration law has changed dramatically over the last 90 years. While once there was only a narrow class of deportable offenses and judges wielded broad discretionary authority to prevent deportation, immigration reforms over time have expanded the class of deportable offenses and limited the authority of judges to alleviate the harsh consequences of deportation. The "drastic measure" of deportation or removal is now virtually inevitable for a vast number of noncitizens convicted of crimes....

These changes to our immigration law have dramatically raised the stakes of a noncitizen's criminal conviction. The importance of accurate legal advice for noncitizens accused of crimes has never been more important. These changes confirm our view that, as a matter of federal law, deportation is an integral part — indeed, sometimes the most important part — of the penalty that may be imposed on noncitizen defendants who plead guilty to specified crimes.

The court provides this analysis in part to respond to Justice Scalia, who was joined by Justice Thomas in a dissent that argued that "the Sixth Amendment guarantees adequate assistance of counsel in defending against a pending criminal prosecution. We should limit both the constitutional obligation to provide advice and the consequences of bad advice to that well defined area."

II

Before deciding whether to plead guilty, a defendant is entitled to "the effective assistance of competent counsel." The Supreme Court of Kentucky rejected Padilla's ineffectiveness claim on the ground that the advice he sought about the risk of deportation concerned only collateral matters, i.e., those matters not within the sentencing authority of the state trial court. In its view, "collateral consequences are outside the scope of representation required by the Sixth Amendment," and, therefore, the "failure of defense counsel to advise the defendant of possible deportation consequences is not cognizable as a claim for ineffective assistance of counsel." The Kentucky high court is far from alone in this view.

We, however, have never applied a distinction between direct and collateral consequences to define the scope of constitutionally "reasonable professional assistance" required under *Strickland*, 466 U.S., at 689, 104 S.Ct. 2052. Whether that distinction is appropriate is a question we need not consider in this case because of the unique nature of deportation.

We have long recognized that deportation is a particularly severe "penalty," but it is not, in a strict sense, a criminal sanction. Although removal proceedings are civil in nature, deportation is nevertheless intimately related to the criminal process. Our law has enmeshed criminal convictions and the penalty of deportation for nearly a century, *see* Part I, *supra*, at 1478-1481. And, importantly, recent changes in our immigration law have made removal nearly an automatic result for a broad class of noncitizen offenders. Thus, we find it "most difficult" to divorce the penalty from the conviction in the deportation context. Moreover, we are quite confident that noncitizen defendants facing a risk of deportation for a particular offense find it even more difficult.

Deportation as a consequence of a criminal conviction is, because of its close connection to the criminal process, uniquely difficult to classify as either a direct or a collateral consequence. The collateral versus direct distinction is thus ill-suited to evaluating a Strickland claim concerning the specific risk of deportation. We conclude that advice regarding deportation is not categorically removed from the ambit of the Sixth Amendment right to counsel. Strickland applies to Padilla's claim.

III

Under *Strickland*, we first determine whether counsel's representation "fell below an objective standard of reasonableness." 466 U.S., at 688, 104 S.Ct. 2052. Then we ask whether "there is a reasonable probability that, but for counsel's unprofessional errors, the result of the proceeding would have been different." *Id.*, at 694, 104 S.Ct. 2052. The first prong—constitutional deficiency—is necessarily linked to the practice and expectations of the legal community: "The proper measure of attorney performance remains simply reasonableness under prevailing professional norms." *Id.*, at 688, 104 S.Ct. 2052. We long have recognized that "[p]revailing norms of practice as reflected in American Bar Association standards and the like ... are guides to determining what is reasonable...." Although they are "only guides," and not "inexorable commands," these standards may be valuable measures of the prevailing professional norms of effective representation, especially as these standards have been adapted to deal with the intersection of modern criminal prosecutions and immigration law.

The weight of prevailing professional norms supports the view that counsel must advise her client regarding the risk of deportation. National Legal Aid and Defender Assn., Performance Guidelines for Criminal Representation § 6.2 (1995); G. Herman, Plea Bargaining § 3.03, pp. 20-21 (1997); Chin & Holmes, *Effective Assistance of Counsel and the Consequences of Guilty Pleas*, 87 Cornell L.Rev. 697, 713-718 (2002); A. Campbell, Law

Handwritten margin notes:

no need to determine if direct/collateral

The court neither rejects nor accepts the "direct/collateral" characterization but simply says it doesn't apply here. Do you find that characterization a helpful one in other contexts? Suppose you enter into a limited representation agreement with a client in a civil action and agree only to provide advice on "matters directly related to the case" and warn the client that "collateral consequences may result from your decisions in this action; however, we will not advise you regarding those consequences." Would such an agreement be enforceable? Ethical? Acceptable to most clients?

OF SENTENCING § 13:23, pp. 555, 560 (3d ed.2004); DEPT. OF JUSTICE, OFFICE OF JUSTICE PROGRAMS, 2 COMPENDIUM OF STANDARDS FOR INDIGENT DEFENSE SYSTEMS, STANDARDS FOR ATTORNEY PERFORMANCE, pp. D10, H8-H9, J8 (2000) (providing survey of guidelines across multiple jurisdictions); ABA STANDARDS FOR CRIMINAL JUSTICE, PROSECUTION FUNCTION AND DEFENSE FUNCTION 4-5.1(a), p. 197 (3d ed.1993); ABA STANDARDS FOR CRIMINAL JUSTICE, PLEAS OF GUILTY 14-3.2(f), p. 116 (3d ed.1999). "[A]uthorities of every stripe— including the American Bar Association, criminal defense and public defender organizations, authoritative treatises, and state and city bar publications— universally require defense attorneys to advise as to the risk of deportation consequences for non-citizen clients...." Brief for Legal Ethics, Criminal Procedure, and Criminal Law Professors as Amici Curiae 12-14 (footnotes omitted).

We too have previously recognized that "'[p]reserving the client's right to remain in the United States may be more important to the client than any potential jail sentence.'" St. Cyr, 533 U.S., at 323, 121 S.Ct. 2271. Likewise, we have recognized that "preserving the possibility of" discretionary relief from deportation under § 212(c) of the 1952 INA, 66 Stat. 187, repealed by Congress in 1996, "would have been one of the principal benefits sought by defendants deciding whether to accept a plea offer or instead to proceed to trial." St. Cyr, 533 U.S., at 323, 121 S.Ct. 2271. We expected that counsel who were unaware of the discretionary relief measures would "follo[w] the advice of numerous practice guides" to advise themselves of the importance of this particular form of discretionary relief. Ibid., n. 50.

In the instant case, the terms of the relevant immigration statute are succinct, clear, and explicit in defining the removal consequence for Padilla's conviction. Padilla's counsel could have easily determined that his plea would make him eligible for deportation simply from reading the text of the statute, which addresses not some broad classification of crimes but specifically commands removal for all controlled substances convictions except for the most trivial of marijuana possession offenses. Instead, Padilla's counsel provided him false assurance that his conviction would not result in his removal from this country. This is not a hard case in which to find deficiency: The consequences of Padilla's plea could easily be determined from reading the removal statute, his deportation was presumptively mandatory, and his counsel's advice was incorrect.

Immigration law can be complex, and it is a legal specialty of its own. Some members of the bar who represent clients facing criminal charges, in either state or federal court or both, may not be well versed in it. There will, therefore, undoubtedly be numerous situations in which the deportation consequences of a particular plea are unclear or uncertain. The duty of the private practitioner in such cases is more limited. When the law is not succinct and straightforward, a criminal defense attorney need do no more than advise a noncitizen client that pending criminal charges may carry a risk of adverse immigration consequences. But when the deportation consequence is truly clear, as it was in this case, the duty to give correct advice is equally clear.

Accepting his allegations as true, Padilla has sufficiently alleged constitutional deficiency to satisfy the first prong of Strickland. Whether Padilla is entitled to relief on his claim will depend on whether he can satisfy Strickland's

[Margin note, left column:] Justice Alito criticizes the majority for relying on these sources in determining the standards of the profession because "these standards may represent only the aspirations of a bar group rather than an empirical assessment of actual practice." What is the proper role of professional organizations in influencing the law?

[Handwritten margin note:] objective reasonable std. breached by attorney

[Margin note, left column:] Do you agree with this analysis that the deportation risks are clear? Justice Alito argues in concurrence that nothing in immigration law is a simple matter. Which position do you find more persuasive?

second prong, prejudice, a matter we leave to the Kentucky courts to consider in the first instance.

IV

The Solicitor General has urged us to conclude that Strickland applies to Padilla's claim only to the extent that he has alleged affirmative misadvice. In the United States' view, "counsel is not constitutionally required to provide advice on matters that will not be decided in the criminal case...," though counsel is required to provide accurate advice if she chooses to discusses these matters. Brief for United States as Amicus Curiae 10.

Respondent and Padilla both find the Solicitor General's proposed rule unpersuasive, although it has support among the lower courts. Kentucky describes these decisions isolating an affirmative misadvice claim as "result-driven, incestuous ... [, and] completely lacking in legal or rational bases." Brief for Respondent 31. We do not share that view, but we agree that there is no relevant difference "between an act of commission and an act of omission" in this context. *Strickland*, 466 U.S., at 690, 104 S.Ct. 2052 ("The court must then determine whether, in light of all the circumstances, the identified acts or omissions were outside the wide range of professionally competent assistance").

In sum, we have long recognized that the negotiation of a plea bargain is a critical phase of litigation for purposes of the Sixth Amendment right to effective assistance of counsel. The severity of deportation — "the equivalent of banishment or exile," *Delgadillo v. Carmichael*, 332 U.S. 388, 390-391, 68 S.Ct. 10, 92 L.Ed. 17 (1947) — only underscores how critical it is for counsel to inform her noncitizen client that he faces a risk of deportation.

V

It is our responsibility under the Constitution to ensure that no criminal defendant — whether a citizen or not — is left to the "mercies of incompetent counsel." To satisfy this responsibility, we now hold that counsel must inform her client whether his plea carries a risk of deportation. Our longstanding Sixth Amendment precedents, the seriousness of deportation as a consequence of a criminal plea, and the concomitant impact of deportation on families living lawfully in this country demand no less.

Taking as true the basis for his motion for postconviction relief, we have little difficulty concluding that Padilla has sufficiently alleged that his counsel was constitutionally deficient. Whether Padilla is entitled to relief will depend on whether he can demonstrate prejudice as a result thereof, a question we do not reach because it was not passed on below.

The judgment of the Supreme Court of Kentucky is reversed, and the case is remanded for further proceedings not inconsistent with this opinion.

It is so ordered.

The wisdom of restricting the holding in this case to instances of misadvice is argued thoroughly in this case between the majority and Justice Alito's concurrence. What kinds of arguments can you think of that each side in this debate might raise? Which do you find more persuasive?

Note

Justice Alito and Chief Justice Roberts concurred, but would limit the holding of the case: "In my view, such an attorney must (1) refrain from unreasonably providing incorrect advice and (2) advise the defendant that a criminal conviction may have adverse immigration consequences and that, if the alien wants advice on this issue, the alien should consult an immigration attorney. I do not agree with the Court that the attorney must attempt to explain what those consequences may be."

Problems for Review

1. Walter is in a general practice. He provides criminal defense representation, mostly in traffic violations and some minor drug possession offenses. Recently, Walter was at the courthouse on another case when he ran into Barney, a police officer with whom he regularly worked. He asked what Barney was doing at the court, and Barney told him that he was there because his girlfriend had obtained an *ex parte* restraining order against him, claiming that Barney had beaten her. Barney is there for the full order of protection hearing. He asks if Walter would be willing to help him at the hearing that morning. Walter agrees. He asks the court for a continuance to prepare the case, but the court refuses, saying he should simply go ahead with the hearing.

   He learns that Barney had indeed struck his girlfriend, but that it was in the context of an argument and he had slapped her after she had shoved him in anger. Barney tells Walter he doesn't really care whether he is prevented from having any further contact with her, but he is concerned that if a full order of protection is entered against him, it could be the basis for a criminal charge later. Walter knows from his criminal practice generally that a civil order of protection has limited *res judicata* effect in criminal matters and advises Barney that, if he agrees to entry of the order without admitting the underlying facts, there is very little risk that this will result in criminal charges. So Barney agrees to entry of the order. What Walter did not know, and what any attorney with training in domestic violence law would have been happy to tell him, is that the entry of this full order of protection would trigger a federal law making it illegal to possess a firearm. 18 U.S.C. 922(g)(8) (1994). Since the ability to carry a firearm is essential to Barney's job as a police officer, he is fired.

   Is Walter subject to discipline? Why or why not?

2. Walter also represented Joseph. Joseph is a public school teacher who has been charged with indecent assault (involving an unseemly incident with a student at a school basketball game). Walter advised Joseph that he should just plead guilty and get the incident over with and avoid all the publicity that would result from a trial. Joseph pled guilty, he was allowed to retire from his position by the school, and the court sentenced him to three years' probation. What Walter didn't tell Joseph about the guilty plea is that a criminal conviction would result in the loss of Jospeh's vested teacher pension rights under the state's Public Employee Pension Forfeiture Act.

   Joseph has now petitioned for relief from judgment, arguing that his guilty plea was not knowing and voluntary because of the ineffective assistance of his counsel. He also has filed a complaint with disciplinary counsel against Walter.

Will Joseph likely prevail in his post-conviction action? Will Walter be subject to discipline? *Commonwealth v. Abraham*, 2010 PA Super 104; 996 A.2d 1090 (Pa. Super. Ct. 2010).

24.5 Relaxing the Regulations to Insure Access

Apart from the obvious impact of unauthorized practice restrictions, other core regulations of the profession impact accessibility as well. For example, recall that Comment 3 to Rule 6.2 indicates that "an appointed lawyer has the same obligations to the client as retained counsel, including the obligations of loyalty and confidentiality ..." Yet state courts and legislatures have modified many regulations of even these core duties in order to lower the regulatory costs of representing low and moderate income persons.

An attorney representing an indigent client pro bono or as a court-appointed attorney owes the same ethical duty of competence to that client as does the attorney for a wealthy entity. However, standards of ineffective assistance of counsel and immunity for attorneys in some public positions lessen the risks of liability for attorneys in certain practice areas.

Laws place additional burdens on and even barriers to certain plaintiffs bringing malpractice actions. You may recall from Chapter Six, for example, that criminal defendants must in most states successfully appeal their convictions or prove their innocence as a prerequisite for bringing malpractice claims. Why? There are many policies supporting this rule, but at least one is the recognition that insulating criminal defense attorneys from malpractice makes the practice more desirable—it is a method of keeping costs low. Likewise, some states provide immunity from suit entirely to public defenders. Annotation, *Public Defender's Immunity From Liability For Malpractice*, 6 A.L.R. 4th 774 (1991, 2009 Supp.).

Likewise, the *Strickland* standard for effective assistance of counsel, requiring not only proof of attorney error but also proof that the error prejudiced the defendant's case, may promote stability of convictions. However, the standard has been criticized as a weak guarantee of competent representation. For example:

> Partly as a result of this deferential standard, representation in capital trials remains notoriously poor, especially for indigent defendants. Many states ... rely on court appointments rather than a specialized defense organization to provide representation to indigent defendants. Attorneys appointed under such schemes are frequently underfunded, inexperienced, unsympathetic to their clients, and thoroughly incapable of mounting an effective defense during either the guilt or punishment phases of the capital trial. Adhering to the Supreme Court's admonition that "the purpose of the effective assistance guarantee of the Sixth Amendment is not to improve the quality of legal representation," state courts and lower federal courts have shown extraordinary reluctance to grant relief on the basis of ineffective counsel, even in compelling cases.

Carol S. Steiker & Jordan M. Steiker, Sober Second Thoughts: Reflections on Two Decades of Constitutional Regulation of Capital Punishment, 109 HARV. L. REV. 355, 388-99 (1995).

Other examples of protection from malpractice suits can be found in the family law area, which continues to be one of the areas of greatest unmet legal needs. For example, child support enforcement assistance is available from government-funded attorneys. Even though these attorneys bring actions to establish paternity and collect child support for individuals, by law they do not represent those individuals and cannot be sued in malpractice by them. Why? If child support attorneys had to give each of their clients individualized, competent, and conflict-free representation, we'd need more lawyers — many more lawyers.

Another example comes from guardian *ad litem* representation. The law requires that courts appoint GALs to represent the interests of children in any case involving allegations of child abuse or neglect. While the GAL role is a highly specialized form of representation, requiring advanced training in most states, it is also an area of representation that relies largely on volunteers. Those volunteer attorneys are, in most states, protected by the doctrine of quasi-judicial immunity from malpractice actions by the children they represent. *McKay v. Owens,* 937 P.2d 1222 (Idaho 1997); *Tindell v. Rogosheske,* 428 N.W.2d 386 (Minn. 1988); *State ex rel Bird v. Weinstock,* 864 S.W.2d 376 (Mo. App. E.D. 1993). Several federal jurisdictions who have considered the quasi-judicial immunity issue have agreed. *Cok v. Cosentino,* 876 F.2d 1, 3 (1st Cir.1989); *Myers v. Morris,* 810 F.2d 1437, 1467 (8th Cir.1987); *Kurzawa v. Mueller,* 732 F.2d 1456, 1458 (6th Cir.1984). One of the frequent justifications for this immunity is the fear that qualified attorneys might be unwilling to represent a child if "disgruntled or vituperative parents could hold the guardian *ad litem* personally responsible." *Delcourt v. Silverman,* 919 S.W.2d 777, 785 (Tex.App.1996).

Conflicts of interest rules also affect accessibility. A number of rules of professional conduct have the aim of eliminating or reducing conflicts of interest disqualification when attorneys are working in settings designed to increase access to representation. Look at the following three rules of professional conduct. Each of these rules was expressly adopted to address a concern that "a strict application of the conflict-of-interest rules may be deterring lawyers" from volunteering in these programs. Model Rule 6.5 Reporter's Explanation of Changes, at http://www.abanet.org/cpr/e2k/e2k-rule65.html.

Missouri Supreme Court Rules of Professional Conduct

RULE 4-6.3: Membership in Legal Services Organization

A lawyer may serve as a director, officer, or member of a legal services organization, apart from the law firm in which the lawyer practices, notwithstanding that the organization serves persons having interests adverse to a client of the lawyer. The lawyer shall not knowingly participate in a decision or action of the organization:

> (a) if participating in the decision or action would be incompatible with the lawyer's obligations to a client under Rule 4-1.7; or

> (b) where the decision or action could have a material adverse effect on the representation of a client of the organization whose interests are adverse to a client of the lawyer.

RULE 4-6.4: Law Reform Activities Affecting Client Interests

A lawyer may serve as a director, officer, or member of an organization involved in reform of the law or its administration notwithstanding that the reform may affect the interests of a client of the lawyer. When the lawyer knows that the interests of a client may be materially benefited by a decision in which the lawyer participates, the lawyer shall disclose that fact but need not identify the client.

RULE 4-6.5: Nonprofit and Court-Annexed Limited Legal Services Programs

(a) A lawyer who, under the auspices of a program sponsored by a nonprofit organization or court, provides short-term limited legal services to a client without expectation by either the lawyer or the client that the lawyer will provide continuing representation in the matter:

> (1) is subject to Rules 4-1.7 and 4-1.9(a) only if the lawyer knows that the representation of the client involves a conflict of interest; and

> (2) is subject to Rule 4-1.10 only if the lawyer knows that another lawyer associated with the lawyer in a law firm is disqualified by Rules 4-1.7 or 4-1.9(a) with respect to the matter.

(b) Except as provided in Rule 4-6.5(a)(2), Rule 4-1.10 is inapplicable to a representation governed by this Rule 4-6.5.

Similarly, rules restricting an attorney's economic relationships with non-lawyers are relaxed when those relationships facilitate pro bono representation. Thus, most states have an exception to their prohibitions on fee-splitting with non-lawyers that permits lawyers to share court-awarded legal fees with a nonprofit organization that facilitated the representation. Advertising and solicitation rules also have exceptions for non-profit legal practice. The series of cases beginning with *NAACP v. Button*, 371 U.S. 415 (1963) and extending through *Brotherhood of Railroad Trainmen v. Virginia State Bar*, 377 U.S. 1 (1964), *United Mine Workers v. Illinois State Bar Association*, 389 U.S. 217 (1967), *United Transportation Union v. State Bar*, 401 U.S. 576 (1971) and *In re Primus*, 436 U.S. 412 (1978), limited a state's ability to place restrictions on the manner in which public interest organizations provide legal services to their members and constituents.

Test Your Understanding

The North Carolina Equal Access to Justice Commission, which was established by order of the North Carolina Supreme Court and charged with expanding access to the civil justice system for people of low income and modest means in North Carolina., issued a preliminary report in May 2008. It cited a number of civil legal needs that go unmet in North Carolina. One of these was the need for legal representation in eviction and foreclosure actions. According to that report:

> Legal representation to stop unnecessary evictions and foreclosures prevents homelessness. Evictions under North Carolina law can occur in three weeks. Legal representation can often stop unjust eviction actions or resolve the problems that lead to eviction or foreclosure actions. Abrupt dislocation of families from their homes causes severe stress. Children who have to change schools midyear can lose four months of educational progress, according to at least one study. It can cost as much as $7,000 to move from homelessness back into housing. Families can lose their life savings when they lose the equity in their homes in foreclosures. As little as $200 worth of legal advice and negotiation at the right moment can stop the downward slide toward homelessness and put a family back on the road to residential and financial stability.

INITIAL REPORT, NORTH CAROLINA EQUAL ACCESS TO JUSTICE COMMISSION 26 (May 2008) http://www.ncbar.org/download/probono/nceatjFullSummit Report.pdf

Think of six ways that the state of North Carolina (or your state) could improve the ability of individuals facing evictions and foreclosures to protect their legal rights. Develop one of those ideas into a proposal.

To Learn More

The American Bar Association has a standing committee on *pro bono* and public service. You can find a chart comparing each state's programs and rules along with other useful resources on the topic at the A.B.A. website. http://www.americanbar.org/groups/probono_public_service.html

Chapter Twenty-Five

The Professional Monopoly

Learning Objectives

After you have read this chapter and completed the assignments:

- For a particular area of law of your interest, you should be able to identify alternative legal service providers in a particular area of practice and analyze from both a legal and policy perspective whether and why unauthorized practice of law restrictions should be applied to that legal service provider.
- You should be able to locate and analyze restrictions on unauthorized practice in your state.
- In a situation in which you are called upon to apply a statute that defines the unauthorized practice of law by an attorney, you should be able to interpret the statute, argue for and against its applicability to the facts, argue for and against the validity of the statute as a regulation of legal practice, and use policy reasons to support these arguments.

Rules to Study

In this chapter we will look at some of the rules that govern the relationship of law with other professions, in particular Rule 5.5. One of the frustrations you will face with these rules is that the most important rule—a clear definition of the practice of law—seems to have eluded us.

Preliminary Problem: The Delivery of Legal Services

Identify an area of law in which you might like to practice. Spend a few minutes thinking about the people and entities who seek out the assistance of attorneys in your practice area. What do they want and need? Generate some very specific needs. Now think about where else these clients might go to get this assistance? Think broadly.

Likely you were able to identify a number of alternative legal services providers for your area of practice. For example, let's consider a consumer dispute. Suppose that a homeowner hired an individual to build a fence for her. The fence was poorly constructed and some damage to landscaping occurred. How can the homeowner resolve this problem? She might first try to solve the problem herself. Even if that requires going to court to sue the fence builder, she may represent herself. She might call the local better business bureau or the news station's consumer advocate, where someone (not necessarily a lawyer) might contact the fence builder on her behalf. Perhaps a mediation service could help her and the builder to work out their disagreement. The mediator might be, but in most states need not be, an attorney. Her insurance company might assist her. She might call the attorney general's office or the local prosecutor, but unless there is some fraud or other crime involved, the attorneys there are likely to consider this a purely private matter. If they do take action, it will be on behalf of the state rather than the homeowner. She may be very likely to go to the internet for resources, information, and advice, whether at general legal help sites like www.nolo.com or at more specialized sites. The sources of that information and advice might be industry, government, private attorneys, or even other consumers. You can likely think of even more avenues for the homeowner to address her problem with the builder.

Why would we limit the ability of this homeowner to be assisted by any of these persons or sources? As you read this chapter's materials on unauthorized practice, consider your own list of client needs and the alternative providers of the legal services in your practice area. Ask yourself what the risks and benefits are of allowing these other providers to serve these legal needs.

25.1 Who Are the Gatekeepers to the Profession?

One of the ways to increase the availability of low cost legal services is to permit non-lawyers to provide those services. While a few states have begun to permit independent paralegals to assist in document preparation, most states require non-lawyers to work under the direct supervision of an attorney. What happens if a legislature decides that it wishes to pass legislation permitting non-lawyer delivery of legal services? Many states do have statutes regarding the unauthorized practice of law that purport to define the practice of law. More than half the states have statutes making the unauthorized practice of law (UPL) a crime (usually a misdemeanor). The practice of law without a license can violate other criminal laws, including criminal fraud. Most states provide a civil liability statute for unauthorized practice of law. Additionally, consumer protection statutes and common law doctrines of fraud, abuse of process, and the like all could provide a basis for liability for those engaged in the unauthorized practice of law.

You will recall that nearly all state courts claim the inherent authority to regulate the practice of law and that in many states, that authority is considered to be exclusive to the courts. Nonetheless, even though UPL statutes involve the legislature's regulation of the practice of law, courts often apply these statutes, either as a matter of comity or as a legitimate exercise of the legislature's police powers. Even if a state court does have the constitutional authority to regulate the practice of law, that does not mean the court must necessarily conclude that it has the authority to regulate the *unauthorized* practice of law. The Supreme Court of Montana, for example, dissolved its unauthorized practice commission, concluding that, "this Court has no Constitutional authority to define, generally, what constitutes the practice of law, except within the context of a case or controversy properly before this Court." The Court noted the complexity of the unauthorized practice issue and chose to defer to the executive and legislative branches to address the issue generally:

> [W]e conclude that the array of persons and institutions that provide legal or legally-related services to members of the public are, literally, too numerous to list. To name but a very few, by way of example, these include bankers, realtors, vehicle sales and finance persons, mortgage companies, stock brokers, financial planners, insurance agents, health care providers, and accountants. Within the broad definition of § 37-61-201, MCA, it may be that some of these professions and businesses "practice law" in one fashion or another in, for example, filling out legal forms, giving advice about "what this or that means" in a form or contract, in estate and retirement planning, in obtaining informed consent, in buying and selling property, and in giving tax advice. Federal and state administrative agencies regulate many of these professions and businesses via rules and regulations; federal and state consumer protection laws and other statutory schemes may be implicated in the activities of these professions and fields; and individuals and non-human entities may be liable in actions in law and in equity for their conduct. Furthermore, what constitutes the practice of law, not to mention what practice is authorized and what is unauthorized is, by no means, clearly defined. Finally, we are also mindful of the movement towards nationalization and globalization of the practice of law, and with the action taken by federal authorities against state attempts to localize, monopolize, regulate, or restrict the interstate or international provision of legal services.

In Re Dissolving the Commission on the Unauthorized Practice of Law, 356 Mont. 109, 111; 242 P.3d 1282 (Mt. 2010).

Other courts have taken a broader view of their authority and have held that statutes purporting to define the practice of law do not bind the courts in determinations of unauthorized practice. Perhaps nowhere is the tension between the courts and legislatures regarding control of the legal profession more evident than in Arizona, where battles over permissions and restrictions on layperson provision of legal services has gone on for more than fifty years.

In 1961, the Arizona Supreme Court addressed an action by the State Bar for declaratory relief against title companies and real estate brokerages. The bar contended that certain real estate brokers were engaged in the unauthorized practice of law. The Arizona Supreme Court agreed. *State Bar v. Arizona Land Title & Trust Co.*, 90 Ariz. 76, 87, 366 P.2d 1, 14 (Ariz. 1961). After this decision, an initiative petition was successful in placing on the ballot a constitutional amendment that would give licensed real estate brokers a constitutional right to draft and complete contracts and other documents in real estate transactions. The measure passed and since then, the Arizona legislature has passed a number of statutes providing for lay representation in a variety of other settings. At the same time, the Arizona court has struck down a number of these statutes and has used its contempt authority to enforce its own unauthorized practice standards.

Should courts have the last say in defining the practice of law? In states in which courts assert this power, how far does the court's jurisdiction on these matters extend? Think about these issues in the context of a more recent Arizona opinion addressing the unauthorized practice of law.

In re Creasy

12 P.3d 214 (Ariz. 2000)

Feldman, Justice

This court disbarred Frederick C. Creasy, Jr. on September 16, 1996, for a number of violations of the Code of Professional Conduct and other Rules of the Supreme Court. The most serious involved failure to properly maintain client funds entrusted to him on two separate occasions, failure to adequately supervise a non-lawyer, and failure to assist in the State Bar's investigation of these matters. In the eleven years prior to his disbarment, Creasy received six informal reprimands from the State Bar.

> *What is the significance of the fact that Creasy had six informal reprimands before this case?*

On April 14, 1999, the State Bar received a report from attorney William Shrank regarding Creasy's possible violations of the disbarment order. The submission included the transcript of the sworn statement of a witness taken in what is described in the record as a private arbitration matter involving a claim for underinsured motorist benefits made by Sterling K. Smith against his insurer, USAA Casualty Insurance Company. Smith's USAA policy required him to submit this disputed claim to arbitration.

Along with his wife, Marilyn Creasy, a certified public adjuster and owner of The Legal Shoppe, Creasy "represented" Smith in this arbitration. Shrank represented USAA. At the time of the accident with the underinsured motorist, Smith evidently had some preexisting injuries caused by industrial accidents and covered under workers' compensation. Creasy sought to establish that the automobile accident, rather than the industrial problems, caused specific injuries. During a sworn statement of Dr. Dennis Crandall, Smith's treating physician, and over Shrank's objections, Creasy extensively and probingly examined Dr. Crandall concerning Smith's injuries.

> *Notice how a disbarment order is enforced. Recall that contempt can result in fines and imprisonment.*
>
> *Creasy → Jurisdiction*
> *Arg → Jurisdiction*
> *over non-lawyer*

Based on Creasy's appearance at and actions during the sworn statement, the State Bar filed a petition asking this court for an order directing Creasy to appear and show cause why he should not be held in contempt for violating the 1996 disbarment order by engaging in the practice of law. Creasy appeared in response to our order and the issues were briefed and argued.

Creasy, no longer a member of the bar, contests the jurisdiction of this court to regulate the actions of a non-lawyer. He also denies that he practiced law when he examined Dr. Crandall, arguing that actions that constitute the practice of law before a court are not the practice of law when done in the context of a private arbitration proceeding. Finally, he contends that because he was employed by an insurance adjuster licensed under A.R.S. §20-281 (1990), the Arizona Department of Insurance has sole jurisdiction to regulate his conduct in this matter. We disagree with all three of his submissions.

Discussion

> *Remember that arguments about jurisdiction are arguments about power. Here the underlying question is a separation of powers battle.*

A. Jurisdiction

We first address Creasy's argument that this court lacks jurisdiction over him because he is a non-lawyer. The argument is without merit. As we have previously said:

Article III of the Arizona Constitution creates the judicial branch of government, separate and distinct from the other branches. This court has long recognized that under article III of the Constitution "the practice of law is a matter exclusively within the authority of the Judiciary. The determination of who shall practice law in Arizona and under what condition is a function placed by the state constitution in this court."

In re Smith, 189 Ariz. 144, 146, 939 P.2d 422, 424 (1997) (quoting *Hunt v. Maricopa County Employees Merit Sys. Comm'n*, 127 Ariz. 259, 261-62, 619 P.2d 1036, 1038-39 (1980) (citations omitted).

The court's authority over the practice of law is also based on the creation of an integrated judicial department and the revisory jurisdiction of this court as provided in article VI, sections 1 and 5(4) of the Arizona Constitution. *See Smith*, 189 Ariz. at 146, 939 P.2d at 424. Prior to 1985, the Arizona Legislature prohibited the practice of law by unlicensed persons. *See generally* A.R.S. tit. 32, ch. 2. Effective January 1, 1985, however, the entire title regulating attorneys was repealed; since then the practice of law has been under the exclusive regulatory jurisdiction of this court, governed by the Supreme Court Rules, in particular Rule 31 (a)(3). *See Marchant v. U.S. Collections West, Inc.*, 12 F. Supp. 2d 1001, 1005 (D. Ariz. 1998) (applying Arizona law to hold that debt collector's application for writ of garnishment was unauthorized practice of law). This constitutional power to regulate the practice of law extends to non-lawyers as well as attorneys admitted to bar membership. *See* Rule 46(b); *Marchant*, 12 F. Supp. 2d at 1005 (citing *Anamax Mining Co. v. Arizona Dep't of Econ. Sec.*, 147 Ariz. 482, 484-85, 711 P.2d 621, 623-24 (App. 1985)) (prohibiting corporate officer or employee from representing corporate employer before the Department of Economic Security).

The facts of this case do not require us to determine the extent of our power to regulate "practitioners" who are not and have never been lawyers.

In the situation presented here, our rules specifically apply to both active lawyers and those who have been disbarred. Rule 31(a)(3) states:

> *Privilege to practice.* Except as hereinafter provided in subsection 4 of this section (a), no person shall practice law in this state or hold himself out as one who may practice law in this state unless he is an active member of the state bar, and no member shall practice law in this state or hold himself out as one who may practice law in this state, *while suspended, disbarred, or on disability inactive status.*

(Emphasis added.) We see no reason why we would have jurisdiction over lawyers and not over disbarred lawyers like Creasy. Creasy's case actually presents an even stronger situation for jurisdiction than that of a person never admitted to the bar. On admission, Creasy submitted himself to the authority of the State Bar and this court. He is still bound by the restrictions imposed on him by this court's disbarment order, made under Rule 31, which explicitly prohibits a disbarred lawyer from continuing or resuming practice. His expulsion from the bar in no way frees him from these restrictions. It would be strange doctrine that as a result of being disbarred, a lawyer may not only resume practice but be free of the obligations imposed on lawyers who have not been disbarred.

Given our authority over the practice of law and those who have been admitted to the bar, we conclude that we have continuing jurisdiction to prevent Creasy from resuming the practice of law. We turn, then, to the question of whether he was engaged in the practice of law.

B. The Practice of Law

Creasy argues that his actions during the private arbitration proceeding—unconnected to any pending judicial matter—do not constitute the practice of law. We long ago defined the practice of law as "those acts, whether performed in court or in the law office, which lawyers customarily have carried on from day to day through the centuries constitute the practice of law. Such acts.... include rendering to another any other advice or services which are and have been customarily given and performed from day to day in the ordinary practice of members of the legal profession...." *State Bar of Arizona v. Arizona Land Title & Trust Co.*, 90 Ariz. 76, 95, 366 P.2d 1, 14 (1961).

More recently, we applied this definition to hold that a judge who represented a corporation in contract negotiations and who advised the corporation regarding those negotiations had engaged in the practice of law. *See In re Fleischman*, 188 Ariz. 106, 111, 933 P.2d 563, 568 (1997). As these cases make clear, a person need not appear in a judicial proceeding to engage in the unauthorized practice of law. Creasy concedes that he represented Smith when he took Dr. Crandall's sworn statement but argues that the medical claim evaluation issues at stake did not require the "application of a trained legal mind." *Baron v. City of Los Angeles*, 2 Cal. 3d 535, 469 P.2d 353, 358, 86 Cal. Rptr. 673 (Cal. 1970). He also argues that because his examination of Dr. Crandall occurred in the context of a private arbitration, his actions do not constitute the unauthorized practice of law. We are unpersuaded for the following reasons.

In this case we need not decide whether the *Arizona Land Title* definition should be changed or whether the *Baron* definition of the practice of law is an appropriate narrowing of *Arizona Land Title* or *Fleischman*. Whatever may be the line separating the proper activities of lay people and lawyers in a nonadversary context, even a cursory look at the caption of the proceedings at which Creasy appeared and a sample of Creasy's examination of Dr. Crandall during the sworn statement makes it apparent that Creasy rendered the kind of core service that is and has "been customarily given and performed from day to day [only] in the ordinary practice of members of the legal profession." *See Arizona Land Title*, 90 Ariz. at 95, 366 P.2d at 14. As noted, our cases make clear that a person need not appear in a judicial proceeding to engage in the practice of law. If negotiation of a contract in *Fleischman* was the practice of law, then, a fortiori, Creasy's representation of Smith by examining a witness in an adversary setting involving a disputed claim certainly falls within that definition as well, particularly in light of the nature of the examination, which was no less exhaustive or rigorous than one would ordinarily see during a formal deposition in a judicial proceeding.

We are quite aware of the social, technological, and economic changes that have taken place since our decision in *Arizona Land Title*. In some situations these changes may require us to reexamine our broad definition of the practice of law.

One commentator noted that, after the *Arizona Land Title* case, the definition of the practice of law in Arizona was boiled down to a tautological definition: "the practice of law is what lawyers do." *Jonathan Rose, Unauthorized Practice of Law in Arizona: A Legal and Political Problem That Won't Go Away*, 34 Ariz. St. L.J. 585 (2002)

What changes since 1961 do you think the court has in mind that would justify changing the definition of the practice of law?

This is not the case in which to do so. We do not deal here with the legitimate practice of other professionals, with the preparation or distribution of generic documents and forms for general use, the mere giving of legal advice, or even the preparation of documents for a specific client, the situation in which the "trained legal mind" test evolved. *See Agran v. Shapiro*, 127 Cal. App. 2d Supp. 807, 273 P.2d 619 (accountant not practicing law when preparing clients' income tax returns but engaged in unauthorized practice when preparing application for carry-back adjustment of losses). *See also Fravel v. Stark County Board of Revision*, 88 Ohio St. 3d 574, 728 N.E.2d 393 (Ohio 2000) (non-lawyer holder of "Durable General Power of Attorney" for property owner engaged in unauthorized practice of law when he filed appeal with Ohio Board of Tax Appeals; appeal remanded to county Board of Revision with instructions to dismiss not only because non-lawyer violated Ohio unauthorized practice statute but also pursuant to court's constitutional supervisory power over practice of law).

Our conclusion that Creasy engaged in the practice of law by acting as a public adjuster is supported by the decisions of other jurisdictions. The Illinois Supreme Court held that a suspended lawyer engaged in the unauthorized practice of law when he represented a former client in settlement negotiations against her insurance company even though the insurance company had already admitted liability. *See In re Bodkin*, 21 Ill. 2d 458, 173 N.E.2d 440 (Ill. 1961). Citing *Liberty Mutual Insurance Co. v. Jones*, 344 Mo. 932, 130 S.W.2d 945, 960 (Mo. 1939), for the proposition that adjusters employed by insurance companies do not engage in the unauthorized practice of law, *Bodkin* argued that "his position was the same as that of an adjustor for an insurance company except that he was acting on behalf of a claimant." *Bodkin*, 173 N.E.2d at 441. The Illinois court rejected this argument, distinguishing *Liberty Mutual* on the grounds that the Missouri Supreme Court had

> distinguished between services rendered by an insurance adjuster on behalf of his company and services rendered by one who negotiates a claim against the company…. The court stated … [that] "appellants' lay claim adjusters work only for their several employers, who hire and retain them with their eyes open. When they deal with claimants it is on an adversary basis, not a representative basis implying a fiduciary relation.

Id. at 441-42 (quoting *Liberty Mutual*, 130 S.W.2d at 960).

Kansas [which], like Arizona, has no statute prohibiting the unauthorized practice of law, has reached the same result by approximately the same reasoning. *See State ex rel. Stovall v. Martinez*, 27 Kan. App. 2d 9, 996 P.2d 371 (Kan. App. 2000). The Martinez court held that an insurance claims "consultant" engaged in the unauthorized practice of law by putting together settlement brochures, negotiating settlements on behalf of injured persons, and advertising that he could save claimants the trouble of hiring a lawyer. The court concluded that the consultant offered a service that required knowledge of legal principles and that his financial interest in settling without litigation conflicted with his clients' interest in receiving a fair settlement, thus distinguishing the consultant's work from that done by insurance company adjusters. *See id.* at 375. The court thus enjoined the consultant from further representation. *See id.* Although the injunction was issued under Kan. Stat. Ann. § 50-623, *et*

[Handwritten margin note: Bodkin case → suspended UPL for suspended lawyer in ins. case]

[Margin text:] Critically examine this reasoning. What exactly is the difference between insurance adjustors for insurance companies and Creasy's practice? Is it the nature of what they do or of the clients for whom they do it? Can't lay people hire and retain lay representatives "with their eyes open"?

seq., the Kansas Consumer Protection Act, the finding of unauthorized practice was based on the court's "inherent power to define and regulate the practice of law." *Id.* at 374.

Of course, unlike Illinois, which had no statute authorizing adjusters to investigate or settle claims" on behalf of either the insurer or the insured," the Arizona Legislature arguably has authorized private adjusters to represent claimants against insurance companies. *See* A.R.S. § 20-281(A). However, we still find persuasive the Illinois court's rejection of Bodkin's argument that his actions were merely "administrative" because of his status as an admitted, though suspended, attorney.

The Kansas Supreme Court reached a similar result in a case in which a suspended lawyer continued all his activities except court appearances, finding that his activities were not permissible just because they could have been performed by non-lawyers. *See State v. Schumacher*, 214 Kan. 1, 519 P.2d 1116 (Kan. 1974). The court's rationale was that "some actions which may be taken with impunity by persons who have never been admitted to the practice of law, will be found to be in contempt if undertaken by a suspended or disbarred attorney." *Id.* at 1125. Applying this reasoning to our facts, we believe Creasy, who acted as a representative for his client by examining a witness in an adversarial setting, cannot now claim to have merely engaged in insurance adjusting under A.R.S. § 20-281. *See Bodkin*, 173 N.E.2d at 442. The court held that Bodkin was engaged in the practice of law, reasoning, "It is obvious that settling a case, under these circumstances, required legal skill. It is mere sham … to contend that the acts during suspension were clerical, administrative, and ministerial only." *Id.* Creasy clearly employed legal skill during his examination of Dr. Crandall and cannot now claim he was not engaged in practicing law.

C. Legislative Authority to License Private Insurance Adjusters

Finally, we turn to Creasy's argument that pursuant to A.R.S. § 20-281, the legislature has authorized the licensing of private insurance adjusters and that he is therefore subject only to the jurisdiction of the Department of Insurance. This argument is also without merit. In defining adjuster and setting out licensing requirements in A.R.S. §§ 20-281 and 20-312, the legislature has undertaken the regulation of insurance adjusters. Section 20-281 (A) defines an adjuster as

> any person who, for compensation as an independent contractor or as the employee of such an independent contractor … *investigates and negotiates settlement of claims* arising under insurance contracts, on behalf of either the insurer or the insured.

(Emphasis added.) Creasy acted as an employee of his wife, who is licensed as an adjuster under A.R.S. § 20-312. Creasy's actions during the sworn statement are therefore permissible if we consider only the statute and if they can technically be characterized as only the investigation, negotiation and settlement of claims.

But even if we were so persuaded, the legislature's adoption of A.R.S. § 20-281 cannot authorize Creasy to violate our disbarment order by engaging in activities that constitute the practice of law. *See Marchant*, 12 F. Supp. 2d at

1005 (Rule 31 trumps statutory law because the practice of law is "within the exclusive authority of the judiciary" (citation omitted)). Section 20-281 is intended to regulate insurance adjusters. The legislature has not purported to, nor can it, authorize non-lawyers or disbarred lawyers to practice law. Whether it is within the legislature's power to authorize one to engage in activities that constitute the practice of law while engaging in the business of insurance adjusting is a question we reserve for the appropriate case, if and when brought.

Conclusion

We hold that Creasy has violated Rule 31(a)(3) and the order of disbarment. We thus find him in contempt and order that he immediately cease and desist from any further activities that constitute the practice of law. In lieu of other penalties that might be imposed, Creasy is ordered to pay the costs incurred by the State Bar, plus reasonable attorneys' fees, the amount to be approved by this court on application by the State Bar.

Notes

1. What would be involved if the State Bar wanted to shut down Creasy's wife's business. Since there is no statute prohibiting unauthorized practice and Mrs. Creasy is not subject to an order of disbarment, under what authority would the State Bar be able to bring an action? Recall that the Kansas court used the state consumer protection statute to accomplish this, but could the bar request an injunction based simply on the court's inherent power? Even if the procedural path were clear, the court would then be drawn into a direct clash with the Arizona legislature once again.

2. Creasy was practicing under the authority of his wife, a licensed adjustor. What if his wife had been an attorney licensed in Arizona? Most states allow laypersons to act as paralegals under the supervision of attorneys and, in that capacity, they undertake a variety of tasks that, if they were done outside an attorney's supervision, would be the practice of law. However, many of these same states do not allow disbarred attorneys to act as paralegals. For example, Illinois Supreme Court rule 765(b) provides that "Upon entry of the final order of discipline, the disciplined attorney shall not maintain a presence or occupy an office where the practice of law is conducted." Why should disbarred attorneys be prohibited from undertaking tasks that laypersons are permitted?

3. What if the type of services Creasy was providing were before a federal agency or court? What if federal law authorized lay representation in that setting? The authority of federal courts to control lawyer conduct is independent of state law. *Theard v. United States*, 354 U.S. 278, 282 (1957) (holding that disbarment by a state court is not binding on federal courts). Moreover, federal courts, being creatures of Congress, do not maintain that they have the exclusive power to regulate the practice of law.

   If federal statutes authorize lay representation before federal agencies, the Supremacy Clause requires that those authorizations take precedence over any state laws that would declare that practice unauthorized. *Sperry v. Florida*, 373 U.S. 379, 10 L.Ed.2d 428, 83 S. Ct. 1322 (1963) (non-lawyer could perform tasks incident to the preparation and prosecution of federal patent applications before the U.S. Patent Office from an office in Florida notwithstanding Florida's prohibition against the unlawful practice of law). The federal Administrative Procedures Act, 5 U.S.C. 555(b), permits any person to represent another if allowed by the agency. Examples of other situations in which laypersons can represent individuals in federal agency decision making include the Social Security Administration, Internal Revenue Service, Consumer Product Safety Commission, Department of Labor, and Environmental Protection Agency. *See also The Florida Bar v. Kaiser*, 397 So.2d 1132, 1133 (Fla. 1981) ("Neither The Florida Bar nor the referee have suggested that Kaiser can or should be restricted in any way from practicing naturalization or immigration law in this state even though he is not a member of The Florida Bar, *see Sperry v. The Florida Bar*, 373 U.S. 379, 83 S. Ct. 1322, 10 L.2d 428 (1963), and nothing in this opinion should be construed as suggesting otherwise.").

4. In the United Kingdom and civil law countries, there are no prohibitions on the unauthorized practice of law similar to those in the United States. Thus, attorneys face competition from non-lawyer providers such as accounting firms and banks. In addition, as you considered in the preliminary problem, outsourcing of legal work to common law countries such as India is an increasing trend. To read more about this issue, consider the American Bar Association, Commission on Ethics 20/20 Discussion Draft Regarding Domestic and International Outsourcing, November 20, 2010. www.abanet.org/ethics 2020/pdfs/discussion_draft.pdf. As law practice, particularly in the corporate context, becomes increasingly globalized, how will this difference in approach affect attorneys in the United States?

5. Why do individuals with a law degree engage in the unauthorized practice of law when they can obtain a license? Even as a disbarred attorney, Creasy could have sought reinstatement in order to be able to continue to practice law rather than practice without authorization. Some individuals choose to use their legal education for careers other than law practice. Which of the following careers would place you at risk of the unauthorized practice of law? Should you go ahead and get licensed just in case? Is there any advantage to not having a law license?

    Financial planner—helping clients choose investment plans and setting up those plans for the clients

    Lobbyist for legislative change on behalf of special interest organizations

    Agent for sports or entertainment figures

    Mediator for family law disputes

    Poverty advocate who helps members of the community prepare bankruptcy petitions, immigration applications, and applications for government benefits

    Insurance adjustor

25.2 What Is the Definition of the Practice of Law?

As you saw in *Creasy*, courts have had no small difficulty in defining the practice of law. The ABA Model Rules of Professional Conduct, while prohibiting attorneys from assisting in the unauthorized practice of law, defer to other law for a definition. The American Law Institute, in drafting the Restatement (Third) of the Law Governing Lawyers also was unable to provide a definition, likely because the case law is so conflicting and vague that "restatement" is not an option. RESTATEMENT (THIRD) OF THE LAW GOVERNING LAWYERS § 4 cmt. c (2000) ("definitions and tests employed by courts to delineate unauthorized practice by nonlawyers have been vague or conclusory"). Recently, the American Bar Association Task Force on a Model Definition of the Practice of Law failed to come to agreement on what constitutes the practice of law and instead suggested that states use a balancing test in arriving at a definition of the practice of law based on the state's particular culture and values. AMERICAN BAR ASSOCIATION COMMISSION ON NON-LAWYER PRACTICE, NONLAWYER ACTIVITY IN LAW-RELATED SITUATIONS 136-37 (August 1995). The three factors the ABA suggested were:

1. Does the nonlawyer activity pose a serious risk to the consumer's life, health, safety or economic well-being?

2. Do potential consumers of law-related nonlawyer services have the knowledge needed to properly evaluate the qualifications of nonlawyers offering the services?

3. Do the actual benefits of regulation likely to accrue to the public outweigh any likely negative consequences of regulation?

What do you think of this definition? Try applying this balancing test to the non-lawyer legal services providers you identified at the beginning of this chapter for your area of practice. Does this test explain why some professions and some processes are more open to non-lawyer professionals than others? Consider, for example, accountants, who are given considerable deference in unauthorized practice issues. "Instead of focusing on the different duties of each profession, most courts emphasize the similarities and allow accountants to perform functions that amount to 'legal services' under almost any plausible definition of the practice of law. Accountants have therefore been permitted to engage in a broad range of activities that were once considered to be the 'practice of law.'" Susan B. Schwab, *Note: Bringing Down the Bar: Accountants Challenge Meaning of Unauthorized Practice*, 21 CARDOZO L. REV. 1425 (2000). Why is this so?

The third factor in the balancing test is a cost-benefit analysis. Under this rationale, courts have appeared to create exceptions to unauthorized practice where the restrictions limit the ability of indigent clients to obtain assistance with their legal needs. For example, the Missouri Court of Appeals has held that assisting incarcerated individuals in factual investigation and participation in discretionary, fact-based application procedures is not the practice of law. *State v. Carroll*, 817 S.W.2d 289 (Mo. App. W.D. 1991). In that case, the court reversed a conviction of the defendant for practicing law without a license when the defendant, a layperson, assisted an incarcerated individual in preparing and filing a habeas corpus petition. The Missouri statutes provided that a habeas petition could be signed by the petitioner or his representative. The court interpreted this statutory provision expansively to include lay representatives and to allow those representatives to not only sign the petitions but also assist in their preparation. The court approved lay representation excepting only representation before a court hearing on the petition. The Missouri court was influenced by a similar holding from the Arizona court and quoted with approval that court's rationale for this exception to the unauthorized practice restrictions, "It is a practical realization that one confined to a cell, without ready access to a lawyer, often must depend on his family or friends to have "his body brought before the court" (i.e. "habeas corpus") to determine the legality of his incarceration." *State v. Carroll*, 817 S.W.2d at 291, (*quoting Hackin v. State*, 427 P.2d 910, 911 (Ariz. 1967); *appeal dismissed*, 389 U.S. 143 (1967)).

Attorneys would be unwise to read this exception too broadly. You are not insulated from unauthorized practice charges simply because you do not charge for your services. Even if the person you are representing for free is a family member, your representation may be prohibited as unauthorized practice. A good example of this principal can be seen in the cases holding that non-lawyer parents do not have authority to represent their children in federal court in actions under the Individuals with Disabilities Education Act. Sonja Kerr, *Winkelman: Pro Se Parents of children with Disabilities in the Courts (or Not?)*, 26 ALASKA L. REV. 271 (2009).

What would be the advantages and disadvantages of a proposal that would permit anyone to provide legal services so long as she did not charge to do so?

Researching Professional Responsibility Exercise 25-A: State Definitions of the Practice of Law

In researching any issue of professional conduct, it is tempting to look for the rules of professional conduct (usually found in the court rules in most states) and then consider yourself done. However, as we have seen, even in states in which the supreme court claims the sole and exclusive authority to regulate the practice of law, the legislature may have spoken on the issue and the court may give some weight to that legislation. Accordingly, never simply look for the rule of conduct and stop there. Always check to make sure there is not legislation on the issue you are researching as well.

Practice with the issue of unauthorized practice. What is your state's approach to the issue? Does it have statutory provisions that address unauthorized practice? If you were to use a web search engine, you might find that the Lawyer's Liability Assurance Society Inc. (ALAS) has compiled a list of unauthorized practice of law statutes and rules from 51 U.S. jurisdictions, including the District of Columbia. You can find this posted at several websites. Use a search engine and search for "unauthorized practice of law statutes and rules." While a useful starting point, take care when using compilations such as this and always confirm that the compilation is correct and current by checking the primary source. For example, the ALAS compilation is current only as of 2000. What is the most recent version of your state's statute? Has the court interpreted it?

Test Your Understanding

Look again at the list of providers of legal services you identified in the preliminary problem in this chapter. Are these providers commonly subject to unauthorized practice restrictions? Should they be? Why or why not? Test your understanding of the policies underlying unauthorized practice restrictions with the following problem.

Anne Gutierrez
1000 Main Street
Yourcity, Yourstate

Dear Attorney,

My name is Anne Gutierrez and I need your help. I am the youngest of five children and the only one who lives here in town. I work in the trust department of First Local Bank. When my mother Dolores was diagnosed with terminal cancer last year, I moved into her home to provide her care. During that time, my mother asked me to help her prepare a will. I told her that she should use a lawyer, but mother wanted me to prepare the will because she didn't want a stranger involved in her private affairs. I went online to LegalZoom.com and purchased the will-making document service. Mother told me that she wanted her estate to be divided equally between me and all my siblings, except she wanted me to have the house as payment for the care I had been giving her. The house is our family home. It is beautiful and is probably worth about as much as all of mother's other property and savings combined.

I prepared mother's will using the online service and answered the questions provided there according to my mother's wishes. I did this on my own, though I had talked to my mother about what she wanted. I designated myself as the executor of the estate and divided the property just the way my mother told me to. Mother did not personally use LegalZoom at all (she was not fond of computers) but simply asked me some questions about the finished will. I arranged for the day nurse and a neighbor to act as witnesses and had mother execute the will as directed by the LegalZoom instructions.

Mother passed away a month ago now, and one of my brothers has now challenged the will, asking the court to invalidate the will because it constituted the unauthorized practice of law. He has also threatened to talk to the local district attorney to see if they will prosecute me under the state's unauthorized practice statute. My brother is not a very kind man and I don't take his threats lightly. I would like your advice and assistance, please. How likely is he to win this will contest? The LegalZoom site said their forms were approved in the state. What about his threat of criminal action? Is it really a crime? How can that be so when they sell these forms?

Sincerely,

Anne Gutierrez

How will you advise Anne? Compare your analysis to that of the court in *Franklin v. Chavis*, 371 S.C. 527, 640 S.E.2d 873 (S.C. 2007). LegalZoom is not a hypothetical company, but has been in business for over ten years. Founded by O.J. Simpson defense attorney Robert Shapiro, LegalZoom provides self-help forms for a wide variety of legal transactions, from wills and divorces to business incorporations. A federal class action against LegalZoom claimed that LegalZoom was engaged in the unauthorized practice of law and violated consumer protection laws. After the district court judge refused summary judgment, the case settled. *Janson v. Legal-Zoom.com, Inc.*, ___ F. Supp. 2d ___, 2011 WL 3320500 (W.D. Mo. 2011).

To Learn More

Visit the American Bar Association's Task force on the Model Definition of the Practice of Law at www.americanbar.org/groups/professional_responsibility/task_force_model_definition_practice_law.htm.

Chapter Twenty-Six

Commercial Speech: Advertising and Solicitation

Learning Objectives

After you have read this chapter and completed the assignments, you should be able to:

- Describe the interests at stake in attorney advertising and solicitation.
- Identify and analyze constitutional issues in state regulation of attorney advertising and solicitation.

Rules to Study

We will study the rules governing attorney advertising and solicitation (Rules 7.1-7.5) and the constitutional framework within which those rules operate.

Preliminary Problem

You have decided to open up a practice in which you will offer limited scope representation, sliding scale fees, and other approaches to representation that will make your services much more affordable for middle- and lower-income clients. You intend to advertise on television and on the internet. Design the advertisement you think would attract clients to your practice. Propose other methods of attracting clients.

26.1 The Controversy over Attorney Advertising

Unless you will be on the legal staff of a corporate or governmental entity, you will need to market your practice. Whether your marketing consists of multimedia emails to in-house counsel, presentations on estate planning at the local library, or billboards next to the freeway, you must be sure your advertising is within the regulatory boundaries set by your state.

At one time, reputation was considered the only proper method to develop a client base. Canon 27 of the 1908 ABA Canons of Professional Ethics provided:

> [T]he most worthy and effective advertisement possible, even for a young lawyer, and especially with his brother lawyers, is the establishment of a well-merited reputation for professional capacity and fidelity to trust. This cannot be forced, but must be the outcome of character and conduct. The publication or circulation of ordinary simple business cards, being a matter of personal taste or local custom, and sometimes of convenience, is not per se improper. But solicitation of business by circulars or advertisements, or by personal communications or interviews, not warranted by personal relations, is unprofessional. It is equally unprofessional to procure business by indirection through touters of any kind, whether allied real estate firms or trust companies advertising to secure the drawing of deeds or wills or offering retainers in exchange for executorships or trusteeships to be influenced by the lawyer. Indirect advertisements for business by furnishing or inspiring newspaper comments concerning causes in which the lawyer has been or is engaged, or concerning the manner of their conduct, the magnitude of the interests involved, the importance of the lawyer's position, defy the traditions and lower the tone of our high calling, and are intolerable.

However, by the mid-1980s, a number of factors had combined to open up the door to attorney advertising. Bans on advertising had been challenged on antitrust grounds by the ABA and the Department of Justice and the United States Supreme Court's first amendment jurisprudence had recognized attorney advertising as commercial speech. These legal developments were very controversial then and remain so today. As Professor Stewart Macaulay observed:

> The leaders of the bar who resist advertising and the reformers who champion it agree about broad goals. People should have access to legal services. Consumers gain when quality services are available at reasonable prices. Consumers benefit from accurate and relevant information so they can make informed choices whether to seek a lawyer and which one to contact. On the other hand, consumers lose if advertising deceives them. They lose if the costs of advertising lower the quality of services. They also might lose if the cluster of ideals and attitudes associated with professionalism and fiduciary obligations were replaced by lawyer self-interest or by bureaucratic constraints in a standardized system geared for efficiency....

> [T]he debate about lawyer advertising may draw our attention from the larger question of access and vindication of rights. Advocates for unrestricted lawyer advertising claim it will lower the prices for lawyers' services in the market. This will solve the problems of access without requiring public subsidy. However, the services made available by increased demand created by advertising will not be the time-consuming counseling and "bargaining in the shadow of the law" that lower-income clients need to cope with public and private bureaucracies. Assuming that lawyer advertising succeeds in delivering low cost wills, uncontested divorces and name changes, we can also ask its advocates to show us what it will do for vindicating the rights found in constitutions and reform legislation.

> Some may be content to have the rights promised by the liberal welfare state remain unenforced and merely symbolic. Lawyer advertising may stir up litiga-

tion and trouble.... [Some] worry that true professionalism based on fiduciary duties towards clients will be lost as hucksters sell legal services in tasteless and deceptive ways. On the contrary, reformers tell us, advertising will inform consumers so that they can shop for services. This will promote efficiency and quality while expanding access to those who could not afford representation before. Both positions are overstated and reflect symbolic stances by those who seek to defend professional ideology or champion the simplification or deregulation as the cure for all problems ... Advertising alone is not likely to push the bar into crass commercialism or produce a nation of rational informed clients seeking to maximize utility. Recognizing this, we must be concerned that largely symbolic debates about lawyer advertising may divert us from concern with more pressing issues of access and equality.

Stewart Macaulay, *Lawyer Advertising: Yes But...*, U. Wis. Inst. For Legal Studies: Working Paper 703 (1985) at http://www.law.wisc.edu/facstaff/macaulay/papers/lawyer _advertising.pdf. The controversies that Professor Macaulay identified in 1985 continue today.

No other area of attorney regulation has as many variations among the states. One commentator, reviewing the states' regulation of advertising, observed that "no two states have identical ethics provisions." William E. Hornsby, Jr., *Ad Rules Infinitum: The Need for Alternatives to State-Based Ethics Governing Legal Services Marketing*, 36 U. Rich. L. Rev. 49, 50 (2002). No other area of attorney regulation (other than standards of ineffective assistance of counsel) has generated more United States Supreme Court opinions. In this chapter we will examine the interests in tension in the regulation of attorney adverting. We will examine the three main mechanisms for new client development: referrals, advertisement, and solicitation.

26.2 Getting Clients — Personal Referrals

Even today, in our competitive and diverse legal market, most clients still prefer to find a lawyer by personal referral, from other clients or from attorneys, rather than by relying on advertising. In a 2011 survey conducted for the ABA Standing Committee on the Delivery of Legal Services, when asked how they would locate an attorney if they were in need of representation, 46% of the respondents said they would ask a family member or colleague for the name of an attorney and 34% said they would contact an attorney they already knew or had used before.[1] You want your name to be the answer that is given when someone asks, "Do you know a good lawyer?" It pays, then, to spend extra effort insuring that your current clients are satisfied with your representation. Many of the lessons from this course—about professional communications and work management— are your best advertising.

Indeed, many attorneys find that plenty of business flows from attending to their professional calling "as a public citizen" to "seek improvement of the law, access to the legal

---

1. Debra Cassens Weiss, *Folks Still Find Lawyers the Old-Fashioned Way*, A.B.A. J. (May 2011) at http://www.abajournal.com/magazine/article/folks_still_find_lawyers_the_old-fashioned_way/.

system, the administration of justice and the quality of service rendered by the legal profession." *Preamble*, ABA Model Rules of Professional Conduct, Para. 5 (2004). For many years, solo and small firm attorneys have provided significant pro bono legal service and civic leadership. The pressure of a competitive legal market may tempt you to forsake these unpaid activities in favor of more explicit "client development" activities. While forsaking the professional call to service will be unlikely to subject you to discipline, it's not especially good ethics or good business. Having your name out in the community and being known for leadership, service, and commitment are still top-notch ways to "advertise" and generate referrals of paid clients.

Other methods of generating referrals, besides establishing a strong reputation, are subject to restrictions in most states. Nearly all states restrict attorneys from paying for referrals, with varying exceptions to that rule. Illinois Rule 7.2 provides all of the exceptions that the ABA Model Rule suggests:

Illinois Rules of Professional Conduct
Rule 7.2 Advertising

... (b) A lawyer shall not give anything of value to a person for recommending the lawyer's services except that a lawyer may

(1) pay the reasonable costs of advertisements or communications permitted by this Rule;

(2) pay the usual charges of a legal service plan or a not-for-profit lawyer referral service;

(3) pay for a law practice in accordance with Rule 1.17; and

(4) refer clients to another lawyer or a nonlawyer professional pursuant to an agreement not otherwise prohibited under these Rules that provides for the other person to refer clients or customers to the lawyer, if

(i) the reciprocal referral agreement is not exclusive, and

(ii) the client is informed of the existence and nature of the agreement....

Even some seemingly innocent arrangements can run afoul of the prohibition of referral fees. For example, even if a referral agreement between attorneys involves no exchange of money, but is simply a promise of reciprocal referrals, most states have opined that these arrangements amount to "giving something of value" for a referral. So the seemingly innocent agreement that "I'll send you my tax clients if you send me your divorce clients" can place an attorney at risk if that agreement is an express *quid pro quo*. Likewise, courts have disapproved of agreements with a current client in which the attorney provides a discount on legal fees if the client refers additional clients. Again, you must know your own state's rules on this. You can see that Illinois provides a safe harbor for these types of arrangements in 7.2(b)(4), following the lead of a 2002 amendment to the ABA Model Rules. This particular exception has yet to be adopted by more than a few states, though.

However, even in a state that prohibits these arrangements, attorneys are likely to develop habits of referral within their communities of practice. These practices are not prohibited so long as they are not the result of agreements to make referrals in exchange for other referrals. As you can imagine, it is nearly impossible to distinguish between reciprocal referrals that are a matter of mutual reputation and trust and are motivated by providing clients excellent referrals and those that are a matter of reciprocity, motivated by the desire for market advantage.

In other ways, the lines on referrals can be less than clear. For example, states in which attorneys may not participate in for-profit lawyer referral services, may permit attorneys to have their names listed in "directories" or participate in "cooperative advertising programs." The internet has further blurred these lines. Where is the line between, for example, an on-line referral service and an on-line directory with search functions? Always carefully consider the nature of the advertising arrangements you enter rather than simply relying on labels. Advertising programs are more likely to be considered referral programs if potential clients do not have access to the entire list of participating attorneys; if potential clients contact intermediaries who direct them to a particular attorney or actually set up appointments, rather than simply providing a list of contact information; and if the "fees" for participation in the program vary according to the number of potential clients obtained from participation. If the advertisement looks like a referral service (that is, potential clients may believe they are being "matched" with an attorney who meets their needs), but it is in fact simply a cooperative advertising program, with no effort to screen or match clients to attorneys, the advertising should be clear about that. In all instances of cooperative advertising, on-line directories, or referral services, you should be very clear about what you are getting into and investigate your own state's ethics rules regarding the propriety of these arrangements.

Another vague line is that separating referral fees and legitimate "fee splitting" agreements with other attorneys. Most state ethics permit attorneys who are not in the same firm to split fees only if the split is proportionate to the services performed or if each lawyer assumes joint responsibility for the representation. Some states require that there be both joint responsibility and proportionate fee splitting. States also vary on the degree to which the client must be informed of and consent to these arrangements. Since most courts do not aggressively police proportionate-work fee splitting agreements, it is sometimes difficult to tell whether an attorney is being paid $500 for simply referring a case to another attorney or whether the attorney truly has completed $500 worth of initial work on a case. Some attorneys deliberately exploit this vagueness, entering into explicit referral arrangements with other attorneys in which the receiving attorney agrees to "split fees" with the referring attorney at a set amount, regardless of work performed. These veiled attempts to skirt the rule prohibiting referral fees are not without significant risk. The referring attorney has, in these circumstances, entered into an attorney-client relationship, with all the associated risks of malpractice and conflicts disqualification. The receiving attorney runs the risk of violating the rules on referral fees. If the referring attorney is engaging in more than simply passive referral, but is actually soliciting clients in violation of the rules, the receiving attorney could be subject to discipline for this violation as well.

Even if referrals were without significant restriction, referrals work best for individuals who already regularly use legal services or interact with professionals who use legal services. Individuals who have the fewest resources to hire attorneys are also the very same people who are unlikely to have the contacts that can provide them referrals for attorneys. For these individuals in particular, advertising can play an important role in increasing accessibility. Studies of advertising and its effects on price and accessibility generally demonstrate that advertising can improve accessibility. Some states expressly recognize this role. For example, Comment 3 to Washington Rule of Professional Conduct 7.2, explains, "Television is now one of the most powerful media for getting information to the public, particularly persons of low and moderate income.... Similarly, electronic media, such as the Internet, can be an important source of information about legal services ..." Advertising, however, is regulated even more strictly than referrals.

26.3 Advertising Regulation

In 1968, the ABA Code of Professional Responsibility D.R. 2-101 banned virtually all forms of advertising and solicitation by lawyers. At that time, an appropriate advertisement would have been a business card that looked something like this:

> ### Barbara Glesner Fines
> _____
>
> Attorney and Counselor at Law
> 500 East 52nd Street
> Kansas City, Missouri
> (816) 235-2380

Moreover, it would have been questionable to whom you could give this card. Giving it to potential clients would result in severe sanction, as in-person solicitation was flatly prohibited.

The first challenge to the advertising ban of D.R. 2-101 came in *Bates v. State Bar of Arizona*, 433 U.S. 350, 365, 374-75 (1977). Two attorneys, who had worked for legal aid, decided to start a practice offering middle-income clients routine legal services at low costs. They concluded that advertising was necessary for their practice to succeed. They placed an advertisement, clearly labeled as such, in the newspaper. (The advertisement is recreated on the next page.) The Supreme Court recognized this as commercial speech, for which a flat ban, justified by the need to protect the dignity of the bar or the unique nature of legal practice, could not survive constitutional scrutiny.

Soon after *Bates*, the Supreme Court decided *Central Hudson Gas & Electric Corp. v. Public Service Comm.*, 447 U.S. 557 (1980). That case did not involve attorney advertising but did develop the test for commercial speech regulation that has been applied since then to attorney advertisement. The threshold test is whether the prohibited advertising is truthful, non-misleading speech regarding a lawful activity. Once the court determines that the commercial speech concerns lawful activity & is not misleading, government regulation is constitutional only if: 1) the government has a substantial interest in regulation, 2) that regulation "directly advances" the government interest, and 3) the regulation is "no more extensive than is necessary to serve" that interest.

Two years later, the Supreme Court in *In re R.M.J.*, 455 U.S. 191, 203, 71 L. Ed. 2d 64, 102 S. Ct. 929 (1982) confirmed that the *Central Hudson* test applied to the analysis of restrictions on attorney advertising. These first two advertising cases by the Court involved regulations that directly affected the availability and affordability of legal services. The attorneys in *Bates* wanted to advertise their fees for routine legal services. The attorneys in *RMJ* sought to advertise their areas of practice and the states in which they were admitted. The Court concluded that regulations may not simply state lists of permitted statements and prohibit everything else.

Since these two cases, the history of attorney regulation has been a search for the proper balance between permitting advertising in order to serve these interests of access, affordability, and education and regulating advertising in order to protect against false and misleading information, marketing methods that are manipulative and intrusive, and advertising that harms the image of the profession.

One of the most important interests to be served in regulating attorney advertising is to insure that the information provided by these advertisements is truthful. States have an important governmental interest in preventing false advertising. Some states take a minimalist approach to defining false or misleading advertising. Oklahoma is a good example of this approach:

Oklahoma Rules of Professional Conduct
Rule 7.1. Communications Concerning a Lawyer's Services

A lawyer shall not make a false or misleading communication about the lawyer or the lawyer's services. A communication is false or misleading if it contains a material misrepresentation of fact or law, or omits a fact necessary to make the communication considered as a whole not materially misleading.

Other states, however, are far more aggressive in defining those statements considered to be false or misleading. Florida is a good example of a highly regulatory state. Florida Rules of Professional Conduct provide three separate rules that regulate various advertisements according to the interests sought to be advanced by each. Those categories are advertisements that are: "Deceptive and Inherently Misleading," "Potentially Misleading," and "Unduly Manipulative or Intrusive." Some excerpts from each of these rules give you a picture of the scope of this regulation:

Florida Rules of Professional Conduct
Rule 4-7.3 Deceptive and Inherently Misleading Advertisements

A lawyer may not engage in deceptive or inherently misleading advertising.

(a) Deceptive and Inherently Misleading Advertisements. An advertisement is deceptive or inherently misleading if it:

(1) contains a material statement that is factually or legally inaccurate;

(2) omits information that is necessary to prevent the information supplied from being misleading; or

(3) implies the existence of a material nonexistent fact.

[This first portion of the rule parallels a pre-2002 version of Model Rule 7.1. The ABA deleted parts (2) and (3) of the rule because it was considered overbroad. The Florida rule goes on to provide a list of ten examples of deceptive and inherently misleading ads. These include, in varying degrees of specificity, predictions of success; comparisons to other lawyers; actors; dramatizations; implications that the attorney will use illegal or unethical tactics; testimonials; statements that the Florida Bar has approved the message; or government titles (e.g., judge, senator, etc.) for currently practicing attorneys.]

Rule 4-7.4 Potentially Misleading Advertisements

A lawyer may not engage in potentially misleading advertising.

(a) Potentially Misleading Advertisements. Potentially misleading advertisements include, but are not limited to:

(1) advertisements that are subject to varying reasonable interpretations, one or more of which would be materially misleading when considered in the relevant context;

(2) advertisements that are literally accurate, but could reasonably mislead a prospective client regarding a material fact;

[the rule goes on to provide detailed restrictions on advertising membership in organizations or statements of specialization or certification and restrictions on contingent fee advertisements] …

(b) Clarifying Information. A lawyer may use an advertisement that would otherwise be potentially misleading if the advertisement contains information or statements that adequately clarify the potentially misleading issue.

Rule 4-7.5 Unduly Manipulative or Intrusive Advertisements

A lawyer may not engage in unduly manipulative or intrusive advertisements. An advertisement is unduly manipulative if it:

(a) uses an image, sound, video or dramatization in a manner that is designed to solicit legal employment by appealing to a prospective client's emotions rather than to a rational evaluation of a lawyer's suitability to represent the prospective client;

(b) uses an authority figure such as a judge or law enforcement officer, or an actor portraying an authority figure, to endorse or recommend the lawyer or act as a spokesperson for the lawyer;

(c) contains the voice or image of a celebrity, except that a lawyer may use the voice or image of a local announcer, disc jockey or radio personality who regularly records advertisements so long as the person recording the announcement does not endorse or offer a testimonial on behalf of the advertising lawyer or law firm; or

(d) offers consumers an economic incentive to employ the lawyer or review the lawyer's advertising; provided that this rule does not prohibit a lawyer from offering a discounted fee or special fee or cost structure as otherwise permitted by these rules and does not prohibit the lawyer from offering free legal advice or information that might indirectly benefit a consumer economically

Despite the Florida court's efforts to distinguish between false advertisements and those which are only potentially misleading or are otherwise intrusive, the lines are far from clear in terms of the constitutional review of these regulations. The difference is critical however, because inherently misleading advertisements may be banned outright without having to satisfy the *Central Hudson* three-pronged balancing test. In contrast,

… the States may not place an absolute prohibition on certain types of potentially misleading information, e.g., a listing of areas of practice, if the information also may be presented in a way that is not deceptive…. Although the potential for deception and confusion is particularly strong in the context of advertising professional services, restrictions upon such advertising may be no broader than reasonably necessary to prevent the deception.

In re R. M. J., 455 U.S. 191, 203 (1982).

Despite state regulations that continue to severely restrict and even ban statements that are only potentially misleading, if challenged, these restrictions have been much harder to justify. For example, the Second Circuit Court of Appeals reviewed a range of New York state prohibitions on advertising and concluded that many of them were unconstitutional. *Alexander v. Cahill*, 598 F.3d 79 (2d Cir. 2010), *cert. denied*, 2010 WL 3207570 (U.S. 2010). The law firm in this case, Alexander & Catalano, used print and electronic advertisements. Their advertisements used jingles, slogans ("we'll give you a big helping hand"), special effects (wisps of smoke and blue electrical currents surrounding the firm's name), dramatizations (including a depiction of a courtroom with a judge), and depictions of the attorneys as giants, as superheroes who could run so fast as to appear as blurs, and as attorneys for space aliens. The court reviewed the state's prohibition of nearly all of these forms of advertising and concluded that most could not be justified under the *Central Hudson* test. Theses included:

1. Client Testimonials—The court concluded that testimonials are not inherently misleading. "Testimonials may, for example, mislead if they suggest that past results indicate future performance—but not all testimonials will do so, especially if they include a disclaimer." *Alexander*, 598 F.3d at 92.

2. Portrayal of a Judge—The state argued that the portrayal of a judge in an advertisement was likely to imply that the lawyer could improperly influence a court. The court rejected this assumption, noting that the attorney's advertisement simply showed a judge in the courtroom and stated that the judge is there "to make sure [the trial] is fair." *Alexander*, 598 F.3d at 93.

3. Irrelevant Techniques—The state's regulation prohibited advertisements that "rely on techniques to obtain attention that demonstrate a clear and intentional lack of relevance to the selection of counsel, including the portrayal of lawyers exhibiting characteristics clearly unrelated to legal competence." The court rejected the correlation between an ad with irrelevant aspects and one that is misleading:

> Moreover, the sorts of gimmicks that this rule appears designed to reach—such as Alexander & Catalano's wisps of smoke, blue electrical currents, and special effects—do not actually seem likely to mislead. It is true that Alexander and his partner are not giants towering above local buildings; they cannot run to a client's house so quickly that they appear as blurs; and they do not actually provide legal assistance to space aliens. But given the prevalence of these and other kinds of special effects in advertising and entertainment, we cannot seriously believe—purely as a matter of "common sense"—that ordinary individuals are likely to be misled into thinking that these advertisements depict true characteristics. Indeed, some of these gimmicks, while seemingly irrelevant, may actually serve "important communicative functions: [they] attract[] the attention of the audience to the advertiser's message, and [they] may also serve to impart information directly." *Zauderer*, 471 U.S. at 647. Plaintiffs assert that they use attention-getting techniques to "communicate ideas in an easy-to-understand form, to attract viewer interest, to give emphasis, and to make information more memorable." (Appellees' Br. 36) Defendants provide no evidence to the contrary; nor do they provide evidence that consumers have, in fact, been misled by these or similar advertisements. Absent such, or similar, evidence, Defendants cannot meet their burden for sustaining subsection 1200.50(c)(5)'s prohibition under *Central Hudson*.

Alexander, 598 F.3d at 94.

4. Nicknames, Mottos, and Trade Names—While acknowledging that some trade names could in fact be deceiving, the court rejected that as a justification for a categorical ban.

Rather than ban potentially misleading advertisements, many states instead require disclaimers or disclosures. The Court in *Zauderer v. Office of Disciplinary Counsel of Supreme Court of Ohio*, 471 U.S. 626 (1985) first addressed the requirement of disclosures or disclaimers as a method of regulating potentially misleading advertisements. The attorney in that case had advertised that his fee was contingent on recovery. The state required attorneys who advertised "no recovery/no fee" to expressly state if the clients would still be charged costs. In upholding this required disclosure, the Court stated:

In requiring attorneys who advertise their willingness to represent clients on a contingent-fee basis to state that the client may have to bear certain expenses even if he loses, Ohio has not attempted to prevent attorneys from conveying information to the public; it has only required them to provide somewhat more information than they might otherwise be inclined to present. We have, to be sure, held that in some instances compulsion to speak may be as violative of the First Amendment as prohibitions on speech. Indeed, ... the Court went so far as to state that "involuntary affirmation could be commanded only on even more immediate and urgent grounds than silence."

... Because the extension of First Amendment protection to commercial speech is justified principally by the value to consumers of the information such speech provides, appellant's constitutionally protected interest in not providing any particular factual information in his advertising is minimal. Thus, in virtually all our commercial speech decisions to date, we have emphasized that because disclosure requirements trench much more narrowly on an advertiser's interests than do flat prohibitions on speech, "warning[s] or disclaimer[s] might be appropriately required ... in order to dissipate the possibility of consumer confusion or deception."

We do not suggest that disclosure requirements do not implicate the advertiser's First Amendment rights at all. We recognize that unjustified or unduly burdensome disclosure requirements might offend the First Amendment by chilling protected commercial speech. But we hold that an advertiser's rights are adequately protected as long as disclosure requirements are reasonably related to the State's interest in preventing deception of consumers.

The State's application to appellant of the requirement that an attorney advertising his availability on a contingent-fee basis disclose that clients will have to pay costs even if their lawsuits are unsuccessful (assuming that to be the case) easily passes muster under this standard. Appellant's advertisement informed the public that "if there is no recovery, no legal fees are owed by our clients." The advertisement makes no mention of the distinction between "legal fees" and "costs," and to a layman not aware of the meaning of these terms of art, the advertisement would suggest that employing appellant would be a no-lose proposition in that his representation in a losing cause would come entirely free of charge. The assumption that substantial numbers of potential clients would be so misled is hardly a speculative one: it is a commonplace that members of the public are often unaware of the technical meanings of such terms as "fees" and "costs"—terms that, in ordinary usage, might well be virtually interchangeable. When the possibility of deception is as self-evident as it is in this case, we need not require the State to "conduct a survey of the ... public before it [may] determine that the [advertisement] had a tendency to mislead." The State's position that it is deceptive to employ advertising that refers to contingent-fee arrangements without mentioning the client's liability for costs is reasonable enough to support a requirement that information regarding the client's liability for costs be disclosed.

Zauderer, 471 U.S. at 650-53.

The requirement of disclaimers is an increasingly common approach to the regulation of advertising. Eight states require a disclaimer on nearly all advertisements, whether a simple, but conspicuous, label, "THIS IS AN ADVERTISEMENT" (Kentucky Rules of

Professional Conduct SCR 3.130(7.25) (2008)), or a warning that "[t]he choice of a lawyer is an important decision and should not be based solely upon advertisements" (Missouri Rules of Professional Conduct Rule 4-7.2(f) (2008)). Eighteen states have disclosure requirements for contingent fee advertisements similar to those reviewed by the Court in *Zauderer*. Other common statements that require disclaimers are comparisons with other attorneys, the use of testimonials or endorsements, and statements regarding past results or verdicts.

Federal regulations include disclaimer requirements for attorneys practicing in specific fields. For example, IRS Circular 230 requires those who practice before the IRS to include in all communications with clients the following disclaimer:

> To ensure compliance with requirements imposed by the IRS in Circular 230, we inform you that, unless expressly stated otherwise in this communication (including attachments), any tax advice contained in this communication is not intended or written to be used, and cannot be used, for the purpose of:
>
> (i) avoiding penalties under the Internal Revenue Code or
>
> (ii) promoting, marketing or recommending to another party any transaction or other matter addressed herein.

IRS Circular 230. 31 CFR part 10 (2011).

Similarly, the United States Bankruptcy Code requires bankruptcy practitioners to include in all advertisements the statement, "We are a debt relief agency. We help people to file for bankruptcy relief." The Supreme Court in *Milavetz, Gallop & Milavetz, P.A. v. United States*, 130 S.Ct. 1324, 176 L. Ed. 2d 79; 2010 U.S. LEXIS 2206 (2010), upheld this requirement. The Court held that the disclaimer requirement satisfied the rational basis test that applies under *Zauderer* to regulations of commercial speech that merely compel disclosures (and do not restrict speech). The Court also limited the definition of "debt relief agency" to an attorney providing services to a consumer debtor. The Court noted: "Section 528 also gives Milavetz flexibility to tailor the disclosures to its individual circumstances, as long as the resulting statements are "substantially similar" to the statutory examples. §§ 528(a)(4) and (b)(2)(B)." *Id.* at 1341. Some attorneys have responded to this opinion by including a statement in their advertising that "We are a designated debt relief agency under the United States Bankruptcy Code." What do you think of this implementation of the Court's requirement?

An excellent example of the difficulty in distinguishing between inherently misleading and potentially misleading advertisement and the outer limits of disclaimers can be found in the regulation of specialization advertising. For many years, advertisement of specialization was considered misleading and most states prohibited it until *Peel v. Attorney Registration and Disciplinary Comm'n of Ill.*, 496 U.S. 91 (1990), where the Supreme Court held that a state cannot prevent a lawyer from truthfully and non-deceptively representing that he/she is certified by a third party as a specialist in a particular area of practice. Nonetheless, nearly all states have some type of restrictions or required disclaimers on specialization advertisements. Many states limit the types of specializations or certifications that can be advertised and require disclaimers regarding those specializations. New York Rule of Professional Conduct 7.4(c) for example provides:

> A lawyer may state that the lawyer has been recognized or certified as a specialist only as follows:
>
> (1) A lawyer who is certified as a specialist in a particular area of law or law practice by a private organization approved for that purpose by the American Bar

Association may state the fact of certification if, in conjunction therewith, the certifying organization is identified and the following statement is prominently made: "The [name of the private certifying organization] is not affiliated with any governmental authority. Certification is not a requirement for the practice of law in the State of New York and does not necessarily indicate greater competence than other attorneys experienced in this field of law;"

(2) A lawyer who is certified as a specialist in a particular area of law or law practice by the authority having jurisdiction over specialization under the laws of another state or territory may state the fact of certification if, in conjunction therewith, the certifying state or territory is identified and the following statement is prominently made: "Certification granted by the [identify state or territory] is not recognized by any governmental authority within the State of New York. Certification is not a requirement for the practice of law in the State of New York and does not necessarily indicate greater competence than other attorneys experienced in this field of law."

The United States Court of Appeals for the Second Circuit recently held that much of this provision was unconstitutional. The court's opinion provides a window into the confusion and tensions underlying the regulation of "potentially misleading" advertising.

Hayes v. New York Attorney Grievance Comm. of the Eighth Judicial District

No. 10-1587-cv, 2012 U.S. App. LEXIS 4526 (2nd Cir. March 5, 2012)

Rule 7.4(d) of the ABA's Model Rules of Professional Responsibility permits a lawyer to be identified as a specialist in a particular field of law provided that (1) the lawyer has been certified by an organization approved by a state or accredited by the ABA and (2) the name of the certifying organization is clearly identified. *See* Model Rules of Professional Conduct R. 7.4(d) (2009). 48 states have rules that permit lawyers to identify themselves as specialists. The rules of 32 of these states are similar to the ABA's model rule,[2] although some of these

---

2. See Ala. Rules of Prof. Conduct, Rule 7.4(c) (2011); Alas. R. Prof. Conduct 7.4(b) (2011); Ariz. Rules of Prof'l Conduct, R. 7.4(a)(3) (2011); Ark. Rules of Prof. Conduct 7.4(d) (2011); Cal. Rules of Prof'l Conduct, Rule 1-400(D)(6) (2011); Conn. Rules of Prof'l Conduct 7.4A (2011); Del. Prof. Cond. R. 7.4(d) (2011); Fla. Bar Reg. R. 4-7.2(c)(6) (2011); Ga. R. & Regs. St. Bar 7.4 (2011); Idaho Rules of Prof'l Conduct, R. 7.4(c) (2011); Ind. Rules of Prof'l Conduct 7.4(d) (2011); Iowa R. of Prof'l Conduct 32:7.4(d) (2011); Kan. Rules of Prof. Conduct 7.4(d) (2011); Ky. SCR Rules 7.40 (2011); La. St. Bar Ass'n Art. XVI §7.2(c)(5) (2011); Me. Rules of Prof'l Conduct 7.4(d) (2010); Mont. Prof. Conduct R. 7.4 (2010); Neb. Ct. R. of Prof. Cond. §3-507.4 (2011); Nev. Rules of Prof'l Conduct 7.4(d) (2011); N.H. Rules of Prof'l Conduct Rule 7.4(c) (2011); N.J. Court Rules, RPC 7.4 (2011); N.M. R. Prof. Conduct, 16-704 (2011); N.C. Prof. Cond. Rule 7.4(b) (2011); Ohio Prof. Cond. Rule 7.4(e) (2011); Or. Rules Prof'l Conduct 7.1(4) (2009); Pa. RPC 7.4(a) (2011); S.C. Rule 7.4(a), RPC, Rule 407, SCACR (2010); S.D. Codified Laws §16-18-appx.-7.4(d) (2011); Tenn. Sup. Ct. R. 8, Rule 7.4 (2011); Tex. R. Prof. Conduct 7.4(b) (2011); Utah Rules of Prof'l Conduct, Rule 7.4(d) (2011); Wis. SCR 20:7.4(d) (2011); Wyo. Prof. Conduct Rule 7.4(d) (2010).

require state board or state court approval of the certifying body.[3] Many of the states that have not adopted the Model Rule require any claim of specialization to be accompanied by various forms of disclaimers, such as a statement that the state does not certify lawyers as specialists.[4] Two of the 48 states, Minnesota and Missouri, permit identification of a lawyer as a specialist even in the absence of certification, but require disclosure that there has been no certification by an organization accredited by a state board or court.[5] One state, West Virginia, prohibits lawyers from identifying themselves as specialists except for patent attorneys and proctors in admiralty.[6] One state, Maryland, prohibits identification as a specialist with no exceptions.[7] Michigan and Mississippi have no rules concerning communications about lawyer specialization.

Efforts by states or bar associations to restrict lawyer advertising, particularly ads asserting accreditation in specialized areas of law, inevitably create some tension between legitimate concerns to protect the public from misleading claims and guild mentality maneuvers to stifle legitimate competition in the market for legal services. The ABA has endeavored to steer a course between these competing concerns by establishing standards for accreditation of specialty certification programs. These standards permit a certifying organization to certify lawyers in a field of specialization only if a lawyer has practiced in the specialty for at least three years, spent at least one-fourth of that time in the specialty area, passed a written exam, obtained five recommendations a majority of which are from judges or lawyers, taken at least 36 hours of continuing legal education ("CLE") in the specialty area in the preceding three years, and be in good standing. *See* ABA Standards for Special Certification Programs for Lawyers, §4.06. Pursuant to these criteria, the ABA has accredited the NBTA[8] to certify lawyers as a specialist in the areas of trial, criminal, and family law. *See* http://www.nblsc.us (last visited Jan. 18 2012). The standards of the NBTA for attorney certification as a specialist include at least 30 percent concentration in the field for at least the preceding three years, at least 45 hours of CLE in the preceding three years, ten to twelve references, including at least three judges and three attorneys, being lead counsel in at least five jury trials, and successful completion of a six-hour NBTA examination. *See* http://www.nblsc.us/certification_standards_civil/. A certified attorney is required to apply for recertification after five years. *See id.* The NBTA certified Hayes in civil trial advocacy in 1995 and recertified him in 2000.

Both parties agree that attorney advertising is commercial speech, which may be subjected to restrictions so long as they satisfy the standards set

---

3. See Ala. Rules of Prof. Conduct, Rule 7.4(c) (state bar approval); Ariz. Rules of Prof'l Conduct, R. 7.4(a)(3) (state board approval); Conn. Rules of Prof'l Conduct 7.4A (state court committee approval); Pa. RPC 7.4(a) (state court approval); S.C. Rule 7.4(a), RPC, Rule 407 SCACR (state court approval); Tex. R. Prof. Conduct 7.4(b) (state board approval).

4. See, e.g., Colo. RPC 7.4(d) (2011); Ill. Sup. Ct. R. Prof'l Conduct, R. 7.4 (2011); Va. Sup. Ct. R. pt. 6, sec. II, 7.4 (2011).

5. See Minn. Rules of Prof'l Conduct 7.4(d) (2011); Mo. Sup. Ct. R. 4-7.4 (2010).

6. See W. Va. Prof. Cond. Rule 7.4 (2011).

7. Md. Lawyer's R. Prof'l Conduct 7.4(a) (2011).

8. [The NBTA is now known as the National Board of Legal Specialty Certification.]

forth by the Supreme Court in *Central Hudson*. The four-part test is as follows:

> First, for commercial speech to merit any First Amendment protection, it "must concern lawful activity and not be misleading." Next, the government must assert a substantial interest to be achieved by the restriction. If both these conditions are met, the third and fourth parts of the test are "whether the regulation directly advances the governmental interest asserted" and whether the regulation "is not more extensive than is necessary to serve that interest."

Anderson v. Treadwell, 294 F.3d 453, 461 (2d Cir. 2002) (quoting *Central Hudson,* 447 U.S. at 563-66). In some contexts, a less rigorous First Amendment test applies to governmental requirements that compel rather than prohibit speech. *See Milavetz, Gallop & Milavetz, P.A. v. United States,* 130 S. Ct. 1324, 1339-40 (2010); *Zauderer v. Office of Disciplinary Counsel of Supreme Court of Ohio,* 471 U.S. 626, 651-52 (1985); *In re R.M.J.,* 455 U.S. 191, 202-03 (1982); *National Electrical Manufacturers Assn. v. Sorrell,* 272 F.3d 104, 113-14 (2d Cir. 2001). *But see Riley v. National Federation of Blind of N.C., Inc.,* 487 U.S. 781, 796-97 (1988); *Milavetz,* 130 S. Ct. at 1343 (Thomas, J., concurring in part and concurring in the judgment); *Glickman v. Wileman Brothers & Elliott, Inc.,* 521 U.S. 457, 480-81 (1997) (Souter, J., dissenting).

In two decisions the Supreme Court has considered the constitutional validity of state restrictions on professionals holding themselves out as specialists. *See Peel* and *Ibanez v. Florida Dep't of Business and Professional Regulation,* 512 U.S. 136 (1994). The teaching of these two cases is not entirely clear. In Peel, the Supreme Court considered a prohibition against an attorney's advertisement that stated that he was a civil trial specialist certified by the NBTA. The Court held, 5 to 4, that absolute prohibition of the certification statement violated the First Amendment. *See Peel,* 496 U.S. at 99-111 (Stevens, J., with whom Brennan, Blackmun, and Kennedy, JJ., join); *id.* at 111-17 (Marshall, J., with whom Brennan, J. joins, concurring in the judgment). The plurality opinion was willing to assume, however, that the specialist certification was "potentially misleading," *id.* at 109, and observed that, "[t]o the extent that potentially misleading statements of private certification or specialization could confuse consumers, a State might consider ... requiring a disclaimer about the certifying organization or the standards of a specialty," *id.* at 110. Justice Marshall's concurring opinion noted that the certification statement was "potentially misleading," id. at 111, and also suggested that a state "could require a lawyer claiming certification by the NBTA as a civil trial specialist to provide additional information in order to prevent that claim from being misleading," *id.* at 117.

The opinions in *Peel* differed as to the respect in which a certification might be misleading. For the plurality, it could be misleading "if the certification had been issued by an organization that had made no inquiry into [the lawyer's] fitness, or by one that issued certificates indiscriminately for a price." *Id.* at 102. For Justices Marshall and Brennan, "[t]he name 'National Board of Trial Advocacy' could create the misimpression that the NBTA is an agency of the Federal Government," *id.* at 112, and they stated that a state could require "a disclaimer stating that the NBTA is a private organization not affiliated with, or sanctioned by, the State or Federal Government," *id.* at 117. Justice White also considered the certification statement "potentially misleading" for the reasons stated by Justices Brennan and Marshall. *Id.* at 118 (White, J., dissenting). The Chief Justice and Justices Scalia and O'Connor considered the certification statement "inherently likely to deceive," *id.* at 121 (O'Connor, J., with whom Rehnquist, C.J., and Scalia, J., join, dissenting), in that it "lead[s] the consumer to believe that this lawyer is better than those lawyers lacking such certification," *id.* at 123, and "to conclude that the State has sanctioned the certification," *id.*

Thus, although the absolute prohibition of a certification statement was rejected 5 to 4, at least six members of the Court (the Chief Justice and Justices Brennan, Marshall, O'Connor, Scalia, and White) considered the statement at least potentially misleading, believing that it could be understood to imply state sanctioned certification. And Justice Stevens's opinion for the plurality also indicated that a state "could require a disclaimer stating that the NBTA is a private organization not affiliated with, or sanctioned by, the State or Federal Government." *Id.* at 117.

Four years later in *Ibanez*, the Court, considering a state's censure of a lawyer for truthfully listing herself as a CPA (Certified Public Accountant) and a CFP (Certified Financial Planner), sent a rather different message. Invalidating by a vote of 7 to 2 the censure as violative of the First Amendment, *Ibanez*, 512 U.S. at 143-49, the Court began by emphasizing the requirement from Central Hudson that "[c]ommercial speech that is not false, deceptive, or misleading can be restricted, but only if the State shows that the restriction directly and materially advances a substantial state interest in a manner no more extensive than necessary to serve that interest." *Id.* at 142 (citing *Central Hudson*, 447 U.S. at 566) (footnote omitted); *see Florida Bar v. Went For It, Inc.*, 515 U.S. 618, 625-26 (1995). Continuing, the Court in *Ibanez* noted that "[t]he State's burden is not slight," and that " '[m]ere speculation or conjecture' will not suffice; rather the State 'must demonstrate that the harms it recites are real and that its restriction will in fact alleviate them to a material degree." *Id.* at 143 (quoting *Edenfield v. Fane*, 507 U.S. 761, 770, 771 (1993)). And, said the Court, "we cannot allow rote incantation of the words 'potentially misleading' to supplant the [regulating body's] burden." *Id.* at 146 (citing *Edenfield*, 507 U.S. at 771).

Then, recalling that *Peel* had indicated some tolerance for a disclaimer to avoid potentially misleading statements about certification, the Court stated that *Ibanez* "does not fall within the caveat noted in Peel covering certifications issued by organizations that 'had made no inquiry into [the lawyer's] fitness,' or had 'issued certificates indiscriminately for a price,' " *id.* at 148 (quoting *Peel*, 496 U.S. at 102), thereby using the extreme examples of a potentially misleading certification offered by the plurality opinion in *Peel*, rather than a consumer's possible belief that the certifying organization was affiliated with the government, which had been noted by five Justices in *Peel*. Indeed, the Court in Ibanez invalidated the requirement that a disclaimer state that the certifying agency is not affiliated with the state or federal government "[g]iven the state of the record—the failure of the [regulating agency] to point to any harm that is potentially real, not purely hypothetical." *Id.* at 146. The Court even observed that the detail required in the disclaimer, which also included the requirements for certification, was too extensive to be included on a business card or letterhead or in a yellow pages listing. *See id.* at 146-47.

Thus, we are left to wonder whether to follow *Peel*'s apparent approval of some sort of disclaimer to avoid at least some potentially misleading aspects of a certification statement or to insist, as *Ibanez* did, on a record demonstrating real harms that will be alleviated to a material degree by the challenged disclaimer requirement. Despite this perplexity, we will consider separately the three components of the Disclaimer at issue in the pending case and then turn to the vagueness challenge to the requirement that the disclaimer be "prominently made."

We see no First Amendment infirmity in the required assertion that the certifying organization, i.e., the NBTA, is not affiliated with any governmental authority. Absent this assertion, which is entirely accurate, there would be a risk that some members of the public would believe that New York State or its judicial branch had authorized the NBTA to certify lawyers in their field of specialty. Such a belief might make some people think that this certification is more valuable than a certification conferred by a private organization without official authorization. Avoiding such a possible misconception furthers a substantial governmental interest in consumer education and is not more intrusive than necessary to further that interest. Although the Grievance Committee has not developed a record in support of the possible misconceptions concerning government affiliation, we feel obliged to follow what a majority of the Court said in Peel on this precise subject in a case dealing explicitly with NBTA specialist certification.

The statement that certification is not a requirement for the practice of law is more questionable. It is sought to be justified on the basis that, absent this assertion, there would be a risk that some members of the public would believe that certification is required to practice law, thereby leading them to think that they must limit their choice of state-licensed lawyers to those who have been certified as specialists. This possible belief that certification is needed to practice law is sufficiently strained to require some basis in the record to support it. *See, e.g., Florida Bar*, 515 U.S. at 626 ("'[A] governmental body seeking to sustain a restriction on commercial speech must *demonstrate* that the Harms it recites are real....'" (quoting *Rubin v. Coors Brewing Co.*, 514 U.S. 476, 487 (1995) (emphasis added). Although trial testimony is not required, the proponents of a restriction must either advance an interest that is self-evident or put something in the record to make the required "demonstrat[ion]." No such demonstration is present in the record before us. And the alleged harm is surely not self-evident. It is difficult to imagine that any significant portion of the public observing the thousands of lawyers practicing in New York without certification believe that all of them are acting unlawfully. Because this second statement relies on "mere speculation or conjecture," *Edenfield v. Fane*, 507 U.S. 761, 770 (1993), it does not satisfy the Central Hudson test.

The third required assertion—that certification "does not necessarily indicate greater competence than other attorneys experienced in this field of law"—is even more problematic. Although the assertion might be technically accurate, depending on how "competence" and "experienced in the field" are understood, the assertion has a capacity to create misconceptions at least as likely and as serious as that sought to be avoided by the first assertion. Some members of the public, reading this third assertion, might easily think that a certified attorney has no greater qualifications than other attorneys with some (unspecified) degree of experience in the designated area of practice. In fact, the qualifications of an attorney certified as a civil trial specialist by the NBTA include having been lead counsel in at least 5 trials and having "actively participated" in at least 100 contested matters involving the taking of testimony, passing an extensive examination, participating in at least 45 hours of CLE, and devoting at least 30 percent of the lawyer's practice to the specialized field. *See* http://www.nblsc.us/certification_standards_civil/. These qualifications may reasonably be considered by the certifying body to provide some assurance of "competence" greater than that of lawyers meeting only the criterion of having some experience in the field, and a contrary assertion has a clear potential to mislead. Such a requirement does not serve a substantial state interest, is far more intrusive than necessary, and is entirely unsupported by the record. As such, it cannot survive First Amendment scrutiny.

[The court went on to hold that the requirement that the disclaimer be "prominently made" was potentially void for vagueness.] The judgments of the District Court are reversed, and the case is remanded with directions to enter judgment for the Plaintiff-Appellant declaring the second and third components of the Disclaimer invalid and enjoining enforcement of the first component against Hayes absent clear advance notice to him from the Committee of specific alleged defects in his advertising and an opportunity for him either to know what he must do to comply or to seek judicial review of the Committee's elaboration of the requirement.

Notes

1. What was the court's confusion about the difference in the standard of *Peel* and that of *Ibanez*? Which standard did the court appear to finally apply?

2. How do you decide what to do if you want to advertise in a particular way that the rules of conduct prohibit or restrict and you believe that regulation is unconstitutional? The attorneys in the New York case, like many of the cases challenging attorney advertising, brought a declaratory judgment. This method has the advantage of avoiding any sanction and having clear guidance from the court regarding your actions. Of course, declaratory judgment is not available in either the federal courts or in most state courts unless there is a "case or controversy." "Basically, the question in each case is whether the facts alleged, under all the circumstances, show that there is a substantial controversy, between parties having adverse legal interests, of sufficient immediacy and reality to warrant the issuance of a declaratory judgment." *Maryland Cas. Co. v. Pacific Coal & Oil Co.,* 312 U.S. 270, 273, 61 S. Ct. 510, 85 L. Ed. 826 (1941). So, for example, in the *Hayes* case, the attorney had been sanctioned previously for violating the advertising rules and sought a declaratory judgment to prevent future similar sanctions. In contrast, the attorney's claim in *Geisenberger v. Gonzales,* 346 B.R. 678 (E.D. Pa. 2006), seeking to challenge the Bankruptcy Act's restrictions on attorney advice to clients, was dismissed because the attorney "did not allege that he had suffered, or was about to suffer, any injury in fact. He did not assert that either the United States or the

Commonwealth of Pennsylvania had threatened to enforce the 'debt relief agency' provisions of the BAPCPA against him or that he feared such enforcement in the immediate future."

Another route to challenge regulations is to appeal from the imposition of discipline. For example, the attorney in *In re RMJ* had appealed from a private reprimand for his violation of the advertising regulations. However, the attorney there had not simply violated the rule in the hopes he would not be sanctioned, but his actions were intended to challenge the rule. *In re RMJ*, 609 S.W.2d 411 (1980) ("We are aware, of course, that this is a 'test' case"). The most obvious disadvantage of this route is that, if the appeal is unsuccessful, you will have incurred disciplinary sanctions. Comments to Rule 8.4 provide that "A lawyer may refuse to comply with an obligation imposed by law upon a good faith belief that no valid obligation exists." However, there are almost no cases where this comment has been cited to provide a safe harbor for the attorney who is acting in good faith within that area of uncertainty. *In re Gadbois*, 173 Vt. 59, 786 A.2d 393, 2001 Vt. LEXIS 277 (2001) (discipline inappropriate for attorney who was disqualified from a representation he undertook in circumstances in which law was unclear regarding standard for former client conflicts).

Either route to challenging a rule of conduct is of course very expensive and time-consuming. You can see why many attorneys simply choose to comply with regulations rather than challenge their constitutionality.

26.4 Regulating Solicitation

Whereas courts have struck down flat bans on advertising of various sorts, they more regularly uphold bans on in-person solicitation of paying clients. Mississippi's regulation is a good example of this regulation.

Mississippi Rules of Professional Conduct
Rule 7.3 Direct Contact with Prospective Clients

(a) A Lawyer shall not by in-person, live telephone, or real-time electronic contact solicit professional employment from a particular prospective client with whom the lawyer has no family, close personal, or prior professional relationship when a significant motive of the lawyer's doing so is the lawyer's pecuniary gain.

(b) A lawyer shall not solicit professional employment from a particular prospective client by written, recorded or electronic communication or by in-person, telephone or real time electronic contact even when not otherwise prohibited by paragraph (a), if:

(1) Prospective client has made known to the lawyer the desire not to be solicited by the lawyer or

(2) The solicitation involves coercion, duress or harassment.

(c) Every written, recorded or electronic communication from a lawyer soliciting professional employment from a particular prospective client known to be in need of legal services in a particular matter, with whom the lawyer has no family, close personal, or prior professional relationship, shall include the words, "solicitation material" on the outside envelope or at the beginning and ending of any recorded communication.

(d) Notwithstanding the prohibitions of paragraph (a), a lawyer may participate with a prepaid or group legal service plan operated by an organization not owned or directed by the lawyer which uses in-person or telephone contact to solicit memberships or subscriptions for the plan from persons who are not known to need legal services in a particular matter covered by the plan.

The first case that drew a distinction between advertising and solicitation was *Ohralik v. Ohio State Bar Ass'n*, 436 U.S. 447 (1978). The Court there held that "the State—or the Bar acting with state authorization—constitutionally may discipline a lawyer for soliciting clients in person, for pecuniary gain, under circumstances likely to pose dangers that the State has a right to prevent." That case involved an attorney who went to a hospital to visit and engage as a client an 18-year-old girl who had been injured in an auto accident. The Court differentiated this type of direct, in-person solicitation from advertising in upholding the state's prohibitions:

> Unlike a public advertisement, which simply provides information and leaves the recipient free to act upon it or not, in-person solicitation may exert pressure and often demands an immediate response, without providing an opportunity for comparison or reflection. The aim and effect of in-person solicitation may be to provide a one-sided presentation and to encourage speedy and perhaps uninformed decision making; there is no opportunity for intervention or counter-education by agencies of the Bar, supervisory authorities, or persons close to the solicited individual. The admonition that "the fitting remedy for evil counsels is good ones" is of little value when the circumstances provide no opportunity for any remedy at all. In-person solicitation is as likely as not to discourage persons needing counsel from engaging in a critical comparison of the "availability, nature, and prices" of legal services, it actually may disserve the individual and societal interest, identified in *Bates*, in facilitating "informed and reliable decision making." ... The Rule does not prohibit a lawyer from giving unsolicited legal advice; it proscribes the acceptance of employment resulting from such advice....

> The state interests implicated in this case are particularly strong. In addition to its general interest in protecting consumers and regulating commercial transactions, the State bears a special responsibility for maintaining standards among members of the licensed professions. "The interest of the States in regulating lawyers is especially great since lawyers are essential to the primary governmental function of administering justice, and have historically been 'officers of the courts.'" While lawyers act in part as "self-employed businessmen," they also act "as trusted agents of their clients, and as assistants to the court in search of a just solution to disputes."

As is true with respect to advertising, it appears that the ban on solicitation by lawyers originated as a rule of professional etiquette rather than as a strictly ethical rule. "[T]he rules are based in part on deeply ingrained feelings of tradition, honor and service. Lawyers have for centuries emphasized that the promotion of justice, rather than the earning of fees, is the goal of the profession." But the fact that the original motivation behind the ban on solicitation today might be considered an insufficient justification for its perpetuation does not detract from the force of the other interests the ban continues to serve. While the Court in *Bates* determined that truthful, restrained advertising of the prices of "routine" legal services would not have an adverse effect on the professionalism of lawyers, this was only because it found "the postulated connection between advertising and the erosion of true professionalism to be severely strained." The *Bates* Court did not question a State's interest in maintaining high standards among licensed professionals. Indeed, to the extent that the ethical standards of lawyers are linked to the service and protection of clients, they do further the goals of "true professionalism."

The substantive evils of solicitation have been stated over the years in sweeping terms: stirring up litigation, assertion of fraudulent claims, debasing the legal profession, and potential harm to the solicited client in the form of overreaching, overcharging, underrepresentation, and misrepresentation. The American Bar Association, as amicus curiae, defends the rule against solicitation primarily on three broad grounds: It is said that the prohibitions embodied in DR 2-103(A) and 2-104(A) serve to reduce the likelihood of overreaching and the exertion of undue influence on lay persons, to protect the privacy of individuals, and to avoid situations where the lawyer's exercise of judgment on behalf of the client will be clouded by his own pecuniary self-interest.

We need not discuss or evaluate each of these interests in detail as appellant has conceded that the State has a legitimate and indeed "compelling" interest in preventing those aspects of solicitation that involve fraud, undue influence, intimidation, overreaching, and other forms of "vexatious conduct." We agree that protection of the public from these aspects of solicitation is a legitimate and important state interest....

Appellant's argument misconceives the nature of the State's interest. The Rules prohibiting solicitation are prophylactic measures whose objective is the prevention of harm before it occurs. The Rules were applied in this case to discipline a lawyer for soliciting employment for pecuniary gain under circumstances likely to result in the adverse consequences the State seeks to avert. In such a situation, which is inherently conducive to overreaching and other forms of misconduct, the State has a strong interest in adopting and enforcing rules of conduct designed to protect the public from harmful solicitation by lawyers whom it has licensed.

The State's perception of the potential for harm in circumstances such as those presented in this case is well founded. The detrimental aspects of face-to-face selling even of ordinary consumer products have been recognized and addressed by the Federal Trade Commission, and it hardly need be said that the potential for overreaching is significantly greater when a lawyer, a professional trained in the art of persuasion, personally solicits an unsophisticated, injured, or distressed lay person. Such an individual may place his trust in a lawyer, regardless of the latter's qualifications or the individual's actual need for legal representation, simply in response to persuasion under circumstances conducive to uninformed acquiescence. Although it is argued that personal solicitation is valuable because it may apprise a victim of misfortune of his legal rights, the very plight of that person not only makes him more vulnerable to influence but also may make advice all the more intrusive. Thus, under these adverse conditions the overtures of an uninvited lawyer may distress the solicited individual simply because of their obtrusiveness and the invasion of the individual's privacy, even when no other harm materializes. Under such circumstances, it is not unreasonable for the State to presume that in-person solicitation by lawyers more often than not will be injurious to the person solicited.

Ohralik, 436 U.S. at 455-461.

In a concurring opinion, Justice Marshall expressed concern with the far-reaching scope of the Court's decision. Believing that total restriction on in-person solicitation has a discriminatory impact on less privileged classes of society and on sole practitioners and small firms, and that some solicitation can have the same beneficial effects on public knowledge of availability of legal services as advertising, Justice Marshall expressed reservations that a total ban on solicitation could pass constitutional muster.

What is the difference, then, between advertising and solicitation? Is a newspaper ad providing advice that a particular claim may exist and offering representation to those potentially having such a claim closer to advertising or solicitation for purposes of First Amendment analysis? The Court in *Zauderer v. Office of Disciplinary Counsel of Supreme Court of Ohio*, 471 U.S. 626 (1985) concluded that a letter mailed to the general public, seeking clients for particular types of representation, could not be banned as in-person solicitation:

> It is apparent that the concerns that moved the Court in *Ohralik* are not present here. Although some sensitive souls may have found appellant's advertisement in poor taste, it can hardly be said to have invaded the privacy of those who read it. More significantly, appellant's advertisement—and print advertising generally—poses much less risk of overreaching or undue influence. Print advertising may convey information and ideas more or less effectively, but in most cases, it will lack the coercive force of the personal presence of a trained advocate. In addition, a printed advertisement, unlike a personal encounter initiated by an attorney, is not likely to involve pressure on the potential client for an immediate yes-or-no answer to the offer of representation. Thus, a printed advertisement is a means of conveying information about legal services that is more conducive to reflection and the exercise of choice on the part of the consumer than is personal solicitation by an attorney. Accordingly, the substantial interests that justified the ban on in-person solicitation upheld in *Ohralik* cannot justify the discipline imposed on appellant for the content of his advertisement.

Zauderer, 471 U.S. at 642.

Mailing letters to persons known to need legal services, or what has become known as targeted direct mail, falls somewhere between public advertisements and private in-person solicitation. In *Shapero v. Kentucky Bar Association,* 486 U.S. 466 (1988), the United States Supreme Court held that a state may not categorically prohibit "soliciting legal business for pecuniary gain by sending truthful and nondeceptive letters to potential clients known to face particular legal problems."

> [R]espondent's facile suggestion that this case is merely "*Ohralik* in writing" misses the mark. In assessing the potential for overreaching and undue influence, the mode of communication makes all the difference. Our decision in *Ohralik* that a State could categorically ban all in-person solicitation turned on two factors. First was our characterization of face-to-face solicitation as "a practice rife with possibilities for overreaching, invasion of privacy, the exercise of undue influence, and outright fraud." Second, "unique ... difficulties," would frustrate any attempt at state regulation of in-person solicitation short of an absolute ban because such solicitation is "not visible or otherwise open to public scrutiny."

Targeted, direct-mail solicitation is distinguishable from the in-person solicitation in each respect.

Shapero, 486 U.S. at 475. While categorical bans on this form of solicitation are not permitted, states aggressively restrict the timing and content of these solicitations. In 1995, the Court decided one of the last of its major attorney advertising cases. In *Florida Bar v. Went For It, Inc.*, 515 U.S. 618 (1995), the Court approved a prohibition on sending letters to victims of accident or disasters until after a 30-day waiting period.

Notes

1. Increasingly targeted direct mail is being replaced by electronic solicitations. The court in *Alexander v. Cahill*, 598 F.3d 79, 101-102 (2d Cir. N.Y. 2010) addressed a New York rule that imposed a moratorium on any targeted solicitations, including those conveyed by other media:

   The moratorium provisions in this case extend by their plain language to television, radio, newspaper, and website solicitations that are directed to or targeted at a specific recipient or group of recipients.... The Supreme Court has in some circumstances favored a technology-specific approach to the First Amendment.... Different media may present unique attributes that merit a tailored First Amendment analysis.

   But the differences among media may or may not be relevant to the First Amendment analysis depending on the challenged restrictions.... cf. Shapero v. Ky. Bar Ass'n, 486 U.S. 466, 473, 108 S. Ct. 1916, 100 L. Ed. 2d 475 (1988) ("Our lawyer advertising cases have never distinguished among various modes of written advertising to the general public.").

   In the context before us, we eschew a technology-specific approach to the First Amendment and conclude that New York's moratorium provisions—as we construe them—survive constitutional scrutiny notwithstanding their applicability across the technological spectrum. We focus first on the potential differences among media as to the degree of affirmative action needed to be taken by the targeted recipient to receive the material Plaintiffs seek to send. For many media forms, it is about the same. Thus, to us, the affirmative act of walking to one's mailbox and tearing open a letter seems no greater than walking to one's front step and picking up the paper or turning on a knob on a television or radio.

   It is true that the Internet may appear to require more affirmative acts on the part of the user in order to recover content (and is therefore perhaps entitled to greater First Amendment protection insofar as users are soliciting information, rather than being solicited). But regardless of whether this characterization was once accurate, it no longer is so. E-mail has replaced letters; newspapers are often read online; radio streams online; television programming is broadcast on the Web; and the Internet can be connected to television. *See* Christopher S. Yoo, *The Rise and Demise of the Technology-Specific Approach to the First Amendment*, 91 Geo. L.J. 245, 248 (2003) ("[T]he impending shift of all networks to packet switched technologies promises to cause all of the distinctions based on the means of conveyance and the type of speech conveyed to collapse entirely."). Furthermore, Internet searches do not bring a user immediately to the desired result without distractions. Advertisements may appear with the user's search results; pop-up ads appear on web pages; and Gmail (Google's e-mail service) creates targeted advertising based on the keywords used in one's e-mail. In such a context, an accident victim who describes her experience in an e-mail might very well find an attorney advertisement targeting victims of the specific accident on her computer screen.[9]

States are increasingly responding to these expanded and expanding roles of the Internet. Several already apply existing attorney professional responsibility rules to electronic and Internet advertisements and solicitations. *See* Amy Haywood & Melissa Jones, *Navigating a Sea of Uncertainty: How Existing Ethical Guidelines Pertain to the Marketing of Legal Services over the Internet,* 14 Geo. J. Legal Ethics, 1099, 1113 (2001) ("[I]t can be assumed that Internet use in the context of legal marketing will generally invoke all ethics rules relating to advertising and solicitation."). Texas and Florida have also added language to their disciplinary rules specifically to address attorney solicitation via the Internet. The New York Task Force Report reached the same conclusion. The Report repeatedly stated that "on-line advertisements and websites are not materially different than typical" printed advertisements, and that the rules should be enforced equally across media. (Task Force Report 54-55) In so doing, the Report "demonstrate[d] that the harms it recites are real and its restriction will in fact alleviate them to a degree." *Florida Bar,* 515 U.S. at 626 (quotation marks omitted).... Accordingly, we conclude that even acknowledging that differences among media may be significant in some First Amendment analyses, they are not so in this case.

2. Prohibitions on in-person solicitation in all jurisdictions provide exceptions for family members and former clients. Some, like Mississippi, include close personal friends. Where is the line between an acquaintance and a friend? Does this exception explain why attorneys might solicit on the golf course but not in the hospital?

3. You should be especially careful to avoid solicitation when providing seminars or other public information events. While the states laud the professional effort to keep the public informed about law and legal rights, when these sessions turn into "infomercials," discipline soon follows. It is perfectly appropriate to put your name on information distributed at a public seminar, but avoid encouraging individuals to call you specifically and certainly avoiding providing individualized legal advice at such a seminar. Instead, encourage those who are interested in seeking legal advice to contact an attorney. You may say that you are happy to have individuals call but only if you also suggest that many fine attorneys in your community provide the type of legal services about

9. At present, Gmail's algorithm for placing targeted advertisements next to e-mail messages omits such ads where an e-mail message mentions a catastrophic event or tragedy. See More on Gmail and Privacy, Jan. 2007, http://mail.google.com/mail/help/about_privacy.html. It is by no means certain, however, (a) that Google will continue such a policy, (b) that the algorithm runs without flaws, or (c) that other e-mail providers will exercise similar good taste.

which you are presenting and that participants should feel free to "shop around."

4. Remember that under Rule 8.4, if you can't do something (like solicit clients in person), you can't hire someone else to do it for you. The practice of hiring "runners" whose job is to locate potential clients and solicit their representation violates the rules, even if you call the runners "investigators" and are paying them for gathering documents and evidence. The courts take these schemes very seriously. For example, attorneys who participated in "one of the largest runner-based solicitation schemes in Louisiana" recently were permanently disbarred, even though they did not originate the scheme. *In re O'Keefe*, 877 So. 2d 79 (La. 2004); *In re Laudumiey*, 849 So. 2d 515 (La. 2003). Even attorneys who facilitated the scheme mostly through inadvertence and inadequate supervision of staff were given significant suspensions. *In re Goff*, 837 So. 2d 1201 (La. 2002). Other attorneys have found themselves with criminal convictions for this conduct. *In the Matter of Silver*, 545 S.E.2d 886 (Ga. 2001) (attorney disbarred after pleading nolo to a misdemeanor charge of paying runners for his firm).

   Obviously, this is territory to scrupulously avoid. Train your staff carefully. Many an attorney has been subject to disciplinary action simply because a well-meaning paralegal or secretary did not know that being "part of the team" did not mean going out into the community and "drumming up business."

5. In a companion case to *Ohralik*, the Court held that solicitation undertaken to offer representation in litigation that will express political beliefs and advance civil-liberties objectives rather than for pecuniary gain is not subject to the same analysis as that in *Ohralik*. *In re Primus*, 436 U.S. 412 (1978). Rather, because these types of speech and conduct are closer to the core of the First Amendment, they are to be governed by "pure" First Amendment analysis rather than the more restrictive analysis used for commercial speech. Thus, a state may not categorically ban this non-profit solicitation, but must examine each case to determine, on the facts, whether the solicitation in question actually involved the undue influence, misrepresentation, overreaching, or invasion of privacy that the solicitation rules are designed to prevent. Only in cases where these evils are actually present may discipline be imposed. Justice Rehnquist concurred in *Ohralik* but dissented in *Primus*, finding no basis for a "principled distinction" between the two cases.

   What is the distinction between solicitation for political rather than pecuniary motivation? Is it the presence of a fee? Professor Susan Carle suggests that this distinction, while a clear line, poses its own challenges:

We might also ask whether conflating the notions of pro bono work and work without any fee tends to perpetuate a system in which pro bono or "public interest" law is dominated by two nonrepresentative groups of American lawyers: first, corporate law firms that can afford to let their associates cut their teeth handling pro bono cases and, second, the tiny handful of lawyers able to get work at the few surviving nonprofits engaged in public interest advocacy. Why should only these lawyers shape our nation's public interest agenda? ... What happened to the grass roots public interest litigation model exemplified by lawyers ... who pursue legal work for political and ideological reasons but accept modest fees from clients, when possible, in order to keep their practices afloat?

Susan Carle, *Re-Envisioning Models for Pro Bono Lawyering: Some Historical Reflections*, 9 AM. U.J. GENDER SOC. POL'Y & L. 81, 94 (2001). Would a solicitation rule that applies this broader conception of public interest law be workable, or does that suggestion simply prove Justice Rehnquist's observations?

26.5 Dignity and the Image of the Profession as a Governmental Interest

Throughout all of the cases addressing attorney advertising and solicitation there has been a recurring theme that attorney advertising undermines the image of the profession, and thus the professionalism of attorneys. Justice O'Connor has been the strongest proponent of the position that the interest of the profession as a whole is a governmental interest that justifies significant restrictions on advertising and solicitation. Her dissent in *Shapero v. Kentucky Bar Association*, 486 U.S. 466 (1988) explained this position:

> Relying primarily on *Zauderer*, the Court holds that States may not prohibit a form of attorney advertising that is potentially more pernicious than the advertising at issue in that case. I agree with the Court that the reasoning in *Zauderer* supports the conclusion reached today. That decision, however, was itself the culmination of a line of cases built on defective premises and flawed reasoning. As today's decision illustrates, the Court has been unable or unwilling to restrain the logic of the underlying analysis within reasonable bounds. The resulting interference with important and valid public policies is so destructive that I believe the analytical framework itself should now be reexamined....
>
> Assuming, arguendo, that the removal of advertising restrictions should lead in the short run to increased efficiency in the provision of legal services, I would not agree that we can safely assume the same effect in the long run. The economic argument against these restrictions ignores the delicate role they may play in preserving the norms of the legal profession. While it may be difficult to defend this role with precise economic logic, I believe there is a powerful argument in favor of restricting lawyer advertising and that this argument is at the very least not easily refuted by economic analysis.
>
> One distinguishing feature of any profession, unlike other occupations that may be equally respectable, is that membership entails an ethical obligation to temper one's selfish pursuit of economic success by adhering to standards of conduct that could not be enforced either by legal fiat or through the discipline of the market. There are sound reasons to continue pursuing the goal that is implicit in the traditional view of professional life. Both the special privileges incident to membership in the profession and the advantages those privileges give in the necessary task of earning a living are means to a goal that transcends the accumulation of wealth. That goal is public service, which in the legal profession can take a variety of familiar forms. This view of the legal profession need not be rooted in romanticism or self-serving sanctimony, though of course it can be. Rather, special ethical standards for lawyers are properly understood as an ap-

propriate means of restraining lawyers in the exercise of the unique power that they inevitably wield in a political system like ours.

It is worth recalling why lawyers are regulated at all, or to a greater degree than most other occupations, and why history is littered with failed attempts to extinguish lawyers as a special class. Operating a legal system that is both reasonably efficient and tolerably fair cannot be accomplished, at least under modern social conditions, without a trained and specialized body of experts. This training is one element of what we mean when we refer to the law as a "learned profession." Such knowledge by its nature cannot be made generally available, and it therefore confers the power and the temptation to manipulate the system of justice for one's own ends.... Precisely because lawyers must be provided with expertise that is both esoteric and extremely powerful, it would be unrealistic to demand that clients bargain for their services in the same arm's-length manner that may be appropriate when buying an automobile or choosing a dry cleaner. Like physicians, lawyers are subjected to heightened ethical demands on their conduct towards those they serve. These demands are needed because market forces, and the ordinary legal prohibitions against force and fraud, are simply insufficient to protect the consumers of their necessary services from the peculiar power of the specialized knowledge that these professionals possess.

Imbuing the legal profession with the necessary ethical standards is a task that involves a constant struggle with the relentless natural force of economic self-interest. It cannot be accomplished directly by legal rules, and it certainly will not succeed if sermonizing is the strongest tool that may be employed. Tradition and experiment have suggested a number of formal and informal mechanisms, none of which is adequate by itself and many of which may serve to reduce competition (in the narrow economic sense) among members of the profession. A few examples include the great efforts made during this century to improve the quality and breadth of the legal education that is required for admission to the bar; the concomitant attempt to cultivate a subclass of genuine scholars within the profession; the development of bar associations that aspire to be more than trade groups; strict disciplinary rules about conflicts of interest and client abandonment; and promotion of the expectation that an attorney's history of voluntary public service is a relevant factor in selecting judicial candidates.

Restrictions on advertising and solicitation by lawyers properly and significantly serve the same goal. Such restrictions act as a concrete, day-to-day reminder to the practicing attorney of why it is improper for any member of this profession to regard it as a trade or occupation like any other.... In my judgment, however, fairly severe constraints on attorney advertising can continue to play an important role in preserving the legal profession as a genuine profession. Whatever may be the exactly appropriate scope of these restrictions at a given time and place, this Court's recent decisions reflect a myopic belief that "consumers," and thus our Nation, will benefit from a constitutional theory that refuses to recognize either the essence of professionalism or its fragile and necessary foundations. In one way or another, time will uncover the folly of this approach. I can only hope that the Court will recognize the danger before it is too late to effect a worthwhile cure.

Shapero, 486 U.S. at 488-90.

In *Florida Bar v. Went For It, Inc.*, 515 U.S. 618 (1995), the majority opinion, authored by Justice O'Connor, cited both the justification of consumer privacy and the reputation of the bar in upholding the state's 30-day moratorium on targeted direct-mail:

> We believe that the Florida Bar's 30-day restriction on targeted direct-mail solicitation of accident victims and their relatives withstands scrutiny under the three-part *Central Hudson* test that we have devised for this context. The Bar has substantial interest both in protecting injured Floridians from invasive conduct by lawyers and in preventing the erosion of confidence in the profession that such repeated invasions have engendered. The Bar's proffered study [showing that members of the public view such letters as an invasion of privacy and as adversely affecting their opinions of the lawyers who send them], unrebutted by respondents below, provides evidence indicating that the harms it targets are far from illusory. The palliative devised by the Bar to address these harms is narrow both in scope and in duration. The Constitution, in our view, requires nothing more.

Florida Bar, 515 U.S. at 635.

Notes:

1. What do you think about this justification for restrictions on attorney advertising? Remember your "picture of a professional" from Chapter One? What has shaped that picture? Has advertising played a role in that image? If the "image of the profession" is a significant government interest that can restrict commercial speech, how would that express itself in regulation?

2. Many state prohibitions on advertising that might be characterized as distasteful could be viewed as protecting this interest in the image of the profession. However, when challenged, states do not tend to proffer this justification, but instead rely on the more well-established justifications of avoiding deceptive or misleading advertising. Could the advertisements in *Alexander v. Cahill*, 598 F.3d 79, 101-102 (2d Cir. N.Y. 2010) (depicting attorneys as superheroes, giants, etc.) be constitutionally prohibited on the basis of undermining the image of the profession?

3. One of the recurring issues in all of these advertising cases is the degree of proof that is required to establish that the regulations are narrowly tailored to serve the government interest. In *Florida Bar*, for example, the state provided a survey of members of the public regarding their perceptions of attorney solicitation following accidents or disasters. Should the courts require that all restrictions on advertising be supported by this type of evidence?

Researching Professional Responsibility: Constitutionality of Advertising Restrictions

As you can see, attorney advertising and solicitation is subject to detailed and aggressively policed regulation, regulation that varies considerably from state to state and changes over time. Research your own state's restrictions on attorney advertising. Choose one that you believe might raise issues of constitutionality and then research the case law to determine whether similar restrictions have been challenged and the result of those challenges.

Test Your Understanding

Reconsider the advertisement you prepared at the beginning of this chapter. Using your state's rules, decide whether any part of your advertisement would subject you to discipline. If so, would the imposition of discipline violate your constitutional rights? Ask yourself as to both the ad as a whole and as to each specific statement in the ad:

- Is the statement false?

- Is the statement misleading?

- Are any terms sufficiently abstract that different consumers could have different ideas about what it means, such that some would be misled?

- Do any statements expressly or impliedly compare the lawyer's services with other lawyers' services? If so, can that comparison be "factually substantiated"? Are the terms used in the comparison sufficiently subjective that they would be incapable of verification?

- Are clients likely to have expectations about results that are unrealistic? Don't presume that a "your mileage may vary" statement is sufficient to protect statements that otherwise would create unrealistic expectations.

To Learn More

The ABA has a website dedicated to information on attorney advertising, including a chart that compares the states' regulation of advertising to the Model Rules and reports on current litigation involving state rules. http://www.americanbar.org/groups/professional_responsibility/resources/professionalism/professionalism_ethics_in_lawyer_advertising.html

Another good way to review your own state's advertising restrictions is to read through ethics opinions from your state. Advertising and solicitation restrictions are a frequent topic for discussion in these opinions.

Review of Unit Seven

Practice Context Review

Presume that according to a State Bar Task Force on the Public Defender system, the average caseload for a trial-level public defender in your state is 305 cases. This exceeds by almost one-third the maximum caseload size of 235 cases that was set 15 years ago by the Governor and the State Public Defender Commission. Attorneys, the courts, and the legislature have been proposing a number of measures to address this issue.

The following proposal has been developed by a state legislator. It has three parts:

I. All attorneys in the state would be required to provide 50 hours of free legal representation in municipal ordinance violations. These usually involve misdemeanors that theoretically could involve substantial jail time, but practically almost never do because nearly all cases are resolved through plea agreements. Rules of procedure and evidence are often relaxed so that even attorneys who do not regularly appear in court can master the process in short order.

II. Lay persons would be permitted to represent individuals in parole revocation hearings unless the parole board decided an attorney was necessary in a particular case. Of course parolees do have certain due process rights at these hearings. *Morrissey v. Brewer*, 408 U.S. 471 (1972), however, the right to counsel is a matter of a case-by-case balancing test. *Gagnon v. Scarpelli*, 411 U.S. 778, 790 (1973). Presume that in our state, the right to counsel has been provided by statute but this proposal would modify that statute.

III. One aspect of the costs of the public defender system is raised by conflicts of interest rules. If a public defender has a conflict of interest in representing a client, that conflict will be imputed to all other attorneys in that office and private attorneys will then be appointed or the case will be transferred to another public defender office. Both of these solutions increase the costs, and thereby decrease overall availability, of resources for public defenders. Thus, the third part of this proposal provides that:

> No court shall disqualify an attorney serving as a public defender on the basis of a conflict of interest that is not personal to that attorney but is imputed to that attorney based on the conflicts of interest of other attorneys in the office. The Missouri Public Defender system is directed to implement screening programs for public defender offices in order to reduce the sharing of information among attorneys in cases in which conflicts of interest are present.

What legal issues do these proposals raise and what is the likely outcome if these proposals are challenged in the state courts? Use concrete examples from the rules and the readings to support your position on the proposal.

Multiple Choice Review

1. Attorney lives in a rural county 40 miles from City where she has her principal office. Attorney has a small office in the rural county where she lives and has a secretary there and Friday office hours. The county judge appointed her to defend an indigent on municipal criminal assault charges. The court would provide the usual minimal amount of compensation. Attorney hasn't practiced criminal law for many years and accepting this case would require at least twenty hours of preparation and require her to come to the rural office at least twice on a Wednesday in addition to her usual Friday hours. Attorney asks the court to excuse her from the appointment and remove her name from the list of attorneys who will be appointed in these cases. Is attorney subject to discipline?

   A No, because attorney's acceptance of the representation would be an unreasonable financial burden.

   B. No, because the attorney is not competent to represent a criminal defendant.

   C. Yes, because attorney is seeking to avoid court appointment without good cause.

   D. Yes, because the attorney has a duty to accept pro bono cases.

2. Lucinda Lawyer is licensed to practice law in Florida. After a hurricane swept through the Gulf Coast, many people were left without homes and in need of legal services to assist with their applications for disaster assistance and to negotiate with their mortgage lenders and others. Lucinda is an attorney in a firm that regularly represents Tenth Bank of Florida in its consumer lending work. Lucinda primarily provides estate planning work. The local bar association has asked attorneys to volunteer to help staff an emergency legal aid center in Lucinda's county. Lucinda agrees to help and gives short-term limited legal assistance to many residents and small business owners about their legal rights under their mortgage agreements. One of the clients she helps at the clinic is Frank. She helps Frank read and interpret his mortgage document from Tenth Bank, pointing out several procedures and rights that help him to negotiate with the bank to defer payments. As the clinic makes clear to all clients, Lucinda has no continuing duty to Frank after that meeting. Lucinda knew that her firm represented banks but didn't know that Tenth Bank was a current client of the firm. Later, however, she discovers that one of the partners in her firm has been representing Tenth Bank in foreclosure proceedings against Frank. Is Lucinda subject to discipline?

   A. Yes, because she represented a client in matter that was directly adverse to a partner's current client.

   B. Yes, because it is unreasonable for her to limit the representation to advice without research.

   C. No, because she did not know that Tenth Bank was a current client of the firm.

   D. No, because Tenth Bank was not her personal client.

3. Attorney gives talks to local groups about estate planning. He is careful not to provide legal advice to individuals during the seminars, but provides only general legal information. He distributes a brochure to individuals at the talk with helpful information about estate planning, including worksheets and a glossary of estate planning terminology. The brochures have his name and phone number on the back and a coupon for $50 off the first office visit. Attorney says nothing to the people attending the meeting about his services or the coupon. Is attorney subject to discipline?

   A. Yes, because he has engaged in improper solicitation.

   B. Yes, because coupons are not a proper method of advertising legal services.

   C. No, because Attorney does not provide advice to individuals at the seminars.

   D. No, because Attorney did not individually solicit any client.

4. Bonita Barrister is aware of the significant need for victims of domestic violence to have legal representation. To help assist these individuals, she advises the local shelter that she will accept representation of clients who need assistance in divorce or custody matters. She works with the lay person volunteer to develop a list of criteria for the types of clients she will accept. When the volunteer is conducting the intake interview at the shelter, she also compares the individual's information to the criteria, and if they qualify, she provides them Bonita's business card and tells them that Bonita will represent them for free. Is Bonita subject to discipline?

   A. Yes, because she is assisting in the unauthorized practice of law.

   B. Yes, because she is directing someone to engage in in-person solicitation on her behalf.

   C. No, because she is providing her representation pro bono.

   D. No, because she has instructed the volunteer on specific criteria.

Answers and Analysis

1. The best answer is C under Rule 6.2's standard of "shall not seek to avoid." This is a better answer than D because, while Rule 6.1 does suggest that attorneys contribute pro bono representation, it is a "should" rule and so it is problematic to call it a duty; moreover, attorney is being paid, so it is problematic to call this "pro bono" under the terms of Rule 6.1. A is not correct because the attorney is being compensated and the time required is no more than Rule 6.1 suggests all attorneys should contribute. B is not correct because the attorney is able to make herself competent.

2. The best answer is C. Rule 6.5 Nonprofit and Court Annexed Limited Legal Services Programs provides a more liberal standard for conflicts of interest in these types of representations. A is not correct because Rule 6.5 provides that imputed disqualifications occur only if the attorney knows of the conflict at the time she is participating in the program. B is not correct because limited legal services are permitted under Rule 1.2 and in many states (including Florida) under either state court rules amendments or ethics opinions interpreting Rule 1.2. D is not correct because, if a conflict did apply, it would be imputed to her partner. D ignores the effect of 1.10 if it were applicable.

3. The correct answer is A. Handing out the brochures to generate clients is in-person solicitation. It doesn't matter that the attorney didn't give advice at the seminar itself—solicitation doesn't necessarily involve advice—and it doesn't matter if the attorney didn't solicit any one client individually (in terms of speaking to them) because handing them the brochure in person is a face-to-face solicitation. B is

wrong because there are no restrictions on attorneys discounting their fees, even with a "coupon."

4. The correct answer is C. If this were an arrangement in which the volunteer were sending paying clients, then the correct answer would be B; however, nonprofit solicitation is protected as political speech and so cannot be restrained like commercial speech. A is incorrect because the volunteer is not giving legal advice, only making referrals. D is irrelevant to the analysis of whether the attorney is violating any rules.

Appendix

Advice on Preparing for the MPRE

Many students choose to take the Multistate Professional Responsibility Exam (MPRE) during the same semester they take the Professional Responsibility course. The MPRE takes 120 minutes. It has sixty questions, ten of which are questions the National Conference of Bar Examiners (NCBE) is testing to use on future exams. Your answers on these questions don't count; however, you won't know which of the ten questions is a test question. All the questions are multiple choice, typically paired yes, yes, no, no. The test covers the ABA Model Rules; the Model Code of Judicial Conduct; and "general law" (which is best reviewed by looking over the malpractice, privilege, and agency sections of the Restatement of the Law Governing Lawyers).

To prepare for the MPRE, first, select resources that can help your study. Most students prefer to take the MPRE the same semester they take the professional responsibility course in law school. If that doesn't work for your schedule or you simply want to take the MPRE another time, it is not essential that you take the class to pass the exam. It does mean you must be especially disciplined and thorough in your preparation. The commercial bar services have MPRE preparation courses, which may include outlines, lectures, and sample exams. If you are not especially disciplined in your study or simply want the reassurance of these coaching services, they are likely worth the investment of time and money.

To prepare for the MPRE you need the following materials. You must have a current copy of the Model Rules of Professional Conduct (www.abanet.org/cpr/mrpc/home.html). You must have a current copy of the Model Code of Judicial Conduct (www.abanet.org/judicialethics/approved_MCJC.html). Be sure you have actively read all the rules and comments in both sets of rules. It is also helpful to have access to a copy of the Restatement (Third) of the Law Governing Lawyers (available on Lexis and Westlaw, in some professional responsibility course supplement texts, or in your law library). This is helpful, especially if you are studying for the test on your own, without a class.

Finally, you will want to have some practice exam questions. If you are taking a commercial preparation course, it will provide sample exams. If you are studying on your own, the National Conference of Bar Examiners, has an MPRE Sample Questions VI packet that is available online in pdf form. You can find it at the NCBE website at www.ncbex.org. (currently at www.ncbex.org/assets/media_files/MPRE/MPREVI2002.pdf). Even more helpful is the NCBE online practice exam, which for $24 gives you unlimited access to a practice exam, which provides not only the correct answer but an explanation as to why the answer you chose was right or wrong. You can find this in the NCBE store.

Second, schedule your study. Divide your study into topic themes as tested on the MPRE (see the suggested study schedule below). Allocate a reasonable amount of time to each topic. For each topic area, read the relevant rules and comments and any other materials you have on that topic. Take notes, make an outline, make flashcards, or otherwise work with the materials in whatever way works for you.

If your schedule does not permit sufficient study time without exhausting your mental and physical resources, reschedule something. Each week study the topics for the week. Read the rules or the restatement provisions and any other materials you are using to prepare (notes, outlines, etc.). Highlight, outline, make flash cards, or take any other approach to studying these rules that works for you. Test your understanding of the rules. When you identify gaps in your knowledge, decide whether the problem is incomplete learning (did you simply forget a rule?) or incomplete understanding (did you not understand the rule?). Work on understanding. Read additional materials in your areas of weakness; write out mini-outlines or charts to help visualize your understanding. Work on memory. If there are rules or subject areas you simply forgot, devise memory devices to better capture those rules.

Be sure to study the test as well as the subject and take at least one full-length practice test under test conditions. Review your answers and fill in any gaps in your understanding revealed by your self-testing. Study carefully the questions you answered incorrectly or those which you got correct but were surprised by. Try to identify why you missed the question and see if you can identify any patterns to your errors. Study especially those answers for which you thought you clearly had the answer right and it was not. Work on test strategy. If you consistently made test-taking errors (e.g., overlooking qualifier phrases or second-guessing your answers) devise strategies to address these gaps.

Finally, prepare for the exam day. Get enough sleep. Talk to yourself positively. Locate the test center and identify parking or access issues. Gather your identification and test entrance ticket. Get a passport size photo. Set up a date for a celebration for your completing the exam and another for when you learn you have passed the exam. Take the exam with confidence, knowing you have prepared yourself thoroughly and professionally.

Suggested Study Schedule
Beginning Eight Weeks Prior to the MPRE

Week Eight

Clear your calendar for the date of the exam.

Register for the exam

Read Description of Exam

Study Topics for this Week

Regulation of the Legal Profession (6–12% of the exam)

   A. Powers of Courts and Other Bodies to Regulate Lawyers (class notes)

   B. Admission to the Profession (Class notes & Rule 8.1)

   C. Regulation after Admission — Lawyer Discipline (Class notes & Rule. 8.4)

   D. Mandatory and Permissive Reporting of Professional Misconduct (Rule 8.3)

   E. Unauthorized Practice of Law — by Lawyers and Nonlawyers (Class notes & Rule 5.3, 5.5 & 8.5)

   F. Multi-jurisdictional Practice (Rule 5.5 & 8.5)

   G. Fee Division with a Nonlawyer (Rule 5.4)

   H. Law Firm and Other Forms of Practice (Rules 5.1 & 5.2)

   I. Responsibilities of Partners, Managers, Supervisory and Subordinate Lawyers (Rules 5.1 & 5.2)

   J. Restrictions on Right to Practice (Rule 5.6)

Judicial Conduct (2–8%) — **Code of Judicial Conduct**

   A. Maintaining the Independence and Impartiality of the Judiciary

   B. Performing the Duties of Judicial Office Impartially, Competently, and Diligently

   C. *Ex parte* Communications

   D. Disqualification

   E. Extrajudicial Activities

Week Seven

Study Topics for this Week

The Client-Lawyer Relationship (10–16% of the exam)

   A. Formation of Client-Lawyer Relationship (class notes)

   B. Scope, Objective, and Means of the Representation (Rule 1.2)

   C. Decision-making Authority — Actual and Apparent (Class notes)

   D. Counsel and Assistance Within the Bounds of the Law (Rule 1.2; Rule 1.16)

   E. Termination of the Client-Lawyer Relationship (Rule 1.16)

   F. Client-Lawyer Contracts (Rules 1.4, 1.5, 1.15)

   G. Communications with the Client (Rule 1.4)

   H. Fees (Rule 1.5)

Week Six

Study Topics for this Week

Safekeeping Funds and Other Property (2–8% of the exam)

    A. Establishing and Maintaining Client Trust Accounts (Rule 1.15)

    B. Safekeeping Funds and Other Property of Clients (Rule 1.15)

    C. Safekeeping Funds and Other Property of Third Persons (Rule 1.15)

    D. Disputed Claims

Competence, Legal Malpractice, and Other Civil Liability (6–12% of the exam)

    A. Maintaining Competence (Class notes)

    B. Competence Necessary to Undertake Representation (Rule 1.1)

    C. Exercising Diligence and Care (Rule 1.3)

    D. Civil Liability to Client, Including Malpractice (Classnotes)

    E. Civil Liability to Nonclients (Class notes)

    F. Limiting Liability for Malpractice (Rule 1.8)

    G. Malpractice Insurance and Risk Prevention (Class notes)

Week Five

Study Topics for this Week

Litigation and Other Forms of Advocacy (10–16% of the exam)

    A. Meritorious Claims and Contentions (Rule 3.1 and Rule 11 FRCP)

    B. Expediting Litigation (Rule 3.2)

    C. Candor to the Tribunal (Rule 3.3 and class notes)

    D. Fairness to Opposing Party and Counsel (Rule 3.4)

    E. Impartiality and Decorum of the Tribunal (Rule 3.5)

    F. Trial Publicity (Rule 3.6)

    G. Lawyer as Witness (Rule 3.7)

Week Four

Purchase a review course if you will be taking one

Study Topics for this Week

Client Confidentiality (6–12% of the exam)

    A. Attorney-Client Privilege (Class notes)

    B. Work-product Doctrine (Class notes)

    C. Professional Obligation of Confidentiality—General Rule (Rule 1.6)

    D. Disclosures Expressly or Impliedly Authorized by Client (Rule 1.6)

    E. Other Exceptions to the Confidentiality Rule (Rule 1.6)

Transactions and Communications with Persons Other than Clients
(2–8% of the exam)

    A. Truthfulness in Statements to Others (Rule 4.1)

    B. Communications with Represented Persons (Rule 4.2)

    C. Communications with Unrepresented Persons (Rule 4.3)

    D. Respect for Rights of Third Persons (Rule 4.4)

Week Three

Get a passport size photo taken for admission ticket

Confirm that your calendar is clear for the test date/

Purchase the online MPRE Test available at the ncbe store
  http://www.ncbex2.org/catalog/

Study Topics for this Week

Conflicts of Interest **(12–18% of the exam)**

    A. Current Client Conflicts—Multiple Clients and Joint Representation (Rule 1.7)

    B. Current Client Conflicts—Lawyer's Personal Interest or Duties (Rule 1.8)

    C. Former Client Conflicts (Rule 1.9)

    D. Prospective Client Conflicts (Rule 1.18)

    E. Imputed Conflicts (Rule 1.10)

    F. Acquiring an Interest in Litigation (Rule 1.8)

    G. Business Transactions with Clients (Rule 1.8)

    H. Third Party Compensation and Influence (Rule 1.8)

    I. Lawyers Currently or Formerly in Government Service (Rule 1.11)

    J. Former Judge, Arbitrator, Mediator, or Other Third Party Neutral (Rule 1.12)

Different Roles of the Lawyer **(4–10% of the exam)**

    A. Lawyer as Advisor (Rule 2.1)

    B. Lawyer as Evaluator (Rule 2.3)

    C. Lawyer as Negotiator (Rule 4.1)

    D. Lawyer as Arbitrator, Mediator, or Other Third Party Neutral (Rule 2.4)

    E. Prosecutors and Other Government Lawyers (Rule 3.8)

    F. Lawyer Appearing in Nonadjudicative Proceeding (Rule 3.9)

    G. Lawyer Representing an Entity or Other Organization (Rule 1.13)

Week Two

Attend any review lectures you may have purchased

Take the entire MPRE Online test under test conditions

Study Topics for this Week

Communications about Legal Services **(4–10% of the exam)**

    A. Advertising and Other Public Communications about Legal Services (Class notes & Rule 7.1, 7.5)

    B. Solicitation—Direct Contact with Prospective Clients (Rule 7.3)

    C. Group Legal Services (Rule 7.2)

    D. Referrals (Rule 7.2)

    E. Communications Regarding Fields of Practice and Specialization (Rule 7.4)

Lawyers' Duties to the Public and the Legal System (**2–4% of the exam**)

    A. Voluntary Pro Bono Service (Rule 6.1)

    B. Accepting Appointments (Rule 6.2 and class notes)

    C. Serving in Legal Services Organizations (Rule 6.3)

    D. Law Reform Activities Affecting Client Interests (Rule 6.4)

    E. Criticism of Judges and Adjudicating Officials (Rule 8.2)

    F. Political Contributions to Obtain Engagements or Appointments (Rule 7.6)

    G. Improper Influence on Government Officials (Rule 8.4)

    H. Assisting Judicial Misconduct (Rule 8.4)

Week One

Re-read the instructions for the exam; make sure you have your ticket, photograph, transportation, and #2 pencils ready.

Scan through your notes/flashcards/outlines/highlighting (whatever you have used to study).

Get enough sleep.

Review the questions you got wrong on the online test and read through those Rules one more time.

In taking the test, apply the same principles you have learned about test-taking in other standardized testing situations. Pace yourself on the exam. Be careful you are answering the right question on the answer sheet. Answer every question—there is no penalty for guessing. Don't change your answers.

Be sure you read the call of the question very carefully. For example, here is a typical question:

> Attorney is a criminal defense specialist. He represents defendant in a robbery prosecution. Witness has died and prosecutor wants to introduce deposition testimony. There is a new case that would make introducing the testimony impossible but attorney hasn't been reading lately because he's been busy. He doesn't object to the introduction of the depositions. Defendant is convicted. Defendant probably would have been convicted even if the deposition evidence had been excluded, but there is a possibility that the sentence would have been lower.

This is a relatively easy question if the call of the question is "Was Attorney's action proper?" The answer is no of course not—failing to manage your caseload and failing to stay abreast of the law violate the spirit if not the letter of Rule 1.1. This would have been a much more difficult question with a likely different answer if the question was "Is attorney subject to civil liability?" (No, surely not, because in order for criminal defendants to sue for malpractice, most states require that they be exonerated). It might even be a difficult question if the call of the question was "Is attorney subject to discipline?" because, while the letter of Rule 1.1 appears to make even one act of simple negligence a violation of the rule, some courts hold that simple negligence cannot equal incompetence.

Some key terms in the call of the question you need to have clear are:

1. Subject to discipline: The Model Rules or the Model Code of Judicial Conduct prohibit or require this conduct. Be careful not to answer this as "would be disciplined"—that is a question that includes considerations of whether it is likely that the behavior would result in a complaint, whether disciplinary authorities would act on the complaint, and whether actual discipline would be imposed. Answer these questions without any reference to these discretionary factors.

2. May or proper: Is the behavior something that is neither prohibited nor required by the rules, is not inconsistent with any other part of the rules (preamble or comments); and is not inconsistent with principles expressed in the restatement. These questions are testing the limits of attorney discretion.

3. Key terms relating to regulation outside the rules

   a. *Subject to litigation sanction*

   b. *Subject to disqualification*

   c. *Subject to civil liability*

   d. *Subject to criminal liability*

In addition, be aware of key modifiers in the answers:

BECAUSE—the explanation or theory for the choice.

IF—if clauses add additional facts to the hypothetical—assume these facts are true and then evaluate the answer.

ONLY IF—test whether there is a necessary precondition for the answer to be true.

Some areas are easy to test but hard to answer if you don't study the rules carefully. These include differences in required mental state (know, reasonably believe, pecuniary gain, etc.); differences in whether client agreement is necessary or sufficient and what type of agreement is necessary: consent, written consent, informed consent, or consultation; and rules with multiple factors (e.g. 1.6(b)(2)).

There are some common misconceptions about the rules you should be especially careful to attend to. Do not assume no-harm-no-foul—there is not a general principal that if no harm occurs no violation of the rules has occurred. Likewise, beware no-fee-no-foul—there is not generally a different set of rules for paid versus pro bono attorneys (some exceptions to that idea are in Rules 6.4-6.7 and 7.3). Finally beware of "the client said it was okay"—unless the rule clearly permits clients to waive or consent to the rule violation, it doesn't matter what the client said.

Choose the answer that is the most complete (addresses all parts of the rule—watch for incomplete definitions of determinative rules), the most correct, and is related to the facts (some answers will be a correct and complete statement of the rule, but it will be irrelevant for those facts, and so is incorrect). Be careful of "everybody does it" reactions to answers. Do not answer MPRE questions based on what you think most attorneys actually do—for some rules violations are rampant, and these are exactly the kinds of rules the MPRE likes to test. If two answers seem correct as to outcome and both reasons seem logical—choose the most compelling reason. Remember that the test is testing the lines drawn by the rules, not best practices. For many years, students would hear that the "second most ethical response is correct." The NCBE has tried to eliminate this pattern from prior exams, but remember to keep the outlook of a rule maker, not what the best attorneys would do, and not even what disciplinary counsel would do, but what disciplinary counsel COULD do.

Good luck in your exam preparation and testing.

Index